D0234161

For Christine

A Modern History of the Islamic World

REINHARD SCHULZE

Translated by Azizeh Azodi

I.B.Tauris *Publishers*
LONDON • NEW YORK

New edition published in 2002 by I.B.Tauris & Co Ltd
6 Salem Road, London W2 4BU
175 Fifth Avenue, New York NY 10010
www. ibtauris.com

First published by I.B.Tauris & Co Ltd, 2000

The translation of this work has been supported by Inter Nationes, Bonn

ISBN 1 86064 822 3

A full CIP record for this book is available from the British Library

First edition typeset in Minion by Hepton Books, Oxford
New edition typeset by Wyvern 21, Bristol
Printed and bound in Great Britain by MPG Books Ltd, Bodmin

Contents

List of Maps

Acknowledgements

This book was written between the winter of 1992–93 and the summer of 1993. It is the result of various seminars I held at the universities of Bonn, Bochum and Bamberg. I wish to extend my sincere thanks to the students who participated in these seminars through their papers and discussions. I am particularly grateful to Mr Detlef Felken of C. H. Beck publishing for his untiring efforts in arranging the text of this book and for his many valuable suggestions and Mr Ulrich Haarmann, may agent. I would also like to thank those of my colleagues who, over the last few years, have encouraged and stimulated me in the course of numerous conversations. The making of this book also owes much to the fruitful discussions that took place at the Committee on the Comparative Study of Muslim Societies of the Social Science Research Council (New York).

Preface

The devastating terrorist attacks of September 11, 2001 in New York and Washington once more placed the Islamic world at the very heart of world affairs. It is assumed that the attacks were perpetrated by Islamic extremists linked to the so-called bureau of registration of *jihad* fighters (*sijill al-qa'ida*, known as *al-qa'ida*) created by Osama bin Laden in 1988 during his stay in Afghanistan. On 23 February 1998, bin Laden issued a *fatwa* in the name of a World Islamic Front for Jihad declaring that it was the duty of each individual Muslim to fight and kill Americans according to their capability. Nobody really knows with certainty how many people work within bin Laden's World Islamic Front. Estimates range between hundreds and thousands of combatants acting at different levels of the organization. There exist other smaller *jihad* federations and groups trained in Afghanistan which have been serving in crisis areas such as Chechnya and perhaps also Algeria and which might be related to the network of Afghanistan veterans. All in all perhaps 5,000 sympathisers in the broadest sense might have had contacts with bin Ladin's *al-qa'ida* over the last 13 years. Ladenist sympathisers are probably also active in other Islamic circles – particularly in Pakistan, Egypt and Saudi Arabia – without, however, operating as supporting groups.

These extremists make up only a very small fraction of the Muslim population of the world, currently estimated at over 1 billion. The Ladenists perceive themselves as a small heroic elite of 'True Muslims'. They describe their collective identity as a 'community of fate', formed in the holy war they have been fighting for so many years. Cut off from their social and cultural roots, they see themselves as errant fighters, whose only social reality is the community of *jihad*-combatants, the *mujahidin.* At the same time, they believe themselves to be part of a military avant-garde of the Islamic community and the executive power of a general Islamic will. This they believe is the will of all Muslims, entirely divorced from the notion of will as it is articulated in conventional democratic and social forms.

In contrast to the classical Islamic groups and federations like the Muslim Brothers or the Algerian FIS which could expect to win up to 15% of voters in a parliamentary election during the time of their political ascendancy in the early 1980s, the Ladenists (as most members of the *jihad* movement today) have largely given up on any hope of achieving the kind of social utopia so ardently fought for by their forerunners of the 1970s and 1980s, best typified by the currents behind Khomeini's coup in Iran.

These classical Islamist social utopias were by no means homogeneous. Rather they arose wrapped in any number of ideological colours, assembling socialist, étatist or even fascist world views. Their common ground was made up of nothing but a joint Islamic language and code: Islam itself never determined the ideological world-view of its adherents. It served more as an extremely powerful interpretation foil, which contributed to localise the global ideologies of the 20th century in Muslim communities.

Like every other culture, religious or not, Islam determines neither social nor political activity in the community. Being a complex system of traditions, symbols and rituals, Islam offers the means to interpret the manifold life worlds of all Muslims. On the one hand, the normative content of the Islamic religion relating to God, his last Prophet Muhammad and the Day of Judgement are unconditional. But on the other hand, since very early times, Muslim scholars and exegetes have argued about how to understand the world. The fact that consensus could be reached, however tortuously (and some disputes have taken generations to resolve), meant that Islam managed to do without a centralised normative institution. Consensus had always to be flexible enough to include Muslims living in such different circumstances as al-Andaluz and Indonesia afforded, which in practice meant that consensus mostly confirmed the changing worlds over which it ranged without being responsible for their factual transformation.

Consequently, Islam most importantly represents a means for world interpretation. At the beginning of the 20th century, however, this notion was rejected by the Muslim avant-garde. For them, Islam represented a closed statement about the world, with the correlate that the world and not Islam would have to change should the two be found not to correspond. Naturally, this same Muslim élite would define the terms of correspondence. The world in which these Islamists lived, worked and thought was a one of nation states. In yoking Islam and the world around them, they came to perceive Islam as a social fact, a principle by which to determine the basic patterns of society. Increasingly, the message of Islam (which often supplied nothing but the ethical maxims for social interaction within this world) secularised itself: describing and legitimating social utopias out of its text traditions, while any perception of the hereafter stepped further and further into the background.

At the end of the 1980s, the great ideological narratives had ostensibly spun their tales, fizzled out. Drafting social utopias went out of fashion. As a result, classes and social groups were no longer seen to serve anymore as categories of order. Classical Islamism turned increasingly into a kind of ethical conservatism, based on the assumption that ethical values should be safeguarded in the face of globalization. Politically, it often changed to a purely populist propaganda. The more ideological utopias (both within the Islamic world and beyond) lost their legitimacy to shape the world, the more the term 'culture' or 'civilisation' stepped into the foreground and replaced the term 'society' as the hitherto most important concept of order and social classification. Under the terms of 'culture', the world suddenly seemed decodable at a global level, without having to refer to internal-social processes anymore.

In a sense, globalization re-created 'culture' as an effective and powerful concept of its own in order to newly determine hierarchies on a global level. Former class and later national liberation struggles have now turned into a war of cultures or civilisations. Linguistic usage of the word is illuminating: throughout the 19th century, public discourse repeatedly spoke of cultural wars when addressing the struggle between Church and State (ending, as it did, with the victory of secular ideas). Pluralism reigned and these wars were seen taking place within society at every level. Today we are happy with the notion of a plurality of cultures, but war is always singularised – a direct echo of the global perspective which increasingly dominates our thinking. World wars have become a war of the worlds. This concept, describing a pluralised world arranged and determined by cultures, permits another form of mental world geography: the world is no longer divided into states, whose sovereignty is weakened due to globalization, but into cultures. This idea also fits snugly within the Islamist framework – in fact it defines their world view. Just as in former times Islamists regarded Islam as the best ideal of a society or even as equivalent to society, so Islamists of today understand Islam as a political culture which offers the best structures and concepts with which to order the world.

The functional equivalence of 'culture' to the old term 'society' is striking. Where at one time societies were regarded as a collective determinant of human action, today it is culture. Accordingly, Islam – understood as culture and thus the determinant of action – imposes its law on every Muslim. It is unsettling that those who see Muslims determined by Islam take up exactly the same position the new Islamists use: they also state that Islam ties Muslims together within a community of fate which determines their social and political identity. Some of them think of Muslims forming some sort of closed community based on common religious extraction or origin. Islam in this context is seen as a divine order to be kept independent of any human interference. Myths that describe the evolution of an 'Islamic community of fate' create a new discourse of Islamic history – Islam is more and more ethnicised.

As 'culture' has become increasingly politicized, so social and political action has been interpreted differently. Cultures do not refer any more to nation states; a 'cultural liberation movement' – as bin Laden would probably put it – is not confined to the boundaries of a specific nation state. Former national liberation movements had clear strategic goals, notably the implementation of a social utopia in a certain territory. After having 'stormed the headquarters' (Mao Tse-tung), the victory was achieved.

Nowadays, however, cultures are not constrained by nation states. They are boundless and global. Therefore 'cultural liberation' has no strategic goal within a certain adversary state and there are no more headquarters to be conquered. Instead, it is the symbols of hostile cultures that are identified as targets. The attacks on the World Trade Center in New York and the Pentagon in Washington are cruel examples of this.

Cultures are not based on utopian world-views but refer to concepts of origin and identity which have to be internalized and translated into action. That is why political discourse constantly re-invents these two terms. Islam is just as exposed to political culturalization as other traditions, discourses and religions. Muslims who try to mobilise Islam to gain political advantage can always rely on the effect of the key word culture.

At a time of concern for political correctness, the boundaries of cultural identity are guaranteed. The political culturalization of the world order has created a new explanatory script for social and political events. It is asked whether Islam endorses or promotes suicide attacks, whether Islam unconditionally calls individual Muslims to *jihad* and whether Islam ethically legitimises the use of violence. Humans do not appear any more as responsible for their actions, but as an executive power of Islam – its agents.

But their actions were never determined by normative Islamic systems. On the contrary, their interpretations reformulate Islam. Bin Laden's terrorism is not, for example, the expression of an innate Islamic readiness for violence or self-sacrifice, but the expression of his very specific world-view that rhetorically re-creates the meaning of *jihad*, power and sacrifice. His rhetoric is not conditioned by Islam – it is Islam, within his discourse, that is reconditioned by his rhetoric. In consequence, such a discourse is only successful in places where it helps to give meaning to a social reality.

Surely, this discourse is to be expected from people who consider themselves homeless and betrayed by their parent generation. That they should turn to a new ethical conservatism that believes in a community of fate ordained by Islam is no surprise. The politicization of culture promotes this feeling since it allows people to ignore any critical analysis of their social situation or of their actions by describing them as executors of a greater cultural or religious will.

Bern, November 2001

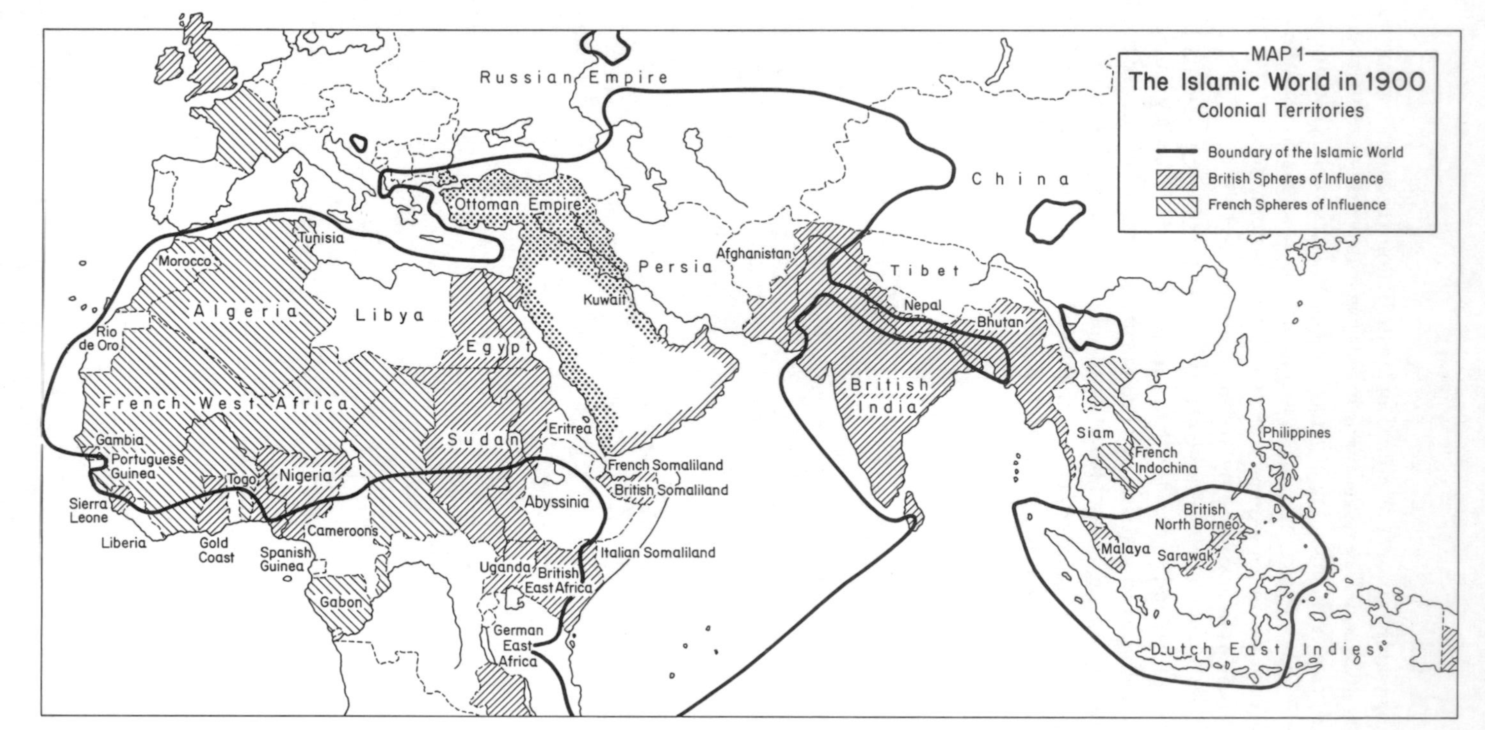
MAP 1
The Islamic World in 1900
Colonial Territories
Boundary of the Islamic World
British Spheres of Influence
French Spheres of Influence
Russian Empire
China
Ottoman Empire
Persia
Afghanistan
Tibet
Nepal
Bhutan
British India
Siam
French Indochina
Philippines
British North Borneo
Sarawak
Malaya
Dutch East Indies
Tunisia
Morocco
Algeria
Libya
Egypt
Kuwait
Rio de Oro
French West Africa
Sudan
Eritrea
French Somaliland
British Somaliland
Italian Somaliland
Abyssinia
Gambia
Portuguese Guinea
Togo
Nigeria
Sierra Leone
Liberia
Gold Coast
Spanish Guinea
Cameroons
Gabon
Uganda
British East Africa
German East Africa

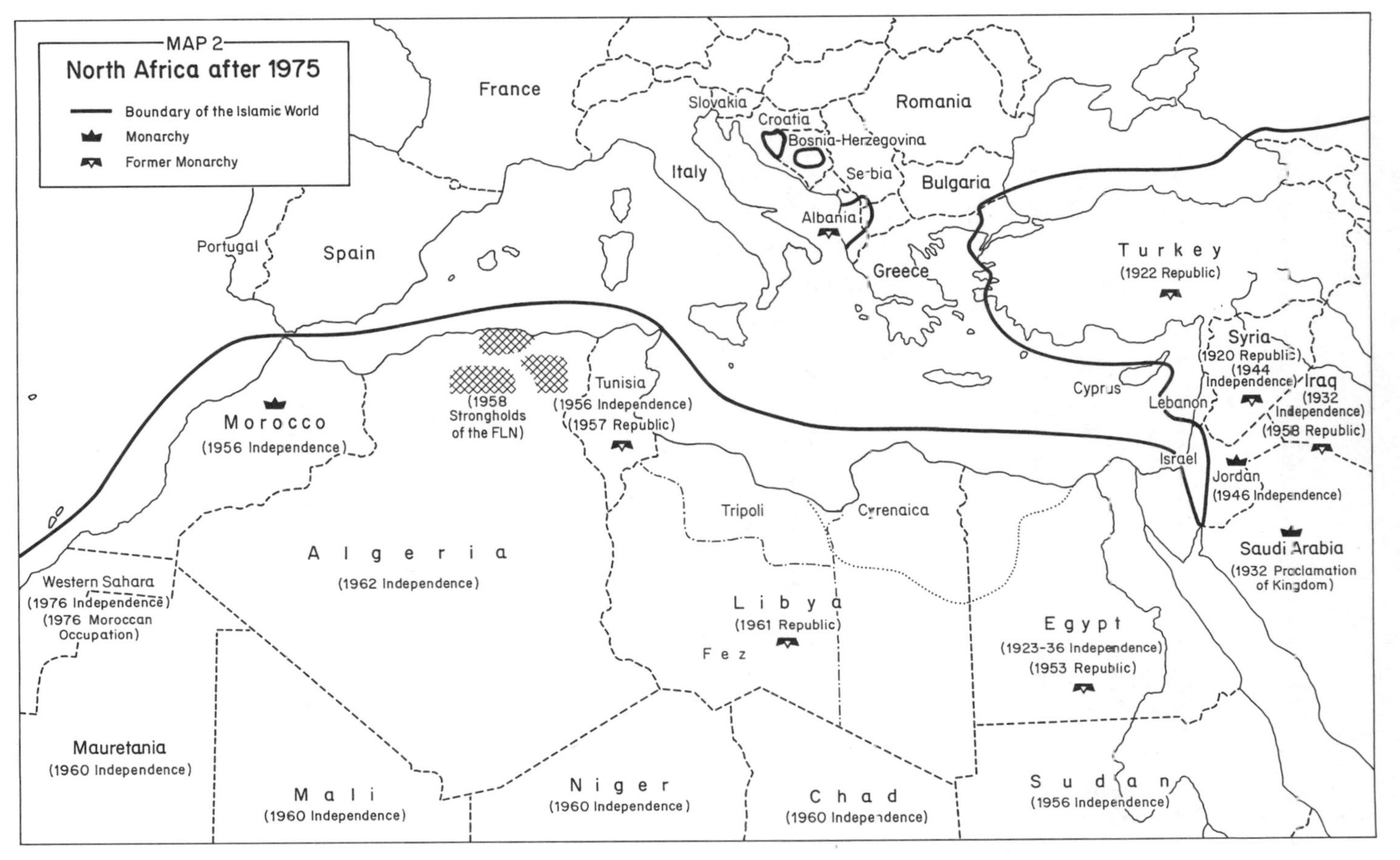
MAP 2
North Africa after 1975
Boundary of the Islamic World
Monarchy
Former Monarchy
France
Slovakia
Croatia
Bosnia-Herzegovina
Romania
Italy
Serbia
Bulgaria
Albania
Portugal
Spain
Greece
Turkey
(1922 Republic)
Syria
(1920 Republic)
(1944 Independence)
Iraq
(1932 Independence)
(1958 Republic)
Cyprus
Lebanon
Israel
Jordan
(1946 Independence)
Saudi Arabia
(1932 Proclamation of Kingdom)
Morocco
(1956 Independence)
(1958 Strongholds of the FLN)
Tunisia
(1956 Independence)
(1957 Republic)
Tripoli
Cyrenaica
Algeria
(1962 Independence)
Libya
(1961 Republic)
Fez
Egypt
(1923-36 Independence)
(1953 Republic)
Western Sahara
(1976 Independence)
(1976 Moroccan Occupation)
Mauretania
(1960 Independence)
Mali
(1960 Independence)
Niger
(1960 Independence)
Chad
(1960 Independence)
Sudan
(1956 Independence)

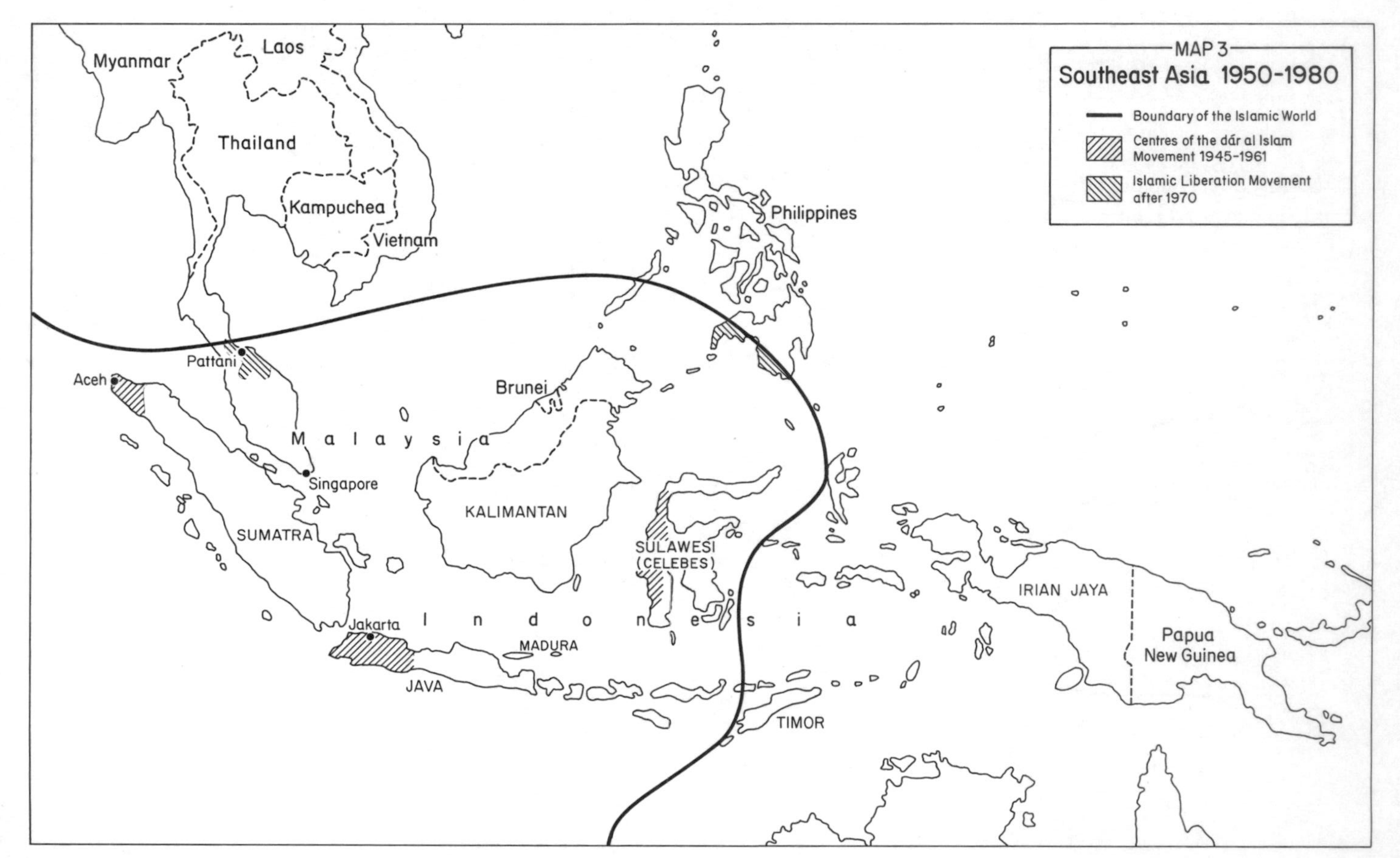

MAP 3
Southeast Asia 1950-1980
Boundary of the Islamic World
Centres of the dār al Islam Movement 1945-1961
Islamic Liberation Movement after 1970
Myanmar
Laos
Thailand
Kampuchea
Vietnam
Philippines
Pattani
Aceh
Brunei
Malaysia
Singapore
KALIMANTAN
SUMATRA
SULAWESI (CELEBES)
IRIAN JAYA
Papua New Guinea
Jakarta
Indonesia
MADURA
JAVA
TIMOR

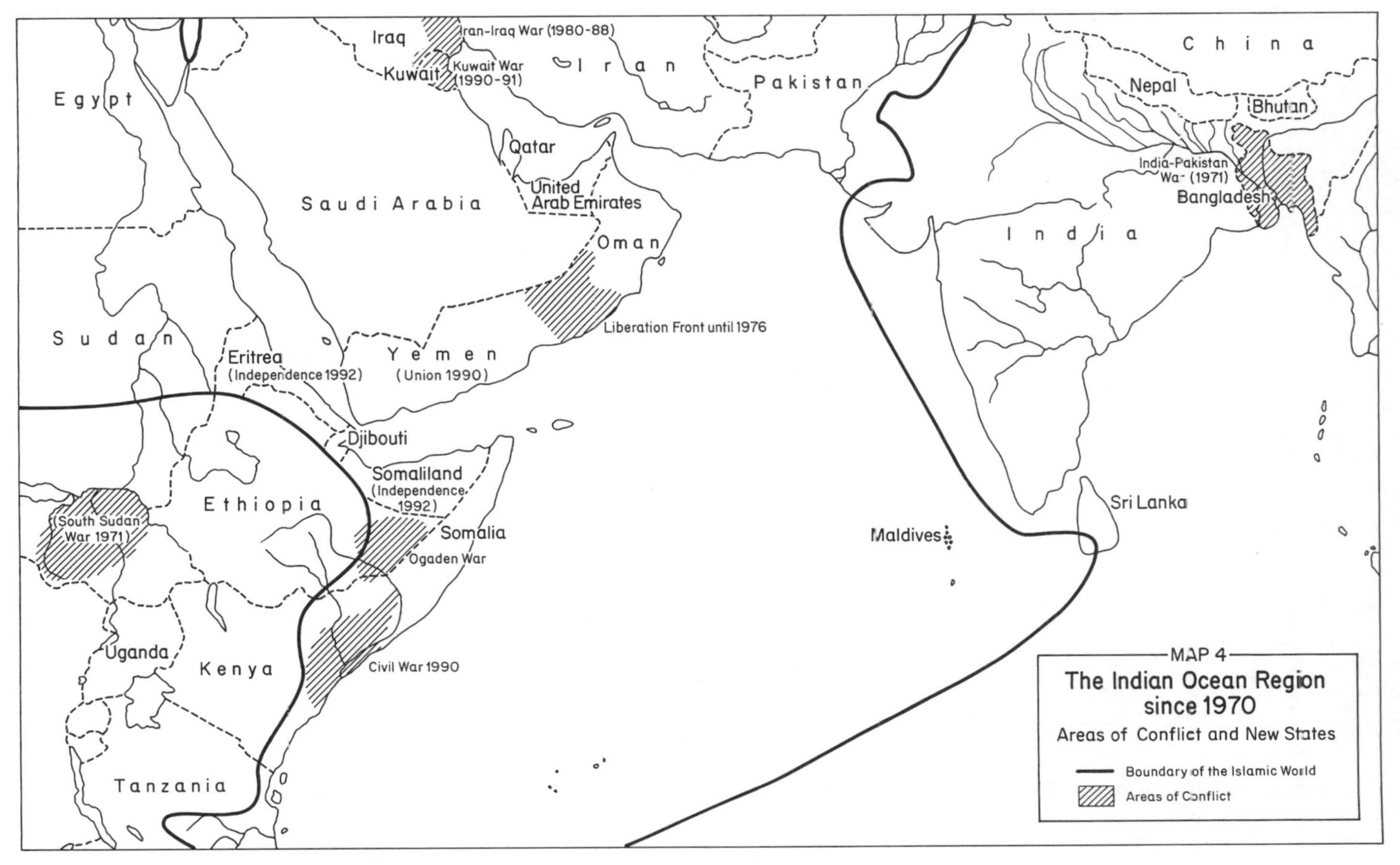
MAP 4
The Indian Ocean Region since 1970
Areas of Conflict and New States
Boundary of the Islamic World
Areas of Conflict
Egypt
Iraq
Iran-Iraq War (1980-88)
Kuwait
Kuwait War (1990-91)
Iran
Pakistan
China
Nepal
Bhutan
India-Pakistan War (1971)
Bangladesh
India
Sri Lanka
Maldives
Saudi Arabia
Qatar
United Arab Emirates
Oman
Liberation Front until 1976
Sudan
Eritrea (Independence 1992)
Yemen (Union 1990)
Djibouti
Somaliland (Independence 1992)
Ethiopia
(South Sudan War 1971)
Somalia
Ogaden War
Uganda
Kenya
Civil War 1990
Tanzania

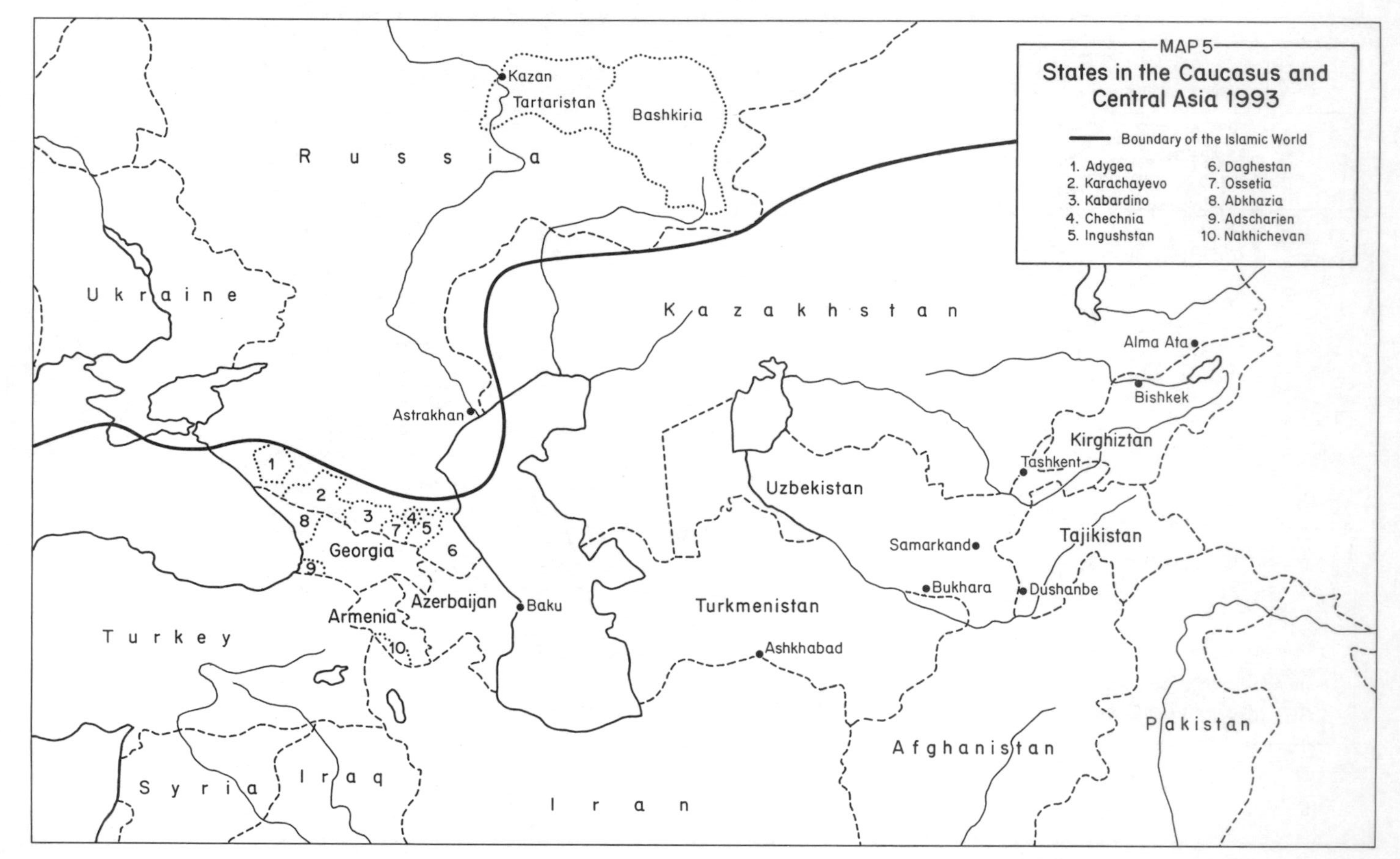
MAP 5
States in the Caucasus and Central Asia 1993
Boundary of the Islamic World
1. Adygea
2. Karachayevo
3. Kabardino
4. Chechnia
5. Ingushstan
6. Daghestan
7. Ossetia
8. Abkhazia
9. Adscharien
10. Nakhichevan
Russia
Kazan
Tartaristan
Bashkiria
Ukraine
Kazakhstan
Astrakhan
Alma Ata
Bishkek
Kirghiztan
Tashkent
Uzbekistan
Tajikistan
Samarkand
Bukhara
Dushanbe
Georgia
Azerbaijan
Baku
Armenia
Turkmenistan
Ashkhabad
Turkey
Syria
Iraq
Iran
Afghanistan
Pakistan
1
2
3
4
5
6
7
8
9
10

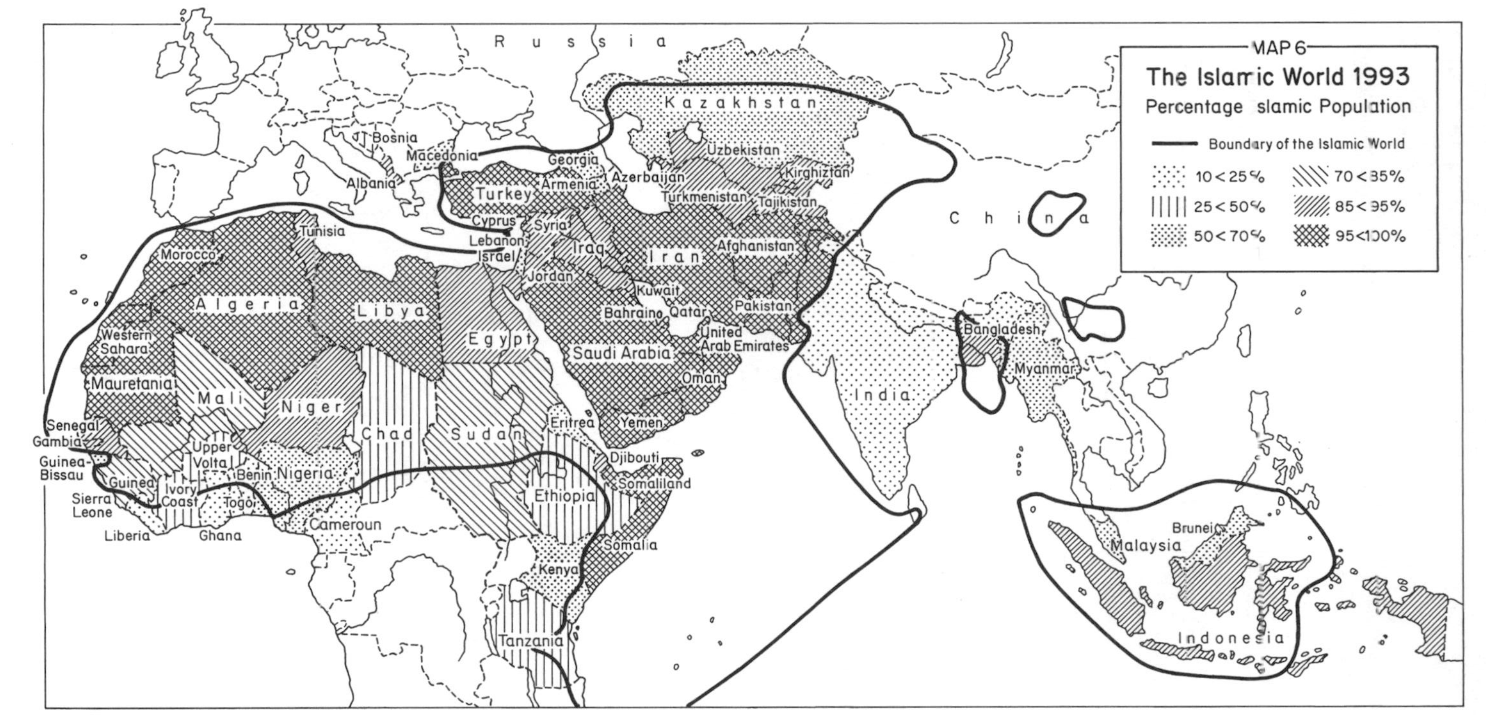
MAP 6
The Islamic World 1993
Percentage Islamic Population
Boundary of the Islamic World
10 < 25%
25 < 50%
50 < 70%
70 < 85%
85 < 95%
95 < 100%
Russia
Kazakhstan
Uzbekistan
Kirghiztan
Tajikistan
Turkmenistan
Azerbaijan
Georgia
Armenia
Bosnia
Macedonia
Albania
Turkey
Cyprus
Syria
Lebanon
Israel
Jordan
Iraq
Iran
Afghanistan
Kuwait
Bahrain
Qatar
Pakistan
United Arab Emirates
Saudi Arabia
Oman
Yemen
China
India
Bangladesh
Myanmar
Malaysia
Brunei
Indonesia
Tunisia
Morocco
Algeria
Libya
Egypt
Western Sahara
Mauretania
Mali
Niger
Chad
Sudan
Eritrea
Djibouti
Somaliland
Ethiopia
Somalia
Kenya
Tanzania
Senegal
Gambia
Guinea-Bissau
Guinea
Sierra Leone
Liberia
Ivory Coast
Upper Volta
Ghana
Togo
Benin
Nigeria
Cameroun

Introduction

The 'Islamic World' is a blanket term. It covers all those countries, regions and societies in which Muslims live together as a majority, and which are historically connected with the development of Islamic culture since the 7th century. This is traditional concept which depends on the notion that Muslims form an cultural unity, and that this unity is of greater significance than the specific traditions of individual countries or social histories. Moreover, it assumes that the Islamic world has a 'unifying bond' in the religion of Islam, that it is a space defined by its inhabitants' unified profession of Islam. Certain cultural geographers even speak of a distinct 'cultural region', which is in addition marked by certain ethnic or – to use an older term – racial characteristics. Other scholars have spoken of a specific 'cultural circle' marked by a 'common Oriental mentality'.

Such a definition of the Islamic world is based on a whole range of historical, social and psychological views that were prevalent in the 1930s and 1940s and it goes much too far. It is plausible, on the other hand, to conceive the Islamic world as a global culture: global because the limits of the Islamic world, insofar as they can be defined at all, cannot be staked out by political or social units, since the Islamic world consists of more than countries and states; and a culture because Islam consists primarily of a network of social relations that are conveyed by communication and symbolic systems and about whose content there more or less exists a consensus. It is precisely this definition that has caused 'the Islamic world' and the corresponding Arabic term *al-umma* (*al-Islamiya*) to become a conventionally accepted concept.

If the Islamic world is described as an independent cultural space or as a global culture, this means that it confronts, say, Europe or 'the Western world'. But while the unity of the West is no longer, after the secularization of the Christian Occident, defined in religious terms, in this definition religion continues to form the fundamental identity of the Islamic Orient. This is usually explained by the fact that the societies of the Islamic world have gone through no process of secularization, because, it is often argued, Islam admits of no separation between religion and state. As a result, a secular West organized into nation states confronts a religious, ethnically differentiated Islamic East.

In the last few decades, and especially after the rise of radical Islamic movements, this view has contributed to a renewal of the idea of the 'centuries-old opposition between Orient and Occident' as a conflict of systems which, 'takes the place of the ebbing East-West conflict', and marks a renewed hostility between 'Islam and the West'.

This interpretation of the relationship between 'Islam and Europe' has had a number of effects in the historiography of the Islamic world. For one thing, it demands that the Islamic world be on principle excluded from the history of modern times because it is bound to a religion which has not traversed the 'politico-ideological process' that made Europe into 'a historical idea'. Since Islam experienced neither an 'Enlightenment, nor a Reformation nor the French Revolution', which made 'religious faith reflexive and unfettering subjective freedom', it is a 'pre-modern culture' and as such it stands outside the modern global community. We may add here that, if it is true, as many would argue, that the modern world represents the second great revolution of human history after the so-called neolithic revolution then, within this framework, the gulf between the Islamic world and the West would be as wide as that between the paleolithic world and advanced agrarian civilizations.

It remains to be seen if there is any truth in these postulates. Curiously, they are repeated again and again, although no one has actually taken the trouble to find out if there is any reality in them from a historiographical point of view. In fact, there are indications that Islamic history did, as early as the 16th century, and on the strength of an independent tradition, participate in elaborating a modern culture, which in many respects shows distinct parallels with European cultural history.

These parallels may come as a surpise. But we can today at last historiographically trace back the achievements of cultural events through the centuries: we can translate the characteristics of modern history from a European into an Islamic and from an Islamic into a European context. A historiography which accepts the translatability of cultures thus makes it possible to reconstruct the communication that actually took place between the Islamic and the European worlds.

Each culture has its own language, in fact culture itself is a language. But just as facts can be differently expressed in various languages without having different meanings, cultures can present specific forms of expression of a historical process which they have in common. In cultural history the point is, of course, to recognize the facts that are differently expressed, rather than to treat the statements themselves as the content of history. We certainly come across cultural expressions which have no equivalent in other cultures; or find that one culture differentiates a fact with considerably greater care because it has acquired more historical importance in its eyes, while simplifying another because it has no precise knowledge of it. But this is merely a problem of cultural experiences. Since facts do not change with their designation, it does not change the basic pattern of translatability,

An important condition for the translatability of a historical fact is synchronism. Languages always communicate on a synchronic level. Although diachronic studies do make it possible to trace back the changes undergone by a given cultural expression within a society, that expression cannot be put into a direct relationship with other cultural languages. Thus it makes little sense to establish a relationship between 7th century Islam and contemporary Western culture, which is what happens when the statement that Islam cannot separate state from religion is made, or that Islam cannot differentiate between collectivity and individuality. This was certainly not an issue discussed in early Islamic dogmatics. But there was no need to discuss it, for in Islam there was no religious power that had to be separated from worldly power, since Islam had no clergy and no priesthood. It is precisely this feature that led to the autochthonous character of Islam, so it would be senseless to burden Islam with a problem of Christian dogmatics. However, at the same time, this hidden conflict between religion and history has also affected the Islamic tradition, so that in the course of time Islamic cultures reached specific solutions for this basic conflict found in all societies marked by revealed religions.

It is equally meaningless to speak of the backwardness of Islamic culture and, for example, try to prove it by comparing the history of Egypt in the 20th century with that of France in the 17th. This point of view disregards what Wolfram Eberhard has called *weltzeit* (universal time), that is, the time that characterizes an epoch-making context. The history of the Islamic world has never moved outside this universal time, otherwise the extensive communication between East and West would never have been possible.

Cultures communicate with one another by using the vocabulary of their own history. This kind of communication has had a lasting effect on the relationship between Europe and the Islamic world and has steadily expanded both vocabularies. But while the European world has up to the present managed to integrate the foreign cultural vocabulary, non-European cultures were, in the colonial context, forced to acquire a European vocabulary of world appropriation and world description which was outside their own tradition. The disruption caused by the colonial period was far-reaching: while itself integrating the foreign vocabulary, the European world prevented the integration of foreign societies. The Islamic world was thus forced to integrate European society without itself being allowed to appropriate European vocabulary.

The cultural effects of colonialism have not been completely realized to this day: up to the 1960s, Muslim intellectuals were convinced that precisely because of their own tradition, they could faultlessly integrate the now dominant European cultural vocabulary. However, this was prevented by Europe's claim that modernism was its own monopoly, a claim which went hand in hand with the pretence that colonialism is civilization, and which was further underpinned by a Euro-centred historiography. Thus the willingness of parts of Islamic societies to receive and integrate European values, norms, and ways of life as a natural process of intercultural communication was not acknowledged.

Basically, Europe persists even today in looking at the Islamic world in this colonial framework. For one thing, Europe has been uwilling or unable to see the Islamic world become secularized in its own image. Indeed the perception of secularism has always ended at the limits established by the European identity. Secondly, in order – among other things – to preserve its own uniqueness, Europe has always described the Islamic (as well as other) worlds in diachronic terms; that is, it has defined an 'Islamic condition' established at the time of the revelation, and looked at Islamic history exclusively in terms of the extent to which it represents a deviation from early Islamic norms.

A typical aspect of the colonial situation is the fact that this European interpretation of Islamic history has been institutionalized and assimilated by the Islamic world as part of the European discourse. This can indeed be regarded as the real source of Islamic fundamentalism. Since any narrative which has the self-emancipation of man as its theme can be seen as an emanation of European identity, the Islamic intellectuals had nothing but historical retrospective with which to explain to themselves the actual condition of self-emancipation in which they lived: Islam in its idealized original form was built up as a counterweight to the European identity, since the use of the European cultural vocabulary by non-Europeans was consistently branded as Westernization or alienation. But this marked the end of the translatability of cultural experiences: thus, for instance, the European Enlightenment could not be brought into connection with what is commonly called Islamic fundamentalism. Colonialism has thus built a trap in which any cultural expression by the colonized can be denounced on the one hand as 'fundamentalism' and on the other hand as 'Westernization'.

Since it was not just intellectual, but also, and perhaps more importantly, social, technical and economic Western phenomena that were imported into the Islamic Orient, the ban on cultural reception brought about a radical split in Islamic societies. Those sections of society which used a European discourse, despite the reproach of 'Westernization', were separated from those sections that either could not or would not use the discourse for cultural or material reasons. As a consequence a split developed between what I call the 'colonial' and what came to be known as the 'traditional' sectors of society, a split which brought about a tension that was to become a crucial characteristic of the Islamic world in the 20th century.

The most important effect of this split has been on historiography itself. Since the principle of untranslatability was maintained, Muslim historians found it impossible to describe their own history with the categories of European historiography. Thus the context of Islamic history lacks all the 'classical terms' of European historiography which describe modern times. We need only mention concepts such as 'bourgeois society', 'the general public', 'territorial state', 'nation state', 'national economy', and 'capitalism'. When they are used, it is very often declared that they are borrowed from the West and are therefore foreign to Islamic culture. The history of Islamic societies, on the other hand, is described with constructions referring to its supposed 'premodern' condition, for instance 'tribe', 'tradition', 'religion', 'clan' and 'collectivism'. All these concepts, which were of crucial importance in the history of the Islamic Middle Ages, thus continue to be used without any compunction in this modern era, which as a result ceases to be modern. The situations they describe cannot be translated into the vocabulary of European history. Thus even history stops communicating.

This leads us to the conclusion that the unity of history has been torn apart in the Islamic world (as in other non-European societies). Here, in contrast with the European world, history as what has already happened, and history as the science of what has happened, are no longer one and the same, but are broken wide apart through the ahistoricism of historiography. It therefore comes as no surprise that it is precisely the period immediately preceding colonialism, that is, roughly speaking, the history of the 18th century, that is elusive and as yet hardly intelligible. The categories of medieval history are obviously inadequate to comprehend the modern pre-colonial Islamic period. But since all categories of modern history are subject to the Western claim to monopoly, they are not applied to 18th-century Islamic history. As a result, text books of Islamic history always describe the early modern era as a period of decadence and cultural decline, or as a finale of so-called Islamic classicism.

Since there no longer exists any conformity between the events of the modern Islamic period and history as a science, we have to consider a fundamental revision of historiography. To do justice to the principle of the translatability of cultures, this revision would have to start with hypothetically applying to the modern history of Islam those categories that have hitherto been a monopoly of Europe and have at the same time created the European identity. If this leads to a plausible and meaningful result which corresponds to events, we may succeed in grasping the multilingual aspect of modernism and also providing the Islamic world with a place of its own in modern history. At the same time, we may realize that the European dialect of modernism is merely one of many cultural dialects of modernism. This multilinguism for the present only leads us to anticipate that modernism is at the same time both specific and universal and that this may be the sign of the 'universal time' which we call modernism.

Universal time is the theme of the present book. It will deal with the history of the Islamic world within the context of the universal time of the 20th century, hence with modernism in the narrow sense of the word, and will treat it as an integral part of world history. But Islamic history is also characterized by the fact that it represents its own world history. This twofold character of Islamic history will be our subject.

As I am mainly concerned with the context of the universal time of modernism, this account will – apart from keeping to a strict chronology – lay particular emphasis on the synchronism of political, social and cultural events which have gone beyond the narrower concerns of countries and acquired general historical significance. I have chosen the political public as the framework for my interpretation and inquired to what extent Islamic culture has contributed to its formation. This by no means signifies that Islam had a unique role in shaping the political public in the countries of the Islamic world in this century. Other cultural points of orientation might be just as meaningful. Thus the history of political modernism in the Islamic world might similarly be described from a comparative point of view based on anthropology, feminism, the history of ideas or social history. If we were to focus on international economy, the societies and countries which are here summed up as 'the Islamic world' might be formed into completely different groups. The overall picture might then look quite different in many respects. But it seems to me that it is legitimate to move Islamic culture as such into the focus of the study, since it has played and continues to play an essential part in formulating the political and social process.

I have intentionally refrained from stringing together studies of different countries. This would have greatly prejudiced the intended synchronism of my enquiry, making no allowance for the temporal context of modernism, which to a greater or lesser extent concerned the Islamic societies – and not only these. References to the history of separate countries and regions are therefore to be understood as illustrations. They are meant to clarify how the political, cultural and social process of 20th-century modernism affected the societies of the Islamic world, how modernism was formed from an Islamic perspective and how communities and individualities left their mark on the histories of various countries.

Since the questions asked in this book always concern the political public, I have dealt predominantly with those factors that have had a great effect over a short period. In so doing, I hope to show that the major primary force of the Islamic world in the 20th century is not Islamic culture (or even 'Islam' itself), but the temporal context of modernism, which has deeply involved the political public in supranational world affairs. As this temporal context is nothing but an aggregate of economic and social changes, which are only indirectly connected with politics, and as it can by no means be compared with what is commonly called the spirit of the age, my investigation is essentially based on factors of economy and social history, although they are only occasionally addressed as such.

The history of the Islamic world in the 20th century is marked by three characteristics which were common to all Islamic societies in varying degrees. It is precisely these three features of 20th-century history which also form the contours of what is today commonly called the Islamic world. They were always present in the temporal context of modernism, which – as emphasized by the interpretation of historical events in the Islamic world – acquired a global character in the 20th century. They determined the political public in Paris and London, as well as in Cairo and Djakarta. The only invariable constant, on which – despite many globalizing ideologies – the modern political public insisted was the territorial state. Even the appeals for the unity of the Islamic world, the Islamic *umma*, had the political effect of confirming the territoriality of the state from which this propaganda issued. Nationalism is thus confirmed as the dominant, extremely flexible 20th-century view of the world, which attributes absolute primacy to the constitution of a society as a territorial state.

1. The Islamic political public was subject to the dogma that the territoriality of a state has to be preserved at all costs. This characteristic of the 20th century (as a temporal context) is confronted with a threefold shift in ideological focus, guaranteeing the preservation of territoriality despite periods of war and crisis. In the first three decades of the 20th century, the state itself formed the ideological focus of the political public of the Islamic world. It was marked by ideologies which saw the state as the subject of the historical process and therefore identified politics with state power. The experiences of the Second World War relativized this view of the state in favour of

ideologies which gave society the rank of a historical subject. Society-oriented ideologies formed the progressive ideals of the political public until the late 1980s. It is only in the closing decades of the century that a further change has taken place, about which one can no more than speculate for the time being. But apparently the homogeneous national culture of society is receding into the background as a point of reference. Instead, there is an accent on references to smaller groups with completely heterogeneous views. In the framework of discussions about civil society, the plurality of group identities is considered as positive and welcomed as a liberation from unitary ideologies. In those areas of the world where a militarization of group relations has become possible through very specific historical developments, there are – from the point of view of civil society – so-called war lords representing group interests.

The third phase of the 20th century, however – again from the point of view of the Islamic world – does not signify an end to territoriality. It is true that certain secessionist movements have been successful, particularly in the former Soviet Union, where historical peculiarities have led to rejections which are now causing violent reactions. But even the armed units of such groups who, as in Somalia, fought with all their might against a United Nations protectorate have only rarely questioned the territoriality of the country.

These three phases have not followed one another in a strict chronological order. In fact all three concerns were at all times present in the opinion of the political public. What allows us to form a sequence is the varying prevalence of each of these political reference points. At the beginning of the 20th century, socialist programmes were already proclaiming the unequivocal primacy of society and trying to influence the political public in Islamic societies; but they met with little success. The ideals of ethnic groups were also represented in the Islamic public at an early stage. In reverse order, the two first phases had a long after-effect: ideologies of state socialism have been popular until recent years, and even the ideal of a revolutionary mobilization of society has not yet faded away. Iran is an example of the continuing conflict between statist, revolutionary and ethnic policies.

The group interests that dominate today's political public do not have any common identity. What constitutes a group as far the history of ideas is concerned is constantly changing. On the other hand, ethnic concerns are clearly gaining in importance. As a result, group characteristics are hardly any longer defined ideologically or in terms of a Utopian concept of progress, but often mythologically: thus a group affiliation is no longer established with reference to a common political aim, but by pointing to a common origin. This can lead to the creation of entirely new identities declared as ethnic. The Islamists of Upper Egypt thus suddenly emerge as champions of an ancient tribal Arab identity of the local population; or what was once Soviet Tajikistan is associated with a national Tajik culture which, from a historical point of view, has never existed. Such mythological traditions have meanwhile gained access to the political public; but it is as yet too early to judge whether they will play a decisive role in the shaping of political modernism and if they will actually be able to replace the unitarian ideologies. But in any case, these group relations are thoroughly rational forms of expression of social and economic processes.

From the point of view of the history of the Islamic world, the political modernism of the 20th century can be divided into three alternating reference points. The shift from state via society to the particular group was closely connected with the world-wide economic processes which preceded each of the changes. The plea for the state in the first decades of the century quite evidently followed the overall conditions caused by the boom of competing world economies in colonialism. The opening of world economies into cooperating systems inevitably led to a new political definition, which was additionally reinforced by the catastrophe of the Second World War. But the problem of what economic processes finally led to the replacement of society as the reference point remains to be answered by future historians. It can be assumed that the loss of sovereignty of nation states in the economic field has meanwhile gone so far that the classic nation state can only be reintegrated by way of particular group references.

2. Islamic culture offered all three stages of the 20th century a powerful linguistic expression. In this respect the history of the Islamic world is closely linked with the history of the Islamic political public. Due to the very specific characteristics of the political public in countries that had once been European colonies, Islamic culture competed to a considerable degree with political cultures that used a European discourse. What we mean here by an Islamic discourse are all media, institutions, linguistic statements and symbols deliberately using a vocabulary and a sign system which convey concepts of the Islamic tradition. The Islamic discourse is thus primarily an outward form and by no means disposes of a specific content. When, for example, 'justice' is discussed in an Islamic context, the Arabic word *shari'a* is used. But this is in fact a neutral concept which, in classical terminology, can also be applied to other religious cultures. However, since the concept *shari'a* also conveys a content involving the history of religion, it appears today as a religious concept. This still does not explain what people who speak about the *shari'a* mean by it. Depending on the context, it can actually mean justice, as well as the Islamic judicial tradition, a way of life, social practices (in the Marxist sense), state authority and the Islamic religion in

general. The same is true of the widely used term *'aqida*. In a neutral sense *'aqida* means any dogmatic system, that is any system of thought that is considered to be true. In the context of the history of religion, it of course means Islamic religious dogmas which describe the teachings of God and of his prophets and the life to come. In other contexts, however, *'aqida* can also mean theory (even in analogy with the Marxist tradition), persuasion, world outlook or ideology. The most important concept of the Islamic discourse as a whole is the *sunna*. In the history of religion *sunna* means, among other things, the traditional way of life of an Arab tribe in pre-Islamic times, and further, the traditional way of life of the Prophet Mohammad and his closest companions, and finally the way of life of the early Islamic community in Medina. In the course of time, the word *sunna* came to be used in the same sense as our 'tradition'. Within the context of Islamic politics, however, it does not denote the immediate historical tradition (custom), but the ideal life of the human being as such. This ideal is said to form the true personality of man. It may be interpreted as the meticulous copy of the way of life of the Prophet Mohammad, as claimed by some religious scholars. But the *sunna* can also mean the purely spiritual 'relationship' of a human being with Mohammad or it can describe an Islamic personality's not yet completed evolution towards the ideal.

A discourse containing Islamic terms and symbols is not necessarily religious. This discerned from the fact that it basically does not communicate with other religions, but with a 'European discourse'. The latter includes – and here I deliberately repeat myself – all the media, institutions, linguistic utterances and applied symbols expressly using a vocabulary and sign system full of the concepts of the European tradition. The European discourse is thus predominantly an outward form and by no means has a specific content. Nor does it necessarily signify that it is religiously neutral.

Both kinds of discourse communicate within Islamic societies and provide a permanent process of cultural translation. This means that Islamic terms and symbols can constantly be translated into 'European' ones and vice versa. This in turn allows for *code switching*, that is, the use of one or the other cultural language of modernism, depending on the context. Islamic parties thus interpreted the leading themes of the 'European' political public with a vocabulary of their own, which gave the outside observer the impression that these parties were religious groups. But in fact, the Islamic and the European discourse became widely assimilated to one another, and it was only with the emphasis of new reference points that they were torn apart. This again gave a dynamic impetus to politics in Islamic countries. The common recourse to an Islamic language also enhanced the awareness of belonging to one and the same 'cultural community'.

What should not be underestimated, however, is the specific dynamic proper to the Islamic discourse. For in the context of generalizing Islamic modes of expression whose aim is social mobilization, the Islamic discourse can be used by other parts of the population in a sense completely different than that originally meant. Since the Islamic vocabulary can always equally be interpreted as religious expression, there always exists the possibility that parts of the population addressed by it feel that it refers to their specific religious views of the world and are hence 'religiously' motivated in their reaction. This can have repercussions on the elites, who frequently take up the religious interpretation of the Islamic discourse and represent it in public.

3. Side by side with the succession of phases dealing with those political reference points that may be defined as pertaining to the history of ideologies, a continuous political conflict between city and country also marked the historical process of modernism in the Islamic world. This conflict is specific to those countries that had experienced an agrarian-capitalistic development in the course of colonialism. The integration of the agrarian sectors of the Islamic world into the international economy promoted cooperation, and even a community of interests, between the landowners and the urban society of the colonial powers. Thus land was distinctly upgraded not only economically, but also politically, as against cities. The classical nationalism of the 20th century was now expressed by the cities striving to become an independent power in the country and to limit, if not entirely abolish, the supremacy of land. This nationalism was fundamentally republican, and was thus also – or especially – directed against the royalist agrarian elites, who, for their own part, were trying to develop their own political and cultural profile by cooperating with the colonial powers. Finally, the conflict between the two sectors became the dominant factor in the development of the political public. Both sides kept trying to upgrade their cultural position by using the Islamic language.

Islamic culture was also politically promoted by a fourth factor: by those urban nationalists who were using an Islamic language were trying to liberate themselves from tradition. In the context of Islamic culture, tradition primarily implied the widespread mystical orders and popular ethnic-religious practices. Irrespective of ideological or social differences, the Islamic political public almost unanimously turned against popular mysticism, in fact mystical culture was in many respects considered as the expression of an altogether negative tradition that had to be discarded. In certain cases, however, the reaction to mystical cultures was regionally differentiated, for they differed from one country to another and from one region to another.

These suggested interpretations are meant to assist the reader in acquiring a better understanding of the historical process in the Islamic world. I would like to allow them a clear advantage over the many theoretical models developed for Islamic societies on the basis of widely differing disciplines. Informative as they may be in their details, they have the disadvantage that historical events as such are frequently faded out or reduced to marginal notes. The 20th century then often appears as a static unit, as opposed to the dynamic modernism of Europe. My aim in the following pages is therefore also to retrace the dynamic happenings and actions in the Islamic world in the 20th century, and to put them into a relationship with what I call the temporal context. I hope that, as a result, the independence of Islamic modernism, as well as the universality of modernism as global time will become visible and intelligible.

In the condensed space of a few hundred pages, justice cannot be done to the manifold historical events in the Islamic world. So I have reluctantly given up the attempt to include the new Islamic minorities in Africa, America, Europe and Australia, although they now have an important voice within the international Islamic political public, a voice which is also heard in traditional Islamic countries. It might equally be said that the Islamic world can hardly be defined at the end of the 20th century by geographical borders. In fact, with the migratory movements of the 20th century, the Islamic world itself is acquiring global dimensions and will, as a result, eventually lose its ancestral geographic identity. But as Islamic cultures on the continents mentioned above have so far had no access to the political public and no part in determining the historical process of these non-Islamic countries, I have decided to limit myself to referring the reader to the works of other authors on this subject.

I have also had to forgo a discussion of such social and cultural aspects of the Islamic world as cannot be treated directly in relationship to the problems broached by this book. These include specific local cultures, mystical cultures and above all, the vast field of Islamic theology and law. On these subjects, too, I refer the reader to other works.

It is only in the more recent standard works in European languages that somewhat greater attention has been devoted to contemporary Islamic history. The first overall account which no longer presents modern times as a mere appendage of the classical history of the Islamic world – usually ending in 1258, the year when the Mongols conquered Baghdad – is the volume *The Central Islamic Lands* of the *Cambridge History of Islam* edited by Peter M. Holt in 1970. A year later, Gustav von Grunebaum published the omnibus volume *Der Islam II. Die islamischen Reiche nach dem Fall von Konstantinopel* (1971). This was followed by Marshall Hodgson's famous and controversial posthumous work *The Venture of Islam* (1974). A more recent, very readable overall account is the voluminous work by Ira M. Lapidus *A History of Islamic Societies* (1988). Lapidus extensively describes the historical process in the countries of the so-called Islamic periphery and discusses the change in the history of institutions more clearly than I have done. For the Arab countries, there are several important general accounts: among the most recent publications are the omnibus volume *Geschichte der arabischen Welt* ([3]1994) edited by Ulrich Haarmann, and Albert Hourani's *A History of Arab Peoples* (1991).

The sources and bibliographical data I have quoted merely serve as documentary evidence or as references to more exhaustive and specific investigations. The books in Arabic, Persian or Turkish listed separately in the bibliography offer only a small selection of the relevant literature and are merely meant as suggestions for those who wish to devote themselves to contemporary Islamic history written particularly in Arabic, but also in Persian and Turkish. As for the titles in European languages, I have tried to show the state of historical research in a representative manner. Many of these works deal with specific subjects and contain further bibliographies on the history of various countries, regions and problems.

CHAPTER ONE

Islamic Culture and Colonial Modernism, 1900–1920

1. THE VISION OF AN ISLAMIC SOVEREIGNTY

Around the turn of the century, Abd al-Rahman al-Kawakibi, a Syrian journalist and lawyer who came from a distinguished merchant family in Aleppo reported the proceedings of an imaginary conference held in Mecca on 23 January 1899, at which Islamic dignitaries from many countries met to review conditions prevailing in the Islamic world and to discuss the possibilities of an international Islamic policy.[1] Al-Kawakibi, invented this conference as a pretext that enabled him to have his protagonists discuss the problems that preoccupied the intellectual Islamic political public in 1900.

The idea of an Islamic community, that would express the historical identity of the *umma*, had been very popular among some Muslim intellectuals in the 1870s. Many Ottoman authors and journalists, such as the distinguished Namiq Kamal (1840–88), had enthusiastically extolled the ideal of the caliphate, of which the Ottoman sultans Abd al-Majid (r. 1839–61), Abd al-Aziz (r. 1861–76), and above all Abd al-Hamid II (r. 1876–1909), had revived after the institution received international recognition at the end of the Russo-Turkish war (1768–74) in the famous peace treaty of Küçük Kainarca. In that treaty, the Ottoman sultan obtained Russian recognition as 'the sovereign caliph of the Mohammedan religion' and was acknowledged as such by the Tatar Muslims on the Black Sea Crimean peninsula. In exchange the Ottoman Empire withdrew its claims to sovereignty over the Crimea, which was annexed by Russia in 1783.[2] The notion of the caliphate, which had been little more than a shadow under the Mamluk rulers of Egypt from 1258 to 1516/17, and was virtually abolished afterwards, was thus re-introduced into international relations. But although in the late 18th century Ottoman historiography produced the legend that the last Abbasid shadow caliph al-Mutawakkil III had conferred the caliphate on the Ottoman Sultan Salim in Cairo, to begin with the Ottoman sultans made little use of the new-found prestige attached to the institution. During the long years of reform (1774–1861), problems of internal policy were distinctly more pressing. Nor, in the sphere of foreign policy, were the Ottomans very keen to use spectacular measures to emphasize their claim to the caliphate, since they did not want to jeopardize the empire's equal status within the system of the European powers of the 19th century by making a point of pursuing a separate Islamic policy.

The Ottoman attempt to create a new order (*tanzimat*) in public administration, which was meant to bring about this equal status, had at first achieved good results. The Ottoman Empire had participated in the Crimean War (1853–56) against Russia as a 'Western power' on an equal footing with France, Great Britain and Sardinia. To give prominence to the caliphate in this context would have meant jeopardizing the Empire's newly acquired place in the 'concert of powers'. Similarly, many Arab, Turkish and Persian intellectuals of the period maintained the belief that they were part of a universal modernism, in which European and Islamic civilizations could compete honourably with each other. Indeed, up to1869 the Islamic world could hardly conceive of assuming a subordinate position with respect to Europe.[3] But after 1869, just as the new Suez Canal was opened and the Egyptian Khedive Isma'il was euphorically exclaiming 'my country is no longer in Africa; we have now become part of Europe',[4] European politicians, journalists and scientists were drawing a radical line between Europe as the bulwark of modern civilization and the rest of the world, including the Islamic countries. Reflecting the attitude of many Europeans, the French pretender to the Bourbon throne, Count Henri V of Chambord wrote in his diary while visiting Egypt in 1861: 'All these Oriental nations only assume the semblance of civilization; at any moment you can see the barbarian reappearing.'[5]

The year 1869 was, then, a turning point in East-West relations. For the first time, European politicians began to perceive that their power in the Orient, which had been built up economically and commercially by European merchants from around 1820, was explicitly political and colonial. Oriental countries were in future to be judged exclusively by their position within the structure of the imperial powers. At the same time, there developed in many Islamic regions a new world outlook in which the break with the 19th-century process of modernism was discussed and re-evaluated and the idea of the unity of Muslims was brought to the fore as a means of countering the unfriendly

European power bloc. To begin with, Ottoman authors wrote with some hesitation about the cause of Islam, about the necessary union of Muslim nations under Ottoman supremacy and about the need to transform traditional Islamic culture into an independent modern culture. The idea of the caliphate had been revived after the 1774 treaty, which had also mentioned the 'Islamic nation' (*ahl-i Islam*), to be culturally represented by the caliphate, and it now came to their aid. But the Ottoman sultan's identity as caliph had to be lent a political function 'from below'. If the caliphate represented a 'nation of Islam', then it could rule Islam politically as an independent sovereign. Thus, side by side with the predominantly Muslim nation states, there emerged the ideal of a homogeneous Islamic community (*umma*), which found a powerful cultural and political expression in the 'Islamic caliphate' of the Ottoman sultan.[6]

Since the 18th century, the division between religious and temporal power had been an established fact, also admitted in the treaty of 1774. The sultanate as the state power and the caliphate as the religious symbol of cultural unity were to exclude one another, even if both functions were combined in one person. When Ottoman intellectuals like Namiq Kamal demanded the restoration of the caliphate, they did not necessarily mean that the separation between religious and state authority should be abolished. Rather, their appeal for an Islamic identity reflected their search for a concept of their own that would represent their ambition as citizens. And the best way to claim a constitutional order was through an Islamic statement. The new political Islamic language provided them with the concepts they required to describe a civic order without raising the suspicion of simply importing and copying European political concepts such as nation, constitution and division of powers.

The definition of the *umma* by the Indian philologist al-Thanawi in 1764 as a unity of religion *or* place shows that the Islam of the time disposed of secular concepts for the *umma*.[7] Religion was not a necessary prerequisite for the definition of a community. The concept *milla* had already been in use in the Ottoman language in the 18th century to describe the Ottoman subjects as a whole by contrast with the *daula*, the dynasty of the Ottomans. The *milla*, in its turn, consisted not only of Muslim subjects, but also of members of other confessions, for instance Christians and Jews who in the 18th, and particularly the 19th century, were granted an independent legal identity which was also called *milla*, or *millet* in Ottoman Turkish.

The political terminology of the 18th and 19th centuries may appear confusing. But it in fact reflects a process which was to lead to the emergence of a secular idea of the state and nation in the Islamic world. Thus the word 'Islamic' was not necessarily meant in a religious sense. In the course of the romantic or positivist interpretations of history and social thought, the idea became popular – in the Ottoman Empire among other places – that the community would only be able to liberate itself from its submissive position if it had an objective and undeniable common interest. The unifying bond (*rabitat-i ittihad*) was primarily Islam considered as a nation. The common language was the religion of Islam and Islamic culture, and the place of union was the Ottoman Empire.[8]

Many Ottoman intellectuals of the late 19th century saw themselves first and foremost as 'Ottomans'. For them the *daulat-i aliya-yi uthmaniya* was not merely the name of the Ottoman dynasty, but a concept of the Ottoman state, which they themselves meant to represent.[9] Thus the concept of dynasty was secularized: *daula* or 'dynasty' had become 'state'. This conceptual evolution can be compared with one that took place in German, which also went through the change in interpretation from the 'state' as the 'court of a sovereign' (*hofstaat*) to the civil state. It clearly reflects the transformation of the Ottoman Empire into a territorial state, which began in the early 18th century.[10] The Arab members of this *daula* of course no longer considered themselves as 'subjects', but as 'citizens' (*muwatin*, earlier *ibn al-watan*, in the 18th century *ibn al-balad*[11]) of Arab nationality, although it remained controversial whether the citizenship referred to the Ottoman Empire or to sovereign Arab countries. This is why the constitutional idea of the state was often ambiguously formulated. The idea of a nation state was universally acknowledged in the 19th century; but there was a question about defining the unity which had brought forth the nation. For the representatives of constitutionalism there were essentially two factors involved: either Islam itself or a specific linguistic tradition, Arabic, one of the Turkic languages or Persian.

Although Muslim authors had by now shown that they were able, like their German or Italian rivals, to master the political language of the 19th century, which was essentially based on French, without coming into conflict with their own Islamic tradition, they did not receive international recognition. One Ottoman author complained bitterly to a Frenchman: 'Do you find that I am quite different from a Frenchman or an Englishman when I talk to you? Do you still think that I enjoyed a European education? Everything I know I have learnt at home. I am subject to Turkish laws and Turkish morals, and yet you have to admit that I am your equal all the same.'[12]

The degradation of Islamic societies into objects of European colonialism after 1870 led to a sadly defiant reaction. Much worse than economic colonialism, which up to this point had been perceived as progress by almost all Muslim intellectuals, were the propagandist statements from Europe implying that all progress was the inalienable property of Europe, which might, if need be, endow other countries with it. The entire cultural framework of progress was to be put at the Orient's disposal as a loan, of which the colonized countries could avail themselves without having their own rights to this culture. Railway construction, the laying of telegraph lines and the development of new irrigation technologies in the Islamic countries were all marked as imports, as made in Europe. Muslims were not even allowed to create modernism on their own. Well-known thinkers such as the French philosopher Ernest Renan (1823–92) consistently argued that Islam was responsible for the fact that the Muslims were unable to develop their own progressive concept.[13] The Islamic world was in this way downgraded into a 'backward culture', a 'culture without machinery'[14] and Islam became the byword for the separation between Europe and the Orient.

Confronted with the accusation that Islam prevented Muslims from sharing equally in modernism, Islamic intellectuals, above all the famous Iranian Jamal al-Din al-Afghani (1839–1897), who considered himself an Islamic cosmopolitan, mobilized the Islamic identity, a process which was in its turn to accentuate the division between Europe and the Orient. The optimism of the years before 1870, when Islamic intellectuals still believed that they could participate in modernism precisely because of their Islamic tradition, had now turned into deep pessimism. As an analogy to Europe's critical perception of 'Islam's hostility to modernism', the Islamic tradition was now put forward as an argument for being different. Corruption, it was argued, had invaded the Oriental world because Muslims had given up Islam and turned to obscure varieties of religiosity such as popular mysticism, magic and witchcraft. The return to the 'pure' Islam of the forefathers (*al-salaf al-salih*) became the target of a new intellectual movement, which was accordingly given the programmatic name of Salafiya. The Salafiya movement was an Islamic variant of late 19th-century classicism. Indeed it is rather appropriate to compare the semantic content of the Arabic word Salafiya with the European concept of 'classicism'. Like classicism, the Salafiya sought a timeless aesthetic and intellectual ideal, derived from an origin that was pure of all temporal circumstances. In the Islamic context this could only be the early Islamic period.

Members of the *ulama* in different areas of the Islamic community now set about to work out a new Islamic theory of modernism. Their major concern was to reconcile modernism with theology and thus provide the Islamic world with an access to the modern world by way of Islamic culture. This theology was meant to be thoroughly idealistic. In the timeless example set by the 'forefathers', its exponents saw an orientation which would make Islam an upholder of progress which, in the spirit of the time, they defined as the most important characteristic of modernism. Islam was to turn towards the future, it was to be a theology that promoted the sciences and conceived the Islamic heritage as its own humanism. They quite logically traced back their ideals to the period of great Islamic humanism of the 10th to 13th centuries, which had also shown the way to European humanism.[15] Even among those of the *ulama* who distanced themselves from the classical Salafiya on theological grounds, this optimism about progress could be sensed. Thus Muhammad Taufiq al-Bakri (1870–1932), the leader of a group of mystical orders in Egypt, wrote a programmatic treatise entitled *The Future Belongs to Islam*,[16] in which he used numerous quotations from authors of the French Enlightenment in order to explain the progressive character of Islam and celebrate it as an ideal for the future civilization of the world.

Inspired by the hope of finding their own independent cultural expression of modernism, the theologists of the Salafiya took the living conditions and cultural practices of their compatriots severely to task. The whole of recent Islamic history was – again by analogy with Western points of view – described as decadent and repudiated. Those of the *ulama* who were committed to tradition were blamed for producing nothing but 'rubbish', while the nationalists, who had broken away from the primacy of Islamic culture and were trying to formulate a political programme, were criticized for their narrow-minded and opinionated policy.[17]

Even outside the narrower realm of Islamic theology, the message of the Salafiya had a stimulating effect. Writers and poets spared no effort to highlight the 'real' Muslim way of life, and abandoned the traditional patterns of literature to proclaim: 'Life is beautiful poetry!'[18] What was real to them was no longer technical progress as such, which many a poet had previously acclaimed, but the country in which they lived. The 19th century as the age of technology seemed to lose its significance for many classicists. Thus the Egyptian journalist Khalil al-Ghawish, the father of an Islamic politician who later became famous, emphatically took his leave from the past century:

> Finally I say that the 19th century has reached its end, and has even gone too far in material matters; it has also shown great shortcomings in cultural matters and in those perfect things that actually make the human being into a real human being. Its ideal of the representations of true happiness has changed, and its hopes are vanishing among worldly trifles and their show. Some may perhaps hope that the 20th century is the guarantor to lead us to that distant aim, although the first signs of this century announce the opposite of such hope. It may be that the signs will change and that the right leadership will surmount temptation. Perhaps the new century will be the evergreen oak which the woodworm will eat from the top, not from the roots. Those who live will see![19]

The scepticism of many a Muslim author about the coming 20th century had its roots in their evaluation of the general political situation. In 1895, the Moroccan historian Ahmad b. Khalid al-Nasiri al-Salawi summed it up as follows:

It is known that at this moment the Christians have reached the apogee of their strength and power, and that the Muslims on the other hand – may God lead them together again and put them on the right track – are as weak and disorderly as they could possibly be. We are, they [the European nations] and we, like two birds, one equipped with wings, who can go wherever he pleases, the other with clipped wings who keeps falling back on earth without being able to fly.[20]

According to al-Kawakibi and a few other authors, the 'despotism' of the Ottoman Empire was, above all, responsible for this general misery. Kawakibi the Syrian saw himself exposed to persecution by secret agents of the empire who belonged to a country-wide network of spys against Arab intellectuals. In 1896, the Egyptian journalist and critic Ibrahim al-Muwailihi (1846–1906) had, under a pseudonym, and after his appointment by order of the Ottoman sultan in 1894 as the under-secretary of state to the Ministry of Culture, written a sarcastic complaint about conditions in the empire. He painted a picture of a country that was ruled by mysterious conspirators, and in which the omnipresent spies of the sultan were constantly watching over the citizens. Censorship was so severe that one journalist could no longer even use the words 'French Republic' because the censor each time inserted the word 'French community' into his text, fearing the power of the word 'republic'. Journalists were not even allowed to mention the successor to the Russian throne, since it might arouse in the sultan the fear of an immediate palace revolution.[21] In any case, added al-Muwailihi, the Ottoman sultan, meaning Abd al-Hamid II, was not a real sultan, but an effeminate tyrant addicted to pleasures and women.

Yet Ottoman policy still found support in the national literatures, which enjoyed a true revival at the turn of the century; around 1900 there was nothing unusual about showing patriotic sentiments and Ottoman inclinations at one and the same time. Even politicians and authors like the Egyptian poets Ahmad Shauqi, Muhammad Hafiz Ibrahim and Ahmad Muharram, or the politician Mustafa Kamil, who considered themselves to be patriots, set great hope in the Ottoman sultanate.[22] But patriotic poems in favour of the state and ruler confronted cutting satirical texts. Others, such as the authors Wali al-Din Yegen[23] and Ibrahim al-Muwailhi, caricatured the Ottoman Empire as a stronghold of the darkest despotism. Yegen, who was deeply committed to the idea of liberalism, saw himself as a free Ottoman citizen, but although Turkish was his mother tongue he confined himself to using Arabic. For some authors Arabic was the most suitable medium to express their longing for freedom and for a new era. This was also true of the Egyptian poets of the 'New School' (*al-madhab al-jadid*) who no longer concealed their national sentiments under a show of attachment to the Ottomans, but expressed them in poetry of a highly subjective, impressionistic kind. The new era, they hoped, would liberate them from the constraints of the old order and confirm them as subjects of society.

However, the old society put up a fight. In 1900, Sultan Abd al-Hamid II wrote in his diary that the weakness of the empire, which was lamented by the followers of the 'New School' like the Ottoman nationalists and their new Committee for Union and Progress, was in fact a 'natural phenomenon' in a state comprising many nationalities. But the 'sick man' – a metaphor brought into play by the Europeans in connection with the 'Eastern Question' – would soon become strong again.[24] However, this could only happen if 'our gentlemen' could acquire a corresponding sense of economy and if men of letters could create an Ottoman ideal which would not merely be a European stereotype.[25] What was probably implied here were the republican ideas which had gradually caught on among Ottoman intellectuals, although they could not publicly express them. For in the end, said the Sultan, 'it is religion which forms the basis for the political and economic structure of the state,'[26] not the sovereignty of the people, as propagated by intellectuals like Ibrahim Shinasi, Namiq Kamal or Ali Su'awi (Suavi) since the mid-19th century.[27]

A small achievement which was enthusiastically celebrated by the pro-Ottoman Arab poets, and which put many an Islamic intellectual in an optimistic mood, was the Ottoman 'victory' over the Greek army in 1897. About 10,000 Greek soldiers landed on Crete in February 1897 to support native rebels against the Ottoman administration. Between 1868 and 1889 Crete had had a semi-autonomous status, but this had been repealed by Sultan Abd al-Hamid II, who wanted to carry out a fundamental administrative reform. Greek irredentists now found an opportunity to take open action against the Ottomans on Crete. Since they achieved no military results, the Greek government found itself forced to open a second front against the Ottomans on the mainland on 10 April 1897. But the Greek army was quickly repulsed by the Ottoman troops. Athens suddenly appeared to be threatened again, but the European powers enforced an armistice which, although not to be regarded as an Ottoman victory, at least did not mean a defeat. Crete was more or less placed under Greek administration until it was formally annexed by Greece in 1912.[28]

After the disastrous defeat of the Ottoman Empire at the end of the first great Balkan crisis in 1876/78, after the French occupation of Tunisia in 1881, the British conquest of Egypt in 1882 and the first Armenian revolts in Istanbul and in Anatolia in October 1895 and in the winter of the same year,[29] this was the first but also the last military success of the Ottoman Empire. But although at the beginning of the 20th century some pro-Ottoman Muslims still believed in a revival of the power of the Ottoman sultanate and the Islamic caliphate, the majority of the Islamic public were of the opinion that the Ottoman Empire had lost its sovereignty over the Islamic *umma* for good.

Politics among the widely divergent public of the Islamic countries now increasingly aligned itself with the realities in the nation states. Political rhetoric, it is true, still demanded some lip service to the Ottomans; but in realpolitik the prevailing policy aimed at having the native elites take charge of the new colonial administrative institutions. The dream of a Pan-Islamic replacement to fill the power vacuum within the colonial states had soon vanished. The Islamic enthusiasm aroused in 1877 by Abd al-Hamid's summons to the 'just war' *(jihad)* against the Russian empire had definitely died down, even if the numerous pan-Islamic publications still printed in the Ottoman Empire after 1900 tried to present a different picture.[30]

Al-Kawakibi did not live to see this distorted form of his vision of a supranational Islamic sovereignty. He died in a mysterious way in 1902, and the rumour soon spread that he had been poisoned by Ottoman spies.

2. THE UPHEAVAL OF 1905–1909: THE NATION STATE AND CONSTITUTIONALISM

The Islamic World Around 1900

At the beginning of the 20th century, Islamic societies were very definitely 'the product of a twofold history'.[31] European politics and economics left their mark on any development within them that impinged on the international terrain of Europe while their internal processes resulted in contradictory trends which made historical events appear in a conflicting light. In addition, the heterogeneity of the Islamic world did not admit of any unified history of the kind which Islamic classicists such as al-Kawakibi would have liked to fall back upon.

In 1900, the Ottoman Empire controlled no more than a small part of the Islamic world and about 10 per cent of the Muslim population:

The Ottoman Population 1884–1914[32]

1884	17,143,859	of which	73.4% Muslims	Non-Muslims
1890	18,400,177	of which	74.4% Muslims	(on an average)
1894	18,450,845	of which	74.0% Muslims	Greeks: 13.5%
1897	19,050,307	of which	74.0% Muslims	Armenians: 6.5%
1906	20,897,617	of which	74.3% Muslims	Bulgarians: 4.4%
1914	18,520,016	of which	81.2% Muslims	Jews: 1.1%

The ethnic distribution of the Ottoman Empire, which had become significant within the framework of nationality policies from about 1750, had made it into a state of many nationalities. Linguistically speaking, in 1900 the Ottoman state ruled over at least fourteen ethnic groups: Albanians; Arabs;Armenians; Bulgarians/Pomacs; Bosnians/Serbs; Circassians; Greeks; Jews; Kurds; Lazes; Macedonians; Roma; Turks and Turkic tribes; Turcomans. The factors determining the cultural affiliation of these nationalities included religious communities – Christian, Jewish, Manichaean, Parsi, local cults – whose distribution only rarely coincided with linguistic borders, but who contributed decisively to the formation of the millet system.

Outside the Anatolian heartland and Europe the regions that still belonged to the Ottoman Empire around 1900 were the Syrian territories of Damascus, Aleppo, Lebanon and Palestine, the Iraqi regions, Kuwait and the Arabian provinces of al-Ahsa, the Hijaz and northern Yemen, as well as the North African provinces of Tripolitania, Cyrenaica and Fezzan. The Rumelian provinces of the empire, in other words the European regions, had dwindled to a few small tracts of land after the Berlin Congress of 1878; only southern Bulgaria (Rumelia proper), Macedonia and Albania still belonged to the empire. Bosnia-Herzegovina and the Sanjak of Novipasar were, like Egypt and the island of Crete, still officially Ottoman, but were politically and militarily administered by Austro-Hungary, Great Britain and Greece respectively.

The Ottoman Empire was marked by an extreme cultural pluralism which was not, however, reflected in political pluralism. A similar situation basically applied to all Islamic societies at the beginning of the 20th century: around the year 1900, about 80 per cent of the total Muslim population were ruled by eleven colonial powers which restricted their cultural heterogeneity within the narrow limits of state sovereignty.[33]

In North and West Africa, France gradually succeeded in extending its colonial empire into the Saharan regions; only the Moroccan sultanate still preserved a formal autonomy. Great Britain controlled the coastal areas of the Arabian peninsula, Egypt after 1882, and – after the defeat of the last followers of the Sudanese Mahdi Muhammad Ahmad in 1899 – the Sudan, as well as the Muslim regions of north and central India and the Malayan principalities. In East India (Indonesia), the Netherlands had consolidated its colonial empire and, in the years 1904–6, added the last independent areas in Bali around the town of Denpasar and Sumatra to its territories. The Muslim Khanates of Central Asia had all meanwhile been subjected to the Russian empire. Even the Muslim regions of Eastern Turkestan (Sinkiang/Uighur) were under Russian influence, although they belonged to China. The United States also ruled over a small part of the Islamic world, having taken the Philippines from Spain in 1898. The only independent territories were the Ottoman Empire, Persia, Afghanistan and Morocco. And even these were often called semi-colonial, since essential parts of their national dealings depended on the decisions of European powers, particularly France and Great Britain.

A Muslim Intellectual Looks at the Islamic World

In the eyes of the journalist Kawakibi, however, the Islamic world consisted above all of Arab regions and cities (Aleppo, Damascus, Jerusalem, Alexandria, Cairo, Yemen, Basra, Najd, Medina, Mecca, Tunis, Fez), of Turkish regions (Anatolia, Crimea, Kazan, Kashgar), of the Persian–Indian region (Kurdistan, Tabriz, Afghanistan, India, Sind), and – as representatives of Islamic minorities – of England and China. He did not include Black Africa, or the Malayan archipelago or Dutch East India. Although by this choice Kawakibi meant to suggest the international nature of the Islamic *umma*, the privileged position he gave to the Arabs of the east, the 'Mashriq', is obvious. The representatives of other Islamic countries, who had presumably participated in Kawakibi's Meccan conference, each supported certain traditions that were part of their local Islamic cultures; these were meant to prove that although Islam had to a certain degree produced a unified culture, regional and local traditions continued to play an important part. The Indian representative, for example, was immediately identified as a member of the Naqshbandiya, a famous mystical brotherhood which had contributed a great deal to the formation of the Salafiya in India.[34] Chinese Islam, appears to have been an unknown quantity even to Kawakibi, for he contented himself with the remark that there Islam was relatively 'truthful' (*hanif*) and had not been weakened by internecine feuds.[35] Even the Chinese had to do their bit to support Kawakibi's plea for an Islamic democracy.

A special role was played in the conference by the representative of Najd, part of the Arabian peninsula which was at the time not under direct colonial administration. Kawakibi described him as the vehement champion of a 'purified' Islam, who especially fought against 'illicit innovations' (*bida'*) and superstitions. He thus deliberately placed him within the tradition of the Wahhabiya, a pietistic 18th-century movement initiated in Najd around 1744–45 by the scholar Muhammad b. 'Abd al-Wahhab (1703–92). The Wahhabiya movement did not at the time have much standing in the Islamic world, since the majority of Muslim intellectuals saw it as the expression of a thoroughgoing desert culture which had excluded all other Muslims from the Islamic umma because they would not follow its pietistic rules and dogmas. Kawakibi, however, was one of the first Islamic intellectuals who tried to integrate the Arab pietism of the Wahhabiya into the classicism of the Salafiya and he made a point of praising his Najdi sheikh's reconstruction of the Islamic *umma* and of presenting him as the true Islamic conscience. For him the quintessential Arab nature, as embodied by the 'free' tribes of Najd, was the guarantor of a 'pure' Islam.

Colonial Powers in the Islamic World (1900)

1. Great Britain	Egypt, Eastern Sudan, Kenya, Gulf Coast, Kuwait, Southern Arabia, Indian territories, Malaya (except for the principalities of Kedah, Kelantan and Terengganu, which were tributaries to the kingdom of Siam), Sarawak and northern Borneo, northern Somaliland, northern Nigeria, northern Ghana – 100 million Muslims.
2. Netherlands	Sumatra, Java, Borneo, Celebes – 30 million Muslims.
3. Russia	The former Turkic Khanates, northern Caucasus - 15 million Muslims.
4. France	Northern and western Africa, Saharan regions, western Sudan, Djibouti, Comores, Indochina – 15 million Muslims.
5. China	Sinkiang, Central China (Hui) – 10 million Muslims.
6. German Empire	Territories in East Africa, Northern Cameroons (Adamaua) and Northern Togo – 3 million Muslims.
7. Austria-Hungary	Bosnia, Novipasar – 2 million Muslims.
8. Italy	Southern Somaliland – 1 million Muslims.
9. Portugal	Coastal areas of Mozambique – 0.5 million Muslims.
10. USA	Southern Philippines – 0.3 million Muslims.
11. Spain	Rio de Oro (Western Sahara) – 0.2 million Muslims.

Total population: at least 160 million Muslims

Independent States

Ottoman Empire:	20 million
Persia:	10 million
Arabian Peninsula: (Najd, Shammar)	5 million
Morocco:	4 million
Afghanistan:	2 million

Total population: ca. 41 million Muslims

After his death, the proceedings of Kawakibi's fictitious congress were republished by Muhammad Rashid Rida, the chief editor of the *al-Manar*,[36] the organ of the Egyptian Salafiya. But essential passages of the 1899 edition were altered because, according to Rida, Kawakibi spoke very poor Arabic and his text often led to 'misunderstandings'. Rida also admitted that he had made additions to al-Kawakibi's text while the latter was still alive, although he was only partially authorized to do so.

The Arabian Peninsula at the Beginning of the 20th century

The Wahhabiya was the supporting pillar of a fairly recent Arab tribal culture which had already given attracted attention in the 18th and 19th centuries. Often mocked by the *ulama* of other regions because of their 'un-Islamic culture', the Arab tribes had found in the Wahhabiya an expression for a new concept of the state which had revalorized their tribal dominion. A number of smaller Arab principalities had already been merged in 1745–1808, and again in 1848–86, under the 'Saudi' dynasty, and were subsequently united as a self-contained territorial domain named after the princely Al Sa'ud family who were to protect the Wahhabi doctrine as a secular power. In the late 19th century, however, the Al Sa'ud were defeated both politically and militarily by the princes of Shammar, the Al Rashid. Officially the principality of Shammar still paid tribute to the Ottoman Empire, so that when in 1886 its troops conquered Riyadh, the Al Sa'ud capital, much of the Arabian peninsula came under the nominal sway of the Ottoman Empire. Only on the southern coast and on the shores of the Gulf, where Great Britain had contracted a large number of protectorates with local principalities between 1824 and 1892, was the situation different. The Gulf emirates, still known at the time as the 'Trucial Coast', as well as Qatar, Bahrain and Oman were administered by the Government of India because they belonged to the British–Indian sphere of influence. The Arabian peninsula was thus by 1900 divided into two clearly distinguishable spheres of influence. The Ottoman Empire – which appeared ready to give up its 'unproductive' Rumelian provinces, and, within the framework of a new 'eastern orientation', relied much more on its Arabian provinces – now controlled not only the Islamic holy sites of Mecca and Medina, but also the important internal Arabian trade from southern Iraq to the shores of the Red Sea. Kuwait and the eastern Arabian province of al-Ahsa became the starting point for a new Ottoman policy directed towards India. The project for a railway from Istanbul to Basra in southern Iraq (the famous Baghdad railway), worked out by German and Ottoman engineers, was meant as a counterpart to the Suez Canal, which, since its inauguration in 1869, had become part of the Western European trade network.

Great Britain tried with all its might to prevent the construction of this railway and, by occupying Kuwait,[37] which had been an independent principality since 1782, it intended to neutralise its utility as well as to secure its hegemony in the Gulf. Internal disputes within the Al Sabah family of Kuwait, which the Ottoman Empire had not at this stage claimed as its own territory, enabled the colonial officers of the India Office to appear as a 'protective power' which could support the Amir Mubarak against his opponents. Thus the Ottomans and the British were lunged into conflict over the tiny territory of Kuwait, again reflecting the geopolitical interests of the European powers.

The hegemonic interests of Great Britain and the Ottoman Empire contributed to the extension of the Kuwait conflict to other parts of the Arabian peninsula. British officials promised the members of the Al Sa'ud, who after their defeat at the hands of the Al Rashid, had been living in exile in Kuwait, logistic support to reconquer their lost territories. Subsequently, in January 1902, the tribal federations led by prince Abd al-Aziz b. Abd al-Rahman Al Sa'ud (died 1953), who was later to become King Ibn Sa'ud, succeeded in occupying Riyadh and in founding a new independent Saudi dominion, the so-called 'Third Saudi State', which was, however, slow to expand.

Hegemonic Conflicts

In other Islamic areas, too, European hegemonic conflicts recurred on a small scale, marking the development of new states. A well-known example is eastern Sudan which, after the British conquest in 1899, came under an 'Anglo–Egyptian' condominium, a kind of joint British–Egyptian administration. The French conquests in western Sudan had met with the violent resistance of the military ruler Rabih b. Fadl Allah, who had established himself in Bornu in 1893 and was not defeated until 1900. In the course of these wars of conquest, French legionaries had penetrated as far as the Sudanese city of Fashoda (Kodok) where, in the autumn of 1898, they had come across British contingents advancing from the east. The conflict over spheres of influence in north-east Africa was settled in an agreement in 1899 under which Darfur, the eastern province of the old Mahdi empire, was joined to Sudan. In exchange, France was given a free hand to occupy the last Muslim empires in North Africa – Bornu, Kanem and Wadai – and to transform them into the military region of Chad.

The state in the Islamic world was, at the beginning of the 20th century, shaped by three crucial factors. Initially, the majority of the colonial states depended on the political, economic and social traditions which had already been decisive in determining a territory before the 19th century. The colonial powers then adapted these traditions to suit their interests and aligned those territories in which older state or ethnic traditions ran counter to colonial interests. Finally, all colonial regions were adjoined to power blocs centred on Europe, so that even local political events, like the conquest of the city of Riyadh, were only possible within the context of international power politics.

This interdependence between local history and European power politics was characteristic of all Islamic societies from the time colonial structures assumed a stable form. Territories that were at this stage conceived as colonial regions formed the nucleus of later national identities. The native elites of these territories were by no means disinclined to accept the results of the colonizing process in their main features. They had found in the new colonial states a political frame of reference which closely corresponded with their fields of social action and was much less hypothetical than the concept of a united Islamic world. For these states disposed of exactly those political institutions in whose power they wanted to share. Through taxation, laws and military power, the colonial administration had secured geographically circumscribed, surveyable areas which, from the 18th century, had often formed the basis for a nation-state identity of the elites. In a curious way, colonialism thus confirmed the tradition of many Islamic societies as principalities, a tradition that had prevailed in the 18th century. In places such as North Africa, where colonial policy kept to the previous state borders, the old place names were essentially preserved. Following the linguistic usage of the 18th century, capital or residential cities provided a name for the country: Algeria (Algiers), Morocco (Marrakesh), Tunisia (Tunis), Misr (Cairo and Egypt), al-Sham (Damascus and Syria), Kuwait. Politically significant regional designations similarly became the names of state territories (Sudan, Yemen, Hijaz, Iraq, Oman). New names were only given to the three provinces of Tripolitania, Fezzan and Cyrenaica (Libya, 1911), which still belonged to the Ottoman Empire, and to Mauretania (the ancient Shinqit region, 1903).

However, politically, the dominant system in the Islamic world around 1900 continued to be the idea of empire, which demanded that the prince also appear as the protector of the faith. This was as true of the British kings as of the Ottoman sultans, who now enhanced their sovereign power with the title of caliph in order to substantiate their claim as protectors of Islam. This concept of the sultanate was at the time only to be found in those countries which were not directly subjected to colonial power: in the Ottoman Empire, in Morocco, Persia, Afghanistan and in the principalities of northern Malaya. Some regions in the colonies were also ruled by sultans, for instance in Nigeria, northern Cameroon, in India and on Java; but here the colonial powers had deliberately preserved the sultanate as an institution in order to reduce costs by using indigenous administrative structures. These small sultanates no longer, however, marked the borders of a nation state, which was placed over them like a bell. The title 'ruler over the faithful' (*amir al-muminin*) – a concept that comes close to the title of some European monarchs as 'defenders of the faith' – was used above all by the Ottomans and the Alavite Moroccan sultans, as well as the Persian shahs of the Qajar dynasty (1779–1925); but the Sultan of Sokoto in northern Nigeria also used this title to make up for his loss of authority through the colonial state by stressing his religious legitimacy.

In most Islamic regions, the nation state identity of the elites had become self-evident by the year 1900. The focus of political conflict was the colonial state, for hardly any of the nationalist movements had irredentist tendencies. Indeed, some Islamic intellectuals complained that the Muslims had had no Garibaldi or Bismarck to produce new state units over and above the limits confirmed or created by colonialism. The impact of nationalism on Islamic countries was, however, primarily confined to domestic politics and largely concerned the question of who had the right to wield power in the modern state. In this context constitutionalism stood at the heart of nationalist demands, a constitutionalism, however, that was mainly directed against the European rule whose power was compared with the power of autocratic monarchs. Thus the nationalist intellectuals first sued for their right to participate in decisions and institutions, but in the course of time radicalized their position and finally demanded the abolition of European rule.

Similar claims were raised by intellectuals in those Muslim countries which were not under the direct or indirect political control of European powers. In such countries, primarily the Ottoman Empire, Iran and Afghanistan, the demand for constitutionalism was directed against sultans who still reigned as absolute monarchs. According to many of the nationalists, state sovereignty should be directly exercised by themselves. They even claimed the right, as did the Ottoman political poet Mehmet Ziya Gökalp (1876–1924), to appear as 'protectors of the faith', since they believed that the function of the caliph had to be carried out by the political will of the Muslims themselves.[38] This point of view had already been adopted in 1887/89 by the Ottoman opposition group the Committee for Union and Progress (Jami'yat-i Ittihad wa-Tarraqi), previously the Society for Ottoman Union (Jami'yat-i Ittihal-i 'Uthmani). To the Committee's supporters, the slogan 'down with the *padishah*', which could be heard in the streets of Istanbul after 1906,[39] signified the assumption of power by the nation; the role of Islam was to express this demand symbolically. In the struggle for constitutionalism, religion was thus subordinated to the political aims of the nation. For this point of view, the partisans of the union could quote important advocates. As early as 1855, the opposition historian Ahmad Jaudat Pasha (1822–95), had written that Islam was in fact ruled by two nations (*millet*), Arabs and Turks, but that the Turks had made the decisive contribution to its civilization.[40] Implicitly, he thus demanded the restoration of national sovereignty by way of Islam.

Constitutionalism and the claim to sovereignty were the central aims of Muslim civil societies which, from about 1860, had begun to detach themselves from the sultan's sovereignty and follow their own, albeit very diverse, political programme.[41] In this connection, Islam primarily formed a linguistic medium in the broadest sense of the word, which was brought into play in the struggle for a programme of citizenship. But from early on Islamic theologians opposed this politicization of Islam, fearing that its use as an ideological tool might immediately endanger the religiosity of the individual believer. Even the co-founder of the Salafiya, the Egyptian mufti Muhammad Abduh (1849–1905), inveighed against the political programmes of Islamic nationalists in Egypt: 'When you state that politics suppresses thought, knowledge or religion, then I belong to those who say: May God preserve me from politics, from the word politics and from the content of politics!'[42]

According to Abduh, politics could not be allowed to 'suppress religion'. It always had to submit to the aim of theology, which was to protect religiosity. Many members of the Salafiya were later to embrace this point of view. However, for the nationalists, who used Islamic symbolism and language, the primacy of politics was an established fact; in their opinion, Islam was not only meant to establish the ethics of an internal, ascetic way of life, as claimed by many pietists; its most important task was to found an independent policy focused on the idea of sovereignty.

Colonial Crisis and Constitutionalism

The restless years between 1904 and 1909 show how deeply the Islamic world had become involved in international events and how much it was influenced by contemporary political developments. It is true that no causal relations can be established, say, between the Russian Revolution of January 1905, the Persian Constitutional Movement of 1906, the nationalist propaganda in Egypt in 1906 and the Young Turk coup in Istanbul in July 1908. But the political climate of the pre-war period in the Islamic countries was not very different from that in the European states. Colonial expansion which, from 1878 to 1896, had brought relative peace to the Islamic countries was evidently threatening to succumb. The 'golden decade' of colonialism (1896–1906) was coming to an end now the world was almost entirely occupied. Countries that were not yet directly controlled had long been divided up among European interests by means of secret agreements such as the 1900–1902 agreements between France and Italy concerning Morocco, which was so far independent, and Ottoman Tripolitania.[43] The events surrounding the Fashoda crisis of 1898–99 had similarly brought about an adjustment between the imperial interests of Great

Britain and France in North Africa. Even the Ottoman Empire had long been divided up on the drawing-board into French, Russian, British and Austro–Hungarian spheres,[44] and Persia under the Qajars was threatened with division into a Russian and a British zone.

Although political colonialism had managed to enforce its sovereign rights, the colonial economy had fallen into a deep recession. For many financiers and merchants the colonial market had become an attractive field for speculation. Their motto was to make large profits as quickly as possible without investing too much of one's own capital on a long-term basis. As a result, less and less European capital was invested in Islamic countries; instead, massive speculation caused a flight of capital back to Europe and threatened to rot the economic foundations of colonialism. The state budgets of the European colonial powers were being drained. In addition, the intricate inner-European power diplomacy (Entente Cordiale 1904) demanded more and more miltary spending, so that the colonies had hardly any public resources at their disposal.

At the same time, the colonial economy, for instance in Egypt, Indonesia or the Ottoman Empire had reached the limits of its development. The cultivation of cotton, wheat, jute and sugar, as well as the extraction of rubber, reached a peak around the year 1904. After 1907, the export prices of silk from Syria fell by about 10 per cent.[45] In addition, the United States intensified its activity on the world market, threatening to do lasting damage to the classical colonial structure. Some contemporary observers, especially those who were directly interested in financial affairs, were already foretelling the end of the colonial era.[46]

The real situation was certainly not quite so dramatic and the foreign trade of the colonial states soon recovered from the speculative crisis of 1905/6. In most Islamic societies, however, the (temporary) standstill of colonial expansion led to grave problems of internal policy. The native elites who, until about 1900, had for the most part been thoroughly optimistic about the process of colonization, viewing it as a specific expression of modernism, now found themselves cheated of its fruits. They saw that the economic development of 'their' countries depended much too directly on the interests of the European powers, and they demanded a 'national stock-taking'. Nevertheless, the social and political structures of most Islamic countries were so firmly embedded in colonialism that, in the opinion of many nationalists, the existence of modern states in the Oriental world depended on whether it would be possible to preserve the colonial structures in a different form.

The great constitutional movement of the years 1905 to 1909 was essentially a political movement to rescue the state at the end of the colonial development boom. Japan had shown in the war against Russia in 1904/5 that a non-European power could triumph over the 'old powers' if it also liberalized itself politically. So the Japanese victory of 1905 was euphorically celebrated even among Muslim intellectual circles, who praised it as a model for the 'victory over the colonial powers'.

Political Ideologies on the Eve of the First World War

The constitutional movement in the Islamic world was supported by widely differing political forces. In each case, however, the various parties aimed at curtailing the power of the sultans or that of the European colonial administrations which had replaced them, and at appointing a native civil government and administration which would claim its own political sovereignty. Three major political tendencies provided the constitutional movement with its decisive orientation. First of all, the representatives of the liberal middle classes came together to demand a constitutional regime, without a simultaneous redefinition of the identity of the state as a whole. They wanted, for example, to preserve the Ottoman Empire as a pluralistic civic regime. For the liberals, the idea of a nation state was primarily based on the conviction that society had to consider itself as a 'historical' nation without throwing into relief any 'objective affiliations' such as religion, culture, race or language. More than almost any other political orientation, the liberals identified themselves with the national market, which to them represented the focus of the state.

On the other hand the second tendency, the urban nationalists, thought of themselves as true 'positivists'. Closely following the theories of the French sociologists Auguste Comte and Emile Durkheim, they considered race, language and history as an 'objective state of affairs' which no member of society could escape. The legitimate authorities in society were, in their opinion, those ideals or characteristics which determine the unity of the nation. To them Islam was in this context a necessary, but by no means sufficient element. The acquisition of political power by the nationalists would put them in a position to reform society on the basis of its 'objective' factors. This was also, fundamentally, the point of view of the Islamic classicists, the Salafiya. For the Salafiya, however, Islam was the superior characteristic of a nation state identity, and they therefore provided Islam with the typical positivist definition of an objective, social state of affairs. This national culture was, as already mentioned, of a thoroughly urban nature.

The third party consisted of those political groups which contemporary literature usually calls 'Islamists'. To them Islam was a mark of revolutionary identity which the people could assume in order to seize power. Islam was viewed as the only true political expression of the people vis-à-vis the ruler. In this sense, the Islamists clearly distanced themselves from traditional Islamic scholarship which saw the preservation of Islamic knowledge and culture as its sole task, for which it believed it was protected by the state. National identity, said the Islamists, could only be achieved in a subjective act of popular rebellion based on Islamic ethical principles. Accordingly, it was the Islamists who most vehemently demanded the unity of religion and state, which would guarantee the people (symbolically represented by religion) sovereignty (symbolically represented by the state). This culture also had its centre in the urban societies; its followers, however, saw themselves as more closely linked to those circles of the urban population who directly suffered the results of the colonial crisis, that is, with artisans and merchants and the 'little people' of the city quarters. Not to be underestimated are the ties of the Islamists with the mystical Islamic orders whose members, with their regional distinctions, had great influence on the everyday world of the 'little people', and whose elites were also to be found in the state administration and in urban bourgeois society.

In the Islamic societies of the late 19th and early 20th centuries there had thus emerged certain political tendencies which showed distinct analogies with the overall pattern of political parties in Europe. There, modernism had brought into being three main currents of political theory (nationalist, liberal-conservative and socialist), which equally manifested themselves in the Islamic societies, although outwardly the use of Islamic language in political matters relativized this analogy by throwing into the debate religious terms that showed no immediate relationship with contemporary political theories. The Islamic linguistic tradition created a synthesis comparable with that found in Zionism which, under the influence of a Jewish linguistic tradition, produced a synthesis of religion and its aspirations to a nation state. In both cases, however, ideological content prevailed over religious symbolism. Islamic culture quite evidently did not raise any barriers against the political theories of modernism; it merely gave them a specific emphasis through the use of religious symbolism, thus determining the accompanying political rhetoric.

Social revolutionaries, nationalists and bourgeois liberals thus represented the real political system in almost all Islamic countries. Although all three groups were involved in the discussions about the new definition of the nation state, they did not simply refer to their particular leitmotif as a measure of their identity. Islam, race and citizenship were rhetorical points of reference, to be sure; but each group had a completely different idea of the respective validity of these concepts. For the radical nationalists, such concepts as race and language were 'objective' realities to which society had to submit if it wanted to become a nation. The liberals, on the other hand, considered the idea of civic freedom as a means to national emancipation – only those who deliberately embraced this principle could become a nation. Finally, the Islamists considered the Islamic human being as the expression of a divine historical will. The moment a human being became aware of his intrinsic Islamic nature, he would find the way to freedom and emancipation from the constraints of the old order.

This picture of society and humanity rounded off the new political ideologies. Islam, race and citizenship as such did not produce any clear political contours, for as concepts they were also important to other groups. Thus an Egyptian liberal like Gurgi Zaidan (1861–1914), who was himself a Christian, could rave about the Arab race, celebrate Islam as a cultural ideal and call for civic freedom without at the same time falling into political syncretism or becoming a social-revolutionary national liberal. Zaidan's cultural and political affiliation manifested itself when he set his ideals of freedom above all other concepts and gave prominence to Islamic history and to the Arab people in their longing for freedom.[47]

Similarly, the nationalists, who belonged for the most part to an Islamic tradition, also created their own Islamic conceptual world. However, unlike the dispersed social-revolutionary or populistic groups, they did not regard Islam as a subjective category of society. The parties of the Young Turks – the term 'Young Turks' was probably coined in 1877 by Khalil Ghanim (1846–1903), a Maronite Lebanese exiled in Paris – immediately adopted the ideas of union and progress as the designation for their secret society. Radical Islamists like the members of the Egyptian 'Islamic Union', who became known for their murderous assaults in 1911, also considered themselves as representatives of the Egyptian nation; but they did not content themselves with maintaining that the nation consists of 'objective' characteristics; instead they summoned society to become the subject of its own history through Islam. This may explain the close affinity at the beginning of the 20th century between Islamists with a social-revolutionary approach and atheistic socialist and communist groups – an affinity which the revolutionaries in Russia made use of after 1917 to celebrate Islam as a socialist-oriented liberation ideology.

These three currents were none other than the expression of a kind of political modernism in the Islamic countries, which had lost all links with direct tradition. The common enemy was tradition, and with it the political system of sultans and colonial lords sanctioned by tradition. Tradition was contrasted with modernism, which was differently understood, depending on the social provenance of the elites. So no matter to what extent Muslim intellectuals used a political Islamic language to express their demands, their political culture was an essential part of colonial modernism.

Constitutional Demands

The constitutional movement marked its first success in Persia in 1906. On 5 June, a year after the revolution in Russia, the opposition movement, led by the liberal Ihtisham al-Saltaneh, carried through its proposal for a constituent assembly. The movement, which counted prominent Islamic dignitaries and merchants among its leaders, and which had first emerged in connection with the 'Tobacco Revolt' in 1890–92, produced a constitutional charter in August 1906 and fought its way to holding elections for a national parliament. The latter, however, was elected according to a very restrictive suffrage of six classes, in which the capital Tehran was distinctly over-represented from a political point of view. Although the electoral laws only admitted 'God-fearing' parliamentarians, its representatives included members of the Qajar court and of the traditional learned society as well as liberal deputies, nationalists and social revolutionaries. The Persian constitutional movement indeed succeeded in creating a large political public, and in drawing into its debates the so far apolitical bazaar, that is, the traditional merchants and traders in Tehran and in other Persian urban centres; but it was not, in the long term, successful. The coup d'état against parliament on 23 June 1908 by Muhammad Ali Shah Qajar with Russian support, showed how little resistance the opposition managed to put up against the old political order. Even the parliament, re-formed in 1909, hardly served to promote the constitutional movement.[48]

The Russian revolution of 1905 also had a direct impact on other Islamic regions. In Azerbaijan there were bloody conflicts between the Dashnaks, followers of the Armenian Revolutionary Federation, and Muslim groups which extended as far as Tiflis and are said to have caused the destruction of almost 300 villages.[49] In these restless months Liberals, Nationalists, Socialists and Islamists were able to form their own organizations and to acquire seats and votes in the local Duma of Baku. Their influence on the events in Persia, and above all in Tabriz where members of the opposition aided by Azerbaijanis stood their ground for a while against the Shah's counter-revolution, was considerable.

In Turkestan, too, the 1905 revolution established the foundations for a new political culture shared by liberals, nationalists and Islamists.[50] Here, as had already occurred in an incipient fashion in Baku, the affinity between Islamists and Social Revolutionaries became apparent, for the majority sided with the Bolshevik faction which had split off from the RSDAP in 1903.

The greatest triumph, however, was celebrated by the constitutionalists of the Ottoman Empire where a series of bad harvests had intensified the economic crisis of 1905–1907. At times the state could not afford to pay its employees their salaries, and promotions had to be put off. In this tense climate, Greek and Bulgarian rebels in Macedonia became increasingly eager to take open action against Ottoman sovereignty.[51] The traditionally powerful Committee for Union and Progress (the Unionists) in Macedonia saw themselves as the only executive power that could control the unrest. In June and July

1908, an armed conflict over Macedonia threatened to break out between the Committee and official Ottoman troops. The Unionists demanded the re-establishment of the constitution, suspended in 1878, and were backed by major demonstrations in Macedonia. Sultan Abd al-Hamid II finally gave in to the pressure and, on 23 July 1908, proclaimed that since the empire had been modernized, there was nothing to prevent a re-enaction of the constitution. The leading Unionists pronounced themselves in favour of an indirect control of the new government, which – with the approval of Abd al-Hamid – was formed by the conservative administrative expert Mehmed Kamil (1832–1913).

The constitutional upheaval of the years 1905–1909 showed that political culture in the Islamic world had for the most part fallen into line with global standards and norms, and that there was little scope for specific regional politics following traditional models. The demand for political sovereignty based on a nation state in which the native elites could participate with equal rights had become a criterion shared by both Islamic and non-Islamic societies.

3. THE YEARS OF WAR, 1909–1919

When, on 5 October 1908, Austro-Hungary took advantage of the revolutionary situation in Istanbul to annex the territories of Bosnia and Herzegovina, which had been occupied since 1878, and when at the same time Bulgaria declared its independence and Greece a day later took possession of Crete, the sovereignty of the Ottoman Empire was directly threatened. The new Ottoman government tried to engage in diplomatic negotiations to rescue its sovereignty in the face of the European powers and found a mediator – though by no means a selfless one – in the German empire. In its negotiations with Austro-Hungary, the empire was able to retrieve the small Sanjak of Novipasar; in addition, Austria declared itself willing to help the empire re-establish its inter-state sovereignty by abolishing the foreign postal service and capitulations. The empire was also to preserve its cultural sovereignty in the Islamic affairs of Bosnia-Herzegovina and could continue to appoint civil judges, legal experts (*mufti*) and teachers of religion in the former parts of the empire. The Ottoman Empire had already lost far more territories in the Balkans than had been the case under Abd al-Hamid; but the exchange of 'land against independence' seemed to have made up for the territorial loss for the time being.[52]

However, depending on their social positions, the political parties of the empire had completely different conceptions of the meaning of independence. For the nationalist Committee for Union and Progress, which had hovered in the background since 23 July 1908, it was primarily a matter of power politics. The liberals, on the other hand, sought to combine the cultural aura of a European identity with a specifically Ottoman tradition. They aspired to a freedom which they perceived as an equal right to participate in international culture and in the international market. Finally, the Islamic circles upheld their own tradition as the mark of a newly obtained Ottoman independence. The abortive coup of 13 April 1909, which was staged by the Islamic popularist Hafiz Darvish Vahdati and which, after its failure, led to the deposition of Abd al-Hamid II on 24 April,[53] pointed to the fact that Islamic policy continued to be an attractive alternative even in bourgeois circles. But because, before the First World War, political power was almost exclusively based on military strength, even Vahdati's coup could only be put down by the intervention of the Macedonian army. The Unionists, however, now established themselves as a political party which could always count on part of the armed forces which thus emerged as mentors of a constitutional system as early as 1909. Accordingly, the Ottoman civil administration (Husain Hilmi and Ibrahim Haqqi, 5 May 1909–29 September 1911) guaranteed the continuance of the armed forces through a budgetary policy which gave them considerable priority.[54]

Share of Military Expenditure in National Budgets

	Ottoman Empire	Total	Egypt
1889	42.1%	7.8 mill. T£	4.2%
1900	39.0%	7.2 mill. T£	5.8%
1908	34.6%	9.6 mill. T£	5.0%
1911	35.7%	12.6 mill. T£	5.8%

The Ottoman Empire, which traditionally gave maximum priority to its military budget, was further militarized after the Young Turk coup d'état on 12 June 1913. In Egypt, however, military expenditure was relatively low. In the Ottoman Empire the armed forces more or less served as a second bureaucracy, called to administer the empire together with the civil authorities. In the Islamic countries controlled by European powers there was also a kind of twofold administration, but here the second authority was provided by the colonial regime itself. The Ottoman Empire's defence of its independence burdened the national budget to such an extent that there was no question of planning a purposeful construction of urgently needed civil institutions.

Militarization and Colonialism

As we have already shown, to dispense with the militarization of the bureaucracy meant formally inviting the colonial powers to 'come into the country'. This was what happened to the Moroccan sultans Mulay Abd al-Aziz b. Hasan and Mulay Hafiz b. Hasan (1908–12). From the time Spanish troops had first entered Morocco in 1860, and French contingents had settled on the Moroccan coast and on the border of Algeria after 1905 in order to emphasise the financial demands of European creditor countries, the Moroccan government had wondered whether the foreign pressure could be met by militarizing the state. The Moroccan sultans, who had only rarely asserted themselves through military power, finally had to realize that without a modernized army there was no way of controlling the country or preventing European intervention. It was by renouncing militarization that they had opened the doors to the colonial powers. And when in 1912 Morocco was divided into a French and a Spanish protectorate and the city of Tangiers was placed under international administration, the European colonial regimes built up a new military administration which was gradually to bring the country under their control. Independence, which had to be defended by a strong military power, and colonial occupation were ultimately no more than two sides of the same coin: for in the pre-war period it was above all important to extend the sovereignty of the state into all social domains, to centralize it and thus to construct an authoritarian nation state. Military, civil and colonial bureaucracy were all guarantors of such a nation state. The military option, however, was only of outstanding importance in the Ottoman Empire. In almost all other Islamic countries, the degree of militarization was relatively low, so that here the foreign colonial administration assumed the task of re-organizing the institutions of the nation state and lending the latter a 'modern' appearance.

Italy in Libya and the Rise of Turkish Nationalism

With the impending French annexation of Morocco, the Italian occupation of Libya was, by 1911, once more conceivable, although officially Italian policy had been to maintain the status quo of the Ottoman Empire.[55] This paradoxical policy, which was closely bound up with the personality of the prime minister Giovanni Giolitti, must have surprised even the Ottoman government. But although Italy's ultimatum to the Ottoman Empire on 26 September 1911, and the declaration of war four days later, led to a certain warlike spirit in Istanbul, the Islamic legitimation of the war against Italy did not achieve a truly mobilizing effect.[56] The beginning of the war coincided with a period in which the Turkish nationalists had begun to assert themselves on the political stage of the Ottoman Empire. Ottomanism had, up to this point, formed the consensus of most of Ottoman parties. Now, under the pressure of nationalist uprisings, even in Albania, which had so far been considered an Ottoman 'homeland', the demand for a 'Turkish native country' (*Türk Yurdu*) could no longer be ignored. In the face of such developments, the Ottoman nationalists had to recognize that the attempt to establish a centralized sovereignty in all the provinces of the empire would necessarily lead to a rebellion by the population concerned.[57]

By the end of November, there was already a military stalemate in Libya, which left the situation open to numerous diplomatic negotiations. The effects of the war on the political situation in the Balkans became apparent as early as December 1911. Despite all attempts at mediation, Ottoman hopes of British support were disappointed and it soon became clear that the Ottoman Empire no longer had an influential diplomatic ally. Italy thereupon escalated the war in the Red Sea (February 1912) and occupied the Dodecanese islands in April and May 1912. From 3 August 1912, efforts to negotiate a peace treaty were finally launched in Switzerland, but at the same time the fighting in Libya intensified, with Italy increasingly claiming a racist justification for it. The political mood in the Arab countries threatened to change. People began to suspect that the Ottoman Empire might even sacrifice its Arab provinces to the European powers. Islam as the 'unifying bond' with which the Ottoman Empire had sought to justify its war was losing its appeal. Efforts at delay did not work and the Ottoman Empire, whose military situation was becoming increasingly precarious with Montenegro's declaration of war on 8 October 1912, finally had to accept Italian terms. The Lausanne treaties, signed on 15 and 18 October, also signified that, in view of its imperialist interests in Africa, Italy was ready to give up intervening in the Balkan conflict, which had reached its climax with Bulgaria, Greece and Serbia declaring war against the Ottoman Empire on the 18 October. Italy's (unkept) promise to give up its position in the Dodecanese can also be interpreted in this light.

The fears of Arab politicians from Syria and Lebanon that the Ottoman Empire might recede to its Turkish territories was reinforced by the Turkification policy of the new administration in Istanbul. After five years of constitutional government, all Ottoman political parties had manoeuvred themselves into a deadlock. With the peace treaty signed in London on 9 June 1913, the empire had been forced to retreat almost completely from Europe. Even Edirne, the second capital, had fallen into the hands of a Bulgarian volunteer corps which wrought havoc in the city. Bourgeois groups held the armed forces under the Grand Vizier Mahmud Shokat responsible for the disastrous conditions. On 12 June 1913, shortly after he was shot by an opposition group, the army leaders under Jamal Pasha raised a revolt in the name of the Unionists, who appointed the Egyptian Prince Mehmed Sa'id Halim Pasha as the new grand vizier.

Turkism, which was now propagated by the government of the Young Turks, oriented the empire to the north east: Azerbaijan, Tataristan and even the remote Turkish regions around Bukhara, Kokand and Samarkand had now assumed greater importance among the Ottoman public than the Arab provinces of the empire. The drive to centralization had, moreover, demonstrated to Arab elites that the Ottoman state now regarded its central administration as an exclusively Turkish affair. Many Arab politicians who had in the past always found a way to Istanbul and into the highest echelons of the administration, suddenly found that their career depended on their support of Turkification. Those who were neither culturally nor socially in a position to support the trend began to increasingly favour a new, local national policy, which they understood as an 'Arab' policy. Abd al-Hamid's principle that religion was the basis for the political and social structure of the state[58] had secured for the Arab elites an additional, albeit limited, source of influence. But now that religion was to step back in favour of national identity, even political Islamic ideas could no longer harmonize the threatening conflict between an Arab and a Turkish hegemony.

Yet around the year 1912 the extent of the colonial interest in the Arab provinces of the empire was by no means clear-cut; on the contrary, a basically pessimistic mood seemed to spread within the European colonies. According to many observers, only forty years after the beginning of political colonialism, the interest in a number of regions was already declining. As already mentioned, the resources of the colonial powers no longer allowed for further expansion. The development of cotton cultivation in Egypt was past its peak and financial expenditure for the colonies was often out of all proportion to the returns. It was only in southern Persia that the discovery of oil deposits opened up new prospects for the colonialists.

The Ottoman Empire in the First World War

The first Balkan War (1912–13) marked the beginning of a ten-year period of war which was to shake the traditional structures of the Islamic world. In 1913 the Ottoman Empire could give up all its Rumelian provinces without jeopardizing its existence; the First World War, however, was to lead to the destruction not only of the empire, but also the centuries-old cultural and political alliance between Turkish and Arab societies.

The events of the war as such need not be discussed here.[59] The covert German interventions against Odessa in 1914, the bloody fights for the Dardanelles in 1915–16, the last Ottoman military triumph in Qut al-Amara in 1916, the Suez offensive in 1916, the gradual conquest of Iraq and Palestine by allied troops in 1917–18, and finally the armistice of Mudros in 1918, have not only occupied historians, but caused such suffering among the civilian and military populations that they are widely remembered in popular songs. On the Ottoman side the war caused about 325,000 casualties. The number of civilians who died from starvation or were killed is unknown, but probably amounted to two to three millions. For the civilian population of Egypt, for instance, the war was no 'minor matter': about one in three men had to do compulsory labour as transport workers or in the construction of fortifications for British or Australian military units.[60] Many Algerian Muslims were used as *spahis* in the trenches of northern France; some of the survivors, uprooted them from their native country, remained in France or even in the occupied areas of the German empire. Even in the German colonies – for instance, in the Cameroons – Muslims were recruited for the German war effort.[61] The great famine in Syria, caused by the British blockade of the Red Sea ports, depopulated entire villages and regions.[62]

The Islamic countries could not remain neutral in the 1914–18 war; they either had to follow the policy of their colonial rulers or join the small group of those loyal to the Central Powers. The Ottoman Empire, which imagined itself to be part of a 'brotherhood in arms' with Germany and Austro-Hungary, tried to act against the division of the Islamic world through intensive Islamic propaganda. Innumerable pamphlets spoke of an Islamic union, legitimised by the just Islamic war (*jihad*) proclaimed by the Ottoman Sheikh al-Islam on 15 November 1914. But counter-propaganda soon pointed out that the government of the Young Turks could well have learnt to use such a vocabulary through German agents. German diplomats like Baron Max von Oppenheim had for some time been recommending the declaration of *jihad* for the benefit of the German and Ottoman Empires.[63] Although Ottoman propagandists often put their Islamic appeals into a local context, trying to take into account the specific situation in, say, North Africa or Russia, they had very little success. Aside from some local expressions of sympathy among a few small intellectual circles, Islamic propaganda was unable to surmount the political and military division of the Islamic world. There indeed arose doubts in the Islamic world over the legitimacy of the Ottoman war, and even over Ottoman cultural supremacy as such.

The economies of Islamic countries were also drawn into international conflicts. This was inevitable if only because of the structure of the world economy, which allowed for no border between belligerent and neutral countries. In the colonial countries, as well as in Egypt and Algeria, there was in addition a new push towards internal colonization. The threat to international shipping routes by naval units of the Central Powers demanded a greater mobilization of economic resources to make the colonies independent both of supplies by their 'mother countries' and of exports.

The Conflict between City and Country

In Egypt, the war economy led to a complete reorganization of the colonial administration and economy, which in its turn was to accelerate the growth of Egyptian nationalism. On 18 December 1914, Great Britain unilaterally declared Egypt to be its protectorate, endowing it by implication with de facto independence from the Ottoman Empire. Besides the colonial administration headed by the High Commissioner Henry McMahon, a military administration was set up under the commander-in-chief of the British troops in Egypt, John Maxwell, who expanded it into the remote areas of the country. This newly organized administration achieved an extensive centralization which in turn supported the political identity of the native elites in whose eyes Egypt was once more becoming an integral whole, which they interpreted as a nation. The separation of the country from the Ottoman Empire on British initiative was therefore generally welcomed by the nationalists,[64] even if a few among them felt nostalgic about the Ottoman period. Modernism demanded going one's own way, rather than being dependent. And in a certain sense, the wartime economy had demonstrated the value of going one's own way: the state could watch more efficiently over economic resources, it could make up for the collapse of the major shipping lines by promoting the development of the domestic economy, and even – as it did in 1918 – by confiscating the country's entire cotton crop. A powerful state was the dream of the nationalists. Like the colonial state, it was to be led from the capital. Cairo, whose population had just reached a million, had become the residence of Sultan Husain Kamil – who had been proclaimed sultan on 19 December 1914[65] – as well as the capital of the colonial administration. But economically and politically the city was powerless. The countryside, through its influential cotton and cane sugar economy, ruled the political mentality of the state. It was only when the interventionism of the wartime economy considerably expanded the decision-making power of the cities to the detriment of the great landowners that the nationalists were encouraged in their hope that they could aspire to be the heirs of colonialism and take over the administration. The interventionism advocated by the nationalists thus acquired a new impetus through the wartime policy of state control.

The First World War, for the first time in the history of colonialism, provoked a political conflict between town and country which was to influence the political destiny of many Islamic societies for a long time to come. While it consolidated the political alliance between the rural areas of the colonies and the urban centres of the mother countries, it at the same time accelerated the detachment of the urban elites from the land. Moreover, the British military administration had for the first time integrated about 3,400 Egyptian villages and towns into a homogeneous administrative system governed from Cairo.

The modern nation state, which was essentially based on a centralized bureaucracy, thus acquired a countenance even in the eyes of the nationalists. The creation of an Egyptian citizenship in 1914 was no more than the legal expression of this new identity. The nationalists now considered even the peasant to be a 'son of the country', (*ibn al-balad*) an expression which, a century earlier, was used exclusively for Egyptian bourgeois society. The fellah who had once been looked down upon became not only an Egyptian, but an archetypal Egyptian viewed by the urban nationalists as the true hero of Egypt.

Such nationalist transfigurations became popular in many Islamic countries during the war years. They were encouraged by the colonial authorities who needed – and succeeded in acquiring – a new definition of the political system to uphold their power. Paradoxically, the second wave of colonization during the First World War created in this way a new sense of belonging, paving the way for the nationalism of the 1920s.

Another feature of the modern nation state, the national market, was, however, persistently undermined by colonial policy. The colonial economy continued to impose customs duties and taxes throughout the territory of the colonial state, as was done in the European nation states; but it allowed for no real internal economic development, since all internal market relations were primarily dependent on the mother countries, into whose national markets they were integrated in different degrees. What is more, the domestic economy almost exclusively supplied military provisions, so that the general population had no share in the new goods produced in the country.

Islamic Nationalism and the Promise of Independence

Urban nationalism was not a phenomenon limited to particular Islamic societies. It was often confirmed by colonial policy itself, which neatly separated colonists and 'natives'. In Algeria, the French colonists first started referring to a special nationality of the Muslim population after 1914, although the northern part of the country, which was divided into three departments, legally belonged to France. In Indonesia, too, the Dutch colonial administration distinguished between natives and foreigners, thus indirectly confirming the nationalist view that Indonesia had its own nationality and hence the right to independence.

Woodrow Wilson's famous Fourteen-Point Declaration of 8 January 1918 was thus interpreted in almost all Islamic countries as a confirmation of their right to independence. When the peace conferences of Versailles and Paris were convened, numerous delegations from widely different Islamic regions travelled to France to demand that the promise of independence be carried out. Among them were also non-Muslim minorities such as Armenians and northern Iraqi Assyrians. But they waited in vain in the conference anterooms and the dozens of 'black books' or 'white books' in which the nationalists tried to describe the dramatic situation in their homelands were ignored. The right to national self-determination celebrated by the victorious powers applied, as they quickly realised, to the European world alone. Thus the newly created League of Nations was appointed as the mandator for the Middle Eastern territories of the Ottoman Empire conquered by the allies in the course of the war. In accordance with the Anglo–Franco–Russian agreement of 16 May 1915, negotiated by Mark Sykes and George Picot – which had long been kept a secret but was published by Russian revolutionaries on 22 November 1917 – and following the Damascus protocol of the same year, the Fertile Crescent was divided into a French and a British sphere.[66] Each region was subdivided into an actual colonial area and a mandate situated inland. The special role of Palestine as a refuge for European Jews and as a geographic focus for the political utopia of the Zionist movement had already been established by the famous declaration of the British foreign minister Arthur James Balfour on 2 November 1917.

Wartime colonialism meant that political identity in the Islamic countries had by this time acquired a thoroughly nationalistic orientation in the sense that the demand for independence was raised on the basis of the social and economic realities created during the previous decades, which were also to determine the borders of the new states. Nationalism did not, therefore, contradict colonialism, but confirmed it in the radical statist form which it had assumed during the First World War. The issue was power and control in the colonial states.

For this reason, the nationalism of the 1920s cannot be differentiated from Islamic political identities. Hardly any politician with an explicitly Islamic approach, arguing within the framework of an Islamic ideology, would now embrace the idea of creating an Islamic superstate of the kind al-Kawakibi had dreamt of. Islamic internationalism had become no more than a refuge for a few of the *ulama* and those Muslim intellectuals who, for various reasons, were either unwilling or in no position to participate in the political conflicts of the colonial state which went on between the nationalists and the colonial powers. Even inveterate Pan-Islamists such as the Egyptian journalist Abd al-Aziz Jawish (1876[?]–1929 had by now wholly embraced the nationalist movement. Jawish continued his campaign for an Islamic national liberation, but he gave up calling for an 'Islamic union'.[67] The Islamic classicism of the Salafiya was thus, for the time being, either nationalized or depoliticized. The Syrian journalist Muhammad Rashid Rida (1865–1935) who had gone to Egypt in 1898 and, after the death of Muhammad Abduh in 1905, acted as the intellectual leader of the Salafiya, also advocated a national orientation. This even led him to support

Jewish immigration to Palestine, which he did not consider as a threat to the Islamic national identity.[68]

Islamic nationalists such as Rida, Jawish and Ziya Gökalp, all men of urban origin, thus joined the urban wing of the national movement. Like the latter, they pleaded for the establishment of a powerful centralized state which would lend the urban centres a new political and economic authority over the nation. Confronting them were the liberals, who were mainly committed to the land where they had their social and economic power basis. The national liberals, prominently represented by the Egyptian Ahmad Lutfi al-Sayyid (1872–1963), also demanded national independence for the colonial state, but also the preservation of close economic relations with the 'motherlands', especially in agrarian matters. The rural communities were thus in favour of strengthening their ties with the colonial powers, while the cities demanded their independence even and especially from the country, and consequently from the colonial powers. For them the concept of 'independence' had become a synonym for liberation from the power of the rural areas.

An Islamic interpretation of nationalism was by no means unusual. Rida, for example, followed the classicist ideal of the Salafiya in conceiving early Islamic history as a model for a modern, urban nation state. He argued for a sovereignty unified by Islam, in which religion was to substantiate the authority of the urban elites over the state. To him religion (*din*) was always a public, and hence a political matter. It was possible to appoint an absolute authority over it, which would no longer be a few established dignitaries like the Ottoman shaikh al-Islam, but vested in all Muslim citizens. However, the claim to sovereignty raised by Rida was not necessarily a democratic one. On the contrary, Rida considered the Islamically legitimized unification of state authority based on the principle of absolute sovereignty as the true essence of a political utopia which would provide Islamic societies with a new modern system. Rida gave nationalism a republican interpretation, thereby differentiating himself from other urban nationalists who did not connect the state system with the aims of nationalism. Besides, it was not Riza's declared aim to found an 'Islamic republic'; this concept was to acquire significance decades later. Rida considered Islam as the realization of a system which in non-Islamic Europe was called – for want of a better term – a 'republic'. He firmly believed in the power of state institutions which would no longer be marked by traditional territorial bonds, but were to be based solely on political ethics. He thus enlarged the nationalists' conception of independence, which was purely concerned with external policy, by adding an internal dimension to it. For Rida independence could only be based on the perfect sovereignty of society, which was legitimized by the absolute sovereignty of God. As representatives of God on earth, human beings were entrusted with this sovereignty for which they were politically responsible.[69] Urban Islamic nationalism was of a highly moral nature: its fundamental idea was based on the concept of justice (*adl*), which had already been the subject of theological debates in the scholastic period. Islamic intellectuals had again and again pointed out that the Western concept of freedom essentially corresponded with the Islamic concept of justice.[70]

Islamic republicanism, which was passionately represented by Rida between 1908 and 1924,[71] was matched on behalf of the landed interest by a no less vehemently represented Islamic liberalism. Liberal nationalists were well able to use Islamic symbolism to present their standpoint and they could refer to the political traditions of the 19th century, when liberal Islamic discourse was taken for granted – a famous figure at that time had been the Indian journalist Sayyid Ahmad Khan who, in a very Anglophile spirit, pleaded for a secular constitutional system. The national liberals now mainly argued in terms of the Islamic concept of freedom, since they believed that the success of their world could only be achieved through the absolute freedom (*hurriya*) of the individual – again a concept which reflected the actual social position of the landed liberals and their need for free access to the world and to the global economy. Islamic liberals had no problem with legitimating their bid for freedom by pointing to Islamic history, for it was obvious to them that the Prophet Mohammad had created the Medina canon by following his own rational criteria and that this canon had nothing to do with revelation. While the classicists argued that the Islamic law is clearly described in the Medina *suras* (chapters) of the Koran and was already established in Mohammad's lifetime as the 'Constitution of Medina', the national liberals replied that these Medina *suras* were of a predominantly historical nature and that only ethical principles could be derived from them.[72] Religion and state, they argued, were two essentially different phenomena: in the state, man establishes laws on the basis of his understanding of his own freedom, while in religion he determines his inner relationship with transcendence.

Islam and the Political Public

Although the contrast between urban and rural politics contributed to a radical distinction between Islamic republicanism and Islamic liberalism, both tendencies were closely related through their common reference to an Islamic identity. While, after the First World War, the majority of the political public in the Islamic countries used a 'European' language to express their various concerns, both wings of the Islamic public now argued in an explicitly Islamic language.

The characteristic division of the political public of the post-war years was thus into two competing spheres which, in accordance with terms that had long been in use, could be described as 'secular' and 'Islamic'. This usage does not, however, in the end do much to advance our understanding of the nature of politics in Islamic societies, since all forms of political action in Islamic modernism were basically secular. More telling are the different cultural terms of reference of the division: Islamic culture represented a network of social relations which was distinctly different from that of 'European' culture,[73] and since culture is primarily transmitted by communication, the two spheres were separated by language. This division, which occurred in all Islamic societies from about 1870, had been highly politicized through the First World War. Only those societies in which the pietistic tribal cultures of the 18th and 19th centuries prevailed (Najd, Cyrenaica, areas of the anti-Atlas in North Africa) were a remarkable exception. Here there had soon occurred a thorough homogenization of the spheres of life in which the Islamically interpreted tribal culture had assumed a highly modern function of social integration.

The public in Islamic societies had thus acquired a very complex, three-dimensional structure, in which the following polar concepts were effective:

Colonial – traditional (social change, change of values)
City – Country (also degree of mechanization of material culture)
Islamic network – European network (linguistic form of the elaboration of the spheres of life).

The weighing and forming of these fields were a matter of time and place and had a lasting effect on the political traditions of each of the Islamic societies. For politics only those fields were decisive which were attributed to the colonial sectors of the Islamic societies, as for example the press, parties and unions. The nationalists shared an urban culture in the new European quarters and created their own network of social relations, using a 'European discourse'. They spoke like Europeans, adopted their fashions, frequented European coffee houses and organized themselves within the same structures as European politicians were wont to do. The national liberals behaved like the nationalists, except that they lived in the colonial framework of the agrarian areas where they had their landed properties. They talked about the export prices of cotton, sugar or jute like the stockbrokers in Manchester, London and Paris. The members of the Salafiya felt that they belonged to the same Islamic network, but like the nationalists they followed an urban culture. Not unlike the Islamic liberals they merely distinguished themselves from their 'secular' competitors by their relationship to the Islamic network.

This typology of the public in the Islamic societies after the First World War is of course very roughly sketched. The specific conditions in each of the countries often produced very independent forms of expression on behalf of this public, leading to the conclusion that the colonial public had been instrumental in creating a rather original, non-transferable national culture. It is true, however, that all Islamic societies of those days shared the structure of a twofold public.

The traditional sectors of the Islamic societies, which had emerged simultaneously with the colonial sectors, also disposed of a very complex cultural structure, but this did not give rise to a powerful public. The old towns and old villages had a close network of social relations, which comprised the 'quarters' or communities, respectively, and separated them from the colonial outside world. Within these traditional worlds the prevailing culture was based on Islam; but there were also merchants or small landowners who regularly used a 'European discourse' and intentionally avoided conventional Islamic symbols.

The making of this three-dimensional structure of Islamic cultures was a rather lengthy process. The First World War had, particularly through the war economy, promoted a political orientation towards statism and thus shaken the already precarious balance between the sectors. So it was merely a matter of time for the invasion of modernism to make itself felt in the Islamic societies.

4. THE PERIOD OF REVOLTS 1919–1923

The End of the Ottoman Empire

The Mudros armistice of 30 October 1918 was at first welcomed with relief in the Islamic world. Almost ten years of war had been disastrous for the Ottoman Empire. Militarily, it is true, the empire had not been defeated. Indeed, in the last month of the war it had conquered the city of Baku in Azerbaijan (15/9/1918) over whose citadel fluttered a red flag with a white crescent, brought into town by the troops of the Ottoman General Enver Pasha. Nor, in November 1918, did Mustafa Kemal,[74] the army officer who would soon be known Atatürk (1881–1938), return to Istanbul a defeated man. But Ottoman society, famished, miserable and worn out by the war, was defeated.

In Istanbul the government led by Damad Farid had quickly accepted the armistice conditions, although these established anything but a victory for the Ottomans. By Article VII the allies were granted the right to occupy any part of the empire if the safety of their troops demanded it. They made liberal use of this privilege. On 13 November 1918, fifty-five allied warships cast anchor in Istanbul, which for the first time since its conquest by Ottoman troops in 1453 had to tolerate the presence of a foreign army. French units occupied the south-eastern parts of Anatolia in 1919 and advanced as far as Afyon in central Anatolia. British marine units established themselves on the Black Sea coast, and Italians occupied the south-western part of Anatolia. Thrace, the rest of Ottoman Rumelia, was already under French control. The entente powers had almost realized one of their war objectives – 'to drive the Ottoman Empire, which has proved completely alien to Western civilization, out of Europe',[75] as they had informed the American government on 11 January 1917

Despite its defeat, the Ottoman Empire for the time being remained a cultural, political and social centre of the Islamic world. In the Libyan province of Fezzan, which was officially a part of the Italian colony of North Africa, Ottoman military units held their position until 1920. Even in Medina, the city of the Prophet Mohammad, Ottoman troops under the self-willed Fakhri Pasha controlled the citadel until 1919.[76] There were also independent Ottoman contingents in the southern Arabian principality of Lahj and in the Caucasus. However, the new Istanbul government – now that the government of the Young Turks had been ousted – dispensed with its military base; for the first time in Ottoman history a civilian administration governed in Istanbul. But by abandoning its military structure, the Istanbul government completely lost control over what was still Ottoman land. At the turn of the year 1918–19, Turkish nationalists set up the first units of the 'Unions for the Defence of Rights' (Müdafaa-i Hukuk Cemiyetleri), especially in the eastern part of the country. In Anatolia volunteer corps were mobilized to fight against the occupation army. Known as 'national forces' (*kuva-yi milliye)*, these corps were partially led by *efe*, 'brigands' who had settled in their local centres which they defended against the threatened occupation by allied troops. Other corps leaders were Ottoman officers who refused to demobilize, as well as nationalist intellectuals and a few notables, especially from the Izmir region which was occupied by Greek troops in 1919.

On 5 May 1919, Mustafa Kemal was sent to Samsun to take supreme command of the 9th army (later 3rd army) and to establish order in Anatolia whose civil administration was also entrusted to him. To this day it remains unknown whether it was on behalf of the Ottoman government or of the Ottoman sultan that he organized the resistance against the occupation troops in Anatolia.[77]

On 14–15 May 1919, Izmir was occupied by Greek troops with considerable logistic support from the Entente powers. The subsequent gradual conquest of Western Anatolia by the Greeks mobilized the heterogeneous rebel groups and volunteer corps. In the east of the country, Kemal called for resistance against the Greek occupation and, under British pressure, was dismissed by the Ottoman government on 23 June 1919. The political break between Istanbul and the Anatolian east was now complete, although Kemal continued to act as the defender of the sultanate and caliphate.

The nationalist congresses convened at Erzerum (23 July–7 August 1919) and Sivas (14–11 September 1919) formed the foundation for a new state power.

These congresses assumed legislative power, with the administration in Istanbul serving as the executive power. Among the major demands of the Anatolian nationalists was the preservation of Anatolia's territory; the 'provinces inhabited by Turks' were on no account to be yielded 'to the enemy'. These included the 'six provinces' which were considered as centres of Armenian settlement and had already been the scene of frequent and violent fights between Armenian and Turkish or Kurdish rebels. Since a rebellion in Van on 17 May 1915, about 400,000 Armenians had been deported from these areas and forced to settle in northern Iraq or in Syria because the Ottoman army feared that the Armenians might, as a result of Russian war propaganda, build up another internal front. In the course of the deportations, there were frequent pogroms, famines and epidemics, causing more than 200,000 Armenian deaths.[78]

The more the nationalist resistance increased, the more violent the reaction of the Entente powers. In March 1920, two months after elections to the last Ottoman parliament, in which the nationalists could have formed a majority, British troops took over the Istanbul police and Mustafa Kemal was indirectly condemned and outlawed by the then Sheikh al-Islam as a 'rebel and renegade'.

The conflict was moving to its climax. In Ankara, which had become the headquarters of the 'representative committee' led by Mustafa Kemal – an organ of the 'Union for the Defence of the Rights of Anatolia and Rumelia' – the Great Turkish National Assembly (Büyük Millet Meclisi), which was meant to represent the executive and legislative power of the Turkish nation, convened on 23 April 1920. Sultan Wahid al-Din (ruled from 28 June 1918), who still resided in Istanbul, was at this point to have a place in the new constitutional system. After his 'liberation from foreign power' – since according to the nationalists, the sultan was being kept in Istanbul as a captive of the Entente powers – he was to join the National Assembly in a capacity to be decided later. This approach had met with the approval of many of the Anatolian *ulama*, who were now declaring that the fight against the Istanbul government, and particularly against the grand vizier Damad Farid, was justified from an Islamic point of view.

Sixty per cent of the National Assembly consisted of urban intellectuals – among them Ziya Gökalp – and professionals, as well as military personnel. These represented what had by this time crystallised as a classical Turkish nationalism, which was gradually leading the country away from its ties with the Arab Islamic world. Their political concepts were interwoven with 'European' ideals. The achievements of the Russian revolutionaries also provided, through the small leftist groups among them, a certain support for the nationalists. The liberal wing was represented by a small group of landowners and merchants who used both an Islamic and a 'European' language. Not to be forgotten were the *ulama* who made up just under 17 per cent of the deputies and were the advocates of the traditional Islamic cultural system.[79]

Even if entirely different political views found their way into the National Assembly, the slogan of liberating the Turkish nation gave it a certain common purpose. To be sure, there was no consensus at all over what was meant by liberation. To many nationalists the important thing was military liberation, and they were even prepared to toy with socialist or communist ideas as long as these contributed to mobilizing against the occupation. In April 1920 Kemal himself made a political overture towards the Soviet government by inviting the Foreign Affairs Commisar Chicherin to join Turkey in forming an anti-imperialist front.[80] The Soviet Union's pro-Armenian and pro-Kurdish nationalities policy prevented a serious rapprochement. Nevertheless a communist corps complete with red flags emerged in Anatolia.[81] And, in the constituent assembly of the first Turkish Communist Party, it became clear that Islamic culture could not be ignored. For participating members of the *ulama*, communism was simply a principle of Islam, and it was occasionally maintained that Lenin himself had acquired his communist ideas from Islam.[81]

Thus the concept of 'liberation' contributed to the association of Islamic and socialist views. A rumour got around that the former general Enver Pasha, who lived in Russia and was a radical partisan of the Unionists, was organizing a 'Green Bolshevik Army' which would arrive in the country for the final liberation of Turkey. A short-lived 'Green Army' (*yesil ordu*) was actually established in Ankara, but it soon turned against the nationalist majority and for a short time caused agitation among the nationalist military leaders. Militant Turanism, a nationalist ideology which aspired to a Greater Turkey and fought for political and cultural solidarity among the Turkish people from the Balkans to China, had been propagated by Enver in his Russian exile. It was thus a combination of red and green, the colours of communism and Islam.

The New Economic Policy introduced in the Soviet Union in 1921 led to a partial political cohesion between the revolutionaries and the bourgeois camp. This circumstance, as well as its implied renunciation of an early proletarian world revolution, which had already been mentioned at the 2nd Comintern Congress, now allowed the Soviet revolutionaries to cooperate with 'bourgeois-national governments' outside Russia, thus paving the way for a treaty of friendship between Moscow and Ankara signed on 16 March 1921. For the first time in history a Russian government guaranteed the existence of Turkey as a nation state. This was also one of the first treaties signed by the new Turkish government with a foreign power.

In the new Turkish constitution of 1 March 1921, the word 'Ottoman' as the name of the state was once and for all replaced by the word 'Turkish'. Thus the Ankara government definitely renounced any cultural and political sovereignty over the 'non-Turkish' territories of the old Ottoman Empire. Ottoman cosmopolitanism decisively fell prey to nationalism. Even those territories which were inhabited by non-Turks such as Kurds, Lazes and Armenians were absorbed into the Turkish national identity, so that from the point of view of the nationalists, the goal of transforming the Ottoman Empire into an independent Turkish state appeared to be accomplished.

Meanwhile, the unity among the Entente powers was crumbling. At a conference held in London, France decided to revise the Treaty of Sèvres signed on 10 August 1920[83] and prepared to recognize the Ankara government. The last phase of the Greco–Turkish war (23 March 1921–11 October 1922) finally ended with the triumphant victory of the nationalists, who had reached Istanbul and repulsed the Greek armies in several battles. The fate of the Ottoman caliphs was thus sealed. Although it was repeatedly rumoured that Sultan Wahid al-Din had backed the government in Ankara and encouraged it to act against the Entente powers, he had to pay for his apparent hesitation. He fled on 16 November 1922 on board a British warship bound for Malta and from there to exile in San Remo. As sultan he had already been deposed when the National Assembly institutionally separated the caliphate from the sultanate and thus officially proclaimed the end of the Ottoman Empire. On 16 November, Abd al-Majid II (1868–1944), a son of Sultan Abd al-Aziz, was proclaimed caliph, but his powers were considerably curtailed. Mustafa Kemal declared that the Turkish people now unconditionally held sovereignty in their hands. By February 1923 the three major demands of the 'national fight' (*milli mücâdele*) seemed to have been realized: political independence from the great powers, sovereignty of the people as the expression of internal political independence, and in some domains economic independence.

The Entente powers paid tribute to this surprising development. At the Lausanne Peace Conference (21 November 1922–24 July 1923) the Treaty of Sèvres was thoroughly revised in favour of the Ankara government. Turkey was granted political sovereignty over the regions it had declared as national territory of the Turks, which included the Armenian and Kurdish provinces although Great Britain was able to secure for itself as a pledge the predominantly Armenian and Kurdish region of Mosul in northern Iraq, and France the district of Alexandretta (Hatay) in northern Syria. The gradual pace at which the Lausanne resolutions were to be implemented also provided the Entente powers with some breathing space. It was not, for example, until 1929 that Turkey acquired full sovereignty in the realm of customs policy while until as late as 1944 it was paying back international debts which it had incurred during the second half of the 19th century.

When on 2 October 1923 the last British troops left Istanbul, the Turkish national army could at last march into the old capital. But Istanbul was no longer to be the capital and on 13 October Ankara was declared the capital of the Turkish state, the constitution of which was established on 29 October, together with the proclamation of the republic. On the same day, Mustafa Kemal was appointed as the first president of the Turkish Republic.

It was the first time in recent Islamic history that urban nationalists had won a victory over an *ancien régime*. The republic symbolized this victory: its ideals – sovereignty of the people and, in a sense, the division of powers – corresponded with the outlook of the urban nationalists, who were completely geared to a 'European discourse'. The power of the sultanate in Istanbul could no longer have had any influence on Turkish intellectuals. Socially divorced from the old power, they dethroned anything sultanic and replaced it with their own sovereignty. The caliphate was not at issue here. Indeed the separation of the caliphate from the sultanate in 1922 can be interpreted as an attempt to protect it from the inevitable downfall of the old order and to rescue it for the new era. The caliphate also had something like an idea of sovereignty about it. According to the contemporary classical interpretation of the Koran 6/165: *huwa lladi ga-alakum hala'ifa l-ardi* ('It is He who has appointed you viceroys [of previous generations] on the earth'[84]), every man was a caliph, that is a deputy of God on earth. This made man the sovereign on earth, within the limits of his membership of a nationality. National sovereignty (*milli hakimiyet*) thus did not contradict the caliphate; in fact the caliphate required the sovereignty of man. Kawakibi had already written about this interpretation of the caliphate, quoting the oft-mentioned prophetic tradition which had only now, with the advent of constitutionalism, acquired its full significance: 'Each of you is a herdsman, and each of you is responsible for his herd.'[85]

The classicist discourse of the Salafiya thus to a large extent coincided with republican doctrine. What remained to be seen was whether the Islamic discourse could be integrated into the 'European'. If that could be achieved, a bridge within contemporary modernism might be built between 'Europeans' and 'Islamists' which would end the dual orientation of the political public and lead to a true 'national' identity. In this respect, the post-war period offered a good starting-point in Turkey, because with the removal of the sultanate, the question of the caliphate could be discussed in entirely new terms. The prerequisite was, of course, the establishment of the independent nation state, which formed the subject of political discussion in almost all Islamic societies after 1918.

Rebellions in Egypt

For the time being, however, other wartime phenomena had left their effects. The war had not only heightened awareness among city dwellers that they belonged to a nation; it had also mobilized other, traditional sectors of society.

In Egypt, peasants and nomadic Arab tribes had their own very specific way of striving for independence. In December 1918, Egyptian city dwellers and landowners had come together to put their demand for independence before the British government. The latter had reacted very negatively and had tried to prevent a small delegation (Wafd) of Egyptian politicians from participating in the Paris peace conferences. When four of the leading Egyptian nationalists, among them the former minister Saad Zaglul (died 1927), were arrested on 8 March 1919 and deported to Malta, the politicized citizens of the colonial society reacted with strikes and demonstrations. The peasant communities thereupon literally picked up the claim to independence and tried to put their own independence into action by announcing their freedom from the colonial society and from urban bureaucracy. In these communal movements numerous social and economic conflicts which had accumulated during the wartime period broke into the open. The strength of the protest of the traditional societies against the colonial state surprised the British as well as the native nationalists. In the confrontations that occurred between 15 and 31 March, at least 3,000 Egyptians were killed, numerous villages were burnt down, large landed properties plundered, railway stations destroyed and railway lines cut off. In early April 1919, the nationalists and the British army managed to recover their control over the country. In the wake of the British units the nationalists, who had temporarily organized themselves around the Wafd as a new national party, for the first time gained a foothold in the Egyptian provinces. They were able to open party offices and thus spread the colonial public over the entire land. It was through the colonial power and the national movement that Egypt was reorganized as a nation state. The colonial society had recovered its sovereignty over the country.[86]

The destruction of remnants of local, non-colonial forms of resistance and the spread of politics to all realms of society had, it is true, been inevitable. For without the unequivocal authorization to act as the executive power of a national will, the national movement would have miscarried. This authorization was obtained by the Egyptian nationalists – as its was by the Turkish partisan Mustafa Kemal – by force; but since there was no independent army available to them, they had no alternative but to use British military force.

The Arab Revolt 1916–1920

Sharif Husain b. Ali al-Hashimi, since 1908/9 Amir of Mecca, and Abd al-Aziz b. Abd al-Rahman (Ibn Sa'ud), since 1915 Amir of Najd and its dependencies (above all, the country of al-Ahsa with the centre of Hufuf) were both in practice governors under the Ottoman Empire. Ibn Saud's annexation of the province of al-Ahsa had been confirmed by the empire in a treaty of May 1914; he himself thereupon temporarily acknowledged Ottoman sovereignty. The Sharif of Mecca, Husain, who like Ibn Saʿud had been able to build up his local power with British support, had since the height of the Turkification policy of the Ottoman Empire (from about 1912/13) entertained hopes of founding a sovereign Arab empire with British military support. For both Husain and Ibn Saʿud, the nation was only conceivable in the form of an empire. They therefore considered sovereignty as a power relating to the personality of the ruler, to be delegated to him by the people in the form of an official homage (*bai'a*). An 'authoritarian state' (W. J. Mommsen) established in this manner would have to show a national identity which for Husain was the Arab lineage whose most 'noble part' was his own family (Al Hashim), which he traced back to the Prophet Mohammad. His counterpart, the Amir of Najd, also saw himself as the defender of the 'noble Arab lineage'. But for Ibn Saʿud the decisive point was not a family history that could be traced back to the prophet, but the prestige of his family within the tribal society of Najd. In addition, the sovereignty of the people as delegated to the prince had to be legitimized in a traditional way. Religious culture was the appropriate means to achieve this end. Just as Husain had, in his own way, substantiated his claim to power through Islam, so Ibn Saʿud had obtained religious legitimacy for himself by restoring the old Wahhabi policy of solidarity in defence and offence, thus compensating for the relatively low position of his family within the tribal society.

The idea of an Arab empire was newly revived by the outbreak of the First World War. Both Ibn Saʿud and Husain hoped that with allied support, they would be able to secure for themselves a leading position on the Arabian peninsula and in the Fertile Crescent. The diplomacy of letters with the British authorities in the form of the British high commissioner in Egypt, Henry McMahon, so keenly pursued by Husain and his son Abdallah, was aimed mainly at international recognition.[87] This 'Husain–McMahon Correspondence' between 14 July 1915 and 10 March 1916 raised the hope, both among Arab politicians, especially in Syria, and in Husain himself, that Great Britain would no longer stand in the way of founding an Arab empire.

A similar kind of secret diplomacy was also conducted by Husain with Arab oppositionists in Damascus and Istanbul, who met in small Arab clubs like al-Fatat ('Youth') or al-Ahd ('the Alliance'), and were closely watched by the Ottoman army in 1915–16. In Ottoman eyes these clubs had been launched by France and Great Britain with the aim of separating the Arab regions from the Ottoman Empire and bringing them under their own control.[88] Some of them had been founded immediately after the miscarried revolution of 31 March 1909, among them the 'Culture Club' (al-Muntada al-Adabi), which was officially tolerated by the Young Turks, and whose mentor was the Syrian journalist and publicist Abd al-Hamid b. Muhammad al-Zahrawi (1855–1916) who was condemned to death by an Ottoman military tribunal in 1916.[89] Others, like 'the Alliance', went back to pro-Ottoman officers and intellectuals who had turned away from the Young Turks around 1911. A co-founder of 'the Alliance' (1913) was, for example, the Egyptian officer Aziz b. Ali al-Misri (1879–1965), who had played a highly ambiguous role in the Arab national movement. After 1911, when among the Young Turks the pro-Turkish triumphed over the pro-Ottoman trend, the political opposition in Syria and Lebanon began to lean towards Arabization. On the insistence of al-Misri, the al-'Ahd union changed its name to the 'Arab Revolutionary Society' and presented the pre-Islamic tribal identity of the Arabs as true descendants of Qahtan.[90] From the Ottoman point of view, the 'Society for Decentralization' (al-Lamarkaziya), which was founded in Cairo in 1910 or 1912, formed the turntable for the Arab national movement; apart from al-Zahrawi, other founding members of this organization were said to include Rashid Rida and a few Christian Syrians.[91]

Ottoman–Arab Societies 1908–1913[92]

1. Ottoman–Syrian Society (Paris 1908)
2. Arab–Ottoman Brotherhood (Istanbul 1908
3. Culture Club (Istanbul 1909)
4. Society of Arab–Ottoman Brotherhood (Cairo 1909)
5. Lebanese Alliance (Cairo 1909)
6. Qahtniya Society (Istanbul 1909)
7. Young Arab Society (Paris 1909 or 1911)
8. Society of Reform (Beirut 1912)
9. Ottoman Party of Administrative Decentralization (Cairo 1912)
10. The Alliance (Istanbul 1913)

Although the Ottoman authorities later treated these Arab oppositionists with great harshness, their political demands were rather modest. They wanted the Arab world to share with Europe in the achievements of modernism, so the Ottoman Empire had to be 'reformed' in order that modern European civilization might become a solid constituent of Arab culture. This somewhat pro-Ottoman construction of Arab nationalism conflicted with that of oppositionists like the 35 Arab deputies who, in 1911, suggested to Husain, the Sharif of Mecca, that the Arabs were prepared to rebel against the Ottoman Empire under his leadership and that Husain would be invested with the caliphate as a result.[93]

The Arab national movement did not offer Husain much back up. For one thing, its social anchorage was inadequate; for another, it was clearly felt as early as 1913 that, for all the Arab rhetoric, the real issue was not the establishment of one Arab nation state, but the independence of separate Arab regions as nation states. In the Arab nationalist movement there thus emerged the political outlines of Lebanon, Syria and Iraq, the economic, cultural and social borders of which had already been drawn in the course of the previous decades.

Even Husain himself did not see his role as the political leader of the entire Arab world. What he was really striving for was the political confirmation of 'his' territory by the international public. The British authorities acknowledged these ambitions to the extent of confirming him as the King of Hijaz in 1916. Where the borders of Hijaz were to be was, however, unclear. For the British colonial authorities, the Hijaz traditionally ended at the Gulf of Aqaba; but the Arab tribes in the north of the country, who supported, Husain demanded at least the incorporation of the districts up to Ma'an in today's southern Jordan, and even the inclusion of Damascus itself.

In the summer of 1917, a real race began between Great Britain and the Mecca powers for supremacy in Palestine and Syria. Edmund Allenby, the commander of the British army, led British troops into Palestine, while Arab troops, sent off by Husain on 5 June 1916 at the beginning of the 'Arab revolt' which had the support of British advisers such as T. E. Lawrence, almost simultaneously marched north.[94] The massive Ottoman defence positions in Palestine delayed both campaigns for a long time. On 9 December 1917, British troops finally conquered Jerusalem, and Haifa fell as late as 23 September 1918. The new advance of British and Arab troops finally encouraged notables and politicians from Damascus to rise openly against the Ottoman garrison (1 October 1918). On the same day Arab troops under Husain's son Faisal, and soon afterwards British troops under Allenby, marched into the Syrian capital. For the Arab nationalists Syria was liberated by an Arab army and political power belonged to the liberators, who immediately tried to establish an Arab civil administration in Syria. Almost simultaneously with the establishment of the National Assembly in Ankara, Arab nationalists in Damascus organized an Arab National Congress which met from 3 June 1919 until 19 July 1920. This Congress, which was led by Faisal, had the function of looking after Arab interests, and to begin with it was taken for granted that Arabia included the whole of the Fertile Crescent. Political sovereignty was for the time being to remain with the National Congress, whose members included a considerable number of former Ottoman deputies.[95]

Faisal's appearance at the Paris Peace Conferences encouraged the Congress to proclaim the independence of 'Arabia' as a kingdom on 7 March 1920: 'We have announced the end of the present regimes of military occupation in the three regions [Lebanon, Aleppo, Damascus], and these are being replaced by a royal constitutional regime, which is responsible to this Assembly [the

Congress] for everything underlying the complete independence of the country.'[96] Faisal was appointed King of the Arabs; his father Husain remained King of Hijaz. The 'new Arab government', which had, as late as 5 October 1916, nominated Husain as 'Sharif and Emir of Mecca', no longer played any part in Damascus because the citizens of Hijaz who had supported this government were unwanted on Syrian territory. The Syrian character of Damascus politics had now become evident. All the same, the Congress had also acknowledged the independence of Iraq, although Iraq and Syria were to form a kind of economic community. Lebanon and Palestine were considered as inalienable parts of Syria.[97]

Rashid Rida had also arrived in Damascus as early as 14 September 1919 to take charge of the reorganization of the legal system under the 'Arab government', and to assume the presidency of the Congress in the name of the Progressive Party, of which he had a very guarded opinion.[98] As anticipated, the Syrian Congress was dominated by two political groups: the urban Progressive Party (Hizb al-Taqaddum) led by the then Syrian foreign minister Abd al-Rahman Shahbandar, and the party of the liberals, the Independence Party (Hizb al-Istiqlal). Rida, as the representative of the Salafiya, must have found it difficult to join either of these groups, since they did not use an Islamic discourse. But as he himself said, he inevitably had to participate in the founding of the Progressive Party, since it represented the political community whose ideals he had shared.[99] Rida's Islamic republicanism, however, met with little response in Damascus. The groups supporting Husain and his son Faisal were too strong and were even ready to include foreign advisers in the government, albeit under the condition that the Sykes–Picot Agreement, which was rumoured to be under negotiation in Paris, would not be concluded.

The intervention of French troops, the devastating defeat of the quickly organized 'regular Syrian army' near Maisalun (24 July 1920) and the bombing of Damascus put an end to the dream of a Syrian nation state. Unlike the Turkish nationalists, the Syrian National Congress was unable to contribute to the kind of social or cultural integration of Syria which might have led to a successful mobilization of the Syrian population against the intervention troops. Besides, Syria was demilitarized, as were most other Arab countries. The urban political leadership thus not only lacked a properly functioning civil administration, but above all real sovereignty over the country. The military power of the ethnic groups was especially significant and the community of the Druzes in the Hauran mountains was to play a crucial role in the resistance against the French occupation in 1925.

The colonial lords, on the other hand, could re-define the states of the Arab countries thanks to their military presence. In 1920 Great Britain separated its new 'mandated territory' of Palestine from eastern Jordan for strategic reasons, and the latter was subsequently renamed Transjordan. Iraq, which from 1920 included the Mosul area – France having renounced its interests in this oil-rich region in exchange for British support in the issues of Alsace-Lorraine and Syria – was 'united' as a British protectorate in 1921.[100] Iraq and Transjordan were put under the formal regency of Husain's two sons Faisal and Abdallah in 1921 and 1922 respectively. The victory of the 'liberals' over the urban nationalists was thereby completed. The monarchy had triumphed over republicanism. When on 28 February 1922 the British protectorate over Egypt was finally cancelled, this country soon afterwards also became a 'kingdom' under Fu'ad I. The old ideal of the sultanate thus lost its political significance for good. Instead, the eastern Arab world now had five new kingdoms (or emirates) – Egypt, Transjordan, Iraq, Hijaz and Najd – a political system that no longer left room for the Islamic division between sultanate and caliphate.

CHAPTER TWO

Bourgeois Nationalism and Political Independence, 1920–1939

1. THE CALIPHATE BETWEEN REPUBLICANISM AND ROYALISM

The Arab nationalists, unlike the Turks of the Ottoman heartland or the Persians, could not oust an 'emperor' from the throne after the war, since the Arab world no longer had an 'emperor'. Thanks to the Turkish nationalist offensive, the Arab countries under Ottoman sovereignty were spared the task of overthrowing the old social system of the sultanate and creating a republican regime of their own. This may also explain why Arab nationalism at first remained true to the tradition of monarchy. Republicanism was limited to Syria, Lebanon and Algeria, where the ideals of French colonial policy had had their effect and in the Muslim regions of post-revolutionary Russia. But there were also a few early instances in which republican ideas were realized in the Arab world independently of the models provided by the colonial powers.

The Tripolitanian Republic

The short-lived Tripolitanian republic was one of the first to be established in the Islamic world.[1] It was co-founded on 16 November 1918 by the Libyan journalist and former member of the Ottoman parliament Sulaiman al-Baruni (1870–1940). Al-Baruni, who had published a periodical called *al-Asad al-Islami* (the Islamic Lion) in Cairo in 1908, saw himself as the proponent of a constitutionalism derived from Islamic history itself.[2] The declaration of independence issued by four equally entitled councillors of state who were appointed to form a government – among them al-Baruni – read as follows:[3]

> In the name of God, the All-Merciful and All-Compassionate! On Tuesday the 13 Safar 1337 (16/11/1918) the Tripolitanian nation decided to crown its independence by proclaiming a republican government commensurate with its great religious scholars, its nobles and notables and the leaders of its honoured fighters, who have assembled here from all parts of the country. The elections to the Tripolitanian parliament have been carried out and the Council of State has been chosen and has begun its task with the proclamation of the republic, which has also been communicated to the Great Powers and to the Italian state.

At a General Assembly in the Mosque of Misallata, the members of parliament and the Council of State swore the following oath:

> I who am laying this my hand on the Holy Koran, swear by God, the Exalted, that I make myself and my belongings a property of this my nation and my Tripolitanian republican government, that I shall be an enemy of its enemy and a friend of its friend and will respect its law' (...)'.

The new Tripolitanian Republic filled a political gap which had opened in the hinterland of the city of Tripoli as a result of the retreat of Ottoman troops. The situation was different in Cyrenaica (Barqa) in Eastern Libya where the mystical-pietistic order of the Sanusiya had asserted itself in the 1840s as a dominant institution since its foundation by Muhammad Ali al-Sanusi (1787–1859). After the death of the 'Great Sanusi', his family promptly established a monarchical system which mainly relied on a closely-knit network of settlements of the order, including the tribal community. But this political model was not popular in urban Tripolitania over which the Sanusiya had not succeeded in extending its influence. Whereas in its power centre in Cyrenaica the Sanusiya could count on the support of more than 40,000 'brothers' and had 49 settlements, by 1920 it had only 18 settlements in Tripolitania with about 3,500 members (compared with 22 settlements in Fezzan and 34 in western Egypt). It was also weakened in Tripolitanian eyes by the decision of the then leader of the Sanusiya, Muhammad Idris, to seek a modus vivendi with the Italians in Cyrenaica and to stop resistance against the Italian troops.

After the end of the war between Italy and Turkey, the urban nationalists had retreated into the Jabal al-Nafusa area and had tried, as early as 1913, to establish a state which would be independent of both the Ottoman Empire and Italy. To this end al-Baruni, who had very good contacts in Europe where he had invested his 'fortune of several millions', had even asked for support from the German Kaiser Wilhelm II.[4] On the other hand, the Ottoman general Enver Pasha had proposed himself as the Tripolitanian viceroy of the Ottoman Empire.[5] All the attempts of the Sanusiya to gain military control of Tripolitania were frustrated by the resistance of the citizens and above all by the ruler of Misrata, Ramadan al-Shtaiwi al-Suwailihi, and in January 1916, the warriors of the Banu Sulaiman had to capitulate to the superior force of the urban unions.

By contrast to the situation in Cyrenaica, the urban nationalists thus succeeded in shaking off the supremacy of the Sanusiya – a victory over the tribal community – and, at the same time, rejecting the royalist system they represented. A negative result of this was, however, that the republicans lacked the support of the great tribal unions who represented a decisive military power and were much more strongly rooted in a mystical culture which promised them power, respect and learning.

After the proclamation of the republic, the nationalists were soon forced to enter into negotiations with the Italian government under Francesco Saverio Nitti, which led to a 'constitutional law' for Tripolitania (1 June 1919). This constitutional law had the peculiarity of extending common citizenship to Arabs and Italians and of recognizing the Islamic law as the civil law.[6] In order to document the independence of the provinces of Barqa (Cyrenaica) and Tripolitania, it also included 'provincial constitutions'. The leaders of the Tripolitanian Republic finally accepted Italian sovereignty and, since the Italians promised to carry out parliamentary elections, reorganized themselves into a National Party of Reform (Hizb al-Islah al-Watani). After the assassination of Ramadan al-Suwailihi, one of the former Councillors of State[7] (August 1920), the entire political leadership of the republic went underground.

The Rif Republic

The republican tradition in Morocco emerged from an ethnic secessionist policy followed by various tribal unions in northern Morocco. After the First World War, French and Spanish colonists had established themselves in the country. The French Consul General Louis Hubert Lyautey, known as Le Maréchal, who was résident général (administrative head of the protectorate) from 1912 to 1925, began organizing a Moroccan–French bilateral administration which was to lead to social apartheid between Europeans and natives. By 1921 the country had been completely 'pacified', at least within the sphere of influence of the French protectorate. Using military support, the colonial administration managed to impose taxes on most of those regions which had already been run as *bilad al-makhzan*, taxable areas, under the Moroccan sultans. Only the tribes of the Middle Atlas resolutely resisted French sovereignty until 1934.

In northern Morocco, the post-war period was marked by secessionist tendencies. One of the spokesmen was Muhammad b. Abdalkarim al-Khattabi (1882–1963) from Agdaira in the neighbourhood of Alhucemas (al-Husaima). After studying law at the famous Islamic university of Fez, al-Qarawiyin, Abdalkarim went to Spanish Melilla as a judge. When the Spaniards conquered the traditional city of Shifshawan in the Rif mountains in 1919, there was growing resistance among Islamic personalities against the policy of the Spanish occupation. Abdalkarim's father spoke up for the opposition, as a result of which his son was removed from office and arrested by the Spaniards in 1920. He escaped from prison to found an independent Berber republic in the city of Annual, and was at times able to summon 100,000 men to its defence. Having carried out a major reform of the army in 1921, Abdalkarim finally succeeded in crushing Spanish troops near Annual in 1923 and gaining control over almost the whole of northern Morocco. He also managed to bring under his sway the 'Lord of the Mountains', Ahmad b. Muhammad al-Raisuni (died 1925), who had defied both the French colonizers and the sultanate at the beginning of the century.[8] Having announced in 1921 that he would liberate 'the whole of Morocco', in 1923 he launched an overhasty invasion of the French protectorate. But in 1925 the French army under Marshal Pétain, which was at times said to have risen to 500,000 men, pushed back Abdalkarim's Kabyle troops before they could reach Fez and Meknes. On 25 May 1926, he was forced to surrender, and was banished to Reunion Island with members of his family.[9]

Abdalkarim's Rif Republic was not only an attempt to found an independent Moroccan state, but also a starting point towards a new non-sultanic regime for the country. The Moroccan Sultan Mulay Yusuf (1912–27), who had been appointed by the French administration on 12 August 1912,[10] was in a certain sense a counterpart to the Ottoman Sultan Mehmed VI Wahid al-Din, who was supported by the Entente powers in Istanbul. The fact that Abdalkarim, unlike Mustafa Kemal (Atatürk), failed to preserve his republic was due to a lack of political representation. Abdalkarim put his full trust in the Berber consultative bodies and dispensed with the task of organizing a national congress which would have included urban nationalists. In addition, he based the legitimacy of the Rif Republic first of all on Islamic tradition and secondly on the solidly established tribal structure of Berber society. Because of this ethnic structure, many members of the Arab communities felt excluded and followed the five-year war merely as observers who sympathized with the rebels. The ethnic framework of the Rif Republic thus undermined the republicanism of the urban nationalists, who for the most part saw their Arab culture much better preserved under the French protectorate than under what appeared to them to be an obscure Berber Republic. Moroccan national policy was accordingly shaped by two factors: on the attempt of the urban population to found a political culture of their own against the traditional order of the country, and on the French colonial administration which, especially under its leader Lyautey, practised a policy of segregation designed to mark off modernism from tradition socially and culturally. Faced with the choice of either adhering to or rejecting political traditions steeped in tribal connections and aristocratic relationships, most city-dwellers showed a preference for French colonial culture. The French language did not present too much of an obstacle, for since the 19th century it had been the language of modernism, as well as a medium of prestige for the Moroccan urban nationalists through which they could communicate directly with the colonial culture.

The at first rather small group of Moroccan Salafiya was therefore closely connected with the colonial culture. This group used an Islamic discourse both to substantiate its social break with tradition and to demand recognition for it. Its main opponents were therefore primarily the traditional sites of Islamic scholarship such as the Qarawiyin University of Fez and the numerous local and regional Islamic centres which went back to settlements of mystical orders and groups.

French colonial officials on the other hand benefited from the decentralization of Morocco, which was rooted in ethnic traditions. At the end of the 19th century, three 'empires of the princes of the Atlas'[11] had succeeded in making themselves independent, each belonging to a Berber tribe (M'tuga, Gundafa and Glawa). After 1908, the small Berber states had gradually been combined into a system of indirect colonial control, forming a strong backing for French colonial policy. From the point of view of the Islamic nationalists who originally belonged to the Salafiya environment, French policy in this way broke the 'colonial consensus' between nationalists and colonists, a consensus which aimed at establishing the sovereignty of a nation state. But as the colonial administration, precisely because of its ethnic policy, regionally limited the development of the country into a nation state, the nationalists found themselves faced with an insoluble contradiction: on the one hand, they saw themselves as members of a 'modern, national society' to which they had won access solely through the colonial administration; on the other hand, the administration was thwarting the development of a nation state through its ethnic politics. When in 1930 the colonial administration granted the Berbers their own judicial power, based on Berber traditions of justice, in the so-called Berber Decree (*dahir berbère*), the colonial consensus was decisively broken. The colonial administration now became the political opponent of the nationalists, in whose view it had abandoned the task of establishing a nation state with a uniform judicial system and had thus destroyed the Moroccan nation state.

The Abolition of the Caliphate

Liberal nationalism, which represented economic liberalism in a culturally integrated society, had been the popular point of view of intellectuals in the Islamic world up to the end of the First World War. However, the political and social revolts of the post-war period strengthened those nationalists who were partisans of statism and believed that political secession from the colonial power was the only way to enforce the recognition of Islamic countries as nation states. Secessionism was keyed to autarchy: the 'strong state' was not only meant to create the basis for a homogeneous economic system, but also to provide for the uniformity of law, education and national culture. The liberal nationalists quite quickly came to terms with the new constitutional monarchies in Egypt, Transjordan, Iraq and Hijaz, while the republican nationalists were able to triumph only in Turkey and, to begin with, in the new Soviet Union. This state of affairs did not essentially change until the international economic crisis.

For the new Turkish republic, integration as a nation state fitted in with the needs of the moment: the Turkish nationalists, who had built a platform of their own by founding the People's Party (Khalk Firkasi),[12] considered Ottoman cosmopolitanism as the cause of the disintegration of the state and now spared no effort to unify Turkish state culture on the basis of a number of principles. Among these two were unquestionable: namely that the state had to be 'Turkish' and that it should be republican. What remained open was the attitude towards public Islamic culture, which had made such a contribution to the cosmopolitanism in the Ottoman Empire. Abd al-Majid II was at this time still officiating as the caliph from the house of Osman, although there was no longer an Ottoman Empire. The hierarchical institution of Islamic scholarship (*ilmiya*) with the Sheikh al-Islam at its pinnacle also remained intact, even if the *ulama* (especially those from the Naqshbandiya entourage) were gradually liberating themselves from this hierarchy and taking part in Turkish national policy.

The abolition of the union in one person of sultanate and caliphate was at first viewed as a good solution by most Islamic intellectuals, for in this way the idea of the nation state could be combined with the ideal of the caliphate. At the same time, the power of the Ottoman sultanate, which the younger Arab nationalists sensed as oppressive, could be separated from the caliphate. Indian Islamic intellectuals like Sayyid Amir Ali (Syed Ameer Ali, 1849–1928) as a result gained fresh hope that the Muslim world might succeed in creating a caliphate which would be free of the narrow limits of a nation state, and whose function would be to symbolically represent the Islamic world.[13] Even Rashid Rida agreed with the proposals of the Turkish press that 'the Islamic world' should be consulted about the question of the caliphate.[14] The abolition of the sultanate thus appeared to revalorize the non-Turkish Islamic world, since from the point of view of Arab nationalists Turkey had given up its claim to political leadership. From India as well as Egypt more and more proposals were advanced for a new political interpretation of the caliphate. There were also questions over the caliph's person, for it was by no means indisputable that the caliph necessarily had to be an Ottoman, or even the learned Abd al-Majid.

These discussions provided the Salafiya with an occasion to search for a completely new definition of the caliphate's function. The caliph was not to be a politician, but a 'scholar', an *alim*, and he was to embody the ideals of classical erudition, that is he was to combine jurisprudence with moral guidance. There was no longer any question of political sovereignty; on the contrary, the caliph had to be democratically minded as an expression of Islamic scholarly culture. Therefore it was the task of the *ulama* to elect the caliph. Rida even thought it imperative to establish an institute for the training of caliphs and the *ulama*.[15] The caliph accordingly had to assume a sovereign function in the realm of culture and education which would correspond with the ideals of reformers rather than those of conservative scholarship, and which would hold good for the entire Islamic world. Thus, in practise, the Salafiya argued for a self-sufficient caliphate without sultanic identity. This idea necessarily meant that the Muslim nation states which acknowledged such a caliphate would forfeit part of the sovereignty they had just won. However, the aim of the Islamic nationalists was to secure for themselves, a field of political sovereignty in the new civic system, now that there was hardly a space that might be assigned to them within the political public of the nation states. This field was the control of an Islamic system of norms and an Islamic public which would rise above the nation states.

The undisguised claim to power of the Salafiya was thus perceived as a challenge by the new Turkish government which was not prepared to yield its sovereign rights and therefore decided to take a leap ahead. In order to reintegrate the power of the caliphate into the state, the office of the caliph, i. e. the caliph as a person, was to be abolished. On 1 March 1924, Mustafa Kemal submitted a proposal to this effect to the Turkish National Assembly. After a long debate, the delegates almost unanimously approved the new law Article I of which reads:[16] 'The caliph has been dismissed. The office of the caliphate has been abolished, since the caliphate is essentially contained in the meaning and concept of government and republic.'

With this law the caliphate was reintegrated into the new Turkish state culture as an 'essential' component of the republican order. At the same time, the Turkish National Assembly declared that it was not prepared to give up the sovereignty represented by the caliphate in favour of an 'overall Islamic' solution. The sovereignty which had been exercised by the caliph as the cultural head of the Islamic community now also devolved upon the republic. In other word, the Turkish republic appropriated sovereign rights which strictly speaking – in the view of the Salafiya – were vested in the caliph: that is, in the fields of civil rights and education. A month later, the Ottoman *shari'a* courts, the office of the *shaikh al-islam* and the Ministry of Justice and Islamic institutions were abolished. The new order was finally laid down on 20 April in a new constitution in which Islam continued to be the state religion for the next four years.

It was not the caliphate, then, but the independent institution of the caliph which was superseded by the Turkish government, which at the same time admitted that the functions of the caliph had been taken over by the National Assembly, and that the state had now irrevocably put an end to any separate religious institutions in the country. On 1 July and 4 October 1926 respectively, Turkey acquired a new criminal and civil law. A few other important innovations in republican Turkey are also worth mentioning: 4 March 1924, the compulsory retirement of most of the *ulama*; 30 November 1925, the closure of all establishments of mystical orders and a ban on Islamic orders;[17] 26 December 1925, the solar calendar declared as the only official calendar; 22 March 1926, a state monopoly on alcohol; 1 September 1926, the introduction of civil marriage at registry offices; 5 May 1927, a ban on religious inscriptions on public buildings; 1 November 1928, the introduction of Latin alphabet.[18]

This process of social and cultural integration was described as the secularization of Turkish society or, in Turkish usage, laicization (*layiklik*). But laicism was much more of a political motto than an analytical concept. For the Turkish state was quite manifestly combining the authorities and sovereign rights that had been institutionally separated in the Ottoman Empire, although subjected to a common control by the palace. The crucial fact was that the Islamic discourse was banned from public in favour of a purely Turkish identity. Thus in 1932 the Koran was for the first time openly recited in Turkish and from 1933 the call to prayer as well as the prayers recited in mosques had to be in Turkish.

The process of secularization begun in 1925 was basically nothing but a thorough Turkification of the old Ottoman society. Some contemporary authors pointed out that 'the Turks have certainly not abandoned Islam. This is an Arab idea. The Arabs, however, do not know what Islam is.' Turkish secularism, they claimed, had revealed the 'Islam of the Koran' and liberated Turkey from superstitious popular Islam and the legalistic Islam of the *ulama*.[19] The Turkish state was hence setting itself up as the guarantor of 'true spiritual Islam'. The criticism of popular Islam and scholasticism was nothing new to the classicists. So it is not very surprising that Turkish religious policy was almost favourably received by the Salafiya,[20] for Turkey in the 1920s actually seemed to be founding a state culture in which the classicist ideals of the Salafiya, the ideas of the urban nationalists and Islamic social-revolutionary and socialist traditions had found homogeneous expression. However, above it all reigned the state, which was henceforth regarded as the only authority of Turkish society. Every policy now became state apologetics – the principle that the state incorporated the absolute sovereignty in society was soon extended to economic realm and condensed into the ideology of statism (*devletçilik*, later *etatism*).

This claim of absolute sovereignty by the state essentially contradicted the concepts of most Islamic political currents. For the ideal of civil independence endorsed by both classicists and revolutionaries was directly threatened by the autonomy of the state. The more deeply the new Islamic nation states committed themselves to a state-centred republicanism or to a constitutional monarchy, the more isolated became Islamic policy in the public eye.

Indian Reactions

Even the claim that a concept of sovereignty was being formulated through Islamic policy was now directly jeopardized. When on the 5–6 March 1924 Husain, the King of Hijaz, proclaimed himself as the new caliph following the initiative of his son Abdallah, the idea of an Arab caliph enjoyed a brief revival; but the fact that a monarch was proclaiming himself caliph all too clearly contradicted the classicists' concept of Islamic sovereignty. No wonder then that Husain's caliphate was only acknowledged by a few of the *ulama* from Palestine, Transjordan and Iraq.[21] The Indian social revolutionary Muhammad Barakat Allah (1859–1927), who had lived in Moscow from 1919 to 1922, having previously led a 'Committee of Indian Muslims' in London,[22] wrote a voluminous text in which he denied Husain's legitimacy.[23] Indeed, the Indian public, which paid particular attention to the question of the caliphate, altogether condemned its 'usurpation'.

In 1912–13, Indian *ulama* and Muslim intellectuals, especially the members of the 'Servants of the Ka'aba' (Khuddam-i Ka'aba) group founded by Mushir Husain Kidwai (1879–1926) in Lucknow in May 1913, had come forward as advocates of an Ottoman caliphate. The All-India Central Caliphate Committee, which convened in November 1919, not only made an attempt to exercise direct influence on post-war international policy, but supported the political organization of Indian Muslims, as well as the Indian opposition against British colonial rule; even Mahatma Gandhi joined the Caliphate Committee.[24] The committee succeeded in founding numerous regional offices in India and in promoting a new interpretation of the caliphate in Europe. Its foremost propagandists were the brothers Muhammad and Shaukat Ali, who soon became the political leaders of the caliphate movement in India. The Indian

Caliphate Committee followed the new Turkish national policy in its essential aspects; but the Indian pro-caliphate politicians could not agree with the abolition of the caliphate, because it meant that they might lose their symbol of sovereignty. However, that would be less tragic than the usurpation of the caliphate by Husain, whose self-proclamation definitely contradicted the concern of the nationalists to make their own decision about the incumbent of this office. They promptly presented the government in Mecca with a declaration demanding that 'a powerful republican government (organized in accordance with *shari'a* laws) be appointed in the Hijaz; this government should be independent in its internal policy, and its external policy should be such as to satisfy the Islamic world and comply with its views regarding the complete and absolute independence of the country – an independence that should be free of external influence, whether overt or covert.'[25] In the eyes of the Indian Committee, republicanism was capable of saving the caliphate; in actual fact there was hardly any political latitude for a construction of this kind.

The Struggle for the Hijaz, 1924–1926

The entry of Arab tribes of the Najd into the Hijaz (1 September 1924) and the occupation of Mecca (13–16 October 1924) marked the beginning of a one-year war between the Hijaz and Najd which was to end with the capitulation of the port of Jeddah on 24 December 1925. By 4 October 1924 Husain had already abdicated both as king and as caliph in favour of his son Ali who used the caliphate as a pawn to win supporters in the war against Najd, if the need should arise. Thus in August 1925 he offered the caliphate to the Egyptian King Fu'ad I, who, after some hesitation, turned him down. At the beginning of January 1926, Ibn Sa'ud had himself proclaimed king of the Hijaz by some of the region's notables.[26]

The conquest of Mecca and Medina had grave consequences.[27] For one thing, it soon emerged that Ibn Sa'ud had not, as originally declared, liberated the Hijaz from the 'usurper' Husain for the Islamic world. Indeed he made it quite clear that the Hijaz was to be an integral part of his new Arab empire. For another, Arab tribes from Najd, who were committed as Ikhwan ('partisans' or 'brothers in faith') to a radical version of Wahhabi doctrine, provoked the destruction of the old cosmopolitan system of the Hijaz by imposing the Wahhabi culture on it as a new compulsory social order.

The Ikhwan movement was a pietistic cult of Arab tribes who, from about 1912, had been made to settle in agrarian colonies, or so-called *hujar*. Ten years after he founded the third Saudi principality, Ibn Sa'ud had through this device tried to break the dominance of the old tribal society in the principality and, by gradually urbanizing the central highland, to build the nucleus of a centralized state system. The tribes who settled in the *hujar* represented, as mentioned, a radical trend within the Wahhabiya. Following the ideal of the Prophet's life, they regarded their colonies as a recreation of the settlements of Muslims who had fled Mecca for Medina in 622 and thus believed the surrounding society to be 'un-Islamic'. Just as Muhammad had returned to Mecca, their emigration was to be followed by a 'reconquest', that is, the by the reappropriation of the lost land on the Arabian peninsula. Between January 1913 and 1920, a total of 70 operational *hujar* villages were founded whose settlers belonged mainly to the great central Arab tribes. But the Ikhwan only emerged as a military asset towards the end of the First World War when separate contingents of their tribes provoked conflicts on the Hijaz and Kuwait borders, where Ibn Sa'ud had allowed a chief of the Mutair tribe, Nayif b. Shuqair, to build his own *hujar* towards the end of 1919.[28] Now the Saudi prince could count on about 15–20,000 'regular' troops. Together with these units he also had at his disposal members of the Wahhabi *ulama* or *mutawi'a* who entered the newly conquered areas to ensure that Wahhabi doctrines were observed and whose major target of attack continued to be popular Islamic piety, which they believed to be a violation of the principle of the absolute oneness of God.

The conquest of the Hijaz was without doubt Ibn Saud's most daring military enterprise. The conquest of the Shammar region in 1915–17 might be explained by the pro-Ottoman attitude of the ruling Al Rashid family; the occupation of the districts of Abha in Asir might also be represented as a 'matter of domestic policy' and as the settling of unsolved border problems. But the occupation of the virtually international areas around the holy cities of Mecca and Medina required a different rationale, especially in view of the fact that both the Hijaz and the Najd had concluded a defence treaty with Great Britain and received considerable subsidies under its terms. At a conference in Riyadh in July 1924 complaints were made against the Hijaz. It was preventing pilgrimages by Muslim tribes from Najd and boycotting the implementation of a public policy in accordance with the *shari'a*.[29] For the first time, the Ikhwan units were engaged on a large scale. Led by their most prominent chiefs, Khalid b. Lu'ayy and Sultan b. Bijad, they advanced at some speed towards Mecca, plundered the city and destroyed all the symbols of the 'heathen' practices of the Meccans.

Ibn Sa'ud had taken advantage of the settlement of the Bedouin tribes, which he had promoted since 1912, to boost his dynastic power. The pietistic Ikhwan movement was, however, by no means willing to put up with the prince's 'realpolitik', which aimed at establishing a central state. The tribes not only saw such a state as a threat to their economic and political independence, but above all as a danger to the tribal system of Najd itself. Ibn Saud's proclamation of himself as King of Hijaz had already curbed the autonomy of the Ikhwan tribes, who had been compelled to withdraw from the Hijaz in 1926. The new king, whose main concern at the time was to have his sovereignty acknowledged by the international Islamic community, was now not only the victor over the Hashimite dynasty, but also the man who rescued the Hijaz from the clutches of radical Wahhabi partisans. The damage Saudi foreign policy suffered through the conquest of the Holy Cities by the Wahhabi tribes did not have any major consequences. Its main critics were the traditional *ulama* of Islamic universities who violently protested against the sacrilege committed at the shrine of the Prophet and at the tombs of the first three caliphs and several of the Prophet's companions. But their political position had meanwhile grown so weak that they were reduced to defending popular rituals at the tombs as Islamic. The Islamic public was meanwhile almost entirely aligned with the Salafiya which, though it believed the behaviour of the Ikhwan to be an improper example of them taking the law into their own hands, thought that the aim of the Wahhabis had to be seen as a whole. And since the Wahhabis, like the Salafiya, pleaded for the repression of traditional cults at Islamic public places, there at least existed a basis for shared political views.

From the early 1920s, Salafiya *ulama* had started to publish the self-testimonies of Wahhabi *ulama* from Najd. Rashid Rida himself edited a collection of such writings in 1924.[30] In accordance with their classicist ideal, the Wahhabiya had found in the medieval Damascene scholar Taqi al-Din Ibn Taimiya (1263–1328) an important advocate for their fight against orally transmitted innovations (*bida'*) that were not admissible from a doctrinal point of view. This revival of Ibn Taimiya's literary tradition soon became a connecting link between the Wahhabiya and parts of the Salafiya.[31]

The conflict that had long been smouldering between traditional *ulama* and apologists of the Wahhabis was now reordered: the Salafiya were able to persuade the Wahhabi state culture in Najd to relativize its radical moralism; in return, the Salafiya began to adopt a friendly policy towards Ibn Sa'ud, which greatly contributed to raising the status of the Wahhabiya in Islamic public opinion.[32]

Rashid Rida now openly approached the new king of the Hijaz. He was soon followed by other prominent representatives of the Salafiya, such as the Druze Amir Shakib Arslan (1869–1946) and the publisher Muhibb al-Din al-Khatib (1886–1969), who came from Damascus but lived in Cairo. This rapprochement did not mean, however, that the Wahhabi and Salafi cultures were blending. This was not possible because not only were they from divergent social environments but also there were extensive theological differences between them. The crucial point was the connection of Ibn Saud's royal regime with the Salafiya, which would inevitably lead to contradictions within the Wahhabi society. In 1926, Ibn Sa'ud dismissed the radical Wahhabi, Muhammad

b. Abdallah Ibn Bulaihid (1867/8–1940), from his function as Great Kadi of the Hijaz and replaced him with a scholar who was one of his devotees and came from the family of the founder of the Wahhabiya, namely Hasan b. Abdallah Al al-Shaikh from Riyadh (1870–1959).

To crown his efforts to achieve international recognition, Ibn Sa'ud called for an international Islamic Congress, which convened in Mecca from 7 June to 5 July 1926. Many prominent Islamic intellectuals, *ulama* and politicians attended in the hope of being able to discuss the political future of the Hijaz. But Ibn Sa'ud, who had originally intended to put this question on the Congress agenda, changed his mind and defined it as a gathering to discuss medical, social and cultural questions connected with the annual pilgrimage to Mecca.[33] The Congress led to a distinct polarization of the Islamic political public. The Salafiya was suddenly split into two political factions, a pro-Saudi royalist and a republican wing with Rida's group from Cairo now partially complying with the Saudi state culture, while other members of the Salafiya propagated Islamic republicanism. The pro-Saudi position was from then on to become one of the major political options within Islamic politics. Confronted with this situation, the republicans considered the deflection of the Rida group as treason and suspected Rida of having received a considerable sum from the king.

Salafiya support was very useful to Ibn Sa'ud. Among the Wahhabi communities in the *hujar* there was unrest, since the tribes had practically been excluded from any exploitation of the conquered regions in the Hijaz. At a conference in Artawiya, a stronghold of the Ikhwan movement, they reproached the king, among other things, for betraying the ideals of the Wahhabiya by introducing new technologies and un-Islamic taxes, and violation of the territorial sovereignty of the Ikhwan by a cession of grazing rights to Jordanian tribes.[34] On 29 January 1927, Ibn Sa'ud summoned the Ikhwan leaders, among them the two rebels Faisal al-Dawish and Sultan b. Bijad, to a conference in Riyadh where they were informed that the Wahhabi *ulama* had almost unanimously rejected their accusations. Thereupon the Ikhwan tribes mobilized to enforce their claims. They were also keen to conquer Iraq, which was in their eyes the country of infidels, and hoped to draw British troops stationed in Iraq and Kuwait into the conflict so that they might simultaneously fight against the mainstay of Saudi sovereignty. It was only with British support that Ibn Saud's loyal units managed, in several engagements, to defeat the Ikhwan. On 12 January 1930, when two of the most important rebel leaders were captured, the conflict finally came to an end.

The Search for a New Caliph

The civil war in Arabia was hardly noticed by the Islamic public. Much more important than these local conflicts was the blatant fact that the different Islamic ideas of the political system could no longer be conveyed through the ideal of a caliphate. In 1926, a last attempt at saving the caliphate, made by traditional *ulama* at a much publicized, but in fact very small conference in Cairo, had run aground. The participating *ulama* had to admit that the public was no longer interested in the issue. Besides, it was no longer clear what function a caliph could exercise in an Islamic world organized into nation states, none of which showed any sign of wanting to give up its sovereign rights. Meanwhile Islamic liberals, foremost among them the militant judge Ali Abd al-Raziq (1888–1966), had begun to campaign for an Islamically legitimized separation between religious and state institutions. Abd al-Raziq's polemic *Islam and the Foundations of Authority*,[35] for which he was expelled by the Azhar University, as well as the new interpretation of the historicity of poetry in the pre-Islamic period and its influence on the Koran by Taha Husain, then Professor of Arabic literature at the Egyptian University,[36] were merely the tip of the iceberg. More and more intellectuals pleaded for a secular modernism based on Islam, which to them had in any case been a reality for a long time. Yet on the one hand Islamic liberals found it very difficult to express their ideas among the local Islamic public which was still dominated by traditional scholarship or by Islamic nationalists. On the other hand, outside this public there was no great need to lend an Islamic foundation to secular modernism, for here a 'European discourse' prevailed which allowed Islam no special role.

2. ISLAMIC NATIONAL POLICY AND THE DE-ISLAMIZATION OF THE POLITICAL PUBLIC

The 1920s marked a political breakthrough for civil nationalism in the Islamic world. Henceforth the nation state order, even in those countries which were still colonies, was steeped in a civil culture in which the 'European' discourse prevailed. The 'Islamic' discourse had by this time almost completely adapted itself to secular modernism: the essence of all things political was the establishment of national sovereignty (*al-hakimiya al-milliya*), a goal the Islamic parties also adopted. However, the social contradiction of modernism could not be overcome in the 1920s. Although nationalists and Islamic partisans both fought for the abolition of independent institutions that limited the sovereignty of the nation state, only a few Islamic countries developed a homogeneous political public in which religion no longer played a functional role, but merely influenced the private sphere. In Turkey, Iran and Afghanistan, as well as in the new Central Asian republics of the USSR, secular modernism became the political issue. In all other Islamic countries, however, the Islamic discourse remained part of public debate. In Algeria and Indonesia, settler colonialism and the accompanying 'civilizing claim' of the colonial powers provoked the mobilization of the Islamic public which, in its fight against colonialism, prevailed over urban nationalism.

The absence of Islamic discourse from public debate was soon perceived and interpreted as 'secularism'. Thus the European discourse used in the Islamic world corresponded with current opinion in the West, according to which secular modernism could only be part of the European discourse and could not be integrated within any other cultural system. This kind of language soon became political. Many nationalists now perceived all varieties of Islamic policy as a challenge to once more combine religion and state within society. In their own turn Islamic activists reflected this linguistic usage and declared that the European discourse was synonymous with secularism and therefore implied a break with the Islamic public. They feared 'secularism' all the more because they felt that their own position in colonial society was threatened. In response, they radicalized their Islamic discourse – as did, especially, Rashid Rida – by deliberately appearing in public in 'oriental clothes', ostentatiously praying in public, and altogether leading an exemplary Islamic life. But all this separated them even more widely from the political public, except for that in emphatically Islamic states such as Najd and Hijaz, which still invested them with an aura of internationalism and public recognition.

Secularism and Islamism were thus political concepts that were formed in the competition for predominance within the political public and that gradually became petrified into a social typology. But for all the rhetoric, both secularists and Islamists followed the same object: the nation state, based on absolute sovereignty, was to represent the crucial authority. Society had to delegate its own sovereignty to the state. Islam and nation were now two interchangeable concepts having an identical function, that of providing an idealistic and factually extra-societal foundation for the authority of the state.

The de-Islamization of the public was an important characteristic of the late 1920s. It was particularly promoted as a political programme wherever urban nationalists had triumphed. This was especially the case in Turkey. But it was also true of those new Asian republics of the USSR in which Muslims lived as a majority. Here the victory of the Russian revolutionaries in 1917 was the initial spark for the enforcement of an urban policy.

Turkestan under Soviet Rule

By Turkestan is meant the region that stretches from the Caspian Sea to the then Russo-Chinese border. After the conquest of Merv in 1884, this region was divided into two Russian general governments (Turkestan and the Steppe) as well as the khanates of Bukhara and Khiva. The two khanates had been forced, in order to preserve their old system, to tolerate considerable loss of territory including the three Zuz sultanates in northern Turkestan (Kichi, Orta, Ulu), the Turkmenian principalities in the steppes, as well as the great Khanate of Kokand which had completely disappeared. Ruled by Russian military governors, the lands of Turkestan were subject to an extensive agrarian colonization which soon led to close economic involvement with Russia.

The ethnic heterogeneity of the region was overlaid by a relatively homogeneous Islamic culture in which Persian and Jagatai played a major role as literary languages. These written cultures lost their significance when the incorporation of members of the social elites into the Russian administration promoted an inclination to recognize and use Russian as a 'cultural language'.

The urban elites, the majority of whom did not identify with the old sultanic regime of Turkestan, for the most part adopted the course of assimilation into the Russian imperial culture. But, like the Algerians, they wanted equal rights to participate in political and social life without having to renounce their own cultural idiosyncracies. The reformists in Turkestan had thus an enemy in common with the Russian democrats and revolutionaries, namely Tsarism. And since Tsarist power in Turkestan had established itself primarily as a military power, the political emancipation of the elites was aimed mainly at establishing a civil system which would guarantee a free political public and an autonomous bureaucracy. This aim was also endorsed by many of the *ulama* who had, as early as 1905, demanded a free Muslim religious administration for Tashkent, the seat of the general government of Turkestan.

There were vastly differing reports on the impact of Russian rule. Muhammad Ali Khalaf, called Madali Tshan, from Andijan in the Ferghana, who had led a horde of Kirgiz and Kipchak rebels against Russian troops in 1898, is reported to have said before his execution:

> The Russians have treated us well. There is more and more wealth everywhere. The Muslims have become rich, but we have paid for it, because the soul of the Muslim has disappeared. The body rejoices, but the soul is corrupted. That is why the voice of heaven told me to liberate the Muslims from this sad wealth which signifies the end of the reign of Muhammad and of his law.[37]

The motif evoked here of the 'decomposition of the Muslim personality' and 'alienation from the self', which was expressed later, especially in Algeria, as *dépersonnalisation*, was picked up both by urban nationalists and by the numerous rebel leaders. But while the latter considered revolt alone as an act of liberation, the urban nationalists expected to work out a polished linguistic, educational and cultural policy for the creation of their 'national personality'.

By 1913, however, champions of a more extensive independence had emerged. The writer Ahmad Baitursun (Aqymet Bajtursyn, 1873–1937), for example, promoted a linguistic policy among the Kazakhs – he first spoke mainly about the Kirghiz – to oppose both the Russian and the widely used Tatar languages.

The urban nationalists were at first unsuccessful and had little chance of playing their part in the great revolt of 1916. On 4 July 1916, Muslim peasants and labourers mutinied against mobilization at the Russian–Galician front and against being forced to supply the Russian colonial troops directly, even though sorely needed wheat imports were hardly arriving from Russia itself. The Russian army had intended to enlist altogether 390,000 Turkestanis to serve in the war. Muslim deserters formed the core of a rebel army consisting of up to 30,000 men which controlled the Ferghana valley until the end of November 1916. In August 1916, when the harsh sanctions imposed by General Ivanov had mobilized almost the entire region around Samarkand against Russian rule, the unrest threatened to spread to the Emirate of Bukhara. Although Cossack troops managed to regain control over Ferghana until February 1917, the political and social break could no longer be mended. Many of the rebel leaders soon became Bolsheviks and founded the Alach Orda government in Tashkent (1917–18), foremost among them Turar Riskul (Ryskulov, executed in 1939) and Alibay Zangil'din (1884–1953).[38] Few rebellions in the early 20th century claimed as many human lives as this uprising which, according to national historians left more than 650, 000 victims.[39]

It was not until after the October Revolution that the urban nationalists started to play a politically influential role. Once the question of power was raised anew by the revolutionary councils, in most of which Russians formed the majority, the nationalists came forward as advocates of territorial autonomy. They saw their claim borne out by Lenin's theses on the 'right to free severance and the creation of independent states', proclaimed by the Russian Social Democratic Labour Party in April 1917. After the fourth Muslim Regional Congress was held in Kokand on 10 December 1917, the delegates established the provisional autonomous government of Kokand and Turkestan, which greatly differed from the City Soviet of Tashkent, a stronghold of Russian revolutionaries since 15 November 1917. From a structural point of view, this congress was similar to the Arab Congress of Damascus. That is, it created a legislative body without having at its disposal an executive body or real state sovereignty. Russian revolutionary troops as well as Cossack counter-revolutionaries could therefore relatively quickly establish themselves in the region. The gradual Soviet reconquest of the independent Islamic regions was launched from Tashkent and in February 1918 Kokand was captured and destroyed.

The great famine of the war years, which claimed more than 3 million victims in Turkestan, made it easier for the Russian revolution to impose its sovereignty over what used to be the general government of Turkestan. On 5 May 1918, a congress in Tashkent proclaimed the 'autonomous republic of Turkestan' within the framework of the Union of Soviet Socialist Republics. The Soviet government of Turkestan soon afterwards tried to form a coalition with the urban nationalists and members of the Russian opposition (among others, the social revolutionaries who were powerful in Tashkent), since the country had been completely cut off from the USSR through the civil war. At the same time, British operations in the Turkmenian regions around Ashkhabad (13 August 1918 to 5 April 1919) tried to split the young republic into two parts and thus indirectly provoked a rapprochement of the nationalists with the Soviet government.

The Basmachi Uprising

Unlike the Syrian nationalists, some of the nationalists in Kokand succeeded, after their defeat in February 1918, in mobilizing native clan leaders and combining their units into a rather efficient troop (later on called Muslim troops or, pejoratively, Basmachi ['robbers']). Until 1924 the Basmachi, though they experienced many vicissitudes, exercised military control over the rural areas of Turkestan (Bukhara and Ferghana). Again by contrast to the Syrian case, the Basmachi leaders soon succeeded in eliminating the urban nationalists. To start with, they divided up their field of operations among six commanders (including the former town-major of Kokand, Irgash Qurbashi, and the police chief of Margilan, Mehmed Amin Bey). These were only able to control the larger cities temporarily and based their decentralized power on villages and communities in which they were recognized as patrons. After 1922, there were more and more signs of a growing ethnic orientation among the Basmachi groups which prevented a unified military command and gradually allowed the Russian expeditionary troops to 'pacify' Ferghana. It was only in Bukhara and in the Samarkand region that they continued to be successful, probably because what was at stake there was the restoration of the old Emirate of Bukhara, and the local Basmachi leaders had been recruited from among the beys who had served the emir for years.

The fact that the power of the rebels was concentrated in small towns and villages created political and social tensions between city and country. The urban nationalists, the majority of whom had a positive attitude to the rebels, feared that the return to traditional ways of resistance might jeopardize the political power which the cities had acquired through the revolution – Samarkand having more than 100,000 and Tashkent perhaps 400,000 inhabitants. The far too obvious influence of the traditionally-minded *ulama* and members of mystical orders confirmed the city-dwellers in the belief that they had to withhold their support from the Basmachi. Some of them, like Abdallah Karimoglu (1896–1938?), fought against the rebels as convinced communists. Others tried to negotiate a peace treaty, which was usually refused. A striking fact is that the Basmachi of Turkestan – unlike those of Bukhara – had, for the most part, dissociated themselves from the old system of the sultanate and at a national congress in Samarkand (April 1922) called the future regime of Turkestan an 'independent Turkestani, Turkish and Islamic republic'.[40]

The splintered rebel front was given a final breath of life by the arrival of Enver Pasha, a man who liked to compare himself with Hindenburg and who, while in Russia, had remained loyal to the politics of the Committee for Union and Progress and had collected together scattered groups of Islamic nationalists and assembled them into a 'League of Islamic Revolutionary Societies' (Islâm Ihtilal Cemyetleri Ittihadi) founded in Moscow. Among those who co-operated with Enver were such personalities as Shakib Arslan, Abd al-Aziz Jawish and the Ottoman defender of Medina, Fakhri Pasha.[41] Enver arrived in Bukhara on 8 November 1921 (at the latest), together with the Bashkiri leader and historian Zaki Walidi (Validov), in an attempt to influence the Basmachi movement on behalf of the Soviet government. However, instead he joined them and in May 1922 was acknowledged by the Basmachi as 'Supreme Leader of the Armies of Bukhara, Khiva and Turkestan'. He in addition supposedly proclaimed himself Emir of Turkestan, and even representative of the Prophet Mohammed.[42] On 4 August 1922, Enver was killed in a gun battle with Soviet soldiers. A year later, in the winter of 1923–24, the Basmachi uprising finally broke down. A general amnesty was proclaimed for a two year period, but after 1926 numerous members of the opposition were arrested as suspected rebels and brought to trial.

By contrast to the situation in Western European colonial states, Russian colonial policy, which was almost exclusively designed by urban nationalists, found no rural allies. The agrarian and nomadic societies were thus excluded from national politics and followed traditional patterns. In this connection, the comparatively 'liberal' Khanate of Khiva (Khwarazm from 1622) and the 'conservative' Emirate of Bukhara (since 1752) played as important a part as ethnic relationships. The many years of Basmachi resistance demonstrated that the old system was considerably more robust than the new republican institutions of 1917 and 1918. With the victory of the urban nationalists over rural resistance in 1924, there began a complete change in political power structures, reaching a climax in 1936 with the final establishment of the borders of the five Soviet Socialist Republics of Kirghiztan, Kazakhstan, Uzbekistan, Turkmenistan and Tajikistan. The new political and territorial borders were based on the views of urban nationalists who sought to canalize the various aspects of Turkestan into clearly demarcated national territories. In so doing they distinguished, for example, between a Kazakh and a Kirghiz nationality, although the two concepts denoted different social conditions rather than ethnic distinctions. In addition, out of a Turkestan traditionally consisting of heterogeneous ethnic groups, there emerged a Tajik national identity which made the Persian elite culture, which had for a long time also left its mark on the Turkophone societies (with the exception of Jagatai-speaking Khiva) into the specific feature of a distinct nationality.[43]

Islamic National Communism in the USSR

In the years between 1918 and 1921, the few Muslim members of the Communist Party managed to set up their own Islamic interest group within the organization. On 19 January 1918, Tatar and Bashkirian nationalists founded the 'Central Commissariat for Muslim Affairs' and Stalin himself appointed Mullanur Vahitov (1885–1918), the leader of the 'Muslim Socialist Committee', as its president. One of his deputies was the leftist socialist Tatar writer Alimjan Ibrahimov (Galimdjan Ibragimov, 1887–1938?), who succeeded Vahitov in 1918 and became the leading figure among Muslim communists after 1920.[44]

When the Russian civil war ended in 1920, four political groups confronted each other in the Islamic regions:

1. The Muslim national communists, who pronounced themselves more and more openly for the proclamation of a Republic of Turan, which was to combine communist ideals with Islamic cultural traditions.
2. The Turkish nationalists who, after 1921, had clearly submitted to the influence of the former Ottoman war minister Enver Pasha.
3. The supporters of the old system, who had found their representative in the Emir of Bukhara. Bukhara was conquered by Soviet troops on 2 September 1920 and – like Khiva – declared a people's republic.[45] The emir Abd al-Sa'id Mir 'Alim Khan first escaped to the east of the country and in March 1921 sought temporary exile in Kabul in order to organize the resistance from there.
4. The Islamic Salafiya movement, which was in the tradition of the Tatar Usul-i Jadid ('New Foundation') movement. As a movement for educational and cultural reform, Jadidism predominated among the Islamic political public in the late 19th and early 20th centuries. After 1920 most of the Salafiya members joined the Communist Party because they believed that it provided a mandate for a comprehensive cultural reform against the old regime.[46]

The integration of the Salafiya into a socialist society presented no major problems. Far more complicated were the national communist programmes devised by Sultan Galiev. Unlike the Salafiya, which saw itself as part of the Soviet intelligentsia, Galiev thought of the entire Muslim population, which was to be represented by an autonomous Islamic communist movement, as part of the world proletariat. The 'metropolitan proletariat' – so Galiev proclaimed in a nine-point declaration in January 1926 – had inherited the mantle of the bourgeoisie and would pursue its agenda.[47] For this reason, no organizational union between the urban and the national Muslim proletariat could exist. Rather, the cultural specificity of the Muslims as a proletariat would have to be preserved in an independent republic of Turan, which would embrace all Turkophone countries as well as Tajikistan. The national communists were also popular with disillusioned followers of Jadidism, who were greatly attracted by Galiev's idea of organizing a Muslim International Association as a counterpart to the Communist International Association. The attraction of a culturally independent communism was indeed very strong. 'Galievism' mainly strengthened the Tatar and Bashkirian opposition groups. After 1928, the success of the Muslim national communists finally led to a far-reaching revision of Soviet policy with regard to the Islamic population. All the party institutions were mobilized to unmask the 'reactionary' character of Islam and to eliminate it from the political public. In November 1928, Galiev was arrested and condemned to forced labour for life. Nothing is known of the circumstances of his death.

As early as 1927, the Communist Party, in a bid to sever any cultural attachment to the Islamic world, had made the use of the Latin script compulsory for all Muslim peoples.[48] For the Party the core problem was Tataristan, which between 1928 and 1933 it attempted to completely de-Islamicize and 'liberate' from any Tatar identity. In 1932–33, it launched a veritable persecution of Tatars of bourgeois origin thus secretly settling accounts with the fact that, in the 19th and early 20th centuries, Tatar society had made a large contribution to bourgeois (as well as aristocratic) culture in Russia.

Islamic discourse was now systematically banned from public discourse, which after 1928 consisted of little else but Soviet politics. A large number of Muslim national communists were arrested, interned or summarily liquidated. Apart from Galiev himself, these included, among others, the Kazakh writer and founder of the Kazakh national party Alach Orda, Ahmad Baitursun; the ideological head of Young Bukhara, Abd al-Ra'uf Fitrat (1866–1938), who had been foreign minister of the People's Republic of Bukhara in 1923 and later professor at Tashkent University; Nariman Najafoghlu Narimanov (1870–1933), founder of the Azerbaijan leftist socialist party Hümmet and a long-time member of the executive committee of the CPSU; the Kazakh prince Ali Khan Bökaikhan (1869–1932), a well-known local historian and co-founder of the

Alach Orda. The Islamic courts had already been eliminated in 1926 and 1927. Islamic schools were closed, among them also the schools of the Usul-i Jadid movement, of which there were about 6,000. Charitable institutions were shut down in 1930, as they were in most other Islamic societies; family rights, which had so far always been a stronghold of Islamic cultural identity, were de-Islamicized by 1926. With the arrest of numerous members of the *ulama* in the early 1930s, the elimination of Islam from public life finally reached its climax. Only a few of the 25,000 or so mosques and almost 45,000 convents of the mystical orders that had previously existed preserved their social functions.

The Islamic regions were thus laid open to Russian colonial settlement. A particularly cruel blow to Muslim communities was the reproach that they were collaborators of the German empire or of Japan. This admonishment, which from 1931 was frequently levelled at them, led to the collective deportation of entire village or tribal communities from their traditional settlements. This factor, in addition to the identification of Islam as 'the most bourgeois of all cultures in the Soviet Union' and the Latinization of the written cultures, which officially started in 1927, contributed to the complete repression of publicly practised Islam. It was only after 1941–42 that a gradual restoration of the official practice of Islam was allowed.

The New Order in Afghanistan

Afghanistan, like Turkey, was a refuge for persecuted nationalists from the Central Asian republics. In May 1923, a number of former Ottoman officers held a conference in Kabul to discuss the future of the Basmachi movement. They were also planning to draw up an ideological programme, for they realised that the movement could not be based solely on a general resentment of Russia. However, there was not enough time to develop a more precise ideological orientation, since it was more important to secure an arms supply from the British and the officers wanted to take advantage of the good relations between Afghanistan and British India and the British government's willingness to provide military assistance to the Emir of Bukhara, who was living in exile.[49] From the Afghan border areas to Tajik and Uzbek Turkestan, they planned to reorganize the Basmachi. The Emir himself had addressed the world from Kabul and demanded that 'Bolshevik goings-on' in Bukhara be stopped.[50] But the Soviet government had already managed to win over those members of the *ulama* who were in favour of reforms. On the occasion of the First Congress of Ulama in Bukhara (May 1924), the authorities persuaded them to draft an appeal against the Basmachi in which they declared that the emir was no longer the head of state, that the Basmachi were nothing but bandits, and that the Muslim population should submit to the will of the Soviet government 'which guaranteed power to the people'.[51] The national communist and president of the council of commissars of Bukhara, Faidallah Khodjaev (1896–1938), who was later executed, declared that the Basmachi movement had lost its political character and should be liquidated.[52]

Afghanistan was both a base of operations of the Basmachi and a place of exile for the Turkestani nationalists, groups whose differences fully corresponded with the political situation in Afghanistan. Under King Amanallah (r. 1919–1928), this country – like contemporary Persia – experienced an extensive de-Islamization of the political public, causing resistance among Islamic scholarly circles. The *ulama* were further provoked when Amanallah introduced a new penal code,[53] which they perceived as a direct threat to their own sovereign rights, for until then judicial power as far as Islamic law was concerned had been theirs, while the tribal leaders were responsible for the common (*'urf*) law. With the establishment of a third legal institution devolving on the state, there would be competition for cultural and political supremacy, as well as for the preservation of regional and social sovereignty.[54]

The exiled nationalists thus found strong support among the new political public centred on the state bureaucracy. The Basmachi, on the other hand, counted on the Turkmenian and Uzbek tribes, who were not prepared to yield their sovereign rights to the state in Kabul. The *ulama* who had fled from Bukhara and Kokand formed a third group of exiles supported by the Afghan *ulama*.

The constitutional movement in Persia (from 1 January 1935: Iran) also had an impact on Afghanistan. Amanallah, who witnessed the fall of the Ottoman sultanate in 1922 and the end of the Qajar dynasty in Persia in 1925, believed that he would have to establish a new system in order to maintain the *ancien regime*. An extensive administrative reform was introduced in order to break the power of authorities in society which might compete with the state, namely the tribes and the *ulama*. The attempt to integrate Afghan social groups into a nation state was thus carried out through the bureaucracy, in which the small but influential Salafiya community also played an active part through its 'mentor', Mahmud Tarzi, the owner of the newspaper *Siraj al-Akhbar* (1911–19). This paper had already played an important role when Amanallah became king in a new colonial society which had gradually tried to assume sovereignty over the country. When, after a three-month war against British India, the country recovered its full independence on 8 August 1919, and the substantial British subsidies were discontinued, the colonial society adopted a bureaucratic constitution, desite its lack of economic institutions. This implied that the desired constitutional system would give rise to a division of powers within the colonial society which would also include the tribal leaders and *ulama*. This constitutionalism 'from above' was, however, vigorously opposed by the historically evolved constitutional system 'from below'. At the great assemblies of the major Afghan tribes and clans (*loya jirga*) the old system was passionately vindicated.

The 'new system', which was symbolized by the change of the ruler's title from emir to shah, was, however, unable to free itself from the dominance of tribal society. It basically remained true to the Pashtun tradition. The Pashtuns, who perhaps made up 40 per cent of the Afghan population, carefully watched over their ancient *jirga* system, the local, regional and supra-regional assembly, and made sure that the power of their 'wise men' (*spin geray*) and khans was not curtailed and that their social code, the *nang* (honour, also called *pushtunwali*), remained intact. It was precisely the *nang* that formed their tribal claim to sovereignty. The Pashtuns therefore only allowed themselves to be integrated into the new system on condition that there would be no change in their social position which appeared to be guaranteed by the fact that, since the early 19th century, the royal family had itself belonged to the Barakzay clan of the Durrani tribe of Pashtuns.

Other ethnic groups such as the Tajiks, Uzbeks and Turkmenians, and particularly the socially outclassed Hazara, who were mainly Shi'i, were excluded from both political systems. They were neither able to acquire a lasting influence in the Great Assembly, nor could they gain a foothold in the small colonial society of Kabul.

The establishment of the 'European' discourse as the dominant form of expression in political matters separated Kabul's colonial society from other communities. Of course, this only made itself felt when the royal regime tried to establish Afghanistan as a nation state and place it under a unified central power, decisively upsetting the balance between the different political traditions. In November 1928, Amanallah was deposed under pressure from the tribes and *ulama*. There followed a brief interregnum by the Tajik 'bandit' Bacha-yi Saqqao, who was enthroned as Emir Habib Allah Ghazi with the support of the former leader of the Basmachi settled in Afghanistan.[55] Amanallah's successor, Nadir Shah (r. 1929–33) partially restored domains that had been under the special authority of the tribes and *ulama* and had himself proclaimed king by the latter on 17 October 1929. In 1931 he revised the constitution to make allowance for this tripartite sovereignty. The new parliament, which consisted of two chambers, was viewed as a stronghold of nationalistic, 'European' discourse, the provincial administrations under the khans were de facto independent and the *ulama* again acquired major fields of jurisdiction. Nadir Shah preserved an extensive right of veto for himself, which made a farce of the constitutional regime. Royal sovereignty thus soon developed into a pure dictatorship of force. In 1933 Nadir Shah was murdered. His son Mohammad Zahir (reigned until 1973) at first assumed the throne together with three of Nadir Shah's brothers and carried on his father's cautious reform policy.

The Preservation of Monarchy in Persia

In Persia the situation had calmed down in 1921. With the conclusion of the Persian–Soviet treaty, under whose terms Soviet troops withdrew from Gilan, and the cancellation of the Anglo–Persian treaty of 1919, which was to have secured Great Britain a monopoly of influence in Persia, the period of rebellion seemed to have ended. The short-lived republic of Gilan, founded in 1920 by nationalists around Mirza Kuchik Khan[56] and social-revolutionary Jangalis ('forest denizens'), had been named a Soviet Socialist Republic on 4 August 1921 but threatened to run aground due to conflicts between communists, social revolutionaries and nationalists. In February 1921, the army under the leadership of Reza Khan, an officer of the Cossack Brigade created in 1879, rebelled against the government and initiated a military dictatorship. On 3 November 1921, it occupied Rasht, the provincial capital of Gilan, and during the same period moved to 'appease' rebellious Turcoman tribes in Khorasan.

To begin with, the new government was nominally led by civilian prime ministers (among others Qavam al-Saltaneh) although Reza Khan appointed himself as minister of war. However, the army had in practise become a guarantor of the power of the nation state. In 1924, it marched into Khuzistan, which had gradually been evacuated by British troops, and abolished the autonomy of the Arab tribes. Here the Shi'i tribal leader Shaikh Khazal had previously availed himself of British support and of his close relations with the Kuwaiti Amir Mubarak to have himself proclaimed 'ruler of Arabistan'. According to the writer Amin al-Raihani, the khan had advocated a well-balanced religious policy and even authorized the outlawed Chaldaeans to build their places of worship.[57] But from the Persian point of view, Khuzistan formed an essential part of the empire, and regional power centres were not to be tolerated. The reconquest of Khuzistan thus completed the recovery of the country's unity. By this time the army had become a 'national army' and the reconquest of the provinces was celebrated as a 'national liberation'.

Reza Khan was a republican. Like Mustafa Kemal he at first considered a republican constitution as the appropriate form of regime to secure a centralized nation state.[58] In October when Ahmad Shah, the last Qajar sovereign, finally appointed Reza Khan as prime minister and was sent into exile in Europe, there was a fair chance that a republic would be proclaimed. Unlike the Turkish nationalists, however, the Persian army lacked a political wing and had not succeeded in convoking a national congress which would depart from the tradition of the old Majlis with its elite members. Without a civilian base a republic was inconceivable. The legitimacy of Reza Khan's military dictatorship was therefore violently attacked by both constitutionalist and conservative members of the *ulama*. Instead, however, of filling the civilian vacuum and exercising their function as a legitimizing authority, these men agreed to acknowledge Reza Khan on the condition that the military regime gave up its republican aims. Thus, on 31 October 1925, Reza Khan deposed Ahmad Shah Qajar and soon afterwards had himself proclaimed by the newly elected Majlis, which included a handful of the *ulama* among its deputies, as the new shah of the Pahlavi dynasty. There were only three opposing votes.

Persia had preserved its imperial regime. But as the country lacked civil integration, it remained a military dictatorship until as late as 1978–79, when it was replaced by a temporarily civilian regime. The new shah deliberately gave himself a military appearance, and the army itself controlled vast realms of the bureaucracy and was in practice the executive body of the various reform edicts issued between 1926 and 1928. The army's extraordinary grasp on power and the lack of civil integration in the imperial regime formed the basis for Iran's specific path in the 20th century.

Islamic Policy in Algeria

In Algeria, French colonial settlement created entirely different conditions for the political activity of the native elites. In 1914, 10 per cent of Algerian society consisted of French, Spanish and Italian settlers. In accordance with older, precolonial traditions, northern Algeria was divided into three departments, which were considered as an integral part of France after 1873. Yet Muslim Algerians were not French citizens. From 1918 onwards, they were to receive full citizenship if they gave up their Islamic traditions, especially the Islamic civil law – the Islamic penal law having been invalidated earlier. The French policy of segregation created a social and cultural divide between the 'European' and the 'Islamic' world which could only be crossed if Muslims renounced their Islamic culture. The adoption of a 'European' discourse was an indispensable requirement for integration into the colonial society. But the 'Young Algerians' were refused any kind of political participation, despite their French education, and despite the fact that they had indeed adopted the 'European' discourse. According to one of the most prominent leaders of the Young Algerian integration movement of the 1930s, Farhat Abbas (b. 1899), the Arab and Islamic empires belonged to the past; he believed his own future to be inseparably linked with France.[59]

To those who achieved integration within Algeria's French society, a public Islamic discourse no longer meant anything. But for those who were denied access to French society the situation was different. Above all, Muslim workers in France witnessed how the policy of segregation was extended into the mother-country. The Algerian proletariat in the cities of northern France, which numbered 100,000 men by 1924, became closely connected with the Communist movement and it was the French Communist party which, on 20 March 1926, promoted the foundation of the Étoile Nord Africaine (ENA) by al-Hajj Ali Abd al-Qadir and led from 1928 by Ahmad Massali al-Hajj (Messali Hadj, 1898–1974).[60] The ENA, which was soon in a position to mobilize over 4,000 activists in France, at first devoted itself entirely to proletarian internationalism, ignoring the cultural differentiation of the Algerian working class.

The real national opposition came from the milieu of the Algerian Salafiya. In the 1920s, the Salafiya, led by the Tunis-trained *alim* Abd al-Hamid Ibn Badis (Ben Badis, 1887–1940), started organizing itself to found Muslim schools and was particularly successful in the departments of Alger and Oran.[61] Unlike the liberals and social revolutionaries of the ENA, it accepted the cultural segregation of Algerian society and gave it an important place in the development of an Islamic political public of its own. The Salafiya, which in 1931 organized itself into the Association of Muslim Ulama, took advantage of the vacuum created by French colonial policy, for outside it there were practically no properly functioning administrative organs or institutions of social assistance. Until 1938, the organization was emphatically non-political: schools and social centres were built, among other purposes to reduce the 'harmful' influence of the mystical orders which were well nigh dominant in Algeria.[62] The policy of segregation had allowed the mystical orders, particularly the influential Tijaniya order from Ain Madi, great latitude and they long remained the most important authority outside the colonial society. It is not therefore surprising that the Society of Algeria Ulama paid little attention to French colonial policy to begin with, but turned vehemently against the orders.

Algeria's identity as a nation state was as divided as Algerian society. Those sections of the elite who definitely wanted Algeria to become part of the French nation and share equal rights with it had no political connections with the Islamic environment. The Islamic public, for its part, wanted to free Algeria from the culture of the mystical orders, and saw no reason to engage in the issues of colonial policy. There was no political link between these two positions and it was not until the late 1930s that the gap between Islamic reformists and Algerian autonomists was bridged.

Indonesian Forms of Islamic Policy

A very similar situation had arisen in the Dutch East Indies which around 1920 had a population of about 44 million and was thus the largest Islamic country under a single political authority. The regions on the archipelago which were under the control of the Dutch East India Company (founded in 1602, liquidated in 1799) were handed over to the Dutch government in 1800. From then on until 1910, the latter extended its colonial possessions to almost all parts of today's Indonesia. The colony remained politically divided. The East India Company, which from the end of the 19th century ran the colony as a private capitalist concern, organized itself into 34 'residences' and three superior governments. Native society was distributed over about 300 principalities. The entire supreme colonial administration, like the five-headed Raad von Indië or the Allgemeene Redenkamer with its seat in Batavia, was exclusively run by the Dutch. Here, as in Algeria, colonial settlement led to an obvious segregation of society.

Dutch colonialism, which controlled the cultivation and export of sugar, tobacco, coffee and tea, as well as the extraction of rubber, oil, tin and other metals, did not, to begin with, create an economically homogeneous country. On Java the traditional economic and social structures could be preserved by continuing to plant rice, which was essential to subsistence, as well as sugar cane, a very profitable crop. The intensive cultivation of rice made it possible to feed a rapidly growing population and numerous immigrants. With the addition of maize and soya beans, the variety of crops was almost complete. The food supply for the population of Java appeared to be secured, while export assets constantly rose with the intensified cultivation of sugar cane. Conditions on Sumatra were quite different. Here classical colonialism prevailed, leading to a drastic reorganization and urbanization of the native society. Instead of subsistence products, export products such as tobacco and coffee were planted while the expansion of rubber plantations promoted the seizure of peasant holdings. But native entrepreneurs soon gained a foothold in the economy of the colonial society and the borders between the world of European colonists and that of the natives threatened to disappear.[63]

From the beginning of the 20th century, the Dutch colonial administration had adopted an 'ethical' or 'clerical' policy, a Dutch variant of the French *mission civilisatrice* which aimed at the de-Islamization of public life. The mission of the colonial administration also included the welfare of the natives and aimed to sever them from their traditional culture and gradually integrate them into Dutch colonial society.

This ethical policy was at first approved in small cultural clubs like the Buddhist-Hindu association Budi Utomo. But colonial society in Sumatra, which had meanwhile become very mixed from a cultural point of view, had assimilated the 'European' political discourse and, from 1911, started to demand the national independence of Indonesia. Here, too, as in other Islamic societies, the conflict between national liberals stemming from the landed aristocracy (*priyayi*) and urban nationalists shaped the political public. In 1920 urban nationalists had founded the first Communist party; but an urban national party was not launched until 1927, by Ahmad Sukarno among others.

The 'Islamic' discourse of the political public became effective somewhat earlier. On 9 November 1911, Javanese merchants under Umar Sa'id Cokroaminoto (1883–1934) had founded an economic interest group called Sarekat Islam, which was opposed to the dominance of Chinese traders in Java.[64] This group was closely connected with the Salafi Muhammadiya association with which the scholar Ahmad Dahlan (1868–1923), who had spent a long time in the Hijaz, cooperated to surmount the power of the Islamic mystical orders, especially in the educational system. More radical Salafi groups were the 'Society for Religious Guidance' (Jam'iyat al-Irshad al-Dini) founded in 1911 by Ahmad Muhammad al-Surkati (born 1873) and the 'Reform of Islam' (Persatuan Islam) launched by the merchant Ahmad Hasan (born 1887).[65] In Indonesia, as elsewhere, the Salafiya opposed the cults of the mystical orders and created a public that was only formally divorced from the 'European' discourse. In other words, it used the very same institutions as the colonists, such as the press, printers, parties, cultural establishments and clubs.

The heterogeneous Islamic culture in Indonesia confronted the Salafiya with particular problems. The mystical orders were not only a manifestation of popular piety which had to be repressed; they themselves had, since the 18th century, fiercely fought against the syncretistic popular culture 'red Islam' (*Islam abangan*) and were considered as the real authors of the archipelago's Islamization. *Agami Islam* and *kejawen* were designations for the typical associations made among peasant communities between traditional cults (for example, that of the rice goddess) which were reflected in social custom (*adat*), and the Islamic legal norms of the *shari'a*. Sultan Iskandar Muda, who ruled the principality of Aceh in Northern Sumatra from 1607 to 1636, is even said to have codified some of the *adat*.[66] The orders, especially the Naqshbandiya, which was reformed in the 18th century, considered themselves as protagonists of a unified Islamic culture which would ban the *adat* and its supporting older mystical orders, such as the Shattariya, from public life. It was above all in Aceh, but also on the island of Madura north of Java, that the orders had been successful. The cultural integration of the peasant communities in these places led to a marked sense of regional allegiance which contributed to long years of warlike confrontation with the Dutch administration. Aceh was to preserve an extensively autonomous status at least until 1961.

The mystical orders formed the backbone of a modern regional Islamic identity, despite the fact that from the point of view of the Salafiya they represented an un-Islamic, false tradition. The modernism of the orders became apparent when in 1926 the scholar Abd al-Wahhab Hasb Allah, a declared opponent of the Wahhabis, founded a political society in Java with the characteristic name of 'Renaissance of the Ulama' (Nahdat al-Ulama). The local and regional merchant class was thus provided with an influential organization to counterbalance the powerful Sarekat Islam.

The triple Islamic culture in South-East Asia, consisting of Abangan, the orders and the urban Salafiya, created specific conditions for the political public. Both the 'European' and the 'Islamic' discourse agreed that these separatist mystical cultures had to be de-politicized, that is, they had to lose their political influence. The orders, however, derived their modern legitimacy from their altercations with Dutch colonists and syncretic communities; a policy directed against the 'old generation' (*kaum tua*) thus necessarily ended in a defence of the colonial state dominated by the Dutch. Here the internal contradiction in the political public became particularly obvious. The field of activity of Islamic and nationalist politicians was deeply divided because of their different aims. The more socialist and nationalist programmes prevailed among the public, the further the prestige of the Salafiya sank. In 1924 the Muhammadiya separated from the Sarekat Islam, when Marxist intellectuals asserted themselves in the latter. Thus the Muhammadiya lost an important ally in the political public, which now increasingly adopted a 'European' discourse.

3. THE WORLD ECONOMIC CRISIS AND THE NEW ISLAMIC MOVEMENTS

In many Islamic countries the unsettled 1920s marked the political breakthrough of bourgeois nationalists, who were essentially de-Islamicized in their public life. Even the 'Islamic' discourse of the Salafiya had to a large extent adapted itself to the 'European' discourse. In some societies, for instance in the Muslim Republics of the USSR, in Turkey or in Indonesia, the partisans of the Salafiya had merged with the state elites and had lost their independent position. They had made an important contribution to the cultural and social integration of the nation states, which from then on represented the only focus of political action in the Islamic countries. Yet the Salafiya had provided a major impulse to the development of secular Islamic modernism. They had contributed to the abolition of independent Islamic institutions and placed the claim to sovereignty of nationalist elites in an Islamic context. In its steadfast fight against tradition, into which it had been driven by the powerful mystical orders, the Salafiya had lent a popular dimension to the Islamic public discourse. But with that its function seemed to be over. The history of the classic Salafiya ended in the late 1920s. Classicism, which had traced back every inner-worldly orientation of religiosity to its ideal origin in the early Islamic period, had given way to a new expressive, late romantic concept of culture in which the state represented the realization of the national feeling inherent in each Muslim. There was practically no more need for a specific Islamic discourse of colonial societies. The argument about the rationalist foundation of modernism in the early Islamic period no longer existed. The positivist, indeed historicist tradition of the Salafiya, which had directly placed it within the context of the European history of ideas and had left its mark on numerous Islamic intellectuals, lost its impact in the 1920s because of the radical changes that occurred as a result of the ideological induration of political discourse. In the late 1920s, the combined ideologies of nationalism, liberalism and socialism produced a stronger impact on the divided world of Islamic societies than the elitist culture of the Salafiya.

The policy of integration in the nation states had familiarized Islamic societies with these ideologies. National politics were thus no longer to be separated from global political discourse. The Salafiya itself had been part of this global tradition, for there was hardly an Islamic country in which it had not been active and had not influenced the political public. Although modernism had found a powerful expression in the Salafiya, specific regional traditions of politics had prevented the Salafiya from establishing itself as the sole organ of Islamic modernism. Local Islamic cultures, often described as 'nationalistic', competed with it for cultural supremacy and were often able to express the 'individuality' of the different Islamic societies much more distinctly.

In some regions of the Islamic world, the spiritual, sometimes even pietistic doctrines of the Salafiya were still effective, marking theological discussions for a long time to come. And the old Salafiya dream of creating a truly international Islamic public in which it could represent the Islamic world almost as an Islamic superstate was kept alive in small circles. Outside *ulama* circles, however, the influence of the Salafiya was no longer felt. In places like Morocco, for example, where the Salafiya devoted itself to national politics, its partisans were often directly associated with the colonial administration, for they considered the state – even if it had been usurped by European powers – to be the executive of social modernism. They were prepared to yield the Islamic claim to sovereignty in legal and social matters to the state as long as it was willing to admit members of the Salafiya into its administration.

The Salafiya's readiness to integrate grew at the same rate as its political influence waned. As long as the nation states, whether under foreign or native rule, were ready and able to integrate, there was little danger of the Islamic public breaking away from the now established 'colonial consensus' and finding its way to new, independent forms of political activity.

An additional characteristic of the political public in the Islamic countries was consolidated in the 1920s. Compared to Europe, the rural areas retained a powerful position. Because of colonialism, the countryside in the Islamic countries had evolved in a way that was very different from the pattern of agrarian development in the Western industrial states. These agrarian sectors underpinned the monarchical system of many nation states, namely Iraq, Transjordan, Egypt, Afghanistan, Tunisia and Morocco, as well as the principalities on the Arabian and Malayan peninsulas. Urban republicanism had so far only been established in Turkey, in the Islamic republics of the USSR, and, under colonial conditions, in Algeria, Lebanon and Syria. Iran had a special status, insofar as the imperial regime actually came from a republican tradition and was thus much more of a representative of the power of the city. It was not by chance that state reforms under Reza Shah were almost exclusively aimed at cities and neglected the countryside. Accordingly, the Majlis in Tehran mainly consisted of urban notables, *ulama* and intellectuals, while in Cairo the reverse was true. Iran – and in a sense Afghanistan too – at first formed 'incomplete' republics, the development of which was 'completed' under radically different circumstances as late as 1979 and 1973 respectively. In other Islamic countries such as India, Indonesia and, above all, the African countries south of the Sahara, the problem of power was not settled, but the sultanic system of local sovereignty continued to exist under a superimposed colonial power.

The International Economic Crisis in the Islamic World

The international recession starting in the late 1920s showed that economically, too, the Islamic world was closely bound up within the structure of global processes. The economic crisis radically curtailed the potential of the nation states to achieve integration. A current theory explained the critical situation in terms of two interdependent crises of one economic system: for one thing, there was a steadily accelerated decline in the prices of primary commodities after 1926, which had lasting effects on the economic situation of Islamic countries which relied on agrarian products; and for another, the collapse of the gold, money, credit and the stock market had a devastating effect on the financial power of the colonial societies. The fall in the prices of primary commodities after their rise in the post-war period came as a complete surprise to the recently stabilized economies of the nation states, and none of these countries had taken preventive measures. To begin with, the urbanization and subsequent industrialization of society promoted by the republican regimes (especially in the Islamic republics of the USSR) mitigated the effects of the agrarian crisis; but even here the collapse of the financial market finally led to considerable inroads into the new industrial sectors.[67] The extent to which the global agrarian crisis affected the economy of the Islamic countries is suggested in the following survey of major exports.[68]

Exports of Selected Islamic Countries 1928–1935

Country/Currency	Commodity	1928	1930	1932	1935
Egypt/1,000 £E	Cotton	45,138	23,788	17,866	26,413
Turkey/1,000 TL	Tobacco	54,196	43,160	27,140	18,950
Indonesia/mil. gulden	Sugar	–	254	–	51 (1937)
Algeria/1,000£	Cereals	18,756	–	–	8,285
Persia/Iran/1,000£[69]	Petroleum	800	1,000	1,300	15,000
Palestine/£	Wheat	949,907	–	359,087	–

Tunisia's exports of wheat dropped to half the previous year's level in 1932–33. The yield of barley, a favourite crop with the native peasants, fell to half its average quantity in 1931. The export of wine on the other hand, the main produce grown by European settlers (*colons*), rose by a third within the same period. Algeria's exports altogether declined by 50 per cent from 1929/30 to 1934/35. For Iraq's transit trade the effects of the crisis were equally dramatic, the figures plummeting from 7 million (1924) to 1.6 million Iraqi dinars.

A direct effect of the global economic crisis was the rapid loss of the native population's purchasing power. This was, of course, particularly felt by those parts of society that had previously been able to afford the relatively expensive colonial commodities. In Turkey the consumption of tobacco, maize and wheat was reduced by 30–34 per cent, although the cost of living had at the same time dropped only by about 17 per cent.[70] In Algeria almost half the sheep flocks had to be slaughtered within one year. The world economic crisis, in other words, led primarily to a major decline in consumption. The impoverishment of the colonial tertiary sector, that is, the sector which lived on all kinds of services, the considerable losses sustained by the great agrarian concerns, and the growing proletarization of the peasant population turned the global economic crisis into a crisis of colonial society as well.

The second colonial crisis after the upheaval of 1905–1908 intensified the process of segregation between colonial society and traditional Islamic communities. Before the global economic crisis, Muslims versed in the 'European' discourse had nevertheless found it possible to earn their living in a manner that accorded with their culture within the tertiary sector of the colonial society. In almost all Islamic countries, the tertiary sector grew steadily in the first quarter of the 20th century. In 1934 1,135,000 people in Egypt and 785,000 in Turkey, or about 6–7 per cent of the population, were employed in the tertiary sector earning, in 1934–35, about 45 and 31 million pounds, respectively.[71] Now, however, the colonial society could quite evidently no longer admit newcomers from the provinces or suburbs into its fabric. Its inability to absorb the labour force was now manifested in a distinct rise in unemployment which, together with the simultaneous growth of urbanization, meant that the situation in the big cities became oppressive.[72]

The integration of urban immigrants into the colonial society depended on their ability to consume. Those who did not have enough money for an expensive life style withdrew to the outskirts of cities and formed the nucleus of the new slums or bidonvilles. The first compact slum in Morocco came into existence in 1934 in Casablanca, the stronghold of Morocco's colonial society.[73]

For the newcomers to the city, detaching themselves from the traditional way of life in the provinces had been a drastic process; but they had found an Islamic precept for it, namely to defame the old order as 'false tradition' and to destroy all the symbols of their cultural affiliation to the 'old system'. This included clothes, linguistic characteristics, manners and, above all, the ritual worship of the local saints which had differentiated the identity of communities from each other. The entire social code was called into question, criticized and repudiated with a view to assimilating the 'European' discourse. But now that they were segregated from the colonial society, the newcomers had no access to its aspirations. They interpreted segregation as refusal, and since they were not prepared to consider it as a personal failure, they argued that the colonial society was also a 'false, un-Islamic system'. The true social code had to be different from both the traditional and the Western code, that is the colonial society. Both the abandonment of the ancestral system and the renunciation of colonial society became the keynote of political interpretations which were entirely conveyed through the 'Islamic' discourse.

The Foundation of the Egyptian Muslim Brotherhood

To begin with, only a few of the newcomers politicized their experiences in this way. These included, as may be expected, students, teachers and members of the liberal professions, a group particularly inclined towards this kind of politicization, since they directly connected their social role with the establishment of a role in the political public. Particularly well-known were the Egyptian elementary teacher Hasan al-Banna (assassinated on 12 February 1949) and his compatriot, the author and journalist Sayyid Qutb (executed on 29 August 1966). Both were born in 1906 and were still studying when the first effects of the global economic crisis were felt in Cairo. For al-Banna, who was born in Damanhur in Lower Egypt and grew up in a lower middle class household, and for his family, the teaching profession was a social ideal. Al-Banna symbolically bought his first books in Damanhur. But it was difficult to obtain the desirable post of schoolteacher in Cairo and he had to content himself with an appointment in Ismailiya on the Suez Canal, which he took up in September 1927.[74]

Sayyid Qutb came from Mush, a village near to the town of Asyut in Upper Egypt and had just arrived in Cairo to study at the teacher's training college (Dar al-Ulum). From the time he was a student, he made contact with the contemporary celebrities of the Egyptian literary scene and was able to publish his first works of literary criticism in various journals (*al-Ahram*, *al-Risala* and *al-Thaqafa*). While Sayyid Qutb had thus managed to gain access to the Egyptian public and, after finishing his studies in 1934, to obtain a post at the Ministry of Culture, al-Banna had already arrived at the boundaries of the colonial society. Politicized at an early age – he experienced the Damanhur revolt of March 1919 as a young boy – he records in his memoirs that he searched Cairo for the remnants of an Islamic public, but found that Islamic institutions had hardly survived in the city. Characteristically, he does not even mention Rashid Rida, who for years had left a decisive mark on Islamic politics in the capital. He also avoids any direct references to his negative childhood experiences, camouflaging them behind a general criticism of tradition and presenting himself as a loyal son of his father, whose authority he acknowledged completely.[75] Sayyid Qutb, on the other hand, had to fight against his peasant origin. His childhood memories were full of bitterness about the 'backward culture' of the countryside, about the superstitions prevailing in it, and the power of the great landowners.[76] When he first started writing in Cairo in the late 1920s, he used the 'European' discourse current among the literati; there was no trace in these early writings of a specifically Islamic expression.

A comparison of the biographies of these two men, who in retrospect emerge as the most important personalities of political Islam in Egypt, points to the different socializing potentials of newcomers in the early 1930s. Al-Banna, the son of a clockmaker, was unable to integrate. He remained rooted in the Islamic discourse and politicized his own misery when he co-founded the Muslim Brotherhood (al-Ikhwan al-Muslimun) around March 1928.[77] Sayyid Qutb, however, did not need this kind of Islamic public. He already had access to Cairo's literary circles. Here authors and critics like Ibrahim Abd al-Qadir al-Mazini (1890–1949), Muhammad Husain Haikal (1888–1956), Taha Husain and Mahmud Taimur (1894–1973), the spokesman of the national literature group 'The New School' (from 1925), were deeply influencing the younger generation. The Egyptian national literature of the late 1920s and early 1930s was a provocation for any intellectual who still explicitly used an 'Islamic' discourse. Indeed one of the radical followers of the new school, the Coptic author Salama Musa (ca. 1887–1958), who in 1929 had just founded his avant-garde journal *al-Majalla al-Jadida*, demanded: 'I would like [Egyptian] literature to be 99 per cent European, and to have it based not on words, as with the Arabs, but on meaning and sense.'[78]

The general de-Islamization of the public in Egypt now even had its effects on Arab identity. In a 'pharaonic' way, both literati and consumers sought to free themselves from the 'Arab blemish' and to become 'Egyptians' by committing themselves to ancient Egyptian culture.

The newcomers who were rejected by the colonial society could only fall back on Islamic symbolism and language to explain their awkward position to themselves and others. This explanation was facilitated by already existing interpretations going back to the Salafiya. For had not the classicists already found an Islamic interpretation for their own experience of departure from tradition? But at the time of the economic crisis there was no longer any ground for optimism about being integrated into the colonial society. What was missing was an expression of the actual social situation of the newcomers from the lower middle class.

Hasan al-Banna's Muslim Brotherhood was but one of many organizations which provided an Islamic interpretation for the retreat from the colonial society by comparing it with the departure of the Prophet Muhammad from Mecca in 622. Departure and separation were from now on to be the leading themes of the small Islamic circle. The aim of Islamic discourse was no longer integration, but to prove that it was subjectively right to be excluded. Because of their conceptual affinity with the Salafiya, these groups will henceforth be called by the collective name of neo-Salafiya.

The neo-Salafiya started out as a small movement of Islamic intellectuals who recognized the failure of the Salafiya *ulama* and sought to found their own independent Islamic public. Many of their partisans had, for a variety of reasons, interrupted their studies at the Islamic universities. For example, the future leader of the Moroccan neo-Salafi 'Independence party' (Hizb al-Istiqlal), Allal Fasi (1919–74), had failed the examination leading to the scholar's diploma (*alimiya*) and now turned bitterly against scholarly culture in the framework of the Moroccan national movement.[79] Others, like the Indian journalist Abu'l-A'la al-Maududi (1903/4–1979), wrote in favour of the new Islamic policy, without themselves joining any group.

The many neo-Salafi groups formed almost everywhere in the Islamic world between 1927 and 1935 show how universally the world economic crisis had affected Islamic societies. In fact, it can even be argued that in such places as Egypt, where the crisis had far-reaching social consequences, the neo-Salafiya assumed a leading role as a cultural reference point. Most of the groups were not political in the sense of the colonial society; an approach to the political public of the nation states only began in the 1930s, in Egypt in 1938. When the Muslim Brothers were established, they therefore purposely avoided any designation such as party, society, order or union.[80]

The early neo-Salafiya was thus a cultural movement. It aimed at creating a social network among the non-integrated and at the same time non-traditional parts of Islamic societies. Social gatherings, mosques, cultural clubs and sports clubs were the nodal points of this network. At the beginning, the groups were also open to mystical Islamic traditions. In mysticism's apparent detachment from the world, a very plausible expression could be found for withdrawing from society. Some poets such as the Indian Muhammad Iqbal (died 1938) actually celebrated voluntarist mysticism as an essential part of intellectual culture. The new groups, however, only accepted a mysticism that differed clearly from that of the traditional dervish orders. The ritual worship of saints and tombs was out of the question, as was the mystically legitimized liberation from a uniform system of social norms. Indeed, the culture of the neo-Salafiya could only be conveyed through a new social code. As long as mysticism contributed to the latter, the Muslim Brothers would welcome it. No wonder, then, that in Syria and Turkey, as well as in the USSR and in parts of India, the reformed, pietistically oriented order of the Naqshbandiya became a reservoir for many neo-Salafi organizations, since this great urban order represented precisely those ethical ideas in which Islamic intellectuals believed.

Not all neo-Salafi organizations were in favour of complete withdrawal. Take, for example, the Society of Muslim Youth (Jam'iyat al-Shubban al-Muslimin) founded in Cairo in November 1927 by Abd al-Hamid Sa'id, a student of law. Sa'id was able to secure the cooperation of prominent Salafiya *ulama* including the Tunisian Muhammad al-Khidr Husain (ca. 1876–1958), who had earlier failed in Egypt, and his friend Abd al-Aziz Gawish, who after his return from Moscow had found no support among the Azhar *ulama* and instead obtained a post in the Egyptian Ministry of Education. The famous historian Ahmad Taimur (1871–1930) was appointed as treasurer, and the publicist Muhibb al-Din al-Khatib as secretary-general.[81] At the founding assembly in Cairo, Sa'id characteristically spoke on the theme 'between two civilizations', describing the social break between the colonial, bourgeois world and the 'Islamically' interpreted world of the excluded.[82] In his article in the first issue of the new journal of the society, the lawyer Yahya Ahmad al-Dardairi stated that a society based on the ethics of the Koran and rejecting the 'blind imitation of the West' was by no means authoritarian, but on the contrary liberal; for the ethics of the Koran were based on the freedom of knowledge and thought, without which there could be no social reform.

According to al-Banna, The Society of Muslim Youth and the Muslim Brotherhood maintained good relations until well into the 1930s. The alliance was arranged by Muhibb al-Din al-Khatib, who also attempted to win over al-Banna to his pro-Saudi orientation by sending him to the Hijaz as a teacher in the winter of 1928. However, the Muslim Brothers of Ismailiya at the time had no contact with Islamic groups outside Egypt. The main aim was the establishment of the organization in the large urban centres, especially in Cairo itself. It was not until October 1932, when the headquarters were moved to the capital, that the organization assumed a structure allowing external contacts.

Islamic Politics and Palestine

The political conflict over Palestine was not taken up by the Islamic public until the late 1920s. Until then, most Islamic journalists and publicists had shown great reserve over Jewish immigration. Indeed, Rashid Rida and a few Palestinian personalities had considered it as a rather positive move. It is true that the early Jewish immigration lacked the character of settler colonialism. In comparison with Algeria, the early Jewish settlers adapted themselves much better to Palestinian society; their main aim had not been the city, but the countryside. Besides, the number of settlers had been, in comparison with Algeria, quite modest.

It was only with the third Aliyah (literally: 'ascent', designating the different waves of immigration into Palestine) from 1919 to 1923, when about 35,000 Jews, mainly from Russia and Poland, settled in northern Palestine, that settler colonialism started. The fourth Aliyah (1924–28) for the most part brought Polish city dwellers into the Palestinian countryside, leaving a lasting mark on the social structure of the immigrant community. Like Haifa, Tel Aviv became a regionally important town with about 40,000 inhabitants.[83]

The 1927–29 economic crisis led to the stagnation and even a decrease in the number of immigrants. Palestine's agriculture suffered a decline of up to 50 per cent in the prices of its products. The price for a ton of wheat dropped from £10.81 (1929) to £6.97 (1931), and that of a ton of oats from £7.66 to £3.03 within the same period. Wheat production itself sank by almost a third, so that the value of the wheat crop was reduced altogether from £949,907 to £359,087.[84] A drought in the spring of 1932 brought the highland additional losses of 80 per cent of the olive crop and 60 per cent of the maize crop. More and more peasants moved to the cities, which had meanwhile also become the aim of the Jewish immigrants.[85] After 1928, the 'fight for the city' came to a head. Both Jewish settlers and Arab nationalists considered the city as their political and social territory. The Arab nationalists' scope for a 'European' discourse, however, had been considerably reduced because it was beset by the 'European' nationalism of a Zionist group who laid claim to the city. Consequently, the 'European' discourse of nationalism was already 'taken'. As in Algeria, the Islamic public in Palestine therefore had another specific task, that of lending expression to the political will of Palestinian citizens. The Arab landed proprietors followed the political principles of the country and emphasized their pro-British, liberal and national views, which were also expressed in an Islamic language.

Even Haifa, the stronghold of the Jewish immigration, now became the focus of internal Palestinian migration. Pressed by the drop in the price of farm products and the 50 per cent decline in salary levels, the only chance of economic survival for the migrants was the new city of Haifa. From 1922 to 1931, the number of Arab inhabitants in Haifa almost doubled (1922: 18,404, 1931: 34,560).[86] Even for peasants from the Syrian Hauran, the Palestinian cities were attractive. Here the unemployment rate among the Arab population came to reach almost 10 per cent in 1931–32.

A political feature that was to be decisive for Palestine's later development was the colonial society's policy of ethnic segregation; for with the gradually evolving Jewish supremacy in the cities, the Arab newcomers were prevented from achieving not only economic, but even cultural integration. In August 1929, with the first peak of the economic crisis, the fight for the city began, symbolically encoded in the conflicts for freedom to perform the rituals at the western wall, the 'Wailing Wall' of the temple district of Jerusalem. The Zionist defence organization, Haganah, which was founded in 1920, soon had the conflict under control, but the Arab protest quickly spread to other Palestinian cities, especially Hebron and Safed, where some Arab rebels even raged among Jewish families who had long been estalished there. During this unrest 133 Jews lost their lives and 116 Arabs were killed as a result of British punitive measures.[87]

The Arab natonalists were at a loss over how to cope with this unrest. They had to realize that their authority over the Palestinian population was infinitesimal. This was a result of the structure of the political public in Palestine. Ever since the Arab nationalists had followed the stipulations of the British mandate of 1920–22 and given up the Great Syrian ideal of a nation state to plead for an Arab nation state in Palestine, their political reference point had become the regime of the British mandate. The concept of independence had clearly receded into the background – in the 1920s the Arab nationalists had become a 'British' party, especially under the influence of the great landowning families al-Nashashibi, Abd al-Hadi, al-Dajjani and al-Khalidi. Meanwhile, the Zionists in Palestine reinforced their organization, which now included a small army.

The Arab Executive Committee, which was mainly dominated by these landed proprietors and was the organ of the national movement until 1934, was unable to represent the interests of the Arab urban population. In the cities, especially in Jerusalem itself (1922: 62,500 inhabitants), prominent residents managed to mobilize the Islamic public agains the Arab Executive Committee. In 1921, notables from the country had unsuccessfully tried to prevent the election of Muhammad Amin al-Husaini (1897–1974) as the Hanafi Mufti of Jerusalem, an office that had been in his family since 1856.[88] On 9 January 1922, al-Husaini also assumed the presidency of the Supreme Islamic Council and steadily consolidated his position in the political public. His family was also represented within the Arab Executive Committee when Jamal al-Husaini (1892–1982) was appointed its secretary. The political background of the al-Husaini family was Islamic. Jamal had participated in the 1926 Caliphate Congress in Cairo, while the mufti soon afterwards had himself celebrated as Palestine's representative by the Islamic World Congress in Mecca. He was by no means a typical follower of the Salafiya, for in Mecca he had argued for the restoration of the domed tombs destroyed by the Wahhabi groups in the holy cities.[89]

The neo-Salafi movement soon found support among the Palestine public. In cooperation with Rashid al-Hajj Ibrahim, the director of the Arab Bank, the rebel of Haifa, the Syrian scholar Izz al-Din al-Qassam (ca. 1894–35), founded the local branch of the Society of Muslim Youth, and now preached on the same lines as the neo-Salafiya. The Society was now also represented in Jaffa (Yaqub al-Ghusain), Nablus (Akram Zualtar) and Amman (Muhammad al-Sammadi).

The neo-Salafi rise in the Islamic public after 1930 became manifest when al-Husaini issued invitations to an international Islamic congress in Jerusalem with a view to protecting the holy sites. The General Islamic Congress of Jerusalem held from 7 to 17 December 1931 reflected the political scene. Through it, the neo-Salafiya found an opportunity to make itself known to the political public, while the Palestinian notables hoped to obtain the backing of other Arab nations. Hardly any important political decisions were reached at the Congress, but it became a significant factor in the representation, and hence the reconstruction, of a broader Islamic public. The Society of Muslim Youth was prominently represented. Its president Abd al-Hamid Sa'id led a high-ranking delegation from Egypt which included the rector of al-Azhar University, Abd al-Wahhab al-Najjar, who travelled to Jerusalem as the society's vice-president. Al-Husaini had been able to enlist such personalities as Rashid Rida, the Tunisian journalist Abd al-Aziz al-Taalibi (1874–1944), Shaukat Ali from India, Abd al-Qadir Mudakkar (ca. 1900–73), a member of the Muhammadiya from Java, and the leader of the Shi'is in Najaf, Muhammad Husain al-Kashif al-Gita (1877–1953). Even communities as yet hardly represented in the Islamic public used the congress in order to attract attention. From Ceylon the university teacher Rauf Pasha was there and delegations arrived from Kano in Northern Nigeria, from Kashgar in Chinese Turkestan and from Yugoslavia.[90] The Tatar Salafi author Muhammad Iyad Ishaqi (Ayaz Iskhakov, 1874–1954), who lived in exile in Berlin, also attended in order to re-establish his relations with the political public.

The political prestige al-Husaini gained through the Congress helped to throw more light on the Palestinian national movement. The al-Husainis founded their Arab-Palestinian Party in 1934, and their opponents, the al-Nashashibi family, followed with the proclamation of a National Defence Party. The manifest rehabilitation of the Islamic public also provoked a reorganization of the 'European discourse' within the national movement. August 1932 marked the creation of the radical nationalist Independence Party (Istiqlal), which almost completely abstained from any Islamic orientation and followed a pan-Syrian policy. It even succeeded in persuading three co-founders of the Society of Muslim Youth from Jaffa to join it.

The neo-Salafiya also managed to consolidate its position. Al-Qassam politicized his group, the Society of Muslim Youth, in Haifa and campaigned for support among the local peasants and the newcomers in Haifa. He summoned them to a just war against the Jewish settlers and actually gained a hearing among some of the peasants in the area. He himself was killed by a British police squad on 20 November 1935.

When the sale of land to Zionist agrarian contractors reached its peak in the year 1935 – in that year 1,225 official transactions were made – the urban nationalists feared that they were losing control over the countryside. They wrote numerous articles warning people about the sellout of Palestine to Zionist organizations and demanded that the sale of land be immediately stopped.[91] Jewish real estate had meanwhile increased tenfold between 1890 and 1933. The sale of land was such a popular, and often necessary step during the depression that even members of prominent Arab families participated in it. Thus Auni Abd al-Hadi (1888–1970), the founder of the Istiqlal party and former advisor to Emir Faisal, participated as a notary in the sale of a large property in April 1929. His brother Afif directly sold parts of the family property to the Jewish Agency in 1929.[92]

Expropriations through Zionist agencies, confiscations of landed property by the British authorities, as well as speculation by Arab landowners themselves, increasingly alienated the peasant communities from the urban population. However, the Arab parties, which had meanwhile increased to six, needed more and more support from the Arab population. In February and March 1936, Syrian city-dwellers went on a fifty-day general strike, thus wresting from the French government extensive concessions towards autonomy. It was also through a general strike that the urban nationalists in Palestine wanted to force the British government to abandon its pro-Zionist attitude. The strike was called in late April 1936, following conflicts between peasant rebels and Jewish settlers and the founding of independent strike and national committees by local nationalist groups. Amin al-Husaini assumed the leadership of a Supreme

Arab Committee to which all six parties belonged and whose task consisted of organizing the strike which was was doggedly continued until October 1936 and only ended after an appeal from Transjordan, Saudi Arabia and Iraq.

The Palestine revolt, which flared up again in the summer of 1937 and which reached its peak in autumn 1938, increasingly developed into an uprising of the countryside against the supremacy of the urban areas.[93] The colonial society, whether Jewish, British or Arab, had lost its authority over the rural areas and it was not until the end of 1938 that British troops succeeded in regaining control.[94]

The great general strike of 1936 had isolated the urban nationalists in two respects. The Jewish society used the strike as an argument for making its economy independent, while the Arab peasant communities split politically from the nationalists. Only prominent Palestinian landowners, such as the Nashashibis, who had resigned from the Supreme Arab Committee in autumn 1937, were able to enlist some of 'their' peasants to act against the rebels. The Islamic discourse of the national movement had factually collapsed in 1938/39. Amin al-Husaini had already fled to Beirut in autumn 1937, and the Society of Muslim Youth had meanwhile for the most part merged with the Istiqlal party.

From Syria, exiled nationalist notables under the leadership of the al-Husainis still tried to exert a certain influence on the political scene in Jerusalem. However, the increasingly powerful Great-Syrian nationalists, above all the Syrian Popular Party founded in 1932 by the Greek-Orthodox teacher Antun Sa'ada (1904–49), made it difficult for them to preserve an independent Palestinian position. Even the Islamic public in Lebanon had been influenced by the Syrians, who dreamt of a Great Syrian empire embracing Lebanon, Transjordan and Palestine.[95]

The Political Transformation of the Islamic Public

In the 1930s the neo-Salafiya failed to create an independent Islamic public which could challenge the superior force of the nationalists. During this decade the ascendant idea in the Islamic world was of a self-sufficient, powerful state: a state that would ensure economic development through a restrictive customs policy and a gradual replacement of agricultural export products by industrial production promoting the home market, and a state that would seek to establish its political sovereignty through repressive measures within society. Inevitably, the urban nationalists' support for this programme provoked the opposition of the agrarian bourgeoisie, which tried to preserve its liberal connections with the world market and with the powers behind it. The neo-Salafi groups were unable to gain a foothold in this political conflict between city and countryside, and so to keep out of the reach of the nationalists they presented themselves as apolitical. Only Morocco was an exception to this pattern. There the neo-Salafiya came forward immediately after 'pacification' in 1934 to demand the establishment of national sovereignty; the movement spared no effort to be recognized as the heir to the now militarily united country and was emphatically political. As a result, it immediately became a national party and for the most part discarded the Islamic discourse.

By 1938, however, political pressure on the constantly growing neo-Salafi groups in Egypt had become so great that they gradually changed into political organizations. Two years earlier, in 1936, the Muslim Brothers had taken a position against the Anglo–Egyptian Treaty of Montreux, which, although returning full sovereignty to Egypt, still allowed Great Britain decisive rights in foreign affairs and security. In response, they had put a fifty-point programme before the public[96] in which they insisted on the 'new Islamic code'. The flourishing Egyptian film industry was to be controlled, sexual segregation was to be intensified and cafés were to be used as centres for Islamic culture.[97] Muslim Brotherhood political speeches abounded in demands for the 'condemnation of party politics', the 'reinforcement of the army', the duty to encourage the creation of groups of young people and to inspire them with enthusiasm for the Islamic moral fight *(jihad)* or the 'propagation of the Islamic spirit in administrative offices'. But according to al-Banna, who had meanwhile been elected as 'general leader' (*al-murshid al-amm*), the Muslim Brothers did not become a political organization until May 1938 when, in the first issue of their new 'political weekly' (*al-Nadir* of 29 May 1938), he defined Islam as 'cult and political leadership, religion and state, spirituality and practice, prayer and fight, obedience and sovereignty, Koran and sword; neither of each of these two (elements) can be separated from the other.'[98] At their fifth council meeting in Cairo on 3 February 1939 the Muslim Brotherhood declared that it would henceforth participate in political discussions with the aim of securing the sovereignty of Egypt on the basis of its Islamic principles. From 1937, the organization had acquired small fighting groups (*kata'ib*) to ensure that the social code was being followed in the city quarters, but they were now also to become effective in the political conflicts to which the political climate lent itself. After the party fights in the years 1936 and 1937, the national conservatives around the judge Ali Mahir, who had an accommodating attitude to the Muslim Brothers, had become stronger. Thanks to the influence of the Mahir family at the royal court, the organization was able to make contacts with the new king Faruq (r. 1937–52) and thus gain a foothold in the political public. Because the king had received religious instruction from the rector of the Azhar University, Sheikh Mustafa al-Maraji (1881–1945), himself a pupil of Muhammad Abduh, this enabled the Brotherhood to penetrate into the centre of Islamic scholarship. In addition, in order to maintain their position of leadership within the Islamic public, they had tried, as early as 1936, to continue the journal *al-Manar*, the organ of the Salafiya, after the death of its owner, Rashid Rida. But they failed and by 1939 were only able to produce a few rather insignificant issues.

The Muslim Brothers were, in the early 1940s, well on the way to becoming a nationalist neo-Salafi party. Their leadership's growing tendency towards integration provoked the protest of some members, who felt it as a betrayal of the old principle inherited from Rida, according to which they alone were authorized to act as an executive, legislative and judicial unit. As early as 1922, Rashid Rida had called for the creation of communities (*jama'at*) which would no longer be subject to the sovereignty of the state, but would themselves exercise all sovereign social rights.[99] Integration within the political public thus inevitably went against the Muslim Brothers' claim to their own sovereignty, a claim raised, up to this point, by their emphatically 'non-political' attitude.

The majority of the Muslim Brothers, however, followed the political leadership's integration programme. At their February 1939 fifth council meeting, it was decided to establish a 'constitutional committee' to examine the Egyptian constitution from the point of view of 'the basic principles of the Islamic system of sovereignty'; a second committee was to rid the Egyptian judicial system of all its 'non-Islamic' provisions. And, finally, the ideological precepts of the Muslim Brothers were to be summarized in a 'brief, handy book', in other words, as a political programme.[100]

The neo-Salafiya did not have a homogeneous political or social programme. It in fact represented – which is what the name neo-Salafiya is meant to convey – the entire range of ideological tendencies that were current in the international political public during the 1930s, albeit disguised in a specifically Islamic discourse. It is very difficult to interpret this Islamic discourse as an independent ideology, even if political demands such as the introduction of the *shari'a* or the split with the West might suggest such an interpretation. The importance of the neo-Salafiya lies, above all, in the fact that, by using an independent Islamic discourse of global ideologies, it was able to comply with the specific needs of the mixed societies in the Islamic world. That is, it was able to comply with the needs of those social groups who already had one foot in the colonial society while the other still lagged behind in the tradition they so hated. These mixed areas can be characterized in terms of the following prototypes:

Sectoral distribution of the Cairo Population around 1930/1940[101]

Traditional urban sector	Mixed area I	Mixed area II	Colonial urban sector
Native economy	Workers in industry and infrastructure	Technicians in industry and infrastructure	Professionals; capital government
Self-supply; traditional supplies	Sectoral trade trade	Inter-sectoral trade	Transurban trade
Repair craftsmen, Coffee-houses etc. Clerks, Healers, etc.	Lower ranks in army, police administration	Middle ranks in army, police administration	Higher ranks in army, police administration
'Part-time' religious functions; mystic orders	*Ulama*, mystic orders; religious students esp. of Azhar	Higher ranking *Ulama*; former Azhar students	Salafiya
Poor folk (*popolino*)	High school pupils	Students; intelligentsia	Foreigners; students; intelligentsia

This illustration of Cairo's population shows two mixed areas within which the neo-Salafiya became active and which are distinguished from one another in terms of social and economic standing. While the members of Mixed area II had sufficient means to adjust their every-day life to the consumption demands and living standards of the colonial society, those of Mixed area I lacked such material resources. From a political point of view, these two sectors differed in their public approach. The members of Mixed area II tried to express their claim to participate in the colonial society by demanding integration within it. The members of Mixed area I, on the other hand, had to provide an ideological expression for their separation from the sphere of colonial society by deliberately disassociating themselves from its values and concepts. Their isolationist tendency, however, had no political effect on the colonial society. They founded no parties and issued few articles in the press. Instead, they formed heterogeneous circles which mainly tried to point out administrative problems in those city quarters that had been 'abandoned by the state', that is, where institutions of maintenance or control run by the colonial society hardly existed.

The ideologies of both types of mixed area could be expressed both in an 'Islamic' and in a 'European' discourse. In Algeria, for instance, where thousands of Muslim workers had contacts with the labour movement in France, it was the 'European' discourse that at first prevailed among the Algerian Communist party and socialist groups. In the 1930s, however, the isolationist trend within the Algerian working classes became 'Islamicized'. The crucial factors were the far-reaching differences between the French communists and the Étoile Nord Africaine (ENA) around Messali Hadj. On 28 May 1933, the ENA had declared Algeria's complete independence as a firm objective of its programme. From October 1935 to June 1936, Messali Hadj stayed in Geneva with Shakib Arslan, one of the leading representatives of the Salafiya, who converted the one-time communist to Islam. From 15 April 1937, the Étoile Nord Africaine became the Parti du Peuple Algérien (PPA) and demanded 'neither assimilation nor separation, but emancipation!' When Messali Hadj finally arrived in Algiers on 20 June 1937, countless partisans were awaiting him with the Islamic green flag. The red flag could no longer symbolize the will for emancipation expressed by the members of the mixed areas in Algiers. Hadj himself had designed the now green-and-white Algerian national flag in 1937 and declared it a symbol of emancipation.[102]

The ideological core of the neo-Salafiya focused on the concept of emancipation. While the integrationists sought to achieve emancipation through an Islamically legitimized adaptation to the colonial society, the isolationists believed that emancipation could only be achieved by the establishment of a different kind of system, that is, an Islamic system of their own.

The two tendencies were also distinguished by their attitude to power. The isolationists believed that they should exercise their sovereign rights in the districts they controlled and also, as an avant-garde, 'export' these rights into other districts. The integrationists, however, saw themselves as legal parties and groups who for the most part acknowledged the state's monopoly of authority, but at the same time wanted to control it.

In European history this typological distinction is well-known. We only have to refer to the different conceptions of the German SA and NSDAP between 1932 and 1934. The same difference also existed within the Communist movement. The neo-Salafiya, which expressed the social conflicts within Islamic societies, thus followed the logic of the global political concepts prevailing in the 1930s and early 1940s. It did not – and this point should be emphasized – represent an independent ideology, but merely an Islamic form of the prevailing political discourse.

Within the Islamic public, from which the neo-Salafiya in its rudimentary form emerged in the 1930s, there appeared in outline the ideological concepts presented in the table below. From this table it can easily be deduced that the isolationist groups were open to social revolutionary or socialist programmes, while the integrationists were more apt to conform with conservative or liberal points of view. This explains why the neo-Salafiya in Algeria was recruited from the old ENA, while the Muslim Brothers in Egypt cooperated with the national conservatives.

The World Economic Crisis and the New Islamic Movements

	Integrationist	Isolationist
Economy	Islamic economy Islamic eonomic ethics based on the *sunna*	New system = Islam,
State	Islamization of existing institutions, recognition of the nation state	New institutions on the basis of an ideal history, the state as *jama'a* ('community')
Education	Islamic education (*tarbiya*)	Islamic culture (*ta'dib*)
Finance	Islamic banks, Islamic insurance	No banks, no insurance
Private property	Islamically justified	Restricted or rejected
Parties	Islamic parties and constitutions, *al-qaumiya al-islamiya* ('Islamic nationalism')	No parties in the classical sense, no participation
Culture	Islamic culture, acknowledgement of scholarly culture	Rejection of scholarly culture
Law (shari'a)	Preservation of the division between law and ethics, i. e. law and politics, *shari'a* as ethical and legal criterion.	Abolition of the division between law and politics, new proofs through the universal *sunna* (= *shari'a*)

The political mobilization of the mixed areas was characteristic of the 1930s. By contrast to the situation in Central Europe, however, in the Islamic world no mass movement emerged because of – and this was the decisive factor – the high degree of organization in traditional Islamic cultures, which strongly opposed the neo-Salafiya's petit-bourgeois claim to hegemony and found important support from old scholarly circles. The radical critique of tradition by both the Salafiya and the neo-Salafiya corresponded to the spheres of life of the mixed societies, but not to those of the traditional communities, which continued to regard the mystical orders as their most essential cultural and social reference point. The network of social relations formed by the mystical orders was in many respects publicly effective and their literature apparently found more readers than the ideological texts of the neo-Salafiya. Due to the annual pilgrimages to the tombs of the founders of orders, as well as the massive participation in processions to commemorate the day of the murder of Husain b. Ali in Karbala in 680 (*yaum al-'ashura*, 10 Muharram of the Islamic era), the orders were always present among the public. In most Islamic countries, they had in fact organized themselves into an up-to-date, hierarchical structure, thus drawing the attention of the colonial society. In Egypt, for example, there were more than 200 recognized mystical orders around 1935.

The mystical culture of traditional communities formed a real bulwark against the hegemonic claims of the neo-Salafiya. No wonder, then, that the neo-Salafiya was unable to gain a foothold in the countryside and had to focus its activities on the rapidly growing mixed areas in the large cities.

Fascism in the Islamic Public

The typological division between isolationism and integrationism primarily describes the attitude of the opposition groups towards the state and towards the political public. At the same time, certain groups could assume completely different ideological positions which might best be described by the traditional European categories of 'Left' and 'Right'. Here the crucial point is the question of sovereignty. While leftist Islamic groups like the neo-Salafiya or the PPA (Parti du Peuple Algérien) attributed absolute sovereignty to society, rightist groups such as the leadership of the Muslim Brothers argued that sovereignty belonged to the Islamic state alone. The leftists saw Islamic society as the subject of history, while the rightists attributed this role to a glorified state.

The Islamic Right was, for this reason, in theory open to the fascist movements of Central Europe. And yet, perhaps surprisingly, this version of fascism found little support in Islamic societies during the 1930s. The ideals of the Islamic Right corresponded more closely to those of Italian fascism under Mussolini with its corporate system of social representation and idealization of history. National socialism, whose racism and anti-Semitism formed an insuperable cultural barrier, was from the very beginning a marginal phenomenon in the eyes of the Islamic world. Yet there were attempts to create fascist groups within the neo-Salafiya such as the 'Society of Young Egypt' (Jam'iyat Misr al-Fatat), an organization of 'green shirts' which, reflecting the prevailing political fashion, was founded by students in Cairo on 12 October 1933. The Egyptian nationalist Wafd Party, founded in 1919, mobilized a similar formation of 'blue shirts' with which it tried to confront the agitations staged by the 'Young Egypt' group. But the Society of Young Egypt was itself no more than a marginal phenomenon among Egyptian parties and was unable to achieve any real influence. As early as 1938 its leader, Fathi Ridwan, had called Adolf Hitler a madman and had repudiated international fascism and by 1944 it had been completely re-organized to dispense with any kind of Islamic discourse and present itself as a purely socialist organization. The 'Young Egypt' group did not, therefore, represent an explicitly fascist programme; it merely acted within a political climate which encouraged fascism. Similarly, when the Parti du Peuple Algérien was banned by the French authorities in Algiers on 26 September 1939, some of its members formed an underground organization called CARNA (Comité d'Action Révolutionnaire Nord-Africaine), which was wholly committed to Italian fascism. But most of the members of the PPA followed the advice of its leaders and retired from public activity and this group also remained an insignificant minority.

A much more spectacular movement was the Khaksar in the Punjab in north-west India. It was founded by the Cambridge-trained academic Inayat Allah al-Mashriqi (1888–1963), who had studied Oriental languages and natural sciences, and who began his political career in 1924 with the publication of his *Tadhkira* ('The Warning'), in which he maintained that man's function was to subdue nature, a path that led to him to become the deified 'superman'.[103] Al-Mashriqi described communism and democracy as the chief enemies of mankind. On a trip to Europe in 1926 he stopped over in Cairo where he unofficially attended the Caliphate Congress. In Germany he is said to have met Hitler and to have been greatly influenced by national socialism, while for his own part he maintained that Hitler had been deeply influenced by his *Tadhkira*.[104] Al-Mashriqi founded the paramilitary Khaksar in 1931 in Ichra in the Punjab. Although the movement followed in the tradition of fascism it could not do without a symbolic Islamic framework and al-Mashriqi even went so far as to incorporate his social Darwinian views into Islamic doctrine. By 1939 Khaksar was able to mobilize almost 400,000 Muslims who believed they were the only legitimate representatives of India and provoked not only the British colonial administration, but also the members of the All India Muslim League. From 1937 the League was led by the Karachi lawyer Muhammad Ali Jinnah who up to 1943 tried to integrate Khaksar into his movement, but did not succeed. The creation of an independent Muslim secular state was, after the Lahore resolution of 1940, at the top of the Muslim League's agenda, and any potential opposition to the future state was eliminated from the very start.

Despite the relative success of the Khaksar movement, European fascism was not accepted in the Muslim world to any significant extent because most Islamic societies lacked the potential for mass mobilization. It was only partially supported by a handful of intellectuals who considered fascism first and foremost as an ally against French and British colonial rule. The state with a strong leader was certainly much favoured by intellectuals with statist views, and the image of Hitler as the ideal leader 'who would show it to the British and French' was so popular that the slogan 'bala misyu, bala mister, fi s-sama Allah al-ard Hitler' ('No, Monsieur, no, Mister, God in heaven, Hitler on earth') could be heard in the streets of Damascus and there were even several attempts to translate *Mein Kampf* into Arabic.[105] The cult of genius, which national-socialist propaganda had pompously associated with the person of Hitler, also appealed to some Arab writers. The Egyptian author Abbas Mahmud al-Aqqad (1889–1964) was particularly fond of the idea. His theory that 'historical genius' was embodied in the Prophet Mohammad and in the first four caliphs entirely corresponded with the prevailing taste.[106] Later, however, he publicly opposed national socialism.[107] Anti-semitism may have occasioned certain resentments against Jews within the Islamic public. Some global anti-Semitic conspiracy theories, paticularly inspired by the Arabic translations of the pamphlet 'The Protocols of the Elders of Zion' (one of the translations was by al-Aqqad himself) were also popular in certain circles. But German policy was so disconcerting to the Palestinian Muslims that they saw themselves as the victims of a 'false friendship', since it was Germany's persecution of the Jews that truly legitimized the Jewish immigration to Palestine.[108]

The attitude towards Italian and Spanish fascism also posed a problem. Shakib Arslan, who still, at this time, lived in Geneva, pronounced himself in favour of a rapprochement with Italy in the early 1930s and thus provoked sharp protest among the Islamic public. In 1935, the Society of Muslim Youth declared that Arslan had betrayed the cause of Islam, since Italian colonialism in Libya had shown what fascism was capable of. In fact, Arslan's rapprochement had coincided with the time when Italian troops under General Graziani had broken the last resistance of the Libyan tribes in a war that must altogether have cost the lives of a million people.[109] The Libyan popular hero, Umar al-Mukhtar, had been publicly hanged on 17 September 1931. Siding with fascism factually meant supporting Italian settler colonialism in Libya. This marked a definite political limit to the acceptance of fascism to which even Arslan had to submit. To avoid a complete loss of his influence among the Islamic public, he revised his pro-Italian attitude in 1935/36. But it was not until 1938, when large-scale settler colonialism began with the *Ventimilla*, the propaganda-induced immigration of 20,000 Italian settlers to Libya, that positive attitudes towards fascism disappeared.

CHAPTER THREE

The Period of Restoration, 1939–1958

1. THE ISLAMIC WORLD DURING THE SECOND WORLD WAR

At exactly the point that signs of impending war in Europe began to emerge, the Islamic world grew strangely quiet. The Islamic public, increasingly influenced by the neo-Salafi organizations, hardly seemed to notice the conflicts in Europe. Furthermore, at least one focal issue of Islamic politics appeared to have been settled when Great Britain stated that the aim of the 1917 Balfour declaration on the creation of a national homeland for the Jewish people had at last been realized, and that the Jews now had a home which would not be further enlarged. The statement gave a positive turn to the suppression of the Palestinian uprising in the autumn of 1938. The Palestinian leaders suddenly found their claim to the land confirmed and were at the same time relieved that the disastrous peasant uprising was over.

The Algerian nationalists, who for the most part used the slogan 'assimilation' to demand integration into colonial society, suffered a serious defeat in 1938 when the French parliament rejected a bill proposed on 30 December 1936 by Léon Blum, the president of the Popular Front government, and Maurice Violette, the minister of state, which would have awarded 20–30,000 'progressive' (*évolués*) Muslims franchise and eligibility. Both the members of the Parti du Peuple Algérien (PPA) and the society of 'French Algerians', whose numbers grown to more than one million, rejected the proposal; the former because it did not go far enough and only granted full civic rights to a minority, and the latter because it recognized non-Europeans as citizens with equal rights.

Numerous demonstrations for and against the bill coloured the political climate until 1938 after which there was a sudden quiet.

The small nationalist groups in Algeria, the Parti National Pour la Réalisation des Réformes (PNRR) in Morocco and the radical-nationalist Tunisian Neo-Destour Party (Parti Néo-Destour), which had split off from the old constitutional party (Destour) under Habib Bourguiba (Bu Rqiba) and decisively marked the 1938 unrest,[1] were unable to sustain the high degree of popular mobilization. In Morocco a real nationalist public had not even emerged. In Indonesia the Sarekat Islam, which had previously counted 360,000 adherents,[2] lost many of its sympathizers when its left wing abandoned the organization in 1926. As ever, the nationalist groups, whether they argued in Islamic or in European terms, had a low level of organization. In North Africa there were perhaps only a few thousand Muslims who were really organized, in Indonesia there were at best 80,000. Even the neo-Salafi groups only slightly raised the level of organization in these societies, although both the Muslim Brothers in Egypt and the Khaksar in India had an impressive membership.

Sequels of War

In the late 1930s, most colonial regimes took advantage of the structural weakness of the nationalist opposition to initiate a policy of colonial restoration which, to a certain extent, was continued during the Second World War. Their aim was to secure and re-organize colonial resources. When the Netherlands were attacked and occupied by German troops in May 1940 and the Dutch government went into exile in London, Indonesia continued to be administered as an integral part of the Dutch colonial system by the government-in-exile. Meanwhile, Winston Churchill pointed out that the war aimed at rescuing and securing the British Empire.[3]

The importance of the colonial powers was apparent at the very beginning of the war. The Islamic world depended upon vital imports from European countries, or as Wilfred Cantwell Smith expressed it: 'A situation had arisen in which the possibility for the Middle East to eat did not depend on its inhabitants, but on the Great Powers,'[4] Indeed in Turkey alone the production of food dropped by 50 per cent between 1942 and 1945.[5] War and crisis were two sides of the same coin in the Islamic world. From 1904–6, 1915–18, 1929–32, and once more in the years 1940–44, the implications of economic involvement in the world market became evident. Trade routes to the cities of Europe were suddenly blocked, shipping tonnages were dramatically reduced and native populations were left with inedible raw materials on their hands. Crisis and war resembled each other in their social repercussions. The war, it is true, led to a rise in international prices, while the economic crisis of the Great Depression had primarily been experienced as a fall in prices; but high prices were of no use to exporters who were unable to ship their goods. Cotton cultivation suffered a dramatic 50 per cent reduction which could only be compensated by the higher international market prices. Similarly, the consumption of wheat in Egypt sank by 40 per cent and that of maize by 16 per cent. By contrast to the situation during the world economic crisis, the prices of wheat, beans and maize rose considerably – in Istanbul as much as tenfold – so that the poorer urban population and rural communities were pushed to the limits of subsistence. The inflation rates of a few selected countries in the year 1944 (1939 = 100) were as follows:[6] Egypt: 293; Iran: 756; Turkey: 350; Algeria: 539 (1949: 2,160).

The war also led to a considerable shortage of consumer and production goods and stimulated urban contractors to satisfy the need for such commodities. While crisis gripped the agrarian sector, cities in the Islamic countries prospered as efforts were made to produce substitutes for imports. A direct result was the nationalization of domestic capital. In Egypt the part played by Egyptian capital in limited companies doubled between 1933 and 1948 while the number of small enterprises, and hence the number of employees in small industries, rose considerably (by 30 per cent and 67 per cent respectively). Large industrial ventures, however, remained in a preliminary stage of development and there was little change in the overall pattern of capital allocation. Nevertheless, the growth of urban capital was matched by a dramatic reduction in agrarian capital and large agrarian banks and mortgage companies lost more than 50 per cent of their capital.[7]

This tendency was by no means specific to Egypt. Once the lines of communication to European cities were cut off, there was a similar development in almost all Islamic countries. The war brought both boom and crisis and promoted the urbanization of Islamic societies. The political public experienced this as a growth of urban self-confidence as against the rural population. No wonder, then, that the war led to a radicalization of urban identities which was publicly expressed as nationalism.

War, prosperity and crisis were by no means marginal phenomena in the Islamic world. Indeed, they were so comprehensive that the Second World War contributed to a fundamentally new orientation of the political public. The events of the war inflicted deep wounds in Islamic societies, especially in the Balkans, in North Africa, in Iraq, and to a certain extent also in India and particularly Indonesia. To a much greater extent than in the First World War, these societies had become non-combatants involved against their will. In Libya, especially in Cyrenaica, the coastal population passively witnessed the frequent deployment of Italian, German and allied troops on the new coastal road (September 1940 to January 1943). Having escaped the carnage of the 1920s, they were pressed into rendering auxiliary services to the powers. In November 1942, Algeria was conquered by American and Free French troops. In August 1941, British and Soviet troops occupied Iran to prevent a presumptive alliance between Iran and the Axis powers and to supply the threatened USSR with allied reinforcements. Albania became an Italian colony on 7 April 1939, only a few years after it had gained its independence. The 'kingdom' of Croatia, newly founded by Italy and the German empire, appropriated Bosnia-Herzegovina, and the Sanjak of Novipasar was annexed by Italian-occupied Montenegro. Between January and May 1942, Japanese troops conquered almost all of Dutch Indonesia, having already in December 1941 occupied the Malay peninsula with its great rubber plantations and tin deposits. The indirect effects of the war were equally momentous. In the USSR, Stalin denounced many smaller Turkish populations such as the Crimean Tatars and Caucasian tribes as collaborators of the Axis powers and had them deported to the east. The Crimea and Abkhazia on the Black Sea coast were for a short time theatres of operation of the Axis powers.

The victims of war among the Muslim civilian population have never been counted. But their numbers, including those who died from starvation, must have been considerable. No indemnification has ever been offered to the countries that were affected and even today the inhabitants of Cyrenaica suffer from the mine fields laid during those years.

Changing Alliances

The events of the war and their aftermath confirmed the nationalists in their conviction that sovereignty could only be enforced against the European powers. The propaganda of the Axis powers, who represented themselves as potential liberators, had elicited only a few positive reactions from them. Yet the polarization of the war led to a particular policy of alliances in the Islamic world. Urban nationalists basically tended to see themselves better represented by the policy of the Axis powers, while the majority of the rural-based nationalists sided with the allies. Among the crucial factors were the diverse economic, social and cultural relations connecting the agrarian elites with the colonial powers, all of which were now fighting against the Axis powers. The urban nationalists, on the other hand, considered the national dictatorships of the Axis powers as political models which reflected their idea of a powerful state. The old political conflict between city and country thus found an international equivalent which marked the political alliances of nationalist parties in the Islamic world from 1940 to 1942. The best-known example of this was the brief interregnum from 3 April to 21 May 1941 of the Iraqi jurist Rashid Ali al-Kilani (1892–1965), who used German assistance to form a 'government of national defence', but whose small military units were quickly overpowered by British forces. Al-Kilani had also tried, though in vain, to win over Abd al-Aziz (Ibn Sa'ud), the King of Saudi Arabia, for an alliance with the Axis powers.

The popular new Egyptian prime minister, Ali Mahir, also tried to implement a policy directed against the Allies and appointed the President of the Society of Muslim Youth, Muhammad Salih Harb (d. 1968), as minister of national defence in his cabinet (18 August 1939 to 27 June 1940). The Syrian Popular Party of Antun Sa'ada and the Egyptian Islamic Socialist Party, which had emerged from the Society of Young Egypt and whose president, Ahmad Husain (b. 1911), is said to have been an 'ardent admirer' of Mussolini,[8] also showed friendship to the Axis powers.

In Algeria the question of alliances was open. The PPA had, as already mentioned, abstained from joining an alliance after its ban in September 1939. The bourgeois nationalists around Farhat Abbas, the speaker of Young Algeria, first turned to General Henri Pétain's Vichy government, which had assumed political control in Algeria with astonishing speed, probably because many French Algerians came from regions under the control of Vichy France and also because Pétain's anti-Semitic propaganda corresponded with the latent racism of many *pied-noirs*, the Europeans in Algeria.[9] To begin with, Pétain enjoyed substantial prestige on both sides in Algeria. He pleased the French Algerians by liquidating French government officials who were suspected of Freemasonry; and he promised the Assimilists a French future by cancelling the Crémieux Decree and admitting a few Muslims into his National Council. (The Crémieux Decree of 1870, which was named after Isaac Moise, called Adolphe Crémieux, granted the Jewish community of Algeria full French citizenship). Farhat Abbas took advantage of the general atmosphere and on 10 April 1941 sent Pétain a report entitled 'L'Algérie de demain', in which he made several reform proposals within the realms of administration, financial matters and schooling. Pétain's reaction was friendly and informal, and he appointed Abbas to the Algerian Finance Commission. Less that a year later, in February 1942, Abbas resigned. General Pétain obviously could not deal with a civilian Algeria. The promised reforms were not carried out, and the wartime economy, which showed the highest inflation rates in the Middle East, considerably aggravated the situation of the Muslims. The short-lived alliance of the bourgeois nationalists with the Axis powers was thus broken.

One India or Two?

A first re-orientation in alliance policy, that is, in assigning nationalist parties their place within the international constellation of conflicts, was promised by American President Roosevelt and British Prime Minister Churchill in the

'Atlantic Charter' proclaimed on 14 August 1941. In the framework of a general definition of the war's objectives, both declared under point three that they would respect the right of all nations to choose the form of government under which they want to live, and they wanted sovereign rights and self-government to be restored to all those from whom they were taken by force.[10] From the point of view of the urban nationalists, the allies, especially the USA, had promised decolonization as an essential war aim. Churchill, of course, saw this differently, hinting that the policy applied only to those countries which had been dominated by the Axis powers, and that a concept such as 'sovereign rights' referred only to the legitimate rule of the colonial powers.

Nevertheless, the nationalists found a new ally in the USA, which from 1941–42 took on the role of custodian of a far reaching anti-imperialism. This was particularly the case in India. The Indian national movement around Nehru, who since 1938 had raised the question of Indian independence in his private contacts with British Labour politicians, including Clement Attlee, believed that its demands were confirmed by the Atlantic Charter. So when on 5 February 1942 the Indian nationalist Subha Chandra Bose launched his propaganda broadcasts against British colonial rule, and when the advance of Japanese troops in South-East Asia became unstoppable, the Americans brought pressure to bear on Great Britain to settle the Indian problem in order to secure the loyalty of at least part of the Indian nationalists.

The Islamic public was deeply divided. The Muslim League had identified itself with the demand made by Muhammad Iqbal, and now vehemently represented by Jinnah, to establish a Muslim state in north-western India. Jinnah pointed out that Islam and Hinduism are not religious in the narrow sense of the word, but represent truly differing and divided social orders: 'Hindus and Muslims belong to two different religious philosophies, social customs and literatures. Thus the Muslims form a nation according to every definition ... and have to have their home, their territory and their state.'[11]

Muslim theologians had, among other things, based their 'two nations theory' on the thesis that Muslims were not permitted to live under non-Islamic rule and must emigrate to their own Islamic territory.[12] No one had yet thought of founding a state which would exclusively use an Islamic discourse. However, Muslims were generally considered to be a nationality of their own and Islam as an ethnic characteristic. A state legitimated in this manner conformed with the 'European' discourse of nationalism. But this was opposed by the Islamic constitutionalists,[13] who had a powerful organization in the Jam'iyat-i Ulama-i Hind (Society of the Ulama of India), founded in 1919. In their opinion, India should be a decentralized, multi-religious state which would pay great attention to the concerns of Muslims. Ideally, the leader of this state should be appointed by an Islamic caliph. Important to them was the preservation of an undivided India whose old religions disposed of a vast cultural and social autonomy. The Muslim League may have had little influence among the population when compared to the Jam'iyat-i Ulama; yet it dominated the Islamic public.

One of the contributors to the journal of the Jam'iyat-i Ulama between 1920 and 1928 had been a young man from the Hyderabad area, Abu'l-A'la al-Maududi (1903–79). The neo-Salafi turning-point of the late 1920s and early 1930s had caught Maududi's attention and encouraged him to give up the Society and found his own journal (*Tarjuman-i Quran*), which he published in Hyderabad from the year 1932. As a neo-Salafi intellectual, Maududi directed all his attention to the Islamization of the nationalists' political discourse. He accepted Iqbal's idea of a Muslim state in north-western India, but at the same time demanded that it should be entirely subject to an 'Islamic ideology'. Maududi was convinced that the state could only be conceived as the expression of a divine sovereignty; Muslims therefore had to organize it in accordance with ideological precepts. From 1939, he criticized the Islamic nationalists of the Muslim League for their lack of 'an Islamic mentality or Islamic habits of thought and for not considering political and social problems from an Islamic point of view.'[14] In March 1938, he accepted an earlier invitation from Muhammad Iqbal and went to Lahore in western Punjab to lead a new Islamic education and research centre, the Islamiya College.[15] Less than a year later, he returned to Pathankot in eastern Punjab to again work as an independent author. On 26 August 1941 when the publication of the Atlantic Charter led Indian nationalists to feel that their hour had come, Maududi called together 75 followers in Lahore to found the neo-Salafi organization the 'Islamic Community' (Jama'at-i Islami), which later became known far beyond Pakistan, and had himself confirmed as *amir*.[16]

The Jama'at-i Islami was in many respects similar to the Egyptian Muslim Brotherhood. However, Maududi's ideological statements bore the mark of the specific conditions of the Indian political public. Unlike the Muslim League, Maududi defined Islam not as the 'ethnic' characteristic of a nationalism, but as an 'ideological party which closely resembles the socialists or communists'.[17] Pakistan was thus to be not a classical nation state, but an ideologically conceived state. Maududi had this principle boiled down to the formula: 'God knows, we don't want a Muslim government; we want Islam to rule, not the Muslims,'[18] and elsewhere added: 'As a true Muslim I have no reason to rejoice that the Turks rule in Turkey, the Iranians in Iran and the Afghans in Afghanistan. As a Muslim I do not believe in the idea of a "government of the people, by the people and for the people". Rather I believe in the sovereignty of God.'[19]

Maududi viewed Islam as an ideology. He thus produced an Islamicized form of ideological thinking which owed its popularity in the 1930s to the following statement: divine will has determined society in its development; but man, who has found his being-for-himself through Islam, has acted autonomously. Determinism and voluntarism thus formed the core of a holistic view of the world which allowed the leaders to act freely, while at the same time considering historical development as predestined. The will to carry out a divine decision turned Maududi into the leader of an 'Islamic revolution' which was to give Muslims a new set of ethics. The 'Islamic state', according to Maududi, must represent a union of ethics, law and politics, it must be the embodiment of God on earth.[20] The specific conditions of Indian nationalism led to the perception of Islam as a complete ideology. Maududi's 'Islamic ideology' later exercised a great influence on the various neo-Salafi groups throughout the Islamic world since it provided a first clear definition of an 'Islamic state'. Most neo-Salafi organizations had previously adopted the nationalist discourse when they addressed the political public. Maududi's Islamic ideology, which he had derived from the Indian situation, could now be considered as a powerful alternative to nationalism.

The idea of an 'ideological state' caused Maududi to move closer to the right. However, as far as the history of ideas is concerned, there are hardly any real connections between European fascist traditions and Maududi's ideologically conceived state. He himself was not impressed by European fascism; on the contrary, his line of thought was closer to that of the Indian left. Maududi's repeated references to socialism and communism show that it was with them, rather than with national conservative circles, that he wanted to associate himself. But unlike the Islamic socialists and communists of the 1920s, including the founder of the influential theological school of Deoband, Abdallah Sindi (1872–1944), he did not consider Islamic society as the subject of history. His focus was always the state. Society was merely a revolutionary device for the establishment of the Islamic state. If we were to look for a typological analogy, it can best be found in Spanish and Italian fascism.

Islam as the Framework for a State Ideology: Indonesia

The years 1941–42 marked a decisive turning-point. With the emergence of the USA as the guarantor of national sovereignty, the nationalist parties had found a new ally allowing them to dispense with their often disastrous ties with the Axis powers. It was for this reason that after the Japanese attack on Pearl Harbour (7–8 December 1941), Indonesian nationalists looked expectantly towards the USA. But on 8 March 1942, when Japanese troops landed in Java, their hopes of a rapprochement with the USA were thwarted. As in northern Sumatra (Atjeh), many welcomed the Japanese as 'liberators', especially when they brought back Sukarno from his exile (since 1936) and gave him a chance to reorganize his national movement. Just as Great Britain tried to make India's national movement into a bulwark against the Japanese threat, the Japanese occupants considered the nationalist movement as a guarantor for their control of Indonesia against the allies. The Japanese military administration particularly promoted the Islamic discourse of the national movement, and did so to such an extent that in 1945 Indonesia corresponded much more with the Islamic ideal of the *santri* (urban intellectuals)[21] than it had in 1942 under the Dutch colonial administration.[22]

The Japanese occupation surprised the highly heterogeneous Islamic public by forcing its numerous parties and groups into a common representative body, the Council of Indonesian Muslims (Madjlis Sjuro Muslimin Indonesia, or Masjumi).[23] This Council included several groups of Salafi *ulama* working together, among them the conservative Nahdat al-Ulama and the Sarekat Islam. The Council was to supervise the reconstruction of an Islamic cultural system while a 'non-European' discourse was imposed in Islamic schools.

The Masjumi was in a sense a successor of the Supreme Islamic Council of Indonesia (Madjlisul Islamil a'laa Indonesia) founded in 1937, but officially dissolved in October 1943, which had first represented the Islamic political public. However, despite their unification through the Masjumi, the political rifts within the Islamic parties could not be overcome. A powerful conservative group confronted the heterogeneous neo-Salafiya, in which Islamic socialists as well as radical isolationists had found their place. Even nationalists using the 'European' discourse had joined the Masjumi. Sukarno, who had again and again fought for a radical de-Islamization of politics, now thought that the union between Islamic and nationalist leaders was as solid as a rock.[24] However, the Japanese managed to win over a few leading Islamic intellectuals who were entrusted with integrating the divergent tendencies. An outstanding role in this connection was played by the president of the Masjumi, the scholar Hasjim Asj'ari (Hashim Ashari) from Eastern Java, who was in addition appointed as president of the new Office for Religious Affairs (Kantor Urusan Agama) on 1 October 1944. Another prominent champion was Kahar Muzakkir ('Abd al-Qahhar Mudakkir), who had already appeared as the representative of Indonesian Muslims at the General Islamic Congress in Jerusalem in 1931. How strongly the Japanese administration was promoting unification is shown by the fact that the members of the Masjumi included the most powerful competitors in Islamic public life, the conservative scholarly organization Nahdat al-Ulama and the urban-nationalist Muhammadiya, both of which had refused to join the Supreme Islamic Council in 1937.[25] In January 1945, a member of the Nahdat al-Ulama was even appointed as commander-in-chief of the paramilitary youth organization 'Party of God' (Hizbullah or Hizb Allah), from which the Indonesian National Army was to be later recruited.[26]

As in India, unofficial negotiations began in September 1944 between Japan and the nationalists around Sukarno. On 1 March 1945, Japan repeated that it supported Indonesia's independence. The members of the Masjumi reacted immediately. On 29 April 1945, they organized a Committee for the Preparation of Independence in Djakarta, later known by the number of its members as the Committee of the Sixty-Two. During the Committee's first session (29 May to 1 June 1945), the foundations for the future identity of Indonesia as a state were laid. This included above all the doctrine of the *pancasila* (*pantja sila*) or 'five elements' of the Indonesian state, a doctrine inspired by Muhammad Yamin and formulated by Sukarno. These five principles are briefly described below, because they reflect a very specific Indonesian tradition of Islamic nationalism.[27]

1. *Kebangsaan* ('nationalism') – what was meant, according to Sukarno, was not a nationalistic chauvinism, but a defensive national feeling of solidarity.
2. *Perikemanusiaan* ('humanism') – Indonesian culture was to be internationalist, but not cosmopolitan, since this would run counter to the national character of the state.
3. *Permusyawaratan* ('consultation'), *perwakilan* ('representation') and *mufakat* ('common decision')[28] – political and social decisions should be taken in accordance with *adat* through constant deliberation and by means of a representative system having the aim of reaching a unified and binding position.
4. *Kesejahteraan* ('social welfare').
5. *Ketuhanan yang maha esa* ('belief in the one and only God') – this principle was later given precedence over all the others.[29]

When on 17 August, three days after the Japanese capitulation, the independence of the Indonesian republic was proclaimed, the effect of this long domestic debate became apparent. The 'European' and the heterogeneous 'Islamic' discourse of the national movement had become so unified that the new republic could be described neither as 'secular' nor as 'Islamic'. The propaganda about the unity of Indonesia in the cultural, political and social realm created a state ideology in which the confession of union became the underlying principle both in the Islamic-theological and in the secular-ideological sense. The state was made to engage in religious ethics without committing itself to any theological or ideological tendency. Unity itself became its ideology.[30]

The military vacuum in Indonesia – British troops only landed in Java on 29 September – made it easier for the nationalists to establish a civil administration in parts of Java and Sumatra and to assume military sovereignty. The Republic of Indonesia proclaimed on 18 August 1945 was hence no phantom of the nationalists, but a political reality. However, the Indonesian government under Sukarno was unable to win over the USA, despite the latter's reserved, but anti-imperialist policy: the USA was now discreetly supporting the efforts of the British and Dutch colonial administration to reconquer the colonial regions they had lost to Japan in 1942.[31]

The Political Turning-Point in Morocco and Algeria

The assimilation of Islamic policy to the programmes of the nationalist public was considerably accelerated by the war. After 1942, even traditional rulers like the Sultan of Morocco, Muhammad V, or the Tunisian Bey Muhammad al-Munsif (Moncef), demanded the restoration of their countries' independence from the French government. Al-Munsif was promptly deposed by the French 'because of his collaboration with the Nazis'. Muhammad V used the nationalist 'Independence Party' (Hizb al-Istiqlal), founded in 1943, as a medium to assert his claims to Moroccan sovereignty. The American support he was promised by Roosevelt at the secret Casablanca Conference (January 1943), as well as the confirmation of Syrian and Lebanese independence by the French government-in-exile (23 December 1943), gave him hope of a quick response to his demand. The Independence Party itself was the result of a nationalization of the Islamic discourse of the neo-Salafiya. One of its founders was the already mentioned Allal al-Fasi who had been exiled to Gabon in 1937 because of his Islamic-nationalist propaganda. His fellow contender Ahmad Balafraj, an urban merchant from Rabat, had been exiled to France. The petition for independence which they submitted, among others, to the sultan and the governor general on 11 January 1944 was refused, and Balafraj and others were again arrested.

It must not be overlooked that the anti-imperialist tenor of American foreign policy under Roosevelt encouraged the adaptation of the Islamic discourse to suit the nationalist public because liberal nationalism had the ear of the USA at the time. This was what the Indian and Moroccan nationalists tried to turn to account.

The leader of the Algerian bourgeois nationalists, Farhat Abbas, also saw this as a chance to obtain backing for his demand of autonomy. After the allied landing in Algiers on 8 November 1942, Roosevelt's personal adviser, Robert Murphy, was the direct interlocutor of the group around Abbas. Encouraged by Murphy, Abbas published his famous Manifesto of the Algerian People ('L'Algérie devant le conflit mondial. Manifeste du peuple algérien') on 10 February 1943. Using an ingenious rhetorical style interspersed with suggestions for reforms, he recommended the foundation of an autonomous, but not independent state in Algeria. The French authorities accepted this manifesto as a 'preliminary paper' and De Gaulle, who after June 1943 directed French policy in Algeria, paved the way for the decree of 7 March 1944, by which the Algerians were granted extended powers in the legislative realm.

But this concession no longer corresponded with political realities. The nationalist public met at the Association des Amis du Manifeste et de la Liberté (AML), founded on 14 March 1944, which was joined by the Salafi Union of Ulama and the underground PPA. The latter, which owed its existence to the adaptation of an Islamic-revolutionary discourse to a nationalist movement, quickly got the upper hand at the meeting. The freedom of nations proclaimed by the United Nations, the establishment of the Arab League in 1944–45 and the attitude of the USA, which continued being pro-freedom, firmly embedded the demand for independence, which the association had raised since March 1945, within the minds of an international public.

Meanwhile the state had in many respects lost its control over society. The war-torn economy, the flourishing black market and the devaluation of money mobilized the urban and even part of the peasant proletariat. Many of the 300,000 Algerian combatants returned to the cities from the theatres of war in Italy and France to find neither social nor economic aid towards re-integration. The PPA of Messali Hadj, who had been recognized by the AML in March as the 'undisputed leader of the Algerian people', tried to prevent the social protest from getting out of hand through the hastily planned proclamation of an 'Algerian government' (19 April 1945). However, the French authorities stole a march on Messali, who had been under police supervision since 1937, and exiled him to Brazzaville in the French Congo. The PPA was nevertheless able to organize demonstrations in Algiers on 1 May, which were violently broken up by the police. On 8 May 1945, the day of Germany's capitulation, serious riots broke out in eastern Algeria, especially in the Sétif area. French troops under General Duval quickly succeeded in controlling the situation; but the Algerians suffered at least 8,000 casualties. The arrest of more than 4,000 rebels and almost 100 death sentences led to the dissolution of the remnants of the PPA, which had been planning a second rebellion for 23–24 May. The *ulama* were also shocked by these repressive measures. The new president of the Association of Muslim Ulama, Muhammad al-Bashir al-Ibrahimi (1889–1965), was arrested with Farhat Abbas. All the Islamic schools were closed. It was not until 9 March 1946 that the French parliament issued an amnesty, which was applied to al-Ibrahimi and Abbas, but not to the arrested PPA militants.

In the spring of 1946, the bourgeois nationalists again separated from the PPA social revolutionaries. Abbas founded the Union Démocratique du Manifeste Algérien (UDMA) and participated in the regional elections of 2

June 1946 winning 640,000 votes. The PPA, however, used the characteristic slogan 'whoever votes is an infidel' (*man intakhaba kafara*) and demanded a boycott of the elections, a demand followed by about 500,000 Algerians.[32]

The Islamic public was particularly preoccupied with the problem of securing a place for an independent Islamic cultural identity within the framework of these political conflicts. As it had already done in the 1920s and 1930s, the Association of Muslim Ulama around al-Ibrahimi made special efforts 'to separate Islam from the French government',[33] that is, to create independent institutions for the Islamic public. According to al-Ibrahimi, the state should stay away from the mosques, it should leave charitable endowments and pilgrimages to be run by an Islamic self-government, it should remove Islamic dignitaries from the civil service (sic) and recognize Islamic jurisdiction as an 'independent authority'. The peculiarity of Algerian politics thus challenged the Salafiya *ulama* to declare themselves constitutionalists. They pleaded for a radical separation between state and religion and for an Islamically legitimized division of powers; but at the same time they denounced the French administration sometimes as secularist, sometimes as 'Christian'. From their point of view, the creation of an independent Islamic public with its own schools, its own press and its own problems meant that the religion of Islam would become the expression of a civil identity for Algeria. So without saying it in so many words, the *ulama* were declaring themselves for an Islamic secularism which was to represent a third alternative between bourgeois nationalists and Islamic social revolutionaries. This brought them much closer to the bourgeoisie around Farhat Abbas than they would openly admit.

The Second World War had almost completely, albeit in very different ways, integrated Islamic politics into nationalism. In Indonesia Islam had made a crucial contribution to the development of nationalism as a unitary state ideology. In India, most Muslim politicians considered Islam as the 'ethnic' feature of an Islamic nationalism, while Maududi's minority position claimed Islam as the very idea of a state. And finally in Algeria (as also partly in Tunisia), the demand of the Islamic public was not state sovereignty, but civil freedom.

2. AN ARAB OR AN ISLAMIC NATION?

Islamic policy had now finally adjusted itself to global models. None of the Islamic political groups, not even those representing an isolationist position, could uphold a political concept that differed from these models. By the end of the 1930s, the idea of a nation state was solidly integrated within the Islamic public. Maududi's efforts at demarcation, which were shared by other Islamic groups of the period, brought his political statements even closer to the global model. Political modernism could no longer be hindered by any kind of Islamic discourse, since political Islam was based on the same escape from tradition as modernism itself. Nevertheless, Islamic intellectuals again and again realized that their political statements found no hearing among the non-Islamic public of the world. Whenever a political programme was couched in Islamic rhetoric, the Western world would react negatively. Applying its own fundamentalist verdict, the West ascribed unalterable characteristics to Islam, which it derived from the early Islamic period and considered as the true essence of the religion. In particular it attributed two characteristics to political Islam. First, an independent Islamic secularism could not exist because 'Islam does not differentiate between state and religion' and Islam, as a 'pre-industrial culture', contradicts 'scientific and technical modernism', as well as the secular identity of the West and of the community of nations.[34] Second, the political interpretation of the *shari'a*, the Islamic law, would result in a social order that had nothing in common with the humanitarian values of the West.

After the Second World War, 'community of nations' and 'human rights' had become catch-phrases which were a serious concern to people who had experienced the horrors of war. Both these ideas were of course also present in Islamic countries which had experienced similar horrors and where hunger, destruction, uprooting, broken families, psychological hardship and flight had left their mark on the memories of numerous communities. But unlike the victorious West, the triumphant Soviet Union, or even the defeated countries of Europe, the Islamic world faced more calamities. The colonial restoration that resulted from the Second World War was beginning to show its effects. As Europe celebrated peace in Morocco, Algeria, Tunisia, Yugoslavia, Palestine, India and Indonesia, the battle had only just begun. We can only speculate about the number of victims of these conflicts, but the Algerian–French war alone caused the death of over a million Muslims, a tenth of the Algerian population. Germany had lost about 8.5 per cent of its total population in the Second World War, Japan 3 per cent and France 2 per cent. Conditions in Algeria came very close to those in the USSR (10.5 per cent) and Yugoslavia (10 per cent).

This wartime experience fostered a specific kind of Islamic policy which continued during the following decades. The Islamic political public considered it a duty to appeal to the principles of the community of nations and human rights, since these had become the constituents of its own identity as well as those of the West and East. But as conflict followed conflict, it discovered that these principles only applied to the West and the East, and that the Islamic world was excluded from them because its people were Muslims and were therefore devoid of Western culture.

The Beginnings of an Arab Policy

The de-Islamization of the political public thus definitely corresponded to a need for international recognition. The efforts of the allied powers to incorporate the Islamic world within a post-war system were accordingly based on a purely 'ethno-cultural' perception of the Islamic world, placed within large geo-political contexts. The structure of the post-war order in the Islamic world thus rested on two pillars. The first was the formation of a regional bloc in the Arab world, as proposed during the preparations for the foundation of the United Nations; by their inclusion within an international security system, the independent Arab states were to be brought together to form a regional coalition. The second was the effort by nationalist circles to turn the Arab nation states into a political community expressing an 'Arab public opinion', without giving up their sovereignty as nation states. An Arab foreign policy of this kind had already been floated at the Palestine Conference in London in 1939, when the Egyptian nationalist Ali Mahir had headed an official delegation. The Egyptian nationalists now felt called upon to develop the outlines of an Arab policy and sought the support of Great Britain for their project. This policy was mainly promoted by former Egyptian–Ottoman officers who had fought on the Ottoman side in Libya in World War I and had entertained friendly relations with Enver Pasha, the Ottoman minister of war. Among them were Aziz al-Misri, the co-founder of the Society of Muslim Youth, Abd al-Hamid Sa'id, an Egyptian–Sudanese officer Muhammad Salih Harb, and, in a prominent position, the pro-Ottoman Egyptian nationalist Abd al-Rahman Azzam (born 1893).[35] The officers all belonged to the war generation and – with the exception of al-Misri – had ardently embraced the Ottoman cause. Strangely enough, three of them held high posts within the Society of Muslim Youth. This society itself was now being increasingly 'Arabized'. Muhammad Salih Harb, its president, thought of it as an expression of the Egyptian claim to leadership in the Arab world against the hegemonic aspirations of the Hashimites, who ruled Transjordan and Iraq. It remains an open question, however, whether these Egyptian attempts to establish a Pan-Arab policy did not at the same time convey an old Ottoman political ideal.

The international, or rather British options for a regional coalition of the Arab world had not overlooked the Hashimites. After the British victory at El Alamein, two alternatives unfolded. The Syrian option consisted of the coalition of the countries of Syria, Lebanon, Palestine and Transjordan into a kingdom ruled by the Hashimites. The Iraqi option, on the other hand, aimed at the political union of the Fertile Crescent in the form of a federation, that is, a coalition between Syria and Iraq, as proposed by the Iraqi prime minister Nuri al-Sa'id.

This regional policy was opposed by Egyptian nationalists of all parties. In the spring of 1943, Mustafa al-Nahhas the Egyptian premier, who had good relations with Great Britain, invited Arab delegations to discuss 'the project of a union of Arab nations'.[36] During the first secret sessions of the delegations in Cairo (June–October 1943) no agreement was reached, which de facto signified an Egyptian victory. Syria and Lebanon resolutely rejected the Hashimite proposals. Saudi Arabia and the Yemen insisted on preserving their sovereignty. The trilateral discussions of experts at Dumbarton Oaks (USSR, Great Britain, USA, 21 August to 28 September 1944; separate discussions were afterwards held with China) confirmed the Egyptian position of creating a league of Arab states in which the individual members would only partially renounce their claims to sovereignty. At the General Arab Congress of Alexandria (25 September–7 October 1944), the delegations of Egypt, Syria, Iraq, Lebanon and Transjordan passed the so-called Alexandria Protocol providing for the creation of the League which, in accordance with British wishes, was to feature a military pact. Saudi Arabia only joined the protocol on 21 January 1945, after it had declared war on Germany.[37]

The League pact was signed on 22 March 1945. Abd al-Rahman Azzam, who had meanwhile become the Egyptian secretary of state, was elected as secretary general, despite the protests of the Iraqi delegation. The extent to which the political public had meanwhile become Arabized is shown by the Cultural Treaty of the Arab League signed on 27 November 1945, in which not a word was said about the Islamic public; instead, there were merely references to the 'Arab civilization'. Saudi Arabia signed the treaty, but at the same time proclaimed that '... the government of Saudi Arabia agrees with the conditions of this treaty, albeit with the exception of what it considers as inconsistent with the *shari'a* of Islam.'[38] Many Arab intellectuals were aware of the problems that would result from a forced Arabization of public life. As a preventive measure, Isma'il Mazhar, the editor of the national-liberal Egyptian journal *al-Usur*, wrote:[39]

> One would wish every Arab to have Islam inspire him to be Arab in his innermost being. His most distinguished example shall be Arab culture and Islamic culture; his world policy shall be the policy of the Arabs and the policy of Islam; ... And if one of us mentions an Islamic union, then he must mean an Arab union in the Islamic spirit; and if one of us mentions the Arab union, then he must mean an Islamic union in the Arab spirit.

The establishment of the Arab League was a prerequisite for the admission of the Arab states to the United Nations and Saudi Arabia, Egypt, Syria, Lebanon and Iraq all participated in the San Francisco Conference (25 April to 26 June 1945) as founding members.[40]

A Trans-national Islamic Policy

Post-war policies in the Islamic world thus fell into line with global processes, since security systems, a careful de-colonization through UN custodians, and a cautious definition of a 'just' world order marked the general political atmosphere. Within the Islamic public the process of globalization was also discernable. The Egyptian Muslim Brothers, who saw themselves as representatives of the Islamic identity, tried to establish branches in other Arab countries through their coordinating office in Cairo. One of the aims of the Muslim Brothers must surely have been to assert themselves in their competition with the 'Arab public'. If they limited themselves to a local Islamic public their organization would certainly been doomed. Their first results were achieved in Syria, when in late 1945 several Syrian neo-Salafi organizations, among them the Syrian Society of Muslim Youth and an older group of Muslim Brothers from Damascus formed the 'Syrian Muslim Brotherhood' under the leadership of Mustafa al-Siba'i (1915–64). On 5 May 1946, the Brotherhood was established in Palestine and joined by the large neo-Salafi groups from Haifa. In November 1946, the Brotherhood opened an office in Amman with the official support of King Abdallah. Even the Islamic liberation movement in the Sudan now found itself following the tradition of the Muslim Brothers. In 1947, the Muslim Brothers formed the 'Society of Islamic Brotherhood' (Jam'iyat al-Ukhuwa al-Islamiya) in Baghdad, which was joined by prominent Iraqi Sunni *ulama*, such as the great Kadi Amjad al-Zahawi (1881–1967) and the Salafi Muhammad Mahmud al-Sawwaf from Mosul (b. 1915). But there were setbacks as well. When Hasan al-Banna tried to establish a branch in Mecca in 1946, the Saudi authorities informed him that the Muslim Brotherhood was inconsistent with the Saudi Arabian law of associations. Moreover, many regional groups did not want to be put under 'Egyptian command' and insisted on their organizational independence. The Islamic network which the Muslim Brothers tried to create after 1945 also touched upon the sphere of international politics. In 1946 al-Banna attended a conference where the question of how the Arab bloc system could be extended to other Islamic countries was discussed. The conference included the secretary general of the Arab League, Azzam, the former Mufti of Jerusalem, al-Husaini, the leader of the Indian Muslim League, M. A. Jinnah, the rector of the Egyptian Azhar University, Mustafa Abd al-Raziq, and King Ibn Saud's adviser of long standing, Yusuf Yasin.[41] This was the first time that the term 'Islamic bloc' (*al-kutla al-islamiya*) was used.

In view of the prevalence of the 'European' discourse in nationalist politics, the Islamic parties tried to steal a march on the nationalists. They saw themselves as the spearhead of national movements and as the true representatives of an Islamic public through which Arab policy was best served. But they could not succeed, since the Islamic parties had no independent Islamic policy to offer beyond their own local context. The Islamic public could present no true alternative to nationalist projects either concerning the question of Palestine or regarding the Muslims of India or North Africa or Indonesia. The political orientation of the neo-Salafiya was always centred on a local social context. In the conflicts within urban societies, the neo-Salafi societies were able to realize their own ideas; but the international public was so strongly 'Europeanized' that a specific Islamic discourse made no real sense. The rhetoric of the Islamic parties on an international level soon ended in appeals to 'the union of the Islamic *umma*'. The kind of union this was meant to be could not be formulated in an Islamic discourse. What seemed more important to them was to establish a community of interests of neo-Salafi organizations which would try to support their claim to be an avant-garde on international grounds. Thus the neo-Salafi organizations put themselves above nation states, claiming a kind of transnationalism. What they wanted to achieve was not the union of the Islamic world, but the union of an Islamic avant-garde which would unite into a supranational *jama'a*. In the political terminology of the Islamic public, a distinction was made between the concept of *rabita* ('alliance', 'league') and *jami'a* (here 'league', 'community'). *Rabita* meant the transnational unification of existing neo-Salafi organizations and groups, while *jami'a* – following the old linguistic usage – signified the union of Islamic states in their diversity. Those who supported the idea of a loose union of states explicitly adopted the concept of *jami'a* when the League of Arab States was founded.

The transnational Islamic policy, which was distinctly influenced by fractions of the Egyptian Muslim Brotherhood, aimed at an assimilation of highly heterogeneous ideologies. After the Second World War, the concept of social justice became the major ideological key-note of the neo-Salafiya. In the context of the boom in nationalist politics, the general Islamic public soon started to see itself as the 'social conscience' of the Islamic world. The neo-Salafiya identified the nationalist concept of freedom with a very specific concept of justice. An oft-repeated formulation was that freedom was the equivalent of justice, and that within an Islamic context, freedom would always mean justice.

When referring to social justice, the Islamic parties kept to the local context and could even formulate their own point of view within nationalist politics while at the same time preserving traditional Islamic rhetoric. Thus the neo-Salafi organizations picked up a theme that had found public recognition after the end of the Second World War. The demand for social justice had also been a crucial factor in the discussions about the United Nations.

A second keynote was human rights, which had been the subject of public discussion since the United Nations Charter had come into force on 24 October 1945. Addressing this question, Islamic theoreticians were able to fill a gap that existed among the nationalist public. From their point of view, discussions of human rights in the Islamic world could only be held in an 'Islamic' way. This meant, as Ibn Badis had already written in an article of 1938, that the question of human rights had to have its place in the debate about social justice.[42]

The nationalist intellectuals for their own part realized that the only way to dispense with a specific Islamic apologetic was to define Islam as the national identity of the Arabs. At the height of the conflict over Palestine, the Iraqi nationalist Abd al-Rahman al-Bazzaz provoked the Islamic public with his thesis that Islam was an 'Arab national religion' and, in the same way as Judaism, formed the foundation for the unity of the Arab people.[43] Later on, al-Bazzaz qualified this thesis,[44] but his arguments remained effective and influenced the future Ba'th Party in Iraq.

However, such theories did not present any danger to the Islamic public, since they had no bearing upon the social order of Islamic societies. Far more significant were socialist and communist programmes which became increasingly popular in the Islamic world around 1947. Communist circles, for instance in Egypt, like the Islamic groups, turned their attention to social questions. In the mixed areas of the big cities, they gained a foothold with astonishing speed, forcing the Islamic public into taking more serious issue with social problems. Discussions about private ownership soon became the crucial point of the debate. Many Muslim Brothers, above all the leader of the Syrian Muslim Brothers, Mustafa al-Siba'i, adopted socialist arguments and loudly declared themselves for an 'Islamic socialism'. In accordance with the neo-Salafi tradition, they idealized socialism by comparing it with conditions in the early Islamic period. The militant Muslim Brother Muhammad al-Gazzali (born 1917) summed up the discussion with the impressive formula 'Brotherhood in religion, socialism on earth!'. He thus alluded to the classic Islamic dichotomy of religion (*din*) and the world (*dunya*), which had long marked the ambivalent relationship between theological dogma (*aqida*) and worldly law (*shari'a*).[45]

The Establishment of New States in the Islamic World

During the first post-war years, four new states were established in the Islamic world, in the process of which the Islamic groups of the neo-Salafiya had to decide to what extent they wanted to take part in the new system of nation states. These new states – 1947 Pakistan, 1948 Israel, 1949 Indonesia and 1951 Libya – were based on entirely different international and local principles, and their Islamic policies were followed correspondingly specific orientations.

Pakistan 1947

After the Muslim League's decision on 26 March 1940 to found a nation state for the Muslims of India in north-western India and in Bengal, British public opinion came to the conclusion that India had to be preserved as a complete state. This objective was also followed by the British Labour government, which endorsed the independence of India in August 1945. In India itself the atmosphere was tense. There were mass protests against the arrest of leaders of the small Indian National Army recruited by Japan in 1942, which had been under the command of Subha Chandra Bose in 1943 and had earned itself a reputation through military actions in north-eastern India. These protests led to the British government's growing willingness to grant India its independence as soon as possible. Political discussions between the Indian Congress movement led by Jawaharlal Nehru (1889–1964) since 1936 – the Indian National Congress had been founded in 1885 as the organization representing Indian citizenship – and the Muslim League further heated the atmosphere. Nevertheless, both organizations for the time being agreed with the British proposal of March 1946 to divide India into a federation of three autonomous zones (Bengal, India, and present-day Pakistan); however, both subsequently tried to change the boundaries of the sovereign territories to their own advantage. Nehru's idea of considering the structure of the federation once independence had been achieved particularly provoked the opposition of the League. The latter went back on its agreement with the British proposal and called for a 'Direct Action Day' on 16 August 1946, leading to the notorious Calcutta massacre in which more than 4,000 Indians were killed. The political consensus was broken. All attempts to preserve India as a centralized state were threatened. Instead, the Congress movement showed itself willing to agree with the partition proposed by the League. On 20 February 1947, the British government declared that India would become independent in July 1948. Mountbatten, the viceroy appointed on 22 March 1947, was to prepare for independence. On 3 June 1947, both sides accepted the partition proposal and a date for independence, which was advanced to 15 August 1947. There were suddenly no more than two weeks to prepare for the change.

The rapid decision of the British government and the self-interested cooperation of both Congress and League made it difficult for Maududi to promote his project for an Islamic state among the public. The unrest which accompanied partition showed that, among the population, Islam played a much greater ethnic and cultural role than Maududi – the founder and leader of the Jama'at-i Islami – had expected. Perhaps he recalled the witticism often repeated among neo-Salafi partisans that Islam was something other than Muslims. Indeed, the Muslims did not behave as Maududi's Islamic ideology had foreseen. About 8.9 million, more than 20 per cent of the Muslim population of the new India, fled to the state of Pakistan; and about 8.6 million Hindus migrated to India. In the local and regional wars that broke out while the states were being formed, hundreds of thousands of people were killed.

Maududi's elite society at first included few members, since in 1944–45 a large number had been excluded for ideological reasons and new admissions involved a very complicated process. The secretary general of the Jama'at-i Islami, Tufail Muhammad, kept very detailed records: 700 members in 1943, 750 in 1944, ca. 400 in 1945, 486 in 1946 and 533 in 1947.[46] After the unrest in Pathankot, the Jama'at escaped to Lahore, because Pathankot had been annexed to eastern Punjab and hence India. The Jama'at had no choice but to seek protection in the state which Maududi often called 'na-Pakistan', that is 'the land of the impure'. The Jama'at's historians soon tried to prove that Maududi had been the real leading light in the foundation of Pakistan, that even Jinnah had admired him and that Maududi's famous formula about the 'sovereignty of God' (*hakimiyat Allah*) corresponded with Muhammad Iqbal's concept of a 'Muslim state'. Staunch followers of Maududi rejected this of course. But the fact remained that the Jama'at took almost a year to adapt to the new conditions in Pakistan and it was not until the spring of 1948, that Maududi finally launched his campaign for an 'Islamic constitution' for Pakistan.[47]

The powerful *ulama* of Deoband, who had declared themselves against the partition of India remained passive. Only a small group around Shabbir Ahmad Uthmani (1887–1950), who supported the nationalist policy of the League, formed a new Society of the Ulama of Islam (Jam'iyat-i Ulama-i Islam) and came forward as the representatives of the *ulama* who had fled from the Deoband Centre of Learning and of Muslim fugitives (*muhajirun*) in general. Both the Deobandis and Maududi now tried to participate in the discussions about Pakistan's new constitution. It was the first time in Islamic history that a state was founded whose national identity was based on membership of the Islamic community. And yet, as Jinnah argued, Pakistan was not meant to be a confessional state, but a state with a constitution which neither conflicted with the *shari'a* nor was completely based on it. A constitution was therefore needed to safeguard an ethnically conceived Islam and make it the identity of the new state. In this sense, Pakistan can be thought of as the first successfully established state of the integrationist wing of the neo-Salafiya. The tightrope act of the League between ethnic policy and civil constitutionalism was to go on until 1956, when the first Pakistani constitution was finally proclaimed.

Israel/Palestine 1948

In 1945, when Musa al-Alami, the President of the Arab Executive[48] and leader of the dispersed Istiqlal Party, was appointed as Palestine's representative at the Arab League, the member states declared that the question of Palestine had become an Arab issue. The League perceived the Arab Bureau as a way to internationalize the Palestinian problem. This made it clear that the problem of Palestine was to be seen exclusively from an 'Arab' perspective; an Islamic discourse about Palestine was hardly possible any longer. Although the former Mufti Amin al-Husaini was still able to secure for his family the authority of the Supreme Arab Committee, his friendly relations with Germany had put him on the losing side in the war and among the Palestinian public he had in this way discredited the Islamic discourse.

Even the Arab nationalists were unable to exert much influence on post-war policy in Palestine. Since, in order to found their own state of Israel, the Zionist nationalists aimed at the independence of Palestine in 1944, the Jewish population, which soon counted 630,000 men, was more and more obviously put under the control of Zionist authorities. From 1945, the Jewish resistance movement consisting of Haganah, Irgun Zeva'i Le'ummi (founded in 1931) and Lehi (for Lohamei Herut Israel, also known as the Stern Gang, founded in 1940) assumed the character of a typical 'national liberation army'. The more forcefully the Zionists demanded the independence of Palestine to form an Israeli state, the weaker became the political position of the Arab nationalists who, after their experiences with the uncontrollable peasant risings of 1937 and 1938, no longer trusted their 'own' population and believed that the Palestinian cause would be better represented by the international Arab public than in Palestine itself.

The Arab national movement in Palestine had not only lost its Islamic public, but was even prepared to attach the Arab regions to Jordan in case the country was to be partitioned – a solution which had been rhetorically rejected in 1947 by both Zionists and Palestinians.[49] In 1921, Abdallah b. Husain, the Emir of Transjordan, had already proposed to Churchill that Palestine and Jordan should be joined together and the immigrant Jews provided with autonomous status. Churchill had vehemently rejected this plan, and in the same way he rejected Abdallah's famous 'Great Syria project', which he submitted in London in 1940 and which became briefly topical again after the establishment of the Arab League in 1945.[50] From 1946 onwards Abdallah, who became King of Transjordan in May of that year, pursued his original plan in a modified form, propagating the partition of Palestine with the Jewish part under Zionist and the Arab part under Hashimite sovereignty in a steady series of contacts with leaders of the Zionist movement. The king had advocates within Palestinian nationalist circles, especially among the al-Nashashibi family, the main competitors of the Husainis for controlling the national movement, and also among the al-Alami family, which included the Palestinian representative at the Arab League.[51] Abdallah's partition plan was essentially accepted by Zionist politicians in November 1947 and by the British government in early 1948, and the United Nations resolution for partition was taken on 29 November 1947. Transjordan's delegation of the Palestine problem to the Arab League was certainly a diplomatic feat. Thus the Palestinian national movement lost the sovereignty over its political terrain, although the Supreme Arab Committee under al-Husaini continued trying to act as the political representative of Arab Palestine.

When in January 1948 Zionist units proceeded to extend their sphere of influence to Arab areas which the United Nations partition plan had not marked out as territories of a future Jewish state, some Arab nationalists, including Abd al-Qadir al-Husaini and Fauzi al-Qawuqji, organized armed units as a 'liberation army'. This was the beginning of the Palestinian civil war. The British authorities remained relatively neutral after the British government had returned its mandate to the UN in 1947 and was preparing for the end of the mandate on 15 May 1948.

By 23 April 1948, about 60,000 Arabs had fled western Palestine for the east and Transjordan; on 15 May, their numbers had risen to 300,000, and an additional 480,000 Arabs had to leave the country on 30 November 1949. All in all, about 60 per cent of the Arab Palestinians, more than the total number of Jewish immigrants, were banished.

In April 1948, the Arab refugees reacted by bitterly complaining against the King of Transjordan and accusing him of inactivity and betrayal. By 15 May Transjordanian troops, including the Arab Legion consisting of 2,000 men, had the whole of eastern Palestine under their control, having successfully prevented the conquest of eastern Jerusalem by Zionist units on 13 May. When the State of Israel was proclaimed in Tel Aviv on 14 May 1948, the Arab League states intervened to 'rescue' Palestine so that it could decide its own future. These formulations were already contained in the resolutions of the League taken between 24 and 30 April. In the summer of 1948, after the armistice resolution of the UN Security Council on 15 July 1948, the League surprisingly decided to entrust the Supreme Arab Committee with the task of setting up a civil administration in Arab Palestine. Amin al-Husaini arrived in Egyptian-occupied Gaza to implement this resolution. On 22 September 1948 the Supreme Arab Committee was proclaimed the 'Government of all Palestine'. A week later, a Palestinian national council in Gaza elected al-Husaini as President of Palestine, which was declared independent on 1 October. The change of attitude of the Arab League was certainly the result of Egyptian diplomacy, because the Egyptian government still feared Hashimite claims of hegemony over Arab policy in Palestine. Al-Husaini's government was as Egyptian as the occupation of eastern Palestine was a concern for Transjordan. Egypt continued to have a foothold in Palestine and administered the Gaza Strip as Egyptian territory. Al-Husaini himself was recalled to Cairo in mid October and put under house arrest. This marked the end of the short-lived sovereignty of the Palestinian government. Jordan, as the country was to be called from 1950, established a civil administration in Eastern Palestine and had its sovereignty confirmed by two national congresses (1 October in Amman and 1 December in Jericho). Thus the already old conflict between Egypt and Hashimite (Trans) Jordan was latently continued on Palestinian territory.

The sovereignty of the 'All-Palestine government' in Gaza initiated a brief but significant rehabilitation of the Islamic discourse about Palestine. In December 1947, the Egyptian Muslim Brothers, together with the Islamic Socialist Party (the previous Young Egypt group) and a few *ulama* of Azhar called for the *jihad* (a just war) for Palestine and secured the protection of the national conservative circles around Ali Mahir and Muhammad Ali Alluba. Already in October 1947, al-Banna had given instructions for the establishment of a battalion (*katiba*) to intervene in the Palestine conflict. He considered himself authorized to do so since he had already successfully acted in favour of the admission of the Mufti Amin al-Husaini to Cairo, and cooperated with Muhammad Salih Harb and Muhammad Ali Alluba in organizing a campaign for the support of Arab Palestinians within the framework of the 'Nile Valley Committee'. The Muslim Brothers and the Society of Muslim Youth could also count on the assistance of the Secretary General of the Arab League, Abd al-Rahman Azzam. Their common interest was to limit the measures to be taken by the Arab states to a minimum and to support the Arab Palestinians with the help of unofficial volunteer groups. From May 1947 to December 1948, there were smaller Islamic groups operating, some of which were led by Egyptian officers, especially in the Negev desert, around Jerusalem and Bethlehem, as well as in the Faluja region (west of the Hebron), where they managed to free an encircled Egyptian detachment.

The actions of the Muslim Brothers in Palestine had two effects: first of all, they showed that they considered themselves as political and military executors of a national Arab will which went beyond national borders; and secondly, they proved themselves as an Egyptian party resisting the hegemonic claims of the Hashimite monarch.

The involvement of the Muslim Brothers with the Palestine question led to the preparation of an internal Egyptian power struggle which reached its height in 1948. From the point of view of the Egyptian government (second cabinet of Mahmud al-Nuqrashi, 6 December 1946 to 28 December 1948), the Muslim Brothers had meanwhile been able to establish a state within the state, with 'their own armies, hospitals, schools, factories and enterprises'.[52] The organization was banned on 6 December 1948. Apart from numerous accusations concerning the militarization of the Brotherhood, it was also blamed for having stirred up peasants and workers against the government. It was even suggested that the palace considered the Muslim Brothers as part of a communist conspiracy. After the assassination of the prime minister by a Muslim Brother on 28 December 1948, there was a growing polarization of the Egyptian public. Hasan al-Banna himself was assassinated on 12 February 1949.

Libya 1951

The foundation of the third new state in the Islamic world after the Second World War was a far less spectacular event. Great Britain now controlled the Libyan coastal provinces of Tripolitania and Cyrenaica, while France had established itself in Fezzan. The exiled urban nationalists, most of whom lived in Cairo or Damascus, had already made preparations in 1929 for a political combination of the Libyan provinces of Tripolitania, Cyrenaica and Fezzan. True to the ideals of urban nationalism, they demanded 'the establishment of a national regime of popular sovereignty for Tripolitania and Barqa (Cyrenaica) under a president elected by the people.'[53] In 1944, just after his release from prison by the Italians, Abd al-Rahman b. Husain Zubaida (1890–1946) founded the first Libyan national party, which was to follow the tradition of the old Tripolitanian republic. Until November 1945, he travelled to numerous Arab capitals both to seek support and to thwart the plans of Sayyid Idris, the leader of the Sanusiya, who had just returned from exile in Cairo. Backed by the Egyptian court and numerous tribal leaders, the latter aimed to proclaim Cyrenaica as an independent monarchy. However, national conservative politicians such as Muhammad Nuri al-Sa'dawi from Khums, who had returned from Saudi Arabia in August 1951, were unable to settle the fundamental regional disagreements among the provinces. In May 1949, following an initiative by the plenary assembly of the United Nations, a joint solution was given preference over partial solutions proposed by Great Britain and Italy. At a 'national conference' in Benghazi attended by representatives of both coastal provinces, Sayyid Idris proclaimed himself Emir of Cyrenaica. However, Great Britain's recognition of his emirate failed to influence the attitude of the United Nations plenary assembly. In a resolution passed on 21 November 1949, Great Britain and France were directed to prepare Libya's independence by 1 January 1952 at the latest. After the proclamation of Sayyid Idris as Libyan king (1950), the independence of the kingdom was declared on 24 December 1951. Under a constitution that remained valid until 1963, the three provinces were granted considerable autonomy.

The nationalization of the Islamic public thus did not even stop in the face of powerful mystical unions. The Sanusiya, which originally performed a specific function within the tribal society of Cyrenaica and thus in many respects resembled the Arab Wahhabiya, was transformed into a Sanusi dynasty. Royalism had carried the day over republican traditions because the Tripolitanian national movement could not wield any social or cultural influence over the poorly urbanized provinces of Cyrenaica and Fezzan. Fezzan, for instance, had long been dominated by the Saif al-Islam clan, which took a favourable view of the French occupation and remained aloof from the Sanusiya. The Sanusiya itself had already lost its powerful position in western Egypt during the First World War. In addition, the military measures taken by the Italian colonial army against the tribes loyal to the Sanusiya in Cyrenaica had destroyed its traditional backing as an order. Internal feuds over the leadership of the order between Sayyid Idris and Muhammad al-Sharif, who was even briefly mentioned as caliph, added to the decline of the order's reputation as the custodian of a specific tribal culture. It was from urban exile – the royalists had gone to Cairo and the republicans to Damascus – that the new political and social foundations for Libya's future regime were developed.

Yemen

Monarchy continued to be the dominant political system in the Arab–Islamic world even after the Second World War, but played no part at all in the newly founded non-Arab states of Pakistan and Indonesia. Up to the early 1950s, it seemed to be a matter of course that constitutional royalty alone could guarantee the political stability of the nation states in the Arab world. Urban nationalists occasionally tried to pursue their republican ideals even in those countries in which royalism was firmly rooted in society. But, as the example of Libya shows, this was particularly difficult in places where the city as a social area was attributed no extraordinary political function.

Another example was the abortive uprising of the urban nationalists in Northern Yemen in 1948. After its definitive and internationally acknowledged severance from the Ottoman Empire in 1918, this country was again ruled by Zaidi imams and their allied tribes, although it possessed an ancient and pronounced urban culture in which non-Zaidi traditions – especially Shafi'i – also marked its social and cultural relations. However, this urban culture remained entirely non-political, making no attempt to create a self-reliant public that would support the political development of the Yemeni state. The opposition to the Zaidi imamate was much more preoccupied with regional, cultural and tribal conditions. The Shafi'i coastal province of Tihama, as well as the city of Taizz, were considered as centres of internal Yemeni opposition. In addition Aden, which had been under British occupation since 1839, formed a centre of urban national politics, because here the exiled nationalists 'under the protection' of the British could openly take up position against the Zaidi imams. The Zaidi administration, for its own part, spared no effort to prevent direct contacts between its subjects and foreign countries, which was one of the reasons why the West thought of the country as 'isolated' and 'backward'. Yet there were intensive trading contacts until well into the 1940s, among others with Italy and Greece.

Internationally the country was protected from direct colonial ambitions by a skilfully worked-out system of 'treaties of friendship', with the USSR from 1928 and the USA from 1946 among others. As a result, the ruler, Imam Yahya (r. 1904–48) thought of himself as a true 'patriot'. He was thus able to justify the lost war against Saudi Arabia in 1934, triggered by the latter's annexation of the Idrisi state Asir, as an anti-colonial defensive war, not least because Great Britain strongly supported the Saudi position. At the same time as this defeat, Yemeni troops trained by Iraqi officers were victorious against the rebel tribes in the north, so that the country was finally pacified by the Yemenis.

It was only now, after the final restoration of state sovereignty over a clearly defined territory, that the urban nationalists spoke up. Some of them were still students living in Cairo and had good contacts with the Egyptian Muslim Brothers and with Algerian political friends, among them an Algerian member in the leadership council, al-Fudail al-Wartalani, who played a decisive role. In 1947, he travelled to San'a in connection with the Muslim Brothers' consolidation of external contacts and met a large number of oppositionists. The Muslim Brothers in Yemen dispensed with the propagation of republican ideas, so that their opposition did not call the Imamate system into question. Instead they attributed to themselves an Imami legitimacy through the Zaidi prince Abdallah al-Wazir, who had joined the conspirators. On 17 February 1948, the oppositionists raised a revolt in the capital and killed Imam Yahya. In the following weeks, Crown Prince Ahmad (reigned until 1962) managed to mobilize the northern tribes from Saudi Arabia against the rebels and to reconquer San'a after a brief siege on 12 March 1948.[54]

The ready cooperation of the Muslim Brothers with the Yemeni opposition showed that members of the Islamic public, who were still influenced by neo-Salafi groups, were more and more inclined to identify themselves with republican programmes. Many Muslim Brothers, above all Muhammad al-Gazzali, compared royalism in the Islamic world with the reign of the Umayyad caliphs (661–750), who from their point of view had put an end to the golden age of Islam.[55] They considered kingship, which still ruled in most of the Arab states (only Algeria, Syria and Lebanon were republics), as an 'illicit', non-Islamic innovation which had to be opposed. Others, however, like al-Banna's mentor Muhibb al-Din al-Khatib, insisted on the legitimacy of kingship in Islamic doctrine and stressed the Islamic character of the reign of the Umayyads.

3. THE 'LIBERAL DECADE' OR THE REVOLT AGAINST THE OLD SYSTEM

The Egyptian Republic

In the summer of 1951, the Egyptian journalist Sayyid Qutb returned to Cairo after a two-and-a-half year stay in the United States.[56] The Muslim Brotherhood had been legalized a few weeks earlier and, under the guidance of its 'general leader' Hasan Isma'il al-Hudaibi (d. 1973), who was elected on 17 October 1951, steered a political course that was more distinctly aimed at integration. In 1949, just as he left for the United States, Qutb had published a booklet entitled *Social Justice and Islam* in which he dissociated himself from the 'European' discourse of socialism and advocated an Islamic interpretation of socialist traditions.[57] This book paved the way for a reinforcement of the isolationist tendencies within the Islamic public, a policy also endorsed by Muhammad al-Gazzali and the enthusiastic critic Abd al-Qadir Auda (executed in 1954). These men saw their political opponents in the supporters of Egyptian royalism and in all monarchies and their representatives. Al-Gazzali inveighed against the Saudi monarchy, against the Wahhabis who had 'subjected themselves like sheep to tyrants and despots', and against *ulama* who 'provided the tyrants with moral support'.[58] Auda even advocated that the *ulama* should altogether be deprived of their authority.[59] The split between the Islamic public and the neo-Salafiya was complete. While the leadership of the Muslim Brothers insisted on a pro-royalist, and, in a broader sense, even pro-Saudi policy of integration, the intellectual dissidents, who had established themselves in the editorial offices of Islamic journals, considered the republican ideas of the Free Officers around Gamal Abd al-Nasir (Nasser) and Muhammad Najib – however partially formulated – to be a promising expression of revolutionary policy. It can be assumed that the Free Officers who overthrew the monarchy in Cairo and established a revolutionary council had been politicized by the dissidents and urged by them to proclaim the republic (18 June 1953). No wonder that the Muslim Brothers formed the only legal political party in Egypt after 1953.

The victory of the republicans, whose arguments were partly 'Islamic' and partly 'European', marked a triumph of the city over the countryside. For the first time in more recent Egyptian history, the urban elites had succeeded in at least officially breaking the power of the countryside and providing the so far incapacitated tertiary sector of the cities with political self-determination. The rapid introduction of agrarian reform (1952–56) was to consolidate urban supremacy and at the same time release rural capital resources for the state. Through confiscations, the sale of land and the nationalization of crown lands, the land reform produced an annual net profit of 5.5 million Egyptian pounds. Yet there were still capital reserves of more than 500 million pounds lying dormant in the countryside, waiting to be released for urban development.[60] Besides, the new regime could count on support from the United States, which continued to pursue an anti-imperialist policy and held a thoroughly positive view of the 1952 coup. One of the aims of Egyptian policy was to expand urban supremacy over the agrarian sector in order to curtail the influence of Great Britain, whose colonial policy had made it an international ally of the countryside.

The Islamic supporters of the revolution did not approve of the military orientation of the regime and saw themselves as the civilian wing of the revolution. In late November, however, there was an abortive coup by isolationist dissidents against the leadership of the Muslim Brothers, who aimed at a compromise with the military regime, and al-Gazzali and other activists had to leave the organization. To underline their demand for an Islamic civilian regime, which was violently rejected by the military, the Muslim Brothers called for an 'Islamic General Congress' in Jerusalem in December 1953. Officially the congress was to discuss the possibilities of strengthening the Islamic orientation in the Palestine conflict. The real point, however, was a quest for international recognition in their feud with the Egyptian regime. The congress did not produce any appreciable results and following an attempt on Nasser's life by an Islamic dissident in October 1954, the Muslim Brotherhood was finally banned for ten years.

Islamic republicanism was unable to assert itself. The members of the neo-Salafiya assembled at the General Congress in Jerusalem had to admit that they represented a minority position among the political public, and that an Islamic civil system had little chance of finding its place between royalists and 'European' republicans.

The Islamic Liberation Party in Palestine

In 1949, at the height of the political crisis in Egypt, Taqi al-Din al-Nabhani (d 1978), a Palestinian judge from Haifa, arrived in Cairo to pursue his study of law at the Azhar University. There he soon joined a circle belonging to the Muslim Brotherhood. In Haifa Nabhani had been close to neo-Salafi groups which had merged with the Muslim Brotherhood but had left the organization in 1952, before the abortive coup of the isolationists against the leadership of the Brotherhood, to found his Islamic Liberation Party (Hizb al-Tahrir al-Islami). In his writings he now turned against any nationalist interpretation of

Islam, repudiated the policy of the Muslim Brotherhood as 'narrow-mindedly reduced to the nation state' and upheld the interpretation of Islam as a perfect legal and social system for all people, transcending the concept of the nation state.[61] Islam itself had to be understood as a perfect ideology which should be the basis for belonging to an 'Islamic state'. 'Citizenship' in the Islamic state, the establishment of which was the duty of every Muslim, was only possible through ideological confession. The former judge again and again stressed the quality of Islam as a philosophy of life which rendered any other ideology superfluous since it contained them all.

Al-Nabhani, who adhered to a strictly rationalistic, indeed scientific interpretation of Islam, wrote:

> In any event, the scientists of communism are the only people who have made a serious attempt to comprehend the significance of intelligence. They were on the right track to grasp the reality of intelligence, but they made mistakes ... Yet they have paved the way for those who will come after them ... .[62]

Nabhani also wanted the Islamic world to be reunited under a caliphate.[63] It was through a constitutional and republican caliphate that he saw the possibility of lending the Islamic state an independent, constitutional status. In 1955, he finally drafted the first version of an 'Islamic constitution', which was to be revised and extensively commented upon later.[64] It would allow Muslims and non-Muslims to obtain 'Islamic citizenship'. In the 'Islamic state', individuals as well as entire states would be able to acquire civic rights if they acknowledged the caliph as the sovereign.[65]

The Islamic Liberation Party was the first attempt by urban nationalists to promote a 'Palestinian identity' in an Islamic discourse. It started out as a cadre party without any great influence on the Palestinian national movement, which resisted both the influence of the Muslim Brothers with their 'Egyptian policy' and the 'Movement of Arab Nationalists' established in 1952, a group of intellectuals for the most part living in Beirut. The Muslim Brothers themselves found a certain support among the *Fida'iyun* (meaning 'those who sacrifice themselves for their fatherland'), first organized by Egypt in Gaza in 1953. These included some Palestinian students from Cairo. The movement of Arab nationalists, on the other hand, was considered as a combination of a 'European' and an 'Arabic' discourse about Palestine. After 1953 the influence of Nasser's partisans grew considerably stronger.

National Policy in Iran 1951–1953

After the victory of the Egyptian army over the old regime, republicanism as the political expression of the growing self-confidence of urban elites led to a kind of euphoria that even Islamic groups could not resist. The Arabism propagated by the military contradicted the Islamic aims of these groups, but since the Nasserist republicans were willing to use Islam as a force of political integration they were able to progressively curtail their influence, the more so because after 1955 the Nasserists also emphasized their civil identity. The emanation of republican euphoria could also, and especially, be perceived in Iran.

When in September 1941 Mohammad Reza Pahlavi succeeded to the throne of Iran as a result of pressure from Great Britain and the USSR, the Majlis, or Iranian parliament, was more powerful than it had been in the past. Major landowners, businessmen and constitutionalist *ulama* formed an energetic opposition to the imperial family, which was still dependent on the army. Several representatives of the Majlis belonged to the Iranian party of labour, the Tudeh, which could boast tens of thousands of members[66] and which in 1944 pronounced itself for granting an oil concession to the USSR. Until that time only the British Anglo–Iranian Oil Company (AIOC), founded in 1935, had owned such concessions. As a reaction to this demand, Mohammad Mosaddeq (1882–1967),[67] the leader of the nationalists in the Majlis, insisted in October 1944 that the concessions granted to Great Britain be withdrawn. Mosaddeq had never concealed his opposition to Pahlavi rule and in 1925 had voted against Reza Khan's bill deposing the Qajar dynasty in parliament.

From 1944, control over oil acquired a clear political connotation as a symbol of national sovereignty. Regional aspirations towards autonomy in Azerbaijan, Kurdistan, or among the Qashqa'i and Bakhtiyari tribes no longer attracted the nationalists who in the past had combined with their own demands for sovereignty. Prime Minister Qavam al-Saltaneh could thus with impunity send the army against the rebellious province of Azerbaijan, which was supported by the USSR. In 1947 he abolished its autonomous status and had its dissenting leaders executed.

In 1949 Mosaddeq reacted against the government's continued policy of granting oil concessions, whether to the USSR or the West – a policy also rejected by parliament – by founding the 'National Front' which consisted of representatives of the traditional Iranian opposition: urban nationalists, merchants, great landowners, Shi'i *ulama* and tribal leaders. The international economic crisis had already shown that with oil production, which started in 1911 after the discovery of deposits at Masjed Suleiman in Khuzistan in 1901, the Iranian political economy was entering upon its own specific course of development. The level of industrialization was considerably increased by the construction of refineries. From 1930, Abadan possessed the world's largest refinery and the oil industry, which employed about 25,000 Iranians around 1950, effectively promoted the development of technological skills. The rural region of southern Iran thus acquired a political significance that differed from comparable areas in Egypt or Algeria, where agrarian production for export had not led to any radical mechanization. Oil promoted the development of an urban culture in the rural region around Abadan, originally a small town which rapidly turned into a large city.

The fact that the Iranian state was only entitled to a proportion of the proceeds of the Anglo–Iranian Oil Company (later British Petroleum) made oil into an even more important (urban) symbol of the quest for political sovereignty.[68] Thus sovereignty could only be acquired by 'nationalizing' the oil industry, an objective that was bound up with the extension of urban sovereignty over the countryside. In this context, Abadan played the role of a bridgehead of urban politics.

On 1 May 1951, immediately after his election as prime minister, Mosaddeq had parliament adopt a law nationalizing the AIOC and forcing British experts to leave the country. The British reaction was swift. When exploratory talks in September 1951 proved unsuccessful, the British government severed relations with the Mosaddeq government and promoted a complete boycott of Iranian oil exports. When Mosaddeq failed to get the better of the conservative opposition to his premiership, led by the speaker of parliament, Imam Jum'e, he resigned on 16 July 1952. Five days later, there was serious unrest in Tehran. The demonstrators demanded the immediate dismissal of the new government of Qavam al-Saltaneh and many of them called for the overthrow of the monarchy. Mosaddeq cleverly stayed in the background to avoid publicizing his relations with the rebels. This was particularly true of his relationship with the leader of the Shi'i neo-Salafiya, Ayatollah Mir Sayyid Abu'l-Qasim Kashani, who had returned from Iraq in 1919 and who, until 1951, had been a member of the neo-Salafi group the Fida'iyan-i Islam established in 1945. The rebellion ended badly for the shah who was forced to re-appoint Mosaddeq as prime minister in order to prevent the emergence of an anti-royalist movement like that in Egypt in Iranian politics.

The politicization and, at the same time, polarization of the Tehran population now reached a new climax. In February 1953, there was danger of a split occurring within the coalition of parties supporting Mosaddeq, since the small Fida'iyan-i Islam under their leader Navvab Safavi were demanding a greater emphasis on republicanism.[69] This tendency was opposed by Mosaddeq, who did not want to lose the court altogether. However, pro-Shah demonstrations lead by the obscure Arya party failed to turn the tide. In the spring of 1953, Mosaddeq managed to stabilize his position; but at the same time, he failed to attract the support of the army, which with American support was preparing for a *coup d'état.* The flight of Muhammad Reza Shah on 16 August 1953 lent a new impetus to republicanism; but the army, traditionally committed to the monarchy, shrewdly mobilized the royalist feelings of many Tehrani citizens. With the crucial support of American logistics and intelligence, it carried out a coup against Mosaddeq's government on 19 August 1953.[70] After hours of street-fighting, pro-army demonstrators gained control of the city. Mosaddeq himself was finally arrested, paving the way for another military dictatorship.[71]

General Zahedi, the military leader of the coup, was not a political brain like General Muhammad Najib, and even less like Colonel Nasser. He had no political programme. His only motive was his unconditional loyalty to his supreme commander, the shah. The latter rewarded him after the coup with an extensive re-armament and modernization of the army, which was to become the best-equipped in the region.

By contrast to Egypt, the republican movement in Iran lacked an executive arm. Mosaddeq had to rely on the prestige of parliament, which had developed into a self-confident institution during the liberal period of the Iranian monarchy (1941–51). However, parliament did not achieve a truly far-reaching integration of society. The communist Tudeh Party formed an independent force in the country, facing that of the army. The body of Shi'i *ulama*, which could have contributed to integration, was torn by deep dissension, mainly due to the radicalization of the neo-Salafiya under Navvab Safavi who re-organized the Fida'iyan-i Islam after the 19 August coup and was viewed as a hard-liner within the Islamic movement. For his own part Mahmud Taliqani (1910/11–1979), originally a partisan of Kashani, decisively promoted the Islamic discourse among Iranian nationalists, corroborated the policy of nationalization by lending it Islamic legitimacy and denied the advantage of an authoritative hierarchy of *ulama*.[72] On the other hand, the conservative *ulama* led by Ayatollah Mohammad Hosein Burujerdi (1875–1961), who taught in Qum and was acknowledged as the 'supreme authority' (*marja'-i taqlid*) of the Shi'i *'ulama*,[73] turned against Mosaddeq's attempt to introduce women's suffrage and welcomed the coup as a restoration of the *ancien regime*.

The End of the 'Liberal Decade'

The quest for political identity during the period of restoration and the revolt against the *ancien regime* had provided the Islamic public with an extensive field of activity. The various neo-Salafi groups had been able to establish themselves as an independent political and social opposition and had in many cases become respected allies of the nationalist movements. The urban culture of the nationalists, which continued to be split into a 'European' and an 'Islamic' discourse, was able to defend itself successfully against the old regime in parts of the Islamic world. But neither the victory (Egypt) nor the defeat (Iran) of the urban nationalists led to a political breakthrough for the Islamic groups. On the contrary, revolutions and counter-revolutions confirmed citizens in their belief that it was only by establishing a strong state that social development could be promoted, and that constitutionalism with its inherent fragmentation of political interests would prevent a purposeful transformation of society in favour of the city. No wonder, then, that both the Egyptian and the Iranian government – however different they were – used the same methods to carry their point against an Islamic policy. As for the subject of 'development', which was now on all tongues, even some Islamic thinkers had tried to contribute to it. However, the Islamic discourse did not appear to correspond with the Western revolutionary ideals of the urban population, although there were hardly any differences between the speeches of the Islamic left around Qutb, al-Siba'i and Kashani and the nationalists. But practical politics brought about a certain shift in ideological focus. Since the urban nationalists had at least conquered the state in Egypt, their thoughts were exclusively centred on the state. Islamic policy, on the other hand, remained committed to society because, despite its alliance with the nationalists, it was excluded from power.

During the 'liberal decade' (1942/7–1952/7), the Islamic public had had the chance to develop its own political profile. It was for the most part republican and nationalistic, frequently with a socialistic orientation, and striving to lend this profile an Islamic expression. But now, at the end of the 'liberal decade', it found itself excluded from the political arena. The angry reactions of radical Islamic groups, as manifested, for example, by the attempts on the lives of Nasser in October 1954 and the Iranian prime minister Hosein Ala (19 November 1955), provided the regimes in Cairo and Tehran with the opportunity to fight against the Islamic public. Without fearing major reactions among the population, political leaders of Islamic groups were arrested, and some of them executed (Navvab Safavi on 16 January 1956; Abu'l-A'la al-Maududi had already been arrested and condemned to death in 1953, but as a result of international protests, the sentence was not carried out); the newspapers of the Islamic opposition were banned and many political cadres were exiled. In December 1953, the mood of the neo-Salafiya at the General Congress in Jerusalem was gloomy, but not desperate. When, however, they again met in Damascus in September 1954, the mood was quite different. The assembled members were now primarily concerned with rescuing their arrested peers and denouncing the policy of the state as 'criminal'.

The freedom of action of the Islamic groups was steadily reduced. Syria soon stopped allowing them into the country. Many expatriate Muslim Brothers who had fled to Saudi Arabia had to fall into line with the local Islamic state culture or keep silent. For Islamic republicans there was virtually no solution except to seek refuge in non-Islamic foreign countries. From Geneva, the former Egyptian Muslim Brother Sa'id Ramadan called for an assembly of his followers; but he must have found the reactions very disappointing.[74]

Saudi Arabia

After the death of King Abd al-Aziz Ibn Sa'ud in 1953, more and more voices in Saudi Arabia called for constitutional reorientation. Those who advocated a re-organization of the state were for the most part *ulama*, intellectuals and merchants from the Hijaz. Having decisively lost their political independence after a last phase of internal opposition (1927–31) these groups had been forced to put up with the Saudi Arabian kingdom established in 1932 and had only reluctantly adapted themselves to the pietistic Wahhabi state culture. But as long as they wielded economic supremacy in the country – the Hijaz was the most important economic region – they could come to terms with their loss of power. Hijazis were in addition given important posts in the public administration and the two factors helped to reduce their political opposition to a minimum. Such was the influence of the 'liberal decade', even in Saudi Arabia.[75]

However, the complicated political and social balance which had prevailed in Saudi Arabia since 1932 was threatened by the new oil economy. On 29 May 1933, Standard Oil of California (renamed in 1944 as the Arabian American Oil Company, ARAMCO) was granted an oil concession.[76] After 1945, the systematic exploitation of the oil fields began in the province of al-Ahsa.

For the first time, the wealth of Saudi Arabia flowed from its eastern provinces instead of the western Hijaz. Hijazi intellectuals, whose elite had almost entirely been interned in Riyadh after the opposition was suppressed in 1932 and 1933, resisted their impending loss of power and emphasized their own interests in a nation state reflecting the formerly independent Hijazi trade market. One of their spokesmen, the writer Muhammad Husain 'Awwad (1902/3–1976), who had been elected as president of the Jeddah Culture Club in 1945, did not hide his anti-royalist attitude. In an article entitled 'Arabic Rhetoric' written in 1946, he said that he had looked in vain for a new poetic ideal in classical Arabic poetry only to find it in Egyptian poetry, in the works of exiled writers and among some 'Christian' (Arab) authors.[78] His rejection of 'classical Arabic poetry' was of course a disguised criticism of the royal family, which flaunted its Arab character, or in other words insisted on a revalorization of the Arab tribal traditions. The Hijazis now sought closer contacts with the Egyptian literary scene, in which al-'Aqqad, Taha Husain and other leading poets were setting the tone.

The Saudi monarchy spared no effort in its drive to centralize the institutions of learning which had so far dominated the judicial system in accordance with Wahhabi dogma, and to put them under state control. After the death of Ibn Sa'ud in 1953, his son Sa'ud b. Abd al-Aziz (reigned until 1961, deposed in 1964) managed to introduce major changes in the country's legal system. Under him the Hijaz lost what was left of its autonomous rights. As a counter move, a large number of Hijazi intellectuals took the opportunity to create a new Islamic public through the medium of the press. This public included partisans of neo-Salafi organizations who had fled Egypt, Syria and Iraq. The Islamic public in Saudi Arabia was thus divided into two autonomous spheres. On one side were the Wahhabi *ulama* who had been able to gain a foothold in the newly founded universities (Riyadh 1957, Medina 1961) between 1954 and 1961, and to make them into strongholds of Wahhabi dogma. On the other side stood the Hijazis, who had only very superficially submitted to the Wahhabi state culture, who dominated the media and who kept close political contacts with other countries, especially with Egypt and South-East Asia.

Saudi Arabian Oil Production 1938–1950[77]

Year	Barrels per day	Royalties paid by ARAMCO to the State in US dollars
1938	135	
1939	10,778	3,200,000
1940	13,866	2,500,000
1941	11,809	2,000,000
1942	12,412	2,000,000
1943	13,337	2,000,000
1944	21,296	2,500,000
1945	58,386	5,000,000
1946	164,229	12,500,000
1947	246,169	17,500,000
1948	390,309	50,800,000
1949	476,736	39,000,000
1950	546,703	56,700,000
(1956)	(341,000,000)	

Meanwhile ARAMCO had built a kind of state within a state in the Dahran (Zahran) area, in which Saudi Arabian workers formed the majority (about 61 per cent of the workers in the oil industry in 1952 were Saudi Arabian citizens), but were in fact second-class citizens. The American staff had villas and clubs built for them, while the workers had to live in barracks. In 1953 they went on strike for the first time, demanding better living conditions. One of the leaders of the strike was Nasir al-Sa'id who, after a term in prison, fled to Cairo and founded a republican opposition to the royal family.[79] After 1955 the political situation in Dahran escalated. A workers' committee was formed, and a 'front for national reform in Saudi Arabia' demanded constitutional reforms and the nationalization of the oil production.[80] Opposition groups were also formed in the Saudi army, but they were crushed in September 1955.[81] A further strike in June 1956 plunged the country into a severe crisis, which the state only managed to control by means of repression and promises.

The Hijazi opposition had hardly any connection with the republican groups in the east of the country. Instead, it put its hopes in Crown Prince Faisal, who was to form the first cabinet in 1958 and whose pro-Hijazi orientation was well-known in the country. Faisal was thought to be capable of arranging a compromise between the various interest groups. He was considered pro-Western, which to the Hijazis meant that he would promote their economic and cultural contacts with the West. Besides, he had led a Saudi delegation at the Afro–Asian Solidarity Conference in Bandung in 1955. This also made him attractive to the republican opposition, which believed it had found international support for its aims at the Bandung conference.

CHAPTER FOUR

Islamic Culture and Third-World Republicanism, 1956–73

1. THE TRIUMPH OF THE THIRD WORLD

Between 18 and 24 April 1955, on the invitation of the Indonesian govenment, the representatives of 29 states met at Bandung to hold the first 'Afro–Asian Solidarity Conference'. This conference marked the first united reaction of the independent African and especially Asian states to the construction of international blocs, a process which had been going on for almost ten years and which had overlapped with the 'liberal decade'. With the conclusion of the Baghdad Pact between Turkey and Iraq on 11 January 1955, which was joined in the same year by Pakistan, Iran and Great Britain and which, after Iraq's withdrawal, led to the creation of CENTO (Central Treaty Organization) in 1958 (dissolved in September 1979), the Islamic world had directly participated in the formation of blocs. From the point of view of the United States, it was to become part of an anti-Communist bastion within which CENTO, as the Middle Eastern equivalent of NATO (North Atlantic Treaty Organization), would complete the military circle around the USSR. The Islamic bloc, which had been claimed earlier by certain Islamic politicians, became, therefore, not an independent authority of internal Islamic relations, but an instrument of the Cold War. Pakistani initiatives to found an international Islamic union were in this context usually denounced as attempts to coordinate the Islamic world with the Western bloc. This criticism came predominantly from Egypt. Nasser, who now felt completely committed to 'positive neutrality', perceived the

Bandung Conference as an opportunity to work against the idea of an Islamic bloc and to assemble the non-aligned states instead into an anti-colonial solidarity union. At the time, even Saudi Arabia was still part of this new movement having, in March 1955, joined with Egypt, Syria and Yemen to protest against the establishment of the Baghdad Pact in a four-state declaration.

Suez 1956

Soon after they seized power in the year 1952, the members of the Egyptian Revolutionary Council tried to fulfil their promise to promote the urban sector. The first land reform had provided the state with some of the capital which had so far been left unused in the agrarian sector. But it was not enough to finance ambitious industrialization projects, including the construction of the Aswan dam. Egyptian capitalists kept aloof. The United States, still at the time Egypt's major ally, promised credits and the supply of wheat and arms only on the condition that Egypt join a common military pact. But this was completely against the ideals of the revolutionary council, and any qualification of its recently acquired sovereignty was out of the question. As for the International Bank for Reconstruction and Development (IBRD), its quid pro quo for the allocation of new loans was to control the Egyptian economy, thus posing a threat to the sovereignty of the state. Nasser's most important ally, the small Egyptian army, required extensive modernization of its arms and equipment to catch up with the superior Israeli army. To neglect the modernization of the army would mean the collapse of the mainstay of the revolution. But at the same time, there was a very real threat of financial breakdown. So when the Egyptian army concluded a 'purely commercial' arms deal with Czechoslovakia in September, the political consensus with the USA was suddenly jeopardized. The USA and Great Britain reacted on the 17 December 1955 with the promise of fresh credits for the construction of the Aswan Dam, after the Egyptian government had given them to understand that it preferred Western assistance to being support from the USSR.

The capital requirements were enormous. To carry out the urbanization and industrialization of the Egyptian economy, an annual minimum of 100 million Egyptian pounds was needed, as the financial expert Husain Khallaf wrote in 1955.[1] That was one-third of the total proceeds of Egyptian agriculture and half Egyptian state finances. The construction sector was booming, but industrial investment was still low Thanks to the approval of a 70 million dollar loan by the USA and Great Britain, plans to build the Aswan Dam went forward; but from the very outset, the urban reorganization of society came to a standstill.

In this difficult domestic situation, the members of the revolutionary council searched for a new orientation in its foreign policy. In March 1956, the British General Glubb was dismissed by King Husain of Jordan as commander-in-chief of the Arab Legion at the instigation of the Egyptians. Two months later, Egypt recognized the Popular Republic of China. With the first step, Nasser made a 'deadly enemy' of the British prime minister Anthony Eden, and with the second he provoked the American government and especially its foreign secretary John Foster Dulles. The fundamental conflict between the USA and Great Britain over the future of the British Empire and decolonization was suddenly silenced by the Egyptian question. When, on 19 July 1956, Dulles cancelled the 1955 credit agreement, the British government was pleasantly surprised and immediately followed suit.[2] Nasser's reaction was not long in coming: on 26 July 1956, the Egyptian government nationalized the Suez Canal, stating that the income from the canal had to make up for the absence of credits. For the Egyptian government, the military occupation of the Suez region caused no problems, since the last British soldiers had left the country in accordance with the Anglo–Egyptian treaty.

By contrast to the situation in Iran three years earlier, the former colonial powers of Great Britain and France, who had secured the lion's share of the income of the Suez Canal, had no political backing in Egypt. Republicanism had solidly established itself in Egyptian society, and potential royalists mainly kept out of sight. Any intervention against the policy of nationalization could come only from outside. The USA opposed a direct restoration of the old colonial regime and pleaded for the internationalization of the canal; at the same time, however, it showed a certain reserve with respect to Great Britain and France.

The often contradictory Middle East policy of the Great Powers contributed to the confusion of the political situation. Dulles had recommended that the problem of Palestine be solved by restoring to it the areas occupied by Israel. France supplied Israel with new planes, but at the same time sold arms to the Jordanian, Iraqi and Lebanese armies. Great Britain again harked back to the old partition plan of 1947. The activities of the Fida'iyun units in Egyptian-occupied Gaza soon led to daily skirmishes on the border between Egypt and Israel.

In October 1956, after the UN Security Council demanded freedom of navigation in the Suez Canal, Israel and France agreed to take joint action against Egypt. Israel officially declared that it would proceed against the Fida'iyun military bases on Sinai; and France saw this as a possibility to have the Suez Canal placed under the sovereignty of the colonial powers again. On 29 October 1956, Israeli troops began the conquest of the Sinai peninsula. On the following day, Great Britain and France demanded an immediate armistice and the withdrawal of troops from both sides of the canal. This would have opened the canal once more to the troops of the colonial powers. On 31 October, French and British planes began to bomb Egyptian cities; on 5 November paratroops finally landed in Port Sa'id which, along with the cities of Suez and Ismailiya was completely destroyed in the military action. Cairo was attacked with incendiary bombs.

However, the old colonial system could no longer be restored. Neither the USA nor the USSR had any interest in the survival of a colonial empire which would jeopardize the formation of the new blocs. The withdrawal of Israel, France and Great Britain was therefore merely a question of time. Israel, whose armies seemed invincible, evacuated its last positions on Sinai on 8 March 1957.

Islam as the Culture of National Liberation

Despite the military defeat, the Suez war ended with a victory for the Egyptian nationalists. On 5 January 1957, they were able to nationalize 371 companies with predominantly foreign capital without provoking a major protest. Three months later, all foreign banks were sold to Egyptian credit banks. The capital of the new Egyptian trust company, which took over the administration of the nationalized companies, grew with corresponding speed to over 58 million Egyptian pounds by the end of 1958. A parallel process was the restructuring of the political public. By building up the National Union as a unity party (28 March 1957, later Arab Socialist Union), a corporate representation of the Egyptian society was created to prevent the country's old parties from again assuming a dominant political position in parliament (National Council, dissolved on 1 February 1958). The 'social question' had now become a socialist programme. After the first nationalizations, Nasser had emphasized the 'socialist' character of the political system. From the Islamic side, the development of an independent socialist programme for the Islamic world had already been demanded and Mustafa al-Siba'i, the leader of the Syrian Muslim Brothers, was at the time celebrating the Prophet Mohammad as the first founder of a socialist state.[3] No wonder that the Nasserists also sought to lend their socialism an Islamic appearance. In certain contexts they deliberately used Islamic rhetoric, aiming at the mobilization of those parts of society which were still mixed areas from a social and cultural point of view and were destined to absorb the intensified process of migration from the country to the city. Until 1954, the majority of these mixed areas had been politically represented by the Muslim Brotherhood. In order to integrate this sector of the population into the new unity party, the Nasserists had to place socialism into an early Islamic context, thus going against their own ideals. The contradiction between the required definition of Islam as socialism and the role of socialism as the logically and historically necessary end of historical development was solved in a social manner. It was for the remnants of the Islamic public, above all the leading *ulama* of Azhar, to interpret Islam from a socialist point of view. Part of the leftist intelligentsia, which returned from exile in 1958, strove to create a 'Third-World identity' for socialism and felt particularly encouraged in this respect by the statements of liberation socialism. Outwardly the Egyptian state ideology now acted as an Islamic liberation socialism which was to be propagated in the Third World. This task was assumed by the Supreme Council for Islamic Matters founded in 1960.

The subjects of 'exploitation' and 'despotism', which played an important part in arguments about socialist liberation, had already been discussed at great length by Islamic intellectuals of the neo-Salafiya. Since the experiences of the Syrian Muslim intellectuals with the centralizing policy of the Ottoman governments after 1900, the 'fight against despotism' (*istibdad)* had become part of the canon of Islamic policy. The Egyptian monarchy, and the policy orientations of the country, were a show-piece of despotism in the early 1950s and were vehemently attacked by Islamic intellectuals.[4] By adopting Islamic rhetoric, the Nasserists were able to win over a large number of intellectuals with neo-Salafi inclinations. This also led them to find a smooth transition from late Egyptian history to their new state ideology, which, since 1958, was closely connected with the movement of non-aligned nations. Even the old scholarly Salafiya movement, which was no longer very active, and in particular the political activist and journalist Jamal al-Din al-Afghani (1839–1897), were now considered as representatives of a new Islamic liberation theology, which was finally endorsed by the rector of the Azhar, Mahmud Shaltut.

The Decline of Royalism

Arab republicanism had an exceptional influence because it managed to combine the urban societies within a homogeneous political culture by integrating European socialist ideologies and corresponding Islamic variants. There were, however, three political groups which could not be integrated from the point of view of the Arab nationalists: the predominantly royalist landed society, the communists and the radical wing of the neo-Salafiya. Since the last two groups were also of urban origin, the nationalists had to choose between forming a coalition with them or fighting them. In Egypt, communists and radical Islamicists were persecuted and often interned together in the notorious Abu Za'bal camp. In Lebanon, Syria and Iraq, however, the nationalists preferred to form a short-lived political coalition with their unloved rivals.

The formation of blocs between Arab countries stimulated a more and more distinct division between the so-called 'progressive' and 'conservative' states, which, depending on their political orientations, were committed to either the Western or the Eastern bloc. The years from 1956 and 1958 represented a transitional period, in which the affiliation with a particular bloc was determined through internal crises. After 1958, however, the Arab world, and the Islamic world as a whole, was split into two blocs. The Western bloc now included all the monarchies (especially Morocco, Libya, Saudi Arabia, the Gulf principalities, Iran, the Malayan Federation); most of the republican states (Tunisia, Egypt, Sudan, Syria, Iraq, India and Indonesia) considered themselves as representatives of a 'positive neutrality' within the structure of the blocs. Although they formed a community of interests with the states of the Eastern bloc, they consistently tried to preserve their political independence, especially for internal reasons. Some states assumed a special position: republican Turkey which, within the framework of the 'liberal decade', had taken its first steps towards an opening of society, continued to see itself closely linked with the Western bloc, if only because of its membership of NATO; Pakistan's adherence to the CENTO pact was partially based on its smouldering conflict with India, whose foreign policy under Nehru had had an abiding influence on the neutrality of the 'non-aligned countries'; and lastly, the Yemen had also experienced a political and economic opening during the 'liberal decade', but because of old social traditions, this had linked it with Egypt.

Lebanon and Syria 1958

A special case was Lebanon, whose political constitution, unlike that of all the other Islamic countries, was based on a contrived system of proportionality which gave a dominant political position to its Maronite minority. In 1942/43, shortly before the country obtained its independence, leading Lebanese politicians had agreed to form a national pact – which was never committed to writing – confirming the claim of the Maronite families to the country's political leadership. The magic formula for Lebanon's political system, worked out by the Sunni Riyad al-Sulh and the Maronite Bishara al-Khuri, stated that Lebanon was an Arab nation, but that its political system was fundamentally different from that of other Arab countries. This was warranted by the political balance between the Christian and Muslim communities. For the parliamentary elections of 1943, the leading families had agreed to divide power in parliament and government at a ratio of six to five. Thus the Christian communities were to be represented by 30 members of parliament, and the Muslim communities by 25. Later these numbers were increased to 54 and 45, respectively. The apparent reason for this was a very doubtful census carried out by the French mandatory government in 1932.

During the 1957 elections, a coalition of urban nationalists tried to overthrow the power of the Maronite establishment. The assassination of the publisher Nasib al-Matni on 8 May 1958, formed the prelude to a comprehensive strike in the non-Maronite cities of Tripoli, Beirut, Tyre and Sidon. The republican government, which particularly relied on the Syrian Popular Party and the Christian Kata'ib Party (Munazzamat Val-Kata'ib Val-Lubnaniya, Phalanx) founded on 21 November 1936 after a Spanish model,[5] reacted to the political boycott of the nationalists by asking for help from the USA, and on 15 July1958 the latter sent the first of a total of 10,000 soldiers into the country. The political boycott soon acquired militant features. During the strike, which lasted for about 160 days, more than 4,000 Lebanese were killed. The army commander Fu'ad Shihab was finally elected as the new president on 31 July. After he entered office on 3 September 1958, the situation calmed down, and in October the last US soldiers left the country.

The strike had led to no decision about Lebanon's internal rule or external affiliation. The urban nationalists did not succeed in shaking off the influence of the old establishment. The Movement of Arab Nationalists (dissolved in 1970), already mentioned in the Palestinian context, which had unsuccessfully tried to assume a leading position in the Lebanese crisis, had meanwhile become a pro-Nasser party in the countries of the Fertile Crescent (Lebanon, Syria, Iraq, Jordan). Its rival for the hegemony of urban nationalism was the Arab socialist Ba'th Party, which had emerged from a discussion group with the programmatic name al-Ba'th al-Arabi (the Arab transmission) founded in 1940 by the Syrian teachers Michel Aflaq and Salah al-Din al-Bitar. This party had been joined by smaller nationalist parties in Syria in 1947 and 1953 respectively. These included in particular the Arab Socialist Party, whose leader, Akram al-Haurani, played an important part in the Syrian army. Haurani had negotiated the close relations between the Syrian Ba'th and the army leaders. He was a typical representative of urban nationalism whose stronghold was the central Syrian city of Hama. A 'fierce opponent of the local great landowning families',[6] he believed that the army was the only means through which he could realize his political ideas. He marked his first success in 1954 by contributing to a coup against the Syrian dictator Adib al-Shishakli. Under the government of Shukri al-Quwwatli, who belonged to the 'old guard' and based his civilian government on agrarian-oriented families such as the al-Azms, the Syrian army was able to gain more and more influence through Ba'th propaganda and was also able to contribute to Syria's close relations with the USSR. The army and its allied Ba'th Party saw in Nasser's Arab propaganda a powerful instrument to rid themselves of the supremacy of the 'old guard' around al-Quwwatli, his prime minister Sabri al-Asali and the latter's deputy Khalid al-Azm. Up to this point, the numerous internal upheavals supported by the army had led to no changes in the distribution of powers.

It was al-Haurani who encouraged the Syrian army to form a common leadership with the Egyptian army. In the framework of the corresponding negotiations, a centralized Egyptian–Syrian union was formed by the armies in 1958. Nasser at first opposed it, since Egypt was not prepared to solve Syria's domestic problems. But the Syrians were successful. On 1 February 1958 the United Arab Republic (UAR) was proclaimed. In the first year of its existence, both sides made an effort to create a balanced system of distributing powers. After a drastic defeat of the Ba'th at the July 1959 election – the party only managed to win 2.5 per cent of the seats in the combined parliament – and the ban of all parties except the Egyptian National Party, the Syrian nationalists withdrew from the UAR government in late 1959, so that having no independent political representation, the country became in pactise an Egyptian province.

An indirect result of the union between Syria and Egypt was that the urban nationalists succeeded in eliminating the Syrian old guard from the political scene. In Lebanon, however, the old elites, with their much deeper social roots, prevented a rigorous nationalization of the urban societies. Instead, the old elites assumed new forms on the basis of their ethnic relationships. The connections among Maronites, Druzes, and later on Shi'is became so dominant that even the urban nationalists had to come to terms with them. Thus the Nasserists sought to ally themselves with the parties led by the Druzes, while communist groups found support among Kurdish and Armenian communities. The neo-Salafi groups, especially the rather powerful Society of the Servants of the All-Merciful (Ibad al-Rahman) founded in 1951 by the Beirut merchant Muhammad Umar al-Dawuq, which maintained close contacts with the Egyptian Muslim Brotherhood, had a positive impact on the elaboration of a 'Sunni consciousness', heightening the feeling of solidarity among those Muslim communities who did not feel they belonged to either the Druzes or the Shi'i.

The specificity of Lebanon and Syria largely consisted in the fact that their urban nationalists had to deal with 'republican regimes' and did not have a monarchy to contend with. However, since the prominent old families had been able to secure for themselves leading positions during the brief period of the French mandate (1920–46), the nationalists found it difficult to fight against their influence. Their short-lived alliance with Egypt enabled the Syrian nationalists to overthrow the prominent families in a roundabout way. But even the Ba'th was now forced to form an ethnic coalition. It did so with the Alawi communities of provincial cities, which, due to their special social position – there were no prominent families represented in them – showed an almost identical interest with the nationalists.[7]

Iraq 1958

In Iraq the coup of the Free Officers around Abd al-Karim Qasim and Abd al-Salam Arif on 14 July 1958 was a direct reaction to the dictatorship of Prime Minister Nuri al-Sa'id (1888–1958). The Iraqi premier had played a decisive role in the modern history of Iraq. He came from a prominent Baghdad family and entered the Ottoman army at an early age. In Istanbul he joined the Arab–Ottoman secret society 'The Alliance', and in 1916 he went over to the army of the Hashimite king of the Hijaz, Husain. From then on, his fate was intimately linked to that of the Hashimites. In 1918 he went to Damascus with Husain's son Faisal, whom he later followed to Baghdad when the British enthroned Faisal as King of Iraq in 1921. Faisal's reign was almost exclusively supported by the landowning families. In the mid 1920s, the Iraqi government, and hence the British mandatory administration, granted the great landowners and tribal chiefs an extensive autonomy in their properties, including fiscal rights and the power to police. The oil economy was secured in 1925, when the oil-rich Mosul area was annexed to Iraq with the help of the British. Seven years later Great Britain granted Iraq its formal independence, though preserving for itself important powers in military and foreign affairs. Under the reign of Faisal's son Ghazi (r. 1933–39), the army acquired increased political importance and became a reservoir of the urban opposition, which, under al-Said's opponent, Rashid Ali al-Kilani, for a short time seized power in 1941.

The 'liberal decade' had hardly touched Iraq, although in 1952 and 1956 there had been attempts to assert liberal positions within the framework of anti-British demonstrations. When in 1954 free elections were prepared by the regent Abdal'ilahi, who from 1939 represented the young king Faisal II,[8] and the Iraqi opposition for the first time found an opportunity to appear in public again, al-Sa'id revoked this step – also in the name of the regent – dismissed parliament and governed with special powers granted to him by a loyal 'parliament'. The political impotence of the nationalist opposition was obvious. The small Ba'th party, which since 1955 had found followers in southern Iraq, especially among Shi'i families, was as incapable as the national conservative or socialist parties to form a powerful counterweight to the monarchy. Meanwhile, the monarchy was gaining in strength through the constantly growing revenues from oil production.[9]

The rate of growth in oil production (17.0 per cent per annum), and even more the corresponding rise of national revenues (31.4 per cent per annum), brought more and more money into the capital and the city increasingly became a magnet for landless peasants. Baghdad had more than 500,000 inhabitants around 1955; but like Cairo before 1952, it was a politically powerless city. Even the many small opposition parties were unable to create strong groupings with roots in the population with any lasting effect. So the Free Officers, who were active from 1952, were able to plot their conspiracy in a small circle. On 14 July 1958 their chance came and in a quick *coup de main*, they managed to gain control over the capital. Finding itself suddenly liberated from dictatorship, the furious population stormed the royal palace and killed the king, his family and the dictator Nuri al-Sa'id. The Free Officers immediately formed an administrative coalition with other nationalist parties and as their first official act they proclaimed the dissolution of the monarchy and its institutions.

Iraq's Oil Production 1946–1958

Year	Millions of Tons	Millions of Iraqi Dinars
1946	4.6	2.3
1948	3.4	2.0
1950	6.5	5.3
1951	8.6	13.3
1953	28.0	49.9
1955	33.0	84.4
1958	35.8	79.9

Republicanism in the Yemen

One of the first Arab rulers to acknowledge the new republican regime under Arif and Qasim was the Yemeni crown prince Saif al-Din Muhammad al-Badr (reigned from May 1955). After the suppression of the 1948 coup, the new Yemeni king Saif al-Islam Ahmad had broken with the isolationist policy of his predecessor and gradually opened up the Yemeni economy and society to foreign influence. Under the leadership of the new crown prince al-Badr, the Yemen had in April 1956 joined the defensive pact between Egypt and Syria, a pact which at the time also included Saudi Arabia. Al-Badr also formed a federal association of Yemen with the new United Arab Republic (2/3/1958). After the experience of the attempted coup of 1948, Yemen's foreign policy had been reoriented. In view of the growing confrontation with the British administration in Aden (Southern Yemen), which continued to tolerate the activities of the Yemeni republican opposition, al-Badr considered it safer to form a close relationship with Nasser's alliance policy. Yemen thus joined the United Arab Republic as a preventive measure. As long as it was a member of the union, the republican movements were deprived of any support from Nasser. That is why al-Badr spared no effort to present himself as the 'Arab patriot' turning against the 'reactionary Arab monarchs', and congratulating the Iraqi officers on their great victory.[10]

The tensions between Yemen and Great Britain grew in the same proportion as nationalist groups in Aden demanded the right to self-determination and the Yemeni government sued for sovereign rights over Aden and the areas under the British protectorate.[11] The Arab League and the Bandung Conference of 1955 indirectly supported the Yemeni claim on Aden. The Union of the Sons of the South (Rabitat Abna' al-Janub) was one of the most important pro-Imamite organizations in Aden which more or less unanimously resisted British attempts to unite six southern principalities (Baikhan, al-Dali, the sultanates of al-Awadil, al-Fadli and Yafi al-Sufla, as well as the Sheikhdom of al-Ulaiqat al-Ulya) in a political union. On 8 February 1959, Great Britain created the Federal Union of Southern Arabian Principalities[12] and further provoked Yemeni resistance. By 1964 all the other southern Arabian principalities joined the Union under British sovereignty, with the exception of the two Hadramautic states of al-Qua'iti and al-Katiri.

2. THE CULTURE OF NATIONAL LIBERATION

Algeria at War

Few of the European colonies in the Islamic world had benefited from the 'liberal decade'. Libya, Pakistan and Indonesia did gain their independence, but in other countries the European powers were not prepared to renounce their sovereignty. Not until the Suez crisis, which marked the collapse of European colonial hegemony and the transition to global blocs, did the urban nationalists of the European colonies make a political breakthrough.

Between 1946 and 1948, the nationalists in Algeria experienced a breath of political freedom. On 16 March 1946, a general amnesty was proclaimed for the urban nationalists arrested a year earlier. But while Farhat Abbas, the leader of the Union Démocratique du Manifeste Algérien (UDMA), and Muhammad al-Bashir al-Ibrahimi, the president of the Algerian Association of Muslim Ulama, were released, members of the Algerian popular party (Parti du Peuple Algérien) led by Messali Hadj remained in internment. The election results of the UDMA also raised the hopes of a large group among the popular party that independence might be achieved by legal means. After his return from exile in Gabon on 13 October 1946, Messali Hadj also voted for participation in electing the Algerian assembly, the representative body of the Muslim Algerians, and founded an electoral community with the name Mouvement pour le Triomphe des Libertés Démocratiques (MTLD). At the first congress of this group in February 1947, a compromise was reached between the legalists and the militants by which the Parti du Peuple Algérien would continue as an underground organization with an Organisation Spéciale (OS), while the MTLD functioned as a legal party. The responsibility for the paramilitary OS was to be assumed, among others, by the Berber leader Husain A'id Ahmad (Hocine Ait Ahmad) and Ahmad Ben Bella.

In the eyes of the leaders of the democratic union, however, the Parti du Peuple Algérien no longer played any part. At his own party's national conference in October 1947, Farhat Abbas declared: 'All colonialists have only one enemy, Abbas and the manifesto!'.[13] But all attempts to bring together the diverging political wings of the nationalists ran aground. Even a new statute for Algeria, which was approved by the French parliament on 20 September 1947, failed to create a united opposition. This statute appeared to benefit only the Algerian *ulama*, for the Algerian assembly was only granted sovereign rights regarding the institutionalization of the Islamic religion and the revalorization of the Arabic language in public administration.

In the following years, thanks to its tight organization the MTLD managed to recruit more and more new members to its various subdivisions. In 1949 it had more than 25,000 members, especially among the younger generation. In April of that year in order to raise money the various sections of the OS began a series of armed attacks, among which that on the post office of Oran, led by Ben Bella, became the best known and made the OS into a true revolutionary organization in the eyes of many young people. However, the as yet indistinct commando structures prevented further victories. As a countermove, the French authorities were able to arrest many of the militants, among them Ait Ahmed who managed to escape to Cairo in 1951.

From 1951 to 1954 the members of the MTLD went through a radical change. More and more of them, particularly among the young, felt that the old guard around Messali Hadj no longer represented them. They complained that the split in the Algerian national movement had impeded progress and that the increasingly Islamic orientation of the 'Messalists', the followers of Messali Hadj, was responsible for the desertion of revolutionary ideals in exchange for an Islamic fiction. It is true that on 5 January 1948, the popular party had signed the 'manifeste d'Abdelkrim', which stood for a far-reaching Islamization of the political public and was supported by other prominent Islamic nationalists such as Hasan al-Wazzani (Moroccan Democratic Party), Allal al-Fasi (Moroccan Independent Party, Istiqlal) and Abd al-Khaliq Torrès (Party of National Reform, Northern Morocco).[14]

Similarly, the French Algerians' racist resentment of the 'Arabs' – '*bicots*', '*bounioules*' or '*ratons*', as they called the Muslims – became more extreme. The 1947 statute was criticized, among others, with the following words:[15]

> The granting of French nationality, which was to create equal rights, seems to have been too rash. It is based more on sentimental and political motives than on the social and intellectual development of a race, which albeit disposing of some characteristics of a cultivated civilization, shows in its social, family and hygienic relations that it still stands on a primitive level.

The achievements of the Nasserists in Egypt may have encouraged the MTLD members who had fled to Cairo to replace political parties in Algeria with a more efficient organization. Young party members pleaded for an independent political executive power of the Algerian people which would give preference neither to the Islamic–Arab Party (PPA) nor to the Berber wing of the national movement with its European arguments. The Berber wing was particularly supported by the members of the Fédération Française, who counted tens of thousands in France itself and had openly renounced the Islamic discourse in 1953/54. On 23 March 1954, four cadre units of the MTLD led by Mustafa b. Bulaihid (Ben-Boulaid, 1917–56), a miller of peasant origin from Aurès, founded the Comité Révolutionnaire pour l'Unité et l'Action (CRUA) as a third force against the Messalists. In June 1954, twenty-two cadres related to the CRUA decided to proclaim an armed rebellion on the 1 November. While the Messalists were still trying to secure their political supremacy over the national movement, the CRUA cadres prepared for rebellion and formed the core of the Front de Libération Nationale (FLN), which they conceived not as a proper political party, but as a 'state party' which would represent the state in the liberated areas.

To begin with, about 4,500 members of the OS formed the nucleus of the armed detachments of the FLN, which was later to be called the Armée de la Libération Nationale (ALN). In the first months after the revolt on 1 November 1954, the FLN did not find widespread support among the population; however, more and more members of the MTLD and even the UDMA joined the liberation front. On 4 November, after Messali Hadj was put under house arrest in Niort in France, the MTLD was dissolved; the Messalists had practically capitulated under the impact of the FLN offensive and the members of the MTLD Central Committee (the 'Centrists') had almost all joined the Front. The remaining party members loyal to Messali Hadj formed their own organization under the name Mouvement National Algérien (MNA), but were no longer able to exercise an influence on the nationalist public. The aim of the FLN 'to restore a sovereign, democratic and social Algerian state under Islamic principles' was kept so inclusive that practically any nationalist could cooperate with it.[16]

We will not discuss the details of the highly varied course of the war up to the Algerian declaration of independence on the 3 July 1962.[17] The long period of war had far-reaching effects on the political and social condition of Algerian society. Up to 1962 the country lost two-tenths of its inhabitants. One tenth, mainly Arab or Berber Algerians, were killed in the war,[18] while almost the entire French Algerian community, which had still made up 10 per cent of the total population around 1955, and 84 per cent of whom had lived in the rich *départements* (later *régions*) of Algiers and Oran,[19] fled or was forced to flee. In the course of the war, entire tracts of land were laid waste, villages were destroyed and the infrastructure was decisively weakened. However, since the war never assumed the scope of regular battles and since the ALN therefore only operated at battalion strength even at the height of the military confrontation from late 1956 to early1959, entire regions were periodically spared. Here both the French authorities and the FLN tried in their turn, after achieving territorial sovereignty, to carry out reforms in the realms of agriculture or education. Both sides hoped that they could thus prevent the peasant population from siding 'with the enemy'. As a result of these efforts it was generally known that some important leaders of the powerful mystical order of the Tijaniya (founded in 1782 by Ahmad b. Muhammad al-Tijani of the southern Algerian Ain Madi) were prepared to cooperate with the French.

In 1960 barbed wire, electric fences and mine fields were used to seal Algeria from Morocco to the west and Tunisia to the east, border areas which had served as deployment and communications zones for the ALN whose activities were thereby drastically reduced. Meanwhile General de Gaulle, who on 4 June 1958 had pronounced his famous words 'je vous ai compris' in Algiers (though simultaneously calling with great pathos: 'Vive l'Algérie Française!'), initiated a phase of political conflict between the FLN and the French government. On19 September, the FLN founded a temporary government (Gouvernement Provisoire de la République Algérienne). But French Algerians soon tried to act against the threatening about turn in French Algerian policy. After de Gaulle had recognized the existence of 'an Algerian Algeria' in 1960, a French Algerian opposition was formed and found strong support within the army. With the establishment of the Organisation Armée Secrète (OAS), with General Raoul Salan as its leader, the numerous anti-Arab commandos of the *pieds-noirs* were bunched together. Salan, who had already fought in Lebanon and Syria in 1920–21, and who had lived for a long time in Laos and subsequently in Senegal as a commanding officer, thought of himself as the champion of the old French colonial empire, which after 1956 had become an anachronism in world politics. The war increasingly became an Algerian civil war fought between 'Muslims' and 'Frenchmen'. When on 11 April 1961 de Gaulle finally acknowledged a 'sovereign Algerian state', the Algerian French pressed for action. On 22 April, the generals around Salan raised a revolt in Algiers. But within three days this last attempt at securing a French Algeria ran aground. As a countermove, the peace negotiations in Evian (20 May–13 June 1961, 7–18 March 1962) paved the way for the political recognition of the provisional government. The OAS reacted with a series of attempts in Algeria and France, but finally had to submit to the armistice proclaimed on 19 March 1962. From 17 June 1962 the guns fell silent throughout Algeria. Following a referendum, Algeria's independence was declared on 3 July 1962.

The victory of the Algerian nationalists marked a defeat for the agrarian capitalism dominated by the French; but in1956 a turning-point within the French colonial system, leading to a political devaluation of the agrarian sector had already appeared. In search of oil deposits of their own – until 1952 France was still up to 90 per cent dependent on oil imports from the Middle East countries – French prospectors in the Sahara met with success.[20] Since estimates pointed to a rapid increase in output, reaching 25 million tons a year by 1962, investment in the Sahara regions, which, according to the statute of 1947 was controlled by the Algerian financial administration, rose out of all proportion in relationship to the agrarian sector. But in 1959, the French had expressed opposition to autarchy in the oil sector; instead, Algerian oil was to be shipped to France through the zone of the French franc zone.[21] This had created a situation in which on the one hand Algeria was granted political independence, but on the other, France was guaranteed economic control based on the domination of its capital over Algerian mineral resources.

The end of the war was thus made possible by a compromise between the interests of the Algerian urban nationalists of the FLN and those of the French economy. This inevitably led to the collapse of the previously strong agrarian sector in Algeria. In addition to uprooted families, there were now new generations of peasants thronging into Algerian cities. The FLN, which had developed into a state party, supported this tendency with an economic planning entirely focused on cities.

After 120 years of French rule there were no longer any clear cultural boundaries between the Algerian French, the *pieds-noirs*, and the Arab, Berber and Jewish Algerians. The French language was so firmly implanted within Algerian urban society that even the FLN wrote most of its publications in French during the war. Political representation, however, was subject to clear social boundaries. These separated 'Algerian French', Jews and Muslims who were each represented in very different proportions in the administrative machinery. Islam thus served as a line drawn within society to differentiate French inhabitants from natives. In a manner similar to developments in India, this led to a certain ethnification of Islam, superimposed upon other ethnic differences, such as that between speakers of the Arabic or Berber languages. Two parties, however, politicized the ethnic dimension of Islam: the Algerian *ulama* who claimed their authority over an Arab Islam; and the Messalists, who celebrated Islam as the expression of social liberation.

Neither tendency was able to assert itself during the war. The prevailing ideology of the FLN allowed Islam only a marginal place, although the affiliation to Islam continued to be essential to the definition of Algerian sovereignty. The FLN considered Islam as belonging to the national programme and accordingly deplored the 'denationalization' of the Algerian people through the suppression of the Arabic language and the Islamic religion. When redefining the Algerian national identity, the FLN had been quick to speak of 'the Islamic principles' upon which the sovereign state was to be built. But in 1956, a change occurred. Islam as the essential component of Algerian culture was ascribed the task of national integration, but it was not to count as the defining feature of Algerian citizenship. The FLN leadership believed that any European could become an Algerian citizen by merely submitting to Algerian laws.[22] The relativization of Islam as the mark of a specific Algerian ethnicity vis-à-vis the Europeans had been an almost inevitable result of the war. But Islam was now replaced by membership of the FLN, which was to mark life in Algeria for years to come, and which henceforth allowed the Islamic public merely a secondary place in society. The Association of Muslim Ulama had already indirectly acknowledged this in 1956 when it officially joined the FLN and secured for some of its members leading positions within the civilian organization. In 1962, however, it was dissolved.

Islamic National Policy in North Africa

The exclusion of the independent Islamic public, which had still been able to exercise a strong influence during the 'liberal decade', had become a general characteristic of urban nationalism. If an Islamic expression of political matters was tolerated, it was only within the framework of the superior state culture. The Algerian revolutionaries, who considered their new sovereign state to be the organic expression of the political and social will of the FLN, had great difficulty in conceding traditional Islamic culture an independent place in public life. Neither the *ulama*, most of whom had taken cover during the war, or had at most spoken out from their place of exile, nor the old established families of the marabouts (*mrabtin*), those holy men whose stronghold had always been the countryside, were acceptable to the revolutionaries as coalition partners.

Among the Algerian emigrants in Cairo, however, there was a growing tendency to lend the national culture an 'Islamic expression'. The best known example is the effort of the Algerian engineer Malik bin Nabi (Bennebi, 1905–78) to present Islam as the ideology of Third World liberation. European modernism was merely to be used as a catalyst to surmount Islamic decadence. Bennebi, who only started publishing in Arabic later in life, predicted that the cultural centre of the Islamic world would shift from the Middle East to Pakistan and Indonesia where, he believed, a 'new human being' would arise as the expression of an 'Asian-African awareness' to confront the influence of the Old World.[23] His plea for a de-Arabized, modern Islam was based on the realization that the Islamic public was in danger of foundering completely in the national cultures of the period of decolonization. This prospect at the same time provoked strong opposition from the neo-Salafiya, most of whom lived in exile in Saudi Arabia. Muhammad al-Mubarak, a leader of the Syrian Muslim Brothers, warned against the de-Arabization of Islam; as an Islamic intellectual, however, he had to simultaneously attack the displacement of the Islamic public from national cultures. The Islamists (*al-islamiyun*) suddenly confronted the 'nationalists' (*al-qaumiyun*) as irreconcilable enemies.[24] The former demanded a radical Islamic discourse of nationalism; the latter tried, on the other hand, to submit nationalism to a general ideology of progress which could be served by Islam as long as Islam itself was making progress. A 'fundamentalist' argument of the ideology of progress in Islam, that is, an argument referring to the idealized dawn of Islam and derived from the canon of theological writings (Muhammad al-Ghazzali) was then just as possible as the renunciation of such a reference (Bennebi).

The Islamic discourse and nationalism basically contained the same message; both were an expression of the attempt to work out a national culture. The conceptual difference was merely the result of a struggle for supremacy; thus both forms of expression of national culture were connected with the formation of political blocs. The structural affinity between 'Islamists' and 'nationalists' necessarily led to all kinds of terminological confusion. The Meccan from Hadramut, Muhammad Ahmad Bashmil (b. 1920) pointed out: 'I distinguish between real Arab nationalism, in which I believe, and the new anti-Islamic movement which has been called 'Arab nationalism."'[25]

Although the Islamists in Mecca and Jeddah tried to propagandize against Third World republican nationalism, most of the national cultures of the Third World were unquestionably following the republican ideal. At the same time, many Arab nationalists found it difficult to accept Bennebi's vision of an Islamic Afro–Asiatic community in which the Arab world would not have a leading role. The end of the colonial empires in Africa put Arab as well as Islamic nationalists to a severe test. Released by the liberation boom of African national cultures in the 1950s, they were forced to absorb the threatening shift of the cultural centre by greater efforts towards integration. Egypt tried, particularly in East Africa and on a regional level, to bring the many Islamic groups and parties into line with the Nasserists. Saudi Arabia, which traditionally enjoyed friendly relations with southern and south-eastern Asia, mainly directed its Islamic policy towards the states of the Malayan Federation.

In most of the new African states which had Muslims as an important part of their population – most of them French-speaking countries which had become independent between 1956 and 1960 (Morocco, Tunisia, Mauretania, Senegal, Guinea, Sierra Leone, Upper Volta [Burkina Faso], Mali, Niger, Nigeria, Chad, Cameroons, Somalia) – the old Islamic order presented a good starting-point for the 'royalist bloc'. Their Islamic publics were still for the most part represented by the old-established prominent families who controlled the widely ramified mystical orders and dominated the countryside. These families, who led the mystical orders of the Tijaniya, Muridiya, Sanusiya and Qadiriya, and had acquired vast territories in the previous centuries, were considered collaborators of French and British colonialism, because as great landowners they benefited from their relations with the world market of the colonial economies. The system of 'indirect rule' by the colonial powers, which to a certain extent tolerated traditional political institutions side by side with the European institutions of power, allowed them to preserve autonomous governments (sultanates) within the colonial states. The sultanic system of regional Islamic sovereignties in West Africa at first prevented the widespread development of an autonomous Islamic nationalism supported by the neo-Salafiya.

Yet already in 1953, the Senegalese Sheikh Abdoulaye Touré (born 1925) had managed to found an 'Union Culturelle Musulmane' in the course of a short stay at the Ben Badi Institute, the university centre of the Algerian Association of Muslim Ulama. Following the tradition of the Algerian Salafiya, Touré, who from 1960 closely cooperated with the Jerusalem General Congress of the neo-Salafiya, conceived Islamic politics primarily as an educational movement. The Cultural Union over which he presided and which gradually organized branches in many West African countries, was to initiate an Arabization of education without, however, 'Arabizing politics'.[26] As in Algeria, the union's Arabizing policy had two goals: the teaching of Arabic was meant to contribute to breaking the supremacy of the French-speaking communities and at the same time checking the effective power of the local and regional Muslim dignitaries and sultans. For their own part, however, the latter tried to lend their traditional legitimacy as rulers a new, contemporary power basis by founding independent Islamic unions. The Sardauna (prince) of Sokota in northern Nigeria, Ahmadu Bello (1909–66), launched a Northern People's Congress in 1949, as well as a society called 'Victory of Islam'. This enabled Bello to politicize his function as leader of the Qadiriya and to provide the Qadiriya with a political organization. Ethnicity also played an important role, since the Qadiriya was predominantly represented by the Fulanis. As a countermove, the Emir of Kano, Muhammad Sanusi, was able to bind the non-Fulani societies more closely to the Tijaniya; he himself was one of the six delegates of the head of a Senegalese branch of the Tijaniya, which was led by the great landowner Ibrahima Nyass.

Nyass (1902–75), who was known as a holy marabout, enjoyed great prestige in the Islamic world. In Senegal, however, reformist members of the Tijaniya who rallied around the Sy family disputed the marabout's leadership within the community. They thought that the marabout system discredited true Islamic mysticism and led only to ignorance[27] and hoped to lend mystical culture a better reputation through the 'Council of Islamic Reform' founded in 1957. For although the old orders in fact exercised a certain social and cultural power and played an important economic role, they had very little credit among the urban societies. When Léopold Senghor became President of Senegal in 1962 and immediately after entering office founded the Fédération Nationale des Associations Culturelles Musulmanes as a parent association of the Salafiya, the leader of the Sy-Tijaniya, Abd al-Aziz Sy, was appointed as its president.

To begin with, the sovereignty of the new West African states did not lead to any major loss of power by the old system. The sultanate was preserved in many countries. Even the orders were allowed to maintain their decisive influence in politics and economics. Thus the national cultures which gave a meaning to the administrative division of French Sudan into territorial states were partially subject to regional Islamic influences; but this influence rarely came to an explicitly Islamic formulation of national movements. Suffice it to mention the Islamic orientation of the national movement in Guinea under Ahmad Sékou Touré (b. 1922) and the pro-Islamic approach of the non-Muslim president of Ghana, Kwame N'Krumah (1909–72), believed to be a disciple of Ibrahima Nyass. Sékou Touré, who prided himself on his alleged descent from the old Keita dynasty, lent his syndicalistically directed leftist-socialist movement a deliberate Islamic orientation. But it was not until 1975, when he reacted to the growing influence of the Islamic public by founding the Islamic National Council, that his liberation ideology was given an Islamic foundation.[28]

The Arabists among the African Muslim nationalities certainly formed a minority, albeit in terms of publicity, an effective one.[29] But in public and cultural life, the 'ethnicists' played a much more important part. They aimed at politically revalorizing the syncretism which was so ubiquitous in everyday life and identifying it as the national panacea. The propagation of a self-conscious '*Islam noir*' went parallel with the concept of *négritude*, which was coined by Senghor and exercised a lasting influence on West African literature. 'Black Islam' was to deliberately dispense with the Arabization of knowledge and instead integrate the regional languages as well as the manifold regional cultures within an Islamic identity. The adherents of '*Islam noir*' were thereby reacting to the often dubious involvement of the Arab–Berber Islamic elite with the French colonial administration; quite a few of them considered this elite as the expression of an Arab racism which was in no way better than that of the French colonial officials.

Regionalism and Revolution in Indonesia

The armistice between the Netherlands and the Indonesian national government, which had been arranged by the Renville agreement in 1948, created the foundation for the international recognition of the sovereignty of the new Indonesian state. Internally, however, the supremacy of the nationalists did not go uncontested, because the radical partisans of the neo-Salafiya saw themselves committed to a national remedy which hardly left any room for their own public. A dissident of the Sarekat Islam, Sekarmaji Marijan Kartosuwiryo (b. 1905), who had founded a training centre for cadres in 1940 and had substantially contributed to establishing the Islamic voluntary corps *Hisbullah*, summoned the Sundanese population in Western Java to fight against the central government in 1949.[30] Unlike the central Javanese countries, Western Java was deeply involved in the Dutch plantation economy. The Sundanese secession in the shape of a *Dar al-Islam*, a 'territory of Islam', which was to form a 'Negara Islam Indonesia', an 'Islamic State of Indonesia', was thus politicizing a colonial tradition which had lent Western Java a different economic and social status. Kartosuwiryo, who was imprisoned in Indonesia in 1962, tried to found an Islamic republican system in which the Koran would form the ethical basis for an independent national culture. Symbolically, the Koran thus confronted the Pancasila, the nationalists' declaration of principles.[31]

A similar success was also registered by the Muhammadiya movement on Sulawesi (Celebes). Kahar Muzzakar (Abd al-Qahhar Mudakkar, b. 1921), himself a member of the Muhammadiya, had in 1942 settled down in the south of the island, and in 1945 became first secretary of a Sulawesi regional party (Kebaktian Rakyat Indonesia Sulawesi). In connection with the war of liberation he founded the Republican Army for Sulawesi, which, thanks to the propaganda of the Muhammadiya, but also to army units which had changed sides, was able to gain considerable support for its fight against the Netherlands, and subsequently against the central government. The small Tomini nation, which in 1941 had fiercely resisted the aggravation of labour conditions on the groundnut plantations and had withdrawn from the control of the central government by 1967, soon became the leading force of the rebellion. In 1955, the Dar al-Islam movement reached its peak when Muzakkar and the rebels, succeeded in creating the foundations for an 'Islamic Republic' of Indonesia on Western Java. It was not until February 1965, when Muzakkar was intercepted by government troops and shot, that the Dar al-Islam guerillas collapsed.

The reason for the relative success of the agitation by the dissidents of the

Sarekat Islam and the Muhammadiya may have been, among other things, the fact that the centralized Indonesian state culture was not able to surmount the colonial differentiation of the archipelago. For the new state was also built up on the principles of the colonial economy, lending the country a certain power on the world market. As a result, colonial traditions continued to prevail in independent Indonesia, and the country had to live on with the contradictions that characterized Dutch colonial rule. These included especially the question about the autonomy of the Aceh region in northern Sumatra. During and after the Second World War, revolutionary *ulama*, all of whom were committed to the neo-Salafiya, had overthrown the power of the traditional princes (*uleebalang*) in Aceh and had been able to build up an urban sovereignty over the country. In 1949 they were not prepared to give up the sovereignty they had acquired to the central government. Under Daud Beurewèh they succeeded in preserving the independence of Aceh. In 1959 the Indonesian government had to recognize the special position of Aceh, which in 1961 became an autonomous republic within the state as a whole and was called Daerah Istimewa Aceh.

After 1952 the Islamic parties, above all the Nahdat al-Ulama, gradually withdrew from the Supreme Islamic Council and opened the way for a differentiated party political representation of the public, which more or less corresponded with their majority ratios and regional characteristics. At the parliamentary elections of 1955, the Islamic parties (above all the conservative Nahdat al-Ulama and the Masjumi, which was backed by the Muhammadiya) won more than 42 per cent of the votes, reaching an absolute majority in their strongholds on Sumatra, Kalimantan and Sulawesi. In 1957 Sukarno tried to neutralise the threat of a division within the Indonesian state with an authoritative act. Together with the traditionally strong Communist Party, he tried to break the power of the Islamic regionalists; these, in their turn, reacted by establishing a 'revolutionary government' under the former prime minister Muhammad Nasir, who was now leading the Masjumi. After almost two years of bitter conflict, the nationalists around Sukarno asserted themselves; at the same time, the Islamic urban public was disposed of. Sukarno also wanted to expand the national culture by integrating the Communist Party into it and proclaimed a new programme called 'Nasakom' which represented an Indonesian variant of the Egyptian national union.[32]

The exclusion of the Islamic public from Indonesian national culture was completely in line with the prevailing political trends of the early 1960s. But by contrast to most Arab countries, the Islamic public in numerous Indonesian countries had developed a very specific character through its ethnic fabric. Its destruction led to the establishment of an authoritarian centralism which could only be legitimized by a socialist ideology of progress. Unlike the Nasserist leadership in Egypt, which did its utmost to prevent the rise of an independent communist public, Sukarno was prepared to cooperate with the Communist Party. In Indonesia the power of the countryside was by no means broken. When after 1962 the central government proclaimed the confiscation of large landed property, the conservative Nahdat al-Ulama, which was traditionally powerful on eastern Java, was able to summon its partisans to open resistance. In late 1964, the political city-versus-land altercation, in which regionalism also played a prominent part, exploded in warlike conflicts between the communists and the paramilitary groups of the Nahdat al-Ulama, who were backed by the army. The radical wings of the Communist Party finally tried to take over the central government by raising a revolt. The Islamic Free Corps on Central and Eastern Java consequently attacked everything urban, which they equated with communism, and slaughtered tens of thousands of ostensible or real communists. Sukarno's downfall was merely a question of time. In December 1965, the army under General Suharto, who had already acquired a dubious reputation in 1962 when he commanded the suppression of Western Irian's rebellion against Indonesian annexation, managed to assume authority over the state and gradually disposed of Sukarno. In the spring of 1967, Suharto was finally appointed as acting president.

Algeria on the Road to a One-Party State

The radicalization of urban policy in Indonesia under Sukarno showed certain analogies in Algeria. In August 1962, Ahmad Ben Bella had seized political leadership through a coup within the FLN and had also tried to institutionalize a socialist centralism by eliminating what remained of the Islamic public. From Ben Bella's point of view, the FLN had indeed fought its way to Algerian independence, but it was not in a position to lend a political meaning to national sovereignty.[33] Ben Bella staked all upon a political development in which priority would be given to the self-government of workers, to industrialization and to building up the FLN as a civilian national party.[34] Conflict with the army was inevitable and was intensified when Ben Bella tried to revalorize the FLN with respect to the army by providing it with a militia of its own. By the end of 1964, he had almost gathered the entire state power in his own hands. The army, which relied on the objectively powerless body of *ulama*, rebelled under Houari Boumedienne on 19 June1965. The spontaneous demonstrations for the deposed head of state could no longer turn the tide. Without much support from the population, the army assumed control over the FLN. The by now almost powerless Indonesian president Sukarno had no choice but to be one of the first to recognize the new government.

Both in Algeria and in Indonesia, the army coups of Boumedienne and

Suharto rehabilitated the Islamic public and provided it with clearly defined functions in the new state system. The Islamic political groups were allowed a scope of activity which enabled the army to lend the national culture a certain Islamic expression. This, of course, presupposed that the Islamic groups recognized the absolute sovereignty of the state and of its supporting parties. In Algeria the regime extended its legitimacy by a forced policy of Arabization; thus instruction courses in schools and universities in some areas were switched from French to Arabic. The Arabic language was equally to be used in public administration. Algerian language policy was also directed against regionalist aspirations, especially on behalf of the Berber parties which, as late as 1965, had openly rebelled against the central government in Kabylia.

3. THE ISLAMIC BLOC AND THE BEGINNING OF SAUDI HEGEMONY

In the year 1960 even Saudi Arabia, the royalist bulwark in the Islamic world, almost fell prey to the republican euphoria. Royalism had only a few powerful representatives. The Sultan of Morocco, Muhammad V, had managed to take the leadership of the national movement and to carry his sovereignty – now as a kingdom – undamaged into independence. The Tunisian Bey fared differently. His credit with the nationalists around Habib Bourguiba was very low. He was unable to prevent the proclamation of the republic in 1958. In South-East Asia, the Malay sultans were able to form a federation in 1957 and adroitly fend off the republican ambitions of the Islamic nationalist parties. The centre of royalism, however, was still in 1960 situated on the Arabian peninsula.

Saudi Arabia and the New Islamic Public

The fears of Hijazi merchants and intellectuals that the new oil wealth might threaten the balance between Saudi Arabian power centres had, by 1956–57, proved well-founded. Helpless, they watched King Saʿud squander the millions of dollars flowing into the treasury. The king's arbitrary approach and his absolute authority over state revenues and spending raised doubts about the survival of the Saudi monarchy. When, for lack of a financial administration, the country plunged into a disastrous crisis and in 1957 the state's indebtedness reached a peak, the Hijazis succeeded on 14 March 1958 in having Crown Prince Faisal, who was well disposed towards them, elected as head of the cabinet. Faisal, who subsequently relied entirely on the experienced Hijazi financial administration, was soon able to stabilize the national budget through a policy of rigorous austerity. This, however, inevitably led to a conflict with the king, who saw himself deprived of an essential part of his sovereignty. Saʿud managed to marginalize the most prominent Hijazi politician, the merchant

Muhammad Surur al-Sabban (1898/99–1972), who had already been finance minister in 1956, and to send him into exile in Cairo. In addition, he found himself inevitably cooperating with a group at court which opposed Faisal, the 'Free Princes' Talal, Nawwaf and Badr, who also tried to repress the influence of the Hijazi merchants by applying a nationalist programme which adopted essential elements from Nasser's Arabism. This led to an astonishing mixture of republican politics and royalist traditions. It may be supposed that the Free Princes (al-Umara al-Ahrar) also represented the interests of the great non-Saudi tribal unions of Najd (among others the Huwaiti), who were anything but well-disposed towards the royal house.

Around the end of 1960 the conflict reached a climax. When Sa'ud categorically refused to sign Faisal's budget, the crown prince had to resign. On 29 December, the king appointed a 'cabinet of the people' presided by Talal Abd al-Aziz. Soon afterwards Talal radicalized his policy, which was directed against the king. He stated that Saudi Arabia had to be changed into a progressive state which would follow the Islamic principles of the Koran, and that the country had to give up its pro-American external and military policy. The prince, however, disposed of no corresponding political instruments to carry out an active programme of this kind. On the contrary, in a constitutional project drafted in 1961, Talal had to politically recognize the Saudi hereditary monarchy. On 11 September 1961, his cabinet was dismissed by Sa'ud. Talal fled to Beirut with three like-minded friends and founded the Arab Front for National Liberation, which appeared to attract some support among the tribes and the Eastern Arabian petroleum workers.

Faisal was again appointed deputy of the king and head of the cabinet. When, on 30 March 1962, he had himself proclaimed regent by decree, the struggle for power in Saudi Arabia was definitely decided in favour of the royalists. The leaders of the Arab Front tried in vain to persuade Nasser to provide military aid for tribes that were willing to rebel.

As an indirect result of the rule of the Free Princes, Faisal had no difficulty in maintaining the Organization of Petroleum Exporting Countries (OPEC) founded in Baghdad on 9 September 1960. A major participant in it was the petroleum minister Abdallah al-Tariqi, who had hardly disguised his sympathies for Egypt and republican Iraq.[35] The cartel, which initially consisted of five countries, was also directed against the hegemony of ARAMCO, which was now even more obviously put under the supervision of the Saudi state. This provided Faisal with a powerful instrument of internal financial administration. He again sought advice from the Hijaz merchants, brought their leading representatives into his cabinet and introduced specific measures to promote the Hijaz. Jeddah gradually became the second capital of the kingdom.

Founding Members of the Muslim World League[36]

Name	Origin	Group	Function
Muhammad Hanifa Muhammad	Ceylon		Mayor
Ahmad al-Bashir at-Tayyib	Sudan		Scholar
Muhammad Fal al-Bannani	Mauretania	*malikiya*	Scholar
Hasanain Muhammad Mahluf	Egypt	*malikiya*	Mufti
Muhammad Sadiq al-Mujaddidi	Afghanistan	*naqshbandiya*	Dignitary
Sa'id Ramadan	Egypt	neo-Salafiya	Jurist
Kamil al-Sharif	Jordan	neo-Salafiya	Diplomat
Ahmad Alonto	Philippines	neo-Salafiya	Politician
Abu'l-A'la al-Maududi	Pakistan	neo-Salafiya	Politician
Muhammad Mahmud al-Sawwaf	Iraq	neo-Salafiya	Politician
'Allal al-Fasi	Morocco	neo-Salafiya	Politician
Ibrahim al-Saqqaf	Singapore	neo-Salafiya	Journalist
Ahmadu Bello	Nigeria	*qadiriya*	Prime Minister
Muhammad al-Amin al-Husaini	Palestine	Salafiya	Mufti
Abu'l-Hasan Ali al-Nadwi	India	Salafiya	Scholar
Abdallah al-Qalqili	Jordan	Salafiya	Mufti
Muhammad al-Bashir al-Ibrahimi	Algeria	Salafiya	Scholar
Muhammad Makki al-Kattani	Syria	Salafiya	Scholar
Ibrahim Nyass	Senegal	*tijaniya*	*shaikh al-islam*
Muhammad b. Ibrahim Al al-Shaikh	Najd	Wahhabiya	Grand Mufti
Abd al-Rahman al-Iryani	Yemen	*zaidiya*	Judge

The Hijazi families were now provided with extensive political opportunities. Since there were meanwhile a considerable number of neo-Salafi emigrants living in the Hijaz, Faisal was able to mobilize them, too, for his foreign policy aims. To cope with the republican opposition in the country, the king tried to internationalize the domestic conflict as far as possible, so as to ensure the loyalty of the Saudi population. At the same time a balance had to be kept between the Wahhabi state culture, which continued to support the royal house, and the Hijazi elites who were striving for political outlets. By founding the Islamic University of Medina (September 1961), Faisal provided the Wahhabis with an important foothold of power within Hijazi society. He at the same time obliged the Hijazis by, on 18 May 1962, founding an 'Muslim World League' (Rabitat al-'Alam al-Islami) through which, together with the neo-Salafi exiles, they could build up an independent Islamic public, not only in the Hijaz but in 'the Islamic world as a whole'.

The League, to which the former finance minister al-Sabban was appointed as secretary-general, saw itself as the forum of an Islamic public directed against Nasserism. Within a relatively short time, some of the prominent leaders of the Salafiya and neo-Salafiya, as well as other Islamic dignitaries, many of whom had been regular participants in the Jerusalem General Congress of Muslim Brothers, were involved in it. It thus had among its members some of the leaders of a dwindling Islamic public who were tolerated as long as they did not show too clear a rejection of royalism. Islamists of an explicitly republican inclination such as Muhammad al-Gazzali, who still lived in Egypt, or Imami Shi'is, were neither allowed nor wanted to join. The Wahhabiya representing the Saudi state culture was only symbolically represented by the Grand Mufti; real power lay in the hands of the members of the general secretariat, which had its seat in Mecca and almost exclusively relied on Hijazi institutions.

A striking fact was that Faisal managed to enlist Maududi's cooperation as speaker of the Pakistani neo-Salafiya. Maududi's interpretation of Islam as vindicating the state and lending government a crucial role certainly appeared to the Saudi ruler as a welcome extension of the rigid Wahhabi doctrine. But since they had invited Maududi, the organizers could not avoid inviting his most prominent opponent, Abu'l-Hasan Ali al-Nadwi. In 1961, al-Nadwi (born 1913) had assumed the leadership of the famous Salafi theological school of Lucknow (northern India), the Nadwat al-Ulama, founded in 1893. He was known on the one hand as a strict advocate of free scholarship, and hence considered a worthy fellow combatant in the eyes of the Salafiya; but on the other hand, he had a generally positive relationship with the Islamic mystical tradition, with which he often openly sided. The fact that this could hardly be reconciled with the ideals of the classical Salafiya did not bother him. On the contrary, his positive recourse to mysticism served his aim of establishing a new basis for the independent position of Islamic scholarship. In addition, he argued for the extensive recognition of a specifically Indian tradition of Islamic culture by the Arab world and as early as 1951 criticized the 'ignorance' of the Arab Wahhabiya about the achievements of the Indian Muslims.[37]

Nevertheless, al-Nadwi was indispensable to the League, for his measured complaint against republicanism fully corresponded with the basic frame of mind of the constitutionally disposed Hijazis. As far back as 1950, in a reference to Muhammad Iqbal, he had emphasized that the kind of republicanism which merely replaced the personal sovereignty of the ruler with the dictatorship of a state president was nothing but a another form of royalism, and could never be brought into harmony with the spiritual aims of Islam. He wrote: 'Royalism, however, is not limited to the existence of a person who is cut out for kingship or a person who exploits kingship; for royalism means that man is to be thoughtful of his fellow man and live by respecting the property of his fellow man.'[38] His words corresponded precisely with the views of most Hijazi intellectuals, who wanted to have a constitutional monarchy established in Saudi Arabia. But since this was denied to them within the country itself – despite Faisal's constantly repeated promises – they hoped to lend their constitutionalism a political expression by forming political and cultural relations with Islamic groups and unions outside Saudi Arabia. Due to its social and cultural heterogeneity, however, the League was unable to create a united public and ultimately it remained within the framework of the kingdom's official foreign policy.

Islam as an Ideology of Social Liberation

During the period of republican euphoria, the various Islamic ideologies lost much of their prestige. The theoretical discourse of the Islamists also declined after the late 1950s, since there could no longer be any question of an independent discussion of guiding Islamic principles in political affairs. Every Islamic statement was set into an imposed political context referring either to Egypt or to Saudi Arabia. The international alignment lurked constantly in the background, so that in the end the Islamic discussion became indirectly bound up with worldwide political constellations. Some intellectuals, above all the lawyer Sa'id Ramadan, who then lived in Geneva, still sought an independent third way between the blocs and obstinately published in the name of a fictitious 'Islamistan'. Most of the Islamists, however, were forced to lend legitimacy to superimposed ideologies or national cultures. Theoretical discussion had thus come to a standstill. In Egypt those authors who still wrote in an Islamic way vied to preserve their identity by couching Third World socialism in Islamic language. They meticulously looked for images from Islamic history which might lend socialism a native look. This tendency was intensified when the Egyptian government under Nasser tried to introduce a socialist development programme. The wave of nationalization in industry and finance, which started in 1961, as well as new attempts to revive land reform, established the framework for an Islamic interpretation of socialism. The prevailing question was that of property and the role of the individual within society. Even the Azhar University had to adopt this trend. Its rector, Mahmud Shaltut (1893–1963), who had become famous for his attempts to obtain Sunni recognition of the Shi'a as the 'fifth Islamic school of law',[39] soon became the mouthpiece of an Islamic Nasserism. In doing so he implicitly recognized the fact that in 1961 the autonomy of Azhar university was definitely broken. Shaltut essentially contributed to introducing a Nasserist Islamic scholarlship which fiercely turned against the 'fossilized' *ulama* and became more and more bureaucratic in the course of the following decades.

The Egyptian government also looked for international allies within the Islamic public. Together with the nationalization of the Azhar, in 1961 it decided on the creation of an Academy for Islamic Studies (Majma' al Buhuth al-Islamiya) which was to function as the 'highest authority for Islamic research' and to undertake the task of judging 'the newly emerging ideological and social difficulties' from an Islamic point of view.[40] However, it took three three years for the academy to begin its work. Not unexpectedly, it had little resonance among the *ulama* in 1964, and it was primarily North African members of the *ulama*, among others Muhammad al-Bashir al-Ibrahimi and the Tunisian Mufti Muhammad al-Fadil b. Ashur, who were willing to join the academy.

By 1962 the Islamic public was acquiring a new, though not independent, function through the alignment of Arab countries. There were signs of a far-reaching change as, both from their Western exile and in Egyptian, Syrian and Iraqi prisons, prominent Islamic intellectuals continued to write about Islamic ideologies. Among the well-known works of this period were, above all, the writings of Sayyid Qutb, who was imprisoned in Egypt from 1954. His programmatic *Milestones*[41] and his populistic Koran commentary[42] were to serve as guides for a new generation of Islamic activists. The state-directed restoration of the Islamic public thus, for the time being, on the whole prevented the political regeneration of the neo-Salafiya, which was not to begin until the early 1970s.

Qutb's more recent works featured three guiding principles. First of all, he aimed at presenting a polar definition of right and wrong in Muslim societies; he wanted to create words that might have the effect of weapons, that is, return to the Muslims their freedom to run their own lives. Secondly, he disqualified the present world of the Muslims as a 'world of ignorance' (*jahiliya*), which he symbolically identified with the pre-Islamic era. And thirdly, he proclaimed – in a completely different sense from Maududi's – the absolute sovereignty of God:

A Muslim does not believe that another beside the One God can be divine, and he does not believe that another creature but himself is fit to worship him; and he does not believe that 'sovereignty' may apply to any of his servants.[43]

In man himself divine sovereignty might become reality through the 'creative appropriation of the image' (*tasawwur*). Man as an individual, not the state, as Maududi saw it, is the deputy of divine sovereignty. By way of artistic and intellectual activity, says Qutb, man will find his way back to the 'Islamic imagination' the supreme expression of which is the Koran itself.

In his more explicit social theory, Qutb presents social man as the autonomous Islamic entity which, through a process of becoming-for-itself, can rise to be the subject of history. In a system of this kind, the *shari'a* is nothing but an 'essential' ethical norm 'befalling' anyone who devotes himself to the Islamic imagination. In a 'dynamic and real process', man, the self-defined[44] subject of history, can create a community without a ruler. Since people to whom the Koran is revealed have the unique privilege of experiencing 'the Islamic imagination', that is, of creatively appropriating the divine image in the text of the Koran, 'Islamic man' has the historical duty of following the dynamic way of development towards a society free from rulers.

Qutb's works, which were still relatively unknown during the 1960s, were afterwards quite arbitrarily interpreted in accordance with Maududistic or anarchistic positions. The ambiguity of Qutb's Islamic ideology is also due to his often self-styled diction and his attempt to create concepts for a new Islamic theory by coining neologisms – which made it difficult for many of his partisans to understand what he really meant. An academic study of his work, which might have clarified his intention, was impossible, since his writings were banned; later on, such studies were mainly carried out by Western Orientalists.[45]

Islamic Dissidents in Iran

Another Islamic intellectual with a very similar point of view was the Iranian author and sociologist Ali Shari'ati (1933–77). Contrary to Qutb, who had himself migrated from his village to the city, Shari'ati represented the first generation of newcomers in the city. In his memoirs *Kavir* ('The Salt Desert') he wrote in 1969–70:

> My father broke with tradition and did not return to the village when he had ended his studies. He stayed in the city [Mashhad] and fought with his knowledge, love and inner effort to preserve himself in the morass of urban life ... I am the result of his decision to stay.[46]

His father, whom Shari'ati admired above all, was one of the few Salafi Shi'i *ulama* who committed themselves to the educational movement and who, by reviewing traditional Shi'i cultural ideals, sought to lend the Koran a privileged position in education.

Unlike Qutb, Shari'ati had had an opportunity to study abroad at a relatively early age. After training as a teacher and briefly attending the Faculty of Literature in Mashhad, he went to Paris in 1960 for a period of five years. It was from there that he observed the upheaval taking place in Iranian society, which, after the fall of the Mossadeq regime, went through a ten-year phase of extensive political incapacitation. Following an economic and financial crisis in 1958 which lead to demands by John F. Kennedy's new American government for basic economic and political reforms under the title 'Alliance for Progress', the old political public was able to take form again. With the temporary political opening of the regime in 1960–61, the National Front was reactivated and various political programmes were discussed among student circles; but their attempt to take their protest into the streets often ended in bloody police acts. Nevertheless, until 1962 Iranian liberal nationalists still had a certain influence on the government. In accordance with the American demands, Ali Amini stood up for a process of social openness and went to Mecca in May 1962 to hold discussions with Faisal about the impact of the new oil economy in both countries. But unlike Faisal, Amini had no support from the court and when he tried to make up for an 80 million dollar budgetary deficit by a 15 per cent cut in expenditure he was forced to resign on 18 July 1962.[47]

The two groups of Shi'i *ulama*, the 'quietists' around the *marja-i taqlid* Burujerdi[48] and the 'activists' around Taliqani and Kashani, were paralysed by Amini's policy of appeasement. Burujerdi died on the 30 March 1961, without an agreement among the *ulama* regarding his successor. Kashani, who was politically marginalized after his release from prison in 1956, shortly before his death in March 1962 suddenly showed a certain interest in mending his bridges with the government. But a land reform launched in 1960, as well as the introduction of women's suffrage – both steps by which the regime tried to win a new social base – met with the violent criticism among the majority of the *ulama*, who saw themselves robbed of their social and cultural authority. Among those who spoke up in these discussions, perhaps in the hope of combining the now vacant leadership of the 'activists' with the unoccupied position of the *marja-i taqlid*, was Ayatollah Ruhollah Musavi Khomeini (1902–89), a teacher at the Qum seminary. In November 1962 Khomeini sent the following telegram to the shah:[49]

> The *ulama* have publicly declared that women's suffrage and the renunciation of the conditions whereby only Muslims are entitled to vote and to be elected are contrary to Islam and to the constitution. If you think that you can replace the Holy Koran with the Avesta of Zoroaster or the Bible or other misleading books, you are mistaken.

After the arrest of Khomeini and about 35 other high-ranking members of the *ulama* on 4 June 1963, and the simultaneous proclamation of a three-day period of official mourning for the death of Pope John XXIII, the participants in a procession on the tenth day of Muharram, the anniversary of the death of the Shiʿi Imam Husain, rose in revolt. Their protest, which lasted for almost a week, ended in a blood bath. Two months later, the regime believed that it had stabilized its power and released two of the *ulama* from prison. But there now occurred a change of attitude in Khomeini's Islamic propaganda. His agitation no longer centred on securing the autonomy of the *ulama*, but on the social and political liberation of Iranian society. He even appeared to have second thoughts about his previous negative approach to women's suffrage. By taking up social themes, Khomeini was addressing a society which he was soon to describe as a revolutionary subject. On 4 November 1964, in the course of discussions about a loan of 200 million US dollars for re-armament and the cession of capitulatory rights to US personnel, he was finally banished from the country. As a countermove, the regime stepped up the militarization of the country. Almost 80 per cent of the income from the oil industry, which rose by 19.5 per cent per year, was now spent on the equipment of the Iranian army consisting of more than 100,000 men, and on developing the state police, Savak.[50]

Shariʿati, who observed these events from Paris, now worked more intensively on a project for a humane and socially just Islamic order in Iranian society. For this he was both admired and criticized; admired among socialist partisans in Iran because he wanted to propagate a link between Islam and socialism, and criticized because he argued too much within the context of Shiʿi dogmatics and thus appeared to exclude the Sunni communities from the process of revolutionizing society. Even today his position in Iran remains ambivalent. To some of the Shiʿi *ulama* he appears as the incarnation of a political syncretism which has distorted Islam, to others as the preserver of the revolutionary identity of the Shiʿa and its claim to side with the oppressed.

In an early work from the year 1955, Shariʿati proposed an alternative way between a bourgeois and a materialistic conception of history.[51] Here, it was already apparent that he considered the Shiʿa alone capable of conceptually combining disparate modern outlooks and philosophical currents. What was specific to Shiʿism was its capacity to combine diverging ideologies, philosophies and sciences within a single world-outlook. Existentialism (Jean-Paul Sartre), mysticism (Louis Massignon) and socialism or sociology (George Gurvitch) represented to him those human fields of experience which – expressed in Shiʿi terminology – corresponded with the basic constituents of human existence.[52]

Shariati's understanding of Islam left the borders of religiosity far behind. His insistence that Islam was now an ideology rather than a religion even led him so far as to re-formulate the Koranic statement 'The religion referring to the One God is Islam' to 'The ideology in our school of thought is Islam'. Like Muhammad Iqbal, he interpreted the Islamic history of creation mythologically, thus describing the evolution of man from his 'spirit/mud reality' to a being resembling God. The 'superior' qualities of the Perfect Man, 'self-awareness, creativity and an autonomous will', related him to God, but he remained an 'emanation' of God. Shi'i Islam alone was capable of forming such a complete concept of man. Westerners had to take Pascal, Marx and Sartre as their models, the (non-Muslim!) orientals the heretic Muslim mystic al-Hallaj (executed in 922), the Zoroastrian rebel Mazdak (5th century) or Buddha. The Shi'a alone possessed the ideal of the Perfect Man in the person of the Caliph Ali, in whom mysticism, equality and freedom were inseparably united.

The Proxy War in Yemen

The new ideas with which Qutb and Shari'ati inspired the Islamic public did not bear fruit until the early 1970s. For up to that point, the national states with their old ideological discourses dominated the scene. Social and political liberation, as Algeria's example appeared to show, was conditional upon strong state sovereignty. Since the latter was mainly understood as military power in those countries where there were no strong civilian urban parties, it was naturally supposed that 'national liberation' could only be successfully achieved by military measures.

The Islamic offensive of the Saudi Arabian prince Faisal hit Egypt at a time when the ideals of a progressive Arab union had run aground through the collapse of the United Arab Republic. Syria, which the union threatened to turn into an economic colony of Egypt, with the Syrian elites no longer having a share in the central power, seceded on 28 September 1961. The new Syrian government under Ma'mun al-Kuzbari, which showed a distinctly civilian character, drew nearer to Saudi Arabia, a fact that was interpreted by Egypt as an act of one-sided support for 'reaction'.

Even royalist Yemen finally withdrew, on 27 December 1961, from its association with the United Arab Republic. Nevertheless, the Nasserists in Yemen had been able to benefit from Crown Prince Badr's brief flirtation with the 'Arab cause' to consolidate their bastion in the Yemeni army. The Yemeni army's traditional relations with Iraq now also showed their effect. Whereas in the 1930s the army had been trained in the latest methods by royalist Iraqi officers, it was now mainly trained by republican officers from Iraq who were largely Arab nationalists. On 19 September 1962 King Ahmad died, and very quickley, on 26 September, Yemeni republican officers around Abdallah al-Sallal saw that there was a chance for a coup against the monarchy. They deployed troops in San'a, occupied the royal palace and proclaimed the Arab Republic of Yemen. The new King Badr and the royal court fled to the north of the country, where they found an albeit not always secure and unconditional support among the Zaidi tribes. The Yemen was now divided into two states. The capital city was ruled by the pro-Nasser army around al-Sallal, on whom the non-Zaidi, Shafi'i elites in the west of the country had set great hopes; in the north, however, the Imam managed to preserve his political sovereignty thanks to his close contacts with Saudi Arabia.

Saudi Arabia reacted promptly to the threatening situation on its southern border. On 4 November, it concluded a defence pact with Jordan and mobilized its troops in the border area around Najran. Egypt responded six days later with a Yemeni–Egyptian defence treaty, which allowed Egyptian troops to be stationed in the Yemen. By early 1963, more than 15,000 Egyptian soldiers had entered the country and reconquered some important places north of San'a. Under the supreme command of Abd al-Hakim Amir (committed suicide on 14 September 1967), who had been governor of the United Arab Republic in Damascus, on 12 and 13 February 1963 Egyptian planes bombed the Saudi border city of Najran. A direct confrontation between Egypt and Saudi Arabia was only prevented by a 'guaranteed subsidy' offered to the Saudi regime by Kennedy.[53]

It was already evident that the republican system had not been able to overcome the old Zaidi constitution. Most of the Zaidi families preserved the privileges and offices they had been granted by the king. The only republican element strictly speaking was the Yemeni army, and even that was often supported by the Zaidi tribes of the north, since the tribes, which had had a decisive share in the conflicts between the Yemen and Saudi Arabia in the 1930s, considered the pact between kings Faisal and Badr as treason. In the summer of 1963, the Shafi'i elites in the western part of the country even contemplated the possibility of seceding and joining Southern Yemen.

But in Southern Yemen, too, that is in the Southern Arabian Federation controlled by Great Britain and in the Hadramautic principalities al-Katiri and al-Qua'iti, there were signs of turmoil. On the day of the San'a coup, Aden, which until that point was a British crown colony, declared that it would join the Southern Arabian Federation. This provoked violent protests from the urban nationalists, who had found political solidarity with the as yet small Socialist People's Party of Abdallah al-Asnaj and were by no means ready to submit to the sovereignty of the Southern Arabian principalities. For them it was beyond question that the independence of Southern Yemen must not have as its consequence the restoration of the Sultanic constitution. Encouraged by the presence of Egyptian troops in Northern Yemen, the Southern Yemeni socialists from Aden founded the National Liberation Front (NLF) in June 1963, and in October of the same year they began their attacks on British military bases.

The Ba'th in Power

From 1962 to 1965 the conflict between Egypt and Saudi Arabia dominated almost all aspects of political and intellectual life in the Middle East. During these years, there was little opportunity to remain neutral or to preserve an independent public which did not contribute to the cold war between the two countries. Outside the Yemen, the conflict developed into a violent diplomatic and intellectual feud. Each side enlisted newspapers and radio stations to propagate its line, calling its opponent a 'stronghold of imperialist reaction' or 'a godless apostate and slave of communism'. The corresponding representation of the enemy image led to the unhindered persecution of political dissidents, who, although often holding different opinions, had to seek the protection of the other side to avoid dropping completely out of sight. The Arab republicans saw themselves fortified by the simultaneous coup of the nationalist Ba'th party in Syria and Iraq in 1963. Abdalkarim Qasim's dictatorship in Iraq was overthrown on 8 February 1963 by an ingenious and bloody coup d'état of a few officers of the Ba'th party; a month later, on 8 March 1963, armed forces in Syria assumed power and helped the Ba'thist Luwayy al-Atasi to assume leadership of the government. Although both coups were carried out by groups from the same ideological milieu, they did not create a homogeneous new national culture.

In Syria a wing of the Ba'th took over which had opposed the voluntary dissolution of the party immediately after the union with Egypt, as advised, among others, by Michel Aflaq. The new Syrian government under al-Atasi was thus unwilling to give way to the resurgent enthusiasm for Nasserist ideals in the Syrian cities. Indeed it spared no effort to preserve Syria as a sovereign state, despite the propaganda for an all-Arab ideal, an attitude accepted by Egypt through its diplomatic recognition of Syria. In its internal policy the new government followed a careful course of compromise. Although the partisans of a civilian government under Nazim al-Qudsi were excluded, they were not exposed to direct persecution. Even the Syrian Muslim Brothers, who had for the first time experienced a growth in power under the civilian government and had even briefly supplied a prime minister, Muhammad Ma'ruf al-Dawalibi, from their midst, were able to continue their activity in their strongholds, Hama and Aleppo. But the policy of nationalization provoked resistance. In January 1965, followers of the Muslim Brothers openly rebelled against the Syrian state, but were unable to bring about a decisive change in domestic policy. The first three years of Ba'th supremacy in Syria marked the attempt at a complete invasion of the political and administrative machinery by the Ba'th party and at making the latter into a predominantly Alawite party. On 23 February 1966, radical members of the Ba'th rebelled against its traditional leadership and created a basis for consolidating its power.

The Ba'th's rise to power in Iraq was a considerably bloodier, more contradictory process. Qasim's dictatorship triggered a furious reaction by the Ba'th militia who, in the first months after the coup (1958), gave chase to anything that appeared to be communist.[54] The militia of the Iraqi Ba'th was eliminated in November 1963 by the army leadership under Abd al-Salam Arif, who remained in power until April 1966. The military character of the regime could not be disguised by the civilian government under Abd al-Rahman al-Bazzaz. Nevertheless, national conservative circles around al-Bazzaz managed for almost a year (September 1965 to August 1966) to protect the Iraqi economy from excessive statism. Unlike conditions in Syria, they were at the same time able to recruit Islamic circles as a support for their national culture by emphasizing the inseparable bond between Arabism and Islam. The presidencies of Abd al-Salam Arif and his brother Abd al-Rahman (1966–68) were marked, as in Syria, by a crucial re-organization of the Ba'th. However, the ambitious Arabist and socialist programme was preserved, as was the Ba'thist sense that, as the carriers of a historical will, they fulfiled a mission. The power centre of the Iraqi Ba'th now shifted from the Shi'i communities to the surroundings of the city of Tikrit situated half way between Baghdad and Mosul. The party's general secretary, Ahmad Hasan al-Bakr (1912–82), a career officer who came from that area, had already been head of the government in 1963, but had been forced to resign because of the intrigues of his interior minister Ali Salah al-Sa'di who led the notorious Ba'th militia. The party's power centre increasingly shifted towards Sunni families from Tikrit, although a Shi'i elite continued to adhere to it and was admitted into its subsequent cabinets. This confirmed the astonishing flexibility of the Ba'th; despite or perhaps even because of its pan-Arab advocacy, it promoted the development of political and social regionalism. For example, the founders of the Iraqi branch of the party around Fu'ad al-Rikaki represented Shi'i families who were extremely loyal to one another, while the Tikrit families around al-Bakr and later Saddam Husain (b. 1937) appropriated the Ba'th so that they might also acquire a political means to power. The arguments within the party thus mainly reflected regional conflicts over national culture and control of the wealth of the state. The more clearly regional interests came to the fore, the more powerfully the Ba'th was used as a political instrument. No other party appeared able to represent these particular interests since they were too closely connected with social classes.

The Ba'th only had a real chance of assuming power where public life was marked by currents of regionalism and particularism. This was precisely the case in the ethnically heterogeneous countries of Iraq and Syria. Since the Ba'th was thus closely linked to regionalism, and patently assumed an ethnic character, any attempt to join Iraq, Syria and possibly also Egypt under a unified state sovereignty seemed utopian. Thus all Nasser's attempts to persuade Iraq and Syria to form a new union were doomed to failure, and even the theoretically possible alliance of Syria and Iraq within the Ba'th party proved essentially impossible.

The process of regional coordination lasted longer in Iraq than in Syria. It was not until the 17 July 1968 that the Ba'thist army around al-Bakr managed to overthrow President Arif and, in a second coup on 30 July 1968, to eliminate all internal rivals from the newly founded revolutionary command staff. In the long run, the Ba'th proved to be the only political party which was able to secure the coherence of Syria and Iraq on a long-term basis by means of a dictatorship based on particular interests.

4. THE DECLINE OF THIRD WORLD REPUBLICANISM

The first signs of a decline in the Nasserist ideals of Third World republicanism made themselves felt as early as 1964–65. Nehru's death on 27 May 1964, the conflicts in Indonesia, as well as the overthrow of the Sudanese General Abbud by a civilian opposition movement on 26 October 1964, had led to the disintegration of the alliances that were important to Nasser. The radicalization of national liberation movements in South Yemen and Algeria, and of the regionalist Ba'th party, deprived Egypt of further allies. Faisal had had himself enthroned as the new Saudi king on 29 March 1964 and now appeared as spokesman of the Arab cause. External political difficulties contributed to the division and increasing polarization of the Nasserist national culture in Egypt. That culture had, firstly, to take into account the growing need for a radicalization of socialist discourse, because even the nationalist elites were increasingly open to the new socialist ideology of liberation which was connected not with the USSR but with such names as Mao Tse-tung, Ho Chi Minh and Che Guevara. Secondly, Faisal's Islamic offensive demanded the re-activation of a political ideology marked by Islam. The first conference of the Academy of Islamic Studies, which was convened in Cairo in 1964, was to assume the initiative. At the very beginning of the conference, the 82 delegates from 40 states decided to open the 'doors of free argument' (*bab al-ijtihad*) within the realm of Islamic law in order to achieve a flexible adjustment of Islamic norms of justice to new political factors. The Egyptian regime was thus returning to an essential characteristic of the Salafi and neo-Salafi tradition. The Islamic classicists had fought for decades to abandon the commitments to the Islamic schools of law on which jurists had insisted since the early Middle Ages. In Islamic jurisprudence, the decision to recognize the schools of law as the only legal authority – a decision for which there is hardly any historical proof – and to reduce free jurisdiction to a minimum, was considered as 'closing the door to free argument'.

The attempt by the Nasserist state apparatus to use Islamic discourse to legitimize socialist programmes almost inevitably brought with it a need to reactivate free interpretation (*ijtihad*). With this step the Egyptian regime at the same time responded to Faisal's advances among the Islamic public.[55] The secretariat of the Academy for Islamic Studies sought support even in those parts of the Islamic world which for some thirty years had almost no contact with Islamic scholarly centres in Egypt and Saudi Arabia, particularly the Islamic regions in the USSR. The presence of the mufti of Central Asia, the Uzbek Ziiya' al-Din Babahanov (Papachanov), who embraced official Soviet religious policy and interpreted Islam as a guarantor of social order,[56] managed to bring back Soviet Muslims into the international Islamic public for the first time in many years.

The Egyptian regime even made a gesture of goodwill towards the partisans of the Islamic groups. Sayyid Qutb, who after ten years of detention had become a symbolic figure of Islamic resistance against Nasser's regime, was released from prison and even allowed to publish his latest writings in Egypt.

A New Palestinian National Policy and the Six-Day War

The altogether more limited terrain for an Arab nationalist state ideology was once more enlarged through the foundation of the Palestine Liberation Organization (PLO) on 1 June 1964. But even among the nationalist public, the process of ideological differentiation which had taken place in the 1960s had such a lasting effect that pro-Nasserist circles could no longer form a national movement clearly committed to the Arab cause within the Palestinian context. After 1963, the movement of Arab nationalists turned distinctly towards leftist socialist liberation ideologies. The leadership of the Palestinian Liberation Front (Harakat Tahrir Filastin, Fatah) was now firmly in the hands of Yaser Arafat, who was personally responsible for the close connections between the Fatah and the Egyptian Muslim Brothers. Fatah had been founded in 1958 by Palestinians living in Kuwait, a centre of Palestinian opposition. To begin with its members mainly consisted of Palestinian activists who followed the tradition of the Muslim Brotherhood or al-Nabhani's Islamic Liberation Party. But soon former Ba'thists joined Fatah, so that the political spectrum of the resistance movement gradually shifted to positions that were not explicitly Islamic.

At the same time the national conservative Arab politicians who had been able to stay on the West Bank of the Jordan continued to play an important part and dominated the Palestinian political public in Jordan. The influence of Palestinian personalities in the West Bank on many prominent families in Jordan had indeed played a major role in King Husain's (r. 1953–99) succesful defence of the Hashimite monarchy against a republican opposition which had tried, as late as 1957, to force the country into an alliance with Egypt.

In this dense medley of royalist, Islamic and leftist socialist groups there was hardly any room for the champions of an Arab policy with Nasserist tendencies. When in January 1965 Fatah proclaimed an armed struggle against Israel, Egypt found itself completely isolated. Even in the Palestinian Liberation Front initiated by Egypt and led by Ahmad al-Shuqairi, a pro-Egyptian attitude was by no means the rule. The Front believed itself to be the legitimate successor of the Palestinian government of 1948 and many nationalists, including the aged former Mufti of Jerusalem, Muhammad Amin al-Husaini, had in 1958–59 unsuccesfully demanded that Egypt acknowledge the Palestinian movement as a state, in the same way as it had recognized the Algerian National Liberation Front. Since then the 'struggle for Palestine' had grown into a 'Palestinian national movement' which resisted the dominating influences of an Arab policy.

Egypt tried to regain control over Fatah, and although it found allies, especially among the Palestinian intellectuals living in the Gulf, the autonomy of Palestinian nationalism could no longer be prevented. Meanwhile, more than 60 paramilitary acts carried out by Fatah units up to October 1965 under the code name al-Asifa, most of them directed against irrigation works that carried water from the Jordan to the arable lands in the Negev, alarmed Israel. Since Jordan and Syria were at the same time trying to divert the waters of the river Jordan, Israel reacted with carefully planned military measures. In the autumn of 1966, the situation threatened to escalate when the new Ba'th regime in Syria openly supported guerilla activities.

The conflict over Israel soon became a symbolic fight for hegemony among Arab countries. Saudi Arabia, which had tolerated the Egyptian foundation of the Palestine Liberation Front at the first Arab summit conference in 1964, tried to label it as a struggle between Islam and Zionism. Following the logic of its own state ideology, Egypt saw it as a unique opportunity to lend Arab nationalism fresh impetus after it had lost almost all its bastions through regionalist or leftist socialist movements. To prove that Egypt was able to defend Arab sovereignty, on 18 May 1967 Nasser delivered an ultimatum demanding the departure of United Nations troops from the Sinai peninsula, and stationed his own troops there. The Egyptian government must have been mainly interested in enforcing an economic boycott against Israel as a way of emphasizing the solution of the Jordan problem. With the comment 'Let them come!'[57] Nasserist journalists reacted against fears that Israel's armies might be provoked to a retaliation through the stationing of Egyptian troops on the Israeli border.

In the end even Nasser was unable to arrest the inherent dynamics of the escalation. Lacking any coherent international agreement, the Egyptian and Syrian armies merely relied on the efficacy of the 'Arab cause'. There was no further coordination but a hastily composed Egyptian–Syrian supreme command, which Jordan was also forced to join on the 30 May in order to avoid a nationalist rebellion. Hardly anyone knew what was to be achieved by a war against Israel.

It was altogether different as far as the State of Israel was concerned. The situation had never been so favourable to Israel; with a well prepared strike, the country's security situation could be changed decisively. Yet even the well-informed Israeli army did not predict a success as easy as the one that followed the outbreak of the war on 5 June 1967. In a matter of six days, Israeli troops managed to conquer the Sinai peninsula, Western Jordan and the Golan Heights. On 8 June, in one of the greatest tank battles in history, the Egyptian army suffered a crushing defeat which also detroyed the dream of a pan-Arab national culture. The disaster of June 1967 affected all the Arab states involved. Saudi, Iraqi, Moroccan and Algerian units had been hastily stationed in Jordan and Syria, but even they were unable to stop the advance of the Israeli army. Their defeat thus quickly became a defeat for the Arabs.

At the same time, domestic conditions in most of the Arab republican countries had largely undermined the relationship between state and society. In the autumn of 1965, peasant communities in Egypt had vehemently resisted the agrarian policy imposed on them; the aftermath of the war in northern Yemen which had gone on since 1963 had caused a deep chasm to appear between society and state. There was not enough money to finance the promised development of the urban sector, since the Egyptian government was increasingly militarizing its power and therefore constantly raising its military budget. In addition, Egypt was unable to fund a new agrarian policy which might have reduced the need to purchase wheat, three million tons of which had to be imported in 1967.[58] Following a wave of assassination attempts in the autumn of 1965, the government arrested a large number of communists and Muslim Brothers, including Sayyid Qutb who was executed as a 'brother of the devil'[59] on 29 August 1966.

Nationalist Arab politics had ended up by renouncing social sovereignty. Thus the war of 1967 was by no means a defeat of the Arab societies, which had participated, for all practical purposes, as cannon-fodder in a fight for the sovereignty of a state from which they were becoming estranged. Paradoxically, however, for a brief period the war had once more saved the old national Arab regime. Nasser's offer to resign immediately after the armistice was rejected by an enormous number of demonstrators in Cairo. In the pathos of defeat, society and state were re-united. The victims of the war – apart from the soldiers – were above all the Palestinians for whose sake it had ostensibly been waged. During the first four months of Israeli occupation, more than 250,000 people, a fifth of the total population, left their country.[60] Eastern Jerusalem was annexed by Israel immediately after the armistice. The vast majority of Palestinians now lived in the camps of Lebanon, Syria and Jordan or emigrated to the Gulf states. But in none of these countries were they able to realize their dream of a sovereignty of their own. In Jordan, as in the Israeli-occupied areas, they were second-class citizens; in Lebanon they soon became involved in the internal struggles for national and territorial predominance; and in Syria they were subject to strict police supervision.

The Assertion of Saudi Hegemony

For more than ten years, the public of the Islamic world had been marked by the various nationalist and often socialist movements promoting a specific Third World path between global political blocs and looking for an ideal republican system. The Arab–Israeli war of 1967 can be considered as the end of a period of approximately four years in the course of which Third World republicanism lost its international dominance. In many Islamic countries, this period brought an end to the development ideologies based on the Bandung idea and favouring powerful state intervention to strengthen urban society. The readjustments on the international finance market triggered by the rapid rise in oil production suddenly made any economic development conducted by the state appear as an anachronism. The expensive and often ambitious development projects which continued to follow classical theories of modernization could no longer be financed. In 1970 Egypt already had debts exceeding 1.6 billion US dollars, and Iran owed 2.2 billion dollars. The promotion of urbanism promised by the nationalists led to an unprecedented migration from country to city.

The market completely adapted itself to the oil producing countries, which suddenly disposed of capital reserves that together amounted to many times more than the budgets of the non-oil-exporting countries of the Third World. The share in international trade of the entire Middle East region, including Turkey, Iran and North Africa had amounted to around 5 per cent since 1948.[61] In 1970, more than 80 per cent of the oil production in the Middle East belonged to five countries: Saudi Arabia, Iran, Libya, Kuwait and Iraq. In the same year Saudi Arabia, Kuwait and Libya earned more through their oil exports than the entire sum of Egypt's burden of debt. With this capital, the oil countries could act freely on the world market and import goods in quantities which Egypt and other countries had never experienced. The wealth produced by oil went against any development ideology which still believed in a 'powerful state' and thus also undermined the attraction of Arabism, which was closely connected with utopian theories of progress.

For the present, however, the members of the public bureaucracy, who through the predominantly urban development plans disposed of great powers, were by no means prepared to abandon their ideological tradition. As directors in nationalized industries, in state-controlled trade and banking and in the various organizations which exercised price control and subsidised consumer goods, they were in a position to exercise political power despite the general lack of capital. More often than not they were solidly organized in single state parties, through which they were integrated within a network of communications encompassing the whole of society. As long as their privileges were not curtailed, the urban nationalists faced no serious political danger. And yet important changes were already ocurring. Some members of the 'second stratum', as Leonard Binder described the new bureaucrats, had doubts about the competence of the state to introduce development plans and criticized state-controlled measures in the realm of external trade and international capital movements. They feared that a rigid adherence to traditional ideological models might undermine market relations with financially powerful countries, and they therefore demanded a gradual opening of the state and economy. This attitude became more widespread as the volume of capital in the Islamic world grew through intensive oil production. The turn towards the international market naturally provoked a change in attitude towards those countries which now dominated the market as capital giants, principally Saudi Arabia.

In August 1967, the Arab heads of state and government met in the Sudanese capital Khartoum for a (fourth) summit conference. Faisal managed to present Saudi Arabia as the moral victor while Nasser had to acknowledge Saudi Arabia's new supremacy and promise the withdrawal of the remaining Egyptian troops from the Yemen. The centre of power in the Islamic world had now definitely shifted from Egypt to Saudi Arabia. Faisal responded to Nasser's subjugation by announcing that he would support Egypt and Syria with an annual subsidy of 329 million US dollars, which he would raise from the oil-exporting countries.[62] The 'front-line' countries were thus to be allocated barely 7 per cent of Arab oil revenues.

The Withdrawal from the Yemen

When on 1 September 1967 Egypt and Saudi Arabia agreed on 'peace for the Yemen', there was an outburst of indignation among Yemeni republicans; but during the preliminary peace talks of Harad (November 1965), which were to confirm the agreements of Ta'if and Jeddah (August 1965), the Egyptian delegation had already tried to force the republicans to make a settlement.[63] For a short time, the establishment of an 'Islamic Yemeni state' was accepted by all four contracting parties. However, this project ran aground for internal and external reasons. Now, after losing the June war, Nasser was prepared to give up all his positions in the Yemen. Al-Sallal was deposed before the Egyptian withdrawal (9 December 1967), and Qadi Abd al-Rahman al-Iryani was proclaimed as the new head of state of the Arab Republic of the Yemen. Iryani, who had long been active in the national movement, stood for an emphatically Islamic interpretation of the conflict. His approach had already been acknowledged by the Muslim World League in 1962, when he was elected as one of its founding members. There were also changes on the royalist side. King Muhammad al-Badr was politically marginalized at a popular congress in Sa'da in June 1968. The Zaidi tribes appointed Saif al-Islam Muhammad al-Husain, the commander-in-chief of the royalist troops, as the new head of state. But since he could not be confirmed as an imam, that is as a king, by the people's congress, there arose tendencies even among the royalists to mitigate the old lines of conflict. Al-Badr, however, was able to continue influencing the political attitude of the northern Zaidi tribes from his Saudi exile.

Al-Sallal's overthrow had been the first direct result of the new relationship between Egypt and Saudi Arabia and was interpreted by the Arab nationalists as Egypt's symbolic break with its old ideals. As a countermove, Saudi Arabia managed to exert its influence on a new Islamic public which was now, as Arab national cultures threatened to collapse, faced with a very different environment. Faisal's aim was to restructure the relations of the Arab and Islamic world both on an official and an unofficial level. The official level implied securing Saudi hegemony through the establishment of an Islamic community of states; on an unofficial level, the Muslim World League was to contribute to re-modelling and uniting what remained of the Islamic public and setting it on a Saudi Arabian course.

The Saudi campaign made itself felt at a time of student unrest in Cairo in the summer of 1969. For the first time in years, oppositionists openly appeared as 'Muslim Brothers' and demanded a more definite fight against left-wing socialist and communist activities. Since the Egyptian government continued to maintain close economic relations with the Eastern bloc – after all, the Aswan Dam had been completed with Soviet help in 1967 to the point where it could provide Cairo with electricity – and new projects for the development of heavy industry were tackled with the USSR (May 1969), the opposition's demand was also indirectly aimed at the Egyptian government. As a countermove, Saudi Arabia also stepped up its economic aid to Egypt. An important point of contact were the approximately 500,000 war refugees who had to be integrated. Their willingness to accept Saudi Arabia as their new promised land grew accordingly.

The chief opponents of the Islamic groups supported by Saudi Arabia were the leftist socialist and the Arab nationalist movements. The leftist socialists had gained great prestige with their proclamation of the Arab People's Republic of Yemen on 30 November 1967; but it took some time until both the republican nationalists of the 'Front for the Liberation of Occupied South Yemen' (FLOSY), who had their strongholds in Baikhan and Wahidi and whose leader al-Asnaj operated from Northern Yemen, and the royalists in the sultanates were definitely neutralized. Although the new socialist government in Aden gave the Southern Arab Federation the name 'Yemen', there was as yet no mention of the union of the two Yemens.

The Success of the PLO

The problem of Palestine contributed to the expansion of the Islamic public. Immediately after the Egyptian defeat in the June war, voices were to be heard blaming Arab nationalism for the loss of Jerusalem. In a lecture held at the Unity Club in Mecca, Abu'l-Hasan Ali al-Nadwi, the president of the Indian Nadwat al-Ulama (Society of Ulama), said that the Arabs had not deserved to be victorious because they had waged the war against Israel in an un-Islamic spirit.[64] Ahmad al-Shuqairi, an intimate friend of Nasser's, was removed from his post as leader of the Palestine Liberation Organization on 24 December 1967 and replaced by the Islamic traditionalist Yahya Hammuda, who provided the first signs for the subsequent hegemony of Fatah within the PLO. Once Fatah joined the PLO in 1968, and once Yaser Arafat was elected as its president at the Palestinian National Congress in February 1969, the fate of Egyptian hegemony over the Palestinian national movement was decisively sealed.

Jerusalem soon became a symbol for the invigorated Islamic public, which was moving on three entirely different levels. First of all, the propaganda of the Muslim World League in Mecca, which was closely associated with the Hijaz culture, created a transnational orientation which was altogether committed to the Islamic world, while at the same time embodying the ideological and theological positions supported by the League. These were in turn an expression of the Islamic groups bunched together within the League of which the most important was still the neo-Salafiya, who, from their Meccan exile, tried to regain their influence over their national cultures.

The second level concerned the national cultures themselves. The Islamists assumed a more definite position than in the past against those traditional Islamic cultures in which different mystical ideologies prevailed, and whose representatives had often contributed to excluding the majority of the population from the context of national politics. Moroccan maraboutism, for example, continued to act as an effective barrier against the political mobilization of the population. In this sense the neo-Salafi groups were following a path previously trodden by nationalist movements, for they too were mainly concerned with assuming power over the national cultures.

The third level concerned the claim, particularly by Saudi Arabia, that an international Islamic community of nations could be founded without directly calling into question the sovereignty of the nation states. In October 1968, a community of this kind had been proposed in outline at an Islamic conference at Rawalpindi in Pakistan. But it was not until the al-Aqsa mosque in Jerusalem was set on fire by an Australian fanatic on 21 August 1969 that an initiative to form a new international Islamic community of nations was taken. At a summit meeting of Islamic heads of state in the Moroccan capital Rabat (22–25 September 1969), Faisal successfully promoted the creation of an 'Organization of the Islamic Conference' (Munazzamat al-Mu'tamar al-Islami, OIC) with the support of the Moroccan King Hasan II. It took almost another three years for the OIC to be officially established in the 'Jeddah Pact' at the first Islamic Conference of Foreign Ministers in 1972. But in 1969 it was already clear that Saudi hegemony had to be accepted, however grimly, within the Islamic world, though it is true that it went no further than the adoption of an Islamic form of expressing international policy.

The transformation of the Arab national movement for Palestine into a Palestinian national movement was completed with the creation of state structures in the refugee camps in Lebanon and Jordan. The conflict over state sovereignty which immediately broke out was once more mitigated in Lebanon in 1969 by a settlement arranged by Nasser between the Lebanese government and the PLO. The escalation of the guerilla warfare between Israel and Palestine, which also led to targeted military attacks on Jordan, Lebanon and Egypt, raised the question, especially in Jordan, of the extent to which royal power could still exercise sovereignty over the country. Under the threat of a republican revolution carried out by the Palestinian *Fida'iyun*, King Husain mobilized his army to defeat the armed units of Palestinians. In a war lasting several days (16 to 27 September 1970) the sovereignty of the Palestinians in Jordan ended in a bloodbath ('Black September'). It was only in Lebanon that the PLO and other socialist Palestinian parties managed to preserve a certain degree of sovereignty, perhaps, among other reasons, because Lebanese society had meanwhile become used to the ethnic fragmentation of sovereign power.

Islamic Republicanism in Libya

With the overthrow of the Libyan King Idris by an army officer, Mu'ammar al-Qaddafi, on 1 September 1969 and the Sudanese army's coup against the civilian government on 25 May 1969, the classical Arab national policy, which prided itself on being 'socialist', staged another spectacular appearance. The coup in Libya was of particular importance insofar as a monarchy was here overthrown by Arab nationalists, whereas a decade later the Iranian empire would be brought to an end by Islamic revolutionaries.

The fall of the monarchy in Libya coincided with a period in which Libyan oil production was sporadically rising. In 1970 the state earned more revenues from oil exports than Saudi Arabia (1,351 mil. US dollars against 1,214 mil.).[65] However, by contrast to Saudi Arabia, the oil economy in Libya brought considerable change in traditions of social organization. The old tribal ties were unable to prevent the rush towards the cities and oil fields and as early as 1956 the southern Libyan region of Fezzan was exclusively inhabited by the elderly.[66] The monarchy could not adapt itself to the rapidly changing cultural and political attitudes of the migrants, with the result that the army around al-Qaddafi found it easy to obtain social recognition for their coup.

However, from the first years after the coup, it was evident that even the Libyan revolutionaries could no longer do without an Islamic form of expression. Within three weeks, Qaddafi declared: 'Those who have usurped the wealth of this people and sucked its blood do not believe in socialism, the socialism of Islam; but the conscious, noble and revolutionary nation will never accept an alternative to social justice.'[67] In 1972 the 'introduction of the *shari'a*' was officially proclaimed. This was the first time that a military regime so clearly adopted an Islamic discourse.

Thus Libya was the first country in which an Islamic republicanism was able to prevail against the old royalist system. But until the early 1970s there were apparently only small, politically insignificant Islamic parties which might have provided Qaddafi's roughly formulated Islamic republicanism with a broader ideological identity. The time-honoured Sanusiya, which after 1930 had been transformed into a royalist system, had eliminated almost all competing Islamic groups, so that no independent Islamic public was formed. Nationalism was represented by a relatively small layer of urban workers and army members who had severed their ties of loyalty to the Sanusiya at a time when the neo-Salafi public had virtually ceased to exist, and whatever was left of it depended on Saudi Arabia. This led to the very specific development of political Islam in Libya which was strongly influenced by Qaddafi himself and was centred on national sovereignty. The revolutionary identity of Libyan state Islam was manifested in the foundation of the Islamic Missionary Society (Jam'iyat al-Da'wa al-Islamiya) established on 13 May 1972; but there was as yet no programme that might have provided the Libyan Islamic ideology with clear contours.

The pietistic, ascetic substantiation of the 'socialist and anti-imperialist' tradition in Libya found a certain analogy in the Algerian National Charter, which was proclaimed by Houari Boumedienne, the President of the Revolutionary Council, on 5 July 1976 as a result of a popular referendum.[68] The National Charter, in which the creation of a socialist society was laid down, acknowledged Islam as an essential means towards revolution. The Islamic creed, it said, could only manifest itself 'through a more intensive fight against imperialism and through a decisive commitment to socialism'. Revolutionary Islam was 'militant, unostentatious [and] marked by a sense of justice and equality', as well as a 'bulwark against the de-personalization' of Algerian society.

CHAPTER FIVE

The Ascendancy of Islamic Ideologies 1973–1989

1. THE CRISIS OF THE YEARS 1973 AND 1974

The Start of Political Secession

Third World republicanism collapsed mainly as a result of structural factors. An economic and social development that was centred on the city demanded more from the economy than it could provide. The nationalists' vision of society as an 'ideal city' necessarily excluded the traditional sectors and subjected the agrarian communities to the dictate of the city. Although the urban nationalists had acquired sovereignty over domestic affairs, their power was constantly diminished by lack of capital, and borrowing had plunged the state into a maze of dependences. Inadequate capital was thus increasingly invested in those sectors of society which were considered to be strongholds of the nationalists: the army, public administration and industry. Objects of prestige now also served to document the sovereignty of the state in those realms of society which otherwise remained undeveloped. For example, the Aswan Dam in Egypt supplied electric power for the industry of Hilwan in 1972, but in the immediate vicinity of the dam neither tea nor sugar could be found.

The state increasingly isolated itself from those realms of society which did not fit into the nationalists' world view. As a result, different political forms of expression developed outside the nationalist strongholds. Mobilized and politicized by republicanism, the members of the mixed areas sought a political expression that would reflect their social situation.[1] Since their spheres of life were split into a 'traditional' and a 'colonial' realm, they had to use a kind of 'social code switching'. 'Traditionality' primarily concerned the overall social and economic realm of reproduction, namely family life, everyday experiences and habits, forms of accommodation, cults and cultivating techniques, as well as a division of labour and linguistic norms. We could use the term 'private' instead of 'reproduction', but in my view this concept narrows down the economic character of the tensional structure. The colonial realm was marked by areas of production in the broadest sense of the word, that is, above all by work and its surrounding social fields such as paid employment, bureaucracy, forms of state authority and the political public. However, the values and ways of life of the colonial sector could not be communicated to the sphere of reproduction, for its meagre earnings were inadequate. Thus the workers at a refrigerator factory in Cairo might produce the goods of the colonial sector; but they could not afford these goods themselves. Living within the mixed areas thus implied the daily experience of a segmented reality.

The code switching resulting from this 'split subject' situation created a social tension that could only be adjusted by the state's promise of participation in the wealth produced by society; this promise, which appeared plausible – the Egyptian government, for instance, had guaranteed every high school graduate a steady job – raised hopes among the members of the mixed areas that they would some day adapt their 'traditional' sphere of life to the values of the 'colonial' sectors. This may also have been a reason for the urban nationalists' astonishing ability to mobilize the population.

After 1967, however, this had become an empty promise; indeed, the lack of capital in the 'colonial' sectors accelerated the process of social and economic segregation which had already been evident in the international economic crisis of 1928–32. In addition, the colonial sector began to retreat. The state increasingly renounced its sovereignty over certain districts and regions which in the eyes of urban nationalism were 'unproductive'. Around 1970 the 'traditional' and 'colonial' sectors began to drift apart. In the former, the system of social and economic support, a monopoly of the state, reached the point of collapse. Because the process was slow, those involved only gradually became aware of this ominous situation. Since the state could no longer make up for the discrepancy, many were forced to either take the plunge into 'traditional life' or into 'the colonial world' by either traditionalizing their field of production or colonializing their private life. Since poverty tends to lead back to tradition, while wealth tends to the colonial mode, the financial resources of the members of the mixed areas determined their future, which in either case had to involve a solution of the structure of tension.

Urbanization in the Islamic World, 1960–1988

Inhabitants (including suburbs)	1960	1980[2]	1988[3]
Algiers	600,000	1,748,000	3,000,000
Amman	210,000	1,232,000	972,000
Ankara	453,000	1,877,000	2,845,000
Baghdad	850,000	3,205,000	3,844,000
Cairo	2,500,000	5,084,000	13,200,000
Dacca	556,000	3,400,000	7,015,000
Dakar	374,000	1,250,000	1,500,000
Damascus	120,000	1,156,000	2,951,000
Djakarta	2,913,000	6,500,000	8,200,000
Karachi	1,115,000	5,103,000	9,376,000
Khartoum	120,000	561,000	1,600,000
Mogadishu	74,000	500,000	600,000
Nouakchott	6,000	150,000	450,000
Rabat	160,000	841,000	1,287,000
Riyadh	150,000	1,250,000	2,900,000
Tehran	1,513,000	4,712,000	6,042,000
Tripoli (Libya)	140,000	1,000,000	2,195,000

In the 1970s politics in the mixed areas contributed to a certain polarization within the political public, which no longer strove towards the old ideals of republicanism. The typical political expression of the mixed areas consisted of forms of an Islamic view of the world. In the nationalist strongholds the reaction was a radicalization of the political field because some members of the intellectual elites refused to tolerate the abandonment of major parts of society and demanded a social-revolutionary programme. On the other hand, elites who were closely connected with the state were committed to a kind of regionalism, which was meant to preserve the social and economic unity of their strongholds by referring to 'inalterable' ethnic features. Three ideological models henceforth marked political events in the Islamic world: Islamic, regionalist and social-revolutionary programmes. What they all had in common was the concept of political secession, which expressed the separation between society and state.

The Secession of Bangladesh

Muhammad Ayyub Khan (1907–74), the authoritarian leader of Pakistan from 1958 to his overthrow on 25 March 1969, had also assumed the presidency of the Muslim League in 1963. This time-honoured organization was destined, among other things, to ensure the political union of Pakistan through a superior national culture based on no other ethnic condition but Islam. In the years of classical republicanism, Ayyub Khan managed to expand this framework by limiting the political representation of Pakistani society to 'fundamental democracy' which, for a while, prevented particular interests within the state from competing with his regime. However, the 1965 war over Kashmir between India and Pakistan was a turning-point. In 1966, after the resignation of Foreign Minister Zulfikar Ali Bhutto (1928–79), a resistance was formed in West Pakistan (the provinces of Sind, Baluchistan, Punjab and the North West Frontier had by this time been brought together under a central administration). On 30 November 1967 Bhutto rallied the opposition by founding the Pakistan People's Party (PPP), an explicitly socialist party committed to Islamic principles.[4] A few days later, a rift occurred within the East Pakistan National Awami Party (NAP), which had been founded in 1957 as a collective union of the Bengali national movement and had a considerable number of supporters, even in West Pakistan. The old NAP was a leftist socialist party which had also stood for the re-establishment of the four provinces of West Pakistan. But in 1967, the conflict between regionalists and socialists had come to the fore and had finally led to a split in the party. In West Pakistan, following parliamentary elections in 1970 and 1971 the NAP secessionists had to acknowledge their lack of influence with the population although they continued to canvass for the autonomy of Baluchistan and the Pashtu North West Frontier until the party was banned in 1975.

Developments in East Pakistan took a different course. Here the leftist socialist wing of the NAP under Mujib al-Rahman (1922–75) had been converted into the Awami League in 1966. Al-Rahman, who had so far pleaded for a political compromise between Pakistan and India, was known as a radical socialist and Bengali nationalist who had been arrested several times for his views. Between 1966 and 1969, he managed to develop the Awami League into the leading political force of East Pakistan. The Bengali nationalists soon saw themselves at the vanguard of civil resistance to the dictatorship of Ayyub Khan who, in the face of growing Bengali hostility to the army in West Pakistan, was eventually forced to resign in favour of General Yahya Khan. The latter tried in vain to oppose Bengali nationalism through the restoration of the old system of the five provinces, which had come into force on 1 July 1970. The winners in the parliamentary elections of 1970 and 1971 were the Awami League by an absolute majority in East Pakistan and the PPP of the former foreign minister Bhutto in West Pakistan.

The PPP, which was vehemently opposed to giving up the centralized state system, now came forward as the main opponent of the Awami League, whose members were involved in the frequent massacres of Ayyub Khan's followers (from 15 March 1971), most of whom were Biharis.[5] Yahya Khan, who had been commander-in-chief of the troops in East Pakistan in 1962, tried to break the militant resistance of the Bengali nationalists with elite troops; but their cruel acts against the civilian population only aggravated the conflict. On 25 March 1971, two days after the proclamation of Free Bengal (Bangladesh), a real civil war began in which the government troops only gradually managed to regain power in the cities. After the grave disaster of the flood of 12 November 1970, in which about 300,000 people are estimated to have perished, the war and a cholera epidemic caused countless further casualties among the Bengali population. Several millions of Hindus fled to neighbouring West Bengal to escape the conflicts between the government troops and the secessionists. In July and August, there were growing indications to the effect that India under Indira Gandhi would intervene in favour of the hard-pressed Bengali nationalists. After numerous skirmishes, Indian troops marched into East Pakistan on 22 November 1971 and forced back the Pakistani government troops, which, having failed to build up a second front in the west, had to surrender on 16 December 1971. Mujib al-Rahman proclaimed the independence of West Pakistan for the second time, which was now guaranteed by India. After the withdrawal of the Indian troops, the sovereignty of Bangladesh was officially proclaimed on 26 March 1972.

The New Reconstruction of the Islamic Public

The defeat of Pakistan's army forced Yahya Khan to resign on 20 December 1971 in favour of Bhutto, who cleverly managed to use the failure of pan-Pakistani nationalism to create a new state ideology in which the Islamic public would play a prominent part. The Islamic Advisory Council (later called Advisory Council of Islamic Ideology – Islam Nazariyat Kaunsil)[6] was now able to present the fruits of many years of work, which had up to this point attracted little attention among the Pakistani public. Pakistan's civil law was largely adapted to the Islamic discourse and some aspects of the law were readjusted. The new constitution of 1973 strengthened the authority of the council, which, by Islamizing the 'colonial' sector's social code, tried to prevent the 'traditional' urban sectors from breaking away from the control of the state. By contrast to the situation in Libya, for example, members of the *ulama* in Pakistan supported the state's policy of reintegration by contributing to the creation of new institutions for the Islamic public. Bhutto's policy of social and cultural reintegration thus aimed, on the one hand, at recruiting the urban nationalists by underscoring the socialist component of Pakistan's national culture, and on the other hand at addressing the mixed areas, whose loyalty was to be secured by a predominantly Islamic discourse. This strategy preserved the dual structure of the political public, with its 'European' and 'Islamic' discourse. The state would continue to exercise sovereignty over the Islamic ideologies, but with the *ulama* acting as mediators. By contrast, in Libya Qaddafi insisted on being personally acknowledged as the authority on Islam.

The first achievements in the reconstruction of the Islamic public took place before the political crisis of the years 1973–74. Signs of a political emancipation in the mixed areas emerged most clearly in those Islamic countries in which Third World republicanism had established a state-oriented ideology of social development. In the royalist areas – with the exception of the special cases of Afghanistan and Iran – the Islamically legitimized monarchies seemed to be more successful at integrating the mixed areas into their national culture, and there were few signs of the establishment of an Islamic public that did not depend on the state. In these countries, the opposition was still committed to republicanism, although it increasingly adopted ideological elements of liberation socialism.

The death of the Egyptian President Nasser on 28 September 1970 marked the end of personal ties of loyalty for many officials of the Arab Socialist Union. As early as 1971, a growing competition for power began within the party organization which greatly affected the different realms of social order. Leftist socialist groups tried to stand their ground against the more dominant national conservative currents around the new head of state Anwar al-Sadat (1918–81). Al-Sadat, whose political career had begun within the milieu of the Muslim Brotherhood, had already been represented as the 'Islamic conscience' of the Nasserists. On 15 May 1971, he managed to eliminate the left-socialist wing of the Arab Socialist Union while the Soviet Union's support for India during the war for East Pakistan allowed him to gradually sever his political ties with that country. Party members who were committed to him, such as the long-time governor of Asyut, Muhammad Uthman Isma'il, mobilized Islamic groups to take action against the leftist socialist opposition and thus helped small Islamic groups like the al-Jama'a al-Islamiya ('Islamic Community') to gain public recognition. However, independent Islamic groups, especially among the Cairo students, were persecuted by the state as 'reactionary organizations'.

The Islamic student movement in Egypt, which emerged as a result of a profound conflict over the curriculum and conditions prevailing at the universities, and which from December 1972 gained influence outside Azhar University, formed one pillar of the new definition of the Islamic public. A second, no less important pillar, consisted of secessionist tendencies which had their main stronghold in the provinces of Minya and Asyut. The collapse of Egyptian national culture in 1970–72 thus created a space for regional and social secession. In the new suburban quarters of Cairo, which the urban nationalists had designed and built up with great enthusiasm, the members of the Islamic student movement found the social conditions which would broaden the Islamic political public. In these overpopulated areas there was now a greater lack than ever of those institutions which marked an urban culture. Although the inhabitants lived in modern concrete apartments, electricity and water supplies were poor. There were few shops, traffic facilities or recreational centres and the state had no presence. As had been the case during the world economic crisis of 1928–32, the newcomers faced a cultural situation in which they could neither live within their traditional context nor with the achievements of modernism. The absence of history and tradition called for a new fundamental motive for existence in these suburban ghettos. The absence of the state as an authority providing subsistence and protection left a great chasm to which the Islamic university avant-gardes were able to lend expression. They lent a meaning to the social separation from colonial society by symbolically comparing the latter with the pre-Islamic period of ignorance (*jahiliya*). Even the fact that these new citizens had broken away from the traditional structure of their origins was given an Islamic interpretation as the true and necessary abandonment of a false Islam.

The Islamic student movement was rarely strong enough to mobilize entire districts. Far more important was the spread of a new Islamic feeling of life and a corresponding Islamic code which would declare the experience of these new citizens a social norm and render code switching superfluous. This was precisely what the nationalists had been unable to achieve, for their ideologies of political development were always aimed at a steadily growing integration of the population within a national culture, a goal they lacked the economic means to achieve.

The mobilizing force of the Islamic student movement was nevertheless capable of forming Islamic political groups which could act as an avant-garde in areas supporting direct action against the centres of political power. An influence that should not be underestimated in this context was that of the Islamic Liberation Party of Taqi al-Din al-Nabhani, which had meanwhile grown on a supra-regional level, and whose isolationist programme was particularly attractive to students, because it assigned an extraordinary role to scientific and technical intelligence within the context of Islamic policy.

Transnational Complexities

A further impulse towards the reconstruction of the Islamic public came from Saudi Arabia. In the early 1970s, members of the mixed areas had begun to migrate to Saudi Arabia and to the Gulf States, which had become independent in the years 1971 and 1972. In 1970 more than 225,000 migrant workers went from Yemen to Saudi Arabia, from Syria 40,000, from Jordan/Palestine 50,000 and from Lebanon 30,000. In the same year, 345,000 foreign labourers benefited from the expanding market in Saudi Arabia. Another 121,000 lived in Kuwait and about 80,000, most of them Egyptians, in Libya. By 1975, the total number of foreign Arab workers in the oil exporting countries had grown to 1.295 million.[7] The repercussions in the migrants' homelands were considerable. Money transfers, which rose from 104.2 million US dollars (1972) to 2.695 billion US dollars (1980), provided the families of the migrants with a new prestige and new consumer possibilities, allowing them to buy at least some of the consumer goods of the colonial sector and to gradually furnish their homes with the goods of the modern consumer society.[8] Furthermore, the flows of money were followed by social and cultural assets which were marked by the Islamic national cultures prevailing in the oil regions. Many of the migrants saw these modest new riches as God's reward for a pious life and their newly strengthened pietistic attitude was in its turn assimilated by the societies of the mixed areas. However, since the money allowed a certain upward mobility into the consumer society, it also enhanced the integrationist political trend in the Islamic public, so that there emerged an increasingly clear division between radical isolationists and moderate integrationists.

The latter were further encouraged by transnational Islamic institutions. From 1972 the Muslim World League of Mecca believed that its main task was to place the Islamic public, which was nationally and regionally disunited and marked by specific national cultures, into a transnational relationship which would lead to an extensive harmonization and assimilation of the corresponding political and ideological statements. The coordination of the numerous integrationist Islamic groups, who often acted very informally, was achieved by available institutions of social welfare (mosques). These institutions at the same time provided missing social and cultural services in the mixed areas, especially in the realm of education.

The League was also able to gain new allies on a formal level. In the summer of 1973, its secretary concluded an extensive treaty of cooperation with the rector of the Azhar University, Abd al-Halim Mahmud (1910–78), thus liberating the university from the narrow constraints of Nasserist national culture.[9] In addition, the increased number of Muslim students and migrant workers in Europe were provided with a supra-regional representation of interests through the foundation of an Islamic Council of Europe which was used by the League as a vehicle of direct influence. In late 1972, even the *ulama* of Riyadh, who were much more committed to the Wahhabi tradition, tried to gain a foothold in the transnational Islamic public by convening a World Youth Conference.

State Reactions, the October War and the Oil Boom

The transnational complexity of the Islamic public contributed to the fact that only a small proportion of the many Islamic groups committed to the neo-Salafiya remained independent and were able to give fresh incentive to social and regional secessionism. Also preventive measures by the nation states soon curtailed the nascent achievements of the newly developing Islamic public. The Egyptian government under Sadat, which spared no effort to counteract the threat of losing its sovereign national culture, at first re-activated its old plan to form an Arab confederation, in which this time Syria, Libya and the Sudan were to participate (17 April 1971).[10] Syria had just escaped its self-inflicted isolation after the coup of Hafiz al-Asad on 13 November 1970. In February, Asad was appointed as the first Alawi president of Syria. To begin with, he aimed at an international rehabilitation of the Syrian Baʿth regime, which had been branded as leftist, by sidetracking the advocates of 'socialist transformation' around the former chief of staff Salah Jadid and the civilian apparatus of the party.

Qaddafi, however, tried to use Sadat's internal balancing act by accentuating the idea of unity, and insisted on a political union between Egypt and Libya. When Libyan demonstrators tried to destroy the Libyan–Egyptian border constructions on 18 July 1973, the Egyptian army intervened and thus prevented the project of federation from being carried out.

As a second step, Sadat tried to assume the leading role in the Palestine question. In a surprise attack on 6 October 1973, 70,000 Egyptian soldiers crossed the Suez Canal. At the same time, a Syrian army of 40,000 men advanced on the Golan Heights. While the Egyptians managed to occupy a 5 to 15 kilometre wide strip on the east bank of the canal, the Syrian units gradually had to give way. Israeli troops thereupon advanced to within 40 km of Damascus. The Soviet Union's logistical aid to Egypt and Syria on the one hand, and that of the USA to Israel on the other, soon led to a military pact confirmed by the armistice of 26 October 1973.

The October war was waged from all sides as a 'limited war'. Although the Israeli air force bombed targets in Damascus, operations were on the whole reduced to the attempt to secure individual military positions. Similarly, Sadat's rhetorical slogan, that Egypt aimed to reconquer the entire Sinai peninsula, was not meant seriously. Besides, the military aid of the other Arab states remained very limited. Although Jordan did send troops to the Golan Heights, it opened no third front in the Jordan valley. Equally cautious were the actions of the Palestinian guerillas in south Lebanon. The great powers, the USA and the USSR used the conflict for a large-scale show of force. On 25 October, American armed forces all over the world were alerted after intelligence services discovered that similar steps had been taken by the USSR.

When the members of OAPEC (Organization of Arab Petroleum Exporting Countries) Abu Dhabi, Iran, Iraq, Kuwait, Qatar and Saudi Arabia announced a rise in crude oil prices on 16 October 1973, and shortly afterwards stopped supplying oil to the USA and Holland because of their support of Israel, it became clear that the political conflicts within the framework of the fourth Arab–Israeli war were directly related to global economic developments triggered by the upheaval on the energy market. The OPEC states had already, on 14 February 1971, managed to enforce a 21 per cent price rise, mainly through Libyan pressure. They thus made up for the competitive advantage which Saudi Arabia had briefly enjoyed through its unilaterally negotiated 20 per cent rise in prices with ARAMCO. The price of a barrel of Arabian Light rose as follows:[11]

Increase in the Price of Arab Oil 1970–1980

Date	$ per barrel	Saudi Arabia	
1. 1. 1970	1.42	1970	1,214 mil. $
1. 1. 1971	1.42	1971	1,885 mil. $
1. 1. 1972	1.45	1972	2,745 mil. $
1. 1. 1973	1.83		
16.10.1973	4.89	1973	4,340 mil. $
1. 1. 1974	9.31	1974	22,574 mil. $
1. 1. 1975	11.00		
1.12.1977	12.75	1977	36,900 mil. $
1.12.1978	12.06		
1. 7. 1979	14.16		
1. 1. 1980	26.83	1980	84,466 mil. $
1. 4. 1980	31.28 (average price)		
1. 1. 1981	31.50	1981	101,813 mil. $
1. 1. 1982	30.00 (standard price)		

Since the demand for crude oil had risen considerably with the economic boom in the industrial countries, the latter tried to counteract the pressure of OPEC by their own means. An example was the International Energy Agency founded in November 1974, which aimed at the development of new oil fields outside the OPEC hegemony and for the exploitation of atomic energy. The large oil concerns nevertheless benefited from the rise in prices, since they earned an average of 20 per cent of the profits. The rise in oil prices accelerated the restructuring processes within Islamic society. The corresponding rise in the migration of foreign workers to the Arab world from countries like Pakistan and later the Philippines brought with it a rise in the sum of foreign transfers, which in turn had its repercussions on national markets. The entire communication system in the Islamic world, consisting of a complex of migrations, media and capital transfers, was more and more directed towards the Arab Gulf countries. Libya became a second focal point in this system, while Iran played no decisive part in it despite the profits that accrued to it through the movement of oil prices.

The Policy of Economic Opening

On 8 April 1974, the Egyptian President Sadat announced the leading principles of an economic and political opening (*infitah*) of the country in an 'October paper'.[12] This officially rescinded the principles of the planned state economy which had been the core of Nasser's policy after 1962. Among the reasons for this about turn among the ruling elite of the Arab Socialist Union were the demands of landlords to recover lands which had been expropriated after 1962. This marked the first sign of life after years from the politically excluded agrarian sector. Encouraged by the changing conditions on the global financial markets as a result of the rise in oil prices, they called for private capital in order to render their economic concern competitive again. After all, the cotton crop, which still amounted to 60 per cent of the value of Egyptian exports, had been pledged to the USSR, which, together with other countries of the Eastern Bloc, had guaranteed credits amounting to 1.2 billion US dollars for development projects. Egypt's financial dependence on the USSR had grown through military aid amounting to almost 3 billion US dollars.[13] The threatened loss of internal sovereignty was even more closely connected with the condition of Egypt's public budget. To escape this danger and to receive a share of the new capital from oil production was one of the aims of the 'opening'.

The political change was slow to begin with. Only a few families benefited from the return of their land. These, however, were to provide the backbone of a revived Wafd Party. Through its name, this party tried to continue the tradition of the old Wafd, which had emerged in 1919 from the alliance of the nationalist delegation (Arabic Wafd) at the peace conferences of Versailles and Paris. After the legalization of political parties in 1977, the new Wafd became the forum of national conservative policy in Egypt. Since the legal framework for the direct investment of Western as well as Saudi capital was now improved, there soon arose an independent economic and financial sector opposing the government's state capitalist directives.

The more capital that flowed into the country in different ways, the greater the rift between the new wealth and the old poverty. Some 40 per cent of all Egyptian households were living below the (Egyptian) poverty line around

1975. On the one hand, bourgeois society was emancipating itself from the power of the state and seeking political forms of expression for its autonomy, which included the opening of the press to opposition opinion. On the other hand, there was growing hope among the inhabitants of the mixed areas that they might obtain a share of the colonial society's consumer goods through migration. To be sure, the number of those who were economically and socially excluded from both migration and the home market, and who remained dependent on subsidized prices for food and cheap lodging, which they were guaranteed during the Nasserist period, was considerable.

The *infitah* policy was a logical result of the state's withdrawal from the sectors of the mixed areas, which were not profitable and were at the same time expensive to maintain. It was thoroughly Western in orientation and aimed at an extensive rehabilitation of the state in the eyes of the West. The policy offered bourgeois society new perspectives, enabling it, once more, to assume its place in the international arena, and to renew its commercial and cultural relations with the West, though in so doing it distanced itself more and more from its 'own' society. In this framework the state no longer acted as an authority that guaranteed a balance of interests, but instead promoted the internationalization of bourgeois society.

Egypt's *infitah* policy, which to a crucial extent depended on the conditions set by the World Bank and the International Monetary Fund, was adopted in the following years by other Arab and Islamic states as a model of development (among others by Tunisia, Algeria, Sudan and Syria); thus Egypt remained true to its claim to be the avant-garde of Arab policy.

To counteract the threatened secession of entire sectors of society and geographical regions, the policy of openness demanded a new strategy of social and cultural integration. This was provided in the first instance by the growing willingness of the members of the mixed areas to adapt to the new values which had flowed into their country along with capital, and which were conveyed in an Islamic discourse. These values (domesticity, economy, a renunciation of alcohol, gambling and extravagant clothes, an openly demonstrated piety, and voluntary activities of all kinds) were of a predominantly ascetic nature and had little in common with the hedonism of bourgeois society. Ascetic models of life in the reproductive realm soon became an expression of a new social standard and state policy found itself forced to gradually integrate these values into the national culture. The law 'for the protection of values from dishonour' and for the appointment of a tribunal to protect values, which was proclaimed on 15 May 1980, represented the first step in this development. Since the scale of values was strongly influenced by the Saudi-dominated Islamic public, the Islamic discourse now became dependent on norms propagated by Saudi Arabia. This was also true of the institutional realm.

The Egyptian *ulama* could hardly avoid the hegemony of the Saudi Islamic public and often had to follow the rules established by the institutions in Saudi Arabia. The Academy of Islamic Studies in Cairo, for instance, which had just tried to emancipate itself from the sovereignty of the state, was forced to cooperate more closely with the Muslim World League in Mecca.

Islamic Avant-Gardes in Egypt

Yet radical isolationist Islamic groups were unable to mobilize the population which lived beyond the gulf dividing them from the rich, perhaps, among other things, because the increased capital flow was raising new hopes of participation in the consumer goods of the colonial sector. The isolationist groups suddenly saw themselves forced to act in order to emphasize their claim to be the avant-garde of the 'Islamic movement'. The Muslim Brotherhood no longer offered them a political forum, for once the Muslim Brothers were set free from the internment camps in 1971, the organization's political leadership, which was still banned at the time, accentuated its integrationist course. In April 1974, a year after the death of their leader al-Hudaibi, they published a declaration calling on the Muslim Brothers to support Sadat's *infitah* policy and to side with the state to fight the isolationists.[14]

One of the Muslim Brothers freed in 1971 was the student leader Ahmad Shukri Mustafa (1942–77), who came from the Asyut province. Around 1973 he was co-founder of the Association of Muslims (Jama'at al-Muslimin). In the student quarter of Asyut, al-Hamra, he propagated the departure from 'false society', the formation of 'Islamic cells' in the shape of rather large housing communities, and the establishment of an Islamic code to serve as a sign of belonging to Islam. This group soon became the most important student union in Egypt and in 1976 was even able to surpass the Egyptian student congress.

A different path was chosen by the members and sympathizers of the Islamic Liberation Party, who rallied around the activist Salih Abdallah Sirriya (1933–74) from Haifa. Sirriya had come to Cairo via Jordan and Iraq (1972–73) and there tried to create a platform of his own in the wrangle over the succession to the party founder al-Nabhani, who died in 1973. His insurgent policy had drawn the attention of certain members of the Heliopolis Military Academy in Cairo. But on 18 April 1974, the attempt by conspirators to murder Sadat during a visit to the Academy failed amidst the hail of bullets from the presidential guard.[15]

Although the action of the Sirriya group was considered by most Islamic groups to be sectarian and amateurish, to the public it was a symbolic uprising of the Islamic avant-gardes. As long as these groups focused their activity mainly on the leftist socialist opposition, which had once again demonstrated against the *infitah* policy in January 1975, they went unmolested by the authorities, since they also contributed to liberating the student body from the framework of Nasserist and communist policy. After 1976, however, there was a complete change in the orientation of both the Islamic community and the Islamic avant-gardes. Ahmad Shukri, who adopted a very populist interpretation of the ideas of Sayyid Qutb, challenged the state, as well as the integrationist Muslim Brothers, with his watchword, the fight against 'apostasy', by which he meant both the state perceived as the new 'pharaoh', and the Muslim Brothers who cooperated with the 'pharaoh'.

On 18 and 19 January 1977, countless inhabitants of the mixed areas in Cairo rebelled against rises in the price of subsidized food and consumer goods. The city poor attacked shops and hotels, barricaded themselves in their quarters and fought violent street battles against the police and the army, in which many lost their lives. Although the Islamic avant-garde had no influence on the rebellion, the government held them, together with the 'communists', responsible for the unrest and reacted with severe measures of repression. Shukri saw this merely as a confirmation that the state had fallen into the hands of 'pharaoh'. On 3 July 1977, the Jama'at al-Muslimin kidnapped the former minister for charitable endowments and Azhar scholar Muhammad al-Dahabi. In a communiqué, the kidnappers demanded the liberation of political prisoners and an amnesty, the payment of 200,000 Egyptian pounds and the publication of a declaration in the Arab and European media. When the Egyptian government refused to carry out these demands, al-Dahabi was shot dead on 7 July.

2. ETHNICITY AND THE COMPLETION OF ISLAMIC IDEOLOGIES

The new definition of national cultures in the Islamic world, which became necessary with the collapse of Third World Republicanism, made it possible to re-establish the Islamic public, but at the same time provoked secessionist tendencies on various levels. In each of the Islamic countries, the character of this secession depended on specific historical conditions marked by its national culture. The following are examples of the principal types of secession:

1. The secession of East Pakistan as Bangladesh combined leftist socialist ideologies with nationalist programmes.
2. The secession of Islamic groups in Egypt was marked by the extreme conditions of the infitah policy and was subject to social and/or regional factors.
3. The secession of the Palestinians at first in Jordan, and from 1973 in Lebanon, which fell within ethnic fields of conflict.
4. Ethnic secession increasingly marked the activities of the numerous

liberation movements.

Since the nation state had so far not really been called into question by any secessionist tendency, the issue of who should exercise sovereignty in it was always the focal point of political mobilization. It was by acquiring political power in the nation state that the specific interests of the secessionists found an executive organ. Since the international arms market enabled virtually every party to acquire arms, secessionism was nearly always tantamount to threatening the power monopoly of the state.

In all regional movements, ethnic views of life, often mythologically conceived, have played a crucial part. They were for the most part directed against a dominant society whose culture was Islamic, so that Islam had no specific mobilizing function, unless the regionalist movement denounced the majority society as un-Islamic. It was, of course, a different matter with movements directed against non-Islamic majority societies. Here the Islamic culture often served as a sign of one's own ethnicity even more highly rated than language (for instance on Mindanao in southern Philippines or in southern Thailand).

The reasons for the progressive politicization of ethnic characteristics in the 1970s were, of course, different in each specific case. There was, nevertheless, a growing tendency among societies to identify themselves exclusively by means of characteristics that had so far played no part in the definition of national cultures and had normally produced no more than a vague regional consciousness. Now, however, there was a decisive change in the socio-psychological reference. Instead of class, society or state, which had represented the main characteristics of classical national cultures, the references in the political world became group, community and myth. There have been many arguments over whether these new references of political identity are of a primordial nature or whether they represent a new form of political instrumentalization.[16] It is true that regional movements had previously politicized non-political commonplace judgments about other cultures and reinforced traditional images of the enemy; but the relatively simultaneous emergence of 'ethno-politics' leads to the assumption that this already announced the end of classical national cultures based on the utopia of progress. Thus regional movements contrasted sharply with the neo-Salafiya Islamic movements which, precisely because their ideologies were keyed into written culture, wanted to adhere to their nation state identity. For the initiators of transnationally, or even universally oriented Islamic ideologies, these regional movements must have been an abomination, for their basic argument clearly revealed mythological features and thus attributed a secondary place to Islamic modernism. When in 1975, Mohammad Reza Shah Pahlavi celebrated the 2500-year-old existence of the Persian empire in an ostentatious ceremony among the ruins of Persepolis, when he sat down on the Peacock Throne and abjured the old tradition of sovereignty based on the Safavid dynasty (1501–1732), the mythical argument also cropped up in a national culture and provoked the protest of the *ulama.* The minimal consensus of Iranian national culture, which was based on a Safavid symbolism of sovereignty and culture, was suddenly deeply disrupted. In the end, some members of the Islamic avant-garde also availed themselves of a mythological argument – albeit with a negative reference – when like Qutb after 1974, they denounced the Egyptian state as a 'pharaoh'.

Yet the Islamic public could not ignore the fact that after 1973 the political opposition increasingly represented ethnic elements, and that in some cases, Islamic culture was explicitly used as an ethnic characteristic. Implicitly, this attribution had already existed. Thus the Ba'th may without doubt be thought of as the political expression of an Alawi (Syrian) or early Shi'i, and later a regionalist Sunni (Iraq) ethnicity. But 'European' discourses were by far more predominant than Islamic presentations of ethnicity, .

Principle Ethnic Groups in the Islamic World (circa 1980)[17]

Arab	140,693,000	Somali	7,564,000
Bengali	137,603,000	Hui	7,543,000
Punjabi	57,221,000	Oromo	6,984,000
Javanese	52,715,000	Tatar	6, 980,000
—— 46.4% ——		Tajik	6,708,000
Urdu	48,878,000	Nilotic	5,610,000
West Turkic	38,134,000	Baluchi	4,339,000
Persian	24,697,000	Lur	3,690,000
Sudanese	24,414,000	Sudanese	3,070,000
Hausa	20, 151,000	Nubian	1,870,000
—— 64.8% ——		Cushitic	940,000
Malay	16,814,000	Brahui	740,000
Azeri	15,060,000	Dardic	670,000
Fulani	14,885,000	Tcherkess	235,000
Uzbek	14,828,000	Lazic	80,000
Pathan	14,701,000	Pamiric	30,000
Kurdic	13,000,000	Total	740,686,000
Berber	11,700,000	—— 88.5% ——	
Sindhi	10,688,000	Others	96,524,000
Madurese	10,346,000	—— 100% ——	
Yoruba	8,885,000	Total	837,210,000
Kazakh	8,220,000		

Ethnicity and Liberation Movements in the Islamic World

The oil-producing states of the Islamic world were at the centre of the crisis of the years 1973–74. From here the processes of economic upheaval spread out in waves and, depending on economic and social conditions in individual countries, adapted themselves to and even began to dominate each country's history. Since these revolutionary processes were directly connected with the Islamic state culture of the Gulf States, in particular that of Saudi Arabia, their effect was a far-reaching revalorization of the Islamic public, which finally redefined the geographical space of Islamic history. Of particular importance was also the fact that within the Islamic public additional weight was attributed to those societies that had so far been considered as 'lying at the periphery of the Islamic world'. This revalorization of peripheral Islamic societies as against the Arab, Persian or Turkish centre began to show as early as 1972 when the Malay prince and former prime minister Tunku Abd al-Rahman was elected secretary general of the Organization of the Islamic Conference (OIC). When his successor, the Egyptian diplomat Muhammad al-Tihami (1974–76), completed his term of office, another representative of the 'periphery' was elected to this post, namely the Senegalese Ahmadu Karim Gaye (1976–78).

Another consequence of the processes of economic and cultural integration during the period of oil prosperity was the foundation of the Islamic Development Bank by the member countries of the OIC in 1973–74.[18] At its second summit conference in Kuala Lumpur (11 December 1973–9 January 1974), the OIC had, in addition, devoted much attention to the growing economic importance of East and South-East Asia. Through a special fund created by the representatives of the Fifth Islamic Conference of Foreign Ministers (June 1974) at Kuala Lumpur, the Muslim minorities were to be granted a share in the new oil prosperity.[19] At this point only the Islamic states directly interfered with the concerns of the periphery. Thus, from 1972 and 1977, the OIC was the only mediator in the conflict between the Philippine central government and the Muslim rebels on Mindanao and the Sulu Archipelago.

The following regional movements established themselves in the early 1970s as liberation fronts operating with relative success in the Islamic world:

1. The Moro National Liberation Front, MNLF.[20] The MNLF was formed on 21 September 1972 by rebel units which began operations in 1968, when President Marcos of the Philippines imposed martial law on the southern provinces. Through the creation of a new Moro nationalism, the ethnic borders between Muslim groups (especially from Maranao, Samal and Tausug) were to be eliminated and the latter were to be brought together to form a 'Bangsa Moro', a Moro nation. The earlier conflict between Muslim ethnic groups and the Christian central government flared up again in 1970, when Marcos

encouraged Christian Filipinos to occupy large estates in the Cotabato region.

2. The Pattani United Liberation Organization (PULO) in Thailand. Established on 22 January 1968,[21] the PULO primarily represented the interests of a section of the approximately 2 million Malay–Thai Muslims in the southern provinces of Pattani, Narathiwat, Yala and Satul. The Muslim separatists also relied upon the traditional social strata which clearly distinguished between the urban cultures of the 'reformists' (*khana mai*) and the sultanically oriented 'traditionalists' (*khana kau*). A third factor which came to the fore in 1974 within the framework of the new Islamic public was the Dakwah movement, which had a neo-Salafi orientation.
3. The National Liberation Front FROLINAT in northern Chad. Formed as early as 1966, after 1972/73, the Front splintered into a multitude of rival groups when the Libyan revolutionary leader Qaddafi tried to enforce his own political interests by mobilizing the Islamic identity of the Tebu[22] and Arabs against the predominantly Christian central government under N'garta (François) Tombalbaye (1918–75). The jurist Hissene (Husain) Habré, who had joined FROLINAT in 1971, rejected any identification of the Liberation Front with the concerns of the Tebu and founded a militia of his own under the name Forces Armées du Nord (FAN); the son of the spiritual leader (*derdai*) of the Teda, Goukouni Weddei (Gukuni Wadday), who closely followed Libya, reacted by forming the Forces Armées Populaires (FAP). FROLINAT was unable to overcome the clan structure governing the Tebu societies; as a countermove, however, it contributed to politicize the clans, and after 1975 it achieved the overall political sovereignty of the confederation of clans and was supported by various militias. In this situation, every attempt to restore the sovereignty of the central government with the aid of France ran aground.

The MNLF and PULO obtained observer status with the OIC in 1972 and 1976 respectively, demonstrating the willingness of the liberation movements to renounce their traditional leftist-socialist political programme in favour of an emphasis on their Islamic identity which joined them to the international public. Almost all liberation movements in the Islamic world underwent this change of direction between 1973 and 1978, thereby announcing the decline of the classical ideology of liberation socialism. The Islamic discourse emerged more and more distinctly as the true guarantor of the political survival of liberation movements in the Islamic world. Up to the mid-1970s, all liberation movements had adopted a socialist programme, often showing a close ideological affinity with Central and South American liberation movements which identified state power with compradores who supported world-wide imperialism. This ideological argument had now given way to a rather more defensive world view with a reference to Islam.

The Western Saharan POLISARIO can only indirectly be linked with this field. The Frente Popular para la Liberación de Saguía el Hamra y Río de Oro, POLISARIO Front, founded in 1973, grouped together different traditional resistance groups of the Berber Ruqaibat ('Movement of Blue Men') and the Hassaniya nomads, who had fought against the colonial powers of Spain and France (Mauretania) in 1957/58. The northern part of the country (Saguía el Hamra), which was rich in mineral resources, had for a long time been part of Morocco's sphere of interest, while the south (Rio de Oro) was claimed by Mauretania. In 1975, Spain and Morocco came to an agreement regarding the corresponding division of the country after the end of colonial rule (26 February 1976). The POLISARIO thereupon proclaimed an Arab republic, which was entirely committed to the ideals of classical liberation movements. Its orbit of power outside the large refugee camps in Algeria, in which the population of the Western Sahara had been accommodated, shrank continuously after the entry of Moroccan troops into the north of the country, although it was left a politically sovereign territory in Rio de Oro through a peace treaty with Mauretania (5 August 1979).

A Change of Perspective in the Political Domain

The early 1970s heralded a far-reaching change of perspective in the politics of the Islamic world. The nation state as a political ideal gradually receded into the background, although it continued to serve as a point of orientation. Other perspectives had now gained crucial importance. For one thing, there was a growing interest in an 'ethnic view' of politics, which might include smaller segments of society; and for another, the political public developed a sharper 'social eye' which paid great attention to the social secession within national cultures and also involved a 'gender perspective', insofar as, for the first time, it granted women an independent, albeit separate public life. The interpretation of social identity had thus broadened to a considerable extent. Hardly anyone was now prepared to explain his own social reality by using such concepts as 'Arab', 'Egyptian' or 'socialist', or to subscribe to views of the world in which these characteristics played a prominent part. As a result there was also a change in forms of political expression. A crucial function was hence attributed to Islam, which, being politically unburdened, could lend this new interpretation a powerful expression. In such countries as Lebanon or Israel, where the secession took place along traditional religious lines, Christian or Jewish identities could assume a similar function. This change of perspective went far beyond the classical change of paradigms which have so often determined the outlook of great ideologies. Nor was it phenomenon specific to the Islamic world; on the contrary, it reproduced a cultural process of a universal character, applying to countries like the USA or the USSR, as well as to Morocco or Afghanistan. However, while the change of perspective in the industrial countries almost exclusively took place within the framework of a civil society,[23] and thus only rarely assumed a militant character, many Islamic societies had been exposed to an extensive process of militarization mainly unleashed by the enormous import of arms. The political peculiarities of many countries in the Islamic world had fostered the import of arms, because countries like Iran, Turkey, Iraq or Saudi Arabia considered a strong army to be the most important means of preserving their power. Social and ethnic secessions legitimated this militarization, which in its turn intensified the secession, so that in the end the secessionists themselves operated outside a civilian identity. The extent of militarization after 1973 is illustrated by the following survey:

Arms Exports to Various Countries (millions of US dollars)[24]

Country	1972–1975	1980–1983	Military Expenditure 1972–75 & 1980–83[25]
Morocco	56	1,263	5,996
Algeria	167	3,480	7,991
Afghanistan	173	467	8,761
Pakistan	828	1,507	11,576
Syria	5,777	9,360	13,477
Libya	1,600	9,424	15,303
Turkey	848	1,404	17,929
Egypt	4,043	4,208	24,592
Israel	3,485	3,925	39,478
Iraq	3,307	12,673	54,264
Iran	4,907	3,284	57,806
Saudi Arabia	1,221	9,492	94,316
Others	1,629	9,204	34,389
TOTAL	28,041	69,691	385,878

The highest rates of increase in military expenditure, which are not recorded above, are those of the smaller Gulf States. Between 1972 and 1983, they rose by more than 7,100 per cent in the United Arab Emirates and about 653 per cent in Qatar – figures that point to an undreamt of level of armament in the Gulf States, which in these years accounted for more than 65 per cent of overall military expenditure in the countries of the Near and Middle East. The armament of the old conflicting parties Israel, Egypt and Syria, on the other hand, remained on a comparatively steady, albeit higher than average level.

Not to be underestimated are the informal arms imports into the countries of the Islamic world, which contributed to the arming of the secessionist movements. Since most arms imports were made by countries which disposed of foreign exchange reserves from oil production, huge amounts of capital flowed back into the industrial countries, so that the arms market performed an important function in balancing the world economy. Oil and arms were two products of the world economy which were in many respects connected with one another, and which also played a role in shaping political trends. The oil price boom of the years 1973 and 1974 was directly followed by an arms boom. Iran's military expenditure, for example, rose by 141 per cent in 1974, and more than 30 per cent of its hastily revised Five-Year-Plan (1973–77) was earmarked for military purposes.

Although in most countries of the Islamic world arms expenditure usually amounted to only 3–5 per cent of the gross national product – exceptions were Saudi Arabia with 13.5 per cent, Israel with 12.6 per cent, Egypt with 8.9 per cent, Syria with 8.8 per cent and Libya with 8.3 per cent – the impact on the political disposition of society was momentous, for there was no democratic control of military affairs. The appropriation of military power by secessionist social or ethnic groups was directly promoted through intensive armament, since any civilian control of authoritarian regimes was hardly possible.

The War in Lebanon

After 1958, the year of the abortive coup against the supremacy of the Christian-Maronite families, the demographic ratio between Christians, Druzes and Muslims in Lebanon had continued to change to the disadvantage of the Christians. The leading position of the Maronites in Lebanese politics, which was based on the demographic proportions of the major religious communities agreed upon in 1943, and which had made Lebanon into a confessional state, had become an anachronism from the point of view of the Muslims and Druzes. With the immigration of Palestinians in 1967/68 and above all in 1970/71, and with the formation of armed Palestinian units, the demographic proportions upon which the pact was based had definitely disappeared.

While in 1969 it had once again been possible to preserve the country's status as a nation state through a safety net guaranteed by Egypt, in May 1973 the predominantly Christian Lebanese army was no longer a match for the PLO in small skirmishes; Maronite parties, especially the Kata'ib, now built up private armies to 'protect the country against the loss of its sovereignty'. The usurpation of armed power by the political parties had already considerably weakened the authority of the state. The conflict escalated when on 14 April 1975 Maronite units attacked a PLO bus in Ain al-Rummama, a working-class suburb of Beirut, after two bodyguards of the president and founder of the Kata'ib, Pierre Jumayyil (1905–84), were murdered by unknown people. In the first phase of the war that followed, the main confrontation was between Palestinian and Maronite units. The Palestinian fighters were soon supported by leftist nationalist and Druze parties under the leadership of Kamal Junblatt (ca. 1917–77), who also saw the PLO as a means to overcome confessionalism. The Christian party around the nationalist conservative President Suleiman Franjiyeh tried to achieve peace by introducing an extensive constitutional reform, but this was prevented by a coup by the predominantly Maronite army and units of the Kata'ib, who also enforced the dismissal of Franjiyeh and his replacement by Ilyas Sarkis. The Kata'ib, which was commanded by Bashir Jumayyil, the son of Pierre Jumayyil, occupied Beirut on 12 May 1976 and, among other things, laid siege to the Palestinian camp of Tell al-Za'tar, which was destroyed on 12 August. Thereupon the anti-Maronite coalition, presently joined by Syrian intervention troops, reacted with a counter-offensive and succeeded in breaking the military preponderance of the Christian parties.

During this first phase of the Lebanese war, the ethnic boundaries had already become evident; they corresponded in many respects with the boundaries of social strata, which granted the Maronite families a privileged position derived from their traditional supremacy over the mountainous regions (Mount Lebanon). The urban nationalists, who were now much more openly committed to leftist socialist principles, tried to demonstrate their lack of ethnic attachment; however, even Kamal Jumblatt's progress party – especially under his son Walid – essentially remained a Druzes organization. The PLO obviously thought of itself not as a Lebanese, but as a Palestinian party which claimed its own sovereignty in the country. The Christian partisans around the family of the great landowner Franjiyeh, who had their stronghold in northern Lebanon (Zgarta), for their own part considered the Syrian intervention as an effective instrument against the pretensions of the rival Maronite families.

There were two years of bitter fights between the predominantly Maronite volunteer forces (among others the Forces Libanaises and the Résistance Libanaise) and the remains of the Lebanese army on the one hand, and Palestinian units and Syrian intervention troops on the other. The result was a military stalemate brought about by Syria in 1977. When the Maronite units threatened to succumb, Syria rescued Maronite society by a change of fronts in a small enclave north of Beirut. Thus Lebanon was divided into a confederation of sovereign social and partially ethnic parties, although the economic unity of the country was not jeopardized and in the end the centralized financial system as well as parts of public administration survived the war unharmed.

Islam and the Restoration of the Nation State: Malaysia and the Sudan

The growing secessionist tendencies could not be countered with military force alone, because that would necessarily have led to a civil war in which hitherto non-politicized social and ethnic interests would have been mobilized. In Lebanon, the long years of institutionalized separation between religious creeds, and the attendant division of powers (the president had to be a Christian, the prime minister a Sunni Muslim, etc.), had led to the absence of any institution that was still interested in keeping up an interdenominational, and hence inter-ethnic national culture. The situation was different, however, in those states which still had institutions of national culture, and thus in some way continued to use a nationalist discourse. For them the new definition of national culture was almost necessarily concomitant with the development of military sovereignty. Since this new definition could no longer be brought into line with the discredited 'European' ideologies, the call for an Islamic interpretation of national culture became more and more audible. Supported by the growing influence of the Islamic public and the gradual process of institutionalizing Islamic propaganda through countries such as Saudi Arabia and Libya, neo-Salafi organizations demanded an Islamic change in politics with increasing frequency.

Islamic Policy in Malaysia

By 1975, the pressure of the Islamic public was felt everywhere. Malaysia's leading political party, the United Malay National Organization, resolved to adopt an emphatically Islamic form of expression to achieve the re-integration of Malay society after the bloody conflict between Muslim Malays and the Chinese minority between February and May 1969, and after the suppression of the communist guerillas of the Malay National Liberation Army. The prime minister Tun Abdarrazzak (1970–76) and his successor Datuk ibn Husain Onn (1976–81) pleaded for an extensive opening, especially towards Saudi Arabia, and supported the Dakwah movement of the neo-Salafiya, which was very active in Malaysia.[26] Tunku Abd al-Rahman, the former prime minister and later secretary-general of the Islamic Conference Organization, had created an Islamic welfare society which worked together with the older All Malay(si)a Muslim Missionary Society led by the founding member of the Muslim World League, Ibrahim b. Umar al-Saqqaf (Alsagoff). The party in power, the United Malay National Organization, also included a strong scholarly wing which cleverly managed to integrate the Islamic public within the European discourse of the nationalists.

In 1972 Datuk Asri, a leader of one of Malaysia's Islamic parties (Partai Islam sa-Malaysia, PAS), was admitted into the Malaysian federal government, which was led by a National Front (until 1977). In 1974 a Foundation for an Islamic Mission (Yayasan Dakwah Islamiah Malaysia) was organized at the federal level, acquiring a semi-official status under Prime Minister Onn. The nationalization of the Dakwah movement, which reached its climax under Prime Minister Datuk Seri Mahathir Mohamed (from 1981), was also directed against the Islamic parties which were emerging with increasing self-confidence (especially the neo-Salafi Angkatan Belia Islam Malaysia, ABIM) and often supported the PAS in the elections. The Dakwah was an independent expression of the reconstruction of the Islamic public in Malaysia. Yet there were also impulses from outside. The missionary work initiated by the Muslim World League in 1975 through a Supreme World Council for Mosques (founded 25 September 1975) also had the task of training emissaries who were to propagate an Islamic way of life in the 'peripheral' countries.[27] Members of this council included the controversial chief minister of Sabah, Tun Mustafa ibn Harun (until 1975), and his successor Abd al-Rahman Ya'qub.[28]

Political Particularism in the Sudan

Sudan was a special case, since here the traditionally powerful old clerical cultures had led to the emergence of Islamic parties which did not belong to the neo-Salafiya. For many years the most important was the Umma Party (Hizb al-Umma) of the Ansar movement, which was led by descendants of the Sudanese Mahdi Muhammad Ahmad. In March 1970, the Ansar[29] entrenched themselves around their then leader Hadi b. Abd al-Rahman al-Mahdi on the Nile island of Aba, with which the party was traditionally connected, and proclaimed an independent government. However, government troops rapidly reconquered the island, and al-Mahdi was killed. His nephew Sadiq b. Siddiq al-Mahdi was now acknowledged as the imam of the Ansar and tried to take underground action against Ja'far Numairi's government. Numairi had meanwhile come under the pressure of the communist party, which demanded a stronger socialist orientation. On 19 July 1971, the CP rebelled, but Numairi's government was reinstated a few days later with the energetic help of Libya. At the same time, the secessionist efforts of non-Muslim Sudanese ethnic groups in the southern part of the country became stronger.

Numairi realized that the integration of the urban Islamic public was the only possible way of building a bulwark against the ethnic secessionists, the national conservative clerical parties, and the leftist socialist groups who were particularly powerful in the army and in the trade unions. On 14 April 1973 a new constitution was enacted in which Islam was proclaimed as the state religion and Southern Sudan was granted internal autonomy. There were also minor concessions. The rector of the new Islamic university of Omdurman (since 1975), Kamil al-Baqir, was granted extensive powers within the political public. As a representative of the Sudanese neo-Salifiya, he sat in the Supreme World Council of Mosques of the Muslim World League, which thereby gained great influence in Sudanese politics. In July 1976 a coup by the traditional parties miscarried. But after pressure by Saudi Arabia and the USA, which had lifted the arms embargo against the Sudan in 1976, Numairi was finally prevailed upon to call a 'conciliatory conference'. The participants included representatives of the Sudanese neo-Salafiya around the jurist Hasan al-Turabi (born 1932), who was dean of the Faculty of Law of the University of Khartoum from 1964 and had for years held a leading position within the Muslim Brotherhood, and members of the Umma Party. This enabled the Islamic oppositionists of the Ansar, as well as the Muslim Brotherhood, to again appear in public. Al-Turabi and al-Mahdi were now able to return from their exile in London in August and October 1977 respectively.

Through the gradual admission of an Islamic discourse, Numairi succeeded in, above all, lending his regime a civilian character. He himself avoided appearing in an officer's uniform and liked to be seen in Islamic garb. In 1977, he also tried to improve relations with Egypt, among other things because he regarded Libya as a supporter of the abortive coup of July 1976 and thus wanted to secure the aid of Egypt – and consequently of the USA – as protective powers. The anti-Libyan attitude of his regime also attracted the Chadian rebel Hissene Habré, whose units were now operating from the Sudan against their rival Weddei who was supported by Libya.

New Fronts: the Conclusion of Peace between Egypt and Israel

In the winter of 1976/77, the first effects of the Egyptian infitah policy manifested themselves. Foreign capital could once more be invested in the country almost without hindrance, prospectors of the major oil concerns were busy concluding treaties covering all its oil deposits, and consumer and capital goods were pouring into the Egyptian market from the Western world. Egypt had meanwhile returned to a liberalized market economy. To the satisfaction of the state bureaucracy, however, the tertiary sector which consisted of the whole public administration, education and transport remained in its control. The parallel political opening that came with infitah had given a new shape to the party scene. Out of the Arab Socialist Union, independent political platforms had emerged, soon filling the classical party spectrum. The process of social secession, however, also showed its effects. When subsidies were stopped, more and more people were excluded from the consumer market whose goods were far too expensive for them. The state – following the prevailing financial principles of the World Bank and the International Monetary Fund – was to leave their provision more and more to the discretion of the market. On the 18 and 19 January 1977 the first great urban revolts in recent Egyptian history broke out. The final impetus for the rebellion was provided by drastic rises in the price of subsidized goods.

Such urban revolts were now almost periodically accompanying the political process in Egypt. There were also signs of a move towards social secession in the agrarian milieu. Since the peasant revolts of Kamshish in 1966, when landless peasants and tenants had turned against the Nasserist bureaucracy during the land reform, the countryside had been quite peaceful. But from 1975, when Egyptian peasants began migrating to the Gulf States and almost two million of them went into service in Iraq as farm hands and builders, money from the oil boom flowed into Egyptian villages. Those peasants who for social or economic reasons were unable to benefit from this affluence isolated themselves more and more from the state, which they held responsible for their inadequate maintenance. Tourism, which was now beginning to flourish, also had its effects, by re-directing goods to the centres of tourism in Upper Egypt and creating shortages in the places that were far away from the tourist routes.

Sadat tried to fight the disintegration of Egyptian society with a foreign policy initiative. Once more the Palestine problem served as a catalyst, and grave internal problems in Saudi Arabia also came to his aid. On 25 March 1975, the Saudi King Faisal was murdered by his nephew Faisal b. Musa'id, among other reasons to take revenge for the 1966 occupation of the television station in Riyadh, when a relative of the assassin had been killed by Saudi security forces.[30] Saudi Arabia, which had so far played a controlling role in the Palestine problem, was plunged into internal conflict after Faisal's death, since the balance of social and cultural forces he had so skilfully constructed in the country threatened to collapse. The Wahhabi *ulama* around Abd al-Aziz b. Abdallah Ibn Baz suddenly found an opportunity to win back lost ground and now pointedly propagated their pietistic views. The inefficient King Khalid was hardly capable of preserving the cultural and social balance which was so essential to the Saudi Arabian monarchy, and thus indirectly encouraged Wahhabi critics to confront the all too evident support of the national culture through the Hijaz. In Medina, the Islamic university was made into a stronghold of the Wahhabi opposition, at which even radical partisans of the neo-Salafiya, especially from European minority societies, were allowed to study. The opposition thus formed was to provoke one of the most critical phases of the history of the Saudi monarchy in November 1979.

The death of Faisal enabled Sadat to again seize for Egypt the leading role in the Palestinian problem, which he did in a very self-willed fashion. In the summer of 1977 he proclaimed that he would travel anywhere to serve the

Palestinian cause. By the autumn, contacts between Egypt and Israel, which had improved considerably since the January and September 1975 agreements of partial withdrawal had developed to a point where nothing stood in the way of Sadat's visiting Jerusalem. On 20 November 1977, he delivered his famous speech in the Israeli Knesset, without, apparently, having consulted the other Arab parties to the conflict. The ensuing peace talks at Camp David (August 1978 to March 1979) culminated in the Egyptian–Israeli peace treaty of 26 March 1979.[31]

The Egyptian president had used political rhetoric reflecting an Islamic, and what is more, an interdenominational religious humanism. This led to a decisive rehabilitation of the Islamic discourse among the political public. Although, in terms of content, Sadat's ideas could hardly have been shared by an Islamist, the president succeeded in winning over the authorities of the Azhar University. The peace process was analysed and endorsed from several positions according to Islamic maxims of law. The rector of the Azhar, Abd al-Halim Mahmud, also issued a declaration in which he approved the two draft treaties of Camp David and on 9 May 1979, after his death, it was approved by the committee of legal counsellors of Azhar.[32]

The peace diplomacy of Sadat and of the Israeli Prime Minister Menachim Begin was repudiated by most member states of the OIC at the Islamic Foreign Ministers' Conference at Fez (6–11 May 1979). Saudi Arabia tried to disparage the treaty as a 'Zionist manoeuvre' in which Sadat had acquiesced.[33] But despite this attitude, the kingdom was unable to preserve its hegemony in the Palestine question. Syria, Iraq, Algeria, Libya and South Yemen formed the nucleus of a new Arab rejectionist front in which the old split between republicans and royalists was revived.

Sadat's principal aim of mastering the internal political situation and reinforcing the authority of the state through a symbol of governmental power had been achieved. In 1978, the president had his policy ratified by referendum. At the same time, he emphasized his willingness to cooperate with the Islamic public and sought to get in touch with the great institutionalized and powerful mystical orders, which he wanted to use as a counterweight against the neo-Salafiya.

The Islamic Revolution in Iran

The newly Islamic political public was more than ever ideological. For most of the Islamic groups and parties, the heterogeneous Islamic discourse had matured into an ideological language in which current social and cultural problems could be expressed far more precisely than in the dated forms of political diction. The Islamic enthusiasm was based above all on a highly developed ideological perception of these problems and on the conviction that Islam, due to its modernity, was capable of replacing obsolete ideologies.

A characteristic of the newest Islamic policy to emerge was the ideological instrumentalization of Islam. Unlike the *ulama*, who thought of themselves as the custodians of theological, legal or mystical doctrines, Islamic intellectuals had developed Islam into a many-sided ideology in the strict sense. As an ideology, Islam no longer competed with other religions, especially Christianity and Judaism, but with secular views of the world. From their point of view, the answering of theological questions was merely Islam's secondary function. Islam was to be primarily a unitarian, compact system of explanations and norms for society (or the nation); hence it was to describe both the historical development of the human community (or nation) and the utopian aims of the historical development of mankind.

In the early 1970s, however, a change of perspective occurred. The conventional idea of Islam as an ideological language in which socialist or more generally republican traditions could be formulated within a specific context gave way to the idea that Islam itself was in a position to represent the perfection of all ideological thought. The claim to perfection was by no means unknown to Islamic theologians. They, too, interpreted Islam as the conclusive and latest revelation of the One God, in which all other monotheistic religions were merged and therefore dissolved. Islam, according to the *ulama*, was the perfect form of expression of human existence, because it represented the innate human nature as such. The rediscovery of this principle and its translation into ideological and political views of the world formed the essence of a process of change which reached its climax in the late 1970s. Thus the decline of classical ideologies was procalimed at a very early stage in the Islamic world.

From this point of view, Islam appeared as the perfection of all ideological thought. The Islamic avant-gardes did not deny the legitimacy of the old ideologies; on the contrary, they considered them as decisive for the non-Islamic world as the monotheistic religions. But since Islam contained the pivotal ideas of all Western ideologies and in addition the solutions to their inherent contradictions, which were due to their 'inadequacy', the different variants of these ideologies were contained in Islam, which would finally neutralize them. All ideologies would almost necessarily lead to Islam, so that Islam would become the final and definitive ideology.

The historico-philosophical interpretations corresponding to these views were based on the idea that, in a teleological sense, the world would end in a homogeneous condition in which humanity would be shown its intrinsic, innate meaning through the historical process. As a result, Islam was no longer bound to a particular class construed as a historical subject, but made humanity itself the historical subject of its own liberation. The Islamic public was, however, as already mentioned, divided over the question of whether the liberating authority should be the state or society.

The new interpretation of Islam, which was mainly supported by intellectuals, was thus to regard it as the universal ideological concept which could overcome all other ideologies and lend human existence a conclusive meaning. This interpretation came as a collective relief, because it once again made Islamic culture appear superior to Western ideologies, which it could criticize and surmount. The critique of the West was no longer defensive, but offensive. Islamic intellectuals considered the ideological struggle of the West as no more than a helpless attempt to prevent the failure of modernism with inadequate devices.

Among the Islamic public this change of perspective promoted the development of a specific Islamic political language, which was sometimes used in refined treatises on the philosophy of history, and sometimes in populist pamphlets serving both as a justification for the Islamic state and as a celebration of the Islamic revolution. This language acquired radical forms in intellectual discussions in Iran, where the gap between a military dictatorship disguised as an empire on the one hand, and bourgeois society on the other, had steadily deepened in the years after 1973. The *ulama* in Iran who, unlike those in most other Islamic countries, participated intensively in political discussions, managed to lend the ideological claim of perfection a (Shiʿi) theological foundation. A person who made a name for himself in this connection – aside from the already mentioned Mahmud Taliqani – was Ayatollah Murtaza Mutahhari (born 1919/20), who came from the Mashhad area and taught in Qum. In his work *Motives for Materialism*, Mutahhari discussed the theological foundation of a homogeneous Islamic ideology.[34] The propaganda of such men finally had its effect even on social groups who had not so far been politicized.

However, there were still two competing political trends in Iranian society. On the one hand stood the old political patterns of conduct which had marked the upheavals of 1953 and 1963 and which reappeared in forms of social interaction by the urban nationalists who were always trying to establish a 'National Front' as a centre of opposition. On the other hand, the Islamic discourse had now, after the far-reaching upheavals of the early 1970s, thoroughly emancipated itself from the advocates of a National Front and established its own political public, which was to surmount the ideological ideas of the old generation.

Social secession had acquired much greater dimensions in Iran than it had in other Islamic countries. The unsuccessful land reform had intensified the urbanization of Iranian society. It is true that industrialization had economically and socially absorbed a certain number of new city dwellers; but as in Egypt, the state was unable to manage the social integration of the large number of new city dwellers. Capital was invested in ambitious and expensive projects and in arms, only rarely reaching the newcomers in the cities, who received practically no social or economic support. The southern quarters of Tehran were thus gradually cut off from the north, the political and economic centre, and as a result tried to become independent.

A striking fact was that the Islamic language here served as an expression of independence, because social secession was also accompanied by a symbolic departure from the linguistic usage of the rich northern inhabitants with their European lifestyles. This secession created a competitor for the old political generation. The radicalization of the new city dwellers was proportional to their secession, so that around 1978 there were two autonomous political publics opposing the regime. In addition, there was a growing tendency towards ethnic secession, which was particularly felt in the Azari area around Tabriz and among the southern Iranian tribal confederations. Finally, a completely independent, proletarian, and, as far as Iranian politics were concerned, atypical public emerged in the oil enclaves of Abadan and Ahwaz, intensifying the heterogeneity of the opposition.

Ayatollah Khomeini, who was exiled to Najaf in Iraq from October 1965, was one of the first of the Iranian *ulama* to recognize the threat to the *ulama* of an autonomous ideological re-interpretation of Islam. There was indeed a danger that a new interpretation of Islam as a universal ideological concept might force the *ulama* to abandon their jurisdiction over Islamic culture to the intellectuals. Only through an independent re-interpretation of the political role of the *ulama* was it possible to prevent their impending loss of authority. This required an independent emphasis on Islam. Until his exile, Khomeini had dispensed with formulating an independent Islamic political programme. But in the course of the conflict for hegemony over the Islamic public, Khomeini worked at a new Islamic concept which was to change quietistic Shi'ism into an aggressive political theology. As a new institution, he promoted the creation of a *vilayat-i faqih*,[35] a 'government by jurists', which was to be responsible to the Iranian *ulama*, of whom there were almost 100,000. This institution was to act as a trustee of the sovereignty of God, until the awaited last imam of the Twelver Shi'is, Muhammad b. al-Hasan, who had vanished around 874, returned from his 'great seclusion' (*ghaiba*). The institution was to run parallel to the civil order and assume the character of an Islamic government (*hukumat-e islami*).

In 1971, as the radical change in the Islamic public was gradually making itself felt, Khomeini edited the lectures he had delivered in January and February 1970 to publish a book entitled 'The Islamic Government', which later became known in its Arabic version as 'The Islamic State'. In it he for the first time clearly advocated[36] an Islamic republicanism and, above all, gave the politically incapacitated and economically starving bazaar of Tehran a new political orientation. Islamic republicanism altogether bore the character of a great social compromise. It satisfied both the urban nationalists, for whom it secured an extensive autonomy through the assumption of classical republican forms of representation, and the Islamic revolutionaries and secessionists, who aimed at a completely new definition of the social system. Iran's traditional national culture was as much supported through the Islamic orientation as the culture of the *ulama*, who were for the first time granted executive and consultative power. The propaganda for an Islamic republicanism made it possible to present the Iranian empire as a corrupt and obsolete system without directly criticizing the state's military power. It was hence more and more strongly personalized: on one side the Shah and his 'clique', on the other Khomeini and his 'reactionary and bigoted *ulama* friends'.

In 1977, when the Iranian economy could no longer cope with the food crisis, there were more and more attempts among the urban nationalists to reactivate the 1906 constitution and give bourgeois society a share in authority. At the same time, the Islamic opposition succeeded, at the turn of the year 1977–78, in exploiting the frustration of the population over the economy. In the strikes that took place from November 1977 to February 1978, high-ranking members of the *ulama* played a crucial part and were also able to gain the support of the low-ranking mullas.

There was, of course, no question of a unified Islamic opposition. Although the Islamic language did convey the dominant political trends, it did not produce a real political union. Urban social reformism was mainly represented by Mahmud Taliqani, who also helped to form relationships between the National Front and the *ulama*. The revolutionary left had laboriously, and amidst many internal divisions, settled into the People's Mujahidin (Mujahidin-e Khalq),[37] an Islamic guerilla organization. The Azari and Khorasani regionalists found an Islamic advocate in the liberal scholar Muhammad Kazim Shari'atmadari (born 1905). In this politicized situation, conservative politicians and *ulama* had little opportunity to influence the public. They had relied too much on the institutions of the regime and were now left without an effective organization. Even the reverence some people still showed to the aged Shi'i dignitary al-Khu'i in Iraq could not improve their desolate situation.

For a short time it looked as though the political emancipation of bourgeois society in Iran might be carried out peacefully. At the end of Ramadan, the month of fasting, more than 100,000 Tehranis demonstrated on 4 September 1978 for the reinstatement of the constitution of 1906 or the overthrow of the shah. After further demonstrations, the regime imposed martial law on 8 September, and on the same day suppressed a demonstration, killing, it is claimed, more than 3,000 people. Khomeini, who was expelled from Iraq on 6

October 1978 because of his propaganda activity and had settled near Paris, now called for the overthrow of the monarchy. In the succeeding weeks, the opposition grew into a popular rebellion against the regime. In ever renewed demonstrations, hundreds of thousands of people were mobilized. The demonstrations themselves soon assumed a ritualized character. Manifestations of mourning and penance were brought into line with Shiʿi traditions. Again and again the situation was compared with the 'suffering of the Shiʿi imams'. The twelve imams of the classical Shiʿa (therefore also called the Twelver Shiʿa or Imamiya) had all died an unnatural death, with the exception of the last, Imam Mohammad al-Mahdi, who according to Shiʿi theology had vanished in 874. The Shiʿa, also called the 'party of Ali', constantly emphasized the idea of mourning for their imams and of repentance for the fact that in 681, the year of the murder of Ali's son Husain, the Shiʿi partisans had not taken resolute action against the murderers to revenge the killing of Husain. In the Islamic Revolution vengeance for Husain was thus taken symbolically and in retrospect.

Meanwhile, the inhabitants of the deprived quarters of Tehran appropriated the things they needed for their daily subsistence: electricity lines that led over suburban shanties without supplying them were tapped, warehouses were plundered and the water supply was re-organized. Workers in Abadan went on strike and demanded better pay, better provisions and better accommodation. On 3 January 1979, the shah tried to split the National Front from the opposition by dismissing the military government and appointing a civilian government under Shahpur Bakhtiar, the co-founder of Mosaddeq's National Party. The Shah's third departure on 16 January 1979, after those of 1953 and 1963, brought no appeasement. On 1 February, Khomeini was able to return to Tehran and appoint a revolutionary government. Khomeini endorsed the appointment of Mehdi Bazargan (born 1905), a social reformer and political colleague of Taliqani, as the head of government (until November 1979).[38]

During the ensuing months the institutions of the revolution (among others the revolutionary courts and the revolutionary guards) were organized and integrated into the apparatus of the Islamic Republican Party (IRP), so that the leadership of the revolution was established as an independent party with a strong informal executive power. The ideologically rather unspecific Islamic discourse of the revolution was now mainly supported by the mobilized Iranian mixed societies and contributed to the gradual elimination of competing Islamic parties.

3. ANNI HORRIBILES IN THE ISLAMIC WORLD, 1979–1989

The Islamic Revolution in Iran and the victory of the Sandinistas in Nicaragua in July 1979 raised hopes of a far-reaching restoration of Third Worldism in which Islam appeared as a specific expression of a new liberation culture. To begin with, the Islamic revolutionaries did their best to be true to this image, renouncing too close an identification of their revolution with the ideals of Shi'i scholarship. Above all, the revolution was presented to the world as a milestone in the liberation of the deprived, and celebrated as the guarantor of a new, transnational Islamic identity. The Islamic world was to become the spearhead of a newly invigorated anti-imperialism, which was symbolically expressed by the occupation of the American embassy in Tehran.

Egypt and Iran appeared to have exchanged their political roles. While until 1979 Iran was the foremost ally of the West and of Israel within the Islamic world, this function was now assumed by Egypt. Ironically, as Iran was conducting a referendum which acknowledged the Islamic Republic as the form of the state in March 1979, Sadat was, in putting his signature to the Camp David treaty, moving in a direction that was diametrically opposed to the revolution. Sadat himself pointed out this exchange of roles when he invited Shah Mohammad Reza Pahlavi to Cairo in March 1980, after the latter had fallen ill, and when he honoured him with a national funeral after his death on 27 July 1980. Iran, on the other hand, assumed the role of a candidate for hegemony in the Islamic world and thus became the most important rival of Saudi Arabia.

However, all attempts to propagate the Islamic Revolution as the rebirth of a Third World republicanism were doomed to failure. It soon became evident that the revolution ultimately served the reintegration of the Iranian nation state, which consequently continued the hegemonic policy followed by the Shah. No new latitude was offered either to regionalist movements among the Kurds, Azaris and Turcomans, or to the Arabic-speaking population of the oil province of Khuzistan. Among the Islamic public, the image of Iran thus appeared contradictory: on the one hand, the hegemonic aspirations of the new state were very critically observed, and on the other, the revolution appeared as the symbolic beginning of a new Islamic self-assurance. Nevertheless, the image of the Islamic Revolution was on the whole positive until 1982. To most Islamic groups outside Iran, the revolutionary proceedings of the avant-gardes and their attempts to form a unified Islamic front were thoroughly acceptable.

The Crisis of Mecca in 1979

The revolution in Iran was the first climax of the Islamic fin de siècle. The year 1979 partially coincided with the year 1399 of the Islamic era, which had been re-introduced as the official calendar in Iran a year earlier. A new century was approaching, and turns of centuries regularly prompted chiliastic expectations in the Islamic world. If Islamic cadres were to be believed, this was to be the century of Islam. According to the new variant of traditional eschatologies, the impending apocalypse of modernism was to end in a realm of justice headed by a true leader (*mahdi*), representing the final stage of human history before the Last Judgment. In the popular culture of Iran, these ideas were, moreover, connected with the awaited return of the Hidden Imam, who would convert the temporary Islamic Republic into a true empire of men and humanity. Thus the Islamic constitution of the republic would last only until the return of the Hidden Imam.[39]

The Islamic turn of the century was also used by the political opposition in Saudi Arabia. In Medina, the stronghold of the Arab Wahhabiya, several students had already, after the assassination of Faisal in 1975, formed a plot against the royal family and had sought for a leading personality who could lend the Wahhabi opposition the right image. A member of this group, Juhaiman b. Muhammad al-Utaibi (ca. 1940–79), who had served with the National Guards for eighteen years, suggested that the previous rector of the University of Medina and then president of the Saudi Dar al-Iftah (chief legal office), Ibn Baz, might be won over as a leader. The group simply called itself the Ikhwan, i.e. 'brothers' (in the spiritual sense), though without wishing to suggest any connection with the Ikhwan movement of the 1920s.[40] Al-Utaibi was a radical critic of the Saudi monarchy, although he did not directly advocate an Islamic republicanism. Rather he saw the revival of Wahhabi pietism as a political programme that might lead to establishing a new system other than a republic or monarchy. The revival of the traditions of the Prophet Muhammad (*sunna*) would necessarily give rise to a system of this kind, in which neither the *ulama* nor the rulers would be entitled to a special social position.

The Saudi Ikhwan must have had considerable backing from circles which even today have not been definitely identified. The names of the rebels who were subsequently arrested or executed point to the fact that the adherents were recruited from socially excluded tribes, Muslim immigrants, mainly from the Yemen and Pakistan, and students from the University of Medina. At what time this group took to chiliastic fanaticism is equally unknown. Some time around 1978 (1976?) al-Utaibi declared himself as the emissary of the prophet of the end of time (the *mahdi*) Muhammad Abdallah al-Qahtani, who his sister had identified in a dream as a 27-year-old student from Medina. Muhammad Abdallah was no doubt named after he was identified as the *mahdi*, for according to orthodox tradition this was the name the *mahdi* would bear, albeit without the addition of al-Qahtani, which referred to the mythical ancestor of the Arabs. From 1976 Al-Utaibi is said to have written a series of circular letters on al-Qahtani's behalf, which he was able to publish in Kuwait and in which he called for the overthrow of Al Sa'ud.[41] Soon afterwards he was arrested with 98 of his followers in Riyadh, where the group had assembled around 1976. Through the intercession of Ibn Baz, however, they were released.[42]

For a while no more was heard of the Ikhwan. Utaibi apparently planned to announce the *mahdi* at the end of the pilgrimage month in 1399, that is, on 20 or 21 November 1979. In the course of that month, more than 1,000 Ikhwan had gone to Mecca and mixed with Iranian pilgrims, who were for the first time able to celebrate the victory of the Islamic Revolution within the framework of the Haj.[43] On the morning of 20 November, the heavily armed group occupied the holiest sanctuary of Islam in Mecca and entrenched itself in the numerous buildings surrounding the Ka'aba. According to official information, the rebels disposed of the most modern – ostensibly Soviet – weapons. Other observers declared, however, that their weapons were obsolete, and that the rebels had accumulated them from the remainders of stockpiles which had entered the country from the Yemen wars.[44] After two weeks of siege and the engagement of foreign, especially Jordanian elite troops, the last of the 170 rebels finally had to surrender.

This incident plunged the Wahhabi *ulama* into a deep crisis. By contrast to Iran, they were forced to side openly with the monarchy, although the radicals around Ibn Baz and Salih ibn Lahidan must have found the ideas of the rebels by no means unappealing. Ibn Baz himself declared that the event had caused great damage and that the rebels had been wrong to choose someone as a *mahdi* themselves, although this was only possible through divine signs. In addition, the rebels had sworn an oath of allegiance to the *mahdi* and had carried arms in the shrine.[45] A different reaction was shown by the Hijazi politicians and *ulama*, as well as loyal partisans of the royal family. To them the rebels were new Qarmatis, that is identical with those Shi'i groups who had carried off the Black Stone of the Ka'aba in 929. Although the Saudi authorities did their best to play down the political aspect of the occupation, they at the same time tended to put the 'new Qarmatis' on a level with communists.[46] This seemed opportune if only because, through the occupation of Afghanistan by Soviet troops in December 1979, communism's role as the 'principal opponent of the Islamic world' was confirmed.

At about the same time, unrest broke out among the Shi'i minority in the eastern Saudi Arabian province of al-Ahsa. On 27 November 1979, the Shi'i communities of al-Ahsa decided that they would henceforth openly hold the Shi'i procession to commemorate the death of the Imam Husain (Ashura) in the style of the Islamic Revolution. The insurgents occupied factories and destroyed banks, especially in the city of al-Qatif, and demanded the proclamation of an Islamic Republic. Three days later the rebellion, which had no connection with the revolt in Mecca, was violently suppressed. But soon afterwards, on 1 February 1980, Shi'i groups again demonstrated their sympathy for Iran, when they protested against the Saudi regime on the anniversary of Khomeini's arrival in Tehran.

The Saudi government, which had so far shown restraint over the question of the Islamic Revolution, now mobilized its entire propaganda apparatus against Iran. The Iranian revolutionaries promptly reacted, identifying Saudi Arabia as the stronghold of an 'American' Islam and the centre of apostasy. The Cold War had returned as an Islamic cold war. The Islamic discourse had now become the essential medium of the conflict for hegemony in the Islamic world.

Even Libya tried to pursue a foreign policy geared to an Islamic public. On 2 December 1978, Qaddafi declared that the *sunna* of the Prophet Muhammad should no longer be regarded as the source of Islamic law. Saudi Arabia, whose national culture was based precisely on an idealization of the *sunna* through the culture of Wahhabi *ulama*, interpreted this as a direct attack and mobilized the Muslim World League to dissuade Qaddafi from taking the step. The latter, however, aggravated the conflict and went against the Islamic tradition by idealizing the Prophet Muhammad as a 'shepherd', banning polygamy and maintaining that the holy sites of Mecca and Medina were under American control and the pilgrimage should be replaced by the call to fight for the liberation of Mecca.[47] In October 1982, the conflict grew increasingly critical when the committee of the most eminent *ulama* in Saudi Arabia declared that Qaddafi was a heretic and an apostate.

The War in Afghanistan

In the autumn of 1979, the Saudi authorities had already come to believe that Afghanistan might be the scene of a radical conflict over the primacy of an Islamic system. Through the Islamization of the political public, the Islamic world had been drawn into numerous fields of conflict and was now fragmented into circles, each of which was directed by a different patron. In 1980 the Iranian circle was still the most effective, though not the most powerful. It was the circle which primarily served as a guide for those Islamic groups who wanted social secession. The Saudi circle still had a powerful economic base. Numerous Islamic countries, above all the monarchies of the Gulf States, Morocco, Sudan, Pakistan, Indonesia and Malaysia had submitted to Saudi hegemony and benefited from the patronage of the royal house. On an informal level, Saudi Arabia also managed to exert an abiding influence on integrationist Islamic parties and groups through the activities of the Muslim World League. The Libyan circle mainly incorporated West African Islamic communities. The fourth and last circle consisted of the remnants of a diffuse leftist-socialist public which continued to rely on the patronage of the USSR. Iraq, South Yemen and Afghanistan were the only Islamic countries which still upheld the old tradition of Third World republicanism. Somewhat lost in this complex political landscape were states such as Syria, Algeria and Mauretania, whose national culture was still marked by the old republicanism without, however, explicitly seeking the patronage of the USSR. No less isolated were those Islamic countries which, like Egypt, Tunisia or Turkey, were seeking an entirely Western orientation.

Afghanistan was one of the last Islamic countries in which the republicanism of the urban nationalists sought to overthrow the old monarchical structure. When, on 17 July 1973, the former Afghan prime minister and nephew of King Zahir Shah, Muhammad Da'ud, overthrew the monarchy and proclaimed an Afghan Republic, the overall conditions for the urban nationalists were already very poor. Da'ud propagated a reform programme focused on Kabul, with the essential purpose of building up an urban industry and infrastructure. Road building was also planned in order to connect regions that were not already linked to the centre and thus expand the state's sovereignty. Da'ud was thus promoting the reform concept he had demanded as the prime minister of Zahir Shah.

In order to secure state authority, the army was strengthened by an intensive officers' training course in the USSR. Among these officers were the insurgents who on 27 April 1978, a few days after the assassination of the ideologue and oppositionist Mir Akbar Khaibar, overthrew Da'ud in a bloody coup. These officers were associated with the Democratic People's Party founded in 1965, which had originally been a classical republican people's party but had split in 1972 into a rather nationalistic, 'popular-democratic' (*parcham*, 'banner') and a leftist-socialist 'Leninist' wing (the *khalq*, 'people').[48] Only Muhammad Taraqi (1916–79), who represented the Khalq, was able to unite the two wings temporarily in 1977, but he had to admit the self-willed speaker of the Khalq, Hafiz Allah Amin, into his new government. Until 1973 the Parcham wing had had a positive attitude towards Da'ud's coup. But after his policy of 'opening' in 1976, the Parcham again detached itself from the camp of the urban nationalists. The party was largely identified with the political tradition of the Pashtuns (or Pakhtuns, the largest ethnic group in Afghanistan); only the leftist socialist wing represented a mixed ethnic society in which loyalty to superior tribal confederations was rarely expressed.

The principal means of achieving the sovereignty of urban nationalism was a thoroughgoing land reform, which officially came into force on 1 January 1979 and six months later was considered to be complete. The wave of expropriation met with violent resistance by the landlords, who were now increasingly joining the resistance groups. The conflict between Pashtuns and non-tribal Afghans was the main factor behind the overthrow of Taraqi in September 1979. Amin temporarily took over the affairs of state and acted mercilessly against the representatives of the old ethnic and political parties. He tried to rid himself of Taraqi's leftist-socialist tradition and to escape the growing pressure from the USSR with the help of Pakistan. However, the Parcham wing under the Tajik Babrak Karmal succeeded in recovering their power with Soviet help. On 27 December 1979, Karmal was proclaimed president. The furtive Soviet intervention, which had already started in November 1979 and reached its climax on 24 December 1979 with the invasion of large units of troops, was lent legitimacy by requests for help from Afghan politicians and by the Soviet–Afghan treaty of friendship concluded shortly before. The almost 100,000 Soviet soldiers first of all had to put an end to Amin's dictatorial acts and secure the power of the urban nationalists.

The fact that this actually required so great a number of troops showed that the Afghan state had lost control over large parts of the country since the fall of the monarchy in 1973. The power structure in Afghanistan was based on a traditional system consisting of a balance of interests between the tribal confederations and ethnic groups on the one hand and the urban society on the other. This system had collapsed and had particularly accentuated secessionism when the nationalists tried to carry out reforms in order to spread their own views on the country as a whole.

Resistance against the nationalists, which mainly followed ethnic factors, rapidly adjusted itself both to an Islamic language, whereby Islamic nationalists also played a major role, and to traditional cultural characteristics such as membership of the powerful mystical brotherhoods of the Naqshbandiya or Qadiriya. Afghanistan's manifold ethnography promoted an equally manifold Islamic public. Supported by the armament of the *qaum* ('group'),[49] independent territories were formed, each of which identified itself with a party whose leader, in his turn, represented the ensemble of the cultural identities of the *qaum*. Thus the Tajik professor of philosophy and leader of the Jam'iyat-i Islami-yi Afghanistan (Islamic Society of Afghanistan), Burhan al-Din Rabbani, was the representative of the Pandjir in northern Afghanistan, because – like the local population – he belonged to the Sunni–Persian culture of the Naqshbandiya. In this way, smaller ethnic segments were assimilated to a superior *qaum* identity, finally leading to the emergence of a small separate state led by Rabbani.[50] The Hizb-i Islami ('Islamic party') of the journalist Yunis Khalis was the organ of a *qaum* which was connected with the scholarly culture of the Hugyani and Gadran tribes of the Pashtus and also represented the interests of the Pashtus of Kabul and Qandahar. Other traditionalist Islamic groups were the Harakat-i Inqilab-i Islami (Movement of the Islamic Revolution) of Muhammad Nabi Muhammadi, who appealed to Pashtu *ulama*, especially in south-east Afghanistan, whose influence had been weakened by the urban nationalists; the Jubha-yi Najat-i Milli (National Liberation Front) led by Sibgat Allah Mujaddidi as the forum of the Naqshbandiya in southern

Afghanistan; the Mahaz-i Islami ('Islamic Front') under the control of the royalist Pir Sayyid Ahmad Kailani and representing the interests of the old establishment and the Qadiriya of the south. Unlike Mujaddidi and Muhammadi, both of whom called for loyalty towards the *maulawi*, the *ulama* strictly speaking, Kailani counted on support from the *pirs*, that is, the local mystical masters who did not directly depend on the *ulama*.

The decision to join a certain resistance movement was by no means final; only the large tribal unions were more or less loyal, and even here there were constant conflicts between the old khans and the *maulawis*. In the Pashtu society around Kabul, in which a vital tribal organization hardly remained, alliances often changed.[51] The war itself brought about a far-reaching re-organization of Afghan society, which had crucial effects on loyalties. None of the individual *qaum* parties believed in a true restoration of the nation state, but all were trying to lend secession an autonomous expression by appealing to a notion of the state, so that over the following nine years there was no coordinated attack against the centre, Kabul. Between 1980 and 1984, and from 1986 to 1988, Soviet and Afghan government troops tried to break the power of the *qaum* unions in various offensives. However, the segmentation of political sovereignty made this virtually impossible. The Islamic fighters (*mujahidin*) were not waging a classical guerilla war which aimed at conquering the centre of liberated areas, nor could the government occupy urban centres to break the power of the regional leaders, since the latter operated, for all practical purposes, as an autonomous body and at all events coordinated their actions in loose resistance unions. For its own part, the war promoted the cohesion of the local population with the *qaum* unions. Even the Afghan government in Kabul, which could count only on the loyalty of the non-tribal urban population, gradually became the representative of an autonomous *qaum*, consisting of members of the state administration, the army and an urban middle layer.

From 1980, Saudi Arabia which, as we have observed, viewed Afghanistan as the scene of a decisive battle between Islam and communism, tried to build up a clientele of its own. Many Saudi politicians feared an infiltration of the Islamic public by atheist groups and therefore welcomed the execution of members of the Tudeh party in Iran, through which the Iranian leadership confirmed its anti-communist attitude.[52] Similarly, the Saudi publicists violently attacked the Taraqi regime, which it accused of trying to root out 'Islam in Afghanistan'.[53]

An ally of Saudi foreign policy was, to begin with, Mujaddidi, a Naqshbandi scholar and passionate teacher who had gone to Mecca in 1973 and had worked there with the general secretariat of the Muslim World League. A little later Mujaddidi spent four years in Copenhagen where he headed the Islamic centre of the League. After the Mecca crisis in 1979/80, when the Wahhabi tradition could again assume a decisive position within the Saudi public, Saudi Arabia supported the Pashtu activist Gulb al Din Hikmatyar who had founded a small Hizb-i Islami (Islamic party) and, unlike Rabbani, used a distinctly Islamic discourse which in many respects corresponded with the Saudi national culture. Over the years Hikmatyar's party was built up by Saudi and Pakistani instructors into a powerful military force, intended not only for the defence of a *qaum*, but – unlike other guerilla groups and perhaps also because Hikmatyar appealed mainly to the urban nationalists.– for the conquest of state power.

Ethnic Groups in Afghanistan[54]

Ethnic Group	Number	Per Cent
Pashtus	6,000,000	42
Tajiks	3,527,000	25
Uzbeks	1,300,000	9
Turkomans	380,000	3
Hazara	1,160,000	8
Persians (Farwisan)	600,000	4
Aimaq	478,000	3
Baluchis	238,000	2
Others	600,000	4

The war in Afghanistan claimed more than a million lives, and many millions had to leave the country as town and countryside were laid to waste. Meanwhile, there was a growing tendency towards the ethnification of the various *qaum* unions, so that in the late 1980s the resistance was defined by the five most powerful ethnic groups, the Pashtus, Tajiks, Uzbeks, Hazara and Turkomans. In addition, there were the confessional groups of Sunnis and Shi'is (Hazara).[55] The war finally led to the collapse of urban society, which around 1989 was almost exclusively reduced to the stronghold of Kabul.

The War between Iran and Iraq

Oil has often preserved a state by making available to it huge financial reserves with which it can develop its sovereignty far beyond the traditional forms of state authority. When, as in Afghanistan, such resources were lacking, the urban nationalists had little chance of maintaining their power for any length of time. The regime of the Iraqi Ba'th party was, however, able to benefit from oil wealth precisely at a time when it needed to assert its power in the early 1970s.

From 1973 to 1979, the value of goods imported into Iraq increased six-fold, showing that the regime was in a position to guarantee the subsistence of the population within a certain framework and thereby to heighten its prestige as a public supplier. At the same time, the Ba'th consolidated its political control over society. The party was transformed into a massive organization geared towards the leadership with tentacles reaching into the smallest social units. The proportion of the urban population in Iraq rose to almost 70 per cent by 1980, and the number of people working in public services doubled in the 1970s. The private sector survived only in the building trade and the transportation system.

The consolidation of the state was accompanied by rapid rearmament (mainly supplied by France, the USSR and the USA) and by the development of the security service. The Ba'th's nationalist ideology, which glorified Iraq as the 'land of the Arab nation', made it possible to achieve the political integration of much larger sections of the population than the shah had managed in Iran. Those which were unwilling to be integrated, such as large groups of Kurds or the Shi'is from the southern provinces, who liked to show themselves as the civic conscience of Iraq, were often mercilessly persecuted. The ideal of a strong state, which was identical with the strong man, seemed close to realization when in July 1979 Saddam Hussein replaced the then head of state and government al-Bakr both as secretary general of the Ba'th and as commander-in-chief of the army.

Saddam Hussein was helped by the economic boom of 1978/79, the latest in a series of booms in the country's oil economy, which was fuelled by the collapse of Iran's oil exports after the revolution, the resulting huge rise in oil prices and Iraq's ability to take over the Iranian output quotas. The Ba'thi state had sufficient means to absorb the effects of domestic migration through public subsistence measures and thus reduce the tendency to social secession.

Externally, too, the Iraqi regime had been able to strengthen its position in the second half of the 1970s. When, on 6 March 1975, an agreement was made in Algiers to resolve border problems with Iran on the Shatt-al-Arab, Iraq seemed to have become a bulwark against the hegemonic aspirations of the shah who had not relinquished Iran's claim to the island of Bahrain, although he had shelved the matter. The shah's role as the gendarme of the Gulf after the final withdrawal of the British troops in 1971, – carried out, for example, through his military aid to the Sultan of Oman when the latter was hard-pressed by a liberation movement – had by this time ended. Instead, a strange entente now emerged between Iran and Iraq who together fought against the ethnic secessionist efforts of the Kurds and the emancipation attempts of the Shi'i *ulama* whose political wing in Iraq was represented by Baqir al-Sadr.

The Islamic Revolution abruptly changed the situation. Iraq suddenly saw itself facing a country which on the one hand adopted the hegemonic claims of the Iranian empire, and on the other legitimated them on Islamic grounds, thus influencing the Shi'i population of the Gulf. The Iranian call for emancipation through an Islamic revolution was also heard among Islamic opposition groups in Iraq, especially al-Sadr's Da'wa group. Although the overall impact of all this was not as great as the regime had feared, from the point of view of the Ba'th, any Iranian revolutionary propaganda was in competition with its own attempt to secure sovereignty both socially and regionally in all realms of society.

Muhammad Baqir al-Sadr was a typical representative of the new Shi'i Salafiya. His interest lay in the Islamic substantiation of modernism through a critique of prevailing philosophical and economic trends, to which he devoted himself at length by writing two books with the expressive titles *Our Philosophy* (1955)[56] and *Our Economy* (1961).[57] He repeatedly protested against the attempt of the state to undermine the autonomy of the Shi'i *ulama*, but at the same time accused the *ulama* of having 'neglected the revolutionary character of Islam' in their reform movement, which was limited to the theological colleges, and by their propaganda activities. Like Sayyid Qutb, Sadr defined Islamic dogmatics as 'the theoretical basis of the nation', but he differed from Qutb in considering it at the same time as the 'constitutional basis of the nation'.[58] When Khomeini was expelled from Najaf in October 1978 because his propaganda was also dangerous to the Iraqi regime, the *ulama* around Sadr reacted seriously and considered the move as a proof of the Ba'th's attempt to break their power. In the spring of 1979 Sadr was put under house arrest, and on 7 April, after an abortive attempt at the life of the foreign minister, Tariq Aziz, he was executed. Shi'i rebels responded with a bombing campaign which led to the deportation or internment of numerous Shi'is who were unable to prove that they had lived on Iraqi territory for several generations. At the same time, the government authorities began 'to clear' the old quarters of Najaf and Karbala. In truly Haussmannian style, the houses around the great mosques were torn down, and squares and avenues were built to prevent any rebellion in inaccessible, narrow old streets.

Meanwhile, relations between Iran and Iraq had dramatically deteriorated. Iraq demanded that the Iranian government grant the Kurds, the Baluchis, and especially the Arabs of Khuzistan their autonomy. The March 1975 Algiers treaty was now practically revoked on both sides, and on 22 September 1980 Iraqi troops invaded Iran.

The nine-year war that followed was undecisive. The initial victory of the Iraqi army in Khuzistan came to nought in 1982. As a counter move, Iranian troops managed to advance as far as the Baghdal-Basra road and to conquer the oil fields of the Majnun islands. In steadily renewed offensives, they for a short time reached the suburbs of Basra (1986/87). But on the whole, there developed a stubborn trench warfare, which devastated much of the southern region of Iraq and the province of Khuzistan. The number of victims can only be roughly estimated, but on both sides about 400,000 people must have perished.

At the beginning of July 1988, the Iranian president Ali Khamenei declared during a Friday prayer that the Iranian armed forces had missed several opportunities to crush the Iraqi armies, and that 'weakness' and the lack of a clear goal had been the cause for the failure of their many offensives. Khamenei thus admitted that Iran had not, for some months, made any major territorial advances, and had again and again given the Iraqi army the opportunity to reorganize itself. The latter had used poison gas in the land war against the Iranian troops and against the rebellious Kurds, and had thus destroyed the morale of the Iranians. The war had meanwhile extended to the Gulf itself. In the so-called tanker war, both the Iranians and the Iraqis had attacked ships on their way to the oil terminals. The USA and other European powers had taken over the protection of neutral navigation and were thus directly involved with the events of the war. Between April and July 1988, by which time more than 500 ships had been destroyed or damaged, the tanker war reached a new climax. On 17 and 18 July 1988, the Iraqi President Saddam Husain and the Iranian leader of the revolution Khomeini indicated that a continuation of the war was senseless and that they would in principle agree to Resolution 598 of the UN Security Council. Following tough negotiations, the armistice came into force on 20 August 1988 and was actually observed. Iraq and Iran immediately started to rebuild their oil terminals, and a few days later were able to resume their oil export. The Iraqi army now turned against the rebellious Kurds in the northern part of the country, tens of thousands of whom had to flee from their wrecked villages and towns into Turkey.

The war had brought no material advantage to either Iran or Iraq. But it stabilized the internal political situation in both countries. Both regimes strove to present their political leaders as heroes of supernatural dimensions to whom the population had to show perfect loyalty. Their secret services monitored this loyalty down to the most minute detail. It is true that the Iranian leadership was able to present Iran as the victim of aggression not only against its country, but also against Islam, and thus to motivate the population to fight. This was somewhat difficult for the Ba'th. Saddam Husain presented Iraq's fight as a second Qadisiya (the place where in 637 the Arab tribes confederated by Islam and their followers had dealt the troops of the Sassanid Persians a crushing defeat). But Husain's bold reference to the ancient Arabs and his attempt to identify himself with the Babylonian ruler Nebuchadnezzar brought him little sympathy. More important from an international point of view was his position as a 'bulwark' against the Islamic revolution, which brought him support from the Gulf States, and also from Saudi Arabia and many Western industrial countries. The latter considered Iraq as a guarantor of the free oil trade and, above all, an almost unlimited market for arms as well as industrial and consumer goods. Iran's image, on the other hand, was so bad after the occupation of the American Embassy in November 1979 that there were no open discussions about business deals of the kind.[59]

The Impasse of Islamic Movements

While until 1979 a large number of Islamic groups set great hope on the influence of the Iranian Revolution, the years 1981/82 brought a rather pessimistic mood within the Islamic public. The Iran–Iraq war led to a restoration of Iranian national culture, which no longer took its bearings from an Islamic internationalism, but demanded a national Shi'i interpretation of the revolution. On the one hand, this led to a revalorization of the hitherto mainly apolitical Shi'i communities in Lebanon. The Shi'is had by this time become the largest religious community in Lebanon and represented 30 per cent of the population (compared with 25 per cent Maronites and about 21 per cent Sunnis). The region of Jabal Amil in southern Lebanon had long been known as a stronghold of Shi'i scholarship. The largely impoverished Shi'i communities in Lebanon for the first time acquired a representation of interests when the Iranian-connected Shi'i *alim* Musa Sadr (1928–78?), who came from a Lebanese family, organized a Supreme Shi'i Council in 1967. After the beginning of the civil war, he founded a new political party in 1975, known by the acronym Amal (or 'hope', for Afwaj al-Muqawama al-Lubnaniya, 'Lebanese Resistance Brigades'), which became an important military power only after the retreat of the Palestinian units from southern Lebanon in 1982. The spectrum of Shi'i groups was expanded in 1982 by the foundation of the Islamic Amal run by Iran and the Hizb Allah ('Party of God') closely connected with it. These political and military organizations mobilized the Shi'is who had been pushed off to Beirut from the south and east by the Israel–Palestine war in 1982.

On the other hand, the newly emphasised Shi'i aspect of the Iranian revolution promoted a rapprochement between Iran and the Ba'th regime in Syria, which was now also interpreted as Shi'i, despite the name 'regime of terror' given to it by various Islamic groups, notably by the Syrian Muslim Brothers. The Islamic movement in Syria, which in October 1980 had established a common resistance council in Tadmur as a reaction against the protest movement of March of the same year, and especially against the massacre of Muslim Brotherhood prisoners, tried to turn this revolutionary enthusiasm into a civilian resistance against the regime of the Ba'thist Hafiz Asad.[60] In February 1982 it decided that the time had come to proclaim a rebellion in the central Syrian city of Hama. But being isolated, the Islamic rebels could not withstand the military pressure of the central government for any length of time. A few days later, the old city of Hama was razed to the ground, and several hundred, perhaps several thousand inhabitants were massacred without any open intervention by the Iranian leadership.[61]

To Saudi Arabia the new Shi'i direction assumed by the revolution was a welcome, if unexpected change, for now the old anti-Shi'i resentments of the Wahhabiya could be turned to political profit, and Islamic groups could be won over for a new association with Saudi Arabia. Reactions to the massacre at Hama all shared the same tendency: disappointment over Iran's attitude. After 1982 the Islamic revolutionaries in Tehran could only preserve their influence in reduced spheres of the Islamic public.[62]

Even before the great majority of the Islamic public had turned away from the revolution in Iran, small Islamic groups in Egypt believed that the signs for a direct attack on the 'Pharaoh' were auspicious. In the autumn of 1980, the mood in the Asyut province in Upper Egypt had changed. The Islamic revolutionary cells that had already been active there for several years believed that the strained relationship between the Coptic and Muslim communities of the province could be used for propaganda and other purposes. They themselves were for the most part connected with the student milieu as more than 60 per cent of the members of cells calling themselves *jama'at* ('communities') or *jihad* ('rightful war') groups in Asyut were students. They were even capable of fomenting ethnic resentments in their families, so that the most trifling incident would suffice to stir up a revolt in a village, a small town or a city quarter in Asyut. By the autumn of 1981, anti-Coptic unrest had even spread to the suburbs of Cairo.[63]

The rebellious province of Asyut had found an effective expression in the Islamic propaganda of the *Jama'at* and its emirs to break away – as early as 1974 – from the sovereignty of Cairo. The Islamic secessionists, for their part, had a willing ear in the rebels of Asyut and obtained considerable support from the local public. In September 1981, the Egyptian government tried to counteract the Asyut secession by a massive wave of arrests, which included the leader of the local 'Islamic community', Muhammad al-Islambuli. The latter's brother, Khalid, saw this as a direct attack by 'Pharaoh' on the Islamic movement and decided, together with a few political friends, to assassinate the president and thereby trigger the revolution (at least in Asyut).[64]

The ideological preparation for this project was carried out by Abd al-Salam Faraj Atiya, an electrician by trade, who in September 1981 circulated a text under the momentous title 'The Just War – an Absent Duty'.[65] Faraj belonged to the Cairo group of the *jihad*, of which the Asyut rebels did not have a very high opinion. Indeed Faraj's text could hardly be considered a worthy successor to Qutb's famous *Milestones on the Way*. Faraj, who was paraphrasing and modernizing a legal opinion of the medieval theologian Ibn Taimiya,[66] tried to identify the ruling class of Egypt with the 'Tartars' who – according to Ibn Taimiya – had outwardly adopted Islam but in reality fought against the Muslims. By comparing current events with a medieval situation, Faraj broke with the attempts of Qutb and the Qutbists around Shukri to re-interpret Islamic movements in terms of the philosophy of history.

The assassination of Sadat on 6 October 1981 by Islambuli and his fellow combatants did not lead to a general revolt. It was only in Asyut that the Islamic activists were able to seize power for three days, but they soon had to surrender to the superior strength of the state. Their hope that the Egyptian population would join the insurrection was not fulfilled, just as a year later in Syria the activists were ti find themselves isolated.

The fight for supremacy over the Islamic public in Egypt was won by those groups who pleaded for a far-reaching Islamic integration of society and who soon obtained a solid position within the Egyptian party spectrum as worthy representatives of a national–conservative trend. First of all the Egyptian Muslim Brothers, who until 1986 were led by the integrationist Umar al-Tilimsani (1904–86), sought tactical coalitions with newly established parties, since they themselves were not yet officially admitted. They first aligned themselves with the Wafd Party (re-admitted 1978/1984), which also represented the interests of the rural bourgeoisie and landowners and vehemently fought for economic liberalism and against the remnants of Nasserism.[67] The integrationist policy of the Muslim Brothers was thus also determined by the basic conditions of the *infitah*, because for the first time in their history they also increasingly aimed at the agrarian middle classes, who had so far hardly played a part in the Islamic public.[68] Now that the capital influx from the Gulf States exercised a greater effect on village and small-town communities and was accompanied by an Islamic change of values, the Muslim Brothers were appreciated even by small and medium landowners. However, their cooperation with the Wafd Party was short-lived. Already at the 1987 elections the Muslim Brothers formed a coalition with two urban parties, the Socialist Labour Party (a continuation of Young Egypt of the 1930s) and the Socialist Liberal Party.

The political opening of the Muslim Brothers and the money transfers from the Gulf States stimulated the rise of a new industrialism which was entirely committed to Islamic ideals. In some cities, especially in the lower Egyptian Delta provinces, businessmen established Islamic banks and enterprises geared to the conditions of Saudi, Kuwaiti and other financiers of the Gulf region. They also restored the complex system of the Islamic charitable endowments (*waqf*) and supported intellectual and scientific endeavours to establish an

Islamic economic system.[69]

In view of the success of the integrationist wing of the Islamic public, which was at no time truly willing to protect radical Islamists, the latter found it difficult to continue asserting their position. Neither the unrest which again and again accompanied the government's incisions into the network of social support, nor the extravagant propaganda of the Islamic revolutionaries in Iran, helped to provide the radical isolationists with a noteworthy place in society.

The Failure of Islamization in the Sudan

The Sudanese head of state Numairi saw himself in 1983 as a devout, charismatic Islamic leader who had been purified by spiritual experiences and was now compelled to call for the Islamization of society.[70] When in September of that year he issued three decrees which were meant to represent the beginning of a far-reaching 'compliance with the *shari'a*', radical Islamic groups had reason to be hopeful. Although it did not suit the isolationists for the state to appear as an authority on Islamization, or that the process was to draw major support from Saudi Arabia, the Islamic *obbligato* accompanying Numairi's infitah policy finally allowed the urban Islamic public to play an important part in political events. The leader of the Sudanese Muslim Brothers, which since 1948 had been organized as the Islamic Liberation Movement, was Hasan al-Turabi. He had meanwhile risen to the rank of chief state counsel and he tried to present Numairi's Islamization as a victory against the traditionally powerful parties of the great religious orders. But these civilian Islamic parties, which could rely on a solid network of loyalties and held a particularly powerful position in the provinces, also enjoyed public recognition. The National Party under al-Mahdi and the Democratic Unionist Party of the Hatmiya order under Muhammad Uthman al-Mirghani soon dominated public opinion The structural conflict between the urban nationalists and the agrarian national liberals thus acquired in the Sudan a thoroughgoing Islamic colouring. The urban nationalists realized that the only way to oppose the growing influence of the national liberals was to form an alliance with the regime and they therefore supported Numairi's attempts to stabilize his dwindling power.

However, the Sudanese Muslim Brotherhood did not form a homogeneous front. Its three main movements were the moderate, 'pragmatic' groups around Turabi, the more radical, rather social-revolutionary avant-gardes around Babakr Karar, and the purists around Ja'far Sheikh Idris. These developed what were in some respects very different programmes for Islamic revival in the Sudan. Thus, even after Numairi's spectacular announcement of the three essential principles for a new Islamic legislation, the oppositional character of the Sudanese Muslim Brothers was basically preserved, although Islamization meant that certain of its members were absorbed into the state.[71] Turabi, who in 1964 had established his own Front of the Islamic Charter, basically followed Sayyid Qutb's populist image of society. However, he broadened Qutb's ideas through an interpretation based on the philosophy of history by recognizing the contradiction between the absolute quality of transcendence and the relativity of history as a tensional structure to which Islam was also, or indeed particularly, subjected. Like most Islamic intellectuals, Turabi saw early Islam as the primary model; but at the same time he pointed to the historical relativity which had already marked this early epoch. In his opinion, historical relativity had also determined Islamic law and jurisprudence. Turabi therefore turned against conservative interpretations of Islamic theology, indeed against Islamic theology in general, since he considered theology to be hostile to reforms. Turabi's utopian attitude established Islam as an ethical principle which derived its legitimacy from an absolute reference to transcendence. Reform was a 'concern of God', and therefore mankind must not avoid it. And reform demanded that absolute truth be separated from things that were, historically, always changing, so that a new path to religious truth could be opened, especially through the criticism of traditional concepts of law.[72]

The Islamization of the political public reached its climax in 1984 and was greatly applauded at various conferences of Islamic parties and groups. It was generally believed that the Sudan was the first country into which a new Islamic system had been introduced without a revolution. Yet at the same time the economic impact of the Sudanese infitah policy was making itself felt. The foreign debt tripled between 1978 and 1985 to reach 10 billion US dollars, and the rate of inflation after 1983 was over 60 per cent. There was a rapidly growing tendency towards secession within the population, and steadily increasing parts of the state apparatus refused to be loyal. In 1984, Numairi reacted to the growing unrest with an Islamically legitimized emergency decree, which the Islamic parties viewed as a sign that the government was not interested in a new civil Islamic system. In January 1985 the conflict came to a head when Numairi accused the Muslim Brothers around Turabi of preparing a coup, and had him arrested together with many of his followers. The Islamic University of Omdurman thereupon became a centre of resistance, but the protest soon became independent. At the end of March 1985 the situation escalated. The poor in the cities of Khartoum and Omdurman openly rebelled, and from 1 April the whole of the state bureaucracy was paralysed by strikes. On 6 April, Numairi was finally overthrown by a commando unit under General Abd al-Rahman Suwar al-Dahab.[73]

With a few exceptions, the reputation of the Islamic policy of 'Imam' Numairi was poor. His attempts to interpret the Islamization of the state as a purely judicial matter and to reduce the observance of the *shari'a* to a series of symbolic legal actions – such as the ostentatious elimination of alcohol or the use of corporal punishment – by no means corresponded with the ambitious ideas of Islamic intellectuals. When, on 18 January 1985, Mahmud Muhammad Taha, an aged Sudanese engineer and the founder in 1964 of a mystical–pietistic union called the Republican Brothers, was executed for apostasy because he had 'abandoned Islam'[74] through his pacifist propaganda, many sympathizers turned their back on the Sudan. Saudi Arabia alone remained true to the regime. Not only did high Saudi authorities, including the Muslim World League, welcome Taha's execution,[75] in 1985 they even granted asylum to Numairi officials.[76] For the next four years Sudan was again ruled by a civilian government, which continued to promote the Islamic discourse among a large public, even if many of Numairi's Islamization attempts were left out.

Bread Riots in the 1980s

The efficacy of the ideological utopias of Islamic movements diminished after 1985. The Iran–Iraq war, the suppression of the rebellions in Egypt and Syria, the victory of bourgeois society against the Islamically legitimized dictatorship of Numairi, and especially the growing willingness of the integrationist wing of the Islamic public to follow the national-conservative tradition of granting the highest priority to the nation state – all these factors had thoroughly shaken the faith in an independent position for Islamic ideologies. Equally momentous were the consequences of conflicts over the economic principles of the 'new Islamic order'. In Cairo several financiers and businessmen who organized their enterprises in accordance with the much propagated rules of Islamic economy had turned out to be quite normal speculators and had altogether discredited the idea of an Islamic economy. In addition, social and ethnic conflicts were radicalized and often transformed Islamic movements into ethnic or social parties whose only common characteristic appeared to be secession from the state. The bread unrest in Egypt in the early 1980s had already shown that the majority of the rebellious urban poor were not interested in submitting to an Islamic leadership. It was only in the mixed areas that the Islamic groups still had a following to speak of.

In the Sudan, Islamic students had tried to take up the main theme of the bread crisis within the framework of the revolt against Numairi. Their principal targets were the International Monetary Fund and the World Bank, which were branded as the main cause of Sudan's misery. This, however, brought them only limited support from the mobilized city poor.[77]

The International Monetary Fund and the World Bank played a considerable part in the bread riots which shook many Islamic countries between 1984 and 1988. In the course of a thoroughgoing reform of the enormous foreign debts of many Third World states, countries such as Tunisia and Morocco had made an agreement with the IMF by which they had to adopt drastic reductions in the subsidy of basic foodstuffs within the framework of conversion loans. Between 1972/74 and 1982/84, the per capita production of food had dropped in almost all Arab countries, in some cases dramatically: in Algeria (21 per cent),[78] Tunisia (16 per cent), Northern Yemen (16 per cent) and Iraq (15 per cent). It had risen only in Lebanon (about 45 per cent), Jordan (36 per cent) and Syria (23 per cent).[79] Food imports over the same period had on average doubled (more than the average in Morocco, Tunisia, Sudan, Iraq and Syria) and absorbed up to 83 per cent of export earnings (Egypt).[80] However, world market conditions made it difficult to cut off food imports. Arms and wheat continued to be the main goods exported by the industrial states to many countries of the Islamic world. But after 1983, reduced oil incomes no longer allowed the oil-producing countries to provide major subsidies, since their budgets ran, or threatened to run, at a deficit.[81]

These and other factors created the conditions for a structural food crisis, which in poor counHries, and particularly in times of drought, led to disastrous situations. Especially affected were the African countries of Chad, Sudan, Ethiopia and Somalia.

The first wave of protests against this compulsory policy of austerity reached North Africa in the winter of 1983/84. In December 1983, the peasants of southern Tunisia protested against the low prices of dates and against the announcement by the Mzali government that bread prices were to be doubled from 1 January 1984. This protest was joined at the beginning of January 1984 by the inhabitants of the city of Qafsa who, as early as 1980, had almost unanimously rebelled against government policy, and had been energetically supported by Libyan propaganda. The revolt soon expanded to the industrial city of Kasserine and to Tunis itself. Not until mid-January was the army in a position to calm the situation, after the USA had promised Tunisia military aid if need be.

In the same month, a student strike against higher university fees in Marrakesh, the southern royal city of Morocco, provoked a rebellion which was also directed against the austerity policy. On 9 January 1984, Marrakesh was like a city in open revolt and, as in Tunisia, government buildings, banks, shops and hotels were the rebels' targets. Two days later, the riots spread to north-eastern Morocco where the coastal city of al-Husaima became the centre of an armed uprising which was also started by protesting students.

From 19 to 22 January 1984, rebels were in almost complete control of the city of Titwan. Both Habib Bourguiba and King Hasan II had to revoke the price rises because of the unrest, only to enforce them again under more favourable circumstances a few months later. Both also availed themselves of the occasion to attribute responsibility for the revolts to Islamic groups, although their participation must have been rather marginal. On 30 July 1984, thirteen death sentences were pronounced against members of the Moroccan Organization of Islamic Youth. In Tunisia, ten young people had already been sentenced to death on 26 May without any proof that they were connected to an Islamic group.[82]

The Re-evaluation of Islamic Ideologies

The decade of wars and crises from 1979–89 brought about a gradual detachment of Islamic intellectuals from hitherto traditional ideological patterns. It appears that, within the Islamic world, the political public quite soon proceeded to discard their ideologies; in other words, their belief in the utopian perfection of ideologies through Islam began to yield to the idea of the 'social and democratic mission' of Islam as the way to accomplish modernism, and indeed to surmount it. The main characteristic of this process appeared to be the recognition of social and cultural pluralism which from 1985 could be found in various attitudes of Islamic intellectuals. It is hardly surprising that this re-evaluation of ideologies took place primarily in the French-speaking areas of North Africa where French 'post-modernist' philosophy was easily accepted.[83] In the academic and student milieu of the Maghreb states, in which the classical Islamic neo-Salafi organizations had never found strong backing, intellectuals who pleaded for an extensive renunciation of ideological concepts and ascribed to Islam the role of liberating the individual rather than society soon made themselves heard. Modernism was now conceived not so much as 'Westernization', but as a universal process which was relativized through culture. The task of the political public would now be to point out the polyvalence of modernism by emphasizing cultural relativism, and thus to reject the claim of the Western world to have a monopoly in defining the values of modernism. Crises and wars were no longer interpreted as the result of imperialist intervention, but as the structural problem of modernism itself.

The re-interpretation of Islam in a post-modernist fashion was, of course, largely the preoccupation of an academic minority. Nevertheless, the cultural relativists enjoyed a growing influence in the Islamic parties of the Maghreb which had been established around 1973 and now opposed the classical positivism of older Islamic movements. Islam was no longer considered as an objective, social state of affairs, but as a hermeneutic process of interpretation. This demanded a departure from the conventional idealistic approach of locating political utopia in an idealized reconstruction of the early Islamic period. It demanded recognition of the polyvalence of the Islamic tradition itself, which was inevitably rendered ambiguous by the political declarations of the present.

One of the first Islamic intellectuals to cautiously allude to this revaluation was the Tunisian teacher Rashid al-Ghannushi (Gannouchi). Having studied in Syria in the early 1970s, al-Ghannushi established a small circle called 'Movement of the Islamic Tendency' (Mouvement de la Tendance Islamique, Harakat al-Ittijah al-Islami, MTI) in 1981. Within this far from homogeneous group of academics and students, Islamic 'social-democratic' positions (represented, for instance, by Hamid al-Naifar who turned his back on the MTI in 1987) were also acknowledged. Al-Ghannushi himself, as well as his fellow combatant, the university teacher Abd al-Fattah Muru (Mourou) from the Islamic Zaituna University, began by advocating a relativization of the basic classical Islamic ideologies: a rejection of polygamy, a recognition of the division of powers on the basis of Islamic maxims of law, a revaluation of the *jihad* concept in favour of an 'intervention d'humanité', a recognition of the state's monopoly of power, as well as the separation between the inalienable right of worship and the public Islamic right, which was attributed the character of 'guiding principles'. It is striking that by renouncing the monopoly of Islam – that is Islam's claim to ideological leadership – al-Ghannushi exposed the Islamic public to free political competition in society. He legitimized his revaluation of political Islam by a multitude of references to Islamic intellectual history, tried to establish a philosophical argument which was greatly despised by the neo-Salafiya, and largely dispensed with the utopian idealization of the early Islamic period.[84] By 1987 the MTI had managed to become a leading political force in the Islamic public. In the student strikes of 1987, it played a crucial role, especially after al-Ghannushi and other leaders of the party were arrested in March of that year. However, smaller Islamic groups such as the Tunisian Islamic Liberation Party were also able to recruit new members.

In September 1987, there were a series of lawsuits against Islamic student leaders, but they ended in relatively 'mild' sentences. Bourguiba wanted to intervene in the undecided lawsuits, but he was overthrown by his prime minister, General Zain al-Abidin Ibn Ali (Ben Ali) on 7 November. Although Ben Ali tried to emphasize the civilian character of the new regime and have it confirmed by parliamentary elections in April 1989, Islamic parties such as the MTI were prohibited. Nevertheless, al-Ghannushi was pardoned on 14 May 1988. The IMF and the World Bank were equally generous and granted the government a new credit amounting to 270 million US dollars. Militants of the Islamic Liberation Party staged spectacular demonstrations against the government, which the latter turned to account by opposing the Islamic public. The MTI now organized itself as the Party of Tunisian Regeneration (Hizb al-Nahda al-Tunisiya), but was not allowed to participate in the elections.

Most Arab men of letters were unable to understand the imperturbable optimism of the Islamic public. Both in the Maghreb and in Egypt, writers reacted with biting sarcasm against the radical political and social change of the period of 'opening', exposed the asceticism of the political public as a farce and devised constructivist social satires about the subliminal hedonism of society. The hedonistic private life of the individual and the ascetic public appearance of society seemed so far apart to them that one could speak of a secession of the subject.[85]

CHAPTER SIX

Islamic Culture and Civil Society, 1989–1993

1. A MYTHICAL REVIVAL OF NATIONALISM?

The Collapse of the Ideological World

From our present perspective it is not really possible to analyse the factors that ultimately led to the collapse of ideological world views. A complete answer lies neither in pointing to the failure of the classical progress-oriented ideologies, nor can it be attributed simply to the loss of the old global political orientation with the collapse of the Eastern bloc. It has indeed been shown that, during the period when Islamic ideologies were asserting themselves, their disintegration was already being planned and partially discussed. Could it be that the move towards a post-ideological period was merely a fashion which took hold of the Islamic world, just like the internationalized cult of commodities? Is modernism consequently an 'open universe' which, once born, can boundlessly expand without collapsing as a result of internal contradictions?

For the time being, any conjecture can only be speculative. And yet we should bear in mind Alexander von Humboldt's warning: 'There is always an early anticipation preceding a later knowledge'. So if the collapse of the essentially positivist ideologies of the 19th and 20th centuries does in fact mark an epistemological turning point, and if this leads to an entirely new definition of intellectual activity and thus also of the political public, then it might be expected that mythical forms of thought that are opposed to ideology will develop an undreamt of potency. Ideologies in the narrow sense of the word had acquired importance in the Islamic world by the 18th and 19th centuries and finally asserted themselves as the dominant political view of the 20th century. Ideological thought or, in this context, the thought of Islam as ideology, was essentially different from the classical religious experience of the world. It aimed at the utopian perfection of human existence in this world through the recognition of axioms and norms which were accepted as established, unquestionable principles of social development. Ideological thought is consequently always utopian and derives its arguments from a radical critique of the past and present. Mythical thought, on the other hand, does not seek a utopia, but a common origin. This origin cannot be approached by any direct historical reference; it can only be substantiated by a number of different, historically non-verifiable stories. It is this ethnic perspective which plays a crucial role in mythical thinking. Since the ethnicity of a group or society can hardly ever stand the test of critical historical verification, but instead represents the momentary consciousness of belonging to a group, the multiplicity of mythical thought, which eludes criticism, becomes the identifying factor.

In this connection there also arises a question about the meaning ascribed to the concept of religion. The difficult relationship between religion and ideology, which has so persistently marked the forms of expression of Islamic history in the 20th century, suddenly appears obsolete, or indeed antiquated, in this context. Will religion, now that it is marked by this state of dependence through the new mythical argument of the world, be lumped together with ideologies? And will both religion and ideology be suspended by myth operating in the intellectual and political sphere?

It is too early to decide whether the post-modern concept of the world, which attributes an important role to myth, is nothing but a storm in the teacup of intellectuals, and whether we are confronted with no more than a cyclic revival of classical patterns and value systems. However, the cultural–historical development in the Islamic world provides some indication that the period of upheaval after 1989 is more than a reconstruction of the old system on a different level.

The new academic discourses of political Islam in the North African countries and among North African intellectuals in France met with no immediate response from the general Islamic public. The active and important groups in these countries simply dispensed with reformulating the ideological substance of their views and for the most part contented themselves with making programmatic populist statements which already belonged to the traditional stock of the Islamic public. 'Leftist Islam', which was promoted by some Egyptian and Tunisian intellectuals and explicitly took its bearings from Sayyid Qutb and Ali Shari'ati,[1] was meant to close the gap between radical 'secularists' and

'Islamists', and hence between a 'European' and an 'Islamic' discourse. However, it had no prospect of appealing to a majority.

The political propaganda of the Islamic parties mobilized the heterogeneous mixed areas of urban societies, gave social and ethnic secessions a powerful expression and occasionally legitimized the use of force by small groups of activists. Within the context of the wars in Lebanon and Afghanistan, Islamic propaganda even served as the sign of belonging to a specific group. But all this failed to provide the intellectual development of the Islamic public with fresh impetus; indeed its capacity for innovation was often directly denied during the period after 1979. Among the determining factors were probably the experiences of the 1980s, which showed that the primacy of society postulated by the leftist Islamists had created no way of intervening in the various instances of social unrest. Indeed the rightist Islamists, who demanded the primacy of the state and – following Maududi – could only conceive of an Islamic identity in an 'Islamic state', saw their power growing as social disintegration showed its radical effect on various spheres of life.

There can be no doubt that the Islamic political public was drifting to the right. This, however, led to its further nationalization, for the Islamic state could only be based on the nation state. Political Islam retained its antagonistic function as an expression of social or ethnic secession. But as the example of Afghanistan shows, the general conditions supporting the nation state were so deeply rooted that once the war was won, even radical secessionists pronounced themselves for the nation state.

The Islamic public thus came to declare itself for a new nationalism with more pronounced ethnic characteristics which would contribute to the ethnification of Islam. The cyclic revival of nationalism in the 20th century began in the Islamic world in the late 1980s. However, because of the breakdown of the ideological patterns of orientation created by the East–West conflict, the new nationalism had to show a different identity. In this context, Islam was to acquire an important function by contributing to the provision of a mythical foundation for the specific ethnicity of the nation state. This meant that the conventional ideological forms of expression of political matters had to yield to a new mythical substantiation of Islam.

The revolutionary regime in Iran, which, due to the war with Iraq, had been forced to restore its national culture, re-established its new mythical legitimation with astonishing speed. Helpful in this respect was the creation of a new Shi'i collective identity in which mythical leitmotifs could be tangibly and impressively formulated. It is true that, from the outside, Iran still appeared as an ideological state with specific national interests; but Islamists were well aware of the fact that, although the Islamic Revolution had created a republican system, it had produced no real change in the institutional make-up of that system which might differentiate it from Western patterns. Ten years after the revolution, Iran already appeared as an oddity.

By the end of the 1980s, the vision of a utopian reorganization of the Islamic world on the basis of the primacy of the state or society was upheld by only a few Islamic intellectuals. But there was no new intellectual foundation for political Islam. No wonder, then, that the populists in the Islamic political public found a way to express their social dissatisfaction by means of an Islam reduced to a few symbols. The Islamic *shari'a*, already reduced by ideologists to an Islamic system of correct behaviour, now appeared as nothing more than a legitimation of appropriated power.

The Upheaval in Israel/Palestine

Until 1987, the Islamic public in the West Bank and the Gaza Strip had adapted to the routine of Israeli occupation. The Islamic Liberation Party was free to sell its publications, the Muslim Brotherhood was treated well by the Israeli administration, and various graffiti inscriptions read: 'No to the Palestinian revolution! An Islamic revolution!'

The issue of Palestine seemed to focus on Lebanon, where after the 1982 war the Palestinians could still, in small enclaves, preserve a measure of autonomy. The Palestinians in the occupied territories were, it seemed, almost forgotten. In 1987 the PLO had, after years of internal conflict and various splits in the wake of the war of 1982 – above all, the revolt of the pro-Syrian Abu Musa in May 1983 – drawn together and was on the point of changing into a national political party.

In December 1987, however, a tragic traffic accident on the border of the occupied Gaza Strip changed this situation. An Israeli military vehicle ran into several Palestinian cars, and four Arab workers were killed. In the nearby Jabaliya refugee camp there were spontaneous demonstrations against the Israeli occupation, and a few days later protests were staged in the refugee camps and towns of the West Bank. On 19 December 1987, the revolt spread to East Jerusalem, where it assumed the character of a social rebellion. The intricate system of Arab–Jewish cohabitation collapsed within a few days. The mobilized Palestinians virtually called for secession from Israel through a far-reaching economic, political and social boycott which was soon ritualized and organized by a rapidly formed leadership, and by popular committees.

In this spontaneous uprising, which had something in common with the heterogeneous social resistance of previous years, the PLO played a less important part than it had expected, even though many Palestinian politicians and demonstrators assured the PLO of their loyalty. Faisal al-Husaini, the son of the Palestinian activist Abd al-Qadir al-Husaini, tried to arrange an alliance between the United National Command, the leadership of the uprising, and the PLO; in fact, however, it was only at the beginning that the Command saw itself as the mouthpiece of the PLO. Although at the height of the rebellion on 15 November 1988,[2] the Palestinian National Council had proclaimed an 'independent Palestinian State', by 1989 the Command looked like the executive of a 'state of Palestine' and thus indirectly provoked the PLO.

The local authorities, especially in the Gaza Strip, considered the uprising as a proof that the Palestinian population had, for the first time, and independently of the PLO, taken the political initiative. This promoted the politicization of the 'Islamic Gathering' (al-Mujamma' al-Islami), which had so far almost exclusively limited itself to educational and missionary work in the strict tradition of the old Salafiya, and had in many respects been supported by the Israeli government. The Islamic Gathering controlled numerous social welfare organizations, as well as mosques and private schools in the Gaza Strip and was supported in these activities by Jordanian associations such as the Supreme Islamic Council. Under its leader Ahmad Yasin the Islamic Gathering fought for an Islamic interpretation of the revolt and for the formation of groups of activists who were known by the name of 'Islamic fighters' (*al-Mujahidun al-Islamiyun).* Here populist forms of Islamic ideologies were actively supported. Soon the influence of the Islamic public had grown to such an extent that an Islamic resistance movement (Harakat al-Muqawama al-Islamiya, Hamas), which made its first statement in December 1987, was formed and contested the PLO for leadership. Hamas, which was clearly supported by the Muslim Brotherhood and which, in its charter (August 1988), described Palestine as a country founded by Islam, followed a thoroughly integrationist course. Thus Yasin often demanded that elections be held on the West Bank and Gaza Strip, knowing full well that Hamas would have far more votes than the PLO. On the other hand, there were several small groups under the common name of Islamic Jihad (al-Jihad al-Islami), who followed an isolationist course and also demanded separation from the Christian Palestinians. The Palestinian liberation movement Fatah tried to counteract the influence of Hamas by using Islamic themes and symbols in its propaganda. It also pointed to the fact that it had, as early as 1981, tried to locate its struggle within the context of classical Islamic history as the rightful Islamic war.[3]

The Israeli army was unable to break the civil resistance. By 1992 more than 1,200 Arab Palestinians had been killed and tens of thousands interned for various periods. Even the ban of Hamas on 28 September 1989 and the arrest of 200 of its leading personalities – among them Ahmad Yasin himself – did not succeed in weakening the Islamic public. On the other hand, the conflicts between Hamas and the National Command often had a demobilizing effect, since Hamas also demanded the right to deal with 'collaborators'. Nevertheless the two parties managed to build up an executive power independent of Israel in parts of Palestinian society. Meanwhile the mobilization of Palestinian youth who, within the milieu of Islamic groups for the first time distanced themselves from the nationalists of their parents' generation, generated tension within many Palestinian families.

However, the pressure on the PLO continued, and the secession of major parts of Palestinian society often threatened to elude the control of both the PLO and Israel. The radicalization of the upheaval, for which the Islamic parties were mainly responsible and which was further intensified by severe Israeli measures, for the first time created a certain common interest between the PLO and the Israeli government and both sides tried to de-escalate the revolt. However, there were as yet no political and diplomatic ways to make a point of this evolving community of interests.

The final impetus towards a complete reorganization of Palestine–Israeli relations came from outside. With the end of the East-West conflict, the Palestine question lost its international political importance. Now at last it seemed possible for Russia and the USA to cooperate towards final peace negotiations, unencumbered by bloc interests and allied strategies. On 18 October 1991 the American secretary of state James Baker and his Soviet counterpart Boris Pankin met in Jerusalem and announced a peace conference, which was inaugurated before the end of the month, on 30 October in Madrid.

However, the numerous negotiations that were in this way set in motion only started to move ahead after the victory of the Labour Party at the Israeli parliamentary elections of 23 July 1992. For the first time since 1977, the Labour Party in alliance with the recently founded MERETZ bloc became the strongest power in the country (with 44.2 per cent of the votes). The new government under Yitzhak Rabin was now ready to take up the famous formula 'land for peace' and temporarily stop the development of Israeli settlements in the occupied territories. This radically changed the climate of the negotiations, which was further improved when, on 9 August 1992, the Israeli government rescinded the ban on contacts between Israeli citizens and the PLO. As a result, informal talks between Israeli politicians and representatives of the PLO became possible and were held from January 1993 in strict secrecy, mainly in Norway. On 24 March 1993, Ezer Weizman, an advocate of dialogue with the PLO, was elected President of the State of Israel. A month later, the Israeli government agreed to the appointment of the nationalist Faisal al-Husaini, who had close contacts with the PLO, as leader of the Palestinian delegation at the peace conferences. Rabin had, moreover, declared that Israel would aim at a peace treaty based on the resolutions of the Security Council of the United Nations (especially Resolution 242).

After tough negotiations, the PLO and Israel concluded a skeleton agreement on 19 August 1993 whereby the Gaza Strip and the city of Jericho were granted limited autonomy. The agreement was on the one hand to ensure further negotiations towards a lasting peace treaty, and on the other hand to lead to limited self-government for the Palestinian population of Gaza and Jericho as a starting-point towards a more clearly determined autonomy of the West Bank and Gaza. The agreement practically amounted to an institutionalization of Palestinian internal policy, which was to be provided with legislative and executive power through a parliamentary council and a police of its own. On 9-10 September 1993, the era of peaceful coexistence finally began with the mutual recognition of Israel and the PLO, which led to the signature of an autonomy treaty on 13 September in Washington.

Opposition to the autonomy agreement was shown both by the Israeli and by the Palestinian population. However, the most violent opponents – aside from the Israeli settlers on the West Bank – were those Palestinian groups who had their strongholds in Lebanon, Syria and Jordan. They agreed to build up a new rejection front which was to include Islamic and leftist-socialist organizations whose membership of the PLO was now 'suspended'. But this opposition could not prevent the celebration of the agreement as a milestone not only in Arab-Israeli relations, but above all for the emergence of a new civic consciousness in Arab societies. Even Hasan al-Turabi, the militant leader of the Sudanese Muslim Brothers, appealed to Hamas not to reject the agreement and called for discussions between the PLO and the Islamists.

The militant acts of radical groups of Israeli settlers and Hamas activists only briefly delayed the conclusion of a comprehensive treaty on Palestinian autonomy in Gaza and Jericho. On 4 May 1994, Yitzhak Rabin and Yaser Arafat celebrated the treaty in Cairo as the first step towards a comprehensive peace treaty. Arab Palestine had now become a reality even in a political sense.

The End of War in Lebanon

On 13 May 1992 Ilyas Harawi, the President of the State of Lebanon, appointed the lawyer Rashid Sulh as the country's new prime minister. Almost seventeen years after his first term as prime minister (1974–75), there was once more a member of the Sunni Sulh family at the head of the Lebanese government; the war began and ended with him.

As the following survey will illustrate, the seventeen years of war had thrown almost all political groups into direct conflict with one another at least once. Due to the great dissociation of the warring parties from the Lebanese state, which functioned only as an economic entity, and the short-term aims of most of the military campaigns, hardly any observer believed in the re-establishment of a Lebanese nation state. The division of Lebanon into an Israeli and a

Syrian zone of occupation or influence[4] had indeed been the only concrete outcome of this war with its numerous separate conflicts:[5]

1. April 1975–March 1976: Palestine–Maronite war
2. March 1976–June 1976: Muslim–Druze war against the Maronites
3. June 1976–October 1976: Syrian–Maronite war against Palestinians – secession of southern Lebanon under the 'Free Lebanon' army of Sa'd Haddad (died 1984)
4. March 1978–November 1978: Syrian–Maronite war
5. November 1979–June 1982: Shi'i–Palestinian war – mobilization of the Hizb Allah
6. June 1982–September 1982: Palestine–Israeli war – occupation of Beirut by Israeli troops
7. 1983: confrontation between Syria and Palestine
8. October 1982–February 1984: Druze–Maronite followed by Shi'i–Maronite war
9. August 1984: Israeli-Shi'i conflict and secession of the city of Tripoli under the pro-Iranian Sheikh Sa'id Sha'ban (al-Tauhid al-Islami)
10. 1985: Palestine–Christian conflict over Sidon – Amal in coalition with the Christians of Jazzin
11. March 1985–June 1985: Palestine–Shi'i war over West Beirut – beginning of the 'camp war' (until January 1988)
12. January 1986–October 1986: Rebellion of the dismissed leader of the Forces Libanaises, Ilyas Hubaiqa, against the Christian–Maronite Supreme Command (Samir Jaja)
13. May 1986–September 1986: Shi'i-Palestinian confrontation in Beirut and Sidon
14. February 1987: Shi'i–Druze conflict
15. March 1988–May 1988: War between Amal and Hizb Allah in south Lebanon and Beirut
16. February 1989–September 1989: Syrian war against the Maronite volunteer corps under Michel Aun
17. December 1989–January 1990: second war between Amal and Hizb Allah and renewed Palestinian confrontations in Sidon.

On 22 October 1989, Saudi Arabian and American diplomats succeeded in having the warring parties come to a far-reaching political compromise in the Saudi city of Ta'if, which included a slight change in the Lebanese constitution. The Christian and Muslim parties were each to have a 50 per cent share in the political power of a centralized nation state and Syria was granted important security guarantees for its interests in Lebanon under condition that it withdrew its troops within a certain period. But the Druze and Shiʿi parties came away practically empty-handed.

The Hizb Allah and – on behalf of the Christians – the radical Maronite party of Michel Aun were violently opposed to this arrangement. Almost another two years passed before an extensive disarmament of the contending parties (with the exception of the south Lebanese parties of Christians, Shiʿis (Hizb Allah) and Palestinians) was carried out by a newly formed Lebanese army supported by Syria. From September 1991, most of the militia organized themselves as political parties, and even the PLO was once more accepted as a interlocutor by the Lebanese government. In May 1992 a general strike in Beirut, lasting several days, brought home the fact that after seventeen years of war, social and economic conditions had deteriorated to such an extent that ethnic and secessionist conflicts receded into the background. The surprising end of the Lebanese war was thus also a result of economic disaster. Until 1984 the Lebanese economy had survived the war more or less unharmed. The Lebanese pound was relatively stable, and emigration, which between 1975 and 1978 involved more than 200,000 people, remained on a relatively low level until 1983/84 (35,000 p. a.). After 1984, however, inflation led to the collapse of the economy. The value of the state-guaranteed minimum wage fell by 1987 to 38 US dollars per month (1982: 250 US dollars) and between 1985 and 1989, more than 570,000 people turned their backs on Lebanon.

The confessional system was not given up because of the war. The cabinet introduced by Rashid Sulh on 16 May 1992 again consisted of twelve Christian and twelve Muslim ministers, among them Nabih Barri (Amal), Walid Junblatt (Druze), Ilyas Hubaiqa (pro-Syrian Maronite party) and George Saʿada (Kata'ib). In the first parliamentary elections after the war, which were boycotted by most Christian parties, Amal and the Hizb Allah emerged as victors among the Muslim parties. The restoration of civil order finally led to the beginning of a vast resettlement project in which countless exiled families could return to their ancestral villages and towns. In October 1992, President Harawi formed an entirely new cabinet after consultations with Syria which, with a few exceptions, no longer included the traditional militia leaders. The southern part of the country, however, continued to be the deployment zone of Israeli troops, Palestinian units and militias of the Hizb Allah, and in July 1993 the country was once again the scene of military confrontation.

Afghanistan and the New Central Asian Republics

The radical change in the USSR finally brought about the much desired departure of Soviet troops from Afghanistan. On 15 February 1989, the last units left the country, abandoning it to the rebels and the Kabul government under the Pashtu Muhammad Najiballah, who had seized power in May 1986 and was elected president at a General Assembly on 30 November 1986. Najiballah, who had already approved the retreat of the Soviet troops in 1988, tried to oppose secessionism by promising the commanders of the *mujahidin* regional autonomy. However, they refused his offer and the war continued. Until 16 April 1992, government troops and various rebel units engaged in fierce battles. As a result, the Kabul government lost control over almost all the country's other cities. When at last the new government of the Russian Federation and the USA agreed to stop arms deliveries, Najiballah's power virtually collapsed and on 16 April 1992, as a result of pressure from the army and the rebels, he was forced to resign. The Jam'iyat-i Islami under the Tajik commander from the rebellious Pandjir region, Ahmad Shah Mas'ud (b. 1953), was now able to make its influence felt. The 50 men appointed in Peshawar to form an interim government on 25 April – five representatives each for the ten major rebel groups – agreed to elect the political leader of the Jubha-yi Najat-i Islami, Sibjat Allah Mujaddidi, as the new president. Only the Hizb-i Islami of Gulb al-Din Hikmatyar resisted and engaged in violent conflicts with Mas'ud's units prior to the arrival of the new government in Kabul. On 28 June 1992, Mujaddidi handed over his power, as stipulated in the Peshawar agreement, to the provisional president Burhan al-Din Rabbani. Hikmatyar's statist Hizb-i Islami was by no means willing to abandon control to 'the Tajiks' or 'the Uzbeks' (Abd al-Rashid Dustum, the 'Lord of the North') and stepped up its attacks on Kabul. In the provinces, the Khans were meanwhile organizing autonomous sovereignties and thus challenging the new Kabul government, which wanted to extend its sovereignty over the entire country.

Rabbani was in a way continuing the military policy of Najiballah, as was Hikmatyar, who now tried to identify himself as the champion of 'true Islam' against the 'renegades' of Kabul. The nationalism of the three major parties to the war (Pashtuns, Uzbeks and Tajiks) referred to a united Afghanistan, although with the exception of Hikmatyar's Hizb-i Islami, in the 1980s all had presented themselves as secessionist ethnic parties. The war, which had led to the transformation of the *qaum* movements into ethnic nationalist parties, continued because no side was prepared to give up Afghanistan as an ideal of the nation state and allow for actual secession through a complete political reorganization of the country. Islam, which had lent a powerful expression to the resistance against Najiballah's regime, receded into the background as a political factor. It is true that under Najiballah, Afghanistan was organized as an 'Islamic republic' in May 1990, and that two years later the *shari'a* was introduced; but this in practise led to no results, since the institutions of the state and of the autonomous regions exercised their own authority and were no longer influenced by Islamic symbolism.

The war between the resistance groups now completely centred on the capital Kabul. But no side succeeded in making a military breakthrough. Two peace treaties (signed in Mecca on 7 March 1993 and in Jalalabad on 19 May 1993) mainly served to stabilize the division of regional power by forming a government which embraced all parties to the conflict. However, the regions for the time being remained largely autonomous.

As in Afghanistan, political Islam in the new Central Asian and Caucasian republics was also oriented to ethnic nationalism. The states with a Muslim demographic majority, which had acquired their sovereignty independently or within the Russian Federation between September 1991 and March 1992, considerably enlarged the horizon of the Islamic public.

It is true that the major Islamic organizations had been well aware of the Muslim republics of the USSR since the 1960s; but scepticism prevailed. In the eyes of most Islamic observers, the cultures of these republics were so strongly dominated by the mystical orders that they discredited the claim of Islamic ideologies to count as a modern national culture. In addition, the obvious willingness of their *ulama* to cooperate with the institutions of the Soviet Union was considered as a sign that they would not necessarily profess an Islamic identity once they became independent.

The Muslim states of the USSR were in fact not independently or newly created as 'Islamic states'; indeed, their national culture was established entirely within the framework of the institutional and political conditions created under the rule of the USSR. In some cases, the re-establishment of political parties which had already existed before the Soviet conquest of 1920/24 suggested the continuity of a national political culture which was independent of the USSR. But since the nationalists in the suddenly independent republics by no means wanted to acknowledge the fact that their states were really the product of Leninist and later Stalinist minority policies, they had to resort to sometimes invented, and often mythical traditions to provide their state with the history it lacked. For instance, the nationalist Tajik historiographers would – as they had already done in the 1920s – trace back a specific Tajik national identity to the Islamic Middle Ages, and celebrate the famous Islamic philosopher Avicenna (Ibn Sina, d. 1037) as the representative of an age-old Tajik culture. The Azari nationalists in Baku, the capital of Azerbaijan, also assumed a specific Azerbaijani history in an attempt to free themselves of the embrace of the Pan-Turkists, who considered the Azaris as a homogeneous constituent of the Turkish nation.

The New Muslim Republics in Central Asia and the Caucasus

Country	Population (millions)	Area (1,000 sq. km)	Major ethnic groups	Sovereignty asserted	Confirmed independent status	Political affiliation (2001)
Kazakhastan	14.927	2,717.3	Kazakhs (41%) Russians		16.12.91	CIS
Turkmenistan	4.77	488.1	Turkomans (74%) Russians	23.8.90	27.10.91	CIS
Uzbekistan	24.406	447.4	Uzbeks (74%) Russians Tajiks	19.6.90	31.8.91	CIS
Kirghizstan	4.865	198.5	Kirghizes (57%) Russians Uzbeks		31.8.91	CIS
Baschkiria	4.015	143.6	Tartars (28%) Bashkirs (20%) Russians (38%)	29.10.90		Russian Fed.
Tajikistan	6.237	143.1	Tajiks (62%) Uzbeks (24%) Russians	25.8.90	9.9.91	CIS
Azerbaijan	7.5	86.6	Azaris (85%) Armenians Kurds	29.9.89	18.10.91	CIS (since 1993)
Tataristan	3.7	68	Tatars (48%) Russians (43%)	12.6.90	21.3.92	Russian Fed.
Daghestan	2.12	50.3	Avars (27%) Darginians (15%)	?	?	Russian Fed.
Chechnya	0.8(?)	16.6	Chechens (75-90%) Russians	27.11.89	1.11.91	Russian Fed.
Ingushstan (G'alga'ai Monn)	0.32(?)	2.7	Ingushes Russians Chechens	30.11.91	16.6.92 Secession from Chechnya	Russian Fed.
Karachayewo-Cherkessia	0.433	14.1	Cherkessians Karachais (31%) Russians	?		Russian Fed.
Kabardino-Balkaria	0.786	12.5	Kabardines (47%) Russians Balkarians	?		Russian Fed.

Northern Ossetia	0.663	8	Ossetes (62%) Russians	?		Russian Fed.
Adygea	0.449	7	Adygeans (30%) Russians	?		Russian Fed.
Abkhasia	0.3	8.6	Abkhas Georgians Russians	1990	30.9.93 Secession from Georgia	Russian Fed.

The national cultures of the newly independent republics in the Caucasus and Central Asia were, to begin with, the concepts of urban elites who often managed to condense heterogeneous ethnic characteristics which traditionally tended to incorporate modes of living and life styles, forms and uses of speech, as well as economic roles, into a state ethnicity. Whether or not the new national cultures, which were mainly handed down from the old establishment and were based on Soviet institutions, could preserve the coherence of a nation state was, however, an open question. In those places where the representatives of the old system were overthrown by Islamic-democratic parties (Tajikistan, Azerbaijan), this coherence was particularly jeopardized.

Conflict particularly threatened to break out in Tajikistan, where the harmonious transition towards an independent republic with a corresponding national culture was not immediate-ccessful. On 7 September 1992, Islamic parties had managed to remove the state president (Abdar) Rahmon Nabijev, a member of the old nomenklatura who had been elected in October 1991, and had appointed the speaker of parliament, Akbar Shoh *Iskandarov*, as transitional president. Iskandarov remained in office for two months. His Islamic-democratic coalition government had to resign after bloody conflicts with Nabijev's followers and yield to a government of the Tajik Popular Front headed by Safarali Kandzayev. In mid-December 1992, the new government re-conquered the capital city of Dushanbe from the Islamic rebels, whereupon the warlike conflicts between the Islamic opposition in the southern and eastern part of the country (Badakhshan) and the government troops supported by Russia started to escalate. Nabijev, who died suddenly in late April 1993, was followed as president by the politician Imam Ali Rahmanov, who was now described as a member of the resistance. By the summer of 1993, when the conflict threatened to escalate in the southern part of the country, more than 30,000 men must have fallen victims of the war in Tajikistan.

The Islamic civilian government in Azerbaijan, which, after the presidential election of 7 July 1992, was headed by Abulfas Elçibai, the leader of the Popular Front, was unable to end the war against Armenia over Nagorni Karabagh, an Armenian autonomous region in Azerbaijan.[6] The conflict between Armenia and Azerbaijan, which had been smouldering since 1988, had escalated into open warfare immediately after a referendum of the Armenian population in Nagorni Karabagh, which pronounced itself almost 100 per cent in favour of complete independence. In the course of several years of warfare, Armenia managed to open several land corridors towards Karabagh and thus to prevent the conquest of the region by Azerbaijani government troops. Ethnic conflicts in Azerbaijan had already been noticeable when in the late 1980s Armenian families were again and again attacked by Azeri militants in the industrial cities around Baku and Sumgait. In June 1993, Elçibai, who championed a radical nationalist policy, had to flee from the capital to escape rebellious troops. With the support of army commanders, power was subsequently assumed by the former first secretary of the Azerbaijani Communist party, Gaidar Aliev, who belonged to the old nomenklatura.

2. THE ISLAMIC WORLD AFTER THE END OF THE EAST–WEST CONFLICT ANOTHER CONFLICT OF SYSTEMS?

On 14 February 1989, the Iranian revolutionary leader Ayatollah Khomeini issued his famous sentence (*fatwa*) on Salman Rushdie to the Iranian media. The text read:[7]

> 'In the name of God!
>
> 'To Him we belong, and to Him we shall return' [Koran, *sura* 2/156]. I inform the pious Muslims of the entire world that the author of the book 'The Satanic Verses', which was written, printed and published against Islam, the Prophet and the Koran, as well as its publishers who know its [the book's] content, are sentenced to death. I call on every zealous Muslim to kill them immediately wherever they can find them, so that nobody else will dare offend the holy values of Muslims. Anyone who is killed on this path is – by God's will – a martyr. If someone meanwhile has access to the author of the book 'The Satanic Verses', without having the power to kill him, he must hand him over to the people so that he may be punished for his defamation. Peace be with you, God's grace and His blessing!
>
> [signed by] Ruhollah Musavi [Khomeini] – 25 Bahman 1367 [13 February 1989].'

Khomeini, who was now hailed by Tehran officials as the 'embodiment of

Muslim doctrines and of divine religious standards, by himself an entire nation',[8] was reacting against the external, internal and politico-cultural circumstances of the year 1988, which were disadvantageous to Iran. The armistice with Iraq and the mutual exchange of ambassadors demanded new efforts towards rehabilitating the country and legitimating a settlement with the 'arch-enemy' Iraq. As far as foreign affairs were concerned, Iran was forced to come to a certain understanding with Saudi Arabia, with which it had remained on a 'cold war' footing since 1983. In November 1988, both sides declared their willingness to end their long propaganda war.

Salman Rushdie's novel *The Satanic Verses* was published on 26 September 1988 by the Viking Press in London and caused considerable unrest among Muslim communities first in India, and later in Great Britain. Two Indian parliamentarians (Sayyid Shihab al-Din and Khurshid Alam Khan) started a well-targeted campaign against the book and managed to have the Indian government prohibit its distribution on 5 October. Pakistan, South Africa and Saudi Arabia immediately followed suit. Meanwhile, the rector of al-Azhar University emphatically warned against *The Satanic Verses*, but had to admit that he had only read the passages handed to him by the Egyptian foreign ministry.

To begin with, Islamic societies had reacted cautiously to *The Satanic Verses* which mainly deals with two Indian Muslims who had 'emigrated' to England and described their conflict with mass culture, to which they devoted themselves almost in a trance, only to wake up later in a nihilistic moment. Rushdie's parable of the lost myth of Islam in alien Great Britain commanded little interest outside the Western public, for which the novel had been written. An Iranian reviewer cautiously remarked that 'some critics maintain that *The Satanic Verses* implicitly refers to Iran, or at all events describes a certain reaction of the West to Iran's Islamic Revolution.'[9] In fact the book did not mean anything much to the Islamic public and most Muslim countries had confined themselves to a ban on its importation until December 1988, when the Muslim community of Bradford in England demonstrated against Rushdie himself. On 14 January 1989, several thousand Bradford Muslims participated in a public burning of Rushdie's novel. It was only then that the call to 'execute' the novelist on the grounds that he had 'insulted the prophet' was heard.

The hitherto largely apolitical community of Indian and Pakistani Muslims had suddenly discovered Islam as a medium of protest against their social and cultural misery – which, incidentally, had been described in *The Satanic Verses.* But while Rushdie saw Islam as a parable for the world, the Bradford demonstrators discovered it as a medium through which to find an equitable place in the world. The spark ignited Muslims in Pakistan and India: on 12 February, the day before the formulation of Khomeini's *fatwa*, five demonstrators were shot in front of the American embassy in Rawalpindi in Pakistan. Among the wounded was the leader of the Society of the Ulama of Islam (Jam'iyat-i Ulama-i Islam), Molana Fadl al-Rahman. Even the Pakistani prime minister Benazir Bhutto was not spared by the protests. The demonstrators called her a 'witch' accompanying the 'devil' Rushdie in his 'crusade' against Islam.

Once the author, rather than the book, was the focus of events, and demonstrators from Rawalpindi, Srinagar, London and Bradford found that they had recognized the West, and especially the USA, as their true opponent, the Iranian leadership started to react. To Khomeini – or to his environment – the Rushdie case provided a promising means of recovering the initiative within the general Islamic public. With the publication of the *fatwa*, Iran's ideological and theological isolation was suddenly broken. The crucial factor was not so much the legal character of the verdict. Most Islamic jurists expressed serious doubts as to whether Khomeini could legitimately issue a written statement of this sort. The *fatwa*, they argued, far exceeded the kind of judgment that was customary among jurists because it contained a verdict, indeed a summons, to kill. Though Khomeini had the right to express a legal opinion which among the Shi'a had a high status, this could not amount to a verdict, which could only be pronounced by a court. Besides, Khomeini was not entitled to appoint the Muslims as a whole as executives of his 'verdict', for executive power was represented by the state alone as the administrator of justice. Consequently, the ethical content of Khomeini's statement could be approved; but it could not replace a regular court procedure. Since, in accordance with classical Islamic jurisprudence, this procedure could not be carried out *in absentia*, the Islamic public had to content itself with the moral condemnation of the text of the novel.

If Saudi authorities in particular appreciated such an opinion of the case, others pointed out that, in accordance with Wahhabi doctrine, the Saudi legal system had removed the distinction between ethical guidance in legal matters (*ifta'*) and legally binding verdicts. Indeed, the highest Saudi legal expert, Ibn Baz, always considered his statements as legally binding verdicts. It was also pointed out that on 26 June 1983 the Mufti of Jerusalem, Sa'd al-Din al-Alami, had issued a legal opinion in which he outlawed the Syrian president Asad and called on every Muslim to kill him immediately, wherever possible.[10] By contrast to the public authorities,[11] small neo-Salafi groups considered Khomeini's verdict as a direct summons to act. Islamic Jihad in Palestine and the Hizb Allah in Beirut, as well as the 'Islamic Community' (al-Jama'a al-Islamiya) in Egypt, which was now led by Umar Abd al-Rahman, declared themselves ready to carry out the verdict. Abd al-Rahman (born 1939) was considered by the Egyptian public as the spiritual author of Sadat's assassination and as the *mufti* of the Egyptian Jihad groups. Following several arrests, he went to the al-Fayum oasis in 1989 where he was joined by hundreds of students and other sympathizers. On 7 April 1989, his groups demonstrated their strength. Benefiting from the popularity of Khomeini's verdict, thousands went out into the streets of the capital of al-Fayum province and protested against the 'un-Islamic regime' of Cairo.

On the whole, public response to Khomeini's verdict in the Islamic, and especially the Arab world was insignificant. It was far too obviously connected with Iranian political interests, which were felt by many Islamic groups to contribute to the division in the Islamic community. The moral indignation was without doubt great, but hardly anyone was interested in turning it into a political protest. Arab Muslims in particular interpreted Khomeini's act as a transparent attempt to raise his prestige in the Islamic world by exploiting Islamic feelings of self-respect.[12]

Khomeini's trick did no more than briefly raise Iran's prestige within the national Islamic public. The Libyan revolutionary leader Qaddafi quickly pointed out that 'religious circles were capitalizing on the matter for a fight against Pan-Arabism, because they are jealous of the fact that the Arabs are the true imams of the Muslims.'[13] Nor was Saudi Arabia interested in taking part in the matter which was brushed aside by the foreign minister Sa'ud al-Faisal with the following words:[14]

> The kingdom refuses to be involved in such a marginal and imaginary conflict. Even if the kingdom recognizes the pain felt by Muslims because of the publication of the book, it does not consider it as the most dangerous provocation confronting the Muslims. Every attempt to aggrandize the problem makes Islam an easy prey for those who want to destroy or attack it.

Iran nevertheless insisted on presenting the Rushdie affair at the 18th Islamic Foreign Ministers Conference in Riyadh, which it wanted to turn into a forum to demonstrate the re-awakening of its international Islamic responsibility after the Gulf War. But the Iranian delegates representing the Iranian 'Islamic Propaganda Organization' (Munazzamat-i A'lam-i Islami) did not score the success they expected. Rushdie was discussed under the subject of 'culture' and not, as Iran had desired, under 'politics'.

Saudi Arabia continued to keep its distance from Iran. After all, the Wahhabi *ulama* still considered the Shi'a as a heretical sect, and the Iranian *ulama* for their own part defied all attempts at appeasement by polemicizing against the Wahhabiya as the stronghold of heretical reaction and an 'American Islam'. The great pilgrimage conflicts of the 1980s were not forgotten. Between 1983 and 1988, there had been constant confrontations with Iranian pilgrims in Mecca, who tried to turn the pilgrimage into a political demonstration against the USA and Israel, and Saudi security forces and in July 1987, hundreds of

Iranian and other Shi'i pilgrims were killed as a result.[15] Two years later, there were still obvious tensions between the Saudis and the Iranians. After Khomeini's death on 3 June 1989, his son Ahmad and his appointed successor, the then president Ali Khamenei,[16] tried once more to magnify the hostile image of Saudi Arabia in order to present themselves as the worthy successors of the revolutionary leader. Two bomb attempts in Mecca (11 June 1989) and the execution of 16 Shi'i Kuwaitis in Mecca (20 September 1989) contributed to a further deterioration of the relations between Iran and Saudi Arabia.

New fronts emerged when on 9 March 1989 Saudi Arabia officially recognized the Afghan Mujahidin government. At the Islamic Foreign Ministers' Conference in Riyadh, Iran and the PLO abstained from voting when Saudi Arabia proposed the admission of the government-in-exile into the Organization of the Islamic Conference. Syria, Iraq, Libya and Northern and Southern Yemen voted against. These countries formed the core of the old anti-royalist front. But classical positions in the Arab-Islamic world were beginning to crumble.

Reversed Fronts: The War for Kuwait 1990–1991

In the summer of 1989, Iraq's President Saddam Husain launched a political rehabilitation of the Hashimite royal family who had ruled over Iraq until 1958, and emphasized the Islamic aspect of Iraq's national culture. This enabled him to build up a new alliance with Jordan, which was to be important later on in the war for Kuwait, for it enabled Iraq to evade the economic boycott imposed on it. The posture of Islamic victory which the regime now propagated all over the country, casting it in concrete to form innumerable monuments, was meant to connect the desired rehabilitation of Iraq's market economy after the Gulf War with the continuation of the Ba'th dictatorship. By contrast to the international trend, the opening-up of the Iraqi economy was not followed by a political liberation of civil society. The Islamization of the Ba'thist-dominated public was thus meant to compensate for the open economy and emphasize the 'civilian' character of the regime. Due to the enormous costs of the Gulf War (for Iraq about 452.6 billion US dollars and Iran 644.3 billion US dollars[17]), the liberalization of the economy was an indispensable prerequisite for the preservation of state power and for re-equipping the armed forces, on which twice as much money was spent as on the reconstruction of the ravaged cities in the southern part of the country.

Meanwhile, Iraq remained deeply encumbered with debts: the Gulf states, including Saudi Arabia, had claims to the tune of over 60 billion US dollars, the USSR 10 billion US dollars and the Western industrial states over 30 billion US dollars. Even if the Gulf States and the USSR had possessed the means to collect these debts, the Iraqi economy was unable to raise such sums, Nor did the oil reserves provide the regime with reassurance of a long-term financial recovery. The only true victor was the Iraqi army, which still had more than a million men under arms in 1988. To demobilize this army would have involved the danger of a typical post-war revolution. So the army was supported and re-equipped and a new opponent was soon found for it. Following disputes with the Gulf States over oil prices, the Iraqi government felt affronted when the Kuwait 'parliament' included Iraq's debts to the Emirate in its budget.

Iraq maintained that it had fought the war against Iran 'in the name of the Arabs', and demanded both the cancellation of its debts and compensation through drilling rights in the northern Kuwaiti oil fields. Kuwait, whose income from foreign investments in 1986 for the first time exceeded its oil revenues, and was therefore less interested in an increase in oil prices, was not prepared to comply with the Iraqi demands. To corroborate its claims on Kuwait's oil, the Iraqi government maintained, as it had already done when Kuwait had become independent in 1961, that the country had always been a province of Iraq.

On 16 July 1990, the Iraqi foreign minister Tariq Aziz lodged a claim on Kuwait with the Arab League and at the same time brought the following four accusations against its neighbour: Kuwait had extracted Iraqi oil in the Rumaila fields; it had built military installations on Iraqi land; it had prevented an equitable rise of Iraqi oil incomes through its low-price policy, and it had, like the United Arab Emirates, refused to cancel the Iraqi war debts.

Iraq and Kuwait: Oil Revenues Per Head of Population 1980–1988 (in US$)[18]

Year	Iraq	Kuwait
1980	3,917	12,856
1981	1,511	9,542
1982	1,366	1,292
1983	1,292	6,208
1984	1,453	6,367
1985	1,648	5,972
1986	864	4,263
1987	1,437	3,839
1988	1 ,000	3,220

As 30,000 soldiers of the Iraqi elite units assembled on its border, the Emir of Kuwait reacted by convoking the National Assembly. By this time the USA's Middle East Task Force had been put on alert. Saddam Husain considered

Kuwait's economic policy as a 'declaration of war', and, after negotiations broke down in Jeddah on 2 August 1990, ordered his troops to march into Kuwait.

On 10 August, twelve Arab states of the anti-Iraq alliance attended a summit conference in Cairo, encouraged by the United Nations Security Council. All other states except Libya abstained from voting. Saudi Arabia, which considered itself in the front line against Iraq, summoned all its political resources to recruit the Arab and Islamic states for this alliance. In the course of the further intensified boycott by the member states of the alliance (there had meanwhile been the UN Security Council resolutions 661 of the 6 August, 667 of the 16 September against embassy occupations in Kuwait, 670 of 25 September and especially 678 of 29 November – 'all necessary means for the realization of the UN resolutions until 15 January 1991'), the USA and its allies prepared a major offensive against Iraq, which started on 16 January 1991 with an air offensive in cooperation with 28 states. Shortly afterwards, the Saudi Arabian jurist Ibn Baz made a legal statement declaring that the circumstances allowed the participation of 'infidels' in a *jihad* (just war).[19]

After numerous bombing raids, the allies launched a five-day ground offensive on 23 January 1991, leading to Iraq's complete withdrawal from Kuwait. As in 1988, the Iraqi army now turned against the rebellious Kurds in the north of the country. The population of southern Iraq, which had practically seceded from Baghdad's sovereignty, was also hard-pressed by the Iraqi army, although the latter did not succeed in recovering complete control over the region.

Although internationally isolated, Saddam Husain was still able to improve his prestige within the Islamic world. Above all, his Islamic-nationalist appeal to those who felt 'suppressed by imperialism' led to a short-lived renaissance of a Third-World identity. The Rushdie case, the massive attack against Iraq which cost the lives of 150,000 men, and the obvious interest of the West in securing the stability of the Gulf principalities to safeguard the local oil reserves, had created a distinct anti-Western frame of mind. The losers in this situation were those who had hoped for political liberalization through peaceful change. They were confronted with the fact that Western policy always prevailed over internal political processes in the Islamic world, and that, as a result, Islamic partisans of the political opening-up of civil society and of participation in the state fundamentally distanced themselves from 'Western models'. Many Islamic intellectuals now realized that the time had come to form a new political-Islamic bloc. On one side was the united West–East world which had created the United Nations Security Council as an instrument of 'global supremacy' for itself, on the other the Islamic world which alone continued to represent the ideals of 'Third-World revolutionary anti-imperialism'.

Major parts of the Islamic public readily accepted the idea of a new formation of blocs between Islam and the West. They felt that all the states of the Islamic world were 'siding with the West' (only the PLO, Jordan, the Yemen and Libya, with their highly specific interests, had temporarily showed sympathy for Saddam Husain) and that Muslims deserved an Islamic identity of their own that would be independent of the regimes which dominated them. The formation of blocs, which was stimulated by the events of the years 1989 and 1991, thus symbolically separated the Muslim population from their 'pro-Western' regimes. However, the protest that was expressed in this way against the lack of participation in political power did not lead to direct constitutional demands, since these appeared to be discredited by the policy of the West.

The new formation of blocs was culturally oriented and had no national political counterparts. There were neither alliances nor inter-governmental treaties to lend it any specific contours. Unlike the 1960s, when in terms of realpolitik two great blocs were facing one another in the Islamic world, the new formation involved a process of cultural division between the Western world and Islam, the creation of a heuristic basis through which events in the Islamic world could be interpreted and understood. The ideological blocs of the Cold War were thus replaced by cultural blocs which effectively determined Islamic policy.

The Plea for an 'Open Islamic Society'

Early in 1991, a group of intellectuals from Mecca and Jeddah wrote a declaration on the creation of a 'modern Islamic State' in Saudi Arabia and in May or June sent it to King Fahd.[20] In it, they demanded an extensive reform of the Saudi legal and administrative system and reminded the king of his frequent promises to establish a democratic and constitutional system. It was indeed in the context of the war over Kuwait that the king had again spoken of the possibility of appointing a deliberative assembly.[21] In this declaration, the signatories demanded:

> ... the establishment of a regular system for providing legal information (*fatawa*), whereby the infallible orthodox religious laws which are unalterable and have been incorporated in the mediating texts of the Koran and the Sunna should be borne in mind. Everything else, including the religious judgments of *ulama* and jurists, as well as the opinions of exegetes and the legal opinions and opinion-makers, represents nothing but human efforts aiming at an understanding of legal texts; all this, on its part, is influenced by the personal understanding of those who do it, and by their aptitude for knowledge and learning, whereby each [opinion] is dependent on time and place. As a result, they are subject to temptation, error and debate. Therefore learned men have unanimously agreed that nobody may claim the right for himself alone to know the true intentions of God in the Holy Book and those of his prophet or to

assume the authority to issue laws and impose them on the entire nation.[22]

These very cautious, but essentially resolute claims for the establishment of an 'open Islamic society' (*al-mujtama' al-islami al-maftuh*) were an initial attempt by civil society to make itself heard. After the re-conquest of Kuwait in February 1991, the latter had lost an important bastion, where until 1990 they had normally published their criticism of the state and of the Wahhabi national culture. In this sense, the conquest of Kuwait had provided the king with the welcome concomitant effect that the internal political opposition lost its essential chance of self-expression.

The Wahhabi *ulama* of Najd, who had to deal with the major problem of reconciling the presence of American troops with their basic pietistic approach, reacted promptly. In a letter to King Fahd, members of the Committee of Grand Ulama (Ha'iat Kibar al-Ulama) declared, with explicit support from Ibn Baz, that the situation indeed required the establishment of a council 'to discuss internal and external matters'. The ethical principles of national culture had to be strengthened; the role of the *ulama* had to be newly defined by an expansion of their authority; and 'competent legal committees' had to examine the conformity of state regulations with the *shari'a*. In addition, they demanded that 'the public law corporations be unified and granted effective and complete independence to extend the jurisdiction of the judge to include everyone, and to organize an independent institution to supervise the execution of legal verdicts.'[23]

The constitutionalism of the jurists differed, of course, from that of the Hijazi opposition. While the latter demanded a democratic system in the Islamic tradition based on the division of powers, the Wahhabi *ulama* stated that they alone could control state policy by means of the juristic competence vested in them.[24]

Algerian Strivings for Democracy

The demands of the Saudi opposition for the establishment of an 'open Islamic society' had far greater resonance among the Islamic public after 1990 than those of the radical Islamic visionaries who, within the context of Iranian politics, were still dreaming of an 'Islamic world revolution' and 'the liberation of the oppressed of all countries'.[25] The Leninist revolutionary ideals still concealed behind these Islamic slogans no longer found any support within civil society. Instead, such slogans as 'pluralism', 'openness', 'democracy' and 'freedom of movement' were making the rounds, and were now deliberately derived from the ethical tradition of Islam. Even Islamic jurists eagerly participated in the expression of an Islamic liberalism which had been fiercely attacked by prominent Islamic authors only a few years earlier.[26] With the decline of ideological views of the world, the classical political Islam of the neo-Salafiya also lost much of its political influence.

Hopes for social openness through Islamic liberalism were present in Algeria, Tunisia and Morocco as early as 1988. Some writers now believed that monarchy would offer far better initial conditions for a 'completion of the bourgeois revolution' than a republican regime. These authors seemed to lay stress on the following: the bourgeois revolution in the Islamic world had been interrupted by long years of supremacy on behalf of the 'petty bourgeoisie'; to complete the revolution and thus finally grant the liberal bourgeoisie its breakthrough to power on a constitutional basis was the main task of the Islamic public. This required no Islamic ideological programmes, but an Islamic formulation of bourgeois identity. The latter, for its part, could not be attained by copying Western bourgeois cultures, but by engaging in a new essentialist contemplation of Islam, which would safeguard the values of bourgeois society far better than the Western critics of modernism who were tangled up in their doubts about themselves. Islam was thus considered as the true achievement of modernism. The West attempted to surmount modernism through wordy constructions of post-modernism, but Islam could fill the Islamic world with meaningful content.[27] So it was the task of the Islamic public to achieve the emancipation of civil society as an autonomous, heterogeneous and multiform relationship between citizens and state.

But it was clear, above all in North Africa, that the 'European discourse' was also naturally striving for predominance within a civil society on its way to liberation. Ethnic parties also increasingly gained in influence when, in 1988, the Algerian leadership pleaded for social openness and declared its readiness to give up the FLN's monopoly over power. The crucial factor behind this decision was, without doubt, the disastrous economic condition of the country. With a foreign debt that amounted to half its gross national product, the government could not provide the population with its basic needs. Instead, numerous small Islamic welfare organizations worked to assist and support people, particularly in the underprivileged new settlements of the large cities. The youth protests of November 1986, which spread all over eastern Algeria, showed how necessary the establishment of such civil institutions were in Algerian society and in July 1987, the Algerian government finally passed a law admitting the creation of independent associations.

But the tension in Algeria did not ease. On 4 October 1988, grave unrest kindled, among other things, by renewed attempts of the ruling FLN to carry out austerity measures in order to curb the economic crisis, broke out in Algiers and soon spread to other northern Algerian cities. The government had to admit that more than 150 people had lost their lives in the revolts and more than 7,000 had been arrested. Now that the youth protests threatened to spread over the entire country, Islamic intellectuals called openly for an extensive economic, social and political reform of the system.

The central bureaucracy had manifestly failed, and with it the FLN party of unity which had so often claimed to represent the whole of the Algerian people. On 23 February 1989, the Algerian president Chadli Bendjedid tried to improve his position by introducing constitutional reform, but at the same time had to tolerate a loss of power by the FLN, since the new constitution, approved in a referendum by 73 per cent of the votes, allowed for the formation of parties independent of the state. The first such party to appear in public was the Front Islamique du Salut (FIS), which was officially acknowledged on 16 September of the same year. By January 1990 more than 20 others had been established, among them three additional Islamic parties. The FIS had already, by the autumn of 1989, established itself as a powerful opposition to the FLN, and proved during the earthquake of 29 October that it alone was in a position to provide direct aid to the afflicted population. The numerous positions represented by the Front were as yet still able to state their specific political demands without succumbing to a unified Islamic discourse.[28] The FIS thus started out as a reservoir of Islamic opposition in which a rightist-conservative wing only gradually managed to assert itself under the educationalist Abbasi Madani. The spokesman of the FIS was now the Friday prayer leader Ali Ibn al-Hajj (Belhadj) who, unlike Madani, openly worked for a statist Islamic policy following Maududi's principles, and who appeared as the populist speaker of the 'angry' Algerian youth. Ibn al-Hajj, who still had close personal connections with the young generation, thus also had the support of Algerian students, almost 50 per cent of whom came from families without a steady income.[29]

The non-Islamic opposition formed four major parties: the Parti Social-Démocrate (led by Abd al-Rahman Ajrid), the Rassemblement Pour la Culture et la Démocratie (a Berber party led by Sa'id Sa'di), the Front des Forces Socialistes (Hocine Ait Ahmed, Berber tradition) and the Mouvement Démocratique en Algérie (Ahmad Ben Bella[30]). At the local elections held in June 1990, the FIS emerged as the clear victor. It now controlled 32 of the 48 provincial councils and more than half of the community and city councils. The fight for supremacy over the expanding civil community continued unabated and split the political public into two symmetrical camps: between 28 June and 12 July, an Islamic parent federation of trade unions was formed, while at the same time independent socialist trade unions were also being registered. Both sides were able to mobilize almost 100,000 demonstrators. In July 1991 the conflict came to a dramatic head after the Madani government had more spokesmen of the FIS, as well as 700 militants, arrested. In this tense political situation, large numbers of the Islamic public were radicalized and, pointing to the events in the war over Kuwait, demanded that the importation of 'Western political models' of democracy be stopped.

In the repeatedly postponed parliamentary elections of 26 December 1991, which were to be carried out in two ballots in accordance with the French electoral system, the FIS finally won 188 direct mandates (out of 430), while the non-Islamic parties together took only 33. In the second ballot, scheduled for 16 January 1992, an overwhelming victory of the FIS was feared. Already on 2 January 1992, more than 150,000 panic-stricken demonstrators demanded the cancellation of the second ballot. The FIS, which was sure of its victory, shortly afterwards published a new electoral programme in which a further radicalization of the Islamic viewpoint was demanded. This included the separation of sexes in schools and the absolute observance of the 'Islamic law'. On 11/12 January 1992, an army coup removed Bendjedid from office, dissolved parliament, and on 9 February established martial law. This military coup, which could also rely on support from leading members of the FLN, only provoked a short-lived alliance of most of the political parties, among them between party organizations of the FLN and FIS.

The new Algerian government under the previous commander of the FLN, Muhammad Boudiaf (Bu Diyaf), a former partisan of Messali Hadj, now resolutely proceeded against the Islamic opposition. All the communal administrations dominated by the FIS were dissolved, and the FIS itself was banned on 29 April 1992. After the assassination of Boudiaf by security officials, the new president Ali Kafi, also a former partisan of Messali Hadj, stepped up the campaign against the FIS. Abbasi Madani and Ibn al-Hajj were sentenced to 15 years of prison and a large number of Islamists were taken to internment camps. At the same time, the government tried to involve FIS dissidents in political responsibilities. One of them, Sa'id Guedi, even became a member of the cabinet.

In the following months, Islamic policy was largely repressed in public. Radical splinter groups reacted by taking up an 'armed fight' against the regime, which could only rely on part of Algerian civil society, and propagated a 'second national war of liberation'. But when Islamic militants intensified their attacks on army and police centres and, from the spring of 1993, even acted against civilians who argued in an explicitly non-Islamic manner, the influence of the independent Islamic public was virtually broken. Nevertheless, their discourse had its effects. Both Ben Bella and the politically re-emerging Yusuf Ben Khedda, who had replaced Farhat Abbas as prime minister of the FLN government in exile, now regularly couched their political programmes in an Islamic language.

The FIS mainly symbolized the Algerian society's settling of accounts with the FLN. Since the FLN hardly acted as a party from an institutional point of view, its integration within society was extremely tenuous. It was only under Boumedienne (d. 27 December 1978) that the FLN had had a positive function of integration. Bendjedid, on the other hand, was considered as the upstart representative of an elite which had no nation of its own. The 'nation without an elite', with an unemployment rate of almost 20 per cent, considered the FIS as the only force which could give it a certain cultural and political sovereignty within the state.[31] The elite which supported the state, on the other hand, seemed to refuse to support the nation and thus confirmed the schism in Algerian society created by the FLN. Meanwhile, no account was taken of the Berber parties of Kabylia, where neither the FIS nor the other bourgeois groups had found any major support.

3. THE END OF THE HOPE FOR ISLAMIC SOVEREIGNTY

A New Royalism?

The dream of an 'open Islamic society', in which the sense of belonging to a civil society would be underpinned by a native discourse, soon vanished in those countries in which long years of military dictatorship had in practice caused the urban elites to be 'without a nation'. However, the transition to an Islamically authorized party pluralism went more smoothly in countries like the Yemen, which was officially united on 22 May 1990, and in which the elites and 'the nation' lived together within a close network of relationships. When the consensus between the elites of Northern and Southern Yemen broke down in the spring of 1994, the groups associated with them also split up, siding either with the 'north' or the 'south'. At the beginning of May 1994, the contention escalated and acquired the dimensions of an armed conflict. The fact that the Islamic discourse still had great appeal was demonstrated by the military coup in Sudan on 30 June 1989; here the army around Lieutenant-General Umar Hasan Ahmad al-Bashir had overthrown the three-year-old civilian regime of Sadiq al-Mahdi and arrested all the members of the government. On 17 November leading politicians, among them al-Mahdi and Hasan al-Turabi, were released. To begin with, the revolutionary council under al-Bashir tried to reach a compromise with civilian society. But the established parties proved unwilling to collaborate with the army. The University of Khartoum, traditionally the stronghold of the 'European discourse', became the centre of opposition. The national party of al-Mahdi even contacted the South Sudanese national liberation army led by Colonel John Garang, which it had previously opposed, in order to form a front against the military regime. In May 1990, a national committee began to work out the political framework for a new social system based on Islam. The government had its new course approved on 30 June at a mass meeting in Khartoum and recruited the Muslim Brotherhood around Hasan al-Turabi as an ally 'to re-introduce the *shari'a*'. The 22 March 1991 was named as the target date on which the *shari'a* was to be proclaimed in the northern regions of the country. A year later, Bashir declared that so-called 'basic conferences' by 'democratic groups' were to be organized in order to create an entirely new political system of civil society. In the throes of the crucial war against the rebels in southern Sudan and the hardly improving economic situation, there thus took place a gradual Islamization of the political public which controlled the regime. In this situation Turabi thus had the privilege of exercising a momentous influence on shaping the Sudanese national culture as the *éminence grise* of the military regime. On 17 October 1993, Bashir appeared to have achieved his goal. He announced the dissolution of the Supreme Military Council, had himself appointed as president of the state and proclaimed new elections within a reasonable space of time.

An Islamic sovereignty, as might be deduced from Sudan's example, could only be created by the state. But this definitely defeated the purposes of civil society, which did not want democracy to be granted 'from above', but saw itself as a mixture of different political and non-political institutions and organizations and tried to defend the interests of its citizens against the power of an ideological one-party state. That is why even if a state-imposed Islamization of the public – as in Sudan or Pakistan – could politically bind the 'nation', it would be at the expense of the state's 'elites'.

The Islamic monarchies were much better off. Since princes and kings legitimized their sovereignty through Islam and at the same time offered the elites a civil system of relations through the court, they could always find a compromise between 'people' and 'elite', between an Islamic and a European discourse. That was how the Jordanian King Husain overcame the rise of Islamic parties between 1989 and 1992 without major problems, even though the Muslim Brotherhood's coalition had more than a third of the seats in parliament after the 1989 elections. The Moroccan King Hasan II also succeeded in achieving this adjustment. When slogans against monarchy were heard at a mass demonstration in favour of Saddam Husain during the Kuwait war, Hasan II let it be known that 'his heart was with the Iraqi people, but his head with the coalition troops'.[32] From the perspective of domestic politics – and it must be pointed out that almost all the reactions to the Kuwait war concerned domestic policy – this signified that the king was 'emotionally' siding with 'the people', but 'rationally' siding with the 'elites'. This classical dual function of the monarch played a crucial role in the early 1990s. Above all, the symbols of monarchy seemed to be better at representing national integration than a republican regime. It is true that surges towards restoring the royalist system were only sporadically to be noticed around 1992. But when Saddam Husain rehabilitated the Hashimites in 1989, he laid the foundations for developing his own family's reign into a dynastic system.

But it was precisely the Islamic political public, which was now predominantly committed to an open society and saw itself as the only group authorized to represent civil society, which clearly pronounced itself for a republican system. Even a caliphate was considered out of the question by most Islamic groups, since they attributed the principle of sovereignty to society alone (or to the state as such) as the deputy of God. An Islamic kingdom combining the sovereignty of civil society with the symbol of monarchy was theoretically difficult to imagine and was in practice not discussed.[33] Among the forecasts discussed for the future of the political system in the countries of the Middle East – foreign-trade-oriented 'authoritarian democracy', domestic trade policy tending towards populist control by the mixed areas ('Islamic Republic'), or decentralized bourgeois democracy aiming at an adjustment between foreign and domestic trade[34] – there was no mention of restoring the monarchy.

The Ethnification of Islam: War in Bosnia-Herzegovina

When in 1963 the Republic of Bosnia-Herzegovina adopted a new constitution, it was observed that 'there are Serbs, Croats and Muslims living in Bosnia-Herzegovina'. Thus the Muslim Bosnians (Bosniaks), the majority of whom followed the tradition of the Bogomils, were for the first time granted an independent identity, based not on linguistic criteria, but on criteria referring to their 'sphere of life'. Being-a-Muslim was interpreted by the majority of the Yugoslav population as an independent form 'of living', where the religious content was attributed no specific role. Five years later, the Muslim Bosnians were, for the first time, recognized as a nation by the communist Yugoslav union. A lower-ranking identity as a 'nationality', which was applied to Hungarians and Albanians, was not considered by the central government, because the Muslim Bosnians could not be linked to any other nation state. From 1971, the 'nation' of 'Muslimani' was officially recognized; thus a tradition based on a religion and a sphere of life had become an ethnic category, which in the censuses of 1971 and 1981 was extended to other Yugoslav republics. Oddly enough, the Yugoslav government thus went back to the Ottoman *millet* system, which had marked the legal and administrative independence of religious communities since the 18th century, and which was now applied for the first time to Muslims.

Among the absurdities of the national regulations in Bosnia-Herzegovina was the fact that the Muslimani were not entitled to their own national institutions, but had to share them in a fixed proportion of one-third with the

Serbs and Croats. As in Lebanon, the Muslims were thus politically underrepresented, since they amounted to at least 50 per cent of the republic's population. Besides, Muslim politicians soon complained that the Serbs and Croats already had an independent state and that therefore – according to the principles of Yugoslav national culture – they actually ought to count as mere nationalities within Bosnia-Herzegovina.

In the 1970s the Yugoslav government tried to segregate the Muslimani from the international Islamic public, because they saw the politicization of a hypothetical nation of Muslims as a threat to the nation state system of Yugoslavia. As a result, every attempt by Islamic circles to form an independent Islamic public among the Bosnians was denounced as a 'pan-Islamic' or 'fundamentalist' threat.

Muslims in Yugoslavia 1981–1988[35]

Republic/ Region	1962	1981	Population %	1988
Bosnia-Herzegovina	847,000	1,850,000	48.5	2,200,000
Serbia	137,000	270,000		300,000
Kosovo	830,000	1,350,000	82.2	1,560,000
Macedonia	317,000	450,000	26.0	700,000
Montenegro	58,000	150,000	20.5	160,000
Total	2,189,000	3,650,000	18.3	5,000,000

The collapse of the Yugoslav Federation in 1991/92 at first brought very little change in the internal condition of the Republic of Bosnia-Herzegovina. The Bosnian government prepared a referendum about the independence of the state as a whole without any particular ethnic specification. It was nevertheless boycotted on 29 February and 1 March by the Serbian population, which amounted to one-third of the population as a whole. On 8 April 1992, a day after the international recognition of the new state, the first fights broke out between the hastily assembled army of Bosnia-Herzegovina and the Serbian separatists, who first fought within the framework of the Yugoslav national army, and from 5 May as the Serbian army of the Republic of Bosnia-Herzegovina. The objectives of the Serbian units were unclear at the beginning of the war. To all appearances, the political leadership of the Serbs around Radovan Karadzic was trying to seize power in the capital city, Sarajevo, by military means and to preserve the country as a constituent state of Yugoslavia. However, when on 3 July 1992 a 'Croat state of Herceg-Bosna' was proclaimed for the Croat population around the city of Mostar, the fear of a territorial division of the country caused bitter fighting over the ensuing months. This led to a breakdown of the national consensus in Bosnia-Herzegovina, which was based on the proportional balance of nationalities. The president of the state, Alija Izetbegovich, who for years had appeared in public as a declared Muslim and had been co-founder of the Muslim Party of Democratic Action, continued to demand a united secular state for Bosnia-Herzegovina, in which Islamic culture would guarantee a modern, civil and European order. But with the foundation of the Serbian Republic, which claimed more than two-thirds of the state's territory for itself, there began a further phase of ethnicizing Islamic culture. This was further intensified by the radicalization of the political public due to the numerous Serbian, and later also Croatian massacres of the Muslim population. The initial coalition of Bosnians and Croats broke up in the spring of 1993 for one year, because now even the leadership of the smallest population group in the country (around 17 per cent) demanded an extension of its sovereign territory. The mutual expulsions, which were euphemistically called 'ethnic cleansings', led to extensive social and cultural upheavals in the country, including the regions which had not yet become involved in the war.

The international Islamic public showed very little reaction to the war in Bosnia-Herzegovina. At an Islamic foreign ministers conference held on 19 June 1992, 47 member states of the OIC discussed military action against Serbia, should there be no other way to settle the conflict. They then submitted to the mediation attempts of the United Nations Security Council, which still aimed at preserving the centralized state.

The Loss of National Sovereignty: Somalia

Somalia was for a long time looked upon as a typical example of an ethnically homogeneous state in the Islamic world, especially under the government of Siad Barre (1969–91). The 1978 Ogaden war against Ethiopia, which ended in a disastrous defeat of the Somalian army, was the climax of a pan-Somali national movement which was also active among the Somali tribes living in Kenya. However, the independence proclaimed in 1977 of the Somalian Afar and Issa in French Djibouti already showed that the pan-Somalian idea propagated by the Union of Somalian Youth in the early 1960s had run aground on the borders set by the colonial powers. The Kenyan Somali tribes (mainly belonging to the Darod) were also unwilling to submit to the policy of the urban nationalists who pursued a strict republican-socialist course until 1976/77. The war led to considerable shifts of power within the Somali tribal cultures which formed the agnatic foundation of Somali society. The once powerful Mijertein of the Darod, who controlled the north-eastern provinces, were now confronted by the Maheran (also Darod), who, for their own part, had been forced to fall back from the border areas of Somalia to Ethiopia because the refugee Marod tribes from Ogaden were seeking land and shelter.

To forestall a typical post-war revolution, Barre now based his authority on the power of the refugee Western Somalian Ogaden fighters (mainly Hawiya, but also Darod), who were being settled in Mogadishu and were threatening conflict with the confederation of the locally dominating tribes. As free Samals (nomadic herdsmen) they felt superior to the Sab (dependent tribes, mainly of peasant origin, but also including townsmen) who were split into small groups. The latter disposed of the agriculturally rich regions around the capital city of Mogadishu. The geographically split-up settlements of the Sab tribes (especially Dikhil and Rahanvein) between Mogadishu, Beled Uen, Xuddur, Baydhabo and Marka formed the traditional line of retreat in times of drought and famine, since here there was sufficient rainfall for farming. Due to the immigration of tribes from the southern and eastern parts of the country and the frequent confiscations of land from peasants, the economic and social conditions of the native tribes, especially those of the non-Somali Migdaans, became increasingly precarious, so that they migrated to the capital city.

Famines, poor harvests, and an economic assistance which focused on the capital city of Mogadishu and the cities of Kismaayo, Berbera and Hargeysa, without taking any account of the major local and regional tribes, soon destroyed the Somali national consensus construed by Barre. By 1982, there were three different liberation fronts operating in the country, who were committed to the specific interests of the tribal unions (especially the Mijertein). At the same time, they represented a rational form of resistance against the regime of Barre and his state party, the Somalian Socialist Revolutionary Party. Logistically supported by Ethiopia, these liberation movements, which were particularly active in the northern part of the country, served as a pretext for the USA to provide massive military aid to Somalia. The country not only represented Western strategic interests in its conflict with Ethiopia, but was also assumed to possess important oil reserves.[36] The resistance movement was supported by almost all the tribes, except those who traditionally considered themselves as allies of Barre. Towards the end of 1990, however, there were indications to the effect that the Hawiya tribes north of Mogadishu would have the upper hand.

On 29 January 1991, Ali Mahdi Muhammad (Abgal/Hawiya) was appointed as interim president and confirmed at several 'conciliatory conferences'. But already in 1991, the specific dynamics of the tribes who were mobilized by war, famine and mismanagement no longer admitted of any national culture which could have motivated the majority of the Somali tribes. In the rebellious north of the country, the Somali national movement (Dir, Ishaq) proclaimed the

Republic of Somaliland on 18 May 1991 and thus confirmed the colonial division of the country into a British and an Italian part. In (formerly Italian) Southern Somalia, however, a desperate civil war was raging among the large tribal unions until early 1993. Triggered by the violent struggle for dividing up the meagre resources of the country, this war led to the break-up of the traditionally significant tribal solidarity in favour of entirely new clan structures. The most important rival of the president was Muhammad Aidid (Habr Gedir Air/Hawiya), whose troops were able to conquer parts of the capital city of Mogadishu.

In view of the disastrous food situation, the United Nations Security Council decided on 27 July 1992 to organize an air-lift to deliver food to Somalia. From September 1992, these deliveries were to be protected by military contingents. In January 1993, larger US units finally landed, officially to ensure the distribution of foodstuffs. From the point of view of the meanwhile strongest rebel groups around Muhammad Aidid, however, this was merely an attempt to convert Somalia into an international colony and secure the hoped-for oil reserves. Other Somalian parties openly sided with the actions of the UN troops, and yet others tried to assume a neutral position. The rebels now for the first time resorted to an Islamic language to legitimize their resistance to the UN troops. In 1993 Somalia clearly lost its sovereignty. The remaining urban nationalists now either hoped for a military appeasement through the UN or for a re-formulation of the Somali national culture through the spread of an Islamic expression.

Islam and Group Nationalism

The attempt of the urban elites to preserve nation state sovereignty in Bosnia-Herzegovina, Afghanistan, Tajikistan and Somalia after the collapse of their national cultures was suffused with strong secessionist tendencies. Paradoxically, however, they referred to the former territorial constitution of 'their' state, which they wanted to preserve despite, or precisely because of, secessionism. The murderous fight for Mogadishu thus not only represented a 'post-revolutionary fight for division', but proved how deeply the idea of the nation state was embedded even among the secessionists. Secessionism thus steadily inclined towards a new nationalism. This was indirectly confirmed by the astonishing stability of the economic foundations of the territories of states, which was moreover corroborated by international diplomacy. It is true, however, that the traditional forms of expression of political matters could hardly lead to a compromise between secessionism and nationalism. Take, for example, the cases of Imam Ali Rahmanov in Tajikistan or Gaidar Aliev in Azerbaijan: They both belonged to the old apparatus and represented the old, classical nationalism of city-dwellers based on the ideal of progress. Yet their seizure of power provoked the secession of those regions of their states which had been strongholds of popular fronts and had suffered most in the past from the economic results of progressive policies. On what basis the reintegration of the societies destroyed by the war will succeed is an open question. In none of the examples we have presented here could Islamic culture be used as a means to resolve the paradox between secessionism and nationalism.

The vision of an Islamic sovereignty which would be in a position to end wars and disarm conflicts by restoring Islamic cosmopolitanism has remained a dream. It is often lamented that the creation of a 'unity in multiplicity' based on Islam has not been achieved; that the elites of Muslim societies have been far too ready to appeal to the United Nations or to the West for help in cases of conflict, and thus to sign away to the West their recently acquired sovereignty. And with the wars, the cultural sovereignty of the Islamic world has also perished.

The Islamic public, which since circa 1989 had increasingly lost its ideologies, has indeed been unable to solve its inter-state conflicts, since it is itself nothing but the result of these conflicts. The 20th century has created an Islamic public which is strictly dependent on the nation state. Every attempt to mobilize the *umma* politically as a 'solid, uniting bond' and to use it as an instrument for solving conflicts has been unsuccessful because this is not the function of the Islamic public. Some Islamic intellectuals have as a result stubbornly demanded the cultural secession of the Islamic world from the West. Under the slogan 'It is time to repudiate man-made ideologies', they have pleaded for a new 'Islamic system of the world', which is to be part of a new global order, but at the same time necessarily separate from it.[37]

But precisely in this context it has become apparent that the 20th century had not been able to create any unified Islamic history. Historical events and the Islamic reception of them, which provided the *umma* with the rank of an interpreting horizon, were widely different.

And yet the history of the 20th century as a whole has contributed to the formation of a transnational Islamic identity which often sharply contrasts with the various 'native' histories of nation states. Within the global context, Islam has threatened to become an ethnic quality which competes with traditional forms of ethnicity. The ethnification of Islam may well replace the ideological character of the Islamic public which has prevailed for most of the decades of the 20th century. Essentially, Islamic ideologies represent no more than an Islamic interpretation of global ideologies. Even the ethnification of Islam would not therefore create a true specificity; on the contrary, it would correspond with a further globally effective ethnification of the political public. Since, from the 18th century onwards, the political public has itself been closely associated with the concept of ideology, the character of politics may itself undergo radical change and the public will acquire new characteristics which are no longer comparable with classical ideological modes of thought and interpretation. The two crucial features of the political public over this period have been the state and society, and this is true of the Islamic world as well. Through the process of ethnification, a new system of references has been created in politics, in which the (mythically substantiated) group functions as the third characteristic. How group loyalty is to alter Islam and what modes of thought and interpretation are to characterize the group will be shown by history. All that appears to be certain is that the Islam of the 21st century will have little in common with that of the 20th century.

The ideological interpretation of Islam, which has extensively secularized Islamic cultures, has already led to a far-reaching transformation of religion. The 'World' has supplanted the 'Beyond' and destroyed all religiosity based on the transcendental. Religion has thus become a symbolic form of the appropriation of the world in which all religious content has been used as a metaphor for worldly existence. With the disintegration of ideologies, there has emerged a growing tendency to stop interpreting Islam as a social state of affairs in a positivistic sense, and instead to re-integrate it hermeneutically within mankind. This leads to a 'genealogical concatenation' of Islam which is to provide the individual person in his group with an 'escape' from the separation between him or herself and the world.[38] In this context, Islam becomes a 'community of fate' which is to counteract the cultural uprooting of the Muslim elites. The new 'group nationalism' on a local, regional or extra-regional level was in many respects anticipated by the Islamic movements of the 1880s. It is precisely here that the modernism of the Islamic public asserts itself.

EPILOGUE

Islamic Culture and Civil Society, 1989-2001

Post-Islamism

Classical Islamism had already reached its apogee in the late 1970s and early 1980s. The Islamic revolution in Iran bore striking witness to the successful mobilization of an Islamic discourse featuring the utopian reorganization of society. Soon, however, Islamic discourse showed signs of turning away from utopian ideas and its function, which consisted of expressing social utopias in an 'Islamic' language, also declined. After 1989, the classic Islamic discourse disappeared altogether, giving way to a multi-functional 'post-Islamism'. Post-Islamism implies that the Islamic discourse had assumed a great number of interpreting functions within the public. Any political, social or cultural question could be 'Islamically' articulated without necessarily representing a definite ideological statement. This led between 1989–98 to a broad spectrum of Islamic interpretations whose only common denominator was the use of a repertoire of symbols and concepts handed down by Islam. The loss of an ideological pattern provoked a shift in the function of Islamism from the interpretation of the 'world at large' to more concrete spheres of life.

The disintegration of the mono functional character of Islamic discourse – which might here be qualified by the prefix 'post' – is itself another manifestation of a global pattern. Within the framework of the great recession of the years 1989–98, extensive changes in the structure of national and global economic processes confronted all political institutions, marginalizing both national markets and many nation-state institutions. Particularly affected were those political traditions which underpin the idea of the nation state. Since these could no longer be justified by ideological objectives and since the functions of the nation state were at the same time subject to a distinct process of erosion, new values for nation states were thrown into relief. The idea of culture, which acquired a political connotation in the 1990s, offered an effective concept, since it served to associate experiences based on different spheres of life with the 'overall interest of the state'. This new nationalism, primarily defined through a cultural concept, was to protect both the nation states and their institutions from globalization. Both on behalf of the state and within particular groups, culture was chosen as a collective identity which no longer had a utopian connotation, but functioned as a 'commemorative culture'.

In the 1990s, most nation states found themselves suspended between globalizing and localizing strategies. This means that the classic state had to yield more and more functions both to global institutions and to local groups. In the Islamic world, the dominant political tendencies were those which sought to achieve a re-integration of society by means of democratization and participation. In certain countries, however, where the political system allowed for no true participation of groups in the state – either because the state was dominated by a group, or because it sought to achieve its re-integration through radical nationalist strategies – the fragmentation of society threatened to end in war.

The Fragmentation of Politics in Algeria

Algeria is perhaps the country in which localization processes have led to the most profound fragmentation. This can be measured by the number of victims claimed by the so-called civil war which began around 1994: reliable sources quote 60,000 casualties, most of whom were civilians. Fragmentation affected all political and social realms including the Islamic opposition. The traditional Algerian system of military resistance, the Armée Islamique du Salut (AIS), was undermined by the engagement of independent paramilitary organizations under the name Groupes Islamiques Armés (GIA) which in 1994 became independent under Emir Sharif Gusmi, who had himself proclaimed as caliph.

After 1995, there were therefore two military tendencies: the AIS strategy to attack state institutions by military means, and the GIA actions which no longer distinguished between state and society and were mainly concerned with the extermination of anti-GIA movements. The more violence became part of people's everyday experience, the more it was used as a category of action for the enforcement of group interests.

In September 1997 the AIS, increasingly weaker, announced a unilateral armistice, leading to a certain relief in the area for some time. But before long, groups who were close or similar to the GIA infiltrated the area and assumed the initiative with well-aimed attacks at the suburban population and villagers whom they viewed as opponents. By the summer of 1998, the AIS had almost completely lost its combat capacity. Nor could the GIA units hold their military predominance, although some of them were extending their sphere of activities to villages beyond the border with Morocco in autumn 2000.

In the capital city of Algiers, there were steady attempts after 1995 to promote the 'democratic re-integration' of the country. This policy, called for by the civilian opposition, was initially successful and in January eight political parties agreed to form a 'platform for a political and peaceful solution of the Algerian crisis' in San Egidio, Italy. The government responded with a new campaign of legitimation. Between November 1995 and June 1997, presidential elections, a constitutional referendum and parliamentary and municipal elections were held, with the army apparently drawing 40–60 per cent of the votes in the latter.

More crucial, however, was the regime's attempt to proclaim a homogenous Arab national identity. With the law of July 1998, which proclaimed Arabic as the only national language, conflict with the non-Arab-speaking population, especially the Berber groups, became inevitable. This conflict had been smouldering at a local level since 1980, when a ban by the authorities on a literary reading in the Kabyle language led to the outbreak of serious disturbances in Tizi Ouzou. In May 2000, a youth was shot dead by police in the course of an event marking the twentieth anniversary of these 1980 clashes. After months of argument about the status of the Berber languages in education, the Algerian president, 'Abdal'aziz Butafliqa signified his willingness to give Berber culture and language official recognition on 4 October 2001.[1]

The government's attempts to find a 'civil consensus' were also aimed at Islamist groups and they had some success in September 1999 with a 'reconciliation pact' promising amnesty to the armed Islamist rebels. According to official figures, around 1,200 GIA fighters handed in their weapons, but it is estimated that 5,000 GIA supporters are still in the field.[2] Since summer 2,000, these latter have in fact intensified their operations to intimidate opponents, directed above all at the families of 'renegades' and AIS supporters. Attempts at reconstructing political participation could do no more than cover up the process of fragmentation in Algerian society, indeed in view of the language policy of the regime, further fragmentation is to be expected. What is being negotiated is the participation of parties in power, but since the parties no longer deal with social conflicts, the result is a vacuum.

The Islamic discourse which prevailed in the war in Algeria between 1992 and 1998 was therefore marked by two tendencies: on the one hand it produced a mythically legitimated 'community of fate' among Islamic fighters (*mujahidun*), and on the other it established itself as the expression of a truly democratic order (as represented by Mahfuz Nahnah and his Mouvement Pour une Société de la Paix, MSP). Between these two spheres there was practically no communication.

Islamic Democratization in Iran

In Iran, on the other hand, the Islamic democrats managed a truly spectacular revival. On 23 May 1997 Sayyid Muhammad Khatami was elected as the new president with 69 per cent of the vote. He had the support of young people and women; this alone showing that the young had acquired new political power. Unlike Algeria, the post-revolutionary Iranian youth was not a source of potential recruits for an Islamic guerilla movement, but solidly integrated within the Iranian political structure. The establishment of the revolution were bitterly defeated. The results were institutional conflicts between the party of the new president and the 'old guard' around Ayatollah Khamenei and Natiq Nuri. A major part was played by the media – with sharp exchanges in a journalistic feud between 'old' and 'young' the norm. The judiciary also played a special part. More often than not the conflict between partisans of the 'old' and the 'young' was settled at court – an example being the trial of Tehran's mayor Gholam Hosein Karbaschi (June 1998) for alleged corruption and misappropriation. The position of the judicial authorities became stronger as they sought their 'independence' in this discourse and attempted to establish their function as an autonomous third power of the state.

The conflict between the Iranian revolutionary establishment and the new generation has not been decided at the time of writing (summer 2001). Khatami was re-elected president on 8 June 2001 but the reformers did not manage to fill key positions with their own followers.[3] Moreover, the power of the old revolutionary establishment was visible in the run-up to the election when a number of liberal publications were banned and critical journalists, academics and artists were arrested. Since the Iranian government was clearly unwilling to resolve the argument between the reformers and the old establishment, the main emphasis of their policies shifted to questions of economic development and the reorganization of the administration.

After almost twenty years of Islamic republican rule it is evident that Islamic discourse has not created new economic realities. There was a successful reconstruction of the economy after the eight-year Iran–Iraq war, but without any substantial improvement in the living conditions of the poor or middle classes. The legitimacy of the 'grand Islamic idea' is not called into question, but has certainly been put on the back-burner. Islamic discourse, which mainly used high-flown rhetoric to deal with general, often abstract concepts, has been pushed into the background.

The Crisis in Indonesia

The 'Asian Economic Crisis', triggered by massive speculative attacks against the Thai currency and by dubious real estate transactions, ushered in the end of the Suharto era. Between July 1997 and January 1998 the Indonesian economy lost almost 40 per cent of its value. At the same time, European and American investment capital was withdrawn. The disaster hit the middle classes in particular, whose purchasing power, relying mainly on credit, was considerably impaired by the high prices and whose real income dropped by an average of 40 per cent. Resistance against Suharto's regime, whose family had enriched themselves by 40 billion dollars, was thus also supported by the activists of the middle classes, i.e. the students. Up to 1996–7 the regime had always managed to create divisions in the three official parties so that they would represent no real danger. Now they were in unknown territory: with new opposition from student unions, independent trade unions and those social groups who resented the Chinese and the nouveaux-riches. The pressure of the international monetary institutions on the economic policy of the Suharto regime contributed to the heated atmosphere. To prevent a coup by the 'social wing' of the army Suharto resigned on 21 May 1998, a week after the great Djakarta rebellion, and handed over power to his vice-president Habibie. The latter hesitantly co-operated with the democratic movement, organizing negotiations about new international credit, announcing elections for 1999, and finally by even promising a political solution for the East Timor question. During the short presidency of Habibie, further far-reaching changes took place in Indonesia: the military withdrew from politics, there was a relaxation of restrictions on political parties and the first steps towards the decentralization of political power. In October 1999 the Indonesian parliament was compelled to recognise the independence of East Timor.

Major Islamic parties such as the Nahdatul Ulama, which had at least 35 million adherents in 1997, kept aloof or, like the Muhammadiya (28 million members) promised their unlimited support to the democratic movement without, however, lending it a specific Islamic legitimacy. Within the opposition, the Islamic discourse played a certain part whenever a conflict with the nouveaux-riches was at issue. On 10 October 1996, when Catholic churches and schools were attacked in Situbondo (East Java), these acts were ascribed Islamic legitimacy. But an independent Islamic policy was no longer to be expected, either from the opposition or on behalf of the government.

All the more surprising, then, was the election of K. H. Abdurrahman Wahid, the former leader of the Nahdatul Ulama and later founder of the Party of National Revival as fourth president of the Republic in October 1999. In response to the new distribution of power in the Indonesian Parliament, he had to accept Megawati Sukarnoputri, the leader of the Indonesian Democratic Party and daughter of the first president, Sukarno, as vice president. His hapless period as president – accusations of corruption and his ineptitude in dealing with separatists and ethnic conflicts – came to an end on 27 July 2001, after he was impeached in parliament. Megawati Sukarno succeeded him as president of the largest Islamic state. Her first public pronouncements suggested that she did not intend to pursue a new version of her father's old nationalist policies, but was seeking to achieve social reconciliation through emphasis on the decentralization programme, a strengthening of the institutions of civil society and economic reforms.

The New Islamic Jihad Movement

These examples from Algeria, Iran and Indonesia show that the old political interpretations which programmatically formulated an Islamic discourse no longer suited the social and economic conditions of the late 1990s. Any Islamic social utopia had become meaningless. This radical change was even acknowledged by Islamic opinion leaders who had attained powerful positions in state and society during the 1970s and early 1980s, for example Hasan al-Turabi, the unofficial chief ideologist of the Sudanese regime. The *shari'a* was more and more frequently described as an ethical principle without any direct penal relevance; democratic legitimacy was theoretically acknowledged; the volonté général was no longer derived from its cultural postulate, but from its identification with a process of opinion-formation and democratic legitimation. The Islamism of Sudanese national culture thus became part of the global discourse about the economy, participation and democracy.

Al-Turabi's move away from a classic Islamist ideological position towards an attitude based on conservative values was shared by a number of other leaders of Islamist groups. In the 1990s his generation became part of the global discourse on pluralism and the opening-up of society to wider participation. Since this globalized discourse only appealed to the elites, to whom these values made sense in terms of their life-style, the 'opening-up' was actually detrimental to social integration. Many social groups who did not find themselves supported by the globalizing economy, started mobilizing their own opposition using Islamic symbolism. Therefore classical Islamic discourse no longer ensured reintegration, and it thus lost one of the essential functions which had legitimized it well into the 1980s.

The new Islamist opposition comes mainly from the children of activists of the old Islamist groups who dissociate themselves from their parents' generation because they are unwilling to accept their conservative values. They believe that Islam, binding Muslims together in a community sharing a common destiny, is what gives them their social and political identity. Islam is seen as a divinely ordained order independent of man, who must submit to its laws. Islamic history is correspondingly revised to fit in with this, being exploited to provide a mythical grounding for the Islamists' image of themselves as 'noble, solitary warriors'.

The war against the Soviet occupying forces in Afghanistan was the first testing-ground for this new attitude. In the early 1980s 'Azzam was one of the first Arab volunteers who went to Pakistan to fight. In 1984 he established a contact point for volunteers in Peshawar and urged the setting-up of a *jihad* organization. In total perhaps some 20–30,000 volunteers went to Afghanistan via this bureau. One of them, the son of a Saudi building contractor born in Riyad in 1957, was

Osama bin Laden, who joined the Islamist opposition in Saudi Arabia. A significant section of this movement demanded a return to the original values of the Arab *wahhabiya* and vehemently criticized the abandonment of *Wahhabi* puritanism by Saudi society.

The Saudi authorities did their utmost to channel this opposition in the direction of Afghanistan, encouraging its members to 'fight for Islam' there. Bin Laden left the country in this way and in 1986 he set up his first training camp for volunteers, trying to sever his links with 'Azzam's bureau.[4] He must have had considerable success, for he established an independent registration office for volunteers (*sijill al-qa'ida*, known as *al-qa'ida*) only two years later, financed by his considerable private fortune.

The Gulf War of 1990/91 led to a new mobilization. Bin Laden, who had returned to Saudi Arabia in 1989, looked on, powerless, as American troops were stationed in his country. He and other opposition activists regarded this as the occupation of Islamic soil by 'forces of the unbelievers' and protested against the Saudi rulers who had permitted the occupation.

After the turbulent events of spring 1991, bin Laden left Saudi Arabia and returned to Afghanistan. There he increased his dissemination of anti-Saudi and anti-American propaganda and was active as president of a welfare committee for veterans of the Afghan war. Assuming his commitment to Afghanistan had gained him sufficient prestige to occupy an important political position in Kabul, bin Laden attempted, after the capital had been taken by *mujahidin* units in April 1992, to act as mediator between the discordant parties. However Hikmatyar, who until then had been well-disposed towards bin Laden's volunteers, rejected the new coalition in Kabul and distanced himself from the 'Wahhabis', as bin Laden's men were often termed. After this setback, bin Laden left the country and settled in the Sudan, reorganizing his network from there.

Initially this network was grounded in a new unified Islamist discourse, using categories of Islamic history even more than before and centering on the following key principles:

1. The conservative orientation of the classic Islamist groups was now designated as *irja'* . This term comes from eighth-century discussions within Islam, according to which the faith expressed itself first in personal conviction, making religious practices not conclusive: the verdict on Muslims who did not act as Muslims being 'postponed' (*irja'*). From the mid-1980s this term was used by *Wahhabi* puritans to denounce Islamist parties.[5] In the following years the concept spread amongst extreme Islamist groups demanding an 'Islam of action'.
2. At the same time this discourse drew a line between itself and those Islamists who recognized their members alone as 'true Muslims'. In the discourse these were identified as *mukafira*, that is, 'people who pronounced other Muslims unbelievers'.

3. Finally, Islamist supporters of a pluralist Islamic polity based on the principles of representation and participation were denounced as 'democrats'.[6]

This new consensus produced a discourse for which bin Laden tried to create an organizational structure. Following the preaching of 'Azzam ('*Jihad* and the rifle alone: no negotiations, no conferences and no dialogue'[30]), he demanded the militarization of this community of discourse, at the centre of which was a revitalized, globalized *jihad* concept.[7]

The militarization of the discourse produced results but it was only after the Saudi authorities withdrew his citizenship in spring 1994 that bin Laden started to actively recruit followers. Certain indications suggest that as early as 18 July 1994 supporters of bin Laden were involved in the attack on the Jewish community centre in Buenos Aires, during which 85 people lost their lives. Bin Laden refrained from openly supporting such actions. The climate changed with the bomb attacks in Riyad in the spring of 1995. Both the Saudi and American authorities demanded bin Laden's expulsion from the Sudan where he had been based from 1992. The Sudanese government accordingly declared bin Laden *persona non grata* and he turned to his old Afghanistan contacts. The 1996 attack on the American marine base in Eubar in Saudi Arabia and the devastating 1998 bomb-strikes on the American embassies in Nairobi and Dar es Salaam show that bin Laden's 'declaration of war' did not go unheeded. On 23 February 1998 bin Laden, amongst others, published a *fatwa* which declared the struggle against and killing of Americans to be the personal duty of each and every Muslim.[8]

In the meantime, the political and military situation in Afghanistan underwent a profound change, triggered by the religious colleges. During the war against Soviet occupation, the network of Deoband schools in Afghanistan had attracted young Pashtuns who, because of the war, were cut off from the urban culture of Kabul and hoped to improve their prospects. Many of the students interrupted their courses from time to time to take part in *mujahidin* operations against Soviet troops. When in the summer of 1994, the conflict escalated between the three big warring parties in Afghanistan, the leaders of the independent Pashtun units armed graduates and students who then took part in the war under the name they gave themselves of Taliban. (Persian plural of the Arabic word *Talib,* here used in the sense of 'graduate of a theological college'). In August 1994 Mullah 'Umar was elected emir of the 'Taliban Movement' which had considerable success in mobilizing the population. Many Pashtuns saw in it an organization that would deliver them from the years of warfare and pioneer a new civil order in Afghanistan – a defining characteristic of their new concept of social organization was the politicization of a non-urban, rural outlook among the Pashtun population. Within a short time the Taliban had taken control of the southern provinces of Afghanistan and on 26 September, they assumed power in Kabul.

The Taliban achieved a spectacular reconstruction of Pashtun politics, overcoming the internal tribal segmentations by a radical emphasis on Islamism. But the list of 'sixteen regulations' which they published in December 1996, considered as a sign of the Islamism of the new Afghan social system, revealed other motives.[10] The regulations included measures against the failure to 'wear a veil', against music and singing in public and against cutting one's beard. The point was the eradication of certain cultural symbols because the actual fight of the Taliban was not against a social order, but against all non-Pashtu ethnic groups, especially Dari or Tajik-speaking groups. The Islamism of the Taliban thus signified the cultural formulation of a specific Pashtu claim of sovereignty and so their policy was successful wherever the population could more or less conform to a Pashtu group identity.

It was through Yanis Khalis, the Movement's patron in Kandahar, that bin Laden established contact with the Taliban, gaining space to rebuild his old *al-qa'ida* group. The Taliban's doctrines made sense as a system of belief for the local, rural Pashtun population, but bin Laden had a vision of a global movement for Islamic cultural liberation. Seldom had local and global visions come into such close proximity with each other as here in Afghanistan. The Taliban continued to develop ever more radical Islamic cultural policies from 1999–2001, leaving bin Laden alone, provided he kept out of Afghanistan's internal affairs.

Thus in Afghanistan a coalition of two different Islamic discourses was established: the Taliban's local Islamic view of the world, together with the global vision of the new Islamist *jihad* movement. The September 11 attacks by nineteen Arab *jihadis*, in which over 5,000 people lost their lives, demonstrated the strike power of the new movement. The remarkably small group, probably recruited by *al-qa'ida*, believed their action would initiate the 'cultural liberation' of the Islamic world. This 'war of liberation' has no strategic goal within a specific country, there is no longer a headquarters that can be taken. In its place are just symbols of the 'enemy culture' which is to be destroyed.

The response in the Islamic world was muted. The supporters of the devastating attacks will have hoped for at least more than a few demonstrations in Pakistani, Indian or Indonesian cities. Compared with the mobilization of the Muslim world in 1989 by the Salman Rushdie affair, the expressions of support were meagre. Even when the Afghani Taliban proclaimed a *jihad* at the beginning of October and bin Laden once more disseminated a corresponding call, [11] there were scarcely any public declarations of sympathy. The Iranian president, Khatami, specifically emphasised that the Islamist terrorists had placed themselves outside Islam; whilst also urging restraint in the military measures against terrorism.

After Afghanistan, Chechnya was the second largest recruitment area for the new Islamist *jihad* movement. But until the middle of the 1990s the conflict there between separatists and the Russian central government was completely unrelated to the movement, the two sides being divided solely along ethnic lines. After the withdrawal of Russian troops following the first agreement between Moscow and Grozny, in May 1992, the political situation in Chechnya remained unstable. The president, Dudaev, attempted to counter these internal conflicts by Islamizing the symbols of political life, in the hope that reference to Islam would strengthen the cohesion of the heterogeneous groups within the population. At the same time an effort was made to give clearer expression to Chechen collective identity, to which end in January 1994 the state was renamed Chechen Republic Ichkeria.

In November 1994 the situation worsened once more when opposition groups from the north, supported by Russia, made an attack on Grozny which, however, failed. The defeat of this revolt set off the first Russian–Chechen war (December 1994–August 1996). From the beginning of 1996 the conflict was increasingly Islamized on the Chechen side. They recruited foreign fighters and a Russian Muslim union recognized Chechen resistance as a *jihad*. These logistical and rhetorical reinforcements made it possible for the Chechens to besiege Grozny on 6th August 1996, the day Boris Yeltsin took office as Russian president. The recapture was completed by the end of August and a new truce agreed.

The peace treaty of 12th May 1997 with the Russian Federation was seen as *de facto* recognition of Chechen sovereignty by the Russian Federation, since in international law peace treaties can only be signed between sovereign states. As in Afghanistan, however, the destruction of Grozny and other Chechen towns also meant the destruction of the urban culture in which Chechen nationalism was grounded. And as in Afghanistan, a new Islamic culture with agrarian, tribal features emerged, giving political force to the world of the ordinary Chechen.

The neighbouring Republic of Daghestan similarly saw the formation of local Islamic authorities, as some sixty enclaves or villages organized themselves communally, largely on the basis of *shari'a* law. In August 1999 the leaders of these enclaves accelerated their drive towards independence – the Russian government therefore mobilized almost 100,000 troops, starting the second Chechen war on 23 September 1999. The Russians quickly occupied the northern plain, but Grozny, now completely destroyed, was only taken after weeks of artillery bombardment. At the time of writing (autumn 2001) all attempts to restore order have been unsuccessful.

The new civilian government set up by the Russians on 12 June 2000 under the mufti, Kadyrov, only managed to assert its authority to a limited extent, having to contend with opposition within its own ranks. What was remarkable was that with the traditionalist, Kadyrov, the Russian government was giving the *'ulama'* a new political role. The Russian government maintained that 250 Chechen imams and various former field commanders supported Kadyrov.[12] Such statements contained implicit recognition of the old tribal constitution and the *'ulama'* as the institutions on which Chechen society rested. The ideological lines in the Chechen conflict were increasingly resembling those in the Afghan civil war. Islamist groups, being mainly urban in outlook, had no place there – only those Islamist groups which felt committed to the new *jihad*, had a part to play in this conflict, as long as they restricted themselves to military operations. The ideal to which these *jihadis* felt committed was formulated as follows by 'Azzam in the course of a speech recorded on video:

'A small group: they are the ones who carry their beliefs for the Islamic Umma. And an even smaller group out of this small group: they are the ones who sacrifice their worldly interests, in order to act out these beliefs. And an even smaller group out of this elite: they are the ones who sacrifice their soul and their blood, in order to bring victory to these beliefs and goals. They are the elite of the elite of the elite.'

Palestinian Autonomy

On the international front work has continued on the peace process and considerable progress was achieved in various agreements (including the Oslo Agreement of 1995 and the River Wye Memorandum of 1998). By 1999 there were three items remaining: the status of Jerusalem; the return of the Palestinian refugees; and the future of Israeli settlements in Palestinian areas. But the peace processes which had been drawn up in the international arena proved unsuitable to local conditions in Palestine. The fragmentation of political power made the state's monopoly of force empty rhetoric.

On 28 September 2000 the situation escalated once more. A short visit by the then leader of the Israeli opposition, Ariel Sharon, to the Temple Mount was followed by violent clashes between the Israeli army and Palestinian demonstrators. The Israeli view was that Palestinian organizations had used the visit as an opportunity to call for the uprising they had been planning for some time. However that may be, it is striking that the uprising came exactly five years to the day after the signing of the Palestinian/Israeli interim agreement, which specified a transition period of five years for the solution agreed in it. After only a few days this uprising was seen as the continuation of the first *intifada* of 1987–1993.

The new bloody conflict has once more marginalized civil society. Not only are the traditional opponents facing each other again, the confrontation between the Israeli military and the Palestine Authority's militia has brought new players onto the field, in line with the increased militarization of all parties. Both sides recognized the military nature of the uprising in their political rhetoric. The Israeli side talked of the 'war against the Palestinians' (not, be it noted, against Palestine, since Israel recognises the autonomous authority, but not the state of Palestine) while the Palestinian side saw itself as 'at war' with Israel. At the time of writing, all attempts to contain the conflict have failed.

Since the election of Ariel Sharon as prime minister, the scope for peace initiatives has been further reduced. Israeli politicians used the September 11 terrorist attacks on New York and Washington to justify their anti-Palestinian attitude by declaring they were fighting Islamic terrorism. On the Palestinian side there were sporadic pro-bin Laden demonstrations, but only the Palestinian 'Islamic *jihad*' showed a definite positive attitude to bin Laden.

Prospects

Globalization, which changed the world into a gigantic market, expounded by a neo-liberal economic policy, no longer admits of any homogenous Islamic approach. However, the subject of 'globalization' alone, and the cultural strategies to master it, can still be articulated as specifically Islamic. This means that – as always – Islamic political programmes contain no message of their own regarding society, and that the interpretation of social or cultural problems through an Islamic discourse can no longer be regarded as the great 'narrative' of the world which competed with 'Western' narratives of great social utopias until well into the 1970s. With the loss of meaning, such narratives of the world (for example nationalism or socialism), we are left with a world constructed on cultures (based on myths rather than utopias). The Islamic discourse is inevitably also adapted to this global scheme, so that now the cultural concept has moved into the centre of perception and Islam is mainly interpreted as a 'culture'.

This interpretation, which we will call post-Islamism, has found two prominent expressions: on the one hand, intensive intellectual efforts are today being made to liberate the Islamic discourse from its Islamic chains and to construe a cultural Islam in which the values of globalization (free market, media interlocks, civic rights, rule of law and civil society) are solidly implanted. A characteristic of these intellectual efforts is the sharp criticism of the traditional attributes symbolizing Islam. Thus the prophetic tradition (*sunna*), which has played a major role in the classical Islamic discourse, is attributed less and less importance; instead, hermeneutics of the Koran receives greater attention so that a new ethical institution reflecting the post-modern world may be derived from them.

On the other hand, there are Islamic interpretations of those localizing processes which represent, as it were, the counterpart to globalization. The reduction of people's social reference areas, the suspension of historical or utopian identities in favour of an identification with media information, and the virtual or real freedom of movement of every person all over the world provokes, as it were, a new locally related interpretation of the world. The world itself becomes ambiguous: the great world portayed by the media and the small actually experienced world. Just as the Great New World can be Islamically interpreted, so the small world can also be culturally identified as Islamic. However, the multitude of small worlds no longer allows any homogenous Islamic statement. Thus post-Islamism establishes itself as a new dominant framework of orientation in which the classical utopian views of the world no longer have their place.

Chronology

1898	First issue of the Egyptian journal *al-Manar*, the mouthpiece of the Islamic classicists
1901	Discovery of large oil deposits in Persia, beginning of oil economy in the Middle East
1902	Establishment of the Saudi monarchy in Riyadh
1905–1911	Constitutional movement in Persia
	Partition of Bengal causes a division of the political public between Muslims and Hindus
1906	Foundation of the Muslim League in India
1907	French occupation of Casablanca after the first Morocco Conference
1908	Revolution of the Young Turks in Istanbul – annexation of Bosnia-Herzegovina by Austria-Hungary
1909	Abortive populist counter-revolution, deposition of Sultan Abd al-Hamid II
1911	Foundation of the Sarekat Islam in Java
1911–1912	Ottoman–Italian war
1911–1917	Persia becomes de facto British and Russian protectorate
1912–1913	First Balkan War
1912	Morocco becomes French and Spanish protectorate, respectively.
1912	Foundation of the Muhammadiya in Java
1913	Putsch of the Young Turks in Istanbul
1914–1918	The Ottoman Empire sides with the Central Powers in the First World War.
1914	Egypt becomes a British protectorate

1916–1918	Arab revolt against Ottoman military rule in the Hijaz, Palestine and Syria
1917	Coming to light of Anglo–French plans for a partition of the Fertile Crescent. The Balfour declaration about plans for the establishment of a Jewish home in Palestine
1917–1924	Conflicts between nationalist and socialist parties in Central Asia. Revolt of the Basmachi in Turkestan
1918	Proclamation of the Yemeni imamate as a kingdom
1918	Tripolitanian Republic
1918–1920	Arab rule in Damascus, 1920 as a Hashimite monarchy
1919–1922	Rebellion in Egypt, climax of the independence movement
1919–1925	Caliphate movement in India
1919–1923	Turkish war against allied occupation troops
1920	French occupation of Lebanon and Syria
1920	Final independence of Albania
1920–1924	Hashimite Kingdom of Hijaz
1921	Coup d'état of Reza Khan in Persia
1921/1923	Appointment of Hashimite rulers in Iraq and Transjordan (emirate until 1946) by Great Britain
1921–1926	Rif Republic in northern Morocco
1922	Abolition of the Sultanate by the Great Turkish National Assembly
1922	Proclamation of the Kingdom of Egypt, 1923 independent
1923	Peace Treaty of Lausanne: re-establishment of Turkish sovereignty
1923	Spectacular severance of the Albanian Muslims from the authority of the Ottoman *sheikh al-Islam* and from the caliphate
1924–1933	Abolition of the caliphate in Turkey, extensive de-Islamization of the political public
1924–1926	Hijazi–Saudi war, conquest of Mecca
1925	Proclamation of Reza Khan as Shah of Persia
1925	Druzes revolts in Syria
1926	Proclamation of the Republic of Lebanon under a French protectorate
1926	Foundation of the Algerian Étoile Nord Africaine
1926	Foundation of the Indonesian Nahzat al-Ulama
1927–1931	War between Saudi government troops and rebel tribes (*ikhwan*). Suppression of separatist movements in the Hijaz
1928–1934	International economic crisis
1928	Official foundation of the Egyptian Muslim Brotherhood and the Society of Muslim Youth. The beginning of the neo-Salafiya movement
1928	Albania becomes a kingdom after three years of republicanism
1929	Militant conflicts between Jewish colonists and Palestinian parties
1931	Proclamation of the *Dahir berbère* in Morocco by the French

	colonial authorities – segregation of Berbers and Arabs
1931	General Islamic Congress in Jerusalem
1931	Defeat of the last resistance groups in Libya by Italy
1932	Proclamation of the Saudi Arabian Kingdom
1932	Independence of Iraq
1934	Conclusion of the *pacification* in Morocco – beginning of the Moroccan National Movement
1934	Foundation of the Tunisian Néo–Destour party
1936/1937	Establishment of Egypt's sovereignty (with limitations)
1936–1939	Strike movement and revolts in Palestine
1938	Failure of the French assimilation programmes in Algeria
1939	Italian occupation of Albania
1941	Declaration of the 'Atlantic Charter'
1941	Proclamation of the republic in Syria and Lebanon
1941	Foundation of the Islamic Community in northern India
1942–1945	Japanese occupation of Indonesia
1943	Negotiation of the (unwritten) national pact in Lebanon
1943	Japanese foundation of the Masjumi in Indonesia
1945/1949	Independence of Indonesia
1945	Foundation of the League of Arab States
1946	Complete sovereignty of Syria and Lebanon
1947	Partition of India and Pakistan
1947–1957	'Liberal Decade' in the Islamic world
1948	Proclamation of the State of Israel, first Arab–Israeli war
1949	Assassination of the leader of the Egyptian Muslim Brothers, Hasan al-Banna
1949–1961	Dar al-Islam movement in various parts of Indonesia
1950	Foundation of the Islamic Liberation Party in Israel/Palestine
1951	Foundation of the Kingdom of Libya
1951–1953	Nationalist government in Persia, restoration of the Pahlavi reign
1952	Nationalist coup in Egypt
1953	Proclamation of a republic in Egypt
1954–1962	Algerian war
1955–1979	Baghdad Pact
1956	Suez crisis, second Arab–Israeli war
1956–1960	Independence of Morocco, Tunisia, Sudan and Mauretania
1957–1967	Arab Cold War
1958	Overthrow of the monarchy in Iraq
1958–1961	Union of Syria and Egypt to form the United Arab Republic
1958–1969	Authoritative sovereignty in Pakistan
1958–1964	Authoritative sovereignty in the Sudan
1959–1965	Authoritative sovereignty in Indonesia
1960	Military coup in Turkey
1960–1971	Independence of most Islamic countries in sub-Saharan Africa

1961	Independence of Kuwait
1962	Foundation of the Muslim World League
1962	Recognition of the Algerian Republic
1962–1971	Overthrow of the kingdom in the Yemen, proclamation of a republic, civil war
1963	Rebellions against the reign of Mohammad Reza Shah in Iran
1963	Foundation of Malaysia after the accession of Sabah and Sarawak into the Malayan Federation
1964	Collapse of the Arab sovereignty in Zanzibar
1965	Massive persecution of the Muslim Brotherhood in Egypt
1965–67	Civil War in Indonesia
1967	Third Arab-Israeli war
1967	Independence of South Yemen, from 1970 as a People's Republic
1967–1970	Secession of Biafra in Nigeria
1968	Coup of the Ba'th Party in Iraq
1969	Republican coup in Libya
1969/1972	Foundation of the Organization of the Islamic Conference
1969–1985	Military rule in the Sudan
1971	Foundation of the United Arab Emirate, independence of Qatar and Bahrain
1971	Secession of East Pakistan, war between India and Pakistan
1972	Beginning of the *infitah* policy in Egypt
1972–1982	First climax of migrations to Europe and the Gulf States; consider able growth of the Muslim population in Western Europe
1972–1975	Rebellion in Oman
1973	Fourth Arab–Israeli war
1974	Turkish occupation of northern Cyprus
1974	Beginning of the rise of the Islamic public
1975–1991	Civil war in Lebanon
1976	Moroccan–Mauretanian treaty about the partition of Western Sahara
1977–1979	Military coup in Pakistan, proclamation of the 'Islamic system'
1978/1979	Peace negotiations between Egypt and Israel
1979	Islamic Revolution in Iran
1979	Islamic revolt in Mecca
1979–1989	Soviet occupation of Afghanistan
1979–1991	Climax of the power of Islamic ideological parties
1980	Military coup in Turkey
1980	Revolt of the *mahdi* Mai Tatsine in Northern Nigeria
1980–1988	War between Iran and Iraq
1981	Assassination of the Egyptian President Sadat
1982	Rise of the Muslim Brothers in Hama (Syria)
1982	Beginning of the Islamization of the Malaysian state culture
1983	Military coup in Nigeria

1983–1985	Islamization in the Sudan, overthrow of Numairi's regime
1986	Struggle for power in South Yemen
1986	First nationalist demonstrations in Alma Ata (Kazakhstan)
1988	Nagorno-Karabagh conflicts between Armenia and Azerbaijan
1988	Beginning of political liberalization in Algeria
1988	Beginning of first Palestine *intifada*
1989	Foundation of the Islamic Salvation Front (FIS) in Algeria
1989	Death of the Iranian revolutionary leader Khomeini
1989–1991	Declarations of sovereignty/ independence by 14 'Muslim' states of the former USSR – 6 states join CIS, 6 remain within the Russian Federation
1990	Union of the two Yemeni states
1990–1991	Iraqi occupation of Kuwait followed by allied defeat of Iraq
1991	Beginning of open warfare between Azerbaijan and Armenia
1992	Victory of the Afghan Islamic parties over the central government
1992/3	Civil war in Tajikistan
1992/3	Peace Conferences about the Palestine question
1992–1993	War over Bosnia-Herzegovina
1992	Military coup against the supremacy of parties in Algeria
1992–1993	UN protectorate in Somalia after civil war
1993	Climax of the war between Georgia and Abkhazia
1993	Civil war between Islamist groups and government forces in Algeria
1993	Official end of the first *intifada* in Palestine
1993	Oslo Accords signed in August
1993–1994	Autonomy status for Gaza and Jericho in the occupied territories
1994–1996	First Russian-Chechen war
1993	Mobilization of the Taliban in Afghanistan
1994	Civil war in Yemen
1995	Israel's Prime Minister Rabin assassinated
1995	Beginning of terrorist activities by followers of bin Laden
1995	Peace Treaty between the Russian Federation and Chechnya
1995	Israeli-Palestinian Interim Agreement, Washington 25 September
1996	Muhammad Khatami elected president of Iran
1997–1998	Economic crisis in South-East Asia
1998	Fall of Indonesia's President Suharto
1998	Bombing of American embassies in Nairobi and Dar es Salaam
1999	Repression of the Islamic rebellion in Daghestan (Russian Federation)
2000	Beginning of the second Russian-Chechen war
2000	Occupation of Grozny by Russian forces
2000	Beginning of the second *intifada* in Palestine
2001	Terrorist attack in US, 11 September on the World Trade Center and the Pentagon with civilian planes hijacked by Islamist extremists
2001	US creates alliance including many Muslim states for war of retaliation against al-qa'ida, bin Laden and Taliban regime in Afghanistan. US and British air strikes commence 5 October

Glossary

ʿAbbāsids	Arab caliphate dynasty ruling in Iraq 750–1258, and symbolically in Cairo 1258–1516.
ʿāda, ʿadat	Common law, as *adat* extensive legal system in South-East Asia.
Ahl-i Islam	Ottoman designation for Muslims.
Āl	Clan, family (esp. in the Arab peninsula).
ʿAlawīya, ʿAlawites	Extreme Shiʿi group probably originating from Baghdad. They developed in the 10/11th centuries and today live mainly in Syria. Formerly called Nusayris.
Alevites	From the 19th century, common name for the Shiʿi group of the Qizilbash in Anatolia; originally related to the Twelver Shiʿis, the Anatolian (Arab, Turkish and Kurdish) Alevites have developed an independent form of worship.
ʿālim, pl. *ʿulamāʾ*	'Scholar' in the narrow sense, within the context of Islamic traditions of learning, esp. in the field of theology.
amīr	'Prince'
Amīr al-Muʾminīn	'Prince of the Faithful', title of religious sovereignty.
ansār	'Helper', originally designating the tribes in Medina who supported the prophet Mohammad.
ʿaqida	Dogmatics', in the contemporary political language also 'theory'.
ʿĀshūrā (yaum al-)	The tenth day of the month of Muharram of the Islamic year 61 (10/10/680), on which Husain, the son of the caliph Ali and leader of the Shiʿi party, was killed; also a voluntary day of fasting for Sunnis.

ba'th	'Mission', name of the homonymous Syrian–Iraqi party.
bid'a, pl. bida'	Within the context of classic Islamic law, an 'innovation' that is not based on tradition; mainly used in a negative sense as 'unauthorized innovation'.
da'wa/dakwah	'Summons', 'invitation' (to the correct understanding of Islam), in South-EastAsia mainly written as *dakwah.*
daula,	pl. *duwal*Originally 'turning-point', later 'change of dynasty', then 'dynasty', then 'dynastic rule' and finally 'state'.
dīn	Koranic concept for 'religion', but also 'law-court' and 'cult'
Druzes	Islamic group going back to the tradition of the Sevener-Shi'i Fatimids and first emerging in Egypt in the 11th cent.; since the Middle Ages mainly living in Lebanon.
fatwa, Turk. *fetva*	Judicially non-binding legal information by a mufti.
ḥākimīya	More recent Arabic term for 'sovereignty'
Ḥanafīya	Originally an Iraqi Islamic legal tradition attributed to Abu Hanifa (699–767), which became widespread as an Ottoman legal tradition in modern times.
Ḥanbalīya	Islamic legal tradition and moral-theological school attributed to Ahmad b. Hanbal (780–855), which won recognition in the urban centres of Damascus and Baghdad, as well as on the Arab Peninsula.
hijra	'Emigration' of the Prophet Muhammad to Medina in 622; also beginning of the Islamic era.
hujra, pl. *hujar*	Settlement of members of the Ikhwan and their tribal groups in Central Arabia after 1912.
ibn al-balad	Previous designation for 'country-man', then 'citizen'; later only 'genuine native' without legal connotation.
iftā'	Legal information system
ijtihād	Method of Islamic jurisprudence in dealing with a case which calls for 'summoning up' one's own intelligence.
ikhwān	'Brothers (in faith, in spirit, etc.)'
imām	'Leader', esp. spiritual leader of the Shi'a from the family of Ali.
jahilīya	'Ignorance', which in the Islamic tradition signifies the pre-Islamic period; in contemporary political language it also means 'the un-Islamically living Islamic world'.
jamā'a	'Community', which is reached by consensus.
jāmi'a islāmīya	Arabic version for 'Pan-Islam'.
jihad	'Striving' (on the way to God), in the mystic sense 'inner purification', in the politico–legal context the 'righteous war'.
khān	Princely title especially used in non-Arab countries, later often replaced by shah.
Khatmiya	Mystic order in the Sudan, founded by Muhammad 'Uthman al-Mirghani (died 1853), who considered himself as the 'accomplisher' (*khātim)* of the culture of mystic orders.
khedive	Persian princely title; 1867–1914 official title of Egyptian sovereigns.

khilāfa	'Caliphate'.
mahdī	Emissary of God announcing the end of time.
Mālikīya	Islamic legal tradition from the Hijaz attributed to Malik b. Anas (715–795) and especially widespread in North Africa.
Mamlūk	Mameluks, orig. military slaves who held eminent offices in the Middle Ages; in the 18th century, the ruling elite in Egypt, Syria, Iraq, et al.
Marabout (mrabit)	'Holy Man' (North Africa); in the early Middle Ages the term designated the inhabitant of a *ribāṭ* ('fortified town of a community of religious combatants').Inmodern times, a non-belligerent client of a North African tribe responsible for religious instruction and arbitration.
Maronites	Syrian–Christian religious community united with Rome. They are traced back to the monk Maron (died 423), but have only formed an independent community since the 8th century; united with Rome since1181.
milla	Koranic concept for religion (Koran 7/88f., 18/20) and confession (2/120); hence, later on, religious community.
millet	Ottoman variant of *milla*, used esp. since the 18th and 19th cents. to refer to a nationality with a specific confession.
māulwī, maulawī	Title of a scholar in India and Afghanistan.
muftī, Turk. müftü	Mufti, someone who gives legal advice.
muhājirūn	'Emigrants': Originally the Muslims fromMecca who emigrated to Medina with Muhammad in 622; also the Indian Muslims who emigrated to Pakistan in 1947/48.
Murīdīya	Mystic order founded by Ahmad Bamba (1850–1927) in Senegal ca. 1880.
muwāṭin	Current Arabic term for 'citizen' since the 19th century, replacing the earlier *ibn al-waṭan.*
Naqshbandīya	Important mystic order attributed to Baha' al-Din Naqshband (d. 1388). It was several times reformed in modern times (also as Khalidīya important in the Ottoman Empire and Tataristan) and in that form clearly emphasized the lawful mystical practices and teachings in a pietistic sense.
neo-Salafīya	Neologism (Arabic *al-salafīya al-jadīda*),designating the Islamic political public which emerged since ca. 1930, independently of scholarly circles.
pasha	Honorary and official title abolished in Turkey in 1934 and in
Egypt in 1954.	
Qādirīya	Hierarchic, heterogeneous mystic order traced back to the Baghdad mystic Abd al-Qadir al-Jilani (died 1166).
pīr	Designates a 'Holy Man' in India, Pakistan, Afghanistan and the Turkestan region.
qaum	'People' connected by traditions (cf. Koran 12/3
millata qaumīn	'religion of people'; in tribal society, a tribal group; in a secular

	sense 'nation', as well as 'group with equal social princples and interests'.
rābiṭa	'Bond' or 'alliance' based on common interests.
Shāfi'īya	Iraqi – and later especially Egyptian – legal tradition attributed to the legal dogmatist al-Shafi'i (767–820), which became particularly widespread in Lower Egypt, in the Arab Fertile Crecent, in the Arab Peninsula and in South-East Asia.
Shāh	Persian royal title, used esp. in Persia (Iran), Afghanistan and the Ottoman Empire.
Shaikh al-Islām	Title of the highest-ranking mufti in the Ottoman Empire; in Africa (Senegal) also generally used for the most acknowledged scholar.
salaf sāliḥ	The 'old ancestors', i. e. the group of culturally leading Muslims of the first century of the Islamic era.
Salafiya	Since 1884, current name adopted by this classic Islamic cultural movement; also implies the group of Islamic *'ulamā'* committed to this movement.
Sanūsīya	Mystic order, founded by Muhammad b. Ali al-Sanusi (died 1859); the centre of this order was for a long time in Cyrenaica.
sharī'a'	Way', Arabic concept for 'law', esp. for Islamic legal traditions; derived from it is the concept for 'Islamic law'.
sharīf	'Nobleman', descendant of the family of the Prophet Muhammad.
Shī'ā	To begin with, 'party' of Ali, Muhammad's son-in-law and the 4th caliph against the 'party' of Mu'awiya; secondly, theological school, and finally heterogeneous Islamic religious community which, in a very distinct manner, acknowledges the imams as the spiritual successors of Ali (and hence also of Muhammad).
sulṭān	Widespread royal title, now obsolete.
sunna'	Tradition', 'traditional way of life', 'behaviour'; in the Koran (e.g. 33/38 & 62) also referring to God, i. e. the way in which God acted earlier (i. e. before his revelations to Muhammad. Later on it implied the tradition and way of life of the Prophet and of some of his companions).
tanẓimāt-i khairīya	The 'benevolent arrangements' of 19th-century Ottoman governments for a comprehensive reform of the legal, administrative, educational and military systems.
taqlīd	'Commitment' to the authorities of Islamic legal traditions, often understood as the opposite of *ijtihād* in Islamic jurisprudence.
Tijānīya	Mystical order in North Africa founded in 1781/82 by Ahmad b. Muhammad al-Tijani (died 1815) among the Western Algerian Ain Madi. Autonomous traditions esp. in Senegal, Niger and Nigeria.
'ulamā'	Pl. of *'ālim*.
Ummayads	Arab dynasty of caliphs (661–750).

umma islāmīya	'Islamic community', today mainly a term for 'Islamic world'
usūl-i jadīd	Classicist (Salafi) culture of Tatar *'ulamā'* and intellectuals in the late 19th and early 20th centuries.
Wahhābīya	Pietistic movement in the Arab peninsula attributed to Muhammad b. 'Abdalwahhab (1703–1792).
waqf	Religious 'endowments'.
Zaidiya	Shi'i legal tradition recognizing the imamate of Zaid b. Ali (d. 740); attested as a national tradition from the 9th century; firmly established in the Yemen since 893.

Notes

1. Cf. E. Ehlers, 'Der Islamische Orient im Lichte der Geographie', in: E. Ehlers et al., *Der Islamische Orient. Grundlagen zur Länderkunde eines Kulturraums*, Islamische Wissenschaftliche Akademie, Cologne, 1900, pp. 1–9.

2. See the Islam scholar Jörg Kraemer, who follows in the tradition of Ernst Troeltsch, *Das Problem der islamischen Kulturgeschichte*, Niemeyer, Tübingen, 1959, p. 16 ff., 46. This particular image is very popular today.

3. I have borrowed this characterization of global culture from Immanuel Wallerstein's comments on world economies, see Wallerstein, *The Modern World System, I: Capitalist Agriculture and the Origins of the European World Economy in the Sixteenth Century*, Academic Press, New York 1974, 1st chapter.

4. The *umma* is also a traditional concept. In Islamic theology, Muhammad's *umma* was described, in accordance with the Koran (Koran 3/110), as the 'best community' of humanity in the divine plan of creation, so it means an 'Islamic religious community'. It is distinguished by obedience to the ultimate commands of the revelation (Islam). The Muslims united in the *true* faith form the *jama'a* ('community'). On the multiple Koranic meanings of the word *umma*, which in fact describes a community with a common characteristic (language, religion, et al.) see also R. Paret, 'Umma', in EI IV, pp. 1015-1016. On the historical context, see Albrecht Noth, 'Früher Islam', in Ulrich Haarmann (ed.), *Geschichte der arabischen Welt*, Beck, Munich 1986, pp. 11–100, here p. 35 ff.

5. Claus Leggewie, *Alhambra – Der Islam im Westen*, Rowohlt, Reinbek bei Hamburg, 1993, p. 7.

6. See especially Bassam Tibi, 'Im Namen Gottes? Der Islam, die Menschenrechte und die kulturelle Moderne', in Michael Lüders (ed.), *Der Islam im Aufbruch?*

Perspektiven der arabischen Welt, Piper, Munich, 1992, pp. 144–61, here p. 160.

7. Cf. Reinhard Schulze, 'Das Islamische 18. Jahrhundert. Versuch einer historiographischen Kritik', in *Die Welt des Islams* 30 (1990), pp. 140–59.

8. I am grateful to the Egyptologist Jan Assmann from Heidelberg for pointing out the relevance of cultural translation.

9. Dale Eickelman, *The Middle East. An Anthropological Approach*, Prentice Hall, Englewood Cliffs, N. J., 1981; Michael Gilsenan, *Recognizing Islam. An Anthropologist's Approach*, Croom Helm, London 1982; Ernest Gellner, *Muslim Society*, Cambridge University Press, Cambridge 1981; Clifford Geertz, *Islam Observed. Religious Developments in Morocco and Indonesia*, The University of Chicago Press, Chicago, 1968.

10. E. g. Fatima Mernissi, *Le Harem Politique; le Prophète et les femmes*, Albin Michel, Paris 1987; id., *Beyond the Veil. Male–Female Dynamics in a Modern Muslim Society*, Schenkman, Cambridge, Mass., 1975 [2 Indiana University Press, Bloomington, Ind., 1987].

11. Such works are mainly of an earlier date, e. g. Walther Braune, *Der islamische Orient zwischen Vergangenheit und Zukunft. Eine geschichtstheologische Analyse seiner Stellung in der Weltsituation*, Francke, Bern 1960; cf. also Wilfred Cantwell Smith, *Islam in Modern History*, Princeton University Press, Princeton, N. J. 2 1957 and Gustav E. von Grunebaum, *Studien zum Kulturbild und Selbstverständnis des Islams*, Artemis, Zurich 1969.

12. Attempts at this in Ira M. Lapidus, *A History of Islamic Societies*, Cambridge University Press, Cambridge, 1988. A more extensive comparative social history of the Islamic world in the 20th century ought to be written.

13. By way of introduction see Charles Issawi, *An Economic History of the Middle East and North Africa*, Columbia University Press, New York, 1982.

14. Thus for instance the readable description by Malcolm E. Yapp, *The Middle East since the First World War*, Longman, London 1991.

15. In this connection, the valence of the concept of groups in recent Islamic history would have to be examined. A more recent analysis is that of Georg Elwert, 'Nationalismus und Ethnizität. Über die Bildung von Wir-Gruppen', *Das Arabische Buch*, Berlin 1989. [Ethnizität und Gesellschaft. Occasional Papers Nr. 22]. I use this unwieldy sociological concept to convey the widely used word *qaum* (of Arabic origin).

16. Reinhard Eisener, 'Auf den Spuren des tadschikischen Nationalismus', in *Das Arabische Buch* 1991 [Ethnizität und Gesellschaft. Occasional Papers Nr. 28].

17. That is, according to an 18th-century German definition, 'handing down is like a story known by hearsay, which has nowhere been written down by a proper writer, or human observances, of which nothing is contained or announced in the Holy Scriptures'. Cf. Reinhard Schulze, 'The Birth of Tradition and Modernity in 18th and 19th-Century Islamic Culture', *Studia Islamica* (forthcoming).

18. Especially James Piscatori, *Islam in a World of Nation-States*, Cambridge University Press, Cambridge 1986.

19. Especially Werner Ende/Udo Steinbach (eds), *Der Islam in der Gegenwart. Entwicklung und Ausbreitung – Staat, Politik und Recht – Kultur und Religion*, Beck,

Munich 1984, 21989. But there exists no modern history of Islamic theology.

20. Carl Brockelmann, *Geschichte der islamischen Völker und Staaten*, Munich 1939, 21943, reprint Olms, Hildesheim, 1977, updated under the title *History of the Islamic Peoples*, London 1980 [New York 1944].

21. Ulrich Haarmann's discussion in WI 32 (1992), pp. 281–4, serves as an introduction to this voluminous work.

CHAPTER ONE

1. Abd al-Rahman al-Kawakibi, *Umm al-qura wa-huwa dabt mufawadat wa-muqarrarat mu'tamar al-nahda al-islamiya al-mun'aqid fi Makka al-mukarrama sanat 1316*, Beirut: Dar al-Ra'id al-'Arabi 1402 [1982], first published under the title *Sijill mudhakkirat jam'iyat umm al-qura ay dabt mufawadat* [etc.], Port Sa'id o. J. (1899).

2. Gabriel Effendi Naradounghian, *Recueil d'actes internationaux de l'Empire Ottoman*, I–IV, Paris: Cotillon, Pichon 1897–1903, I, pp. 319–34. In article 3 (*ibid.*, p. 332), it is stipulated: 'Quant aux cérémonies de religion, comme les Tartares professent le même culte que les Musulmans, et que S. M. le Sultan est regardé comme le souverain Calife de la religion mahométane, ils se conduiront à son égard comme il est prescrit par les préceptes de leur loi, sans cependant compromettre par là leur liberté politique et civile, telle qu'elle vient d'être établie.'

3. Christian Arab authors often stated the contrary; they had previously warned against too naive an emphasis on the equality of civilization between East and West. Cf. Rotraud Wielandt, *Das Bild der Europäer in der modernen arabischen Erzähl- und Theaterliteratur*, Beirut/Wiesbaden, Steiner 1982, pp. 131 ff.

4. Here quoted from Sabry, *La Révolution égyptienne* (...), I–II, Paris 1919/1921, I, p. 79.

5. Comte de Chambord, *Journal de voyage en Orient 1861*, Paris 1984, p; 245.

6. V. Bartol'd, 'Khalif i Sultan', *Mir' Islama* (St. Petersburg) I (1912), pp. 203–26, 345–400.

7. Muhammad A'la al-Thanawi, *Kashshaf istilahat al-funun*, Calcutta 1863, I, p. 91: '*Umma* is said of any group of nations [Persian] and therefore it is said: the *umma* is a unity in which they are grouped in accordance with religion, time, place or the like [Arabic]'; at Thanawi distinguishes [in connection with the *shuruh al-mishkat fi kitab al-iman*] between the *ummat al-da'wa* ['nation of summons'], established on the sending of a prophet, and the *ummat al-ijaba* ['nation of consent'] established on the will of the faithful.

8. Ottomanism would soon be violently criticized by Arab classicists, cf. Farah Antun, 'al-Jami'a al-'uthmaniya', *al-Manar* 13 (1328/1910–11), pp. 857, 933.

9. The designation of the 'sublime state' as 'Ottoman' basically started in the 19th century. The classical self-designation was simply: *mamalik-i mahrusa*, i.e. 'the [divinely] blessed countries [of the Ottoman Padishah]'.

10. On the establishment of territorial states in the Islamic world in the 18th and 19th centuries, see also Reinhard Schulze, 'Geschichte der islamische Welt in der Neuzeit (16–19 Jahrhundert)', in Albrecht Noth, J. Paul (eds), *Der Islamische Orient: Grundzüge*

seiner Geschichte, Cologne 1994.

11. The earliest Arabic concept for 'citizen of a territorial state' must have been *ibn al-balad*, which appeared around 1720 in Syria and Egypt. *Balad* originally meant 'city' in the sense of a centre of political power. In the 18th century, *balad* was understood *pars per toto* as denoting the 'entire country', in the centre of which was a large city, i. e. the 'capital'. The expression can thus be translated as 'native'. Around 1820, when the Ottoman language came back into favour in the Arab world, the word *watan* [originally Arabic in the sense of 'dwelling-place'] replaced *balad*; *watan*, a concept often praised in poetry, had a strong emotional nuance: the romantic longing for the *watan* was omnipresent in literature. This suggested a connection with the French *patrie*; thus *watan* became synonymous with 'fatherland'.

12. P. de Lacretelle in: *Journal des Débats*, édit. Hebd., 5/1/1923, quoted from: Un Africain [anonymous], *Manuel de politique musulman*, Paris, Ed. Bossard 1925, p. 31.

13. Renan's lecture on this subject, 'L'Islam et la science', held at the Sorbonne on 29 March 1883 [published in the *Journal des Débats*, 18/5/1883], aroused violent criticism from some Islamic intellectuals. See among others Albert Hourani, *Arabic Thought in the Liberal Age. 1798–1939*, Oxford 1962, pp. 120 ff.

14. Georges Balandier, 'Die koloniale Situation: ein theoretischer Ansatz', in Rudolf von Albertini, ed., *Moderne Kolonialgeschichte*, Cologne 1970, pp. 105–24, p. 105.

15. The best study on classical Islamic humanism is George Makdisi, *The Rise of Humanism in Classical Islam and the Christian West, with Special Reference to Scholasticism*, Edinburgh 1990.

16. *al-Mustaqbal li-l-Islam*, Cairo, al-'Umumiya.

17. Thus the Egyptian Mufti of the time, Muhammad Abduh, quoted in Muhammad 'Abduh, *al-A'mal alkamila*, ed. Muhammad Ammara, vols I–VI, Beirut: al-Mu'assasa al-Arabiya 1972–1974, here III, pp. 178–9 and idem, *al-Islam wa-l-nasraniya ma'a l-'ilm wa-l madaniya*, ed. Muhammad Rashid Rida, Cairo: al-Manar 1341 [1923/4], pp. 99–105.

18. J. Brugman, *An Introduction to the History of Modern Arabic Literature in Egypt*, Leiden-Brill 1984, p. 95.

19. Khalil Afandi al-Jawish in: *al-Diya* (Cairo) 3 (1900/01), p. 266.

20. Ahmad b. Khalid al-Nasiri al-Salawi, *Kitab al-istiqsa' li-akhbar duwal al-maghrib al-aqsa*, 4 vols, Cairo ([2]Casablanca: Dar al-Kitab) 1312/1894/95; [2]1956, here quoted from *Un Africain*, Manuel, p. 69.

21. Ibrahim b. 'Abd al-Khaliq al-Muwailihi, *Ma hunalika*, Cairo 1896, p. 21.

22. Thus e. g. Mustafa Kamil in: *al-Diya* 2 (1899/1900), p. 279. Cf. Fritzz Steppat, 'Nationalismus und Islam bei Mustafa Kamil. Ein Beitrag zur Ideengeschichte der ägyptischen Nationalbewegung', *Die Welt des Islams*, N. S. 4 (1956), pp. 241–341.

23. Wali al-Din Yegen, *al-Ma'lum wa-l majhul*, I–II, Cairo 1909/11.

24. Al-Sultan Abd al-Hamid al-Thani, *Muzakkirati al-siyasiya, 1891–1908*, Beirut [2] 1402/1982, pp. 78 ff.

25. Ibid., p. 74, 191.

26. Ibid., p. 185.

27. Niyazi Berkes, *The Development of Secularism in Turkey*, Montreal: McGill

University Press 1964, pp. 201 ff.

28. H. Turot, *L'Insurrection crétoise et la guerre gréco–turque*, Paris 1898.

29. The literature about the pogroms against the Armenian population in Anatolia in 1915–16 is very extensive and has led to ongoing controversies between Turkish and Armenian national historiography. Among the striking characteristics of the pogroms is the fact that the Armenian bourgeoisie in Istanbul remained unmolested, that it continued being active in its cultural and national associations and was loyal either to the radical Armenian parties or to the empire, while at the same time the Armenian peasant population underwent mass executions and expulsions, cf. Mesrod K. Krikorian, *Armenians in the Service of the Ottoman Empire, 1860–1908*, London, Routledge, 1978.

30. Thus for example Jalal Nuri [Ileri]: *Ittihal-ï Islam. Islamiñ madisi hali istiqbali. Istanbul: yeñi 'uthmanlï matba'asï* 1331 [1013]: cf. Jacob M. Landau's detailed account, *The Politics of Pan-Islam. Ideology and Organization*, Oxford: Oxford University Press,1992, pp. 8 ff.

31. Balandier, *Koloniale Situation*, p. 109.

32. Stanford J. Shaw and Ezel Kural Shaw, *History of the Ottoman Empire and Modern Turkey*, vol. II: *Reform, Revolution, and Republic: The Rise of Modern Turkey, 1808–1975*, Cambridge: Cambridge Univesity Press, 1977, p. 240 ff.

33. Not specifically mentioned here are the minority areas in America and Europe (emigrants, Islamic communities in the Balkan States and Poland). The numbers quoted are very rough estimates. Democratic development in the Middle East is discussed by Charles Issawi, *An Economic History of the Middle East and North Africa*, New York: Columbia University Press, 1982, pp. 93–117.

34. 'al-Rabita al-naqshbandiya', *al-Manar* 11 (1326/ 1908–09), p. 504. The influence of this order, which was revived in the 18th century, on the development of the *salafiya* must also have been important in Syria and Anatolia.

35. al-Kawakibi, *Umm al-qura*, p. 68.

36. Muhammad Rashid Rida in *al-Manar* 32 (1350/1932), p. 114 ff.

37. Cf. the excellent documentation by B. J. Slot, *The Origins of Kuwait*, Leiden: Brill, 1991, esp. p. 104 ff. The name Kuwait was for the first time recorded on a map by Carsten Niebuhr in 1761.

38. Cf. Uriel Heyd, *Foundations of Turkish Nationalism. The Life and Teachings of Ziya Gökalp*, Luzac, London: Harvill, 1950, p. 92 ff.

39. Bernard Lewis, *The Emergence of Modern Turkey*, London: Oxford University Press, [2]1968, repr. 1975, p. 195. On the political programmes of the party during the revolution, and altogether on the Ottoman party scene, we are best informed by Tarik Zafer Tunaya, *Türkiye'de Siyasal Partiler*, I–III, Hürriyet Vakfi Yayinlari, Istanbul 1984, 1986, 1989, I: Ikinci Meshrutiyet Dönemi 1908–1918, pp. 19–130 [documentation]; III: Ittihat ve Terakki, pp. 303–42.

40. Ahmad Jaudat Pasha, *Tarikh-i Jaudat*, 12 vols, 1301–1309 [1883/84–1891/92, I, p. 14.

41. On the emergence of bourgeois society within the context of the Ottoman civil and court bureaucracy, cf. Carter W. Findley, *Bureaucratic Reform in the Ottoman Empire: The Sublime Porte 1789–1922*, Princeton N. J., Princeton University Press, 1980;

idem, *Ottoman Civil Officialdom: A Social History*, Princeton, N. J.: Princeton University Press, 1989.

42. Muhammad Rashid Rida, *Tarikh al-ustad al-Imam Muhammad 'Abduh*, I–III, Cairo: al-Manar (I) 1350 [1931], (II) [2]1344 [1925/26] (III) 1324 [1906], I, p. 891.

43. Timothy W. Childs, *Italo–Turkish Diplomacy and the War over Libya, 1911–1912*, Leiden: Brill, 1990, p. 6 ff.

44. T. G. Djuvara, *Cent projets de partage de la Turquie (1281–1913)*, Félix Alcan, Paris 1914.

45. Roger Owen, *The Middle East in the World Economy, 1800–1914*, Methuen, London 1981, p. 250.

46. Cf. the example of Egypt in Reinhard Schulze, *Die Rebellion der ägyptischen Fallahin. Zum Konflikt der agrarisch–orientalischen Gesellschaft und dem kolonialen Staat*, Baalbek, Berlin, 1981, p. 97 ff.

47. Zaidan, who came from a Greek Orthodox family, was considered as one of the most important authors of historical novels. Despite his sound knowledge of Islamic history, he had to give up a lectureship at the new University of Cairo because the Islamic establishment would not accept an Arab Christian as teacher of Islamic history. In his voluminous work *Tarikh al-tamaddun al-Islami*, vols I–V, al-Hilal, Cairo, [2]1914, [3]1921, [3]1922, he aimed at an extensive rehabilitation of Arab history by emphasizing the 'Islamic civilization'.

48. Mangol Bayat, *Iran's First Revolution. Shi'ism and the Constitutional Revolution of 1905–1909*, Oxford University Press, Oxford 1991, especially emphasizes the role of the 'secular enlighteners' in the revolution; a standard work is still Edward G. Browne, *The Persian Revolution 1905–1909*, Frank Cass, London, 1966 (1st ed. Cambridge 1910); on the history of the constitution, see Vanessa Martin, *Islam and Modernism. The Iranian Revolution of 1906*, Tauris, London 1989.

49. Tadeusz Swietochowski, *Russian Azerbaijan, 1905–1920*, Cambridge University Press, Cambridge 1985, p. 41.

50. A. V. Pjaskowskij, *Revoljucija 1905–1907 godov v Turkestane*, Izd. Nauk SSSR, Moscow 1985, p. 103 ff.

51. Fikret Adanir, *Die mazedonische Frage. Ihre Entstehung und Entwicklung bis 1908*, Steiner, Wiesbaden, 1979, p. 116 ff.

52. Shaw/Shaw, *History*, p. 276 ff.

53. On 27/4/ 1909, Mehmed V. Rashad was elected as Sultan; he died on 28/6/1918. Abd al-Hamid II retired to Salonica, but had to leave the city at the end of the first Balkan war in 1912 and thereafter lived in Istanbul until 10/2/1918.

54. Owen, *Middle East*, pp.198, 223.

55. Childs, *Italo–Turkish Diplomacy*, p. 71 ff., and Rachel Simons, *Libya between Ottomanism and Nationalism*, Schwarz, Berlin, 1987.

56. In Alexandria, students demonstrated for the Ottoman Empire on 31/10/1911, but they could hardly mobilize more than 100 participants. Great Britain, Foreign Office, 407–177–142, Kitchener to Gray, 2/11/1911.

57. Johannes Faensen, *Die albanische Nationalbewegung*, (commissioned by) Harrassowitz, Berlin, 1980. The Albanian revolts combined regional urban nationalism

with the social protest of the peasants against the population census and against new forms of centralized impositions of taxes.

58. Abd al-Hamid al-Thani, *Mudhakkirati*, p. 185.

59. See the official Turkish version *Birinci Dünya Harbinde Türk Harbi*, vol. I, Osmali Imparatorulujunun Siyasî ve Askerî Hazirliklari ve Harbi Girisi, Ankara 1970. On Iraq: Werner Ende, 'Iraq in World War I: "The Turks, the Germans and the Shi'ite Mujtahids call for Jihad"', in: *Proceedings of the 9th Congress of the UEAI*, Amsterdam 1978, ed. Rudolph Peters, Leiden 1981, pp. 57–71; Augustin Bernard, *L'Afrique du nord pendant la guerre*, Paris 1926; Maurice Larcher, *La guerre turque dans la guerre mondiale*, Paris 1926.

60. Schulze, *Rebellion*, p. 121 ff.

61. Monika Midel, *Fulbe und Deutsche in Adamaua (Nord-Kamerun) 1809–1916*, Lang, Frankfurt a. M., 1990,p. 332 ff.

62. Cf. Linda S. Schilcher, 'The Famine in Syria 1916–1918', in John Spagnola (ed.), Problems of the Modern Middle East in Historical
Perspective : Essays in Honour of Albert Hourani (St. Anthony's Middle East Monographs, No. 26) London 1997.

63. Von Oppenheim's memoir of September 1914 is an eloquent example, see Karl Emil Freiherr v. Schowingen Schabinger, *Weltgeschichtliche Mosaiksplitter, Erlebnisse und Erinnerungen eines kaiserlichen Dragomans*, Baden-Baden 1967, pp. 115–25. Quoted from and altogether concerning this subject: Gottfried Hagen, *Die Türkei im Ersten Weltkrieg. Flugblätter und Flugschriften in arabischer, persischer und osmanisch-türkischer Sprache* […], Lang, Frankfurt a. M., 1990. On the reception see Christian Snouck Hurgronje, 'The Holy War "Made in Germany"' and 'Deutschland und der Heilige Krieg', in ibid., *Verspreide Geschriften*, vol. III, Bonn, Leipzig 1923, pp. 257–84, 285–92.

64. And also by the Azhar, which on 24 November 1914 summoned the Egyptians to support the British rule, cf. *al-Sha'b* of 25/11/1914.

65. Curiously enough, two relatives of the Egyptian ruling family, Sultan Husain and the Ottoman Grand Vizier, were facing each other as political opponents.

66. This also includes the Constantinople Agreement of 18 March 1915 (France, Great Britain, Russia), the secret agreement concluded in London on 26 April 1915 between France, Great Britain, Italy and Russia and the St. Jean de Maurienne Agreement between France, Great Britain and Italy of 17 April 1917, cf. Arnold Toynbee/Kenneth Kirkwood, *Turkey*, New York 1927, pp. 68–70. Italy's role as mandatory power in south-western Anatolia had been established in the secret treaty of St. Jean de Maurienne of 17 April 1917.

67. Abd al-Aziz Jawish, *al-Islam din al-fitra*, Cairo 1987, p. 161 ff.

68. *al-Manar* I (1898), pp. 105–8.

69. On Rida it is still worth reading Henri Laoust 'Le réformisme orthodoxe des "Salafiyya" et les caractères généraux de son orientation actuelle', *Revue des Études islamiques* 6 (1932) 2, pp.175–224.

70. Thus e.g. the Egyptian national conservative pedagogue Rifa'a Rafi' al-Tahtawi (1801–1873), 'Kitab al-murshid al-amin li-l-banat wa-l-banin', in ibid., *al-A'mal al-*

kamila, ed. by Muhammad Ammara, II, Beirut: al-Mu'assasa al-Arabiya 1973, pp. 251–767, here p. 469.

71. E. g. *al-Manar* 12 (1909), pp. 150–9), Rida's speech at a political meeting in Beirut.

72. This 'Community canon of Medina' was an agreement made between Muhammad and the inhabitants of Yathrib, the later Medina, where he and his companions had emigrated in 622. From the classicist point of view, this was the earliest document of an Islamic political idea of a canon. Cf. Albrecht Noth, 'Früher Islam', in Ulrich Haarmann (ed.), *Geschichte der arabischen Welt*, Beck, Munich 1986, pp. 11–100, here p. 31 ff.

73. From now on the attributes 'Islamic' and 'European' will usually appear in quotation marks. These terms are conventionally treated as antonyms, although in fact we are not dealing with mutually contradictory concepts. They really differ neither in content nor in function, but merely through the linguistic forms and norms by which social existence is discussed. In this sense, 'Islamic' and 'European' are languages in the broadest sense of the word, that is, they include linguistic statements, texts and gestures as well as clothes, fashions and social manners. As languages they are translatable: it is quite possible to translate an 'Islamic' cultural statement into a 'European' one. However, this only applies to those fields which correspond with colonial, i. e. modern spheres of life. These languages are discursive insofar as their application leads to various procedures which serve the self-identification of the group through delimitations or exclusions; in addition, these languages are instrumental to forming institutions (press, parties, unions, policies etc.), in which the worldly knowledge expressed in language becomes a power.

74. From here on, Turkish names and expressions which refer to Turkish national culture are written in the Latin spelling established by Atatürk himself.

75. Arnold Toynbee, *The Western Question in Greece and Turkey*, New York 1970, p. 328.

76. Elie Kedourie, 'The Surrender of Medina', MES 13 (1977), pp. 124–43.

77. S. Shaw/Shaw, *History*, p. 342.

78. It is still controversial whether the Ottoman army approved of the pogroms or even organized them. Armenian national historians say that more than 1 million Armenians were killed. As proof for the version that the government of the Young Turks had led the pogroms itself, Armenian nationalists used the faked telegrams of the Ottoman Minister of the Interior Talât Pasha (1874–1921), which were published in 1920 by the Armenian nationalist Aram Andonian in a book entitled 'The Memoirs of Naim Bey, Turkish Official Documents Relating to the Deportations and Massacres of Armenians', London 1920 [French transl. Paris 1920]. They are reprinted in a pro-Turkish, critical inventory in Shinasi Orel, Süreyya Yauca, *The Talât Pasha Telegrams. Historical Fact or Armenian Fiction?* Nicosia: K. Rustem 1983, pp. 147–91.

79. S. Shaw/Shaw, *History*, p. 351.

80. Doju Ergil, *Social History of the Turkish National Struggle, 1919–22*, Sind Sagar Academy O. J., Lahore, p. 116.

81. The 'Red Turkish Regiments' were organized between 1919 and 1921, mainly by

Mustafa Subhi (born 1883), who had fled to Russia after World War I and become the speaker of a Turkish Communist movement.

82. Ergil, *History*, p. 100 f.

83. This treaty had never been ratified by the Istanbul government and therefore could not be carried out politically. It stipulated reducing the Ottoman army to 50,000 men; in view of the numerous members of the volunteer corps and the newly organized nationalist formations, this was not possible.

84. Here in the translation by Rudi Paret, *The Koran*, Stuttgart 1979; what was meant were the earlier generations who had committed sacrilege and were punished by God, see also 10/14, 10/73, 35/39 (10/14 and 35/39 refer to *hala'ifa fi l-ardi*, 'representatives on earth').

85. Abd al-Rahman al-Kawakibi, *Taba'i' al-istibdad*, Beirut 1970, p. 145. This text first appeared in the Egyptian journal *al-Mu'ayyad*. The prophetic tradition is also referred to in Abu Abdallah al-Bukhari, *al-Jami' al-sahih*, I–IX, Cairo, al-Khairiya, 1323 [1905], I, p. 160.

86. Cf. Schulze, *Rebellion*, passim.

87. Rashid Isma'il Khalidi, *British Policy towards Syria and Palestine 1906–1914. Study of the Antecedents of the Hussein–McMahon Correspondence, the Sykes–Picot Agreement, and the Balfour Declaration*, London 1980.

88. *Le Commandement de la IVme Armée* (in Syria), La vérité sur la question syrienne, Istanbul 1916.

89. See Khair al-Din al-Zirikli, *al-A'lam qamus tarajim li-ashhur al-rij'al wa-n-nisa' min al-'arab wa-l-musta'ribin wa-l-mustashriqin*, vols I–VIII, Dar al-'Ilm li-Malayin [8]1989, III, p. 288; *al-Manar* 19 (1319/1919–20), pp. 169–81. Al-Zahrawi was elected as member of the Ottoman parliament in 1908. He was a co-founder of the Party for Freedom and Justice and was President of the first Arab Congress in Paris in 1913. Cf. Amin Sa'id, *al-Thaura al-'arabiya al-kubra*, I–III, Cairo 1933, I, p. 7 ff.

90. This was the Ottoman version; others maintain that the Qahtaniya Society was re-named *al–Ahd* in 1913, Tunaya, *Siyasal Partiler*, I, p. 602.

91. Commandement, *Vérité*, p. 58 ff. This 'Ottoman party for administrative decentralization' was founded in 1912 according to Hourani, cf. Hourani, *Arabic Thought*, p. 282 f. The dates when these small circles were founded are altogether uncertain. For 'the Union' the year 1913/14 is mentioned, and for 'Youth' the year 1911; 'the Union' is said to have replaced 'al-Qahtaniya' (founded 1909). Cf. for example Martin Strohmeier, 'al-Kulliya al-Salahiya' in Jerusalem, Steiner, Stuttgart 1991 (AKM XLIX, 4), p. 53 ff. and Bassam Tibi, *Nationalismus in der Dritten Welt am arabischen Beispiel*, Frankfurt a. Main: EVA 1971, p. 95 ff. The reference most used is Georg Antonius, *The Arab Awakening. The Story of the Arab National Movement*, London 1938; this is also used as a source by Richard Hartmann for his 'Arabische politische Gesellschaften bis 1914', in id. Helmuth Scheel (ed.), *Beiträge zur Arabistik, Semistik und Islamwissenschaft*, Harrassowitz, Leipzig 1944, pp. 438–67.

92. Hereafter Tunaya, *Siyasal Partiler*, I, p. 600.

93. Hourani, *Arabic Thought*, p. 284.

94. Lawrence's often mystifying acts also reflect an internal British conflict: the India

Office, which continued seeing itself as an agent of Arab policy, followed different aims than those of the army leaders around Allenby, who stressed Egyptian interests. As so often in history, Syria was again conquered from Egypt; here the question arises of whether the British advance in Palestine was not also serving the aim to secure an Egyptian hegemony against the Hashimite claims to power.

95. *al-Manar* 22 (1340/1921–22), pp. 390–6.

96. Muhammad Rashid Rida, *Rihlat al-imam* (...), ed. Yusuf Ibish, Beirut 1979, p. 304 f.

97. Hourani, *Arabic Thought*, p. 291.

98. *al-Manar* 23 (1341/1922–23), pp. 235–40.

99. Rida, *Rihlat al-imam*, p. 309.

100. This 'union' was, however, preceded by several months of rebellion in southern and central Iraq (30 June–30 November 1920), in which members of the political groups in Damascus also participated. The rebellion embraced every facet of nationalist and separatist politics: Tribal leaders tried to preserve their land from the consequences of the war between Shammar and Najd. Peasants resisted against the 'Indian' methods of direct colonial rule, and merchants and traders found their market jeopardized by the rigorous methods of the British army. Even the oil fields discovered in southern Persia in 1901 played a major part in the conflicts. The rebellion cost the lives of more than 8,000 Iraqis and 2,000 Britons.

CHAPTER TWO

1. The first modern republic in the Islamic world was the 'Azerbaijan Democratic Republic' proclaimed in Ganja on 28/5/1918 (until May 1920); Turkish–Azerbaijani nationalism rejected a royalist system, since the latter would have been supported by a Persian princely dynasty. Almost simultaneously with the Tripolitanians, the notables of the eastern Turkish city of Kars adopted a pseudo-Republican constitution within the framework of an Islamic assembly at that city after its conquest by Ottoman troops. From April 1919 until October 1920, the city belonged to Armenia due to British intervention, but later it was definitively occupied by Turkish nationalists.

2. Za'ima Sulaiman al-Barudi [ed.], *Safahat khalida min al-jihad*, Cairo: al-Istiqlal al-Kubra, 1964, p. 45 ff.

3. Mahmud al-Shunaiti, *Qadiyat Libiya*, Cairo: al-Nahda al-Misriya, 1951, p. 76 f.

4. Auswärtiges Amt, Politisches Archiv, I A. Tripolis 1 – Allgemeine Angelegenheiten 13, A 2089 pr. 31, letter from al-Baruni to Wilhelm II, dated 4/1/1913.

5. Ibid., A 6379, Constantinople – Foreign Office, 29/3/1913. Cf. also the memoirs of Enver Pasha, *Um Tripolis*, Bruckmann, Berlin 1918.

6. al-Tahir Ahmad al-Zawi, *Jihad al-abtal fi Tarablus al-gharb*, repr. Beirut [1973], pp. 245–9.

7. Hasan Ali Khashim, *Safahat min jihadina al-watani*, Tripoli: Maktabat al-Fikr, 1394 [1974], p. 18 ff.

8. Amin al-Raihani, *al–Maghrib al-aqsa*, (written 1939), Beirut [2]1975, pp. 358–96.

9. He remained there until 1946; he spent the last years of his life in Cairo. Cf. Abd

el Krim, *Abd el Krim-Memoiren* translated by Artur Rosenberg, Dresden 1927.

10. Northern Morocco, which was under Spanish protectorate, was nominally ruled by al-Hasan b. al-Mahdi.

11. R. Montagne, *The Berbers: Their social and political organization*, Frank Cass, London 1973, pp. 64–70.

12. This platform at first only consisted of the manifesto of 8 April 1923, in which Kemal presented his nine-point thesis for the sovereignty of the people and the removal of the sultanate. Text among others in *Tarik Tunaya, Türkiyede Siyasî Partiler, 1859–1952*, Istanbul 1952, pp. 580–2.

13. Ameer Ali, 'The Caliphate: A Historical and Juridical Sketch', *The Contemporary Review* 107/594 (June 1915), pp. 681–94. His best-known book, *The Spirit of Islam*, which he first published in London in 1873 under the title *A Critical Examination of the Life and Teachings of Muhammad*, and of which there have since appeared several revised editions, was published in Istanbul in Turkish in 1922/23 under the title *ruh-u Islam*. S. Wilfred Cantwell Smith, *Islam in Modern History*, Princeton, N. J., 1957, Note 40.

14. Muhammad Rashid Rida, *al-Khilafa au al-imama al-'uzma*, Cairo: al-Manar, 1341 [1923], p. 142 (Collection of articles from *al-Manar* 23 (1341/1922–23), pp. 729–52; 24 (1342/1923–24), pp. 33–64, 98–120, 185–200, 257–72, 345–73); transl. by Henri Laoust, *Le Califat dans la doctrine de Rashid Rida. Traduction annotée d'al-Khilafa au al-Imama al-uzma (Le Califat ou l'Imamat suprême)*, Librairie d'Amérique et d'Orient 1986 [Mémoires de l'Institut Français de Damas VI (1938)]; on the Turkish press see OM 3 (1923), p. 409.

15. Rida, *al-Khilafa*, p. 79 f.

16. Here quoted from Seçil Akgün, Halifelijin kaldirilmasi ve laiklik (1924–1928), Turkan o. J. p. 177 f., Ankara; cf. also Gotthard Jäschke, 'Das osmanische Scheinkalifat von 1922', WI N. S. I (1951), pp. 195–228 and C. A. Nallino, 'La fine del così detto califfatto ottomano', OM 4 (1924), pp. 137–53. Already in the law Nr. 308 of 1–2/11/1922 about the abolition of the sultanate, the caliphate was made subject to the sovereignty of the 'popular government' and defined as 'support of the state'.

17. The abolition of the orders should also be seen in connection with the great Kurdish revolt of February–May 1925 led by the *naqshbandi* Sheikh Sa'id from Piran, who was executed on 29 June 1925. Cf. Robert Olson, *The Emergence of Kurdish Nationalism and the Sheikh Sa'id Rebellion, 1880–1925*, Austin University Press, Austin, Texas, 1989.

18. Cf. Gotthard Jäschke, 'Der Islam in der neuen Türkei', WI N. S. I (1951°, pp. 1–174.

19. Smith, *Islam*, 176.

20. Cf. the *al-Manar* issues of 1924–27.

21. Schulze, *Internationalismus*, p. 70 f.

22. Landau, *Pan-Islam*, p. 195 f.

23. Maulavie Mohammed Bereketullah, *Le Khalifat*, Geuthner, Paris, 1924, esp. pp. 60–2.

24. Cf. Landau, *Pan–Islam*, p. 203 ff., incl. further literature; Gail Minault, *The Khilafat Movement. Religious Symbolism and Political Mobilization in India*, Columbia University Press, New York,1982.

25. Quoted from Landau, *Pan–Islam*, p. 211.

26. Cf. Schulze, *Internationalismus*, p. 72 f.

27. Dirk Boberg, *Ägypten, Najd und der Hijaz. Eine Untersuchung zum religiös-politischen Verhältnis zwischen Ägypten und den Wahhabiten, 1923–1936*, Peter Lang, Bern, 1991.

28. Sa'ud b. Hazlul, *Tarikh muluk Al Sa'ud, al-Riyad 1380* [1961], p. 150 f.

29. bn Hazlul, *Tarikh*, p. 129 ff.

30. *Majmu'at al-hadith al-najdiya*, al-Manar, Cairo 1342 [1923–24].

31. The role played by European Orientalists, especially by the French Orientalist Henri Laoust, in rediscovering Ibn Taimiya ought to be clarified. Apparently Ibn Taimiya, who is now considered as the major source of Islamic thought, was rediscovered in a process of Orientalist–Islamic communication.

32. Werner Ende, 'Religion, Politik und Kultur in Saudi-Arabien. Der geistesgeschichtliche Hintergrund der heutigen religiösen und kulturpolitischen Situation', I, *Orient* 22 (1981) 3, pp. 377–90.

33. S. Martin Kramer, *Islam Assembled. The Advent of the Muslim Congresses*, Columbia University Press, New York, 1986, pp. 106–22; Schulze, *Internationalismus*, pp. 79–85.

34. Text in Ibn Hazlul, *Tarikh*, p. 186.

35. *al-Islam wa usul al-hukm, al-'arabiya 1972*, translated by L. Bercher in REI 7 (1933), pp. 353–91 and 8 (1934), pp. 163–222. Cf. also Friedemann Büttner, 'Die Krise der islamischen Ordnung. Studien zur Zerstörung des Orientierungsverständnisses im Osmanischen Reich (1800–1926)', Phil. diss. Munich 1969, published by the author 1979, pp. 119–50.

36. Taha Husain, *Fi l-shi'r al-jahili*, Dar al-Kutub, Cairo 1344 [1926]; cf. detailed account by Ignacij Krachkovskij, 'Tacha Chusein o doislamskoj poezii arabov i ego kritiki', *Bulletin de l'Académie des Sciences de St. Petersbourg* 7 (1931), pp. 589–626.

37. Joseph Castagné, *Les Basmatchi. Le mouvement national des Indigènes d'Asie Central*, Ernest Leroux, Paris, 1925, p. 7.

38. Martha Brill Olcott, *The Kazakhs*, Stanford, Cal., 1987, p. 119 ff., 129–56.

39. Baimirza Hajit, *Im XX. Jahrhundert*, Leske, Darmstadt 1956, p. 30.

40. Hajit, *Turkestan*, p. 206.

41. Kramer, *Islam*, pp. 70–1.

42. Castagné, *Basmatchis*, p. 50.

43. A clear description of the complex ethno–linguistic context can be found in Bert G. Fragner, 'Probleme der Nationswerdung der Usbeken und Tadshiken', in: Andreas Kappeler et al. (ed.), *Die Muslime in der Sowjetunion und in Jugoslawien*, Markus, Cologne 1989, pp. 19–34.

44. Cf. Alexandra A. Bennigsen/ S. Enders Wimbush, *Muslim National Communism in the Soviet Union. A Revolutionary Strategy for the Colonial World*, University of Chicago Press, Chicago 1979.

45. Somewhat dated and mainly using Russian sources: Seymour Becker, *Russia's Protectorates in Central Asia. Bukhara and Khiwa, 1865–1924*, Harvard University Press, Cambridge, Mass., 1968.

46. Cf. Nadir Devlet, *Rusya Türklerinin Millî mücâdele tarihi (1907–1917)*, Türk Kültürünü Arashtirma Enstitüsü 1985, p. 76 ff.; Alexandre Bennigsen/Chantal Lemercier-Quelquejay, *La Presse et le mouvement national chez les Musulmans de Russie avant 1920*, Mouton, Paris 1964, p. 36 ff.; on the relationship between Jadidism and the Islamic world, see Thomas Kuttner, 'Russian Jadidism and the Islamic World. Isma'il Gasprinskii in Cairo 1908', *Cahiers du monde russe et soviétique* 16 (1975) 3/4, pp. 383–424.

47. Quoted in Alexandre Bennigsen/Chantal Lemercier-Quelquejay, *L'Islam en Union Soviétique*, Payot, Paris 1968, p. 124 f.

48. Ingeborg Baldauf follows the political discussions of Turkish and Islamic circles in Russia and the USSR, respectively, in terms of the highly controversial question of the script reform, i. e. the transition to the Latin alphabet. Ingeborg Baldauf, *Schriftreform und Schriftwechsel bei den muslimischen Rußland– und Sowjettürken (1850–1937): Ein Symptom ideengeschichtlicher und kulturpolitischer Entwicklungen*, Bil. or. hungarica, Budapest 1993/94.

49. In the treaty of friendship signed between Afghanistan and the Soviet Union in February 1921, the independence of Bukhara and Khiwa was implicitly recognized.

50. *Times* of 5 June 1923.

51. *Pravda* of 10 May 1925.

52. *Izvestiya* of 5 October 1924, quoted fr. Castagné, *Basmachis*, p. 73.

53. Cf. the comprehensive work by Jan-Heeren Grevemeyer, *Afghanistan, Sozialer Wandel und Staat im 20. Jahrhundert*, Express Edition, Berlin 1987, p. 172 ff.

54. Leon B. Poullada, *Reform und Rebellion in Afghanistan, 1919–1929*, Cornell University Press, Ithaca, N. Y., 1973, pp. 99–103.

55. The rebellion of Bacha-yi Saqqao reflects the social conditions in the region north of the Salang Pass. Here the peasant population, which formed the majority, had lost almost all connections with the tribal communities and represented the stronghold of the local *naqshbandiya*. The ethnic conflicts of the nineties had already been preceded by Bacha-yi Saqqao's Tajik resistance against the Pashtu sovereignty of the Durrani; cf. Olivier Roy, *L'Afghanistan. Islam et modernité politique*, Seuil, Paris 1985, pp. 86–90.

56. Mirza Kuchik Khan, a scholar from Rasht, had been a member of the Moderate Party in 1909 and had founded a 'Committee of the Islamic Union' with Ottoman support before going underground and, together with a Kurdish tribal leader from Kermanshah and a Tehrani democrat with anarchistic leanings, fighting against the Russian and British occupation troops. Farhad Kazemi, 'Peasant Uprisings in Twentieth-Century Iran, Iraq, and Turkey', in Farhad Kazemi/John Waterbury (eds), *Peasants and Politics in the Modern Middle East*, Florida International University Press, Miami, Flo., 1991, pp. 101–24, here p. 105 ff.

57. Amin al-Raihani, *Muluk al-'arab. Rihlat fi l-bilad al-'arabiya*, Beirut: Dar Jail [8]1987, p. 679 ff. [written in 1924]. This Lebanese Christian author, who travelled through numerous countries of the Arab Peninsula on the invitation of Arab princes, was greatly amused by Khaz'al's traditionalism; at the same time he accused him in veiled terms of organizing poker sessions in his palace and of promoting freemasonry.

58. Cf. Donald N. Wilber's rather friendly description of Pahlavi in *Riza Shah Pahlavi: The Resurrection and Reconstruction of Iran*, Exposition Press, Hicksville, N. Y., 1975, pp. 73–80.

59. Quoted from Lapidus, *History*, p. 687.

60. From now on the names of prominent Algerians will be given in the French spelling used by them.

61. On the process of scolarization see Hartmut Elsenhans, *Frankreichs Algerienkrieg 1954–1962. Entkolonisierungsversuch einer kapitalistischen Metropole. Zum Zusammenbruch der Kolonialreiche*, Carl Hanser, Munich 1974, p. 115, note 182.

62. Report on the 5th Annual Congress of the Society (September 1935) in Algiers, *Sijill mu'tamar jam'iyat al-'ulama' al-muslimin al-jaza'iriyin al-mun'aqid bi-nadi t-tarraqi bi-l-'asima fi sabtambar sanat 1935*, Constantine: al-Matba'a al-Islamiya o. J., pp. 5–72.

63. Lapidus, *History*, p. 753 f.

64. Cf. C. C. Berg in EI[1], IV, pp. 175–81.

65. On Salafite foundations, see Deliar Noer, *The Modernist Muslim Movement in Indonesia, 1900–1942*, Oxford University Press, London 1973, pp. 30–56; Howard Federspiel, *Persatuan Islam. Islamic Reform in Twentieth Century Indonesia*, Cornell University Press, Ithaca, N. Y., 1970; Schulze, *Internationalismus*, p. 68 f.

66. Rudolphe de Koninck, *Aceh in the Time of Iskandar Muda*, Banda Aceh, Pusat Dokumentasie dan Informasi Aceh 1977.

67. D. H. Aldcroft, *Die zwanziger Jahre. Von Versailles zur Wall Street, 1919–1929*, DTV 1978 (Geschichte der Weltwirtschaft, 3), Munich; J. Bouvier, 'Crise mondiale et crise coloniale autour de 1929', *Revue française d'outremer* 64 (1976), pp. 378–85; D. Rothermund (ed.), *Die Peripherie in der Weltwirtschaftskrise: Afrika, Asien, Lateinamerika*, Paderborn 1983; Camilla Dawletschin-Linder, *Die Türkei und Ägypten in der Weltwirtschaftskrise,1929–1933*, Wiesbaden 1989.

68. Egypt: Reinhard Schulze, 'Egypt 1936–1956. Die Nationalisierung eines kolonialen Staats', in Wolfgang J. Mommsen (ed.), *Das Ende der Kolonialreiche. Dekolonisierung und die Politik der Großmächte*, Fischer, Frankfurt a. Main, 1990, pp. 134–67, here p. 143; Turkey: Dawletschin-Linder, *Türkei und Ägypten*, p. 65; Indonesia: *Great Britain, Naval Intelligence Division, Netherlands East Indies*, vol. 1–11, London 1944, II, p. 300 ff.; Charles P. Kindleberger, *The World in Depression, 1929–1939*, University of California Press, Berkeley Cal., 1973, p. 89; Algeria: estimate after Charles Issawi, *An Economic History of the Middle East and North Africa*, Columbia University Press, Berkeley, New York 1982, p. 136. Prices after Linda S[chatkowski] Schilcher, 'Die Weizenwirtschaft des Nahen Ostens in der Zwischenkriegszeit: Der Einfluß der Ökonomie auf die Politik am Beispiel Syriens' in *idem*, Claus Scharf (ed.), *Der Nahe Osten in der Zwischenkriegszeit 1919–1939*, Steiner 1989, Stuttgart, pp. 241–59; also *Naval Intelligence Division, Algeria*, vols 1–II, London 1944, II, pp. 205, 222, 280. Palestine: Kenneth W. Stein, T*he Land Question in Palestine, 1917–1939*, University of North Carolina Press, Chapel Hill, N. C., 1984, p. 143 f.; Tunisia: *Naval Intelligence Division, Tunisia*, London 1945, p. 289; Iraq: *Naval Intelligence Division, Iraq and the Persian Gulf*, London 1944, p. 489.

69. Income of the Persian State, estimated after Eckart Ehlers, *Iran. Grundzüge einer*

geographischen Landeskunde, Wissenschaftliche Buchgesellschaft, Darmstadt 1980, p. 191. Strangely enough, oil as a non–agrarian raw material did not experience any dramatic production drop; however, the figures are misleading since they provide annual averages of more than 5 years and thus extend beyond the economic crisis.

70. According to Dawletschin-Linder, *Türkei und Ägypten*, pp. 128 ff., 146 ff.

71. Alfred Bonné, *The Economic Develipment of the Middle East*, London 1943, repr. 1945, p. 88.

72. The static data regarding urbanization for the years 1927 to 1937 often provide a distorted picture. Thus the urbanization in Egypt for the period from 1927 to 1937 would amount to only 0.71 p. a. [whole country 1.55 p. a.], but from 1937 to 1947, 4.49 p. a. [whole country – 0.98 p. a.!] The statistics have in fact only rarely included the settlers in the informal urban sectors.

73. Cf. Janet L. Abu-Lughod, *Rabat. Urban Apartheid in Morocco*, Princeton, N. J., 1980, p. 160, 330–1.

74. A very personal, but since it was written in 1947, also a very iconographic autobiography is: Hasan al-Banna, *Mudhakkirat al-da'iya*, Cairo: Dar al-Kitab al–Arabi, (ca. 1951).

75. al-Banna, *Mudhakkirat*, p. 44.

76. Sayyid Qutb, *Tifl min al-qarya*, Beirut: Dar al-Shuruq 1393 [1973]: Qutb wrote these childhood reminiscences in 1945 and dedicated them to Taha Husain.

77. Officially, the Muslim Brotherhood was not founded until 11 April 1929, when it was entered in the register of unions, Ishaq Musa al-Husaini, *al-Ikhwan al-Muslimun kubra l-harakat al-islamiya al-haditha*, Beirut: Dar Bairut [2]1955 [1st ed. 1952], p. 23 ff.

78. Salama Musa, *al-Yaum wa-l-ghad*, Cairo: al-Matba'a al-Asriya o. J. [1927?], p. 8.

79. Literature on this in Schulze, *Internationalismus*, p. 203., n. 77; Erwin I. J. Rosenthal, *Islam in the Modern National State*, University Press, Cambridge 1965, pp. 154–78.

80. al-Banna, *Mudhakkirat*, p. 74.

81. G. Kampffmeier, 'Egypt', in: Hamilton Alexander Gibb, *Wither Islam? A Survey of Modern Movements in the Moslem World*, Gollancz, London 1932, pp. 101–70, provides a very optimistic report about this association.

82. al-Banna, *Mudhakkirat*, p. 72.

83.

	Arab population	Jewish population
1918	644,000	56,000
1922	673,388	83,794
1931	861,211	174,610

84. Calculated from Stein, *Land Question*, p.143 f.

85. Cf. Albert Hourani, *A History of the Arab Peoples*, Belknap, Cambridge, Mass., 1991, p. 322 ff.

86. Mustafa Murad al-Dabbagh, *Biladuna Filastin*, Beirut 1965, p. 195.

87. Alexander Flores, *Nationalismus und Sozialismus im arabischen Osten. Kommunistische Partei und arabische Nationalbewegung in Palästina 1919–1948*, Munster 1980, p. 186 f.

88. Cf. Uri M. Kupferschmidt, *The Supreme Muslim Council. Islam under the British*

Mandate for Palestine, Brill, Leiden 1987, p. 78 ff. On the Mufti see Yehuda Taggar, *The Mufti of Jerusalem and Palestine Arab Politics,1930–1937*, Garland, New York, 1986.

89. Schulze, *Internationalismus*, p. 85.

90. Ibid., p. 95 ff.

91. E. g. Filastin of 14 February 1935; *al-Difa'* of 25 March 1935; see also Stein, *Land Question*, p. 138 f.

92. Stein, *Land Question*, p. 231.

93. Cf. Kenneth W. Stein, 'Rural Change and Peasant Destitution: Contributing Causes to the Arab Revolt in Palestine, 1936-1939', in: Kazemi/Waterbury, *Peasants and Politics*, pp. 143–70.

94. On the Arab National Movement in Palestine, see the standard work by Y. Porath, *The Emergence of the Palestinian–Arab National Movement, 1918–1929*, Frank Cass, London 1974 and Y. Porath, *The Palestinian Arab National Movement. From Riots to Rebellion*, Vol. II, 1929–1939, Frank Cass, London 1977.

95. Kamal Salibi, *Histoire du Liban du XVIIe siècle à nos jours*, Paris 1988, p. 310 ff. (English edition: *The Modern History of Lebanon*, London 1965.

96. Reprinted in al-Banna, *Mudhakkirat*, pp. 236–41.

97. There were already cinemas in Cairo before 1914; film production began in 1917; the first great Egyptian silent film produced in 1925 was based on Muhammad Husain Haikal's novel *Zainab* (1913); the first sound film was produced in 1932.

98. al-Banna, *Mudhakkirat*, p. 150 f.

99. Muhammad Rashid Rida, al-Ahkam al-shar'iya, *al-Manar* 23 (1341/1922–23), pp. 729–52.

100. al-Banna, *Mudhakkirat*, p. 259.

101. Reinhard Schulze, 'Islamische Kultur und soziale Bewegung' *Peripherie* 18/19 (1984/85), pp. 60–84.

102. Charles Robert Ageron, *Histoire de l'Algérie contemporaine*, II (1871–1954), Paris 1979, p. 349 ff.

103. Amritsar 1924. Of this work, which was meant to contain ten volumes, only the first one appeared.

104. Discussed in Jamal Malik, 'Al-Mashriqi und die Khaksar', unpublished. MA thesis, Bonn, (1938), p. 35 f.; J. M. S. Baljon, *Modern Muslim Koran-Interpretation (1180–1960)*, Leiden 1961, pp. 11–12, has circulated this story on the basis of a letter addressed to him in 1956 by a partisan of the *Khaksar*; P. Hardy, *The Muslims of British–India*, Cambridge 1972, p. 216, takes up this version again.

105. Cf. the comprehensive work of Stefan Wild 'National Socialism in the Arab Near East between 1933 and 1939', WI 25 (1985), pp. 126–73.

106. See Rotraud Wielandt, *Geschichte und Offenbarung im Denken moderner Muslime*, Wiesbaden 1971, p. 103 ff.; cf. also Werner Ende, *Arabische Nation und islamische Geschichte. Die Umayyaden im Urteil arabischer Autoren des 20. Jahrhunderts*, Steiner, Beirut/Wiesbaden, 1977, pp. 105–7.

107. *Hitler fi-l-mizan*, Cairo 1940; cf. also his radio speeches against Fascism published in 1940, *al-Naziya wa-l-adyan*.

108. E. g. al-Jami'a al-Islamiya v.I.I. 1938.

109. Khashim, *Safahat*, p. 105 ff.

CHAPTER THREE

1. In 1937 the *Néo-Destour* still had more than 400 party offices! It had been founded in 1934 by Habib Bourguiba and Mahmud Matari against the old *Destour* party, in which the *ulama* of the Zaituna University of Tunis were represented. One of the founders of the Destour (1920) was the already mentioned journalist Abd al-Aziz al-Tha'alibi; like others, he pleaded for the re–introduction of the 1861 constitution.

2. Bernhard Dahm, 'Der Dekolonisierungsprozeß Indonesiens', in Mommsen, *Ende der Kolonialreiche*, pp. 67–88, here p. 69.

3. William Roger Louis, *Imperialism at Bay. The United States and the Decolonization of the British Empire, 1941–1945*, Oxford University Press, Oxford 1977, p. IX f.

4. Smith, *Islam in Modern History*, p. 96, n. 4.

5. Sevket Pamuk, 'War, State Economic Policies, and Resistance in Turkey, 1939–1945' in Kazemi/Waterbury, *Peasants and Politics*, pp. 125–42, here p. 129.

6. Schulze, 'Ägypten 1936–1956', p. 230, n. 63.

7. Ibid., p. 153 ff.

8. Helmut Mejcher, 'Der arabische Osten im 20. Jahrhundert 1914–1985' in Haarmann, *Geschichte der arabischen Welt*, pp. 432–501, here p. 478.

9. The anti-Semitic attitude among 'French Algerians' is shown particularly in the 15 penny dreadfuls of 'Musette' (= Auguste Robinet), which circulated in numerous copies after the turn of the century; they were written between 1895 and 1919–1920, especially *Cagayous antijuif*, Algiers 1898; Reinhard Schulze, 'Pataouète in Algerien am Beispiel der Erzählungen von Auguste Robinet (1862–1930) unpubl. manuscript 1980. On the 'French Algerians' see Ghani Merad, *La littérature algérienne d'expression française*, Paris 1976, p. 28 ff.

10. Here quoted from Jürgen Lütt, "'Übertragung der Macht' oder 'Sieg im Freiheitskampf'? Der Weg zur indischen Unabhängigkeit", in Mommsen, *Ende der Kolonialreiche*, pp. 47–66, here p. 53.

11. Jinnah's speech of March 1940, quoted from Anwar Hussain Syed, *Pakistan, Islam, Politics, and National Solidarity*, Praeger, New York, 1982, p. 51.

12. This view had already been held in the early 19th century. In 1920 a legal notice was published which made it a duty for any Indian Muslim to emigrate from India. See Aziz Ahmad, *Islamic Modernism in India and Pakistan, 1857–1964*, Oxford University Press, London 1967, p. 136. Several thousand Muslims followed this summons and emigrated to Afghanistan.

13. A spokesman was the famous Salafite scholar Abu'l-Kalam Azad (1888–1958), who led the *Indian National Congress* from 1940 and later became Indian Minister of Education.

14. Quoted from Ahmad, *Islamic Modernism*, p. 214.

15. Maududi's relationship with Iqbal, who died in 1938, is not quite clear. While Maududi claimed that Iqbal was his master, the Iqbalists vehemently denied any close ideological relationship between the two.

16. Cf. among others Leonard Binder, *Religion and Politics in Pakistan*, University of California Press, Berkeley, Cal. 1961, p. 83 ff. and Kalim Bahadur, *The Jama'at-i Islami of Pakistan. Political Thought and Political Action*, Chetana Publ., New Delhi, 1977, p. 13 f.

17. Quoted from Rosenthal, *Islam*, p. 184.

18. Abu A'la Maududi, *Musalman awr maujuda siyasi kashmakash*, vol. III, Pathankot, Tarjuman al-Qur'an o. J. (ca. 1942), p. 11, 16 f., 37 f.

19. Here quoted from Syed, *Pakistan*, p. 35.

20. Hamid Enayat, *Modern Islamic Political Thought*, London, Macmillan, 1982, p. 99 ff.

21. Clifford Geertz described the *santri* culture as 'scripturalism' and as a 'counter-tradition' directed against *abangan* Islam, see Clifford Geertz, *Islam Observed. Religious Development in Morocco and Indonesia*, New Haven/London 1968.

22. Harry J. Benda, *The Crescent and the Rising Sun*, The Hague: Bandung 1958, p. 187.

23. B. J. Boland, *The Struggle of Islam in Modern Indonesia*, Nijhoff, The Hague, 1970, p. 7 ff. From now on Indonesian names will be written in accordance with the spelling reform of 1972. Certain names such as Soekarno or Masjumi [actually Sukarno and Masyumi] will follow earlier conventions, since the older spelling has come into use.

24. Quoted from Bernhard Dahm, *Sukarnos Kampf um Indonesiens Unabhängigkeit*, Frankfurt a. M; 1966, p. 216.

25. On 7 November 1945, the Masjumi was changed into a political party in which leftist and rightist groups could continue collaborating.

26. Boland, *Struggle*, p. 12 f.

27. Here summarized from Boland, *Struggle*, p. 21 f. An English summary can also be found in George McT. Kahin, *Nationalism and Revolution in Indonesia*, Ithaca, N. Y., 1952, pp. 122–7; cf. Eke Darmaputera, *Pancasila and the search for identity and modernity in Indonesian society: a cultural and ethical analysis*, Brill, Leiden 1988; Olaf Schumann, 'Herausgefordert durch die Pancasila: Die Religionen in Indonesien', in Udo Tworuschka (ed.), Gottes ist der Orient, Gottes ist der Okzident. Festschrift für Abdoljavad Falaturi zum 65. Geburtstag, Böhlau, Cologne, 1961, pp. 322–43.

28. This passage was added later.

29. In the first version, the duty of the adherents of the 'divinity' *(ketuhan)* to follow the Islamic *shari'a* had been dropped upon the proposal of a member of the Muhammadiya, cf. Schumann, 'Herausgefordert', p. 322. The Pancasila were at first placed at the beginning of the 1945 constitution and finally put into force on 5 July 1959.

30. Here linguistic policy also played a major part. In 1918 the Indonesian members of the Volksraad carried their point in having Malay used in parliamentary sessions. Ten years later, the first efforts were made to create an 'Indonesian' language and use it as a colloquial language against the *koiné* Melayu kuno/pasar; and another ten years later Malay was prescribed as the linguistic basis of Indonesian and finally became the state language on 18. 8. 1945.

31. A comparison between the Indian and the Indonesian independence movements is presented by L. Blussé *et al.* (eds), *India and Indonesia from the 1920s to the 1950s; the origins of planning*, Brill, Leiden 1987. A brief documentation is provided by Christiaan L. Penders, *Indonesia: Selected Documents on Colonialism and Nationalism, 1830–1942*, St. Lucia/Queensland: QUP 1977 and J. C. Bijwerk, *Vaarwel, tot betere tijden! Documentaire over de ondergang von Niederlands–Indië*, Franeker: Wever [2]1974.

32. Mohammed Harbi, *Aux origines du FLN: le populisme révolutionnaire en Algérie*, Paris 1975, p. 25.

33. Cf. *al-Basa'ir* 11 (1947) and following issues, reprinted in Muhammad al-Bashir al-Ibrahimi, *Athar al-shaikh* ... I–II, Algiers: al-Shirka al-Wataniya 1398 [1978], II ('uyun al-basa'ir), p. 55 ff.

34. Thus especially Bassam Tibi, Die Krise des modernen Islams. *Eine vorindustrielle Kultur im wissenschaftlich-technischen Zeitalter*, Beck, Munich 1981.

35. Azzam had joined Ottoman officers in Cyrenaica in 1916 and had briefly been adviser to the Tripolitanian Republic. He is even said to have been one of those whom the Tripolitanians had invited to found a republic in view of the inevitable withdrawal of the Ottomans.

36. Cérès Wissa-Wassef, 'La Ligue des états arabes face aux conflits inter-arabes' in *Politique étrangère* 38 (1973), I, pp. 51–83, here p. 54 f.

37. Arab Information Center, *Basic Documents of the League of Arab States*, New York 1955, pp. 5–8; cf. also Muhammad Khalil, *The Arab States and the Arab League*, A Documentary Record, II, Khayats, Beirut, 1962, pp. 53–6.

38. Khalil, *Arab States*, p. 99, n. 1.

39. 'Bilad al-'arab li-l-'arab', in: *al-Muqtataf* April 1945, pp. 309–12.

40. Here the admission years of other Islamic countries (until 1960): 1945: Iran; 1946: Afghanistan; 1947: Yemen, Pakistan; 1950: Indonesia; 1955: Jordan, Libya; 1956: Morocco, Tunisia, Sudan; 1957: Malayan Federation; 1958: Guinea.

41. al-Mu'tamar al-Islami al-'alami, Karachi, 8 pages, here page 8.

42. Abd al-Hamid Ibn Badis, *Athar* ..., publ. by Ammar al-Talibi, Algiers 1968, I/2, pp. 407–9, under point 11.

43. S. Fahmi Jad'an, *Usus al-taqaddum 'inda mufakkiri l-Islam fi l-'alam al-'arabi al-hadit*, Beirut 1979, p. 284.

44. Esp. in his famous Baghdad lecture of the year 1952, 'al-Qaumiya al-'arabiya wa-l-Islam', in: idem, *Min ruh al-Islam*, Baghdad 1959, pp. 179, 185; Translation by S. Haim in WI 3 (1954), pp. 201–19.

45. Muhammad al-Ghazzali, *al-Islam wa-l-manahij al-ishtirakiya*, Cairo: Dar al-Katib al-'Arabi [2]1951, p. 182 f.

46. According to Bahadur, *Jama'at-i Islami*, p. 19 ff.

47. Rosenthal, *Islam in the Modern National State*, pp. 125–53, 181–281. Muhammad Asad, *The Principle of State and Government in Islam*, Berkeley, Cal. 1961.

48. The Arab Executive had been founded in 1920 as the supreme organ of the 'Muslim–Christian Union'. Created in 1918, this organization was considered as the continuation of the older Arab cultural club from Ottoman times and was mainly supported by old-established Palestinian families. Until 1934, the Arab Executive was able

to assert itself as the representative organ of Palestinian nationalists.

49. What is meant here is the Morrison–Grady Plan of July 1946, which provided for dividing the country into four parts.

50. S. Majid Khadduri, 'The Scheme of Fertile Crescent Unity. A Study in inter-Arab relations', in Richard N. Frye (ed.), *The Near East and the Great Powers*, Harvard University Press, Cambridge, Mass., 1951, pp. 137–77, here pp. 141–51, 167–70.

51. Cf. Helga Baumgarten, *Palästina. Befreiung in den Staat. Die palästinensische Nationalbewegung seit 1948*, Suhrkamp, Frankfurt am Main, 1991, p. 41 ff.

52. Quoted from Richard P. Mitchell, *The Society of the Muslim Brothers*, Oxford University Press, London 1969, p. 66.

53. Khashim, *Safahat*, p. 140.

54. A comprehensive description is provided by Ahmed Kaid al-Saidi, *Die Oppositionsbewegung im Jemen zur Zeit Imam Yahyas und der Putsch von 1948*, Baalbek, Berlin 1981. A pro-Zaidi account is found in Amin Sa'id, *al-Yaman tarikhuhu al-siyasi mundhu istiqlalihi fi l-qarn al-thalith al-hijri*, 'Isa al-Babi al-Halabi, Cairo 1378 [1959], pp. 135–49. Sa'id describes the events as a palace revolution fomented by Great Britain.

55. Ende, *Nation*, pp. 91–104.

56. In 1948 he was commissioned by the Ministry of Education to evaluate training programmes and curricula for foreign language lessons in the USA.

57. Sayyid Qutb, *al-'Adala al-ijtima'iya wa-l-Islam*, Cairo 1949.

58. Muhammad al-Ghazzali, *Our Beginning in Wisdom*, transl. by Isma'il R. el-Faruqi, Washington 1953, pp. 70, 75 (written in 1950).

59. Abd al-Qadir Auda, *al-Islam baina jahl abna'ihi wa-'ajz 'ulamahi*, al-Mu'tar al-Islami o. J. [ca. 1950], pp. 73–9.

60. Schulze, 'Ägypten 1936–1956', pp. 162–4.

61. Taqi al-Din al-Nabhani, *al-Daula al-islamiya*, n.p., n.d. [1953], pp. 119–21.

62. Taqi al-Din al-Nabhani, *al-Tafkir*, n.p., n.d. (after 1953), p. 12.

63. Min manshurat Hizb al-Tahrir [Taqi al-Din al-Nabhani], *al-Khilafa*, n.p., n.d. [1953], p. 32 f.

64. Hizb al-Tahrir al-Islami, *Muqaddimat al-dustur au al-asbab al-mujiba lahu*, n.p. ^{2}1382 (1963).

65. Ibid., p. 38, 132 f., 143.

66. In the 1940s the *Tudeh* party had 25,000 members and a great many supporters among the 400,000 workers organized by the trade unions.

67. Educated in France and Switzerland, this lawyer was an administrative expert; he was governor general of the province of Fars until 1921, then for a few months finance minister, then again governor general, this time of Azerbaijan, and finally minister of Foreign Affairs. From 1923 to 1927 he was also a member of parliament, but he was excluded from the political arena in 1942. On these and subsequent events, albeit from a purely political-historical point of view, see Fakhreddin Azimi, *Iran. The Crisis of Democracy (1941–1953)*, Tauris, London 1989, p. 258 ff.

68. Oil thus had the same symbolic content as the Suez Canal had for Egyptian national policy.

69. Sayyid Mujtaba Nawwab Safawi, *Jami'a wa hukumat-i islami*, Qum: Markaz-i

Barrasiha-yi Islami n.d. [1950, [2]1953], p. 59. As far as I can see, Safawi did not yet use the concept *jumhurı-yı ıslamı* ('Islamic Republic') which became current later, but spoke of the *mamlakat-i islami-yi Iran* ('Islamic state of Iran') or more frequently of the *millat-i musliman-i Iran* ('nation of Muslims of Iran').

70. Mosaddeq had already been dismissed by the shah on 13 August 1953.

71. Military rule had already been nominally abolished for Tehran and some provinces in 1957.

72. Cf. Mahmud Taliqani, *Islam wa-malikiyat*, Tehran 1330 [1951], 4th ed. 1344 [1965], transl. as Seyyed Mahmood Taleqani, *Islam and Ownership*, Mazda, Lexington, Kent 1983. Cf. Yann Richard, *Der verborgene Imam. Die Geschichte des Schiismus in Iran*, Wagenbach, Berlin, 1983, p. 109 ff.

73. Cf. Heinz Halm, *Die Schia*, Wissenschaftliche Buchgesellschaft, Darmstadt, 1988, p. 134 f., 152–4.

74. Schulze, *Internationalismus*, p. 120 ff.

75. The 'liberal decade', which preceded the period of the great bloc confrontation, had its effects on the political and social conditions in almost all Islamic countries. It started between 1942 (Persia, Egypt) and 1947 (Turkey) and ended between 1952 and 1957.

76. Cf. Irvine H. Anderson, *ARAMCO, The United States and Saudi Arabia. A Study of the Dynamics of Foreign Oil Policy, 1933–1950*, Princeton University Press, Princeton, N. J., 1981, p.ix. Text of the agreement among others in: *Wizarat al-Kharijiya, majmu'at al-mu'ahadat min 1341–1370/1922–1951*, Dar al-Isfahani, Jeddah, [3]1376/1957, pp. 338–52.

77. From Anderson, *ARAMCO*, pp. 120–1.

78. Quoted from Ahmad Abu Bakr Ibrahim, *al-adab al-hijazi fi n-nahda al-haditha*, Cairo: Nahdat Misr, 1948, pp. 72–3.

79. A description full of personal reminiscences and at the same time containing a bitter complaint against the royal family is Nasir al-Sa'id, *Tarikh Al Sa'ud*, [Part I), o. O [Beirut?]: Manshurat Ittihad Sha'b Aljazira al-Arabiya o. J. [after 1980].

80. Collected descriptions in: Johannes Reissner, 'Die Innenpolitik Saudi–Arabiens', in: Thomas Koszinowski (ed.), *Saudi–Arabien. Ölmacht und Entwicklungsland*, Deutsches Orient-Institut, Hamburg 1983, pp. 83–120, here p. 98 ff. and Aleksej Michailovic Vasil'ev, *Istorija Saudovskoj Arabii (1745–1973)*, Izd. Nauka, Moscow 1982, p. 379 ff.

81. al-Sa'id, *Tarikh*, p. 654 ff.

CHAPTER FOUR

1. Quoted from Anouar Abdel-Malek, *Ägypten: Militärgesellschaft. Das Armeeregime, die Linke und der soziale Wandel unter Nasser*, Suhrkamp, Frankfurt a. M., 1971, p. 156 (English ed. Abdel-Malek, Anouar, *Egypt: Military Society; The Army Regime, the Left and Social Change under Nasser*, New York 1968).

2. Discussed in detail in: William Roger Louis, 'Die Vereinigten Staaten von Amerika und die Auflösung der europäischen Kolonialreiche. John Foster Dulles und die Suez-Krise des Jahres 1956', in Mommsen, *Ende der Kolonialreiche*, pp. 168–94; Marwan R.

Buheiry, 'Anthony Eden and the Arabs: The Failure of a Policy', in id., *The Formation and Perception of the Modern Arab World*, ed. by Lawrence I. Conrad, Darwin Pr., Princeton, N. J., 1989, pp. 171–87.

3. Mustafa al-Siba'i, *Ishtirakiyat al-Islam*, Cairo: al-Qaumiya, [2]1960, p. 195 [1st ed. Damascus: al-Jami'a, 1959].

4. For example, Muhammad al-Ghazzali, *al-Islam wa-listibdad al-siyasi*, Dar al-Katib al-Arabi n.d., [ca. 1952].

5. A parallel Islamic phenomenon was the Sunni al-Najjada movement.

6. Malcolm Kerr, *The Arab Cold War 1958–1964. A Study of Ideology in Politics*, Oxford University Press, London, 1965, p. 11.

7. Cf. Nikolaos van Dam, *The Struggle for Power in Syria. Sectarianism, Regionalism and Tribalism in Politics, 1961–1978*, Croom Helm, London 1979, pp. 31–50.

8. Faisal officially succeeded to the Iraqi throne in 1953, when he was 18 years old. But the regent preserved his power at court.

9. According to Marion Farouk-Sluglett/Peter Sluglett, *Iraq Since 1958*, Routledge, London, 1987 (German edition, *Der Irak seit 1958. Von der Revolution zur Diktatur*, Suhrkamp, Frankfurt a. M. 1991, p. 53.)

10. Sa'id, *al-Yaman*, p. 282.

11. Generally on this subject: R. J. Gavin, *Aden under British Rule, 1839–1967*, London 1975; Fred Halliday, *Arabia without Sultans*, Manchester 1974, pp. 153–90; Muhammad 'Umar al-Hibshi, *al-Yaman al-janubi*, Beirut 1968, pp. 16–63.

12. Declaration of principle in Sa'id, *al-Yaman*, p. 244 ff.

13. Harbi, *Origines du FLN*, p. 30.

14. The Tunisian *Néo-Destour* and the Moroccan Nahda Party had also signed the manifesto; it served as a basis for the 'Committee for the Liberation of the Arab Maghreb', see Harbi, *Origines du FLN*, p. 33.

15. Leon Mugniery 1951, quoted from Frantz Fanon, 'The North African Syndrome' in I. William Zartman, *Man, State and Society in the Contemporary Maghrib*, Pall Mall Pr., London 1973, pp. 74–82, here p. 79; Esprit (February 1952), pp. 237–48.

16. From the FLN declaration of 1 November 1954, here quoted from Alistaire Horne, *Histoire de la guerre d'Algérie*, Albin Michel, Paris 1987 (&st Eng. ed. 1977), p. 98.

17. The war is discussed at length in the works of Horne, *Histoire*, passim, and Bernard Droz/Evelyne Lever, *Histoire de la guerre d'Algérie, 1954–1962*, Seuil, Paris [2]1984; The French point of view is reflected in Pierre Montagnon, *La guerre d'Algérie. Genèse et engrenage d'une tragédie*, Pygmalion, Paris, 1984.

18. This includes people who starved to death. The war caused the death of between 300 and 400,000 Muslims.

19. These two regions together shared 74% of the national income, cf. Elsenhans, *Algerienkrieg*, p. 628, n. 506.

20. Oil was produced before 1956, though in very low quantites: 1948 100 t; 1954 72,800 t; 1960 8.8 mill. t; 1962 20.5 mill. t.; 1964 26.2 mill. t. Elsenhans, *Algerienkrieg*, p. 254, n. 326.

21. The main buyers of the Sahara oil were BP, Shell and Esso (1962: 77%).

22. Monique Gadant, *Islam et nationalisme en Algérie d'après 'El Moudjahid' organe*

central du FLN de 1956 à 1962, L'Harmattan, Paris, 1988, p. 32 f.

23. Malik bin Nabi, *Wijhat al-'alam al-islami* [written 1954/59], Dar al-Fikr 1400 [1980], Damascus, p. 153 ff.

24. When exactly the expression 'Islamists' came into use is not clear; it started playing a political role during the violent journalistic feuds between nationalists and Islamic intellectuals from 1955/56 onwards; Ahmad Muhammad Jamal, *Nahwa siyasa 'arabiya sariha*, Dar al-Thaqafa, Mecca, 1381 [1962], p. 65 ff. In classical Arabic, *al-islami* indicated among other things a member of the poetic class in the early Islamic period (al-Farazdaq, Jarir etc.). Another application of this concept is found with the medieval theologian Abu'l-Hasan Ali al-Ash'ari (died 935), who called a discussion about theological questions *Maqalat al-islamiyin*, 'The Discourse of the Islamics', meaning an unorthodox group.

25. Muhammad Ahmad Bashmil, *al-Qaumiya fi nazar al-Islam*, Beirut 1960, p. 97.

26. Moriba Magassouba, *L'Islam au Sénégal. Demain les mollahs?*, Karthala, Paris, 1985, p. 59 ff.; cf. also Hanspeter Mattes, *Die islamische Bewegung des Senegal zwischen Autonomie und Außenorientierung*, ed. wuguf, 1989, Hamburg 1989, p. 29 ff. A similar function was that of the Subbani community centred in Bamako, Mali, which later joined the union.

27. Cheich Tidiane Sy, *La confrérie sénégalaise des Mourides*, Présence Africaine, Paris 1969, p. 293.

28. Cf. Ahmad Sékou Touré, *al-Islam din al-jama'a*, transl. by Muhammad al-Bukhari, al-Shayi', Kuwait 1977.

29. See René Otayek (ed.), *Le Radicalisme islamique en Afrique subsaharienne. Da'wa, arabisation et critique de l'Occident*, Karthala, Paris 1993.

30. C. van Dijk, *Rebellion under the Banner of Islam. The Darul Islam in Indonesia*, Nijhoff, The Hague, 1981, p. 20 ff.

31. C. O. van Nieuwenhuijze, *Aspects of Islam in post-colonial Indonesia. Five Esssays*, van Hoeve, The Hague, 1958, p. 1770 ff., places the Western Javenese rebellion into an internal functional context with other forms of 'revitalism'.

32. Lapidus, *History*, p. 771.

33. See also Bassam Tibi, 'Der Dekolonisierungsprozeß Algeriens. Vom revolutionären Befreiungskrieg zum Militärregime', in Gerhard Grohs/Bassam Tibi (eds), *Zur Soziologie der Dekolonisation in Afrika*, Fischer, Frankfurt a. M., 1973, pp. 13–79, here cf. p. 32 f.

34. Thus already in an interview in *l'Unità* of 12 August 1962, p. 3, in which Ben Bella pronounced himself for an 'Algerian Arab socialism' which was by no means to be a copy of Nasser's socialism.

35. Taufiq al-Shaikh, *al-Bitrul wa-l-siyasa fi l-mamlaka al-'arabiya al-sa'udiya*, Dar al-Safa, London 1988, pp. 393–5.

36. From Schulze, *Internationalismus*, p. 191.

37. Abu'l-Hasan Ali al-Nadwi, *Muzakkirat sa'ih fi sh-sharq al-'arabi*, Cairo: Jama'at al-Azhar, 1954.

38. Abu'l-Hasan Ali al-Nadwi, *Ma-za khasira al-'alam bi-inhitat al-muslimin*, Dar al-Kitab al-Arabi [6]1965, p. 264 f.

39. His corresponding legal opinion was printed among others in *Risalat al-Islam* 55/56 (1963/64), pp. 14–16. This journal was the organ of the 'Society for the Rapprochement between Legal Schools' founded in Cairo in 1948.

40. Wizarat al-Auqaf wa-l-Shu'un al-Islamiya, Cairo: *al-Azhar Tarikhuhu wa-tatawwuruhu,* al-Sha'b, 1383 [1964], p. 481 ff.

41. Sayyid Qutb, *Ma'alim fi l-tariq,* Cairo 1964; quoted from the 'official' edition, Beirut: Dar al-Shuruq,[10]1403 [1983].

42. Sayyid Qutb, *Fi zilal al-qur'an I–VI,* Dar al-Shuruq, Beirut [8]1399 [1979]. Qutb had already become known in 1939 for his literary studies about the Koran; he apparently started his Koran commentary in the USA and continued it between 1952 and 1954. Cf. Olivier Carré, *Mystique et politique, Lecture révolutionnaire du Coran par Sayyid Qutb, Frère musulman radical,* du Cerf, Paris 1984.

43. Qutb, *Ma'alim,* p. 135.

44. Ibid., p. 173.

45. The new conclusions drawn by Sayyid Qutb have only recently been academically appreciated, cf. Hasan Hanafi, *al-Din wa-l-thaura fi Misr,* Cairo 1988.

46. From the autobiographical notes of Ali Shari'ati, *Kawir,* Mashhad 1349 [1970/71], p. 19, 2nd ed., p. 11; cf. *Ali Shari'ati, On the Sociology of Islam.* Lectures transl. by Hamid Algar, Mizan 1979, p. 16, Berkeley, Cal.

47. As a background cf. Gianroberto Scarcia, 'Governo, riforma agrare ed opposizione in Persia', OM 42 (1962), pp. 731–801.

48. Ende/Steinbach, *Islam in der Gegenwart,* p. 81. W. Ende interprets the position of the *marja'-taqlid* (literally 'appellate authority', see Halm, *Schia,* p. 134, n. 209) as the 'ultimate theological authority to be followed by the believer'; Halm, *ibid.,* is somewhat more cautious than Richard, *Der verborgene Imam,* p. 40, who says that this position probably originated in the 19th century. In many cases, functionaries were members of 'the prophet's family' and therefore bore the title of *sayyid.* Recognized authorities up to the 1980s were, among others, Khomeini himself, the scholar living in Iraq Abu'l-Qasim al-Khu'i (1899–1992), Muhammad Kazim Shari'atmadari (1904–1986) and Muhammad Riza Gulpaygani (born 1899).

49. Quoted from Willem Floor, 'Iranische Geistliche als Revolutionäre – Wunschdenken oder Wirklichkeit?' in: *Religion und Politik im Iran,* ed. by Berliner Institut für vergleichende Sozialforschung, Syndikat, Frankfurt a. M. 1981, pp. 306–36, here p. 318.

50. In general, see Shahrough Akhavi, *Religion and Politics in Contemporary Iran: Clergy–State Relations in the Pahlavi Period,* State University of New York Press, Albany, N. Y., 1980, pp. 91–116.

51. Ali Shari'ati, *Maktab-i wasita,* Mashhad 1335 [1955/56].

52. A special part was played in the Algerian war by the discussions in Paris student circles; it was precisely in this connection that Shari'ati positively responded to Frantz Fanon.

53. For the republican view, cf. Yusuf al-Hajiri, *al-Sa'udiya tabtali' al-Yaman. Qissat al-taddakhkhulat fi shu'un al-shatr al-shamali li-l-Yaman,* London: al-Safa, 1988, p. 68 ff.

54. Farouk-Sluglett/Sluglett, *Iraq*, (German ed.) p. 95 f.

55. The Saudi Muslim World League only caught up with this step in 1985.

56. Diya' al-Din Babakhanov, *al-Islam fi ittihad al-sufyati mustaqill 'an al-daula wa-yatamatta bi-nafs al-huquq ka-l-adyan al-ukhra*, Novosti, Moscow [ca. 1963].

57. *al-Ahram* v. 26. 5. 1967.

58. Mahmoud Hussein [pseud.], *L'Egypte, Lutte des classes et libération nationale*. I. 1945–1967, Maspero, Paris 1975, p. 157.

59. Editors of the journal Minbar al-Islam, *Ra'y al-din fi ikhwan al-shaitan*, al-Majlis a'la li-l-Shu'un al-Islamiya, Cairo 1965.

60. On this subject and on the social consequences of the Israeli occupation policy see Meron Benvenisti, 'Das "Westbank Data Project". Eine Untersuchung der israelischen Politik in Westbank und Gaza-Streifen', in: Jan Metzger (ed.), *Auf dem Weg zur Annexion. Die Zukunft von Westbank und Gaza-Streifen nach zwei Jahrzehnten israelischer Besatzung*, Berlin 1986, pp. 9–108, here p. 14 f.

61. Issawi, *Economic History*, p. 233.

62. Converted at the then current rate ca. 1.3 billion DM, of which 70% were to be paid to Egypt. The donor countries were mainly Saudi Arabia, Kuwait and Libya.

63. al-Sayyid Abdallah al-Husaini, *Mu'tamar Harad watha'iq wa-mahadir*, Beirut: Dar al-Kitab al-Jadid, 1966, see specially p. 33 ff.

64. Text of the lecture of 4 November 1967 in Abu'l-Hasan Ali al-Nadwi, *al-Muslimun wa-qadiyat Filastin*, Beirut: [2]1391 [1971], pp. 81–107, here p. 83.

65. Muhammad Fadil, *al-Naft wa-l-wahda al-'arabiya*, Beirut: Markaz al-Buhuth 1979, p. 10.

66. Frederic C. Thomas, Jr., 'The Libyan Oil Worker', MEJ 10 (1956), pp. 264–76.

67. Mu'ammar al-Qadhdhafi, 'A Visit to Fezzan', in Zartman, *Man, State and Society*, pp. 131–6, here p. 135.

68. Decree Nr. 76–57 of 5 July 1976.

CHAPTER FIVE

1. See the detailed account of Leonard Binder, *In a Moment of Enthusiasm. Political Power and the Second Stratum in Egypt*, University of Chicago Press, Chicago 1978, p. 372 ff.

2. The figures for 1960 are based mainly on census; for 1980, however they are almost exclusively estimates, which for the most part do not include the entire extent of an agglomeration.

3. These are rough estimates.

4. Safdar Mahmood, *A Political Study of Pakistan*, Lahore 1972, p. 129.

5. This mainly Urdu-speaking population of East Pakistan fled from the Indian province of Bihar to East Bengal after 1947; all its members were considered as collaborators of the central Pakistan government. After 1972 most of the Biharis fled to West Pakistan, where they expanded the socially and culturally independent society of the *muhajir*, the 'emigrates'. The Biharis were more closely connected with Islamic written culture than the Bengalis, who were often reputed to have an inclination for

syncretism. Many observers believed that the Biharis 'as an ethnic group' tended towards an Islamism à la Maududi, see for example Duràn Khàlid, 'Pakistan und Bangladesh' in Ende/Steinbach, *Islam in der Gegenwart*, pp. 274–397, here p. 303.

6. In 1962 the Council was attributed an *Islamic Research Institute* with the task of establishing the legal foundations of its work, cf. S. Jamal Malik, *Islamisierung in Pakistan 1977–84. Untersuchung zur Auflösung autochthoner Strukturen*, Steiner, Wiesbaden 1989, pp. 42–64; summarized in id., 'Islamization in Pakistan 1977–1985. The Ulama and their Places of Learning', *Islamic Studies* 28 (1989) I, p. 5–27.

7. According to the statements of the International Labour Organization, quoted fr. J. S. Birks/ C. A. Sinclair, *International Migration and Development in the Arab Region*, ILO 1980, Geneva, pp. 134–5 and Saad Eddin Ibrahim, *The New Arab Social Order. A Study of the Social Impact of Oil Wealth*, Boulder Col., Westview 1982, p. 31 ff. Lower figures are recorded by G. Pennisi, *Development, Manpower and Migration in the Red Sea Region. The Case for Cooperation*, Deutsches Orient-Institut, Hamburg, 1981.

8. Regarding the effects on the agrarian sector of Lower Egypt cf. Georg Stauth, *Die Fellachen im Nildelta*, Steiner, Wiesbaden 1983, p. 202 ff.

9. Schulze, *Internationalismus*, p. 275 f.

10. In this context the United Arab Republic was again renamed the Arab Republic of Egypt on 11 September 1971.

11. Compare with the total receipts of Saudi Arabia. The price quotations for the most part only reflect averages. A more precise discussion can be found, among others, in: Fred Scholz, 'Erdölreserven, Finanzreichtum und Wirtschaftskraft. Die globale Bedeutung der Golfstaaten', in idem (ed.), *Die Golfstaaten. Wirtschaftsmacht im Krisenherd*, Westermann, Braunschweig, 1985, pp. 107–29.

12. Summarized among others by Gudrun Krämer, *Ägypten unter Mubarak: Identität und nationales Interesse*, Nomos, Baden-Baden 1986, pp. 14–31; Mark N. Cooper, *The Transformation of Egypt*, London 1982, pp. 35–82; John Waterbury, *The Egypt of Nasser and Sadat. The Political Economy of Two Regimes*, Princeton Univesity Press, Princeton, N. J., 1983, pp. 123–57.

13. Hamid Ansari, *Egypt, The Stalled Society*, State University of New York Press, Albany, N. Y. 1986, p. 177.

14. According to Olivier Carré/Gérard Michaud, *Les Frères musulmans (1928–1982)*, Gallimard, Paris 1983, p. 109 f.

15. Kepel, *Prophète*, pp. 291–3.

16. Cf. Milton J. Esman/Itamar Rabinovich (eds), *Ethnicity, Pluralism, and the State in the Middle East*, Cornell University Press, Ithaca, N. Y., 1988, as well as Thomas Scheffler (ed.), *Ethnizität und Gewalt*, Deutsches Orient-Institut, Hamburg, 1991.

17. This is at least Ernest Gellner's opinion in id., *Postmodernism, Reason and Religion*, Routledge, London 1992.

18. Compiled from Weekes, *Muslim Peoples*, with corrections by the author. As a mark of ethnicity, self-designation was mainly chosen; the establishment of ethnicity is in many cases based on history (e. g. Azeri, Tajik) and the result of romantic constructions of a 'nationality' from the 19th and early 20th century.

19. The decision for its foundation was taken at the first Islamic conference of Finance

Ministers (22 November 1973).

20. Cf. Reinhard Schulze, 'Der Einfluß islamischer Organisationen auf die Länder Südostasiens – von Mekka aus gesehen', in: Werner Draguhn (ed.), *Der Einfluß des Islams auf Politik, Wirtschaft und Gesellschaft in Südostasien*, Hamburg 1983, pp. 32–54, here p. 45.

21. Cf. Mary F. Somers Heidhues, 'Die Moros in Geschichte, Wirtschaft und Politik der Philippinen', in *ibid.*, pp. 129–40; also including further literature. In addition: Cesar Adib Majul, *The Contemporary Muslim Movement in the Philippines*, Mizan, Berkeley, Cal., 1985, p. 62 ff.

22. Raymond Scupin, 'The Politics of Islamic Reformism in Thailand', *Asian Survey* 20 (1980) 12, pp. 1223–35. The 'Thai Muslims' in the north were not yet politically organized around 1975.

23. The blanket term Tebu is here to be understood as the name for the two linguistic groups of the Daza and Teda. The relatively small ethnic group of the Tedu (ca. 15,000) controls the Tibesti mountains and forms a loose federation of clans, while the two main Dazaga groups, the Daza and the Aza (more than 220,000) dispose of independent clans and dominate the pastures south of the Tibesti mountains. Through the oil boom in Libya, many of the Tedus were freed from their economic and cultural isolation.

24. We will not go too far into the discussion underlying this concept. Normally the French and English expression *société civile/ civil society* is rendered in German by the cumbersome word 'Zivilgesellschaft'. This is basically equivalent with 'bürgerliche Gesellschaft', a term I have used in the German, although it has often been pointed out that 'zivile Gesellschaft' refers to the 'citoyen' while 'bürgerliche Gesellschaft' refers to the 'bourgeois'. The ambiguity of the German word 'bürger' makes it easier to identify the two concepts.

25. Here established after Eckehart Ehrenberg, 'Militär und Rüstung', in Udo Steinbach/ Rüdiger Robert (eds), *Der Nahe und Mittlere Osten*, vol. 1, Leske und Budrich, Opladen 1988, pp. 271–86, here p. 278. The report *World Military Expenditures and Arms Transfer 1972–1982* provided by Ehrenberg often quotes lower data than corresponding detailed studies; thus according to Halliday, *Iran*, p. 94, the import value alone of arms from the USA to Iran in 1972–1974 amounted to almost 7,000 million US dollars.

26. Average for the years 1972–1983; in the years of crises and wars 1981 and 1982, the share of Saudi Arabia was 27%, that of Iraq 20.7% and that of Pakistan 5.2%.

27. The *dakwah* movement (from Arabic *da'wa* 'call', 'invitation [to the true Islam]') can in the widest sense be interpreted as an Islamic cultural movement. In South-East Asia it mainly implies the propaganda for an urban Islam devoid of mystic or *abagan* cultures.

28. See Schulze, *Internationalismus*, p. 283 ff.

29. On Islamic policy around 1965 in the city-state of Singapore, which is independent of Malaysia, see Petra Weyland, 'International Muslim Networks and Islam in Singapore', *Sojourn* 5 (1990), pp. 219–54.

30. The concept *ansar* derived from classical Islamic history actually means the

'helpers' who had assisted the prophet Mohammad and the muhajirun ('emigrants') at their arrival in Yatrib (Medina) in 622. Many 19th century Islamic mystic unions took up this expression again to refer to the direct partisans of their leader.

31. The Saudi authorities represented the assassin as a madman, cf. *Saut* al-tali'a, special issue of 1st April 1975.

32. The corresponding texts can be found in John Morton Moore (ed.), *The Arab–Israeli Conflict*, IV/1, Princeton University Press, Princeton, N. J. 1991, pp. 287–393; Sadat's speech in Jerusalem *ibid.*, pp. 77–88.

33. Text among others in Sabine Hartert, 'Ein ägyptisches fatwa zu Camp David', WI22 (1982), pp. 139–42. Mahmud's attitude was discussed in *ahbar al-'alam al-Islami* (Mecca) 572 (13/10/1978), pp. 4–5.

34. *Ahbar al-'alam al-Islami* 569 (25/9/1978), p. 2.

35. Ayat Allah [Murtada] al-Shahid al-Mutahhari, *al-Dawafi' nahwa l-maddiya*, (translated by Muhammad Ali al-Taskhiri), *Fajr al-Islam*, Tehran, 1402 [1982].

36. This comprehensive concept literally means the 'Delegation of Jurists'; here the spiritual delegation of the Shi'i Imams through Ali or his respective successor serves as a model, see Akhavi, *Religion and Politics*, p. 212 f., n. 7. It may also be understood as the trusteeship of (God's) sovereignty transferred (by Ali via the imams) to the jurists (out of spiritual friendship).

37. Several times translated, among others by Hamid Algar, *Islam and Revolution, Writings and Declarations of Imam Khomeini*, Berkeley, Cal., 1981.

38. Founded in 1965 as a national guerilla organization; in the early 1970s, a leftist–socialist discourse asserted itself, corresponding with the circumstances; in 1975 the guerillas split up into the Marxist Peykar and the (Islamic) People's Mujahidin. Taliqani himself had kept close contacts with the Islamic guerillas. Cf. Richard, *Imam*, pp. 107. Ff., 131 ff.

39. Khomeini had already proclaimed a provisional government from his exile in Paris on 12 January 1979 and had thus emphasized that he had the right to do so. For the general background cf. the standard work of Sa'id Amir Arjomand, *The Turban and the Crown. The Islamic Revolution in Iran*, Oxford University Press, New York, Oxford 1988.

40. Shura-yi Baznigari-yi Qanun-i Asasi-yi Jumhuri-yi Islami-yi Iran, *Ba-ra'ayat-i islahat-i sal* 1367, Tehran: Majlis-i Shura-yi Islami 1368 [1989], p. 20, art. 5.

41. Here there are differences of opinion. James Buchan, 'The Return of the Ikhwan 1979', in David Holden/Richard Johns, *The House of Sa'ud. The Rise and Rule of the Most Powerful Dynasty in the Arab World*, Holt, Rinehart and Winston, New York 1981, pp. 511–26, sees a connection in the fact that al-'Utaibi was born and bred in Saghir, a settlement of the 'Utaiba tribe in Qasim, the centre of the Wahhabiya. In 1927, the 'Utaiba had participated in the Ikhwan movement.

42. His Hijazi patron Yusuf Ba Junaid was named as one of the authors.

43. The circulars were presented by the Lebanese journalist Salim al-Lauzi, who was subsequently murdered, in *al-Hawadith* 1211 (18/1/1980), pp. 15-20. Almost all later reports about the Ikhwan can be attributed to him.

44. In 1979, the Iranians formed the largest contingent with 75,000 pilgrims; the

Saudi authorities had for a long time been inclined to establish quotas for the pilgrimage.

45. This was emphasized by Iranian circles, cf. Muhammad Hadi al-Amini, *Makka*, Maktab Nashr al-'Ilm, Tehran, 1988, p. 314 f.

46. *Majallat Rabitat al-'Alam al-Islami*, 18 (1979), 2, p. 54.

47. *Akhbar al-'Alam al-Islami*, 660 (7/1/1980), pp. 3, 14.

48. Here quoted from *Rabitat al-'alam al-Islami, al-radd al-shafi 'ala muftarayat al-Qaddafi*, RAI, Mecca 1402 [1982], pp. 42–3, 9–18.

49. The names referred to two periodicals of the party published in 1965 and 1966. A third wing was formed by the Sitam-i Milli, which concentrated entirely on re-establishing the national sovereignty of the nationalists and considered the social question as secondary.

50. A *qaum* could mean a clan, a village, an ethnic group or even a professional group.

51. See Olivier Roy, *L'Afghanistan, Islam et modernité politique*, Seuil, Paris 1985 and id., *L'échec de l'Islam politique*, Seuil, Paris 1992, p. 200 ff. (English ed. *The Failure of Political Islam*, London, I. B. Tauris 1993); a survey is also provided by Robert L. Canfield, 'Afghanistan: The Trajectory of Internal Alignments', MEJ 43 (1989), pp. 635–48.

52. Roy, *L'Afghanistan*, p. 207 ff.

53. *Akhbar al-'alam al-Islami* 642 (3/9/1979), pp. 2, 5.

54. *Akhbar al-'alam al-Islami* 644 (17/9/1979), p. 1.

55. Estimates from Weekes, *Muslim Peoples*, p. 882.

56. There were four important Shi'i resistance movements: the Shura-yi Ittifaq-i Islami ('Association of Islamic Unity') of Sayyid Bahashti (peasant Hazara), the Nasr (Victory) Organization as an Iranian-influenced neo-Salafite group within the Hazara, the Harakat-i Islami of Asif Muhsini (trans-ethnic), and the radical Iranian-dominated Pasdaran ('guardians'). The traditional division of the Sunni resistance movements into four 'fundamentalist' and three 'moderate' groups can be best defined by their social positions within the elite culture. Three of the four 'fundamentalist' groups (Hikmatyar, Khalis and Sayyaf (Ittihal-i Islami) belonged to ethnically marked forums of the neo-Salafiya; the three 'moderate' groups were closely connected with Afghan scholarly culture; Rabbani's group with its emphatic connections with the *naqshbandiya* occupied a medium position.

57. Muhammad Baqir al-Sadr, *Falsafatuna*, Beirut: Dar al-Ta'aruf, 1406 [1986].

58. Muhammad Baqir al-Sadr, *Iqtisaduna*, Beirut: Dar al-Ta'aruf, Beirut 1402 [1982].

59. In an appeal from the year 1380 [1961] quoted in *al-Jihad* (Tehran) 116 of 19/12/1983, p. 11.

60. Comprehensive information in Shahram Chubin/Charles Tripp, *Iran and Iraq at War*, Westview, Boulder, Col., 1988.

61. The Islamic front in Syria was represented by three personalities, the scholar Muhammad Abu'l-Nasr al-Bayanuni and the two intellectuals Adnan Sa'd and Sa'id Hawwa, cf. Carré/Michaud, *Mouvement*, pp. 142–51; for further literature, see Gudrun Krämer, *Arabismus und Nationalstaatlichkeit. Syrien als nahöstliche Regionalmacht*, Stiftung Wissenschaft und Politik, Ebenhausen 1987, p. 61 f.

62. On Syria's internal policy see among others Volker Perthes, *Staat und Gesellschaft in Syrien (1970–1989)*, Deutsches Orient-Institut, Hamburg 1990. Published in English as *The Political Economy of Syria under Asad*, I. B. Tauris, London, 1995.

63. Soon after the bloody event of Hama, members of the neo-Salafiya began to denounce Khomeini – and the Shi'a as such – as Koran falsifiers and intriguers. In the eyes of a critic, the Shi'a was nothing but a Jewish sect, which was why Iran was now ready for closer cooperation with Israel, Ahmad al-Afghani, *Sarab fi Iran – kilmat sari'a haula al-Khumaini wa-din al-shi'a*, [Riyadh?] 1402 [1982], p. 59 ff.

64. On the unrest in the Cairo suburb of Zawiyat al-Hamra' cf. Hamid Ansari, 'Sectarian Conflict in Egypt and the Political Expediency of Religion', MEJ 38 (1984), pp. 397–418.

65. A comprehensive account and documentation on the trial against the conspirators around al-Islambuli is found in Rif'at Sayyid Ahmad, *al-Islambuli -ru'ya jadida li-tanzim al-jihad*, Madbuli, Cairo, 1988, esp. pp. 125–66.

66. Among the various, often abridged or distorted editions, we shall only mention Amman, (1981/82); the text received much more attention from the Western public than from the Islamic world, cf. among others Kepel, *Prophète*, p. 186 ff.

67. Taqi al-Din Ibn Taimiya, *Majmu'at fatawa* (...), vol. VI, Cairo 1400/1980, pp. 280–97, N° 517.

68. Krämer, *Ägypten*, p. 81 ff. It should be noted that al-Tilimsani's family possessed a considerable amount of land in Lower Egypt. The new leader of the Muslim Brothers, Muhammad Hamid Abu'l-Nasr (born 1913) continued and intensified this policy, cf. Martin Forstner, 'Auf dem legalen Weg zur Macht? Zur politischen Entwicklung der Muslimbruderschaft Ägyptens', *Orient* 29 (1988), pp. 386–422.

69. Statistic material for the restoration of private landed property in Egyptian agriculture is offered by Robert Springborg, "Rolling Back Egypt's Agrarian Reform", MERIP 166 (Sept.– Oct. 1990), pp. 28–30.

70. Elias Kazarian, *Finance and Economic Development. Islamic Banking in Egypt*, University of Lund, Lund 1991.

71. Gabriel Warburg, 'The Sharia in Sudan: Implementation and Repercussions', 1983–1989', MEJ 44 (1990), pp. 624–37.

72. Cf. among others Nazih N. Ayubi, *Political Islam. Religion and Politics in the Arab World*, Routledge, London 1991, pp. 104–13.

73. Hasan al-Turabi, *al-Din wa-l-tajdid*, Cairo 1984.

74. The latter was closely connected with the *khatmiya* and had been appointed Minister of Defence in March 1985.

75. al-Mukashifi Taha al-Kabbashi, *Tatbiq al-shari'a al-islamiya fi l-Sudan baina l-haqiqa wa-l-ithara*, al-Zahra', Cairo 1406 [1986], p. 39 ff. Al-Kabbashi was the presiding judge at the court of appeal, who had confirmed the verdict against Taha. On Taha cf. among others Annette Oevermann, *Die 'Republikanischen Brüder' im Sudan. Eine islamische Reformbewegung im Zwanzigsten Jahrhundert*, Lang, Frankfurt a. M., 1993.

76. *Akhbar al-'alam al-islami* 909 (21/1/1985), p. 1.

77. Schulze, *Internationalismus*, pp. 377–85.

78. Cf. Eric Rouleau, 'Sudan's Revolutionary Spring', MERIP Reports 135 (Sept. 1985),

pp. 3–10.

79. Between 1954/61 and 1982/89 the per capita production even fell by 59%.

80. By way of comparison: globally, food production per capita dropped by about 5%. From 1980 to 1988 the per capita rates further dropped in Iran, Sudan, and now also in Syria and Turkey.

81. Cf. Joe Stork/Karen Pfeifer, 'Bullets, Banks and Bushels: The Struggle for Food in the Middle East', MERIP 145 (March – April 1987), pp. 3–6.

82. Between 1980 and 1987, the revenues of all OPEC states dropped from $287 billion to $90 billion. The price of crude oil dropped on an average by $18 per barrel; oil production dropped by 50% between 1979 and 1985.

83. The verdicts were later changed to imprisonment for life.

84. The new French philosophy was also eagerly received in post-revolutionary Iran, cf. Michel M. J. Fisher, Mehdi Abedi, *Debating Muslims. Cultural Dialogues in Postmodernity and Tradition*, The University of Wisconsin Press, Madison, Wis., 1990.

85. Out of the multitude of publications by the MTI, we shall merely mention the programmatic work *Harakat al-ittijah al-islami, haqa'iq haula harakat al-ittijah al-islami*, [Tunis] [1983].

86. See Stephan Guth, *Zeugen einer Endzeit, Fünf Schriftsteller zum Umbruch in der ägyptischen Gesellschaft nach 1970*, Schwarz, Berlin 1992, p. 284 ff.

CHAPTER SIX

1. Hasan Hanafi, *al-Yasar al-islami*, Madbuli, Cairo 1981.

2. Oliver Roy, *L'échec de l'Islam*, p. 84 ff.

3 Alexander Flores, *Intifada. Aufstand der Palästinenser*, Rotbuch, Berlin 1988, p. 67 ff.

4. Cf. Baumgarten, *Palästina*, p. 305 ff.

5. Harakat al-Tahrir al-Watani al-Filastini, '"Fatah", al-Jihad al-Islami', n.p., mechanically mimeographed typescript, August 1981, 335 pages.

6. Syria controlled about 60% and Israel 20% of the country.

7. Here compiled from Hanf, 'Libanon-Konflikt', passim, and *Middle East Contemporary Survey* I–XIII [1977–1989], Westview, Boulder, Col., 1979–1991.

8. Also to be mentioned are the ethnic conflicts in Kirghizstan (between the Kirghizes and Uzbeks, 4–7/6/1990), the revolt against the Armenians in Tajikistan (11–12/2/1990) and the conflicts between the Shi'i Mechetes (deported from southern Georgia in 1944) and the Uzbeks in Uzbekistan (1989). In Chechenia–Ingushstan, there was danger of a secession in the city of Naterechnaya in August 1993.

9. The old conflict about Nagorno–Karabagh (from 1921 a part of Azerbaijan) escalated in autumn 1989, when the Azerbaijan Popular Front threatened the autonomous region with a general strike jeopardizing its maintenance. In January 1990 the conflicts ended in the evacuation of more than 30,000 Armenians from Baku to the Central Asian republics. On 19/1/1990 Soviet troops invaded Baku.

10. Text in: *Kayhan* (London), 23/2/1989, p. 1, see also New York Times 15/2/1989;

Arabic text in *Kayhan al-'Arabi* 15/2/1989.

11. Consulate-General of the Islamic Republic of Iran (ed.), *The Islamic Republic of Iran. From Resolution 598 to Reconstruction*, Hamburg 8/2/1990 (file 180 – 10/4818).

12. Cf. the excellent study of the Damascene philosopher Sadik J. al-Azm, 'Es ist wichtig, ernst zu sein. Salman Rushdie, Joyce, Rabelais – der Kampf um Aufklärung" (The Importance of Being Earnest About Salman Rushdie) in: id., *Unbehagen in der Moderne Aufklärung im Islam*, Fischer, Frankfurt a. M., 1993, pp. 9–53.

13. *Kayhan-i Farhangi*, November–December 1988, p. 35.

14. *Ash-Sharq al-Ausat* of 27/6/1983, p. 1.

15. Thus the Jordanian Minister for Religious Affairs, Abd al-Aziz al-Khayyat point blank rejected the summons to kill, cf. *Financial Times* of 7/ 3/ 1989.

16. Cf. detailed account in MECS 1989, pp. 173–7.

17. *Financial Times* of 7/3/1989.

18. al-Yaum al-sabi' (Paris) of 27/3/1989.

19. Cf. from an Iranian point of view Fad al-Qutani, *Majzarat Makka -qissat al-madhbaha al-sa'udiya li-l-hujjaj*, as-Safa [2]1409 [1988], London; Sahib Taqi, *al-Wajh al-akhar li-ahdath Makka al-damiya*, Kayhan, Tehran 1988. Saudi authorities denounced the demonstrators as infidel agitators and propagandists of 'Zionist–Khomeinist ideas', *al-rabita* (Mecca) 275 (February 1988), p. 7 f.

20. We might mention here that Khamene'i had participated in the discussion groups of Ali Shari'ati.

21. Farouk/Sluglett/Sluglett, *Iraq* (German ed.) p. 278.

22. According to Joe Sork/Ann M. Lesch, 'Why War? Background to the Crisis', MERIP 167 (Nov.–Dec. 1990), pp. 11–18, here p. 15.

23. *al-Muslimun* (Riyadh) of 18/1/1991.

24. Here we can only discuss a few aspects of the Gulf War. For more exhaustive information, we recommend the following works: Gert Krell/Bernd W. Kubbig (eds), *Krieg und Frieden am Golf. Ursachen und Perspektiven*, Fischer, Frankfurt a. M., 1991; Werner Ruf (ed.) *Vom Kalten Krieg zur Heißen Ordnung? Der Golfkrieg – Hintergründe und Perspektiven*, Hamburg: Lit. 1991; Peter Pawelka (ed.), *Der Golfkrieg in der Weltpolitik*, Kohlhammer, Stuttgart 1991, with interesting contributions by Gudrun Krämer, Eugen Wirth, Werner Ende, et. al.; Georg Stein (ed.), *Nachgedanken zum Golfkrieg*, Palmyra, Heidelberg 1991. A thorough historical elucidation of the Gulf War is certainly impossible at present. Almost all interpretations are based on journalistic, i. e. 'soft' sources and can thus only throw limited light on the real political background. The actual motives for the actions of the Arab states involved, as well as those of the Western alliance, have so far only been very superficially explained.

25. This declaration bears no date; but since one of the signatories, Muhammad Sa'id al-Amudi, died in February 1991, it must have been written before that time.

26. In November 1990 Fahd had declared that a council of that type would be set up 'in the near future', *Akhbar al-'Alam al-Islami* 1191 (12/1/1990), p. 16.

27. Typescript, June 1991, 2 pages, distributed in June 1991.

28. Cf. *International Herald Tribune*, 6–7 July, 1991.

29. Mimeographed typescript, 2 pages, distributed in June 1991.

30. For a more comprehensive account see Reinhard Schulze, 'Islam und Herrschaft. Zur politischen Instrumentalisierung einer Religion', in Lüders, *Islam im Aufbruch?*, pp. 94–129.

31. E.g. in the probably Iranian preface to an earlier impression of a pro-Iranian (Egyptian?) pilgrim in Mecca, Muhammad Hasan Isma'il, *al-Ka'ba fi qabadat Abi Lahb*, 1404 [1984], p. [3].

32. E. g. Yusuf al-Qaradawi, *al-Hulul al-mustaurada wa-kaifa janat 'ala ummatina*, Wahba 137, Cairo [1978].

33. Discussed at length by Leonard Binder, *Islamic Liberalism: A Critique of Development Ideologies*, University of Chicago Press, Chicago 1988, esp. p. 336 ff.

34. This can only be a very abridged summary of a vast discussion. An initial summary of the discussions is found in the corresponding number MEJ 47 (1993) 2; for more about Tunisia Abdelkader Zghal, 'Le concept de société civile et la transition vers le multipartisme', in Michel Camau (ed.), *Changements politiques au Maghreb*, Paris 1991, pp. 207–28; on Egypt: Gudrun Krämer, 'Staat– und Zivilgesellschaft im Nahen und Mittleren Osten. Das Beispiel Ägyptens', in: Erdmann Gormsen/Andreas Thimm (eds), *Zivilgesellschaft und Staat in der Dritten Welt*, Universität Mainz 1992, pp. 115–37.

35. Until a few years ago, complaints were made that the West was by no means prepared to attribute an independent civil society to the Islamic world, cf. especially Bryan S. Turner, 'Orientalism and the Problem of Civil Society in Islam', in: Asaf Hussain et al. (eds), *Orientalism, Islam, and Islamists*, Amana Books, Brattleboro/Vt., 1984, pp. 23–42.

36. Mustafa al-Ahnaf/Bernard Botiveau/Franck Frégosi, *L'Algérie par ses islamistes*, Karthala, Paris 1991; Ahmida Ayyasi, *al-Islamiyun al-jaz'iriyun baina s-sulta wa-l-rassas*, Dar al-Hikma, Algiers 1992; Abderrahim Lamchichi, *L'islamisme en Algérie*, L'Harmattan, Paris 1992.

37. The social composition of the Algerian student body had not much changed since independence, cf. M'hammed Ibn Mobarek, 'La politique d'industrialisation et le dévloppement des couches intellectuelles en Algérie', *Revue d'histoire maghrébine*, 27/28 (1982), pp. 255–68.

38. Ben Bella returned from his exile to Algeria in 1990.

39. Lahouari, Addi, 'Algeria's Democracy between the Islamists and the Elite', *Middle East Report* 175 (March–April 1992), pp. 36–8.

40. *Le Monde* of 13/4/1991, p. 1.

41. Except of course in the monarchies themselves: the Saudi Arabian or Moroccan historians, for example, emphasized the 'ideal union' between royalty and society.

42. According to Peter Pawelka, *Der Vordere Orient und die Internationale Politik*, Kohlhammer, Stuttgart 1993, p. 170 f.

43. Irena Reuter-Hendrichs, *Der Islam in Jugoslawien*, Stiftung Wissenschaft und Politik, Ebenhausen 1988 (AZ 2577) corrected by V. Strika, 'La communità religiosa islamica della Jugoslawia', OM 47 (1967), pp. 1–46, and Popovic, L'Islam balkanique, pp. 343–65.

44. On US Somalia policy see Peter J. Schaeder, 'The Horn of Africa: US Foreign Policy in an Altered Cold War Environment', MEJ 46 (1992), pp. 571–93. The events in

Somalia after 1990 have so far eluded any historical interpretation. They are mentioned here only because they represent an extreme example of the new group nationalism. All interpretations should be approached with the greatest caution. So far the source material does not allow anything more than a superficial description of the complex developments in the external and internal evolutions of the Somalia conflict.

45. Mahboob Alam Khawaja in: *The Muslim World League Journal*, 21 (July 1993), pp. 46–8.

46. A corresponding appreciation of Islam is expressed by Akbar S. Ahmed, *Postmodernism and Islam. Predicament and Promise*, Routledge, London 1992.

EPILOGUE

1. In this Bouteflika followed a step the Moroccan government had already taken in 1995 which allowed primary-school children to be taught in the local Berber language. (About 14% of the Algerian population speak a Berber language in their everyday communications (especially Kabyl 8% and Shawiya 5%)

2. Peter von Sivers, 'Nordafrika in der Neuzeit', in Ulrich Haarmann, ed., *Geschichte der arabischen Welt*, Munich, 2001, pp. 502–604; this ref. p. 602.

3. Even though there was an election for six of the twelve members of the Council of Guardians in September 2001.

4. The actual break with 'Azzam's bureau (*maktab al-hidamat*) only came after the assassination of 'Azzam on 24. 11. 1989.

5. In 1986 the Saudi scholar, Nafar bin 'Abdarrahman al-halawi (b. 1950) wrote a thesis at Umm al-Qura University in Mecca on the subject of *ia' in Contemporary Islamic Ideology*, thus reactivating the concept for the current political discussion. After disturbances in the central Arabian town of Buraida, al-halawi was arrested by the Saudi police together with the scholar, Salman al-'Auda. Together they had founded the forum of the Wahhabi puritans, the 'Committee for the Defence of Legal Rights' on 3 May 1993 (Geoff Simons, *Saudi Arabia: The Shape of a Client Feudalism*, New York, St. Martin's Press, 1998, pp. 34–6). After the 1994 arrests — the same year in which bin Laden was deprived of his Saudi citizenship — the Committee was reconstituted in London by Sa'd al-Faqih. On 11 March 1996 he left the Committee because of 'irreconcilable differences' and founded the 'Movement for an Islamic Reform in Arabia' (*al-harakat al-islamiya li-l-islah*) which has since represented an important rallying point for the Saudi Wahhabi opposition. Cf. Saad Al-Fagih, *The Rise and Evolution of the Modern Islamic Reform Movement in Saudi Arabia*, London, (around 1995). The Committee, which has since 1996 been under the leadership of Muhammad al-Mas'ari in London, clearly has good contacts with the 'Battalions of the Faithful' who demonstrated in Saudi Arabia in 1995. Their strength can be seen in the fact that at least 150 of their members (others talk of up to 1000) were arrested. Alfred D. Prados, *Saudi Arabia: Post-War Issues and US Relations*, CRS Issue Brief 93113 (2. 12. 1996).

6. The point is made explicitly by the Palestinian activist, Abu Muhammad al-Maqdisi (b. 1959, arrested by the Jordanian police in the early 1990s), in *Nida'ul Islam*, Sidney, 21, 1997/98. The aforementioned Saudi scholar, al-'Auda put these tendencies

together with the term 'foreign ideas', (Salman al-'Auda, *rasa'il al-turaba*).

7. *Nida'ul Islam*, 14, 1996.

8. The members of this community of discourse are therefore often referred to – with both respect and disrespect – as *jihadis.*

9. Published in *al-quds al-'arabi*, 23. 2. 1998.

10. *Les Nouvelles d'Afghanistan* 76 (1997), p.10.

11. Ironically bin Laden used the al-Jazeera television station for this, although the Taliban had specifically declared television 'unIslamic'.

12. Russian Federation, press release of 28. 6. 2000.

Bibliography

Abbreviations

EI = *Enzyklopädie des Islams*, 1–4, Brill, Leiden 1913–1934
EI² = *The Encyclopaedia of Islam*, New edition, Brill, Leiden 1954 ff.
IJMES =*International Journal of Middle East Studies*
MEJ = *Middle East Journal*
MERIP = *Middle East Research and Information Project*
MES = *Middle Eastern Studies*
OM = *Oriente Moderno*
RAI = *Rābiṭāt al-ʻĀlam al-Islāmī* (Muslim World League)
WI = *Die Welt des Islams*

Periodicals

Aḥbār al-ʻĀlam al-Islāmī (Mecca)
al-Ahrām, (Cairo)
Al-Difāʻ (Jerusalem)
Al-Ḍiyā (Cairo)
Filasṭīn (Jerusalem)
al-Jāmiʻa al-Islāmīya (Jerusalem)
al-Jihād (Tehran
International Herald Tribune
Journal des Débats (Paris)
al-Manār (Cairo)
al-Muʼayyad (Cairo)
al-Muqtaṭaf (Cairo)
Muslim World League Journal (Mecca)
al-Muslimūn (Riyadh)
New York Times
Pravda (Moscow)
Risālat al-Islām (Cairo)

Kayhān (London)
Le Monde (Paris)
Majallat Rābiṭat al-ʿĀlam al-Islāmī (Mecca)
al-Shaʿb (Cairo)
Ash-Sharq al-Ausaṭ (London)
al-Yaum al-Sābiʿ (Paris)

Bibliographies and Bibliographical Surveys

Abstracta Islamica, Revue des Études islamiques, 1927 ff., from 1965 independent as *Abstracta Islamica. Supplément à la Revue des Études islamiques.*

Atiyeh, George N.: *The Contemporary Middle East*: 1948-1973. A Selective and Annotated Bibliography, Boston, Mass.: Hall 1975.

Behn, Wolfgang H.: *Islamic book review index*, vol. 1–7, Berlin: Adiyol 1982–1988, vol. 8 ff. Millesville, Pa., Adiyol 1989 ff.

Bernath, Mathias/Karl Nehring (eds), *Historische Bücherkunde Südosteuropa*, vol. 2, part 1., *Osmanisches Reich, Makedonien, Albanien*, Munich: Oldenburg 1988.

Berque, Jacques (red.), *Bibliographie de la culture arabe contemporaine*, Paris: Sindbad 1981.

Centre d'Études pour le monde arabe moderne: *Arab Culture and Society in Change*, Beirut: Dar el-Machreq 1973.

Endreß, Gerhard, *Der Islam*. Eine Einführung in seine Geschichte, Munich: Beck 1991, pp. 247–90.

Haarmann, Ulrich (ed.), *Geschichte der arabischen Welt*, Munich: Beck 1987, pp. 662–76.

Hopwood, Derek/Diana Grimwood Jones (eds), *Middle East and Islam. A Bibliographical Introduction*, Zug: Inter Documentation 1972,[2] 1979, Supplement 1977–1983, ed. by Paul Auchterlonie, Zug: Inter Documentation 1986.

Kornrumpf, Hans-Jürgen, *Osmanische Bibliographie mit besonderer Berücksichtigung der Türkei in Europa*, Leiden: Brill 1973 (Handbuch der Orientalistik, Abt. 1, Ergänzungsband 8).

Lowenstein, Amy C. (ed.), *The Middle East Abstracts and Index*, vols 1–8, Pittsburgh, Penn.: *Northumberland Press1978–1986*, vols 9–13 (ed. James Joseph Sanchez), Northumberland Press, Seattle, Wash., 1987–1990.

Lücke, Hanna, *Der 'islamische Fundamentalismus' in der Rezeption der deutsch– und englischsprachigen Forschungsliteratur unter besonderer Berücksichtigung Ägyptens*, incompl. MA thesis, Bonn University (1992), pp. 226–50.

Pearson, James Douglas (ed.), *Index Islamicus. A catalogue of articles on Islamic subjects in periodicals and other collective publications, 1906–1955*, Cambridge: Heffer 1958; Supplements 1–5, Cambridge: Heffer, 1962–1967, London: Mansell, 1972–1983. [Continued as *The Quarterly Index Islamicus* I ff., London: Mansell, 1977 ff.]

Schwarz, Klaus, *Verzeichnis deutschsprachiger Hochschulschriften zum Islamischen Orient* (1885–1970), Freiburg im Breisgau: Schwarz 1971.

Works in Oriental Languages

ʿAbd al-Hāmid al-Thānī, al-Sulṭān: *Mudhakkirātī al-siyāsīya 1891–1908*, ['My political memories'], Beirut ²1402 [1982] [Ottoman first version of 1919].

'Abd al-Rāziq, 'Alī, *al-Islām wa-uṣūl al-ḥukm*, Beirut: al-Arabīya 1972.

'Abduh, Muḥammad, *al-Islām wa-n naṣrānīya ma'a l-'ilm wa-l-madanīya* ['Islam and Christianity in relationship to science and civilization'], ed. Muḥammad Rashīd Riḍā, Cairo: al-Manār 1341 [1923/24].

Afghānī, Aḥmad al-, *Sarāb fi Īrān – kilmāt sari'a ḥaula al-Khumainī wa-dīn al- shī'a* ['Illusion in Iran – Quick words on Khomeini and the Shi'a religion'] [Riyadh?] 1401 [1982].

[Egypt] Wizārat al-Auqāf wa-l-Shu'ūn al-Islāmīya, *al-Azhār tārīhukhū wa-taṭawwuruhū* ['The Azhar: its history and its evolution'] Cairo: al-Sha'b 1383 [1964].

Aḥmad, Rif'at Sayyid, *al-Islāmbūli – Ru'yā jadīda li-tanzīm al-jihād* [al-Islāmbūlī, – 'A new view for the organization of the "jihād"'], Cairo: Madbuli [1988].

Akgün, Seçil, *Halifelijin kaldırılması ve laiklik* (1924–1928) ['The abolition of the caliphate and laicism'], Ankara: Turkan n.d.

Ālūsī, Maḥmūd Shukrī al-: *Tārīkh Najd* ['History of Najd'], Cairo: al-Dīnīya 1343 [1925], ²1347 [1929].

Amīnī, Muḥammadhādī al-, *Makka* ['Mecca'], Tehran: Maktab Nashr al-'Ilm 1988.

'Aqqād, 'Abbas Maḥmūd al-, *Hitler fi l-mīzān* ['Hitler on the scales'], Cairo 1940.

Arslān, Shakīb, *Ḥāḍir al-'alam al-islāmī* ['The Islamic World at present'], I–IV, "Isā al-Bābī al-Ḥalabī' 1352 [1933/34] [transl. by Ajjaj Nuwaihiḍ, with commentary by Arslān, in Lothrop Stoddard, *The New World of Islam*, London 1921].

——*Li-mādhā ta'akhkhara al-muslimūn wa-li-mādha taqaddama ghairuhum* ['Why have the Muslims lagged behind, and why have others gone forward?'] reprinted Caairo: al-Bashīr [1985, 1st ed., 1930].

——*Sīra dhātīya* ['Autobiography'], Beirut: Dār al-Ṭalī'a 1969.

Ashhab, Muḥammad al-Ṭayyib b. Idrīs al-, *al-Sanūsī al-kabīr 'arḍ wa-taḥlīl li-di'āmat ḥarakat al-iṣlāḥ al-sanūsī* ['The Great Sanusi – explanation and analysis of the support of the Sanusi reform'], Cairo: Muḥammad 'Ātif 1956.

'Auda, 'Abd al-Qadir, *al-Islām baina jahl abnā'ihī wa 'ajz 'ulama'ihi* ['Islam between the ignorance of its followers and the incompetence of its ulama'], al-Muḥtār al-Islāmī [circa 1950].

'Ayyāshī, Aḥmīda, *al-Islāmīyūn al-jazā'irīyūn baina s-sulṭa wa-l-raṣṣāṣ* [The Algerian Islamists between sovereignty and bullets], Algiers: Dar-al-Ḥikma 1992.

Bābāḥān[ov], Ḍiyā' al-Dīn, *al-Islām fi l-ittiḥād al-sūfyātī mustaqill 'an al-daula wa-yatamattā bi-nafs al-ḥuqūq ka-l-adyān al-ukhrā* ['Islam in the Soviet Union is independent from the state and enjoys the same rights as other religions'], Moscow: Novosti no year [circa 1963].

Bakri, Muḥammad Taufīq al-, *al-Mustaqbal li-l-Islām* ['The Future belongs to Islam'], Cairo: Al'umūmīya 1310 [1892/93].

Bannā, Hasan al-, *Mudhakkirāt al-da'wa wa-l-dā'īya* ['Recollections of propaganda and the propagandist'] Cairo: Dār al-Kitāb al-'Arabī (ca. 1951).

Bārūdī, Za'īma Sulaimān al- [ed.], *Ṣafaḥāt khālida min al-jihād* ['Immortal phases of the righteous war'], Cairo: al-Istiqlāl al-Kubrā 1964.

Bashmīl, Muḥammad Aḥmad, *al-Qaumīya fi nazar al-Islām* ['Nationalism from the

Islamic point of view'], Beirut 1960.

Bazzaz, 'Abd al-Raḥmān al-, 'al-Qaumīya al-'arabīya wa-l-Islām' ['Arab nationalism and Islam'] in id., *Min rūḥ al-Islām*, Baghdad 1959 [1st ed. Baghdad 1952, transl. by S. Haim in WI 3 (1954), pp. 201–18].

Birinci, *Dünya Harbinde Türk Harbi*, vol. I, *Osmalı Imperatorlujunun siyasî ve askerî hazırlıkları ve harbi girisi* ['The Turkish War in World War I – Political and military preparations of the Ottoman Empire and entrance into war'], Ankara 1970.

Dabbāgh, Mustafa Murad al-, *Biladuna Filastīn* ['Our country Palestine'] Beirut 1965.

Devlet, Nadir, *Rusya Türklerinin millî mücâdele tarihi* (1907–1917) ['History of the national fight of Russian Turks'], Ankara: Türk Kültürünü Arastırma Enstitüsü, 1985.

Fāḍil, Muḥammad, *al-Nafṭ wa-l-waḥda al-'arabiya* ['Oil and the Arab Union'], Beirut: Markaz al-Buḥūth 1979.

Faraj 'Aṭīya, 'Abdassalām, *al-Jihād al-farīḍa al-ghā'iba* ['The just war – the absent duty'], Amman (1981/82).

Fāsī, 'Allāl al-, *al-Ḥaraka al-istiqlālīya fi l-Maghrib* ['The independence movement in the Maghreb'], Cairo 1948.

Jad'ān, Fahmī, *Usus al-taqaddum 'inda mufakkirī l-Islām fi l-'ālam al-'arabi al-ḥadīt* ['Foundations of progress among Islamic intellectuals in the Modern Arab World'], Beirut: al-Mu'assasa al-Arabīya 1979.

Jamāl, Aḥmad Muḥammad, *Isti'mār wa-kifāḥ* ['Colonialism and conflict'], Mecca: al-Thaqāfa 1374 [1955].

——*Fikrat al-daula fi l-Islām* ['The Idea of the state in Islam'], Riyadh: al-Sa'ūdīya 1406 [1986].

——*Naḥwa siyāsa 'arabīya ṣariḥa*, [Towards a clear Arab policy'], Mecca: Dār al-Thaqāfa 1381 [1962].

Jaudat Pāshā, Aḥmad, *Tārīkh-i Jaudat* [Jaudat's Chronicle'], 12 vols, Istanbul: 'Uthmānīya 1309 [1891/92].

Jāwīs, 'Abd al-'Aẓiz, *al-Islām dīn al-fiṭra* ['Islam – the religion of human nature], Cairo: al-Zahrā 1987.

Ghazzālī, Muḥammad al-, *al-Islām wa-l manāhij al-ishtirākīya* ['Islam and socialist programmes'], Cairo: Dār al-Kātib al-'Arabī '1951.

——*al-Islām wa-l-istibdād al-siyāsī* [Islam and political despotism'], Cairo: Dār al-Kātib al-'Arabī, n.d. [around 1952].

Ḥaddād, Muḥammad 'Alī al-, *Ḥāḍir Ṭarābلus al-gharb* ['Tripoli today'], I, Baghdad: al-Jazīra 1356 [1937].

Hājirī, Yūsuf al-, *al-Sa'ūdīya tabtali' al-Yaman, qiṣṣat al-tadakhkhulāt fi shu'ūn ashshaṭr al-shamālī li-l-Yaman* ['Saudi Arabia swallows Yemen. A history of interventions in the affairs of the northern half of the Yemen'], London: al-Ṣafā 1988.

Ḥanafī, Ḥasan, *al-Dīn wa-l-thaura fi Miṣr*, ['Religion and revolution in Egypt'], Cairo: Dār Thābit 1988.

——*al-Yasār al-islāmī* ['The Islamic Left'], Cairo: Madbūlī 1981.

Ḥarakat al-ittijah al-islāmī, *Haqā'iq ḥaula ḥarakat al-ittijāh al-Islāmī* [Movement of the Islamic Direction: Truths about the Movement of the Islamic Direction'], [Tunis] [1983].

Ḥarakat al-Taḥrīr al-Waṭanī al-Filasṭīnī 'Fataḥ', *al-Jihād al-islāmī* ['The National Palestinian Liberation Movement: the just Islamic war'], mimeographed typescript, n.p., August 1981, 335 pages.

Khashīm, Ḥasan 'Alī, *Ṣafaḥāt min jihādinā al-waṭanī* ['Stages in our national fight'], Tripoli: Maktabat al-Fikr 1394 [1974].

Ḥibshī, Muḥammad 'Umar al-, *al-Yaman al-janūbī* [Southern Yemen'], Beirut 1968.

Ḥusain, Ṭāhā, *Fī l-shi'r al-jāhilī*, ['On pre-Islamic Poetry'], Cairo: Dār al-Kutub 1344 [1926].

Ḥusaninī, al-Sayyid 'Abdallāh al-, *Mu'tamar Harad wathā'iq wa-maḥāḍir* ['The Harad Conference – Documents and Proceedings'] Beirut: Dār al-Kitāb al-Jadid 1966.

Ḥusainī, Isḥāq Mūsā al-, *al-Ikhwān al-muslimūn kubrā l-ḥarakāt al-islāmīya al-ḥadītha* ['The Muslim Brothers – the greatest modern Islamic movement'], Dār Bairūt [2]1955 [1st ed. 1952].

Ibn Bādīs, 'Abd al-Hāmid, *Āthār* (…) ['Works'], ed. by 'Ammār al-Ṭālibī, Algiers 1968.

Ibn Hadhlūl, Sa'd, *Tārīkh mulūk Āl Sa'ūd* ['History of the Saudi Kings'], Riyadh: al-Riyāḍ1380 [1961].

Ibn Nabī, Mālik [Bin Nabī], *Wijhat al-'alām al-islāmī* [written 1954/59] [The course of the Islamic world'], Damascus: Dār al-Fikr 1400 [1980].

Ibrāhīm, Aḥmad Abū Bakr, *al-Adab al-Ḥijāzī fī l-nahḍa al-hadītha* [Hejazi literature within the framework of the modern revival'], Cairo: Nahḍat Misr, 1948.

Ibrāhīmī, Muḥammad al-Bashīr al-, *Āthār al-shaikh* (…) [Works', I–II], Algiers: al-Shirka al-Waṭanīya 1398 [1978], II ('uyūn al-baṣā'ir).

[Islamic Republic of Iran] Ṣḥūrā-yī bāẓnīgārī-yī qānūn-ī āṣāṣī, *Qānūn-i asāsī-yi Jumhūrī-yi Islāmī-yi Īrān, bā-ra'āyat-i iṣlāḥāt-i sāl 1367* ['Constitutional Law of the Islamic Republic of Iran, including the revisions of the year 1367 (1988)'], Tehran: Majlis-i Shūrā-yi Islāmī 1368 [1989].

Ismā'īl, Muḥammad Ḥasan, *al-Ka'ba fī qabaḍat Abī Lahb* ['The Ka'ba in the hand of Abū'lahb'], 1404 [1984].

Kabbāshī, al-Mukāshifī Thāhā al-, *Taṭbiq al-shari'a al-islāmīya fī l-Sūdān bana l-ḥaqīqa wa-l-ithāra* [The application of the Islamic *sharī'a* in the Sudan between truth and instigation'], Cairo: al-Zahrā' 1406 [1986].

Kawākibī, 'Abdal-Raḥmān al-, *Umm al-qurā wa-huwa ḍabṭ mufāwaḍāt wa-muqarrarāt mu'tamar al-nahḍa al-islāmīya al-mun'aqid fī Makka al-mukarrama sanat 1316* ['*Umm al-qurā* – Proceedings of the Discussions and Decisions at the Conference of Islamic Revival held in venerable Mecca in the year 1316'], Beirut: [2]Dār al-Rā'id al-'Arabī 1402 [1982] (1st ed., Port Sa'id (1899)).

——*Ṭabā'i' al-istibdād* ['The nature of despotism'], Beirut: al-Mu'assassa al-Arabīya 1970.

Maudūdī, Abū A'lā, *Musalmān awr maujūda siyāsī kashmakash*, ['The Muslims and basic political difficulties'], vols I–III, Pathankot, Tarjumān al-Qur'ān (ca. 1942).

Minbar al-Islām (ed.), *Ra'y al-dīn fī ikhwān al-shaiṭān* ['The attitude of religion with regard to the devil's brothers'], Cairo: al-Majlis al-A'lā li-l-Shu'ūn al-Islāmīya 1965.

Muhannā, 'Abd al-'Azīz al-, *al-Ṣumāl baina ḥayātaini – binā' al-daula wa-ḥayat al-qabīla* ['The Somalians between two lives: Building a state and leading a tribal life'],

Riyadh: al-Hilāl 1412 [1992].

——*al-Busna wa-l-Harsak, al-qaḍıya wa-l-ma'sat* ['Bosnia Herzegovina – the problem and the tragedy'], Riyadh: al-Hilāl 1412 [1992].

Mūsā, Salāma, *al-Yaum wa-l-ghad* ['Today and tomorrow'], Cairo: al-Maṭba'a al-'Asrīya, no year[1927?].

Muwailiḥi, Ibrahīm b. Abd al-Khāliq al-, *Mā hunālika* ['What is there'], Cairo: al-Muqaṭṭam 1896.

[Nabhānī, Taqī al-Dīn al-] *Min manshūrāt ḥizb al-taḥrīr, al-khilāfa* ['The Caliphate'], n.p., n.d., [1953].

Nabhānī, Taqī al-Dīn al-, *al-Daula al-islāmīya* ['The Islamic State'], no place or year [1953].

——*al-Tafkīr* ['Thinking'], n.p., n.d. [after 1953].

——*Ḥizb al-Taḥrīr al-Islāmī, muqaddimat al-dustūr au al-asbāb al-mūjiba lahū* [Prolegomenon of the Constitution or the reasons leading to it'], n.p. [2]1382 [1963].

Nadwī, Abū'l-Ḥasan 'Alī al-, *al-Muslimūn wa-qaḍīyat Filasṭīn* ['Muslims and the Palestine problem'], [Beirut: no publisher mentioned] [2]1391 [1971].

——*Mā-dhā khasira al-'ālam bi-nhiṭāṭ al-muslimīn* ['What the world has lost through the decline of the Muslims'], Beirut: Dār al-Kitāb al'Arabī [6]1965.

——*Mudhakkirāt sā'iḥ fī sh-sharq al-'arabī* ['Memories of a visitor to the Arab East'] Cairo: Jamā'at al-Azhar 1954.

Naṣirī al-Ṣalāwi, Aḥmad b. Khālid al-, *Kitāb al-istiqṣā' li akhbār duwal al-maghrib al-aqṣā* ['Inquiry into the news about the lands of Morocco'], 4 vols, Cairo ([2]Casablanca: Dār al-Kitāb) 1312/1894/95; [2]1956.

Nawwāb Ṣafawī, Sayyid Mujtabā, *Jāmi'a wa-ḥukumal-i islāmī* ['Unity and the Islamic government'], Qum: Markaz-i Barrasihā-yi Islāmī [1950, [2]1953].

Nūrī [Ileri], Jalāl, *Ittihād-ï Islām. Islāmiñ māḍīsi ḥālī istiqbālī* ['Union of Islam – Past, present and future of Islam'], Istanbul: Yeñī 'uthmānlï Mat'ba'asï 1331 [1913].

Qaraḍāwī, Yūsuf al-, *al-Ḥulūl al-mustaurada wa-kaifa janat al-sa'ūdīya li-l-ḥujjāj* ['Imported solutions and how they have damaged our nation'], Cairo: Wahba137 [1978].

Qūṭānī, Fahd al-, *Majzarat Makka – Qiṣṣat al-madhbaḥa al-sa'ūdīya li-l-ḥujjāj* ['The Slaughter-house of Mecca – the story of the Saudi massacre of pilgrims'], London: aṣ-Ṣafā [2]1409 [1988].

Quṭb, Sayyid, *al-'Adāla al-ijtimā'īya wa-l-Islām* ['Social justice and Islam'], Cairo 1949.

——*Fī ẓilāl al-qur'ān* ['In the shadow of the Koran'], I–VI, Beirut:
Dār al-Shurūq [8]1399 [1979].

——*Ma'ālim fī l-ṭarīq* ['Milestones'], Cairo 1964; Beirut: Dār al-Shurūq [10]1403 [1983].

——*Ṭifl min al-qarya* ['A child from the village'] Beirut: Dār al-Shurūq 1393 [1973].

Rābiṭat al-'Ālam al-Islamī, *al-Radd al-shāfī 'alā muftarayāt al-Qadhdhāfī* [A decisive answer to Qaddafi's lies'], Mecca: RAI 1402 [1982].

Raiḥānī, Amīn al-, *Mulūk al-'arab. Riḥlat fī l-bilād al-'arabiya* ['The kings of the Arabs – Travels in Arab countries], Beirut: Dār al-Jail [8]1987 [written in &924].

——*Tārīkh Najd al-ḥadīth wa-mulḥaqātihī* ['History of the new Najd and its dependencies'], Beirut: al-'Ilmīya li-Yūsuf Ṣadr [1928].

——*al-Maghrib al-aqṣā* ['Morocco'], Beirut [2]1975 [written in 1939].

——*Qalb al-'Irāq. Siyāḥa wa-siyāsa wa-adab wa-tārīkh* ['The upheaval in Iraq – Tourism, politics, culture and history'], Beirut: Bāb Idrīs 1939, [2]1957.

Riḍā, Muḥammad Rashīd [ed.], *Majmū'at al-ḥadīth al-najdīya* [Collection of Najd Traditions'], Cairo: al-Manār 1342 [1923/24].

Riḍā, Muḥammad Rashīd, *Riḥlat al-imām* (...) ['Travels of the Imām ... '], ed. Yūsuf Ībish, Beirut 1979.

Riḍā, Muḥammad Rashīd, *Tārikh al-ustad al-imām Muḥammad 'Abduh* ['Personal story of the Imām Muḥammad 'Abduh'], I–III, Cairo: al-Manār, (I) 1350 [1931], (II)[2]1344 [1925/26, (III) 1324 [1906].

——*al-Khilāfa au al-imāma al-'uẓmā* [The caliphate or the supreme imamate'] Cairo: al-Manār 1341 [1923].

Rif'at Bāshā, Ibrāhīm, *Mir'āt al-ḥaramain au al-riḥlāt al-ḥijāzīya wa-l-ḥajj wa-mashā'iruhū al-dīnīya* [The mirror of Mecca or Hejazi travels, the pilgrimage and its places of worship (...)', Cairo: Maṭba'at Dār al-Kutub al-Miṣrīya 1344 (1925). Photomechanical print, Beirut: Dār al-Ma'ārif, n.d.

Sa'īd, Amīn, *al-Yaman tārīkhuhu al-siyāsīya mundhu istaqlālihī fī-qarn al-thālith al-hijrī*, [The Yemen. Its political history since its independence in the 3rd century of the Hijra'], Cairo: 'Īsā al-Bābī al-Ḥalabī 1378 [1959].

——*al-Thaura al-'arabīya al-kubrā* ['The Great Arab Revolution'], I–III, Cairo: 'Īsā al-Bābī al-Ḥalabī 1933.

Sa'īd, Nāṣir al-, *Tārikh Al Sa'ūd* [History of the Saudis'], [Part I], [Beirut?] Manshūrāt Ittiḥād Sha'b al-Jazīra al-Arabīya, n.p., n.d. [after 1980].

Ṣadr, Muḥammad Bāqir al-, *Falsafatunā* ['Our Philosophers'], Beirut: Dār al-Ta'āruf 1406 [1986].

——*Iqtiṣādunā* ['Our Economy'], Beirut: Dār al-Ta'āruf1402 [1982].

Shaikh, Taufīq al-, *al-Bitrūl wa-siyāsa fī l-mamlaka al-'arabīya al-sa'ūdīya* ['Oil and politics in the Kingdom of Saudi Arabia'] London: Dār aṣ-Ṣafā 1988.

Sharī'atī, 'Alī, *Kawīr* [The desert'], Mashhad 1349 [1970/71].

——*Maktab-i wasīṭa* ['The Median School'], Mashhad 1335 [1955/56].

[Saudi Arabia] Idārat al-'Alāqāt al-'Āmma bi-l-Ḥaras al-Waṭanī, *Jarīmat al-'aṣr, sijill li-mawāqif al-'ulamā' wa-l hai'āt al-dīnīya*, ['The Crime of the century. A record of the points of view of the *ulama* and religious institutions'], Riyadh,al-Ḥaras al-Waṭani 1411 [1990].

——Wizārat al-Khārijīya, *Majmū'at al-mu'āhadāt min 1341–1370/1922–1951* ['Collection of agreements of (...)'], Jeddah: Dār al-Iṣfafānī [3]1376/1957.

Sibā'ī, Muṣṭafā al-, *Ishtirākīyat al-Islām* ['Islam's socialism'] Cairo: al-Qaumīya [2]1960, p. 195 [1st ed. Damascus: al-Jāmī'a 1959].

Sijill mu'tamar jam'īyat al-'ulama al-muslimīn al-jazā'irīyīn al-mun'aqid binādī t-taraqqī bi-l-'āṣima fī sabtambar sanat 1935 ['Records of the Conference of the Association of Muslim Algerian Ulama held in September 1935 at the Progress Club of the capital'], Constantine: al-Maṭba'a al-Islāmīya (no year).

Tha'ālibī, 'Abd al-'Aẓiz al-, *Khalfīyāt al-mu'tamar al-Islāmī bi-l-Quds 1350/1931* ['Inside information about the Islamic Conference in Jerusalem'] Beirut: al-Gharb al-Islāmī 1408 [1988].

Ṭāhā, Maḥmūd Muḥammad, *al-Risāla al-thānīya min al-Islām* ['The second message of Islam'], Omdurman: al-Ikhwān al-jumhūriyūn [1971].

Ṭahṭāwī, Rifā'a Rāfi' al-, *Kitāb al-murshid al-amīn li-l-banāt wa-l-banīn* ['The safe guide for girls and boys'], in id., *al-A'māl al-kāmila*, ed. by Muḥammad 'Ammāra, II, Beirut: al-Mu'assasa al-Arabīya 1973, pp. 251–767.

Ṭaliqanı, Maḥmud, *Islām wa-mālikıyat* ['Islam and Ownership'], Tehran 1330 [1951], 4th ed. 1344 [1965], transl. as Seyyed Mahmood Taleqani, *Islam and Ownership*, Lexington, Kent.: Mazdā 1983.

Taqī, Ṣāḥib, *al-Wajh al-ākhar li-aḥdāth Makka al-damīya* ['The other side of the bloody events of Mecca'], Tehran: Kayhān 1988.

Thānawī, Muḥammad A'lā al-, *Kashshāf iṣṭilāḥāt al-funūn* ['The discoverer of scientific expressions'], Calcutta 1863.

Touré, Ahmad Sékou, *al-Islām dīn al-jamā'a* [Islam – religion of the community'], transl. by Muḥammad al-Bukhārī, Kuwait: al-Shāyi' 1977.

Tunaya, Tarik Zafer, *Türkiye'de Siyasî Partiler* ['Political parties in Turkey'], I–III, Hürriyet Vakfı Yayınlıarı 1984, 1986, 1989.

—— *Türkiyede Siyasî Partiler* 1859–1952 ['Political parties in Turkey'], Istanbul 1952.

Tūrābī, Ḥasan al-, *al-Dīn wa-l-tajdīd* ['Religion and innovation'], Cairo 1984.

Wazīr, Zaid b. 'Alī (ed.), *al-Yaman fī mu'tamar al-'ālam al-islāmī fī dauratihī l-sādisa* ['Yemen at the Sixth Islamic World Conference'], Beirut: Ittiḥād al-Quwā sh-Sha'bīya al-Yamanīya 1965.

Yegen, Walī al-Dīn, *al-Ma'lūm wa-l-majhūl* ['The known and the unknown'], I–II, Cairo: Maṭba'at al-Sha'b [2]1911.

Zaidān, Jurjī, *Tārikh al-tamaddun al-islāmī* ['History of Islamic civilization'], vols I–V, Cairo: al-Hilāl [2]1914, [3]1920, [3]1922.

Zāwī, al-Ṭāhir Aḥmad al-, *Jihād al-abṭāl fī Ṭarāblus al-gharb* ['The just war of the heroes in Tripoli'], repr. Beirut 1393 [1973].

Ziriklī, Ḥair al-Dīn al-, *al-A'lām qāmūs tarājim li-ashhur al-rijāl wa-l-nisā' min al-'arab wa-l-musta'ribīn wa-l-mustashriqīn* ['Prominent people. Lexicon of the biographies of famous men and women (…)'], vols I–VIII, Beirut: Dār al-'Ilm li-l-Malāyīn [8]1989.

Works in Other Languages

Abdel-Malek, Anouar, *Egypt: Military Society; The Army Regime, the Left and Social Change under Nasser*, New York: 1968 (German ed.: *Ägypten: Militärgesellschaft. Das Armeeregime, die Linke und der soziale Wandel unter Nasser*, Frankfurt a. M.: Suhrkamp 1971).

Abir, Mordechai, *Saudi Arabia: government, society and the gulf crisis*, London; New York: Routledge, 1996.

Aboujaoude, Joseph, *Les partis politiques au Liban*, Kaslik: Université Saint-Esprit 1985.

Abu-Lughod, Janet L., *Rabat. Urban Apartheid in Morocco*, Princeton, N. J.: Cambridge University Press 1980.

Addi, Lahouari, 'Algeria's Democracy between the Islamists and the Elite', MERIP 175,

(March–April 1992), pp. 36–8.

—— *Les mutations de la société algérienne: famille et lien social dans l'algérie contemporaine*, Paris: ed. la Découverte, 1999.

Ahmad, Aziz, *Islamic Modernism in India and Pakistan, 1857-1964*, London: Oxford University Press 1967.

Ahmed, Akbar: *Islam Today: A Short Introduction to the Muslim World*, London: I. B. Tauris, 1999.

Ahmed, Akbar S., *Postmodernism and Islam. Predicament and Promise*, London: Routledge 1992.

Ajmar, Laura Cabria/Marina Calloni (eds), *L'altra metà della luna. Capire l'islam contemporaneo*, Genoa: Marietti 1993.

Akhavi, Shahrough, *Religion and Politics in Contemporary Iran: Clergy–State Relations in the Pahlavî Period*, Albany, N. Y.: State University of New York Press 1980.

Akiner, Shirin, *Islamic Peoples of the Soviet Union*, London: Kegan Paul 1983.

Albertini, Rudolf von (ed.), *Moderne Kolonialgeschichte*, Cologne: Kiepenhauer & Witsch 1970.

al-Ahnaf, Mustafa/Bernhard Botiveau/Franck Frégosi, *L'Algérie par ses islamistes*, Paris: Karthala 1991.

al-Azmeh, Aziz: *Islams and modernities*, London: Verso 1996 [1993].

Algar, Hamid (ed.), *Islam and Revolution. Writings and Declarations of Imam Khomeini*, Berkeley, Cal.: Mizan Press 1981.

Ali, Syed Ameer, 'The Caliphate: A Historical and Juridical Sketch', *The Contemporary Review*, 107/594 (June 1915), pp. 681–94.

—— *A Critical Examination of the Life and Teachings of Muhammad (The Spirit of Islam)*, London: 1873, Allen [2]1891, Methuen 1965.

Amin, Samir, *The Arab Nation*, London: Zed 1978; (French ed.: *La nation arabe. Nationalisme et luttes de classes*, Paris: Éd. de minuit 1976).

—— *The Maghreb in the Modern World*, Harmondsworth: Penguin, 1970; (French ed.: *Le maghreb moderne*, Paris: Éd. de minuit 1970).

Anderson, Irvine H., ARAMCO, *The United States and Saudi Arabia. A Study of the Dynamics of Foreign Oil Policy, 1933–1950*, Princeton, N. J.: Princeton University Press, 1981.

Ansari, Hamied, 'Sectarian Conflict in Egypt and the Political Expediency of Religion', *MEJ* 38 (1984), pp. 397–418.

—— *Egypt. The Stalled Society*, Albany, N. Y.: State University of New York Press 1986.

Anon., *La Syrie et le Liban sous l'occupation et le Mandat français, 1919–1927*.

Antonius, Georg, *The Arab Awakening. The Story of the Arab National Movement*, London: Hamilton 1938, [2]1945, repr. New York 1965.

Arab Information Center, *Basic Documents of the League of Arab States*, New York 1955.

Arjomand, Sa'id Amir, *The Turban and the Crown. The Islamic Revolution in Iran*, New York, Oxford: Oxford University Press 1988.

Arnon, Arie (et al.): *The Palestinian Economy. Between Imposed Integration and voluntary Separation*, Leiden: Brill, 1997.

Asad, Muhammad, *The Principle of State and Government in Islam*, Berkeley, Cal.:

University of California Press 1961.
Astigarraga, Isabelle: *Tchétchénie: un peuple sacrifié*, Paris: L'Harmattan, 2000.
Avery, Peter (et al., eds), *The Cambridge History of Iran, vol. 7. From Nadir Shah to the Islamic Republic*, Cambridge: Cambridge University Press 1991, esp. pp. 174–293, 426–56, 608–701, 723–869.
Ayubi, Nazih N., *Political Islam. Religion and Politics in the Arab World*, London: Routledge 1991.
Azimi, Fakhreddin, *Iran. The Crisis of Democracy (1941–1953)*, London: Tauris 1989.
Bagley, F. R. C. (ed. and transl.), *The Muslim World. A Historical Survey, IV: Modern Times*, fasc. I, Leiden: Brill 1981.
Bahadur, Karim, *The Jama'at-i-Islami of Pakistan. Political Thought and Political Action*, New Delhi: Chetana Publ. 1977.
Baljon, J. M. S., *Modern Muslim Koran-Interpretation, (1880–1960)*, Leiden: Brill 1961.
Batatu, Hanna, *The Old Social Classes and the Revolutionary Movements of Iraq. A Study of Iraq's Old Landed and Commercial Classes and of its Communists, Ba'thists, and Free Officers*, Princeton, N. J.: Princeton University Press 1978.
Baumgarten, Helga, *Palästina, Befreiung in den Staat. Die palästinesische Nationalbewegung seit 1948*, Frankfurt a. M.: Suhrkamp 1991.
Bayat, Mangol, *Iran's First Revolution. Shi'ism and the Constitutional Revolution of 1905–1909*, New York: Oxford University Press 1991.
Bechthold, Peter K., *Politics in the Sudan. Parliamentary and Military Rule in an Emerging African Nation*, New York: Praeger 1976.
Becker, Seymour, *Russia's Protectorates in Central Asia. Bukhara and Khiwa, 1865–1924*, Cambridge, Mass.: Harvard University Press 1968.
Behrmann, Lucy, *Muslim Brotherhoods and Politics in Senegal*, Cambridge, Mass.: Harvard University Press 1970.
Benda, Harry J., *The Crescent and the Rising Sun. Indonesian Islam under Japanese Occupation, 1942–1945*, The Hague: Van Hoeve 1958.
Bennigsen, Alexandre A./S. Enders Wimbush, *Muslim National Communism in the Soviet Union. A Revolutionary Strategy for the Colonial World*, Chicago: University of Chicago Press 1979.
Bennigsen, Alexandre and Chantal Lemercier Quelquejay, *Le soufi et le commissaire. Les confréries musulmanes en URSS*, Paris: Seuil 1986.
——*La Presse et le mouvement national chez les Musulmans de Russie avant 1920*, Paris: Mouton 1964.
—— *L'Islam en Union Soviétique*, Paris: Payot 1968.
—— *Sultan Galiev*, Paris: Fayard 1986.
Benvenisti, Meron, 'Das "Westbank Data Project". Eine Untersuchung der israelischen Politik in Westbank und Gaza-Streifen', in Jan Metzger (ed.), *Auf dem Weg zur Annexion. Die Zukunft von Westbank und Gaza-Streifen nach zwei Jahrzehnten israelischer Besatzung*, Berlin: Deutsch–israelischer Arbeitskreis für Frieden 1986, pp. 9–108.
Bérard, Victor, *La révolution turque*, Paris: Armand Colin 1909.
Bergmann, Kristina, *Filmkultur und Filmindustrie in Ägypten*, Darmstadt:

Wissenschaftliche Buchgesellschaft 1993.

Berkes, Niyazi, *The Development of Secularism in Turkey*, Montreal: McGill University Press 1964.

Bernard, Augustin, *L'Afrique du Nord pendant la guerre*, Paris: PUF [New Haven: Yale University Press] 1926.

Berque, Jacques, *Egypt: Imperialism and Revolution*, London: 1972. (French ed. *L'Egypte, Impérialisme et révolution*, Paris: Gallimard 1967).

Bidwell, Robin, *Morocco under Colonial Rule. French Administration of Tribal Areas, 1912–56*, London: Frank Cass 1973.

Bierschenk, Thomas, *Weltmarkt, Stammesgesellschaft und Staatsformation in Südostarabien (Sultanat Oman)*, Saarbrücken: Breitenbach 1984.

Binder, Leonard, *Religion and Politics in Pakistan*, Berkeley, Cal.: University of California Press 1961.

—— *Iran: Political Development in a Changing Society*, Berkeley, Cal.: University of California Press 1962.

—— *In a Moment of Enthusiasm. Political Power and the Second Stratum in Egypt*, Chicago: University of Chicago Press 1978.

—— *Islamic Liberalism: A Critique of Development Ideologies*, Chicago, University of Chicago Press 1988.

—— *The Ideological Revolution in the Middle East*, New York: Wiley 1964, [2]New York: Krieger 1979.

Birks, J. S./C. A. Sinclair, *International Migration and Development in the Arab Region*, Geneva: ILO 1980.

Blussé, L. et al. (eds), *India and Indonesia from the 1920s to the 1950s; The Origins of Planning*, Leiden: Brill 1987.

Bodansky, Yossef: *bin Laden: the man who declared war on America*, Rocklin, Calif.: Forum, 1999.

Boland, B. J., *The Struggle of Islam in Modern Indonesia*, The Hague: Nijhoff 1970.

Bonné, Alfred, *The Economic Development of the Middle East*, London: Kegan Paul 1943, repr. 1945.

Braune, Walther, *Der islamische Orient zwischen Vergangenheit und Zukunft. Eine geschichtstheologische Analyse seiner Stellung in der Weltsituation*, Bern, Munich: Francke 1960.

Brown, Carl L: *Diplomacy in the Middle East: The International Relations of Regional and Outside Powers*, London: I. B. Tauris, 2001.

Browne, Edward G., *The Persian Revolution 1905–1909*, London: Frank Cass 1966 (1st ed. Cambridge 1910).

Brugman, J., *An Introduction to the History of Modern Arabic Literature in Egypt*, Leiden: Brill 1984.

Buchan, James, 'The Return of the Ikhwan 1979', in David Holden/Richard Johns, *The House of Sa'ud. The Rise and Rule of the Most Powerful Dynasty in the Arab World*, New York: Holt, Rinehart and Winston 1981, pp. 511–26.

Buheiry, Marwan R., 'Anthony Eden and the Arabs: The Failure of a Policy', in id., *The Formation and Perception of the Modern Arab World*, ed. Lawrence I. Conrad,

Princeton, N. J.: Darwin Press 1989, pp. 171–67.

Canfield, Robert L., '*Afghanistan: The Trajectory of Internal Alignments*', *MEJ* 43 (1989), pp. 635–48.

Carré, Olivier (ed.), *Le mouvement national palestinien*, Paris: Gallimard 1977.

Carré, Olivier/Gérard Michaud, *Les Frères musulmans (1928–1982)*, Paris: Gallimard 1983

Carré, Olivier, *L'idéologie palestinienne de résistance. Analyse de textes 1964–70*, Paris: Colin 1972.

—— *L'Islam laïque ou le retour à la grande tradition*, Paris: Armand Colin, 1993.

—— *Mystique et politique. Lecture révolutionnaire du Coran par Sayyid Qutb, Frère musulman radical*, Paris: Ed. du Cerf 1984.

Castagné, Joseph, *Les Basmatchis. Le mouvement national des Indigènes d'Asie Centrale*, Paris: Ernest Leroux 1925.

Cayrac-Blanchard, Françoise, *Indonésie: L'armée et le pouvoir de la révolution au développement*, Paris: L'Hartmattan, 1991.

Chambord, Comte de, *Journal de Voyage en Orient 1861*, Paris: Tallandier 1984.

Charnay, Jean-Paul, *Islamic Culture and Socio-Economic Change*, Leiden: Brill 1981.

Childs, Timothy W., *Italo–Turkish Diplomacy and the War over Libya, 1911–1912*, Leiden: Brill 1990.

Chubin, Shahram/Charles Tripp, *Iran and Iraq at War*, Boulder, Col.: Westview 1988.

Cleveland, William L., *Islam against the West. Shakib Arslan and the Campaign for Islamic Nationalism*, London: al-Saqi 1985.

Colonna, Fanny, 'Cultural Resistance and Religious Legitimacy in Colonial Algeria', *Economy and Society* 3 (1974), pp. 233–52.

Commandement de la IVme Armée, Le, *La vérité sur la question syrienne*, Istanbul 1916.

Cooper, Mark N., *The Transformation of Egypt*, London: Croom Helm 1982.

Dahm, Bernhard, '*Sukarnos Kampf um Indonesiens Unabhängigkeit. Werdegang und Ideen eines asiatischen Nationalisten*, Frankfurt a. M.: Metzner 1966.

Darmaputera, Eke, *Pancasila and the Search for Identity and Modernity in Indonesian Society: a Cultural and Ethical Analysis*, Leiden: Brill 1988.

Dawletschin-Linder, Camilla, *Die Türkei und Ägypten in der Weltwirtschaftskrise, 1929–1933*, Wiesbaden: Steiner 1989.

Dawn, C. Ernest, *From Ottomanism to Arabism: Essays on the Origins of Arab Nationalism*, Urbana, Ill.: University of Illinois Press 1973.

De Koninck, Rudolphe, *Aceh in the Time of Iskandar Muda*, Banda Aceh: Pusat Dokumentasi dan Informasi Aceh 1977.

Dia, Mamadou, *Islam et civilisations négro–africaines*, Dakar: Les Nouvelles Editions Africaines 1980.

Dierke, Kai W.: *Krieg und Ordnung: eine Studie über regionale Kriege und regionale Ordnung am Beispiel des Nahen Ostens*, Frankfurt a.M., Bern [etc.], Peter Lang, 1996.

Dijk, Kees van: *A country in despair: Indonesia between 1997 and 2000*, Leiden: KITLV Press, 2001.

Djait, Hichem, *Europe and Islam, Cultures and Modernity*, Berkely, Cal.: University of

California Press 1985.

Djuvara, T. G., *Cent projets de partage de la Turquie (1281–1913)*, Paris: Félix Alcan 1914.

Dorronsoro, Gilles: *La révolution afghane: des communistes aux tâlebân*, Paris: Editions Karthala, 2000.

Drague, Georges, *Esquisse d'histoire religieuse du Maroc. Confréries et Zaouias*, Paris: Peyrounet [1952].

Droz, Bernard/Evelyne Lever, *Histoire de la guerre d'Algérie, 1954–1962*, Paris: Seuil [2]1984.

Dunlop, John B.: *Russia confronts Chechnya: roots of a separatist conflict*, Cambridge: Cambridge University Press, 1998.

Ehlers, Eckart, *Iran. Grundzüge einer geographischen Landeskunde*, Darmstadt: Wissenschaftliche Buchgesellschaft 1980.

Eickelman, Dale F.: *The Middle East and Central Asia: An Anthropological Approach, 3rd ed.*: Upper Saddle River (N. J.): Prentice Hall, 1998.

Elsenhans, Hartmut, *Frankreichs Algerienkrieg1954–1962. Entkolonisierungs-versuch einer kapitalistischen Metropole. Zum Zusammenbruch der Kolonialreiche*, Munich: Carl Hanser 1974.

Enayat, Hamid, *Modern Islamic Political Thought*, London: Macmillan 1982.

Ende, Werner/Udo Steinbach (eds), *Der Islam in der Gegenwart. Entwicklung und Ausbreitung – Staat, Politik und Recht – Kultur und Religion*, Munich: Beck 1984, [2]1989.

Ende, Werner, 'Iraq in World War I: The Turks, The Germans and the Shi'ite Mujtahids' call for Jihad', in *Proceedings of the 9th Congress of the UEAI, Amsterdam 1978*, ed. Rudolph Peters, Leiden 1981, pp. 57–71.

—— *Arabische Nation und Islamische Geschichte. Die Umayyaden im Urteil arabischer Autoren des 20. Jahrhunderts*, Beirut/Wiesbaden: Steiner 1977.

Enver Pascha, *Um Tripolis*, Berlin: Bruckmann 1918.

Ergil, Dogu, *Social History of the Turkish National Struggle, 1919–22*, Lahore: Sind Sagar Academy, n.d.

Esman, Milton J./Itamar Rabinovich (eds), *Ethnicity, Pluralism, and the State in the Middle East*, Ithaca, N. Y.: Cornell University Press 1988.

Etienne, Bruno, *Algérie. Culture et révolution*, Paris: Seuil 1977.

Evans-Pritchard, *The Sanusi of Cyrenaica*, Oxford: Oxford University (Clarendon) Press1949 [and reprints].

Faensen, Johannes, *Die albanische Natonalbewegung*, Berlin: (on commission with) Harrassowitz 1980.

Faksh, Mahmud A.: *The future of Islam in the Middle East: fundamentalism in Egypt, Algeria, and Saudi Arabia*, Westport (Conn.): Praeger, 1997.

Falaturi, Abdaldjavad (ed.), *Der islamische Orient: Grundzüge einer Geschichte*, Cologne: Islamische wissenschaftliche Akademie, 1994.

Fandy, Mamoun: *Saudi Arabia and the Politics of Dissent*, New York: St. Martin's Press, 1999.

Fanon, Frantz, 'The North African Syndrome', in I. William Zartman (ed.), *Man State and Society in the Contemporary Maghrib*, London: Pall Mall Press 1973, pp. 74–82.

Farouk-Sluglett, Marion/Peter Sluglett, *Iraq Since 1958*, London: I. B. Tauris, 1990 (revised paperback edition).

Federspiel, Howard, *Persatuan Islam. Islamic Reform in Twentieth Century Indonesia*, Ithaca, N. Y.: Cornell University Press 1970.

Findley, Carter W., *Bureaucratic Reform in the Ottoman Empire: The Sublime Porte 1789–1922*, Princeton, N. J.: Princeton University Press 1980.

—— *Ottoman Civil Officialdom: A Social History*, Princeton N. J.: Princeton University Press 1989.

Fischbach, Michael R.: *State, Society and Land in Jordan*, Leiden: Brill, 2000.

Fisher, Michel M. J./Mehdi Abedi, *Debating Muslims. Cultural Dialogues in Postmodernity and Tradition*, Madison, Wi.: The University of Wisconsin Press 1990.

Flores, Alexander, *Intifada. Aufstand der Palästinenser*, Rotbuch, Berlin 1988.

—— *Nationalismus und Sozialismus im arabischen Osten. Kommunistische Partei und arabische Nationalbewegung in Palästina 1919–1948*, Münster: Periferia 1980.

Freedman, Amy L.: *Political participation and ethnic minorities: Chinese overseas in Malaysia, Indonesia, and the United States*, New York: Routledge, 2000.

Freitag, Ulrike, *Geschichtsschreibung in Syrien, 1920–1990. Zwischen Wissenschaft und Ideologie*, Hamburg: Deutsches Orient-Institut 1991.

Gadant, Monique, *Islam et nationalisme en Algérie d'après 'El Moudjahid' organe central du FLN de 1956 à 1962*, Paris: L'Harmattan 1988.

Ganiage, Jean: *Histoire contemporaine du Maghreb*, Paris: Arthème Fayard, 1994.

Gavin, R. J., *Aden under British Rule, 1839–1967*, London: Pall Mall 1968, [2]1975.

Geertz, Clifford, *Islam Observed, Religious Development in Morocco and Indonesia*, New Haven: Yale University Press 1968.

Gellner, Ernest, *Postmodernism, Reason and Religion*, London: Routledge 1992.

—— *Muslim Society*, Cambridge: Cambridge University Press 1981.

Gershoni, Israel/James P. Jankowski, *Egypt, Islam, and the Arabs. The Search for Egyptian Nationhood, 1900–1930*, New York: Oxford University Press 1986.

Ghani, Cyrus: *Iran and the Rise of Reza Shah: From Qajar Collapse to Pahlavi Power*, London: I. B. Tauris, 2000.

Ghazzali, Muhammad al-, *Our Beginning in Wisdom* [*min huna na'lam*], transl. by Isma'il R. el-Faruqi, Washington: American Council of Learned Societies 1953.

Gibb, Hamilton Alexander, *Whither Islam? A Survey of Modern Movements in the Moslem World*, London: Gollancz 1932.

Gilmartin, David, *Empire and Islam. Punjab and the Making of Pakistan*, Berkeley, Cal.: University of California Press 1988.

Gilsenan, Michael, *Recognizing Islam. An Anthropologist's Approach*, London: I. B. Tauris 2000 (revised edition).

Gödel, Karl-Heinrich, *Moderne schiitische Politik und Staatsidee nach Taufiq al-Fulaiki, Muhammad Jawad Mujniya, Ruhollah Khomeyni*, Opladen: Leske 1984.

Gohar, M. J.: *Taliban*, Oxford: Oxford University Press, 2001.

Gomaa, Ahmed M., *The Foundation of the League of Arab States. Wartime Diplomacy and Inter-Arab Politics 1941 to 1945*, London: Longman 1977.

Gormsen, Erdmann/Thimm, Andreas (eds), *Zivilgesellschaft und Staat in der Dritten Welt*, Mainz: University of Mainz 1992.

Graevenitz, George von, *Geschichte des italienisch–türkischen Krieges.* Parts 1–3, Berlin: R. Eisenschmidt 1912–1914.

Gregorian, Vartan, *The Emergence of Modern Afghanistan. Politics of Religion and Modernization, 1880–1946*, Stanford, Cal.: Stanford University Press 1969.

Grevemeyer, Jan-Heeren, *Afghanistan. Sozialer Wandel und Staat im 20. Jahrhundert*, Berlin: Express Edition 1987.

[Great Britain] Naval Intelligence Division, *Algeria* vol. I–II, London, 1944 [BR 505 a].

—— *Tunisia*, London 1945 [BR 523].

—— *Iraq and the Persian Gulf*, London 1944 [BR 524].

—— *Netherlands East Indies*, vols I–II, London 1944 [BR 518 a].

Grunebaum, Gustav E. von (ed.), *Studien zum Kulturbild und Selbstverständnis des Islams*, Zurich: Artemis 1969.

—— *Der Islam II. Die islamischen Reiche nach dem Fall von Konstantinopel*, Frankfurt a. M.: Fischer 1971.

Guth, Stephan, *Zeugen einer Endzeit. Fünf Schriftsteller zum Umbruch in der ägyptischen Gesellschaft nach 1970*, Berlin: Schwarz 1992.

Hagen, Gottfried, *Die Türkei im Ersten Weltkrieg. Flugblätter und Flugschriften in arabischer, persischer und osmanisch–türkischer Sprache […]*, Frankfurt a. M.: Lang 1990.

Hairi, Abdul-Hadi, *Shīʿism and Constitutionalism in Iran. A Study of the Role Played by the Persian Residents of Iraq in Iranian Politics*, Frankfurt a. M.: Lang 1990.

Hajit, Baimirza, *Turkestan im XX. Jahrhundert*, Darmstadt: Leske 1956.

Halliday, Fred, *Arabia without Sultans*, Manchester: Penguin 1974.

—— *Iran: Dictatorship and Development*, Harmondsworth: Penguin Books 1979. (German ed.: *Iran. Analyse einer Gesellschaft im Entwicklungskrieg*, Berlin: Rotbuch 1979).

—— *Islam and the Myth of Confrontation: Religion and Politics in the Middle East*, London: I. B. Tauris, 1996.

—— *Nation and religion in the Middle East*, London: Saqi Books, 2000.

Halm, Heinz, *Die Schia*, Darmstadt: Wissenschaftliche Buchgesellschaft 1988.

Hanna, Williard A., *Sequel to Colonialism. The 1957–1960 Foundations for Malaysia*, New York: American Universities Field Staff 1965 [1st ed. 1957].

Hanf, Theodor, '*Coexistence in Wartime Lebanon*, London: Centre for Lebanese Studies and I. B. Tauris 1993.

Harbi, Mohammed, *Aux origines du FLN: le populisme révolutionnaire en Algérie*, Paris: Christian Bourgeois 1975.

Hardy, P., *The Muslims of British–India*, Cambridge: At the University Press 1972.

Harub, Halid: *Hamas: political thought and practice*, Washington, DC: Institute for Palestine Studies, 2000.

Heper, Metin/Raphael Israeli (eds), *Islam and Politics in the Modern Middle East*, London: Croom Helm 1984.

Heyd, Uriel, *Foundations of Turkish Nationalism. The Life and Teachings of Ziya Gökalp*, London: Luzac, Harvill 1950.

Hillel, Daniel J.: *Rivers of Eden: the struggle for water and the quest for peace in the Middle East*, New York [etc.]: Oxford University Press, 1994.

Hodgson, Marshall G. S., *The Venture of Islam. Conscience and History in a World Civilization, vol. 3. The Gunpowder Empires and Modern Times*, Chicago: University of Chicago Press 1974.

Holden, David/Richard Johns, *The House of Sa'ud. The Rise and Rule of the Most Powerful Dynasty in the Arab World*, New York: Holt, Rinehart and Winston 1981.

Holt, P. M. et al., (eds), *The Cambridge History of Islam*, vols 1–2, Cambridge: Cambridge University Press 1970, in four vols 1977.

Holt, P. M., *A Modern History of the Sudan. From the Funj Sultanate to the Present Day*, London: Weidenfeld and Nicolson 1961, 3rd ed. 1974.

Horne, Alistaire, *A Savage War of Peace: Algeria 1954–1962*, Harmondsworth: 1979.

Horten, Max, *Die kulturelle Entwicklungsfähigkeit des Islam auf geistigem Gebiete*, Bonn: Friedrich Cohen 1915.

Hourani, Albert, *A History of the Arab Peoples*, Cambridge, Mass.: Belknap 1991.

—— *Arabic Thought in the Liberal Age, 1798–1939*, Oxford: Oxford University Press 1962. [2]Cambridge: Cambridge University Press 1983.

Hurewitz, J. C., *The Middle East and North Africa in World Politics. A Documentary Record*, I–III, New Haven: Yale University Press [2]1975–1985.

Hussein, Mahmoud [Pseud.], *L'Egypte. Lutte de classes et libération nationale. I. 1945–1967*, Paris: Maspero 1975.

Ibrahim, Ferhad, Heidi Wedel (ed.): *Probleme der Zivilgesellschaft im Vorderen Orient*, Opladen: Leske und Budrich, 1995.

Ibrahim, Saad Eddin, *The New Arab Social Order. A Study of the Social Impact of Oil Wealth*, Boulder, Col.: Westview 1982.

Ingram, Edward (ed.), *National and International Politics in the Middle East. Essays in Honour of Elie Kedourie*, London: Frank Cass 1986.

Iqbal, Muhammad, *The Reconstruction of Religious Thought in Islam*, Oxford: Oxford University Press 1932, repr. Lahore: Ashraf 1962.

Islamic Revolution Organization in the Arabian Peninsula: Al-Haram Revolt, [Tehran?] 1401 [1981].

Israeli, Raphael, *Muslims in China. A Study in Cultural Confrontation*, London: Curzon 1980.

Issawi, Charles, *An Economic History of the Middle East and North Africa*, New York: Columbia University Press 1982.

Jahanbakhsh, Forough: *Islam, Democracy and Religious Modermism in Iran (1953-2000)*, Leiden: Brill, 2001

Jankowski, James P., *Egypt's Young Rebels. "Young Egypt": 1933–1952*, Stanford, Cal.: Hoover Inst. Press 1975.

Jauffret, Jean-Charles (ed): *Militaires et guérilla dans la guerre d'Algérie*, Bruxelles: Editions Complexe, 2001.

Johansen, Baber, *Islam und Staat. Abhängige Entwicklung, Verwaltung des Elends und religiöser Antiimperialismus*, Berlin: Argument 1982.

Johannsen, Margret [et al.] (ed.): *Wege aus dem Labyrinth? Friedenssuche in Nahost: Stationen, Akteure, Probleme des nahöstlichen Friedenspozesses*, Baden-Baden: Nomos, 1997.

Julien, Charles-André, *L'Afrique du Nord en marche. Nationalisme musulman et souveraineté française*, Julliard, Paris 1972.

—— *Histoire de l'Algérie contemporaine, II (1871–1954)*, Paris: PUF 1979.

Kahin, Audrey R.: *Rebellion to integration: West Sumatra and the Indonesian polity, 1926-1998*, Amsterdam: Amsterdam University Press, 1999.

Kahin, George McT., *Nationalism and Revolution in Indonesia*, Ithaca, N. Y.: Cornell University Press 1952.

Karrar, Ali S., *The Sufi Orders in the Sudan*, Chicago: Northewestern University Press 1992.

Kazarian, Elias, *Finance and Economic Development. Islamic Banking in Egypt*, Lund: University of Lund 1991.

Kazemi, Farhad/John Waterbury (eds), *Peasants and Politics in the Modern Middle East*, Miami, Fl.: Florida International University Press 1991.

Kazemi, Farhad, 'Peasant Uprisings in Twentieth-Century Iran, Iraq and Turkey' in Kazemi/Waterbury (eds), *Peasants and Politics in the Modern Middle East*, pp. 101–24.

Kedourie, Elie, 'The Surrender of Medina', MES 13 (1977), pp. 124–43.

—— *England and the Middle East. The Destruction of the Ottoman Empire, 1914–1921*, London: Mansell 1987.

—— *Politics in the Middle East*, Oxford: Oxford University Press 1992.

—— *The Chatham House Version and other Middle-Eastern Studies*, Hanover/London: University Press of New England 1984.

Kepel, Gilles: *Jihad*, London: I. B. Tauris, 2002.

Kepel, Gilles/Yann Richard (eds), *Intellectuels et militants de l'Islam contemporain*, Paris: Seuil 1990.

Kerr, Malcolm, *Islamic Reform. The Political and Legal Theories of Muhammad Abduh and Rashid Rida*, Berkeley, Cal.: University of California Press 1966.

Kerr, Malcolm, *The Arab Cold War 1958–1964. A Study of Ideology in Politics*, London: Oxford University Press 1965.

Khadduri, Majid, 'The Scheme of Fertile Crescent Unity. A Study in Inter-Arab Relations' in Richard N. Frye (ed.), *The Near East and the Great Powers*, Cambridge, Mass.: Harvard University Press 1951, pp. 137–77.

Khalidi, Rashid Isma'il, *British Policy towards Syria and Palestine 1906–1914. Study of the antecedents of the Hussein–McMahon Correspondence, the Sykes–Picot Agreement, and the Balfour Declaration, London*: Ithaca 1980 [St. Antony's Middle East Monographs, II].

Khalil, Muhammad, *The Arab States and the Arab League. A Documentary Record*, II, Beirut: Khayats 1962.

Khoury, Philip S./Joseph Kostiner (eds), *Tribes and State Formation in the Middle East*, London: I. B. Tauris, 1990.

Kienle, Eberhard: *A Grand Delusion, Democracy and Economic Reform in Egypt*, London: I. B. Tauris, 2000.

—— *Ba'th v. Ba'th. The Conflict between Syria and Iraq, 1968–1989*, London: I. B. Tauris 1990.

Kindleberger, Charles P., *The World in Depression, 1929–1939*, Berkeley, Cal.: University of California Press 1973.

Knezys, Stasys & Romanas Sedlickas: *The war in Chechnya*, College Station, TX: Texas A&M University Press, 1999.

Kostiner, Joseph, 'Tribe and State Formation in Saudi Arabia', in Philip S. Khoury/ Joseph Kostiner (eds), Tribes and State Formation in the Middle East, London: I. B. Tauris 1990, pp. 226–51.

Kramer, Martin, *Islam Assembled. The Advent of the Muslim Congresses*, New York: Columbia University Press 1986.

Krämer, Gudrun *Gottes Staat als Republik, Reflexionen zeitgenössischer Muslime zu Islam, Menschenrechten und Demokratie*, Baden-Baden: Nomos, 1999.

Kratochwil, Gabi: *Die Berber in der historischen Entwicklung Algeriens von 1949 bis 1990: zur Konstruktion einer ethnischen Identität*, Berlin: Klaus Schwarz Verlag, 1996.

Krikorian, Mesrod K., *Armenians in the Service of the Ottoman Empire, 1860–1908*, London: Routledge 1978.

Kupferschmidt, Uri M., *The Supreme Muslim Council: Islam under the British Mandate for Palestine*, Leiden: Brill 1987.

Kuttner, Thomas, 'Russian Jadidism and the Islamic World. Isma'il Gasprinskii in Cairo 1908', *Cahiers du monde russe et soviétique 16* (1975) 3/4, pp. 383–424.

Laissy, Michel, *Du Panarabisme à la Ligue Arabe. Préface de M. J. Augarde*, Paris: G. P. Maisonneuve 1948.

Lamchichi, Abderrahim, L'islamisme en Algérie, Paris: L'Harmattan 1992.

Landau, Jacob M., *The Politics of Pan-Islam. Ideology and Organization*, Oxford: Clarendon 1992.

—— *Radical Politics in Modern Turkey*, Leiden: Brill 1974.

Lapidus, Ira M., *A History of Islamic Societies*, Cambridge: Cambridge University Press 1988.

—— *Contemporary Islamic Movements in Historical Perspective*, Berkeley, Cal.: University of California 1983 [Policy Papers in International Affairs, 18].

Larcher, Maurice, *La guerre turque dans la guerre mondiale*, Paris: Chiron 1926.

Laurens, Henry: *La question de Palestine*, Vol 1, Paris: Fayard, 1999.

Legge, J. D., *Indonesia*, Englewood Cliffs, N. J.: Prentice Hall 1964.

Lenczowski, George, *The Middle East in World Affairs*, Ithaca, N. Y.: Cornell University Press [4]1980.

Le Postislamisme: *Revue des mondes musulmans et de la Méditerranée*, 85/86, 1999.

Le Tourneau, Roger, *Évolution politique de l'Afrique du Nord musulmane, 1920–1961*, Paris: A. Colin 1962.

Lesch, Ann Mosely: *The Sudan: contested national identities*, Bloomington [etc.]: Indiana University Press: Oxford: James Currey, 1998.

Lewis, Bernard, *The Emergence of Modern Turkey*, 2nd edition, Oxford: Oxford University Press 1975. 1st ed. London, Oxford UP 1961, repr. 1962, with corrections 1965 a. 1966; 2nd ed. Oxford UP 1968, pb. repr. 1975.

Longrigg, S. H., *Iraq, 1900–1950. A Political, Social, and Economic History*, London: Oxford University Press 1953.

Magassouba, Moriba, *L'Islam au Sénégal. Demain les mollahs?*, Paris: Karthala 1985.

Mahjoubi, Ali, *Les origines du mouvement national en Tunisie, 1904–1934*, Tunis: Publ. de l'Université de Tunis 1982.

Majul, Cesar Adib, *The Contemporary Muslim Movement in the Philippines*, Berkeley, Cal.: Mizan 1985.

Makdisi, George, *The Rise of Humanism in Classical Islam and the Christian West, With Special Reference to Scholasticism*, Edinburgh: Edinburgh University Press 1990.

Malik, S. Jamal, 'Islamization in Pakistan 1977–1985. The Ulama and their Places of Learning', *Islamic Studies 28* (1989) I, pp. 5–27.

Malti, Djallal: *La nouvelle guerre d'Algérie: dix clés pour comprendre*, Paris: Editions La Découverte, 1999.

Mardin, Sherif, *The Genesis of Young Ottman Thought. A Study in the Modernization of Turkish Political Ideas*, Princeton, N. J.: Princeton University Press 1962.

Marsden, Peter: *The Taliban: war, religion and the new order in Aghanistan, Karachi [etc.]*: Oxford University Press; London [etc.]: Zed Books, 1999.

Martin, Vanessa, *Islam and Modernism. The Iranian Revolution of 1906*, London: I. B. Tauris 1989.

Martinez, Luis: *The Algerian Civil War* 1990-1998, London: Hurst, 1998.

Mattes, Hanspeter, *Die islamische Bewegung des Senegal zwischen Autonomie und Außenorientierung*, Hamburg: Ed.Wuqûf 1989.

Maududi, Abul A'la, *Fundamentals of Islam*, Lahore: Islam. Publ., 1980 [1st ed. 1975].

—— *Die Politik und das Öl im Nahen Osten, I–II*, Stuttgart: Klett 1980, 1990.

McDowall, David: *A Modern History of the Kurds*, London: I. B. Tauris, 2000.

Merad, Ali, *Le réformisme musulman en Algérie de 1925 à 1940: Essai d'histoire religieuse et sociale*, Paris: Mouton 1967.

Merad, Ghani, *La littérature algérienne d'expression française: Approches socio–culturelles*, Paris: Oswald 1976.

Midel, Monika, *Fulbe und Deutsche in Adamaua (Nord-Kamerun) 1809–1916*, Frankfurt a. M.: Lang 1990.

Milani, Abbas: *The Persian Sphinx: Amir Abbas Hoveyda and the Riddle of the Iranian Revolution*, London: I. B. Tauris, 1996.

Minault, Gail, *The Khilafat Movement. Religious Symbolism and Political Mobilization in India*, New York: Columbia University Press 1982.

Mitchell, Richard P., *The Society of the Muslim Brothers*, London: Oxford University Press 1969.

Moaddel, Mansoor (ed.): *Contemporary debates in Islam: an anthology of modernist and fundamentalist thought*, Basingstoke: Macmillan, 2000.

Moin, Baqer: *Khomeini: Life of the Ayatollah*, London: I. B. Tauris, 1999.

Mommsen, Wolfgang J. (ed.), *Das Ende der Kolonialreiche. Dekolonisierung und die Politik der Großmächte*, Frankfurt a. M.: Fischer 1990.

Montagne, R., *The Berbers: Their Social and Political Organization*, London: Frank Cass 1973.

Montagnon, Pierre, *La guerre d'Algérie. Genèse et engrenage d'une tragédie*, Paris: Pygmalion 1984.

Monteil, Vincent, *L'Islam noir,* Paris: Seuil 1964.
Morton, John Moore (ed.), *The Arab–Israeli Conflict,* IV/1, Princeton, N. J.: Princeton University Press 1991.
Moussalli, Ahmad S.: *Moderate and radical Islamic fundamentalism: the quest for modernity, legitimacy, and the Islamic state,* Gainesville, Fla.: University Press of Florida, 1999.
Nagel, Tilman, *Staat und Glaubensgemeinschaft im Islam. Geschichte der politischen Ordnungsvorstellungen der Muslime, I–II,* Zurich: Artemis 1981.
Nancy: Berger-Levrault [1927].
Noer, Deliar, The Modernist Muslim Movement in Indonesia, 1900–1942, London: Oxford University Press 1973.
Norton, August Richard (ed.): *Civil Society in the Middle East,* I-II, Leiden: Brill, 1995-6.
Oevermann, Annette, *Die 'Republikanischen Brüder' im Sudan. Eine islamische Reformbewegung im zwanzigsten Jahrhundert,* Frankfurt a.m.: Lang 1993.
Olcott, Martha Brill, *The Kazakhs,* Stanford, Cal.: Hoover 1987.
Olson, Robert, *The Emergence of Kurdish Nationalism and the Sheikh Sa'id Rebellion, 1880–1925,* Austin, Tex: Austin University Press 1989.
Orel, Sinasi/Süreyya Yauca, *The Talât Pasha Telegrams. Historical fact or Armenian fiction?* Nicosia: K. Rustem 1983.
Otayek, René (ed.): *Le Radicalisme islamique en Afrique subsaharienne. Da'wa, arabisation et critique de l'Occident,* Paris: Karthala 1993.
Owen, Roger: *The Middle East in the World Economy 1800-1914,* London: I. B. Tauris, 1993.
Owen, Roger and Pamuk, Sevket: *A History of Middle East Economies in the Twentieth Century,* London: I. B. Tauris, 1998.
Özcan, A., *Indian Muslims and the Ottomans (1877–1914): A Study of Indo–Muslim Attitudes to Pan-Islamism and Turkey,* London: unpubl. PhD University of London, SOAS 1992.
O'Ballance, Edgar: *Civil war in Lebanon, 1975-92,* MacMillan; New York: St. Martin's Press, 1998.
—— *The Palestinian Intifada,* MacMillan; New York: St. Martin's Press, 1998.
Paden, John H., *Religion and Political Culture in Kano,* Berkeley, Cal.: University of California Press 1983.
Pamuk, Sevket, 'War, State Economic Policies, and Resistance in Turkey, 1939–1945', in: Kazemi/Waterbury, *Peasants and Politics,* pp. 125–42.
Park, Alexander G., *Bolshevism and Turkestan 1917–1927,* New York: Columbia University Press 1957.
Pawelka, Peter, *Der Vordere Orient und die Internationale Politik,* Stuttgart: Kohlhammer 1993.
Penders, Christiaan L., Indonesia: *Selected Documents on Colonialism and Nationalism, 1830–1942,* St. Lucia/Queensland: QUP 1977.
Pennisi, G., *Development, Manpower and Migration in the Red Sea Region. The Case for Cooperation,* Hamburg: Deutsches Orient-Institut 1981.

Perthes, Volker, *Der Libanon nach dem Bürgerkriefg von Ta'if zum gesellschaftlichen Konsens*? Baden-Baden: Nomos, 2000.

—— *The Political Economy of Syria under Asad*, London: I. B. Tauris 1995.

—— *Vom Krieg zur Konkurrenz: regionale Politik und die Suche nach einer neuen arabisch-nah östlichen Ordnung*, Baden-Baden: Nomos, 2000.

Peteet, Julie Marie: "Male gender and rituals of resistance in the Palestinian intifada: a cultural politics of violence", in: *American ethnologist* (Arlington, Va) 21 (1994), pp. 31–49.

—— *"Post-partition Palestinian identities and the moral community"*, in: *Social analysis* (Adelaide) 42 (1998), pp. 62–87.

Philby, H. St. John, *Saudi Arabia*, London: Ernest Benn 1955.

—— *Arabian Jubilee*, London: Robert Hale 1952.

Piscatori, James: *Islam in a World of Nation–States*, Cambridge: Cambridge University Press 1986.

Pjaskowskiy, A. V., *Revoljucija 1905–1907 godov v Turkestane*, Moscow: Izd. Nauk SSSR, 1958.

Pohly, Michael: *Krieg und Widerstand in Afghanistan. Ursachen, Verlauf und Folgen seit 1978*, Berlin: Das Arabische Buch [2]1993.

Politkovskaja, Anna: *A dirty war: a Russian reporter in Chechnya*; transl. from the Russian and ed. by John Crowfoot, London: Harvill, 2001.

Popovic, Alexandre, *L'Islam balkanique. Les musulmans du sud-est européen dans la période post-ottomane*, Berlin: In comm. with Harrassowitz 1986.

Porath, Y., *The Emergence of the Palestinian-Arab National Movement, 1918–1929*, London: Frank Cass 1977.

—— *The Palestinian Arab National Movement. From Riots to Rebellion, Vol. II, 1929–1939*, London: Frank Cass 1977.

Poston, Larry: *Islamic Da'wah in the West: Muslim Missionary Activity and the Dynamics of Conversion to Islam*, Oxford: Oxford University Press 1992.

Poullada, Leon B., *Reform and Rebellion in Afghanistan, 1919–1929*, Ithaca, N. Y.: Cornell University Press 1973.

Rahnema, Ali: *An Islamic Utopian: A Political Biography of Ali Shari'ati*, London: I. B. Tauris, 2000.

Randot, Pierre, *L'Islam et les musulmans d'aujourd'hui*, Paris: Ed. de l'Orante 1958.

Rashid, Ahmed: *Taliban: Islam, oil and the new great game in Central Asia*, London: I. B. Tauris, 2000.

Reeve, Simon: *The new jackals: Ramzi Yousef, Osama bin Laden and the future of terrorism*, Boston: Northeastern University Press, 1999.

Reid, Donald Malcolm, 'Cultural Imperialism and Nationalism: The Struggle to Define and Control the Heritage of Arab Art in Egypt', IJMES 24 (1992), pp. 57–67.

Reissner, Johannes, '*Ideologie und Politik der Muslimbrüder Syriens. Von den Wahlen 1947 bus zum Verbot unter Adîb ash-Shishaklî 1952*, Freiburg: Schwarz 1980.

Richard, Yann, *Der verborgene Imam. Die Geschichte des Ṣchiismus in Iran*, Berlin: Wagenbqch 1983.

Rieck, Andreas, *Die Schiiten und der Kampf um den Libanon. Politische Chronik 1958–1988*, Hamburg: Deutsches Orient-Institut 1989.

Riesebrodt, Martin, *Fundamentalismus als patriarchalische Protestbewegung. Amerikanische Protestanten (1910–28) und iranische Schiiten (1961–79) im Vergleich*, Tübingen: Mohr 1990.

Rodinson, Maxime, *L'Islam politique et croyance*, Paris: Fayard 1993.

—— *Marxisme et monde musulman*, Paris: Seuil 1972.

—— *Islam and Capitalism*, Harmondsworth: Penguin, 1974.

Rosenthal, Erwin I. J., *Islam in the Modern National State*, Cambridge University Press 1965.

Rothermund, Dietmar (ed.), *Die Peripherie in der Weltwirtschaftskrise: Afrika, Asien, Lateinamerika*, Paderborn: Schöningh 1983.

Rouleau, Eric, 'Sudan's Revolutionary Spring', MERIP 135 (Sept. 1985), pp. 3–10.

Roy, Olivier, *L'Afghanistan, Islam et Modernité politique*, Paris: Seuil 1985.

—— *The Failure of Political Islam*, London: I. B. Tauris 1993 (Orig. French ed.: *L'échec de l'Islam politique*, Paris: Seuil 1985.)

—— *The new Central Asia: the creation of nations*, New York: New York University Press, 2000.

—— *Vers un islam européen*, Paris: Editions Esprit, 1999.

Ruedy, John (ed.): *Islamism and secularism in North Africa*, London: Macmillan, 1996.

Ruf, Werner: *Die algerische Tragödie: vom Zerbrechen des Staates einer zerrissenen Gesellschaft*, Münster: Agenda Verl., 1997.

Russell, Malcom B., *The First Modern Arab State: Syria and Faysal, 1918–1920*, Minneapolis: Bibliotheca Islamica 1985.

Safdar, Mahmood, *A Political Study of Pakistan*, Lahore: Sh. Muhammad Ashraf 1972.

Saleh, Fauzan: *Modern Trends in Islamic Theological Discources in Twentieth Century Indonesia*, Leiden: Brill, 2001.

Salibi, Kamal: *The Modern History of Jordan*, London: I. B. Tauris, 1998.

—— *The Modern History of Lebanon*, London: 1965 (French ed.: *Histoire du Liban du XVIIe siècle à nos jours*, Paris: Naufal 1988.

Schaeder, Peter J., 'The Horn of Africa: US Foreign Policy in an Altered Cold War Environment', *MEJ* 46 (1992), pp. 571–93.

Scheffler, Thomas (ed.), *Ethnizität und Gewalt*, Hamburg: Deutsches Orient-Institut 1991.

Schofield, Clive H., Richard N. Schofield (ed.): *The Middle East and North Africa*, London: Routledge, 1994.

Schölch, Alexander/Helmut Mejcher (eds), *Die ägyptische Gesellschaft im 20. Jahrhundert*, Hamburg: Deutsches Orient-Institut 1992.

Schröder, Bernd Philipp, *Deutschland und der Mittlere Osten im Zweiten Weltkrieg*, Göttingen: Musterschmidt 1975.

Schuldiner, Zvi: *Between occupation and uprising: the relevance of the Palestinian Intifada for understanding of Israeli society*, [S.I.]: [s.n.] 1999.

Schulze, Reinhard, 'Ägypten 1936–1956. Die Nationalisierung eines kolonialen Staats', in: Mommsen, *Das Ende der Kolonialreiche*, pp. 134–67.

—— 'Der Einfluß islamischer Organisationen auf die Länder Südostasiens' – von Mekka aus gesehen', in: Draguhn, *Der Einfluß*, pp. 32–54.

—— 'Geschichte der Islamischen Welt in der Neuzeit (16. – 19. Jahrhundert)' in: Falaturi, *Der Islamische Orient.*

—— 'Islam und Herrschaft. Zur politischen Instrumentalisierung einer Religion', in Lüders, *Der Islam im Aufbruch?*, pp. 94–129.

—— 'Islamische Kultur und soziale Bewegung', *Peripherie* 18/19 (1984/85), pp. 60–84.

—— 'Kolonisierung und Widerstand: die ägyptischen Bauernrevolten von 1919', in Schölch-Mejcher, *Die ägyptische Gesellschaft im 20. Jahrhundert*, pp. 11–41.

—— *Die Rebellion der ägyptischen Fallahin. Zum Konflikt zwischen der agrarisch-orientalischen Gesellschaft und dem kolonialen Staat*, Berlin: Baalbek 1981.

—— *Islamischer Internationalismus im 20. Jahrhundert. Untersuchungen zur Geschichte der islamischen Weltliga*, Leiden: Brill 1990.

Scupin, Raymond, 'The Politics of Islamic Reformism in Thailand', *Asian Survey* 20 (1980) 12, pp. 1233–5.

Shari'ati, Ali, *On the Sociology of Islam.*, Lectures, transl. by Hamid Algar, Berkeley, Cal.: Mizan 1979.

Shaw, Stanford J. and Ezel Kural Shaw, *History of the Ottoman Empire and Modern Turkey. Vol. II: Reform, Revolution, and Republic: The Rise of Modern Turkey, 1808–1975*, Cambridge: Cambridge University Press 1977.

Shepard, William E.: 'Islam and Ideology: Towards a Typology', *IJMES* 19 (1987), pp. 307–36.

Shindler, Colin: *The Land Beyond Promise: Israel, Likud and the Zionist Dream*, London: I. B. Tauris, 1995.

Simon, Reeva S., Philip Mattar, Richard W. Bulliet (ed.): *Encyclopedia of the Modern Middle East*, New York: MacMillan Reference 1996.

Simons, Geoffrey Leslie: *Indonesia: the long oppression*, Basingstoke, Hants: MacMillan, 2000.

Simons, Rachel: *Libya between Ottomanism and Nationalism*, Berlin: Schwarz 1987.

Sivan, Emmanuel, *Radical Islam. Medieval Theology and Modern Politics*, New Haven: Yale University Press 1985.

Slot, B. J., *The Origins of Kuwait*, Leiden: Brill 1991.

Sluglett, Marion Farouk and Sluglett, Peter: *Iraq Since 1958: From Revolution to Dictatorship*, London: I. B. Tauris, 2000.

Smith, Wilfred Cantwell, *Islam in Modern History*, Princeton, N. J.: Princeton University Press [2]1957.

—— *Modern Islâm in India. A Social Analysis*, London: Gollancz [2]1946.

Snouck, Hurgronje, Christian, 'The Holy War "Made in Germany"' and 'Deutschland und der Heilige Krieg' in: idem, *Verspreide Geschriften*, vol. III, Bonn, Leipzig 1923, pp. 257–84, 285–92.

Souaïdia, Habib: *La sale guere: le témoignage d'un ancien officier des forces spéciales de l'armée algérienne*, Paris: Editions La Découverte, 2001.

Springborg, Robert, 'Rolling Back Egypt's Agrarian Reform', *MERIP* 166 (Sept.–Oct. 1990), pp. 28–30.

Stauth, Georg, *Die Fellachen im Nildelta*, Wiesbaden: Steiner 1983.

Stein, Kenneth W., 'Rural Change and Peasant Destitution: Contributing Causes to the Arab Revolt in Palestine, 1936–1939', in Kazemi/Waterbury, *Peasants and Politics*, pp. 143–70.

—— *The Land Question in Palestine, 1917–1939*, Chapel Hill, N. C.: University of North Carolina Press 1984.

Steinbach, Udo/Rüdiger Robert (eds), *Der Nahe und Mittlere Osten*, vol. 1, Opladen: Leske 1988.

Stora, Benjamin: *La guerre invisible: Algérie, années 90*, Paris: Presses de Sciences Po, 2001.

Stork, Joe/Ann M. Lesch, 'Why War? Background to the Crisis', MERIP 167 (Nov.-Dec. 1990), pp. 11-18.

Stork, Joe/ Karen Pfeifer, 'Bullets, Banks and Bushels: The Struggle for Food in the Middle East', *MERIP* 145 (March-April 1987), pp. 3-6.

Strohmeier, Martin, *al-Kulliya al-Salahiya in Jerusalem*, Stuttgart: Steiner 1991 [AKM XLIX, 4].

Swietochowski, Tadeuzs, *Russian Azerbaijan, 1905–1920*, Cambridge: Cambridge University Press 1985.

Sy, Cheich Tidiane, *La confrérie sénégalaise des Mourides*, [Paris]: Présence Africaine 1969.

Syed, Anwar Hussain, *Pakistan, Islam, Politics, and National Solidarity*, New York: Praeger 1982.

Taggar, Yehuda, *The Mufti of Jerusalem and Palestine Arab Politics, 1930–1937*, New York: Garland 1986.

Thomas Jr., Frederic C., 'The Libyan Oil Worker', *MEJ* 10 (1956), pp. 264–76.

Tibi, Bassam, '*Die Krise des modernen Islams. Eine vorindustrielle Kultur im wissenschaftlich-technischen Zeitalter*, Munich: Beck 1981.

—— *Nationalismus in der Dritten Welt am arabischen Beispiel*, Frankfurt a. M.: EVA 1971.

Toprak, B., *Islam and Political Development in Turkey*, Leiden: Brill 1981.

Toynbee, Arnold, *The Western Question in Greece and Turkey: A Study in the Conflict of Civilisations*, New York: Fertig 1970 (repr. 2nd ed. 1923).

Turner, Bryan S., 'Orientalism and the Problem of Civil Society in Islam', in: Asaf Hussain et al. (eds), *Orientalism, Islam, and Islamists*, Brattleboro, Vt.: Amana Books 1984, pp. 23–42.

Un Africain [Anonymous]: *Manuel de politique musulman*, Paris: Ed. Bossard 1925.

Van Dam, Nikolaos, *The Struggle for Power in Syria. Sectarianism, Regionalism and Tribalism in Politics, 1961–1978*, London: Croom Helm 1979.

Van Dijk, C., *Rebellion under the Banner of Islam. The Darul Islam in Indonesia*, The Hague: Nijhoff 1981.

Van Leur, J. C., *Indonesian Trade and Society*, The Hague: van Hoeve 1955.

Van Nieuwenhuijze, C. O., *Aspects of Islam in Post-Colonial Indonesia. Five Essays*, The Hague: van Hoeve 1958.

Vasil'ev, Aleksej Michailovic, Istorija Saudovskoj Arabii (1745–973), Moscow/ Isd. Nauka 1982.

Vatikiotis, P. J., *The History of Modern Egypt, From Muhammad Ali to Mubarak*, London: Weidenfeld and Nicolson [4]1991.

Vatin, Jean-Claude, *L'Algérie politique: histoire et société*, Paris: Presses de la FNSP 1983.

Vernier, Bernard, *La politique islamique de l'Allemagne*, Paris: Paul Hartmann 1939.

Vogel, Frank E.: *Islamic law and legal system: studies of Saudi Arabia*, Leiden: Brill, 2000.

Voll, John O., *Islam. Continuity and Change in the Modern World*, Boulder, Col.: Westview 1985.

Voll, John O./Sarah Potts Voll, *The Sudan: Unity and Diversity in a Multicultural State*, Boulder, Col.: Westview 1985.

Warburg, Gabriel, 'The Sharia in Sudan: Implementation and Repercussions, 1983–1989', *MEJ* 44 (1990), pp. 624–37.

—— 'From Ansar to Umma. Sectarian Politics in the Sudan, 1914–1945', *Asian and African Studies* 9 (1973), pp. 101–53.

—— *Islam, Nationalism and Communism in a Traditional Society, The Case of the Sudan*, London: Frank Cass 1978.

—— *Historical Discord in the Nile Valley*, London: C. Hurst, Evanston, Ill.: Northwestern University Press 1992.

Waterbury, John, *The Egypt of Nasser and Sadat. The Political Economy of Two Regimes*, Princeton, N. J.: Princeton University Press 1983.

Weekes, Richard V. (ed.), *Muslim Peoples. A World Ethnographic Survey*, London: Aldwych [2]1984.

Weulersse, Jacques, *Paysans de Syrie et du Proche-Orient*, Paris: Gallimard 1946.

Weyland, Petra, 'International Muslim Networks and Islam in Singapore', *Sojourn* 5 (1990), pp. 219–54.

Wielandt, Rotraud, *Das Bild der Europäer in der modernen arabischen Erzähl– und Theaterliteratur*, Beirut/Wiesbaden: Steiner 1982.

—— *Offenbarung und Geschichte im Denken moderner Muslime*, Wiesbaden: Steiner 1971.

Wilber, Donald N., *Riza Shah Pahlavi: The Resurrection and Reconstruction of Iran*, Hicksville, N. Y.: Exposition Press 1975.

Wild, Stefan, '*National Socialism in the Arab Near East Between 1933 and 1939*', WI 25 (1985), pp. 126–73.

Wilson, Mary C., *King Abdullah, Britain and the Making of Jordan*, Cambridge, Cambridge University Press 1987.

Winter, Heinz-Dieter: *Der Nahe und Mittlere Osten em Ende des Ost-West-Konflikts: politische und ideologische Orientierungen der Region zwischen Maghreb und Golf*, Berlin: Trafo Verlag, 1998.

Woodward, Peter, *Sudan, 1898–1989. The Unstable State*, Boulder, Col.: Lynne Rienner 1990.

Yapp, Malcolm E., *The Making of the Modern Middle East, 1792–1923*, London: Longman 1987.
—— *The Middle East since the First World War,* London: Longman 1991.
Zartmann, I. William (ed.), *Man, State and Society in the Contemporary Maghrib,* London: Pall Mall 1973.
Zürcher, Erik J: *Turkey: A Modern History,* London: I. B. Tauris, 1998.

Index of Names and Places